Oliver Cromwell and the English Revolution

Edited by

JOHN MORRILL

with
J.S.A. Adamson
J.C. Davis
Anthony Fletcher
Derek Hirst
Johann Sommerville
David Stevenson
Austin Woolrych

Longman
London and New York

Longman Group Limited,
Longman House, Burnt Mill, Harlow,
Essex CM20 2JE, England
and Associated Companies throughout the world.

Published in the United States of America
by Longman Publishing, New York

© Longman Group UK Limited 1990

First published 1990
Fourth impression 1995

British Library Cataloguing in Publication Data
Oliver Cromwell and the English revolution.
1. England. Cromwell, Oliver
I. Morrill, J. S. (John Stephen), *1946–*
942.06´4´0924

ISBN 0-582-06064-8 CSD
ISBN 0-582-01675-4 PPR

Library of Congress Cataloging in Publication Data
Oliver Cromwell and the English Revolution/edited by John Morrill.
p. cm.
Includes bibliographical references.
ISBN 0 – 582 – 06064 – 8 (csd.)
ISBN 0 – 582 – 01675 – 4 (pbk.)
1. Cromwell, Oliver, 1599–1658. 2. Heads of state – Great Britain –
Biography. 3. Generals – Great Britain – Biography. 4. Great
Britain – History – Puritan Revolution, 1642–1660. I. Morrill, John,
1946–
DA426.045 1990
941.06´4´092–dc20
[B]
89–35960
CIP

Set in ventura 10/12 pt Bembo

Produced by Longman Singapore Publishers (Pte) Ltd.
Printed in Singapore

**Books are to be returned on or before
the last date below.**

OLIVER CROMWELL AND THE ENGLISH REVOLUTION

Contents

Preface

This book has been a pleasure to edit. Every one of the contributors handed in drafts and final versions on time; and every one accepted editorial direction on reshaping of his draft to avoid overlap with others and to ensure as comprehensive coverage of the career of Cromwell as possible. There are still some gaps – foreign policy gets rather short shrift, for example. But I hope we have achieved a wide-ranging survey that combines the particular insights of each of the team with a common sense of the bold yet elusive personality of Oliver Cromwell.

Throughout the book all quotations from original sources have been modernized in spelling and punctuation, and standardized as to capital letters and roman typefaces. In the footnotes, the place of publication of books cited is London unless otherwise stated.

John Morrill
April 1989.

List of abbreviations

The following abbreviations are used throughout the footnotes in the book.

Abbott	W. C. Abbott, *The Writings and Speeches of Oliver Cromwell* (4 vols, Cambridge, Mass., 1937–47).
Burton	J. T. Rutt, ed., *Diary of Thomas Burton, esq., member of the Parliaments of Oliver and Richard Cromwell* (4 vols, London, 1828).
Clarke Papers	C. H. Firth, ed., 'Selections from the papers of William Clarke, secretary to the council of the army', 4 vols, *Camden Society*, 1891–1901.
C. J.	*Journal of the House of Commons.*
E. H. R.	*English Historical Review.*
Gardiner, *History*	S. R. Gardiner, *History of England from the accession of James I to the outbreak of the Civil War, 1603–1642* (10 vols, London 1882).
Gardiner, *Civil War*	S. R. Gardiner, *History of the Great Civil War, 1642–9* (4 vols, London, 1893).
Gardiner, *C & P*	S. R. Gardiner, *History of the Commonwealth and Protectorate* (4 vols, London, 1903).
H. J.	*Historical Journal*
L. J.	*Journal of the House of Lords.*
Ludlow	C. H. Firth, ed., *The Memoirs of Edmund Ludlow* (2 vols, Oxford, 1894).
T. R. H. S.	*Transactions of the Royal Historical Society*
T. S. P.	T. Birch, ed., *A Collection of the State Papers of John Thurloe* (7 vols, London, 1742).

CHAPTER ONE
Introduction

John Morrill

I

Any man who moves on at the age of forty from a life as a provincial farmer and businessman to become by the age of fifty-three Head of State and who is prevented only by his own scruples from accepting an offer from a parliament to have him crowned as king of England, Scotland and Ireland is clearly one of the great men of history. Oliver Cromwell dominates our knowledge and our mental picture of the civil wars and interregnum, of the Puritan Revolution, as surely as Napoleon dominates our view of the French Revolution and Lenin our view of the Russian Revolution. Yet his precise achievement, and the extent of his responsibility for the shaping of events and for the failure of the Revolution, remain matters of great dispute. On 3 September every year, members of the Cromwell Association (and how many other Englishmen have societies founded essentially to commemorate their lives and achievements?) meet by the nineteenth-century statue of Oliver next to the Houses of Parliament to recall his championship of religious liberty and civil liberties and his role in the defeat of Stuart tyranny. Yet there also exists a powerful folk memory of him as a bigot and tyrant, the man who presided over one of the great iconoclasms of English history, a sleighting of castles and sacking of churches, with a destruction of stained glass, wood and statuary equal to if not greater than that of the early Reformation, and the man who butchered the Irish and launched an unequalled assault on the rights of the native inhabitants of Ireland. Yet another image of him is as the man who led the Parliamentarians to victory over the king only to betray the cause from the time of

1

his suppression of popular democratic rights in and around Burford church in May 1649.[1]

In a sense, of course, he was all these things; each is a caricature that exaggerates an important truth about him. Nonetheless it is obviously easier to catalogue his failings and failures than his achievements. His failure to leave as an enduring and irreversible legacy any of the things he held dearest – above all liberty of conscience and 'a reformation of manners' that would turn the people from the things of the flesh to those of the spirit – and the return of political and religious values he associated with a broken past rather than with a glorious future, are very palpable. At best, some toughened seeds were left below the topsoil waiting for a long, long drought to end before blossoming forth again as the liberal values of the nineteenth century; at worst, Cromwell's vision of a particular kind of godly society, in which men and women learnt the self-discipline of obedience to a stern Calvinist God and were rewarded by that stern God with peace and plenty, was a futile vision that died with him. His greatness in that case lay in the integrity with which he clung to a noble but unrealizable vision, not in anything lasting. At the end of an essay on another man – Thomas, Cardinal Wolsey, who rose from humble East Anglian roots to dominate his world – Sir Geoffrey Elton wrote that:

to recognize that [he] contributed virtually nothing to the future is not to discard his present. For fifteen years he impressed England and Europe with . . . his very positive action in the affairs of the world. He often achieved what he set out to do, even if subsequent events showed his aims to have been mistaken and his solutions to have been patchwork. He made a great and deserved name, and his age would have been very different without him. And surely, this is something; surely it is enough.[2]

And surely this goes for Cromwell too. Only (we might add) unlike Wolsey, that achievement was not vitiated by any of the greed or the agglomeration of wealth and pomp that Wolsey insatiably craved. What other self-made ruler with the world at his feet has ever taken less for himself and for his family of what the world has to offer in goods and services?

---

1. This is the thesis of C.Hill's lively and cogent study, *God's Englishman* (Harmondsworth 1972) and the pithy essay reprinted in *The Collected Essays of Christopher Hill* (3 vols, Brighton 1985–86), III, 68–93. For a vigorous rebuttal of this 'pessimistic approach' to Cromwell's radicalism, see W.M.Lamont, 'The Left and its past: revisiting the 1650s', *History Workshop*, xxiii (1987), 141–53.
2. G. R. Elton. *Studies in Tudor and Stuart Politics and Government* (3 vols 5, Cambridge 1974–83), 1, p. 128.

This book concentrates on the nature of the 'great and deserved name' that he achieved in his own lifetime, and on his particular contribution to the age in which he lived. The remainder of this introduction summarizes the main events of his career and lays out some of the manifest paradoxes and ambiguities in his life and career. It was written after the other chapters and seeks to pull together strands which several of the authors have identified. There follows eight chapters on particular aspects of Cromwell's life and career: Chapter 2 looks again at what is known of his formative years; Austin Woolrych and John Adamson look at the very different worlds of Westminster politics and the army billet in which he moved and was reshaped in 1640s. Derek Hirst explores his role as Head of State and David Stevenson his particular role in bringing the three kingdoms of England, Scotland and Ireland into a new relationship. Three chapters explore his mind: Colin Davis looks at his religious faith and deep inner convictions; Anthony Fletcher his public commitment to building a Christian commonwealth, and Johann Sommerville at the ways that he drew upon the intellectual traditions that provided the paradigms within which political action was possible in these decades. In a final chapter, I move away from seeking to make sense of Cromwell's own words and actions and consider how he was viewed by his contemporaries. What did they see as his strengths and weaknesses?

II

Oliver Cromwell's life falls naturally into three sections: his forty years of obscurity in East Anglia, his twelve years as an MP and as a senior officer in the parliamentarian and republican armies, and his five years as Lord Protector of England, Scotland and Ireland.

Those first forty years are the subject of the next chapter. Here we should simply note how, in all respects but one, they were a poor preparation for a public career. Cromwell was a man of humble circumstances. His income fluctuated between £100 and £300 per annum; he held little freehold land and no offices that gave him experience of governing; he had no military training – not even, it seems, in the militia.[3] Huntingdon, where he lived until 1631, and, even more, St Ives, where he lived from 1631 to 1636, were backwaters, although Huntingdon did lie on the Great North Road and

---

3. The evidence presented in Chapter 2 makes the claims sometimes made that he had served in the Thirty Years' War much less probable. The spacing of his children's births in the 1620s and the new information we have for most years in the 1630s make it very implausible.

one of Cromwell's friends, William Kilborne, was the postmaster of the town[4]; so he may have been better able than many minor country figures to keep up with the latest news and gossip from the capital. He spent one year in Cambridge in his teens and seems to have spent three years in London from the ages of nineteen to twenty-two. He was present at the parliament of 1628–29. Otherwise he is not known to have moved more than a few miles from his home until after 1640. The evidence of close links with certain London merchants and with prominent gentry families in Essex, to whom he was related through his mother and through his wife, hint, however, he may have had a more active and mobile life than we have hitherto realized. However, this achievement in the 1640s and 1650s cannot be predicated upon his training as a man of action and administration in his prime years. What the next chapter does suggest is that the nature and scale of the *spiritual* crisis he went through in the period 1629–31 helps greatly to explain his later dynamism. He knew (as we shall see) what it was to be stripped of all those things we take for granted – wealth, reputation, health – so that he could be new modelled by God. In the 1640s he witnessed that which had happened to him happening to England. Just as God had destroyed the illusory values of this world in order to make Cromwell an obedient and justified servant, so now He overthrew monarchy, the House of Lords and the established Church in order that a process of national salvation could take place. Cromwell's long apprenticeship taught him only one thing, but it was to govern the rest of his life: Trust God in all things.

Cromwell was more prominent than most MPs, certainly than most MPs of his humble circumstances, in the early years of the Long Parliament; and he quickly identified himself with those committed first and foremost to reforming the Reformation, to a liberation of the pulpits from the Laudian gag and the cleansing of the churches of surviving and recently reinforced remnants of popery and superstition. More remarkable was his unhesitating willingness to resort to arms to impose a settlement in the summer of 1642. Sent down by the House of Commons to organize the local defence forces in the Cambridge/Ely area, in the face of footdragging by the local gentry, he showed resolve and initiative. With a general commendation from the Houses to mobilize the militias, but without a specific military commission, he gathered together a band of vigilantes whom he used both to seize the Castle at Cambridge with its munitions and, more dramatically, to prevent the plate of the

4. Abbott, I, 69.

Cambridge colleges from being sent to the king at York and to put it to the use of the parliament. C. H. Firth's judgement that 'the promptitude with which he assumed responsibility and anticipated the (Parliament's) orders by his acts was extremely characteristic'[5] seems an understatement. War was not yet declared; he was committing highway robbery; he had no warrant for what he opted to do. He might have been sacrificed by the more pragmatic members of both Houses if peace had broken out.

The king did, however, raise his standard a few weeks later, and Cromwell was commissioned by the earl of Essex as a captain, quickly raising a company of sixty horse in and around Huntingdon. He was present at Edgehill and then returned to Ely and Cambridge to see to their defence and fortification. In the course of 1643 he was promoted to colonel, and took part in at least eight sieges, skirmishes and battles and campaigned in at least nine counties.[6] Similarly in 1644, he was at the major battles of Marston Moor in Yorkshire and Newbury in Berkshire, at a series of successful sieges, and campaigned in eight counties in a rather wider arc in the north and south midlands.[7] In 1645 he was commissioned into the New Model on a series of forty-day to six-month commissions that took him through the south midlands and deep into the south west. His war ended only in June 1646 when he was party to the surrender of Oxford. In the period from June 1642 to June 1646 he was far more of a soldier than an MP: he returned to Westminster for two weeks in September 1642, a week in January 1643, a month in early 1644 and three months in the winter of 1644/45, a total of 20 out of 200 weeks.[8] Military life had had its frustrations – as the succession of charges of incompetence and dilatoriness he brought against colleagues and superior officers shows[9] – but it had its rewards too, especially for a soldier who never experienced defeat and who saw God make their common enemies stumble to the swords of Cromwell's troopers. His brief returns to Westminster and, much more, the nine months he spent there after the end of the fighting were an altogether more dispiriting experience, as John Adamson shows in Chapter 3. Life in

---

5 C. H. Firth, *Oliver Cromwell and the Rule of the Puritans* (Oxford, 1900), p. 75.
6. There is an exceptionally helpful itinerary and set of maps of his campaigns in P. Gaunt, *The Cromwell Gazetteer* (Gloucester, 1987), pp. 225–30. His 1643 campaigns were principally in East Anglia and Lincolnshire, but included sorties into Nottinghamshire. For fuller discussion of this paragraph, see Chapter 4 below.
7. Gaunt, *Gazetteer*, pp. 225–30; below, pp. 97–101.
8. Gaunt, *Gazetteer*, pp. 225–30.
9. See below, pp. 59–63 and 99–102.

the Palace of Westminster and in St Stephen's Chapel had all the bickering and none of exhilaration of life in the army camp. It brought on the next great crisis of his life, the agonizing choice of loyalties which spanned the period April to December 1647. It is clear that he tried desperately hard to unite army and parliament, even if it meant purging both; and the aim of maintaining that unity was to reach a settlement with the king. But when choices had to be made and loyalties betrayed, he saw that loyalty to a particular parliament was no more unconditional than loyalty to a particular king. God's will was manifest in his saints, who were concentrated in the army.

Cromwell seems not to have doubted that a settlement had to be made with the king until after the outbreak of the Second Civil War in early 1648. He threw his weight behind the *Heads of the Proposals*, drawn up by his army colleague and son-in-law Henry Ireton, in the summer of 1647; and at the time of the Putney debates in November he would not contemplate any thought of a settlement without Charles. As C. H. Firth wrote of Cromwell, it was the king's flight from the army to Carisbrooke and the revelations of his intrigues with the Scots that 'showed him on what a rotten foundation he had based his policy'.[10] On 3 January 1648, it is reported that he announced that 'parliament should govern and defend the kingdom by their own power and resolution and not teach the people any longer to expect safety and government from an obstinate man whose heart God had hardened'.[11] By the time of the Scots invasion, Cromwell was clear that God was willing His servants to administer justice to the king. As one army statement arising from a prayer meeting had declared:

it is their duty, if ever the Lord brought them back to peace, to call Charles Stuart, that man of blood, to account for all he had shed and mischief he had done.[12]

Cromwell's view of the Second Civil War and of the Scottish invasion was unambiguous:

This [is] a more prodigious treason than any that had been perpetrated before: because the former quarrel on their part was that Englishmen might rule over one another; this to vassalize us to a foreign nation. And their fault who hath appeared in this summer's business is certainly double theirs who

10. *D.N.B.* xiii, 165. For a fuller discussion of Cromwell's change of perspective in 1648, see below, pp. 76–81.
11. Ibid.
12. W. Allen, 'Faithful Memorial' in Sir Walter Scott (ed.), *Somers Tracts* (13 vols, 1809–15), VI, p. 501.

were in the first, because it is the repetition of the same offence against all the witnesses that God has borne.[13]

'Take courage,' he wrote to the Houses from the battlefield of Preston, 'they that are implacable and will not leave troubling the land may speedily be destroyed out of the land.'[14]

In 1648 he led one half of the New Model against insurgents in South Wales and Yorkshire before joining Fairfax to defeat the invading Scots at Preston. By this stage, Fairfax ran the army as a military force, and Cromwell led it as a political force, informing Fairfax of what was being done or had been done rather than consulting him. But it was on Fairfax's instruction that he led the pursuit of the remnants of the Scots army back into Scotland and occupied Edinburgh. Within months of the king's execution, he was engaged in the conquest of Ireland – a task undertaken with a ruthless efficiency. He returned, the back of the problem broken, ten months later. But within a month he was off again, this time to conquer Scotland. He crossed the Border on 24 July 1650 and remained north of it for just over the year, once more, as in Ireland, achieving what for centuries no English commander had achieved, a clinical military conquest and occupation as a prelude to an incorporative union of the three kingdoms. He returned to England hot on the heels of the last of the Scottish armies. He crushed that army at Worcester on 3 September 1651. After twelve years of almost constant movement and action, he returned to London on 12 September and was accorded a military triumph in the classical mould.[15] He was never to leave London again until his death in 1658. Although the New Model was to export its triumphs to the Continent in the years to come – to give English arms a reputation they had not had since the days of the Black Prince and Henry V, 250 years before – his own fighting days were over.

But there was to be no retirement. Ahead of him lay the restless search for a way to make the freedoms released by the revolution into a reality: how to make the people able to take up the respon-

---

13. Abbott, I, 691 (letter to Robert Jenner and John Ashe, 20 November 1648).
14. Ibid., I, 638.
15. 'A perfect relation of his Excellency the Lord General's reception . . .' in [B.A.] *Another Victory in Lancashire Obtained by Major General Harrison and Collonel Lilburn 12 Sept., Together with the manner of my Lord General Cromwel's coming up and noble reception* (15 Sept. 1651). Printed and discussed in M. Seymour, 'Public Relations in Interregnum England: Aspects of official and unofficial pro-government propaganda, 1649–1660', Univ. of Cambridge, Ph.D. thesis (1986), ch. 5 and appendix IB.

sibilities of freedom. Until they were demystified and able to see for themselves what God willed for them, he must govern on their behalf. Government would have to be 'for the people's good, not what pleases them'.[16] His would be a vanguard State, a State controlled by the godly on behalf of the still unregenerate masses. But the aim must be to spread enlightenment, to make 'all men fit to be called'.[17] To that end, he used the army to drive out the Rump, a body lacking the vision and the vim necessary to institute a programme of political education and spiritual renewal; he called together representatives· of the godly to be a constituent assembly, the born-again leaven in the national lump; he reluctantly took office as Lord Proctector to wheedle the people towards acknowledging their call to be a nation elect by God through a policy of 'healing and settling',[18] and when that proceeded too slowly he sent his senior army officers out into the provinces as major- generals to revitalize the call to personal and collective reformation. Although, as early as 1651, his name was linked to the kingship, he refused the offer when it was formally preferred.[19] In Chapters 5 and 8, Derek Hirst and Anthony Fletcher examine the policies of the Protectorate and Cromwell's personal responsibility for them. Not everything done in his name was done at his instigation or even with his knowledge and consent.[20] He died in office and in harness on 3 September 1658, the anniversary of his two final victories – Dunbar in 1650 and Worcester in 1651. He had come a long way from the modest town house in Huntingdon in which he had grown up and spent his early manhood.

Cromwell was a man of action, not of reflection. He was no intellectual in politics. His personal letters and speeches are suffused with quotations, paraphrases and resonances from scripture. However, although Cromwell had a conventional classical education, one looks in vain for evidence of classical allusions or of patristic and modern theologians in what he wrote or said. Almost the only book,

16. Abbott, III, 583.
17. Ibid., III, 64.
18. Ibid., III, 435.
19. The fullest discussion in C. H. Firth, 'Cromwell and the Crown', *E.H.R.*, xvii (1902), 429–42; xviii (1903), pp. 52–80. The classic text is B. Whitlocke, *Memorials* (Oxford, 1842), pp. 517, 549. But see the recent discovery that one highly-placed person, John Dury, told a German diplomat in the aftermath of Worcester that Cromwell was *'unus instar omnium, et in effectu rex'* = one who is worth all the others put together, and in effect a king: L. Miller (ed.), *John Milton and the Oldenburg Safeguard* (New York, 1985), p. 49.
20. For further thoughts on this see, P Gaunt, '" The Single Person's Confidants and Dependents"? Oliver Cromwell and his Protectoral Councillors', *H.J.*, xxxii (1989)

other than the Bible, that he ever mentioned by name was Sir Walter Raleigh's *History of the World*, which he commended in 1650 to his son Richard.[21] If we take a speech to parliament in January 1655 seriously, when he said that 'what are all our Histories, and other traditions of actions in former times, but God manifesting Himself'[22] then perhaps he did study more than Raleigh. He seems to have been proficient enough in Latin to converse in it with ambassadors.[23] But he was not bookish.

There is overwhelming evidence that he had an impulsive, forthright nature. Once his mind was made up, he acted without flinching. He did not mince words. In 1630 he got himself into serious trouble for an intemperate attack on the mayor and recorder of his home town which caused him to be hauled before the Privy Council and to face humiliation before his neighbours and friends.[24] In the early days of the Long Parliament, his ill-considered outbursts were an embarrassment to those who were attempting an orderly reformation of Church and State.[25] No less than four times in the first three years of the civil war he caused bitter division within the parliamentarian cause by denouncing his peers (the Hothams, the heroes of 1642, when they had barred the gates of Hull – and the armaments stored there – to the king, but who got cold feet about the war in 1643; and Major-General Crawford, an influential Scots professional) and his superiors (Lord Willoughby in 1643, dilatory commander of the Lincolnshire forces, and the second earl of Manchester, Cromwell's immediate superior and officer commanding the forces of the Eastern Association in 1643–44).[26] They in turn countercharged that he promoted not so much godly reformation as religious licence; his troopers, for example, had allowed Ely (of which he was now governor) 'to become a mere Amsterdam'.[27] Later in his life, he showed the same bull-headedness when he used the army physically and precipitously to get rid of the Rump in April 1653, or when he purged the army of dissident elements without stopping to calculate the consequences on several occasions during

21. Abbott, II, 236.
22. Abbott, III, 590.
23. S. Carrington, *The History of the Life and Death of his most serene Highness, Oliver Late Lord Protector* (1659), p. 4.
24. See below, p. 31–3.
25. See below, pp. 45–7, 50–3.
26. See below, pp. 59–63, 99–102.
27. J. Bruce and D. Masson (eds), *Documents Relating to the Quarrel between the Earl of Manchester and Oliver Cromwell* (Camden Society, 1847), p. 73 and *passim*; see below, pp. 100–1.

the Protectorate. He was a man who found it hard to disguise his emotions. Those who give us physical accounts of him speak of a florid intensity: rubicund, demotic, a manic depressive who was usually manic. One of the best descriptions comes from the steward and cofferer of the protectoral Household, John Maidstone:

His body was well compact and strong, his stature under six feet, I believe about two inches, his head so shaped as you might see it a storehouse and shop, both of a vast treasury of natural parts . . . His temper was exceedingly fiery, as I have known; but the flame . . . was soon allayed with those moral endowments he had. He was naturally compassionate towards objects in distress, even to an effeminate measure . . . a larger soul hath seldom dwelt in a house of clay.[28]

He thus not only had a fiery temper. After his victory at Dunbar, he laughed uncontrollably, exulting in his sense of God's presence which had given him victory against the odds.[29] At the end of a long, tense meeting, he could pick up a cushion, throw it at a colleague and flee the room; but it is his dyspeptic loss of self-control and descent into a ranting, uncontrolled fury that is most often remembered. Clarendon recalled that at a committee of the Long Parliament in the summer of 1641, examining riots in the Cambridgeshire Fen, Cromwell bullied the witnesses, interrupted other members of the committee, and rounded on the chairman when the latter reproved him for his conduct:

. . . his whole carriage was so tempestuous, and his behaviour so insolent, that the Chairman found himself obliged to reprehend him; and tell him that if he proceeded in the same manner, he would presently adjourn the Committee, and the next morning complain to the House of him.[30]

Along with this impulsiveness and uncontrolledness went occasional lassitude and hesitation. He was a man who clearly often did not know his own mind, or, as he would have put it, who could not discern the will of God in a particular situation. Often he needed to get his ideas from others. This is most obviously the case in November/December 1648 when he hung back from returning to London as the crisis between the parliamentary majority and the army mounted, in the spring of 1653 after his impetuous dissolution of the Rump, in December 1653 when the Nominated Assembly col-

28. *T.S.P.*, I, 766.
29. Abbott, II, 319. Since the origin of the story is John Aubrey, it must be viewed with some caution.
30. *The Life of Edward, Earl of Clarendon . . . By Himself* (3 vols, Oxford 1827 edn), I, pp. 88–9. This source too must be used with some caution.

lapsed, and again in 1657 when the offer. of the Crown was made.[31] Once he had been given a solution, and more specifically when some external event persuaded him that God had given him a nudge and a wink, he acted decisively, forcefully, unhesitatingly. But it sometimes took time.

More controversial was his persistent claim that he was a reluctant Head of State. In his very last speech, for example, at the bitter dissolution of his second Protectorate Parliament in 1658, he said that

I cannot [but] say it in the presence of God, in comparison of which we that that are here [like] poor creeping ants upon the earth, that I would have been glad, as to my own conscience and spirit to have lived under a woodside, to have kept a flock of sheep, rather than to have undertaken such a government as this was.[32]

Or, as he put it four years earlier, discussing in his first Protectorate Parliament his reasons for setting up the Nominated Assembly in 1653:

As a principal end in calling that assembly was the settlement of the nation, so a chief end to myself was that I might have opportunity to lay down the power that was in my hands. I say to you again, in the presence of that God who hath blessed and been with me in all my adversities and successes, that was, as to myself my greatest end. A desire perhaps (and I am afraid) sinful enough to be quit of the power God had most providentially put into my hand, before he called for it, and before those honest ends of our fighting were attained and settled.[33]

This is not how he struck many of his contemporaries, especially those writing from beyond the Restoration gauze. Richard Baxter is typical of those who saw him as a good man corrupted by power:

Cromwell meant honestly in the main, and was pious and conscionable in the main part of his life till prosperity and success corrupted him. Then his general religious zeal gave way to ambition which increased as successes increased. When his successes had broken down all considerable opposition, then he was in face of his strongest temptations, which conquered him when he had conquered others.[34]

A comparable picture of progressive corruption by the exercise of power comes in a tract published by the veteran republican Slingsby Bethel in 1668.

---

31. These episodes can be seen as the depressive phases in an essentially manic life.
32. Abbott, IV, 729.
33. Abbott, II, 454.
34. *M. Sylvester (ed.), Reliquiae Baxterianae* (London, 1696), Part 1, p. 99.

His want of honour, as well as honesty, appeareth yet further, in that, having, by a long series of pious deportment gained by his dissimulation, good thoughts in his masters, the long-parliament; and, by his spiritual gifts, wound himself into so good an opinion with his soldiers (men generally of plain breeding, that knew little besides their military trades, and religious exercises) that he could impose, in matters of business, what belief he pleased upon them; he made use of his credit he had with each, to abuse both, by many vile practices, for making himself popular, and the parliament and army very odious to one another . . . [all this] being for his own single advancement . . . and leaves him a person to be truly admired for nothing but apostasy and ambition . . .[35]

These charges are all too common in the memoirs of his contemporaries. And yet they never seem sustainable. Those like Edmund Ludlow, Richard Baxter and Lucy Hutchinson who see him as aspiring to the Crown and as betraying the Revolution were never able to explain why he set up the Nominated Assembly in 1653.[36] He had absolute power in his hands and he chose to surrender it; he refused to sit in the Assembly or to serve on its Council of State. He sat back and prayed that it – an assembly of men drawn from 'the several sorts of godliness in this nation'[37] – might find a way to enlighten the whole nation, to make them turn from the things of the flesh to the things of the spirit. He yearned that the people might learn the responsibilities of freedom, might recognise the will of God, be willing to act on it, and thus fitted to govern themselves.[38] When, instead, the godly created not a new Temple of Jerusalem but a new Tower of Babel, he accepted power as Lord Protector, but he rejected the title of king. Similarly in 1657 it was inner conviction that God had overturned the title and office of king ('I would not seek to set up that Providence hath destroyed and laid in the dust, and I would not build Jericho again')[39] rather than calculation of what he could get away with that almost certainly persuaded him to decline the title again.

---

35. S. Bethel, *The World's Mistake in Oliver Cromwell*, in Harleian Miscellany, vol. 1 (1825), pp. 294–5.
36 C. H. Firth (ed.), *The Memoirs of Edmund Ludlow* (2 vols, Oxford, 1894), I, pp. 394–9; II, pp. 20–8; *Reliquiae Baxterianae*, part I pp. 69–72; L. Hutchinson, *Memoirs of Colonel Hutchinson* (Everyman Library edn, London, 1927), pp. 272–5, 293.
37. Abbott, III, 56.
38. See his speech of 4 July 1653 (Abbott, III, 52–66), certainly his finest, especially at pp. 64–5.
39. Abbott, IV, 473. When Joshua and the Israelites were besieging Jericho, God caused them to blow their trumpets and the walls of Jericho came tumbling down, allowing Joshua to occupy it.

What gives the charge against Cromwell – that he was the great dissembler – residual credibility is the quite remarkable number of instances in which he got what he wanted in controversial circumstances and in which his denials of foreknowledge and responsibility strain credulity: his exemption from the terms of the Self-Denying Ordinance[40]; his denial of involvement of the seizure of the king from Holdenby House in June 1647[41]; the significance of his contacts with Robert Hammond, Governor of the Isle of Wight, days before the king escaped and took refuge on the isle in the dangerous days after the Putney debates[42]; Cromwell's deliberate(?) delay in coming south at the end of the Second Civil War so as to arrive in London hours after Pride's Purge, late enough to deny complicity in it but not too late to take advantage of it[43]; the almost certainly false accounts he gave of what the Rump was up to on the morning he dissolved it[44]; the convenient way the major-generals were quietly abandoned just before the presentation of the Humble Petition and Advice, which has led some to argue that he wished to clear the decks for an initiative he would maintain had taken him by surprise.[45]

In each of these cases – and more – Cromwell was the beneficiary of initiatives of which he pleads ignorance. The frustrating thing is that his guilt cannot be conclusively established in any of them. Can there be so much smoke without fire? My personal view is that in this case there can.[46] The balance of the evidence points towards Cromwell's insouciance and impulsiveness and against a calculated cunning and deliberate, brazen hypocrisy. He was hardly guileless. It is unthinkable he could have risen from his humble station in 1640 to be Head of State if he had had Fairfax's naïveté (once over-promoted, the latter became an increasingly *irrelevant* figure politically even while he retained the leadership of the army). But

---

40. See below, pp. 63–5 and 102.
41. Cornet Joyce and radical soldiers seized the king from the custody of troops loyal to the 'Presbyterian' leadership in parliament and conveyed him from Northamptonshire to army headquarters at Newmarket. Three days before the coup, Joyce had visited Cromwell in London. The recent account by Austin Woolrych, in *Soldiers and Statesmen: The General Council of the Army and its Debates, 1647–8* (Oxford, 1987), pp. 106–15, supplants all others.
42. Firth, (ed.), *Ludlow*, I, p.168. See the discussion in Woolrych, *Soldiers and Statesmen*, esp. pp. 269n and 275 and n.
43. D. Underdown, *Pride's Purge* (Oxford, 1971), pp. 116, 119, 121, 148–50.
44. A. B. Worden, *The Rump Parliament* (Cambridge, 1974), pp. 345–63; A. Woolrych, *Commonwealth to Protectorate* (Oxford, 1982), ch. 3.
45. The allegation first surfaced in Firth (ed.), *Ludlow*, II, p. 21.
46. See also below, pp. 114–8 for Austin Woolrych's similar conclusion.

what drove Oliver was a fierce commitment to a cause he believed in, a trust in God that made him openly ruthless and uncompromising, not furtive and conspiratorial. The sense of betrayal experienced by so many of his contemporaries and erstwhile friends lay in this: that in each case he briefly identified their cause as his cause. But as he moved on, he cast each of his friends aside in turn. He was loyal to no-one but God.

Cromwell repeatedly called himself a seeker. He did not know exactly what God's will was for him or for England. He simply believed that God had *a* purpose for England. Just as Cromwell's personal sufferings in the 1620s and 1630s had had a purpose which had only become clear in the 1640s, so England's sufferings in the 1640s had a deeper purpose as yet unrevealed. Cromwell had been called to lead God's new chosen people from under the yoke of popery and tyranny to a new freedom. When the Israelites escaped from slavery in Egypt, it took them forty years in the desert to discover enough self-discipline and obedience to God's call to be allowed to enter the Promised Land, the land of milk and honey. So it was to be for England. The benefits that regicide and the destruction of the old structures and tyrannies of Church and State made possible had to be earned. It had taken the Israelites forty years; it might take the English four, or fourteen or forty or four hundred years. Cromwell could only seek to create transitional structures that would help the people to learn their duty of obedience to the will of God.

Cromwell cared about ends not means; giving substance to a shadow from the future, not sheltering in structures inherited from the past. He was, he said in 1647, 'not wedded or glued to forms of government', or, as he put it in ten years later as he pondered the offer of the Crown, 'not scrupulous about words or names or such things', and he scorned 'men under the bondage of scruples' who could not 'rise to the spiritual heat'.[47] This disregard for propping up the sagging forms of ancient constitutionalism went along with a maverick attitude to existing civil rights. His opening speech to the second Protectorate Parliament was a paean to the triumph of necessity (defined by him[48] as conformity to the will of God) over legalism.

---

47. Quoted in Firth's biography in *D.N.B.*, xiii, p. 183.
48. As in 1653, when he told the Nominated Assembly that their authority 'comes to you by way of Necessity, by the way of the wise Providence of God', Abbott, III, 61.

On the general proposition that the government was constrained by the rule of law, he argued that:

If nothing should be done but what is according to law, the throat of the nation may be cut while we send for some to make a law.[49]

The major-generals and the Decimation Tax, both created on Protectoral authority alone, were 'justifiable as to necessity [and] so honest in every respect'.[50] Arbitrary imprisonment without cause shown or trial by jury was justified as follows:

I know there are some imprisoned in the Isle of Wight, Cornwall and elsewhere,[51] and the cause of their imprisonment was, they were all found acting things that tended to the disturbance of the peace of the nation. Now these principles made us say to them, pray live quietly in your own counties, you shall not be urged with bonds or engagements, or to subscribe to the government. Yet they would no so much as say, we will promise to live peaceably . . .[52]

This restlessness, this refusal to settle for the piecemeal conformity of the nation under his government was at the heart of his inability to generate stability. In 1648, he told Oliver St John:

Let us all not be careful what use men will make of these actings. They shall, will they, nill they, fulfil the good pleasure of God, and so shall serve our generations. Our rest we expect elsewhere: that will be durable.[53]

Cromwell's restlessness did not win him the battle for hearts and minds. It led him to alienate his friends as well as to alarm those who hated the regicide but sought to come to terms with its consequences. A majority of the nation never reconciled themselves to regicide and to the government that was set up in its wake. That majority acquiesced in the face of Cromwell's monopoly of military force, but they never *committed* themselves to this rule. The orthodox puritan minister Adam Martindale took the Engagement oath in 1651 to obey a government without a king or House of Lords, but his tart self-justification for taking it showed the limits of that obedience:

49. Abbott, IV, 275. This was of course the argument used by Charles I to justify non-parliamentary taxation such as Ship Money. The irony was lost on Cromwell but not on many of those he addressed.
50. Abbott, IV, 269. 'Honest' here clearly means 'acting so as to promote the honest interest', promoting godliness.
51. Cornwall = the Scilly Isles, which like the Isle of Wight was outwith the jurisdiction of the Westminster Courts and therefore of the writ of habeas corpus.
52. Abbott, IV, 275.
53. Ibid., I, 644.

. . . they deserve to be tried for fools if they believed that the royalists . . . or the presbyterians which generally were more averse to it, would ever be cordial friends, so as to suffer with or for them, or to help them up if once thrown down.[54]

Such an attitude is emblematic of the feelings of those Cromwell had to win over as his instruments if his godly reformation was to succeed. Their support proved unattainable. Many – perhaps most – of those who exercised authority in the 1650s saw the Revolution of 1649 not as a beginning but as an end, not as a dawn of liberty but as desperate expedient to prevent the loss of traditional liberties either to a vengeful king or to social visionaries like the Levellers. The regimes of the 1650s were progressively less radical than the circumstances that brought them into being. In most respects there was a rush to restoration: of the old familiar forms of central and local government (exchequer, quarter sessions, etc.) and of gentry power in the localities. And there was a silencing of radical demands for land reform or for greater commercial freedom or questionings of social paternalism.

Cromwell was not intellectually rigorous and consistent enough, or not courageous enough, to believe that God might want to overturn social forms as well as political and religious ones. He believed the new godly order would be erected within the context of the existing social order. What needed reformation was the beliefs and actions of individuals. If the gentry governed compassionately in the general interest, if the yeomen work to produce a surplus to be sold at fair prices, if the labourer did an honest day's work for an honest day's pay, and if the destitute took their charity with due humility, then the divine plan would be being fulfilled. There was just enough about Cromwell's concern for the existing social order, for the reform of procedures, rather than anything more fundamental in the administration of justice – 'not that the laws are a grievance, but there are laws that are grievance, and the great grievance lies in the execution and administration'[55] – to permit some of those to whom the 1650s were based upon a politics of regret to work alongside him. But they constantly sought to tranquilize him, to restrain him from excesses of religious enthusiasm, to constrain him with the language of prudence. They tried to do this above all by the offer of the Crown in 1657. This would have placed the shackles of custom and

54. A. Martindale 'Autobiography', *Chetham Society*, 1st ser., vol. 4 (1845), p. 98.
55. Abbott, IV, 274.

ancient constitutionalism upon him. They found that the fire in his belly was not to be extinguished with their sweet talk of settlement.

Yet as he toiled in vain to reconcile faint hearts to him and to persuade them to join him in his trek from Egypt to the Promised Land, he was steadily losing those who, like him, saw the Revolution as a dawn of liberty, an opening up of a new-modelled commonwealth. He turned to different groups of the godly in turn, trying out their scheme for government. But as each form failed to bring *his* vision any closer to realization, he jettisoned or and cast out its proponents. His career from 1649 is therefore littered with his betrayals of those he had previously embraced and called his friends – the Levellers, above all his old friend John Lilburne[56] in 1647–49, the civil republicans in 1651–53, Harrison and the Fifth Monarchists in 1653, veteran army colleagues in 1654, Lambert and the paper constitutionalists in 1657. That very energizing power and that very enthusiasm (in both its senses) with which he took them up, led him to drop them without compunction and without regret when God's will was not being effected by the forms they had proposed to him.

It is this which explains above all his apparent incoherence and his erratic political behaviour – that which led Hugh Trevor- Roper to say that 'no career is as full of undefended inconsistencies' as that of Oliver Cromwell.[57] I would rather say: 'incoherently defended consistencies'. Cromwell struggled in his letters and speeches to make clear that means are always subordinate to ends; forms of government ('dross and dung in comparison with Christ') had to be cast aside if they did not built the Kingdom of Christ. Here is Cromwell at his passionate, his most yearning, his most opaque:

When you were entered upon this Government . . . [I hope for] such good and wholesome provisions for the good of the people of these nations, for the settling of such matters in things of religion as would have given countenance to a godly ministry and yet would have given a just liberty to godly men of different judgments, men of the same faith with them as that you call the orthodox ministry in England, as it is well known the Independents are, and many under the form of Baptism, who are sound in the Faith . . . looking at salvation only in the blood of Christ, men professing the fear of God, having recourse to the name of God as to a strong tower . . . Are these things done? Or anything towards them? Is there not yet upon the spirits of men a strange itch? Nothing will satisfy them, unless they can put their finger upon their brethren's conscience, to pinch them there. To do this was no part of the contest we had with the common adversary; for religion was

56. See below, pp. 261–7.
57. H. R. Trevor-Roper, 'Oliver Cromwell and his Parliaments' in *Religion, the Reformation and Social Change* (1967), p. 346.

not the thing first contested for, but God brought it to that issue at last,[58] and gave it unto us by way of redundancy, and at last it proved to be that which was most dear to us. And wherein consisted this, more than obtaining that liberty from the tyranny if the bishops to all species of Protestants, to worship God according to their own light and conscience? . . . Is it not ingenuous to ask liberty and not to give it? What greater hypocrisy than those who were oppressed by the Bishops to become the greatest oppressors themselves, so soon as their yoke was removed? . . . As for profane persons, blasphemers, such as preach sedition, the contentious railers, evil speakers who seek by evil words to corrupt good manners, persons of loose conversation, punishment from the civil magistrate ought to meet with them, because if they plead conscience, yet walking disorderly, and not according but contrary to the Gospel and even natural light, they are judges of all, and their sins being open, makes them subjects of the magistrate's sword, who ought not to bear it in vain.[59]

Here is the essence of his authoritarian libertarianism.

The people must be free to exercise liberty of conscience without the luxury of being allowed to run to licence. Christian liberty consists of the ability to perceive and to obey the will of God. Government is indeed for the people's good, not what pleases them. For Cromwell, freedom was rooted in a belief that human institutions could be designed to bring men and women nearer to an internalized discipline that made them willingly obedient to a protestant God. He saw himself as accountable not to those he strove to liberate, but to that same God.

In the regicide and its aftermath, therefore, we must recognize the greatest paradox of all. In confronting and destroying Charles I, Oliver Cromwell was concerned not to establish constitutional government, a balanced polity in which those who exercised authority were accountable to those they governed. The destruction of divine right kings was to make room for a divine right revolutionary.

---

58. This sentence is often misquoted to mean that Cromwell, godliest of the godly even in 1642, thought that the civil war was fought for primarily non-religious reasons. The context here makes it clear that what he meant was that the civil war had not begun as a war for religious *liberty*. Cromwell could now see that it had begun as a war to impose an alternative religious authoritarianism. God had taught them humility in matters of conscience.

59. Abbott, III, 585–6 (speech of 22 January 1655).

CHAPTER TWO

The making of Oliver Cromwell

John Morrill

I

For the first forty of his fifty-eight years, Oliver Cromwell lived in obscurity.[1] He and his immediate family can be found in parish records as they were baptized, married and buried. We can trace him from his first family home in Huntingdon, via an unsettled period in neighbouring St Ives to the cathedral city of Ely. We can trace his tax returns. We can glimpse him in local disputes which brought him under the scrutiny of the Privy Council. We have three accounts of what appears to have been his only speech to the parliament of 1628–29. We have a few rich but tantalizingly decontextualized letters. But there is much darkness and the beams of light are pencil thin and of low wattage.

Nevertheless, I want to suggest that his invisibility is itself a clue to his early identity. This chapter will re-examine the shreds of evidence and will suggest that he was a man in humbler circumstances, a meaner man, than has usually been allowed; that he spent the 1620s and 1630s in largely silent pain at his personal lot and at the drift of public affairs; and that any understanding of his later life needs to begin from a rather different sense of that early life.

The firm pieces of evidence about him, along with the more or less malicious stories gathered together by biographers in the decade

1. This essay involves building a model with needles from many haystacks. For much help in finding the needles, and some in assembling them, I am grateful to Tim Wales, a marvellous researcher, and to John Adamson, Michael Berlin, Anthony Milton, Conrad Russell, David Smith, Christopher Thompson and many habitués of the Cambridge University Library tearoom.

or so after his death[2] have given rise to a fairly universal modern image of the young Cromwell: the 'mere' country gentleman of solid but not substantial wealth ('by birth a gentleman, living neither in any considerable height, nor yet in obscurity', as he himself put it),[3] a man of magisterial experience, accustomed to governing local communities if not the nation; a man firmly rooted in an extensive cousinage of families prominent in their criticism of royal policies; a man who sowed wild oats in his youth but who, returning belatedly but wholeheartedly to the firm puritan teaching he had received at the hands of Dr Thomas Beard in the local grammar school in Huntingdon and of Dr Samuel Ward and the tutors of Sidney Sussex College Cambridge, underwent an archetypal puritan conversion experience at some time in the later 1620s; a man whose intuitive egalitarianism made him stand up for the freemen of Huntingdon dispossessed of their rights in the town's new and oligarchic charter in 1630 and also stand up for the rights of commoners against aristocratic fendrainers in the later 1630s.[4]

Very little of this picture survives close scrutiny. This chapter will consider in turn Cromwell's family background and his economic and social status; his intellectual formation; and the handful of key incidents known to us. It will conclude with a review of the circumstances of his return as MP for the city of Cambridge in 1640 and his participation in the debates of the first two years of the Long Parliament.

II

Oliver Cromwell was the eldest (surviving) son of the younger son of a knight. In consequence his social status was very ill-defined and his economic situation precarious. The wealth of the Cromwells rested upon former church lands, and the revival of Oliver's economic fortunes was to rest upon the acquisition of preferential leases on cathedral properties. It may indeed be that some of the obsessive anti-popery of the English landed groups in the 1620s and 1630s derived from a residual fear that their titles to land might

2. I have made little use of two very jaundiced Restoration authorities – James Heath, *Flagellum* (1663, 1674) and Sir William Dugdale, *A Short View of the Late Troubles* (1681). To rely on them, as many biographers have, whenever they are uncorroborated is irresponsible, since they are so unreliable whenever they can be checked. See J. S. Morrill, 'Textualizing and contextualizing Cromwell', *H. J.*, xxxiii (1990), forthcoming.
3. Abbott, III, 453.
4. I think this is a fair summary of the views of Abbott, and of the standard biographies of Firth, Paul, Hill, Howell and others (for details, see p. 283).

become insecure if a popish or popishly-inclined king sought to un-make the Reformation. Charles I's challenges to the holders of former Church property in Scotland and Ireland, and the adumbra-tion of such a challenge in England, would have reinforced the suspicions of men in Cromwell's position.[5]

Oliver's grandfather (Sir Henry) and then his uncle (Sir Oliver) lived in the grand Elizabethan style in his substantial modern house at Hinchingbrook, built on the site of a pre-reformation nunnery, just outside Huntingdon, with a second home deep in the fen at Ramsey, a converted monastery. James VI stayed on several oc-casions at Hinchingbrook since he enjoyed the local hunting. The Cromwells sat in several Elizabethan and Jacobean parliaments, and served on the Huntingdonshire commission of the peace. Sir Oliver's income seems to have been around £2000, placing him in the top ten county families and top one hundred in East Anglia. Maintaining that position proved too much for him, however, and in 1628 he sold off his Huntingdonshire property and moved to Ramsey.[6]

Sir Henry had ten children to provide for; and he could not be overgenerous to younger sons. Oliver's father, Robert, was lucky to be set up as a gentleman in a town house in Huntingdon and a job lot of urban and rural property, to which he added by marriage the impropriation of a neighbouring rectory (which entitled him to col-lect the tithe and sell the right to present to the living). In all, his income was probably around £300 a year, just enough to secure him a place as a JP of the county[7]; and his father's influence was able to secure him a single term as MP for the borough of Huntingdon in 1597. But Robert himself had seven daughters as well as Oliver to provide for, and it is clear that the latter's inheritance from his father was a meagre one. In 1631 he was to sell up all but 17 acres of his inheritance (and all his mother's jointure) for a total of £1800, which represents an annual income of no more than £100.[8] The subsidy rolls confirm his humble circumstances. They divide taxpayers into those who paid *in terris*, on the annual value of their freehold land, and those who paid *in bonis*, on the capital value of their 'moveable goods'. All the wealthiest men paid *in terris*. Oliver's tax assessment in the 1620s was £4 *in bonis*. The figure of £4 was notional, but it

5. See, for example, C. Hill, *The Economic Problems of the Church* (Oxford, 1956), chs 12–14.
6. For his family background, M. Noble, *Memoirs of the Protectoral House of Cromwell* (1787) and J. L. Sanford, *Studies and Illustrations of the Great Rebellion* (1858), ch. 4, are fullest. Abbott, I, ch. 1 summarizes but does not improve on these.
7. Firth, *Cromwell*, p. 3.
8. Sanford, *Studies*, p. 216; Firth, *Cromwell*, p. 28.

appears to confirm an income of no more than £100 per annum. This assessment was similar to that of another forty families at the top of a small and unprosperous market town. [9]

In 1631 Cromwell moved to St Ives. He may have been forced to sell up by financial pressures; but, as we shall see, it is more likely that he was forced out by miscalculation in local politics. At any rate, his standing in St Ives was essentially that of a yeoman, a working farmer.[10] He had moved down from the gentry to the 'middling sort'.

In 1636 his economic fortunes revived with the death of his mother's childless brother. His inheritance consisted not of freehold land but of the reversion of leases held by his uncle from the dean and chapter of Ely. He became lessee of the manor of Stuntney, to the south of the city of Ely, and lay rector (i.e. administrator) of the Church lands and tithes of the parishes of Ely itself and of their out-lying chapelries [11]; and he quickly extended these business interests by becoming lessee of lands owned by Cambridge colleges – Clare and Trinity Hall – near Ely.[12] By 1641 his income had probably risen to £300 per annum, and he appears on the subsidy roll as assessed at £6 *in terris*. He was eighteenth on the list. It is possible that he was invited by the bishop to take over from his uncle as JP for the Isle of Ely and that he refused. [13] In any event, his status was improving.

Despite his connections with ancient riches, Cromwell's economic status was much closer to that of the 'middling sort' and urban merchants than to that of the county gentry and governors. He always lived in towns, not in a country manor house; and he worked for his living. He held no important local offices and had no tenants or others dependent upon him beyond a few household servants. When he pleaded in 1643 for the selection of 'russet-coated captains who know what they were fighting for', and when he described his troopers as 'honest men, such as fear God',[14] this was not the condescension of a radical member of the élite, but the pleas of a man on the margins of the gentry on behalf of those with whom he had had social discourse and daily communion for twenty years.

9. P.R.O., E179/122/213, 215, 216.
10. Sanford, *Studies*, pp. 240–1.
11. R. Holmes, *Cromwell's Ely* (Ely, 1982), pp. 10–14.
12. Ibid., p. 13.
13. 'The notebook of Dr Henry Plume', *Essex Review*, XV (1906), p. 15. Plume, an Essex antiquary, recorded that Matthew Wren proposed to appoint Cromwell, 'but he would not act'.
14. Abbott, I, 256, 258.

All this makes his rise to be Head of State the more remarkable. But it may help us to understand his self-perception as Lord Protector. In that role he never likened himself to the justice of the peace, the Christian magistrate that shaped policy and *interpreted* the law; but to 'a good constable [appointed to] keep the peace of the parish' [15] – a role that lacked initiative and executive authority, and was marked by a formal obedience to the decisions and judgments of others. Cromwell's first twenty years of adulthood were marked by a lack of formal involvement in government. Just wealthy and independent enough to escape the drudgery of parish or town government, he was not wealthy enough to *govern* in the fuller sense.

His economic background may have had one other important consequence. Both in Huntingdon and Ely his income came largely from administering tithes. The attack by Laud on lay impropriators, and specifically on the impoverishment of urban clergy, would have been a particular threat to him in the 1630s.[16] Self-interest, reinforcing and reinforced by his evangelical zeal, would have drawn him to call for ecclesiastical reform. Any attack on the deans and chapters could be expected to bring him the right to preferential acquisition of the freehold of the lands he rented at Ely. On the other hand, his notorious later squeamishness about the abolition of tithes, and concern that lay impropriators should be compensated can surely be related to this aspect of his early life.[17]

Yet this does not get his social standing quite right: he *was* the grandson and the nephew of knights; he married the daughter of a substantial London fur trader and leather dresser who was establishing himself amongst the Essex gentry; he was in close contact with members of his family (such as the cousin married to Oliver St John, chief counsel both to Viscount Saye and Sele and to John Hampden in their ship money cases); he seems to have lived in London in the late 1610s with Lady (Joan) Barrington, another relative of his mother's; and these connections linked him into the circle of the Rich family, earls of Warwick and Holland. He also had his sons educated at Felsted School (founded and still controlled by the Riches).[18] His own education, at the local grammar school at Huntingdon and at Sidney Sussex college, Cambridge, was that of a gentleman. Following his father's death he went to London to study

15. Abbott, IV, 470.
16. Hill, *Economic Problems*, chs 5, 6, 11.
17. Hill, *God's Englishman*, pp. 36, 178–9.
18. M. Craze, *A History of Felsted School* (1947), pp. 27–33, 47–50.

law. No record of his presence at any of the Inns of Court has been found.[19] If he stayed in London until his marriage there in 1621, he stayed far longer than those attending purely to equip themselves with a gentleman's sense of the law (i.e. not long enough to qualify to plead a cause, but long enough to know whether they had a cause worth pleading). Perhaps a career as a barrister was intended and abandoned. It would have made sense to a family in such precarious circumstances. Yet Cromwell never *sounds* or *reads* like a common lawyer. It is thus intriguing to consider the unheeded suggestion of his earliest and most reliable biographer, Samuel Carrington, writing in 1659, that 'his parents designed him to the study of the civil law'.[20] What makes this just credible is the fact that his inheritance was centred around the income from an impropriate rectory and that he already had the expectation of his uncle's extensive ecclesiastical business in and around Ely, both of which would bring him into extended dealings with the Church courts. It is also worth speculating that his later impatience with the procedural obfuscations of the common law and his preoccupations with equity might be connected with a training in civil law.

Cromwell was not, then, as he is often portrayed, the typical country squire: the secure, obscure gentleman who rose from solid respectability to govern England with all the experience and all the limitations of a godly magistrate. His economic and social standing was far more brittle than that implies: his reference to himself as being 'by birth a gentleman, living in neither any considerable height, nor yet in obscurity' takes on a tenser, more anxious patina. His cousinage flattered to deceive. Economic circumstances for much of his early manhood beckoned him to the yoke of husbandry; and political miscalculation seems nearly to have completed the task.

III

Huntingdon does not seem to have been a town much troubled by controversy or division in the decades before 1625.[21] But in the

---

19. It is generally argued that he attended Lincoln's Inn; but the records (and especially the accounts) of Lincoln's Inn are very full, and he is not likely to have been a non-fee-payer or to have slipped through the accounts. The case for his being at Gray's Inn is based on the loss of its records and the presence of some cousins there.

20. S. Carrington, *The History of the Life and Death of His Most serene Highness, Oliver Late Lord Protector* (1659), p. 4.

21. W. Carruthers, *A History of Huntingdon* (1824), *passim*; P. M. G. Dickinson, *Oliver Cromwell and Huntingdon* (Huntingdon, 1981).

early years of Charles I a series of minor convulsions shook the town. Fragmentary evidence suggests that Cromwell was a victim of these convulsions. The ingredients of the drama include: the departure of the senior branch of the Cromwells from Hinchingbrook House and the arrival of the Montagus; the disagreements among the leading inhabitants of the borough about the best way to spend a £2000 bequest; and (as a consequence of these changes) the grant of a new royal charter.

We know next to nothing about Oliver's role in the government of Huntingdon in the 1620s because so few borough records survive. As we have seen, he was essentially an urban landlord with a strong interest in the tithes of the parish of Hartford. He may or may not have been one of the twenty-four burgesses elected by all freemen annually to form the common council; he may even have served as one of the two bailiffs. As one of the leading subsidy-men it is to be expected that this was so; and if Hinchingbrook influence could secure his return as MP in 1628, it could surely have secured his election as a councillor.

That return as MP represents the dying embers of family interest. He was returned with and behind a member of the Montagu family who were in the process of moving into Hinchingbrook.[22] Oliver made little impact on the parliament of 1628–29. The extensive diaries for both the tempestuous sessions report only one speech by him, and the Journals record him as on few committees and never active as a teller. He made no impact at all on the first session which culminated in the passage of the Petition of Right.

His one speech was delivered on 11 February 1629 in the Committee for Religion that was investigating the spread of Arminian teaching and its protection in high places. Much of the burden of the complaint was against Bishop Neile, who had solicited pardons on behalf both of those who had preached Arminianism (Montagu and Cosin) and those who had been imprisoned in the first session of parliament for preaching the subject's unqualified duty of obedience in the matter of the forced loan (Mainwaring and Sibthorpe). The version of the speech most readily available, and the source of much misinterpretation, has it as follows:

Mainwaring – who by censure of the last Parliament for his sermons, was disabled from holding any ecclesiastical dignity in the church, and confessed the justice of that censure – was, nevertheless, by this same bishop's means, preferred to a rich living.

22. E. Griffith, *Collection of Ancient Records relating to the Borough of Huntingdon* (1827), p. 106.

If these be the steps to church preferment, what may we not expect? Dr Beard told me that one Dr Alabaster, in a sermon at Paul's Cross, had preached flat popery. Dr Beard was to rehearse [refute?] Alabaster's sermon at the Spittle, but Dr Neile, bishop of Winchester, sent for him and charged him as his diocesan to preach nothing contrary to Dr Alabaster's sermon. He went to Dr Felton, bishop of Ely, who charged him as a minister to oppose it, which Dr Beard did; but he was then sent for by Dr Neile, and was exceedingly rated for what he had done. [23]

This account has been variously misinterpreted. The first part (in italics above) referring to Mainwaring is specious and was not part of what Cromwell said[24]; and the second part, which Abbott called 'a composite of three slightly different versions of the speech',[25] suppresses the vital information that the Alabaster sermon and Beard's row with Neile had taken place ten or twelve years earlier. Alabaster, an unstable man who had converted to Rome *c.* 1596 and reverted to Anglicanism *c.* 1610 was a minister in Hertfordshire.[26] Neile was involved, as two versions of Cromwell's speech makes plain,[27] because he was, at the time, bishop of Lincoln and therefore responsible for both preachers. Cromwell was therefore presenting the committee with very stale beer.

By the time Cromwell returned from the parliament following its dramatic dissolution, Huntingdon was deeply divided over a new issue: the Fishbourne bequest. Richard Fishbourne had been born in the town in the 1580s and had been apprenticed into the Mercers Company of London. He made a considerable fortune and on his death left money for a variety of charitable uses, including a £2000 gift for his home town.[28] It took three years for the borough's representatives to decide whether the money should be spent entirely for the benefit of the poor (to start a scheme to find employment for

23. Abbott, I, 61–2.
24. It was printed in Sanford, *Studies*, pp. 229–30. Sanford prints the italicized part after the second half, and he gives a source which Abbott misrepresents. The publication of W. Notestein and F. Relf (eds), *The Commons Debates for 1629* (New Haven, 1921) should have shown him that Sanford had a corrupt text. Indeed, as far back as 1882, S. R. Gardiner had shown that 'the remainder of the speech . . . relating to Mainwaring . . . is taken from another speech by another speaker, on a different occasion' (*History*, VII, p. 56n).
25. Abbott, I, 62n.
26. *D. N. B.*; R. V. Caro, 'William Alabaster: Rhetor, Mediator, Devotional Poet', *Recusant History*, XIX (1988), pp. 62–79, 155–70.
27. *Commons Debates for 1629*, pp. 139, 143, both of which make explicit that the sermon was delivered when Neile was bishop of Lincoln (1614–17) and diocesan of both Alabaster and Beard. One puzzle is that Felton only arrived at Ely twelve months after Neile left for Durham.
28. P.R.O., PROB 11/145 fos 461–5.

the able-bodied unemployed) or whether it should be divided between such a scheme and the endowment of a preaching lectureship.

At the heart of the dispute was the position of Dr Thomas Beard. He is usually portrayed as a simple, devout puritan schoolmaster, devoting his life to the education of the children of a small country town.[29] In fact he was a greedy pluralist, living in grand style, ungrateful for his comfortable lot, and interfering in the secular affairs of the borough in ways no self-respecting puritan would have done.

Beard had arrived in Huntingdon as a graduate of Cambridge University, just after Oliver's birth. Within a few years he held three positions in the town, as vicar of All Saints, the central parish where most of the wealthiest inhabitants lived and worshipped, as schoolmaster and as Master of the Hospital, an imposing set of former monastic buildings at the heart of the town, close to All Saints, dominating the market square and providing him with a good income and some of the finest quarters in the town. He also held the living of Kimbolton, a wealthy parish of 600 communicants and already associated with the Montagu family. He supplied Kimbolton with a non-graduate and non-preaching curate. He held this living in plurality and in absence for fifteen years, only surrendering it, in 1610, when he had secured a second parish in Huntingdon itself, St John's, parish of the Cromwells.[30]

Beard's ambitions were clearly not satisfied by these pleasant surroundings. In 1614 he wrote to Sir Robert Cotton, complaining about 'the painful occupation of teaching' and asking for preferment to a Hertfordshire living in Cotton's gift.[31] There is not a shred of evidence that he was ever a nonconformist and his acquisition of a prebend's stall in Lincoln cathedral in 1612 and of a royal chaplaincy at some point in James' reign strongly suggest otherwise.[32] When in 1614 Bishop Barlow suppressed a combination lectureship at Huntingdon, the corporation put up the money to establish a fixed lecture every Wednesday and Sunday morning in All Saints, and appointed

29. *D. N. B.*; Hill, *God's Englishman*, pp. 37–45; Paul, *Lord Protector*, pp. 24–9.
30. W. M. Noble (ed.), 'Incumbents of the county of Huntingdon', *T. Cambs and Hunts Arch. Soc.*, III (1914), 126, 130, 134, 137; C. W. Foster, 'The State of the Church in the reigns of Elizabeth and James I', *Lincs. Rec. Soc.*, xxiii (1926), pp. 280–2; Lincs. Arch. Office, Libri Cleri, 3 (1604) and 4 (1614); *Cal. St. Pap. Dom. 1603–10*, p. 195.
31. B. L., Cotton MSS, Julius c. III, fo. 109.
32. As prebend: *D. N. B.*; as royal chaplain, Mercers Hall, Acts of Court [AC] 1625–31, fo. 276v, copy of a letter from Charles I to the company.

Beard to the post.[33] Although he fell foul of Neile over the Alabaster affair in or around 1617, he never seems to have fallen foul of Laud, although the latter was archdeacon of Huntingdon from 1615–21.[34] At no point was his lectureship attacked, and he died in harness, as full of years as he was of livings, in 1632.

Just how 'puritan' was Cromwell's 'puritan' schoolmaster? He was fiercely anti-catholic, and wrote tracts against popery, with titles like *Antichrist the Pope of Rome; or the Pope of Rome is Antichrist*, and he is notorious for his providentialism. [35] But neither was a puritan preserve. His *The Theatre of God's Judgment* [36] is as much in the tradition of medieval cautionary tales as it is a self-conscious exaltation of the rewards God gives in this life to those He has saved in the next and of the foretastes of hellfire in this life to those who are to be damned. It draws far more on (pagan) classical writers and the Fathers such as Chrysostom and Cyprian than it does on post- reformation sources; it preaches against active resistance in all circumstances and for passive disobedience in terms Elizabeth and James would have approved; idolaters and upholders of ceremonies were to be found only in the Old Testament and the medieval Catholic Church. His other writings, dedicated to Cromwell's highly conformist grandfather and to Bishop John Williams, are firmly anti-catholic but show no concern at the incompleteness of the English Reformation.[37] He looks like a complacent Jacobean Calvinist conformist: not the man to ignite the fire in Cromwell's belly.

When to all this we add that Beard was quite happy to serve as a common councillor or as a JP,[38] thus mingling what to strict Calvinists had to be strictly separated, magistracy and ministry; and when we find that he was, certainly in his later years, the creature of the conformist Montagu family, his credentials as the shaper of Cromwell's puritanism appear decidely unimpressive. The apparent animosity between them in 1630 becomes easier to explain.

33. Report on 'public lectures' in Lincoln diocese, part of Neile's primary visitation in 1614, Lincs. Arch. Off., Dean and Chapter MS. A4/3/43, printed in *Associated Architectural Society Reports and Papers*, xvi (1881), p. 44.
34. For Laud's appointment, see W. Bliss (ed.), *The Works of William Laud* (7 vols, 1847), III, 135; for a donation for the Huntingdon poor, see his will in ibid., IV, 445.
35. See note 27.
36. There were three editions in his lifetime, each longer than the one before (1597, 1612, 1631) and a further revised version after his death (1647).
37. *A Retractive from the Romish Religion* (1616) and *Antichrist the Pope of Rome* (1625).
38. For Beard as a common councillor, see Cambridgeshire Record Office, Huntingdon (= C.R.O. (Hunt.), DDM/80/1983/1; as a JP, Carruthers, *Huntingdon*, appendix, unpag.

We can now return to the foundation of the Fishbourne lecture. It took more than three years for the town to find a suitable piece of land for purchase by the company.[39] There then ensued a twelve-month tussle within the borough and between the borough corporation and the company over the uses to which the endowment should be put. One party in the town, represented by Thomas Edwards, the only man rated *in terris* in the 1628 subsidy roll, [40] attended the Court of the Mercers Company in January 1630 and argued that since Beard already lectured on Wednesdays and Sundays and since there was a further lecture established in Godmanchester within half a mile of Huntingdon (this is important for Cromwell as we shall see), there was no need for any further lecture. The £100 per annum from the endowment should all be used to set the poor on work.[41] This was strongly opposed by a majority on the common council. They sent Recorder Barnard and Dr Beard to ask that £60 a year be spent on the poor, and £40 on a lectureship.[42] A committee of Mercers was sent to Huntingdon, and reported back in favour of the latter. The common council then revealed their main interest (and perhaps what underlay Edwards' opposition). The town wanted the lectureship to be awarded to Beard, thus releasing them from the burden of paying him themselves.[43] This did not impress the Mercers. This was new money and should go to a new purpose.[44] They declined and drew up a shortlist for a lecture to be held on market days (Saturday) and on Sunday afternoons in St Mary's parish at the populous and unfashionable end of town in which Fishbourne had been baptized.[45] Before they could proceed, however, they received a peremptory command to appoint Beard from King Charles I himself:

39. C.R.O. (Hunt.), Huntingdon Borough Records [H.B.R.], box 12, bundle 5, fos 9–10. This is a copy of a responsary by the Mercers, annotated by the Recorder, to a bill entered by the Corporation in 1695 alleging that the right of presentation to the Fishbourne lectureship had always lain with the town and not with the company. I have been unable to locate the original bill in the Court of Chancery.
40. P.R.O., E179/122/213.
41. Mercers Hall, Acts of Court 1625–31, fo. 248r.
42. Ibid., fo. 260v.
43. Ibid., fo. 268v–269r.
44. Fishbourne left money for other lectureships with the express provision that the preachers should not 'have any other benefice or church living with the cure of souls besides', P.R.O., PROB 11/145 fo. 461v.
45. Mercers Hall, Acts of Court 1625–31, fos 274v–277r; C.R.O. (Hunt.), H.B.R., Box 12, bundle 5, fos 18–20.

. . . taking special notice of the good conversation and ability in learning of Dr Beard . . . late chaplain of our dear father and one whom the corporation there much desireth to supply that place . . . to recommend him to their election . . . in our said town of Huntingdon, it being the ancient inheritance of our Crown.[46]

Perhaps the king was seeking to prevent the choice of an unbeneficed lecturer; perhaps he was acting on the advice of the earl of Manchester[47]; or, less likely, out of a genuine regard for Beard. In any event, the latter was clearly no nonconformist or precisian.

The company sent a delegation (two of whose members, Mr Spurstowe and Mr Basse, we shall meet again as friends of Cromwell) to Nonsuch to urge the king to let them make a free choice, and, upon an undertaking to add Beard to the shortlist, they appear to have succeeded.[48] They considered seven candidates and selected one Robert Procter. But they then came up against another obstacle, the bishop of Lincoln. John Williams wrote commending Beard; he stalled over granting Procter a licence, and he proposed a succession of compromises. Meanwhile, the corporation prevented Procter over a period of nine months from occupying his pulpit. Williams attempted to persuade the Mercers to add another £20 a year to the pot and to pay Beard and Procter £30 each. When this was rejected, he said he would license Procter, if 'the company would bestow some gratuity' upon Dr Beard. This was agreed, and after yet more haggling, a lump sum of £40 was paid.[49] In mid 1631, six years after Fishbourne's death, and six months before Beard's death, the first Fishbourne lecture was given in St Mary's. Beard made his feelings clear by publishing a third edition of *The Theatre of God's Judgment* with a dedication to the mayor and aldermen of Huntingdon, who had stood by him, 'in the late business of the lectureship, and notwithstanding the opposition of malignant spirits'.[50]

Was Oliver Cromwell one of the malignant spirits? We do not know. But it is tempting to think so. He and Thomas Edwards were the wealthiest men *not* to be named as aldermen in the 1630 charter[51] (and the 'Mr Edwardes' whom Cromwell described as a friend of twenty to thirty years' standing when he sought a position for him

46. Mercers Hall, Acts of Court 1625–31, fo. 276.
47. As Lord Privy Seal he frequently advised the king on ecclesiastical patronage.
48. Mercers Hall, Acts of Court 1625–31, fos 275v, 277r.
49. Ibid., fos 282r–v, 286v–287r, 291v–292r, 296v, 309v, 317r–318v; Fishbourne Bequest, Accounts 1627–56, fo. 17r.
50. Beard, *Theatre* (1631 edn), preface.
51. For the list of aldermen, see Carruthers, *Huntingdon*, appendix 2 [unpag.]; for the list of subsidymen, P.R.O., E179/122/213, 215, 216.

as clerk (in the Prerogative Court) in 1647 is probably the same man)[52] Cromwell had, or was soon to have, strong independent links with Mercers; he opposed the appointment of Beard and was subsequently a strong ally of theirs when the St Mary's lectureship came under attack and also in relation to the Godmanchester lecture (as we shall see). It seems more probable than not that the affair of the Fishbourne lecture explains Cromwell's bitter attack on the new charter in 1630 and the kick in the groin which Beard delivered him at the height of the charter dispute.

IV

In the spring of 1630, hot upon the heels of the arrival of the Montagus at Hinchingbrook and upon the snubbing of the town by the Mercers, the leading men of Huntingdon petitioned the Crown for a new charter.[53] There is good reason to believe that Cromwell supported this move.

The existing charter dated back to the reign of Richard III, and it vested power in two bailiffs and twenty-four common councillors, all elected on an annual basis by the burgesses. Now, in the words of the new charter:

We at the humble petition of the bailiffs and burgesses of the borough aforesaid, being willing, for the better governance of the said Borough, to prevent and remove all occasions of popular tumult or to reduce the elections and other things and public business of the said borough into certainty and constant order,

reincorporated the borough with a permanent body of aldermen, to serve for life, coopting to vacancies, and a mayor to serve for a year by seniority among the aldermen.[54] The disagreements culminating in the humiliation of the borough by the Mercers must surely have had something to do with the 'popular tumults' which were to be avoided in future and the 'certainty and constant order' which were being sought.

The new charter passed the great seal just as the Fishbourne lectureship was finalized. It established a new body of aldermen, most of whom were inhabitants of All Saints parish.[55] The most notable

---

52. Abbott, I, 431–2. Cromwell speaks of his friend as having been an under-clerk 'about sixteen or seventeen years' (i.e. since 1631), suggesting that he too had left (been driven from?) Huntingdon immediately after the charter dispute.
53. Carruthers, *Huntingdon*, pp. 84–7
54. Ibid., appendix [unpag.]
55. Based on a study of the names in the charter and of the parish registers of All Saints, St John's and St Mary's in C.R.O. (Hunt.).

absentees, if we compare the list with the rankings in the 1628 subsidy roll, were Thomas Edwards, Oliver Cromwell and William Kilborne.[56] It is true that Cromwell was one of five JPs named; but the duties of a JP in a small borough did not compare with those of a county JP, especially where so much jurisdiction was exercised in the mayor's court. Had Cromwell taken up the position (which he did not) he would have had little more to do than a parish constable in the countryside.

What followed is well known. Cromwell and William Kilborne became involved in furious verbal arguments with some of the beneficiaries of the new charter, and uttered what their opponents dubbed 'disgraceful and unseemly speeches' against the mayor and the recorder, as a result of which they were reported to the Privy Council.[57] On 26 November 1630, Cromwell and Kilburne appeared before it, but were remanded in custody for six days. On 1 December 1630, the whole matter was handed over to the Lord Privy Seal, none other than the earl of Manchester.[58] On 6 December he produced a report that exonerated Barnard and the mayor, praised the new charter as 'being authorized by the common consent of the town' and required Cromwell to make an apology for words 'spoken in heat and passion'. His report makes plain that Cromwell was not complaining about the oligarchic nature of the new Charter but about the intentions of the particular clique who had gained power under it. His concern, in Manchester's words, was first that

the mayor and aldermen might now alter the rate of their cattle in the commons; secondly that the mayor and aldermen alone, without the burgesses, might dispose of the inheritances of their town lands; thirdly that it was in the power of the mayor and aldermen to fine men that might be poor £20 for refusing to be aldermen.

Manchester made it clear that 'these things . . . cannot be warranted by the new charter', but he got the aldermen to agree to uphold existing rights on the commons, to undertake not to alienate townlands without the consent of the burgesses and to limit the fines on the reluctant to 20 marks.[59] This fits in with the idea that Crom-

56. Kilborne was the other burgess hauled before the Privy Council for attacking the new charter (see below).
57. P.R.O., SP 16/186/34.
58. Abbott, I, 67–9
59. P.R.O., SP 16/186/34 (full transcript in *Cal. St. Pap. Dom. 1629–31*, pp. x–xi.) The extracts in Abbott, I, 69, are distorting and omit important matter. Sanford, *Studies*, pp. 233–7, is also misleading. His statement (p. 233) that the charter dispute followed an electoral defeat of Barnard by Cromwell is unsupported but has misled others (e.g. Hill, *God's Englishman*, p. 41).

well was demoralized by the seizure of power by a clique which he saw as less paternalistic and more greedy than he and his friends were. He suspected them – following their failure to shuffle off their responsibility for Beard onto the Mercers – of trying to turn the assets of the town to their own profit. It was a personal attack, not a precocious defence of democratic principles: and he lost. Barnard showed his gratitude by having his next son baptized (in All Saints church) 'Manchester Barnard'[60] while Cromwell found his long-term position in his native town in ruins – his finances in tatters, his honour severely wounded, and his future prospects of office non-existent. What may have constituted the dregs of the bitter cup he had to drink was an affidavit sworn against him by Thomas Beard. It is to be found in the earl of Manchester's papers and it alleged that:

Oliver Cromwell esquire and William Kilborne, gent., with a free assent and consent did agree to the renewing of our late charter and that it should be altered from bailiffs to mayor as they did hope it would be for future good and quiet of the town.[61]

The implication is that Cromwell's opposition to the charter followed his discovery that he was not to be an alderman, that he was a bad loser over a matter of personal preferment.

The likeliest hypothesis (it is hardly an explanation) of what had happened was this: that a bitter dispute over the Fishbourne bequest had led to a demand for a more settled charter; that those who had opposed Beard, including Cromwell, were ruthlessly omitted from the new, closed oligarchy, and that he responded in a bitter attack on their opponents, Robert Barnard, Thomas Beard, and behind them, the Montagus.

Within twelve months, Cromwell had sold up and moved five miles to St Ives, to begin a new life as a yeoman farmer.

V

Why St Ives? Probably because there was a suitable tenancy available, and because it allowed him to keep in touch with remaining friends in Huntingdon. He retained a nominal 17 acres of freehold there; his mother remained behind, and one of his daughters, Mary was baptized in St John's parish church in 1636.[62]

60. C.R.O. (Hunt.), microfilm roll 171, parish register of All Saints, baptismal entry for 22 August 1633.
61. C.R.O. (Hunt.), Montagu MSS, DDM 80/1983/1. Abbott, I, 68, is a copy of an inadequate calendar version.
62. Sanford, *Studies*, pp. 241–4; C.R.O. (Hunt.), St John's baptism register, 22 April 1636.

But a further reason for his move to St Ives may have been that an old Cambridge friend, Henry Downhall, had recently become vicar there. Downhall presents us with a problem. The earliest extant letter of Cromwell's is an invitation to Downhall, then a Fellow of St John's College, Cambridge, to be godfather of Richard Cromwell.[63] Downhall, however, was even less of a puritan than Thomas Beard. Although he enjoyed the patronage of the earl of Holland and of Bishop Williams (both anti-Laudians), he voted for Buckingham in the bitter contest over the Chancellorship of the University in 1625, and he was later a royalist army chaplain and was to be dispossessed of his second parish, Toft, in Cambridgeshire, for hiring a curate who 'observed ceremonies'. He was also accused of obstructing the activities at St Ives of the undoubtedly puritan lecturer, Job Tookey.[64]

This forces us back to a reconsideration of Cromwell's spiritual conversion. It is generally acknowledged that this would have occurred between 1626 and 1636, with a recent preference for a date around 1628-30.[65] A letter of October 1638 to his cousin Mrs St John is important testimony:

. . . Yet to honour God by declaring what He hath done for my soul, in this I am confident, and I will be so. Truly, then, this I find: That he giveth springs in a dry and barren wilderness where no water is . . . My soul is with the Congregation of the firstborn, my body rests in hope, and if here I may honour my God either by doing or by suffering I shall be most glad. Truly no creature hath more cause to put forth himself in the cause of his God than I. I have had plentiful wages beforehand, and I am sure I shall never earn the least mite. The Lord accept me in His Son, and give me to walk in the light, as He is the light . . . You know what my manner of life hath been. Oh, I lived in and loved darkness, and hated the light. I was a chief, the chief of sinners. This is true: I hated godliness, yet God had mercy on me. O the riches of His mercy! Praise Him for me, pray for me, that he who hath begun a good work would perfect it to the day of Christ . . .[66]

This is generally acknowledged to be a model description of a calvinist conversion experience: 'Once a man grasped the full assurance of God's promise to him, he would pour out his heart in praise and

---

63. Abbott, I, 50–1.
64. For Downhall, see A. G. Matthews, *Walker Revised (Oxford, 1948), p. 79* (though the original edition, viz. J. Walker, *The Sufferings of the Clergy* (1714), vol. II, p. 230, is fuller); T. Baker, *History of St John's College, Cambridge* (Cambridge, 1869), pp. 199, 498, 487, 625; and C. H. Cooper, *Annals of Cambridge* (5 vols, Cambridge, 1842–53), III, p. 187. For Tookey, see below, p. 36.
65. Paul, *Lord Protector*, pp. 39–42; Fraser, *Chief of Men*, pp. 36–40.
66. Abbott, I, 96–7.

thanksgiving for this unmerited gift; the certainty of his own salvation gave the puritan a tremendous sense of his unrepayable debt to Almighty God', as Robert Paul put it.[67] The contrast between an awareness of having been 'the chief of sinners' and a certainty of salvation despite rather than because of his nature is puritan hyperbole. It is not testimony that Cromwell was a reformed libertine and hitherto an ignorant and non-practising Christian: it is testimony to the shift from formalism and external religion to an inner certainty of a specific call from God that gave an empty life meaning and hope.

Cromwell had had that experience by 1638. It was to dominate the rest of his life. Yet our revision of Dr Beard's views challenges the assumption of a puritan schooling, and his father's will (which contains no reference at all to his Faith or Hope, and alludes only to 'man's life [being] like a bubble of water' before setting out the disposal of his property),[68] combined with the anglican-royalism of his Cromwell relatives, weakens the case for a puritan childhood still further. It is probable that he had not had that conversion experience in 1626 when he wrote to Henry Downhall asking him to be Richard's godfather in a letter utterly lacking in the biblical imagery and thankfulness to God that infused almost every letter after 1638.[69] The evidence that his 'conversion experience' occurred in 1627-29 is not as strong as the evidence that it occurred after 1630. His speech in parliament in 1629 is explicable as the words of a pious protestant but of one not yet assured of salvation; his probable antipathy to Beard's candidacy for a Fishbourne lectureship may point to any number of personal grudges rather than to his being more precise than his old schoolmaster.

The testimony of Sir Theodore Mayerne, the prominent London physician, that he treated Cromwell for depression (*valde melancholicus*) at the time of the 1628/9 parliament, fits well with the idea of a man on the brink of a major spiritual and personal crisis.[70] Bishop Burnet, a surprisingly reliable source in such matters, reported that he had been told that Cromwell 'led a very strict life

---

67. Paul, *Lord Protector*, p. 37. See also pp. 399–400 where Paul analyses the biblical references and shows Cromwell to have been drawing on both the Geneva Bible and the Authorized Version. From 1640 onwards he drew almost exclusively on the Authorized Version. Perhaps he was having a flirtation with the Geneva Version in the 1630s before reverting to the text he already knew well.
68. P.R.O., PROB 11/130, quire 78, fo. 115.
69. Paul, *Lord Protector*, p. 39.
70. Sir Henry Ellis, *Original Letters Illustrative of English History*, 2nd ser. (4 vols, 1827), III, p. 248.

for about eight years before the wars' (which would mean 1631 if Burnet – a Scot – was counting back from the Bishops' Wars, and 1634 if he was counting back from the outbreak of civil war in England).[71] If this is correct, then the man responsible for his conversion would have been either the lecturer at St Ives, Job Tookey, who was suspended by Williams in 1635[72] and whose son was immediately afterwards awarded an exhibition by the Mercers Company to complete his studies at Emmanuel College, Cambridge[73] (and we shall soon see why Cromwell is likely to have been behind this award) or Dr Walter Welles, another preacher with whom Cromwell had close ties (and, once more, someone we shall shortly meet again). If Cromwell's conversion followed rather than preceded the personal crises of 1630–31, it would not have prevented his being a conformist Christian or supporter of social discipline in Huntingdon. But it would make his outburst against Mayor Walden and Recorder Barnard a cry of baffled pain rather than the ill-considered haughtiness of a Zeal-in-the-Lord Busy.

VI

We know little about Cromwell in the 1630s. He delayed payment of the fine imposed upon him in 1631 for failing to take up a knighthood on the occasion of the king's coronation (a fine levied on all those with £40 per annum from freehold land).[74] How ironic that it should fall upon a man adjusting from gentry to yeoman status! He seems otherwise to have lived in St Ives without incident, paying his ship money, attending to family and business concerns. We get a glimpse of him from later reminiscence, attending church, generally wearing 'a piece of red flannel around his neck as he was subject to inflammation of the throat'.[75] (This story is perhaps confirmed by Cromwell's own statement, made in a law suit arising from the administration of his uncle's will in 1636 that he was 'sickly'.[76])

71. G. Burnet, *History of My Own Times* (ed. O. Airy, 2 vols, 1897–1901), I, p. 121.
72. *Cal. Comm. Compg. Delqts.*, II, pp. 877–8, 1527; J. Hacket, *Memoirs of the Life of Archbishop Williams* (1715), p. 152.
73. Mercers Hall, Acts of Court 1631–37, at the General Court on 10 Nov 1635.
74. The best account is in *Cal. St. Pap. Dom., 1629–31*, p. xiv. Abbott, I, 71 is misleading in implying that Cromwell was the last man in Huntingdonshire to comply and that 'his composition [may have been] paid by someone else'. This has misled others into even more extreme statements (e.g. Hill, *God's Englishman*, p. 43,). In fact the commissioners sent down to Huntingdon summoned 35 men before them: 15 appeared, 11 failed to appear, and 8 – Cromwell probably the last of them – paid up without appearing (i.e. to avoid having to appear).
75. Noble, *Protectoral House*, I, p. 105n.
76. P. R. O., C3/399/163.

After his uncle's death, he moved to Ely, and to the administration of dean and chapter properties. There too we only have occasional glimpses of him: a letter to London about a lectureship in 1636[77]; an account of his activities in relation to Fen drainage in 1637[78]; and the letter to Mrs St John in 1638.[79]

Too much has sometimes been made of his support for the commoners in the fens against the consortium of Dutch engineers, noble Adventurers and local gentry who were draining the Fen in a large area including Ely.[80] Those involved included at least two of his cousins. (His own immediate family had been active supporters of fen drainage around Huntingdon in his boyhood.[81]) There is not a shred of evidence that Cromwell, then or later, was opposed in principle to the drainage, which would result in the creation of many thousands of acres of rich arable land at a time when many thousands of the poor elsewhere in the country could barely survive a poor harvest; but like the uncle from whom he inherited his Ely property, he was probably worried by the levels of compensation offered to the commoners whose livelihoods were threatened by the drainage. In 1653 he is reported to have said:

the drainage of the fens was a good work, but that the drainers had too great a proportion of the land for their hazard and charge, and that the poor were not enough provided for.[82]

There is no reason to doubt that this was his attitude in 1638. His involvement is known from a single, uncorroborated aside in a paper to the privy council that discusses the deployment by a local JP of 'crowd of men and women armed with scythes and pitchforks,' to oppose one of the Drainers' agents who had tried to drive the JP's cattle off the fen. The report continues:

it was commonly reported . . . that Mr Cromwell of Ely had undertaken, they [the farmers] paying him a groat for every cow they had upon the common, to hold the drainers in suit of law for five years, and that in the meantime, they should enjoy every part of their common.[83]

77. Abbott, I, 80–1.
78. Abbott, I, 102–4.
79. Abbott, I, 96–7.
80. The most reliable accounts are in M. Wickes, *Oliver Cromwell and the Drainage of the Fens* (Huntingdon, 1981) and K. Lindley, *Fenland Riots and the English Revolution* (1982), pp. 95–6, 104, 115–9.
81. Sanford, *Studies*, pp. 253–6.
82. Cited in Wickes, *Fens*, p. 4.
83. Abbott, I, 103.

There is no supporting evidence that he made the offer, and none that anyone took him up on it. A report that he was also a spokesman for commoners at a meeting with Drainers at Huntingdon comes only from a totally unreliable source.[84] His prompt action in parliament in 1641 to secure a Commons' committee investigation of a riot at Somersham and his rough handling of Montagu witnesses at the committee was probably intended not to halt the drainage but to balance a one-sided report by the earl of Manchester's friends to a Lords' committee. It may even have been a settling of the old score from 1630.[85] It was a sneer in the royalist press in 1643 that first gave him the title 'Lord of the Fens' (=a nobody).[86]

As in the case of the Huntingdon Charter, the claim that the fen disputes show Cromwell to be a precocious upholder of popular rights does not really stand up. But – by the late 1630s – he was a precocious puritan.

VII

In 1636, Cromwell wrote a letter to his 'very good friend Mr Storie, at the sign of the Dog in the Royal Exchange'. In it, he wrote that:

Among the catalogue of those good works which your fellow citizens and our countrymen have done, this will not be reckoned for the least, that they have provided for the feeding of souls . . . Such a work as this was your erecting the lecture in our country; in which you placed Dr Welles, a man for goodness and industry, and ability to do good every way, not short of any I know in England; and I am persuaded that sithence his coming, the Lord hath by him wrought much good amongst us . . . surely, Mr Storie, it were a piteous thing to see a lecture fall [when it is] in the hands of so many able and godly men as I am persuaded the founders of this are, in these times, wherein we see they are suppressed, with too much haste and violence by the enemies of God His truth . . .[87] You know, Mr Storie, to withdraw the pay is to let fall the lecture; for who goeth to warfare at his own cost? I beseech you therefore in the bowels of Christ Jesus, put it forward, and let the good man have his pay.[88]

Who is Dr Welles and where was his lecture? He has been regularly and wrongly identified as Dr Samuel Wells, later an army chaplain.[89]

84. Dugdale, *Short View*, p. 460.
85. Abbott, I, 130–2, is superseded by Lindley, *Fenland Riots*, pp. 115–9.
86. Ibid., p. 96; Fraser, *Chief of Men*, p. 56; The title was bestowed in the royalist newspaper *Mercurius Aulicus* in November 1643.
87. This may well be a reference to Williams' suppression, just three months earlier, of Job Tookey's lectureship at St Ives, and to the constant threat to the Fishbourne lecture in Huntingdon (see below, pp. 41–2).
88. Abbott, I, 80.
89. As by those who follow Abbott, I, 81n. A check of the most elementary sources

It is widely and wrongly assumed that he was a lecturer in Huntingdon. In fact, he was almost certainly Dr Walter Welles, lecturer in Godmanchester, just half a mile from Huntingdon. We know next to nothing about the lecture itself and little more about Walter Welles beyond what he tells us about himself in a flurry of letters dated from Godmanchester in 1630-31.[90] In one of these letters, Welles reveals that he studied in Leiden, and internal evidence dates his presence there to the early years of the seventeenth century. (Certainly he does not seem ever to have studied in Oxford or Cambridge.[91]) We have no idea when he arrived in Godmanchester, other than that it was by 1630, and we know that he was still there in 1635, and it seems that he was still there in June 1635, when he appears as a witness on the will of a Godmanchester gentlemen.[92] The letters he wrote in 1630-31 are to two interesting people: Samuel Hartlib and John Dury.[93] Hartlib was a Polish emigré who arrived in England in 1628 to set up an experimental school in Chichester based on Baconian principles, and who spent the next thirty years 'in relieving his fellow refugees, encouraging lay piety, and in disseminating useful information interfused with messianic speculations'.[94] John Dury was the son of a Scots emigré minister in the Netherlands (and a friend of Welles in his own right) who was involved in the 1620s and 1630s in a plan for pan-protestant reunion. In that connection, Hartlib arranged for

would have shown that this could not be so. Samuel Welles was baptized in 1614 and was still at university without an MA, let alone a doctorate, in 1636.

90. G. H. Turnbull, *Hartlib, Dury and Comenius* (Liverpool, 1947), pp. 16–19, 67, 127, 134–40. I am grateful to Dr Mark Greengrass and to the Hartlib Papers Project at the University of Sheffield for a photocopy and transcript of the most important of these letters, to Hartlib, and dated 13 Sept. 1630. (Sheffield Univ. Lib., Hartlib papers 33/3/1–2.)

91. No Welles (or Wells or Weld) with a doctorate who looks plausible can be found in J. and S. A. Venn (eds), *Alumni Cantabriensis* (4 vols, Cambridge, 1922–27) or J. Foster (ed.), *Alumni Oxoniensis* (4 vols, Oxford, 1891–92). Christopher Wells, vicar of Water Eaton in the north of Huntingdonshire, is styled 'Sacrae Theologiae Professor' [i.e. doctor of divinity] in his letter of presentation in 1629 (L.A.O., PD/1629/51), but he has no other link to Cromwell or the Mercers.

92. P.R.O., PROB 11/168 fo. 380. One further puzzle is that the Godmanchester subsidy roll for 1628/9 includes 'Job Tookey, clericus' [P.R.O., E179/ 122/216]. We know that the vicar of Godmanchester was John Wybarne (*V. C. H. Hunts.*, II, p. 296; Noble, 'Incumbents', 100). The likely explanation is that Tookey owned freehold land in Godmanchester although his lecture was clearly in St Ives.

93. H. R. Trevor-Roper, 'Three Foreigners: the Philosophers of the Puritan Revolution', in *Religion, the Reformation and Social Change* (1967); Turnbull, *Hartlib, Dury and Comenius*.

94. Trevor-Roper, 'Three Foreigners', pp. 249–50. Cf. G. H. Turnbull, *Samuel Hartlib* (Oxford, 1920), pp. 16–18.

him to come to England. Welles' letters show him to be close enough to the heart of this reforming group to be able to write a letter to Hartlib critical of some aspects of Dury's scheme, and able to ask for a copy of the manuscript of his commentary on St Paul's epistle to the Colossians.[95] Welles' close involvement with the Hartlib circle is also indicated by his reference to several well-wishers among the east midlands gentry, his apparent close links with the firmly Calvinist James Ussher, archbishop of Armagh,[96] and his promise to discuss Dury's scheme with Bishop Williams, 'a very wise gentleman and very able to promote this cause . . . he favours all good businesses; but how far to trust him, I know not'.[97] Williams' penchant for radical chic and for treachery was never better expressed. In the 1630s, both Hartlib and Dury caught the imagination of some of the most prominent anti-Laudian peers and gentry – prominent among them the earls of Warwick and Bedford and their clients and colleagues Oliver St John and John Pym.[98]

We do not know whether Cromwell's links with Welles preceded or followed his departure for St Ives. Nor do we know on behalf of whom he is writing. We can be fairly sure that 'Mr Storie' is George Storie, a Mercer with strong New England ties.[99] In a postscript, Cromwell asks to be remembered to 'Mr Basse, Mr Bradley and my other good friends'.[100] Mr Bradley cannot be identified, but Mr Basse is almost certainly the Mercer sent as one of the company's representatives to attend Charles I over the nomination of Beard to the Fishbourne lectureship.[101]

It seems likely that the Godmanchester lecture was tied up in some way to the Fishbourne lecture. There was a separate Fishbourne charity in Godmanchester – ten shillings a year to support four poor widows – and the revenue for this bequest came from a piece of land

95. Turnbull, *Hartlib, Dury and Comenius*, p. 230.
96. Sheffield Univ. Lib., Hartlib MS 33/3/1b–2a
97. Turnbull, *Hartlib, Dury and Comenius, p. 236.* For Welles' inclusion in a list of petitioners on behalf of Dury which reads like a roll-call of 1630s puritanism, see B. L. Sloane, MS 1465, fo. 2.
98. Trevor-Roper, 'Three Foreigners', pp. 256, 258. The links are strongest with the Warwick circle. See also B. L. Addit. MS 4276, fos. 176.
99. J. K. Hosmer (ed.) *Winthrop's Journal* (2 vols, New York, 1908,, I, p. 64; *Records of the Court of Assistants of Massachusetts Bay, 1630–92* (1904), II, pp. 117–19.
100. Abbott, I, 81.
101. Mercers Hall, Acts of Court 1625–31, fo. 275; J. R. Woodhead, *The Rulers of London* (1965), p. 25 and P.R.O., E179/251/22, E179/272/36, show him to be a liveryman in the company living in Cheapside.

in the neighbouring parish of Hartford, of which Cromwell was lay impropriator.[102]

There are other elusive links. Thomas Edwards referred to the Godmanchester lecture when he opposed Beard's appointment.[103] Perhaps the Godmanchester lecture was a by-product of Beard's unpopularity with some in the 1620s (Welles and Beard lectured on the same days and at the same times). More likely, individual Mercers undertook to support Welles after the threat to silence the pulpits in Huntingdon.

With the death of Beard, the All Saints lecture appears to have lapsed. That left the Fishbourne lecture on Saturday mornings and Sunday afternoons. The first lecturer, Robert Procter, died or left after only a few months and was replaced by Dionice Squire, of whom little is known other than that he was lecturer at St Leonard's, Shoreditch, in the 1620s and was left £30 in Fishbourne's will.[104] This appointment alarmed both Williams and Laud: the Mercers had set up the lecture 'with a proviso . . . that upon any dislike they have of him, he shall at a month or a fortnight's warning, give over the place, without any relation to bishop or archbishop'. Laud consulted the king who ordered the lectureship suppressed: 'for I would have no priest have any necessity of a lay dependency.'[105] Williams assured Laud that the lectureship would be suppressed until the Mercers agreed both that the bishop should approve their nominee and that the bishop alone could silence the man appointed.[106] It has always been assumed that the lecture was thereupon suppressed; but it was not so. Squire died within weeks of Williams' letter to Laud, and yet the company proceeded to a new and particularly controversial appointment, John Poynter.[107] He had been in trouble with High Commission for holding a lectureship while unlicensed in London (he was discovered soon after Laud arrived in that diocese) and he had recently been a lecturer in Warwickshire in the midst of a particularly godly circle.[108] Despite this, and despite holding a lec-

102. *V. C. H., Hunts.*, III, p. 296.
103. Mercers Hall, Acts of Court 1625–31, fo. 248r.
104. P.R.O., PROB 11/145, fo. 464.
105. *Laud's Works*, V, p. 321
106. Ibid., VI, pp. 348–52.
107. His selection (in 12 August 1634) is discussed in Mercers Hall, Acts of Court 1631–37, fo. 131r. During the interval, the company paid for seven short-listed lecturers to preach to them (Mercers Hall, Fishbourne Bequest, Monies Received and Paid, 1627–56, fo. 34r).
108. P. Seaver, *The Puritan Lectureships* (Stanford, 1970), pp. 176, 179, 246–7; *Calamy Revised*, pp. 397–8; A. Hughes, *Politics, Society and Civil War in Warwickshire, 1620–1660* (Cambridge, 1987), p.73.

tureship without holding a living – in direct contravention of the instructions regarding lecturers issued in 1633[109] – he remained in post until after Williams himself had been sequestered from his bishopric and locked in the Tower in 1638.[110]. Only then was the Fishbourne lecture suspended. Cromwell's continuing connection both with Huntingdon and with the Mercers is confirmed by a cryptic entry in the Mercers' register[111] for early 1640 recording a visit by Cromwell and William Spurstowe (one of those the company sent to the king to lobby against Beard in 1630, and one with decidedly puritan leanings).[112] The visit was expressly to help to get Poynter reinstated.

It seems improbable that it was purely coincidental that some Mercers were privately funding the Godmanchester lectureship when the public lecture at St Mary's was threatened with suspension; and that Cromwell's name crops up so frequently in connection with the company. But the evidence gives out on us. Too many pieces of the jigsaw are missing for its overall shape to be determined.

Cromwell's friends among the Mercers had connections into the circle of alienated magnates around the earls of Bedford and Warwick and Viscount Saye and Sele who were prominent in obstructing the Personal Rule in Church and State, who were active in puritan colonial ventures, and who were planning to bring Charles' government under strict aristocratic control if and when the opportunity provided itself.[113] Cromwell's own links look strongest with Warwick, whose power base lay in Essex. The Barringtons (close political allies) and the Bourchiers (tenants on one of their manors) were at the heart of that circle, and Cromwell hinted in his letter to Mrs St John that family patronage had procured places for his sons at Felsted School (with its strong Warwick connections. Warwick's close personal interest in the school and other hints in Felsted sources

109. E. Cardwell, *Documentary Annals of the Reformed Church of England* (2 vols, Oxford, 1839), II, p. 178.
110. The suspension seems to have lasted for six months in 1638 and for a further eighteen months from Michaelmas 1639 to early 1641 (P.R.O., SP 16/390/25 and 25.I; SP 16/540/403; and Mercers Hall, Fishbourne Accounts 1627–56, *passim*.
111. Mercers Hall, Acts of Court, 1637–41, fo. 203r–v.
112. M. F. Keeler, *The Long Parliament* (Philadelphia, 1955), pp. 346–7. Spurstowe was clearly linked to the parish of St Stephen's, Coleman Street and to its godly ministers John Davenport and John Goodwin. He was a major investor in the Massachusetts Bay Company (V. Pearl, *London and the Outbreak of the Puritan Revolution* [Oxford, 1964],pp. 75, 169, 194n).
113. For a major reassessment of this question see, J. S. A. Adamson, 'The Baronial Context of the English Civil War', *T.R.H.S.*, 5th ser., XL (1990), forthcoming.

strengthen the connection).[114] There are also links between Cromwell and Viscount Saye and Sele via the schoolmaster of Felsted, Martin Holbeach, and via the St Johns.[115] As John Adamson shows below,[116] that is the group with whom he was to closely associate from 1642 onwards. He may have been completely on the fringes, an obscure cousin of some close friends of great men. But, piling speculation on speculation, what has survived may just be the fragmentary remains of a more central role within one or both circles. For we have yet to confront the greatest of all puzzles of his early life: his return to parliament as burgess for the city of Cambridge in the elections of 1640.

VIII

Ever since 1558 (and probably from much earlier) only two types of men were returned as burgesses for Cambridge: the majority were senior members of the corporation, including recorders; a minority were nominees of successive High Stewards of the town, invariably the Lord Chancellor or Lord Keeper.[117] In the 1620s, for example, Lord Keepers Bacon and Coventry had nominated the clerk of the Privy Council, Thomas Meautys (and in 1626 Coventry had also secured the second seat for his secretary). More often than not the recorder held the other seat.[118]

Cromwell's return to both parliaments in 1640 – in the spring as an apparently uncontested partner for Meautys, in the autumn in a contest in which he and a puritan councilman, John Lowry, defeated the Lord Keeper's brother as well as Meautys – is thus very surprising. No evidence throwing light on this contest appears to survive in the local records.[119] We know that he was made a freeman of the borough on 7 January 1640 [120] (after the election was called and

---

114. Craze, *Felsted*, pp. 27, 50–64. Sons of tenants were given priority at the school under the deed of foundation. It seems plausible that this would be extended to the sons of daughters of tenants; the hint in Abbott, I, 97, seems to be to Masham influence.
115. Ibid.; Holbeach's family came from Saye manors near Banbury.
116. See below, pp. 55–65.
117. P. Hasler (ed.), *History of Parliament: the House of Commons 1558–1603* (3 vols, 1981), I, pp. 121; *V.C.H., Cambs.*, III, pp. 68–76.
118. Ibid.; J. K. Gruenfelder, *Influence in early Stuart Elections 1603–1640* Columbus, Ohio, 1981), pp. 5, 23n.
119. The story told by Heath, *Flagellum*, pp. 81–2, was discredited by Cooper, *Annals of Cambridge*, III, pp. 296–304. Abbott's assertion (I, 109) that the election was 'hard fought and bitter' is pure fabrication.
120. Sanford, *Studies*, p. 267.

before the writs arrived). But it is surely too glib to say, as W.C. Abbott did, that:

He was now forty years old, at the height of his vigour and capacity, hardened by active outdoor life, a man of substance and position, well-known in the community, with wide relationships through his family, business and church associates. He had much experience as a landowner and grazier, as a burgess of Huntingdon and a member of parliament, as a lessee of cathedral lands and in the fen dispute. He had developed his talents as a speaker . . . to this he joined a a sense of leadership, deep sympathy with those who seemed to him oppressed, and confidence in his cause and himself.[121]

In fact he was an estate manager only recently recovered from a spell as a yeoman, with a troubled medical record and less credentials for eloquence and as an upholder of the oppressed than this assumes. He had neither the substance, nor the record of achievement, to be able to stand on his own account for parliament. It is hard to think of any other MP with an income as low as £300 who was not either a councilman serving for his own borough or a client imposed on a borough by a noble patron. The absence of any letters (other than those of Lord Keeper Finch) in the borough records makes it seem unlikely that he was nominated by a peer.[122] In any case the city would probably have resisted direct attempts by 'strangers' to interfere. It may just be the case that it was not the patronage brought to bear on his behalf, but the patronage that his return would bring to the town that explains his election. Cambridge had many grievances, especially against the university (for tuning its pulpits, for example). It might hope that these grievances could be addressed in parliament. If so, it would be faced by the opposition of the Chancellor of the University, the earl of Holland, no friend to the Laudians, but a courtier and a man jealous of the privileges of the university. If Cromwell was perceived as a man who could pull strings with Holland's elder brother, the earl of Warwick, his return becomes more explicable. There is one shred of evidence which, if it is reliable, gets us beyond the circumstantial into a definite connection. But it is from an unsatisfactory source, a day book compiled in the 1690s.[123] The author, a dissenter broadly sympathetic to the

---

121. Abbott, I, 109–10.
122. Cooper, *Annals*, III, 296–9, 303–4.
123. B. L., Addit. MS 4460, fo. 74v. The catalogue describes this as 'extracts from the day books of Dr Henry Sampson, 1693–8', and gives Sampson's immediate informant as the nonconformist minister John Howe.

memory of the parliamentarian cause, recorded the following story, which he may have heard from Oliver St John in his old age[124]:

> . . . the true cause of the calling the Long Parliament thus: at the dissolution of the former short parliament the members both Lords and Commons had a great opinion that the king's affairs ere long would necessitate him to call them together again, therefore such as resided about London met together frequently and gave intelligence by Mr Samuel Hartlib and Mr Frost to those in the country of affairs. Ere long, they gave a more general summons to come all up, who not only came themselves but brought up also such country gentlemen as they could confide in, amongst the rest Mr Oliver St John brought with him Mr Oliver Cromwell, the first public meeting this gentlemen ever appeared at. They agreed to send down a petition to the King at York, subscribed by twenty Lords and above 40 Commons to pray him to call a parliament, that 2 Lords and 4 Commons of their number should carry it down, the Lords pitched upon the earl of Essex and Lord Howard of Escrick, the names of the Commons I have forgotten but Cromwell I am sure was the last & Essex plainly refused to go.

The late dating and the uncertain source make this highly suspect. Yet some of the detail – such as the references to Hartlib and Gualter Frost, and the unexpected prominence accorded to Howard of Escrick – gives it plausibility. The background to the petition of the twelve peers and the secret meetings that preceded the petition (in which both Warwick and Saye took leading roles) was not widely reported in the late seventeenth century. It is a tantalizing source, but can only be offered here as a spur to further thought and research: a suggestion and no more.

IX

This thesis about Cromwell's links with the leading oppositionists in the late 1630s can be taken forward by looking at his actions and contacts in the first two years of the Long Parliament. In fact, the evidence points two ways. In the next essay, John Adamson argues that 'there is little evidence that Cromwell was an effective collaborator, much less a client, of any major figure in either house', and he portrays him as a loner, a man who met with little success in his gauche interventions into the high politics of 1641. Such an interpretation clearly carries much weight.[125] But it is possible to put a slightly different gloss upon his evidence, one which fully acknow-

---

124. Between this and the following (connected) entry about the Attempt on the Five Members, Sampson records: 'this from my Lord Chief Justice St John's own mouth'.
125. See below, pp. 51–2.

ledges Cromwell's incompetence while still seeing him as jobbing
for a powerful faction.

Cromwell was immediately visible and at the heart of controversy
in the Long Parliament. In its first week he presented John Lilburne's
petition for a review of Lilburne's conviction and sentence for printing and distributing unlicensed (puritan) pamphlets; he was added to
the powerful committee – including Pym, Hampden, Holles and St
John – already investigating the case of the first of the 'puritan' martyrs of Star Chamber, Robert Leighton; and to a series of other
committees investigating ecclesiastical tyranny and innovation.[126] In
all he sat on eighteen committees in the first session of the Long
Parliament.[127]

How did this come about? Why should Lilburne entrust a man
who had hardly ever spoken before with his petition unless he was
seen as someone with powerful friends? Was the case of so controversial a firebrand deliberately handed by someone of importance to
someone not too closely identified with him? We should remember
that Lilburne was flogged and incarcerated for helping to promote
John Bastwicke's *Letany* and that Bastwicke's petition to both the
Short and Long Parliaments was introduced by Pym.[128] Bastwicke
may also have been at the centre of the struggle for power at Colchester between the factions of the earl of Warwick and Sir John
Lucas.[129] Was it Cromwell's own idea to move the second reading
of the annual parliaments bill (which became the Triennial Act)?[130]
It also seems unlikely that a loner and a wholly unreliable member
would be found so prominently involved in the bill for the abolition
of episcopacy root and branch in May 1641 (he and Sir Henry Vane –
another Massachusetts link and a man very close to oppositionist
leaders – handed a draft to Sir Arthur Haselrig who briefed Sir Ed-

---

126. W. Notestein (ed.), *The Journal of Sir Simonds D'Ewes from the beginning of the
    Long Parliament to the opening of the trial of the Earl of Strafford* (New Haven, 1923),
    p. 19; *C.J.*, II, 24, 44, 52, 54, 56. It should be added that the cases of the puritan
    victims of Star Chamber were soon forgotten or laid on one side.
127. Firth, *Cromwell*, pp. 48–9
128. J. Maltby (ed.) *The Short Parliament Diary of Sir Thomas Aston*, Camden
    Society, 4th ser., xxxv (1988, p. 109; Notestein, *D. Ewes*, p. 4. For Bastwicke's
    close ties with Lilburne, see F. Condick, 'The Life and Works of Dr John
    Bastwicke', Univ. of London Ph.D. thesis, 1984, pp. 90–4, 147.
129. Ibid., pp. 57–60, 317–26. For Bastwicke's links with Dury (from his days in
    Leiden), and Hartlib, ibid., p. 40.
130. Notestein, *D'Ewes*, p. 196. It had been introduced six days earlier by William
    Strode (ibid., p. 188n).

ward Dering who actually introduced it).[131] It was Cromwell who flew kites that the earl of Essex be appointed as Lord General *by ordinance* in August 1641 and October 1641 (though without getting anywhere), but whose return to the subject of parliamentary control of the militia in January 1641 led to the setting up of the committee that produced the Militia Ordinance.[132] Certainly many of his speeches were counter-productive. His contemptuous comments on episcopacy in February 1641 almost led to him being called to the Bar of the House – a kind of parliamentary excommunication, as D'Ewes saw it, usually reserved for those who challenged the rights of the Houses to act *ultra vires*.[133] His intemperate outbursts against the Montagus' witnesses in the Fenland disputes' committee also almost led to his getting into trouble.[134] He had all the appearance of an unguided missile not really under ground control. Such a missile could be useful when ideas were to be floated: a kind of parliamentary forlorn hope. He was a man who could be trusted not to waiver on committees concerned with the destruction of Laudianism and on other issues on which the House of Commons was not divided. But, as his intemperacy in the February debates on root and branch reform made clear, he was not to be trusted when tact, sensitivity and gradualism were required. Thus on issues essential to the reformers progress but likely to be deeply divisive, he kept (was kept?) silent. He did not speak in the debates on Strafford, on the Grand Remonstrance, on the Militia Ordinance (once it was up and running), on the Nineteen Propositions.

X

By the spring of 1642, Cromwell was one of those 'violent spirits' given to 'agitation' and 'asperity' who so alarmed the conservative, respectable puritan-parliamentarianism of Sir Simonds D'Ewes.[135]

---

131. Sir Edward Dering, *A Collection of Speeches* (1642), p. 62; Abbott, I, 128–9.
132. W. H. Coates (ed.), *The Journal of Sir Simonds D'Ewes from the first recess of the Long Parliament to the withdrawal of King Charles from London* (New Haven, 1942), p. 145; W. H. Coates, A. S. Young, V. F. Snow (eds.), *The Private Journals of the Long Parliament, 3 January to 5 March 1642* (New Haven, 1982), pp. 67, 551–5. *L.J.*, IV, 625–7.
133. Notestein, *D'Ewes*, 339–41.
134. Abbott, I, 130–2; Edward Hyde, *The Life of Edward, Earl of Clarendon* (3 vols, Oxford, 1761), I, p. 78.
135. V. Snow and A. S. Young (eds), *The Private Journals of the Long Parliament, 7 March 1642–1 June 1642* (New Haven, 1987), pp. xxiii.

There was a notable increase in his prominence.[136] As the country slid into civil war, he was one of those who grasped nettles, took the initiative, as Austin Woolrych shows in his account of how Cromwell energized the militias of his home counties. The years of doubt and depression, impotent impulsiveness and provincial obscurity, lay behind him. In 1642 Cromwell was no republican, and probably not a religious libertarian. He would still have believed that an authoritarian national Church could be created, answerable to God's will. He could still look to the Scots as exemplars. The war was to change all that. But while other godly men who went to war to reform the Reformation fell away in despair as puritanism disintegrated and as parliamentary tyranny came to replace royal tyranny, Cromwell became ever clearer as to his task. If God willed the destruction, the overturning of all the landmarks of Church and State, then his trust would not be shaken. He had told Mrs St John that:

I live in Mesheck (which they say signifies *prolonging*; in Kedar, which signifieth *blackness*: yet the Lord forsaketh me not. Though He do prolong yet He will (I trust) bring me to his tabernacle, to His resting place. My soul is with the congregation of the firstborn, by body rests in hope . . .[137]

If the speculations in this chapter are at all reliable, Cromwell went through a dark night of the soul in the years 1629–31: he was stripped of all the pretensions and all the comforts of rank, honour and standing. Yet God had then shown him the purpose of that suffering, had taught him to trust Him. In a sense, what Cromwell had gone through in those vital years was what England was to go through in the years around 1649. Then, too, there was a descent into a national hell as old certainties collapsed and structures crumbled. Cromwell's view of God's plan for England was to remain malleable and ever-changing. But his knowledge that God *had* a plan for England and that he was part of that plan sustained him through war in three kingdoms and through a political career that brought him via regicide to the very edge of the throne itself. The personal faith of the man who was to be Lord Protector of England, Scotland and Ireland had been forged in the crucible of a deep personal crisis that is almost but not completely lost to us. The records of his making tell us little: but they tell us enough.

---

136. Ibid., p. xviii.
137. Abbott, I, 96–7. The reference to Mesheck and Kedar is to Psalm 120v. 5 (biblical wildernesses) and to 'the congregation of the firstborn' is to Hebrews 12 v. 23 (in the Geneva translation) and means the elect of Christ.

CHAPTER THREE

Oliver Cromwell and the Long Parliament

J. S. A. Adamson

I

'I profess I could never satisfy myself of the justness of this war,'
Cromwell wrote in 1644, 'but from the authority of the parliament
to maintain itself in its just rights, and in this cause I hope to approve
myself an honest man, and single-hearted.'[1] In 1644, in the midst of
the civil war, when God's 'providences' lit the way for Israel in her
struggle against the Midianite, the Long Parliament and 'the cause'
had seemed in self-evident harmony. Yet it was preservation of 'this
glorious cause' that ultimately led Cromwell to bring that parliament
to its peremptory end[2]: 'the whole weight of this cause', he assured
Barebone's Parliament in 1653, '. . . did hang upon' his dissolution
of that assembly.[3] The cause and the authority of the Long Parliament had apparently become irreconcilable. Thereafter, successful
parliamentary management consistently eluded the Lord Protector.
Time and again he threatened and admonished, hectored and cajoled.
Each attempt to invoke the authority of parliament to buttress
the protectoral regime ended in failure and recrimination, and
Cromwell's wrathful invocations of divine displeasure.

Cromwell's attitudes to parliament and its authority were formed
not as Lord Protector, but as burgess for Cambridge – the con-

1. Abbot, I, 292: Cromwell to Colonel Valentine Wauton, 5 Sept. 1644, I am grateful to the editor and to Dr Blair Worden and Professor the Earl Russell for
   reading and commenting upon an earlier draft of this essay; Mr Christopher
   Thompson also kindly provided a number of valuable suggestions and references.
2. *Declaration by the Lord General and the Council on the Dissolution of the Long Parliament* (22 April 1653), printed in S.R. Gardiner (ed.), *Constitutional Documents
   of the Puritan Revolution 1625–1660* (Oxford, 3rd edn, 1906), p. 402.
3. Abbott, III, 56: speech to Barebone's Parliament, 4 July 1653.

stituency he represented in the Long Parliament until 1653. How did the experience of that parliament shape his attitudes to its powers and 'the cause' which it claimed to champion? How did his career as a parliament-man affect his career as a soldier? And can we explain what is perhaps the central paradox of Cromwell's career: that the burgess for Cambridge, who rose to power as the servant of the Long Parliament, who repeatedly affirmed his subservience to its authority, should come to be the executor of its dissolution – the act which seemed later to have troubled his conscience far more than the execution of the king.

II

Cromwell's transition from nonentity to statesman in the Long Parliament owed as much to the managerial skill of his parliamentary allies as it did to the providential dispensations of Jehovah. He came to Westminster in November 1640 without reputation, with little parliamentary knowledge, and with apparently meagre instincts for its acquisition. During the 1630s, he had been on the fringes of the aristocratic puritan circle of the earl of Warwick, Viscount Saye and Sele and Lord Brooke; and he had connections by marriage with such influential MPs as Oliver St John – Saye's counsel in the Ship Money case of 1637 – and John Hampden.[4] From the start of the session the resolutions he espoused, and the issues he spoke to, were closely congruent with the agenda of godly reformation promoted by the 'interests' of such magnates as the earls of Essex, Warwick and Bedford, and by Viscount Saye and Sele – the figure who was to be, at least until the regicide, perhaps his most effective parliamentary ally. As early as August 1641, it was Cromwell who moved for the appointment of Saye and the 5th earl of Bedford as guardians of the Prince of Wales[5]; and as the crisis over control of the militia loomed during the winter of 1641–42, it was Cromwell who urged, earliest

4. S. J. Weyman, 'Oliver Cromwell's Kinsfolk', *E.H.R.*, VI (1891), 48–60. The notes in the B.L. of the anecdotes of John Coppendale of Morley (the son of one of Fairfax's officers) relate the story that St John brought Cromwell to a meeting of the 'commonwealth' peers – including Bedford, Essex, Warwick and Saye — during the autumn of 1640. This is plausible; but as the story dates from after 1690, it is impossible to accept it without further evidence to support it. B.L., Add. MS 4460 (Birch MS), f. 74v. Cf. above, pp. 44–6.
5. B.L., Harl. MS 6424 (diary of John Warner, bishop of Rochester), fo. 89v–90 (9 Aug. 1641). Anthony Fletcher, *The Outbreak of the English Civil War* (1981), pp. 58–9. For other nominations to offices of State, see *L.J.*, IV, 355.

and loudest, that supreme military command should be vested in the earl of Essex.[6]

For the godly in both houses, such men were the natural leaders of reform. During the early years of the Long Parliament few, if any, saw the likely outcome of the conflict with the king as the creation of a *parliamentary* government. Regular parliaments would provide a check on the executive. But when a settlement was eventually reached – either by negotiation or by war – men such as Cromwell expected power to reside in a reformed Privy Council, and expected that council to be largely composed of the greater nobility and their clients and allies: men such as Essex, in whom Cromwell sought to repose the kingdom's military power, and Saye, in whom he tried to vest the education of the future king. Cromwell had experienced, to his cost, the power of the nobility in the localities and at Westminster in disputes with the Montagus of Kimbolton, earls of Manchester, in the early 1630s; he was to experience it again in 1644. Political realism dictated a respect for their influence, and a desire to work with like-minded members of the House of Lords was a hallmark of Cromwell's parliamentary career. In 1649 he berated the purged House of Commons as 'mad' for abolishing the House of Lords; in 1657 – when he was courting the support of the nobility for the Protectorate – he could deride the Rump Parliament for having arrogated to itself 'the authority of the three estates'.[7]

With the managers of two of those estates in the Long Parliament – with such men as Pym and Strode in the Commons, and Essex and Saye in the Lords – Cromwell pursued common ends, and was fired by a common puritan zeal for godly reformation. Yet before the outbreak of the war, there is little evidence that Cromwell was an effective collaborator, much less a client, of any major figure in either house. Nor was there any reason to suppose anyone should want Cromwell's collaboration. His turbid and lachrymose rhetoric (dropping 'tears down with his words') attracted attention from early in the session.[8] He added his voice to the demand for annual parliaments, seconding a bill which had been introduced by William

6. W. H. Coates (ed.), *The Journal of Sir Simonds D'Ewes [12 Oct. 1641–10 Jan. 1642]* (New Haven, Conn., 1942), pp. 97–8 (6 Nov. 1641).
7. Bodl. Lib., MS Clarendon 34, fo. 73v. Abbott, IV, 487–8. *The Character of the Late Upstart House of Lords* (1659), pp. 31–4. Among those peers whom Cromwell summoned to his 'upper house' were Saye, Wharton, Warwick and Manchester.
8. G. S. [Sir Giles Strangeways?], *A Letter from an Ejected Member . . . to Sir Jo: Evelyn* (16 Aug. 1648), p. 6.

Strode.[9] He discoursed on the barbarities inflicted on such puritan 'martyrs' as Leighton and Lilburne. But he was, as Hyde later remarked, 'little taken notice of'.[10]

Hyde's remark requires qualification. After the Irish Rebellion, and the change of mood it brought in its wake, the House appears to have regarded Cromwell's plain-speaking zealousness with a more indulgent eye. Yet what distinguishes many of Cromwell's early parliamentary initiatives was that he frequently spoke as a lone voice, ineffectively seconded, if at all. And he met with little success. Lilburne had to wait until 1646 – when his case was taken up by Cromwell's friend, Lord Wharton – before his Star Chamber fine was discharged and compensation awarded him. Leighton was still waiting for compensation in 1647, and it is doubtful whether he received compensation at all.[11] Cromwell's motion to appoint Saye and Bedford as guardians of the Prince of Wales failed for want of a seconder. And his own support as a seconder could prove to be a questionable asset. In October 1641, the younger Sir Henry Vane's attempts to trump up charges against thirteen bishops – thereby excluding them from the House of Lords – almost foundered on the legal scruples provoked by Cromwell's naive revelation of the political motivation for the charge. Sir Simonds D'Ewes, who was at first in favour of Vane's motion to sequester the bishops from the Lords, felt constrained to speak against the motion after Cromwell's bungled and undiplomatic speech as its seconder.[12]

Other interventions reveal an ability to misread the mood of the House, and to jeopardize his parliamentary initiatives through simple errors of tact. Cromwell's motion that the Commons should appoint John Moore to write a reply to a libel by Sir Edward Dering (in which Cromwell was among those defamed), was made without any consultation with his intended author, and at the end of an arduous day's debate. It earned from Moore the terse reply that 'I conceived

9. W. Notestein (ed.), *The Journal of Sir Simonds D'Ewes* (New Haven, Conn., 1923), pp. 188n, 196–7. See also, Pauline Croft, 'Annual Parliaments and the Long Parliament', *Bull. Inst. Hist. Res.*, LIX (1986), 155–171.
10. Edward Hyde, earl of Clarendon, *The History of the Rebellion*, ed. W. D. Macray (6 vols, Oxford, 1888), I, 419 (Book IV, §§ 51–2).
11. *C.J.*, II, 903, 974; H.L.R.O., MP 13/2/47. D. Butler, *The Life and Letters of Robert Leighton* (1903), p. 45. (I owe this last reference to Miss Sheila Lambert.)
12. Coates (ed.), *The Journal of Sir Simonds D'Ewes*, p. 40. For the political background to the attempts to remove bishops from the House of Lords, see J. S. A. Adamson, 'Parliamentary Management, Men-of-Business and the House of Lords, 1640–49', in C. Jones (ed.), *A Pillar of the Constitution: the House of Lords in British Politics 1640–1784* (1989), pp. 21–9.

that the gentleman . . . did not dream that it was now near seven of the clock at night, or else that he would not at this time have made such a motion . . . for . . . I have other things to print of more public use and benefit than the confutation of Sir Edward Dering's speech could be'.[13] Rebuffs and disappointments abounded. The Root and Branch Bill for the abolition of episcopacy, on which Cromwell laboured with Vane and Sir Robert Harley during the first six months of the parliament, was never even sent up to the Lords. His optimism, reported by Hyde, in November 1641 that 'very few would oppose' the Grand Remonstrance – the catalogue of Charles I's misdeeds during the Personal Rule – was shattered when the motion to approve it produced one of the most rancorous debates of the session.[14]

Where Cromwell met with his first real successes was in the preparation for war. From as early as May 1641, the parliamentary diarists note Cromwell as among the members most concerned with parliament's vulnerability to the royal army not yet demobilized after the Scottish war of the previous year. The survival of parliament, and the godly reformation which Cromwell hoped it would effect, depended on its ability to ensure its defence. The army plot of May 1641 – in which the king appeared complicit in a conspiracy to use the army to overawe the parliament – moved him to support the creation of a defensive league, a Bond and Association, 'as was in the 27th year of Queen Elizabeth', to resist any attempt to overthrow parliament or the protestant religion by force.[15] And in the months between November 1641 and March 1642, Cromwell appears as an MP profoundly disquieted by the leniency shown to the plotters, and the favour men such as John Ashburnham and Will Morray continued to enjoy with the king. Cromwell complained that almost all the plotters had been released from the Tower on bail; he desired that their bail should be revoked and that they be remanded back to prison forthwith. His seconder on this occasion was Arthur Goodwin, the father-in-law of Lord Wharton, one of Cromwell's life-long friends in the House of Lords.[16]

---

13. W. H. Coates, A. S. Young and V, F. Snow (ed.), *The Private Journals of the Long Parliament: 3 Jan. to 5 Mar. 1642* (New Haven and London, 1982), p. 293 (hereafter abbreviated as *P.J.*, [I]).
14. Clarendon, *The History of the Rebellion*, I, 419 (Book IV, §§ 51–2). The text of the Grand Remonstrance is printed in Gardiner, *Constitutional Documents*, pp. 202–32.
15. B.L., Harl. MS 477 (John Moore's diary), fo. 28r–v (3 May 1641). The proposal for a Bond modelled on the Elizabethan precedent was made by Peard.
16. Coates (ed.), *D'Ewes's Diary*, p. 80; Goodwin was also Hampden's key ally (an

Indeed, to Cromwell, it was impossible to believe that the king had renounced the policy of using military force to violate the 'privileges of parliament' while such men as Morray and Ashburnham continued to enjoy royal favour and regard. Cromwell's anxieties about the army plotters and the use of force against parliament follow a parallel course to that of his proposals that power over the militia be in the hands of a Lord General who would uphold the authority of parliament. Two days after discovering that Ashburnham and his co-plotters were at liberty, Cromwell moved that the earl of Essex might have 'power to assemble at all times the trained bands of the kingdoms . . . for the defence thereof'.[17] In January 1642, in the days following the king's abortive attempt to arrest the five members and Lord Mandeville, all doubt as to the king's willingness to use force against the parliament was removed. On Cromwell's motion, a committee was established to consider the means of putting the kingdom into 'a posture of defence'. This committee was to produce Militia Ordinance, placing the military forces in the hands of the 'well affected' nobility of the kingdom, and precipitating a conflict over military control in the localities during the summer of 1642 which drove the nation into open civil war.[18]

When Cromwell returned to Cambridge to prepare for war in the summer of 1642,[19] he could point to his role in the creation of the Militia Ordinance as his signal parliamentary success. For all the rebuffs and humiliations of the previous two years at Westminster, the hopes of godly reformation as yet imperfectly realized, the Militia Ordinance enshrined his objective that the armed forces of the kingdom should be in the hands of those who would use them to uphold the authority of parliament. That was the principle which lay at the heart of what Cromwell referred to in 1644 as 'the cause', the principle which he had worked to establish in legislation over the winter of 1641–42. Both facts were fraught with irony for the future. The cause represented of course a broader programme of reform: the removal of coercive jurisdiction from the clergy; liberty

observation I owe to Professor the Earl Russell). For Cromwell's continuing concern over those associated with the plot, see his report from the House of Lords on 2 March 1642 concerning the examination of William Morray, one of the Grooms of the Bedchamber implicated in the Army Plot and in the Scottish 'Incident' during the king's stay in Scotland over the late summer. *P.J.* [I], 496.

17. Coates (ed.), *D'Ewes's Journal*, pp. 97–8 (6 Nov. 1641).
18. *P.J.* [I], 67, 551–5 (appendices H and I); *C.J.*, II, 379–80, 406, 432. *L. J.*, IV, 625–7.
19. *C. J.*, II, 674, 680, 720, 734; *L. J.*, V, 214. For Cromwell's role in the preparations for suppressing the Irish Rebellion, see *L.J.*, V, 241, 229–30.

of conscience within defined limits; parliamentary appointment of the great officers of state; and a reformed Privy Council. But the success – indeed, the possibility – of these reforms was contingent on maintenance of parliament's authority by force of arms. 'Religion', as Cromwell was later to remark, 'was not the thing at the first contested for.'[20]

III

From the time he took charge of the defence of Cambridge, in August 1642, until the royalist threat was finally extinguished at Worcester in September 1651, Cromwell's experience of the war alternated between two radically different environments. Attendance at parliament in Westminster alternated with service in parliament's armies in the field. Indeed, after he left Westminster in 1642, Cromwell was never again to spend so long a period in attendance at the House of Commons. Service in the field occupied him from August 1642 to January 1644; from February to November 1644; from March 1645 to July 1646; and despite the end of the war, he was with the army again for much of the period from April to December 1647. Military service against the royalist risings of the Second Civil War occupied him from April to November 1648; and except for a brief period in the summer of 1650, he was away from Westminster again fighting against the Irish and Scots from July 1649 to September 1651. Parliament was forcibly dissolved nineteen months later, in April 1653.

This catalogue represents more than the difference between Westminster and the field of battle; between civilian comfort and the austerities of the campaign. They were more than different physical environments, in which the role of the parliament-man was traded for that of the soldier. For between the two worlds there was a major disjunction between the success which met Cromwell's military enterprises and the failure which, in general, attended his parliamentary undertakings. Moreover, his experiences of life as a parliament-man and as a soldier with the army were correspondingly matched by profoundly different *spiritual* states, profoundly different apprehensions of what Cromwell spoke of as the nearness of God. In the field, the epic of Israel's redemption advanced bloodily and gloriously to its prophetically ordained end. Israel's cause was the parliament's cause. Cromwell's sense of certainty in the 'evidences'

20. Abbott, III, 586 (speech of 22 Jan. 1655); in context 'religion' here means religious liberty of conscience.

of the Lord's blessing grew with every successful skirmish, every battle won.[21] God was almost palpably immanent. There was the 'very signal appearance of God Himself . . .'. 'The Lord is very near, which we see by His wonderful works.'[22]

It was otherwise at Westminster. In place of the certitudes of battle, the assurance of victory through the 'mercy' of the Lord of Hosts, there were the equivocations and compromises, concessions and procrastinations, that were the stuff of parliamentary life. Brief and effective words of command were replaced by prolix and often fruitless debate. Proposals disappeared without trace amid the luxuriant undergrowth of committees and commissions. At Westminster, God was 'mock[ed]' with 'fine tricks'.[23] The 'ideological schizophrenia' Dr Worden has discerned in Cromwell's temperament – the subjective tension between the conservatism of his social and political instincts, and the 'spiritual radicalism' engendered by his introspective puritan piety – had its objective correlative in his disparate experiences of political and military life.[24] Cromwell led, quite literally, two parallel lives.

If Cromwell's parliamentary career was one undertaken in the interstices of military employment, how did military service affect and influence his standing and conduct in the Commons? What was Cromwell's experience as a parliament-man? And how did that experience inform his momentous decision, in April 1648, shortly after he survived an assassination attempt, to 'turn at God's reproof'? Whence followed his endorsement of the army's resolution to bring Charles I to account for the blood he had shed; and ultimately the purge of parliament, and the regicide.[25]

Military service endowed Cromwell with reputation and esteem in the Commons which contrasted sharply with the scant regard he had been accorded hitherto. 'Now he began to appear to the world',

21. Blair Worden, 'Oliver Cromwell and the Sin of Achan', in D. Beales and G. Best (ed.), *History, Society and the Churches: essays in honour of Owen Chadwick* (Cambridge, 1985), pp. 125–6.
22. Abbott, III, 54; II, 103–4.
23. Abbott, I, 430: Cromwell to Fairfax, [*c.* 12] Mar. 1647.
24. Blair Worden, *The Rump Parliament 1648–1653* (Cambridge, 1974), p. 69.
25. Christ Church Muniment Room. Oxford, Browne Letters (Evelyn collection), Box A–C: 'Φ' [i.e. William Pretyman] to Sir Richard Browne, letters of 6 and 13 April 1648. Worden, 'Oliver Cromwell and the Sin of Achan', p. 131, citing Abbott, II, 340 (l. 5); William Allen, *A Faithful Memorial of that remarkable Meeting of many Officers of the Army* ([27 April] 1659); Austin Woolrych, *Soldiers and Statesmen: the General Council of the Army and its Debates 1647–48* (Oxford, 1987), pp. 332–6.

Whitelocke noted in the summer of 1643, Cromwell's first campaigning season in the field.[26] London newsbooks extolled his talents as a commander. Conscious of the fruits of publicity, Cromwell cultivated links with John Dillingham, a former client of Lord Montagu of Boughton and editor of *The Parliament Scout*.[27] 'Reputation', Cromwell reminded the Committee of the Eastern Association, 'is of great advantage in our affairs.'[28] But in this respect Cromwell was an anomaly among his fellow soldier–MPs. Figures such as Hampden, Stapilton, Waller or Nathaniel Fiennes in the Commons, or Essex, Warwick and Brooke in the Lords, were all men of major influence in the parliament *before* they undertook service in the field. Cromwell's 'reputation' – both inside and outside of parliament – was the consequence of his military success. Although he rapidly became as familiar a figure in the newsbooks as Stapilton or Waller, in the early years of the war he did not enjoy influence in the Commons that was in any way commensurate with his renown as a commander in the field. At Westminster he had few allies, and fewer friends. 'If you lay aside the thought of me and my letter,' he wrote to Oliver St John, in September 1643, 'I expect no help.'[29]

The combination of this relative weakness in the Commons, and his military renown in the field, had a major effect on Cromwell's position in parliament. Through Oliver St John, Cromwell was drawn into the aristocratic political circle of St John's former patron, Viscount Saye and Sele, Lord Wharton, and their allies in the Commons: men such as the younger Vane (with whom Cromwell had collaborated on the Root and Branch Bill), Sir John Evelyn of Wiltshire, Saye's son Nathanial Fiennes, Henry Darley and John Gurdon. This group held to an interpretation of the cause which was close to Cromwell's own: the necessity for an 'absolute victory' over the king[30] as the prelude to the creation of a reformed and godly Privy Council, an Erastian Church settlement which permitted toleration of Independent congregations, and the holding of frequent parliaments. All this depended upon parliament winning that 'absolute victory', so that negotiation could begin from a position of over-

26. Bulstrode Whitelocke, *Memorials of the English Affairs* (4 vols, Oxford, 1853), I, 209.
27. John Lilburne, *Ionahs Cry out of the Whales Belly* (1647) p. 8 (B.L., E400/5); A. N. B. Cotton, 'John Dillingham, Journalist of the Middle Group', *E.H.R.*, XCIII (1978), 819–21.
28. Abbott, I, 256.
29. Abbott, I, 259: Cromwell to St John, 11 Sept. 1643.
30. Cf. Abbott, I, 287.

whelming strength. Effective military strategy was essential to the success of their political strategy. Cromwell and the political interest of Viscount Saye shared a common purpose. And that common purpose in secular politics was underpinned by a shared and intense puritan piety.

Such was the cause for which Cromwell fought. From the autumn of 1643, the time – in Whitelocke's phrase – that he 'began to appear to the world', Cromwell's political fortunes were intimately connected with those of Saye's and St John's parliamentary interest. As we shall see, Saye's patronage secured Cromwell's first appointment to parliament's powerful executive, the Committee of Both Kingdoms; this interest defended him in his dispute with the earl of Manchester over the winter of 1644–45; this same interest remained loyal to the New Model during 1647 when a precipitate disbanding of the armies threatened 'speedily and certainly' to 'reinvest the king with all'[31]; and it was Saye and Wharton who introduced legislation in the Lords to give the *Heads of the Proposals* legal force. This was the group which upheld the cause during the 1640s. All that changed in 1648. It was Cromwell's conviction in that year that this group had 'withdrawn' their 'shoulders' from the Lord's work through 'fleshly reasonings'[32] – that they had abandoned the cause of God – which led him to break the alliance which had hitherto sustained his parliamentary career. Characteristically, after the cataclysm of 1648–49 had occurred, Cromwell was to spend the last four years of the Long Parliament trying to piece together this alliance's shattered fragments.[33]

Like his faith in the 'providences' of God, Cromwell's faith in parliament had its origins in personal experience. From the first year of the civil war, his attempts to promote a more effective prosecution of the war in East Anglia dovetailed neatly with the efforts of the Saye and St John interest at Westminster to advance that policy nationally. Parliament was the means by which both sought to effect the necessary changes of personnel. At the local level, Cromwell wished to supplant the incompetent commander in Lincolnshire, Lord Willoughby of Parham, a protégé of the earl of Essex, with a commander who would ensure a more effective management of the

31. [Viscount Saye and Sele], *Vindiciae Veritatis* (1654), p. 42. Cf. John Rushworth to Ferdinando, Lord Fairfax, 9 June 1647: B.L., Add. MS 18979 (Fairfax corr.), fo. 238.
32. Abbott, I, 697; II, 189–90; cf. Zechariah, VII, 11.
33. Abbott, II, 189–90; Worden, *Rump*, p. 72.

war. At Westminster, Saye and his allies sought to curtail the powers of the commander-in-chief, Essex, suspecting he was opposed to bringing about that 'absolute victory' upon which their war-aims depended. In parliament, these two strategies converged in the last week of January 1644. Cromwell launched a stinging attack on Willoughby for indiscipline among his troops, fiscal mismanagement, and a dismal record of military failure. After a short but acrimonious tussle, Cromwell's motion that Willoughby 'might be ordered to stay here and to go no more' to Lincolnshire was approved. In place of the deposed Willoughby, the earl of Manchester was appointed to command[34] – part of a general campaign to reorganize the administration of the Eastern Association under the earl's control. For the moment, at least, Cromwell and Manchester were collaborating; their relationship had yet to be poisoned by the fierce controversy over the treatment of religious nonconformists within the army, a debate which was to rage over the summer and autumn of 1644.[35]

But the incident of Willoughby's removal from command had wider ramifications. Willoughby owed his commission to, and had been defended by, the Lord General, Essex. His dismissal had focused attention on the fact that it was Essex, not the parliament, to whom Willoughby was responsible for his conduct of the war, exactly at the time when Saye was planning to introduce legislation that would permanently usurp Essex's supremacy of command. Saye's bill for this new committee – to be composed of members of the two houses meeting with the Scots Commissioners as a 'Committee of Both Kingdoms' – was introduced on 1 February, the day Willoughby was committed to custody for challenging his successor to a duel.[36] Although the bill provoked a lengthy legislative battle in both houses, it became law three months later. And among the four-

---

34. B.L., Harl. MS 165 (D'Ewes's diary), fos. 230v–31r; *C.J.*, III, 373; *L.J.*, VI, 414. The local background to the incident is discussed in Clive Holmes, 'Colonel King and Lincolnshire Politics, 1642–1646', *H.J.*, XVI (1973), 451–84; and *idem*, *The Eastern Association in the English Civil War* (Cambridge, 1974), pp. 107–9.
35. Holmes, *Eastern Association*, pp. 108–9; cf. B.L., Add. MS 18779 (Walter Yonge's diary), fos 49v–50. (I am grateful to Mr Christopher Thompson for generously making available to me his transcription of this diary.)
36. *C.J.*, III, 503–4; David Laing (ed.), *The Letters and Journals of Robert Baillie* (3 vols. Edinburgh, 1841–42), II, 141; Gardiner, *Civil War*, I, 305; *L.J.*, VI, 405, B.L., Harl. MS 166 (D'Ewes's diary), fo. 64. Holmes, 'Colonel King and Lincolnshire Politics', pp. 458–9. See also, B.L., Harl. MS 2224 (Lord Robartes's notes of proceedings), fo. 15v: examination of Lord Willoughby, 3 Feb. 1644; *Mercurius Britanicus*, no. 32 (15–22 April 1644). For Willoughby's dependence upon Essex, Bodl. Lib., MS Tanner 62, fo. 232: Willoughby to Essex, 6 Aug. [1643].

teen members of the Commons appointed to the new committee was Oliver Cromwell. Significantly, he, like his colleague Oliver St John, owed his nomination not to the House of Commons, but to the House of Lords, where the list of members had been drawn up by Viscount Saye.[37]

This pattern of bi-cameral cooperation was replicated the following winter, with strikingly similar parliamentary tactics. The central issue remained the same: placing management of the war in hands that would ensure the prosecution of an 'absolute victory'. Without that, the cause – at least as defined by Saye, Cromwell and their allies – was doomed. As in the parliamentary manoeuvres that displaced Willoughby and established the Committee of Both Kingdoms, the moves to displace Essex and to 'new model' the army in the winter of 1644–45 began with an attack on an individual commander by Cromwell in the Commons. Debate was then focused on the general question of the conduct of the war.

The political manoeuvres which gave rise to the Self-Denying Ordinance – removing members of both houses from all civil and military offices, and deposing Essex as commander-in-chief – had their origins in the political initiatives of Cromwell's and Saye's opponents. During the autumn of 1644, Cromwell had been accused of commanding a regiment of Independents which would not fight if Presbyterianism was established in the Church.[38] At the same time Essex's men-of-business in the Commons – Robert Reynolds, Holles and Stapilton – had established a committee to 'consider of all the offices and places of benefit bestowed by the parliament . . . and to begin first with the places conferred upon members of each house'.[39]

---

37. His name follows St John's in the text of the bill: *C.J.*, III, 504; the text is printed in Gardiner, *Constitutional Documents*, pp. 273–4. B.L., Add. MS 18779 (Yonge's diary), fo. 61. Cf. the remarks of Dr Valerie Pearl who has argued unconvincingly that the measure was not intended as an attack on Essex's supremacy of command ('Oliver St John and the "Middle Group" in the Long Parliament: August 1643–May 1644', *E.H.R.*, LXXXI (1966), 511–15).

38. *The Parliament Scout*, no. 68 (10 Oct. 1644), p. 546. Baillie, *Letters and Journals*, II, 229–30. *Mercurius Civicus*, no. 79 (28 Nov. 1644), p. 731; *Perfect Occurrences*, no. 16 (29 Nov. 1644), pp. 2–3. A. N. B. Cotton, 'Cromwell and the Self-Denying Ordinance', *History*, LXII (1977), 219–20.

39. B.L., Add. MS 31116 (Whitaker's diary), fo. 174. *C.J.*, III, 695. For these three collaborating to defend Essex's interests, see Longleat House, Wilts., Whitelocke MS IX, fo. 27. Reynolds was a stalwart ally of Essex: he had opposed the Committee of Both Kingdoms bill in the Commons in February; in December, it was he who moved that Essex be excluded from the provisions of the Self-Denying Ordinance. B.L., Add. MS 31116 (Whitaker's diary) fos 113v, 180; *C.J.*, III, 726.

It was clearly intended to deter those who owed to Parliament their lucrative civil offices and perks – such boons as Saye's occupancy of the palatial Arundel House, and Vane's treasurership of the navy – from turning their attentions to Essex and Manchester who enjoyed their military offices by the same authority.

Cromwell's assault on his superior officer, the earl of Manchester, in November 1644 was a comprehensive political attack. It charged him with an 'averseness' to seeing the war fought to a definitive victory, a reluctance to press home the attack on the king's forces. From its beginning, the charges were also an implicit attack on the earl of Essex – a point which Cromwell made explicit in the Commons on 9 December.[40] Realizing himself to be under fire Essex managed the counter-attack on Cromwell from behind the arras. His allies in the Commons were summoned to a meeting at Essex House on 1 December. Only the consideration of 'the interest Cromwell had in the parliament and the army' deterred Holles and Stapilton from pressing ahead with impeachment proceedings against him in the lower house.[41] Mindful of this political 'interest', an alternative strategy was devised. In place of impeachment proceedings (which had to begin in the Commons), the attack on Cromwell was pressed home on the following day (Monday, 2 December), in the Lords.[42] Manchester's case against Cromwell had been meticulously prepared. The earl had been provided with 'leaked' copies of the evidence Cromwell planned to use against him[43]; and he retaliated with the (almost certainly false) charge of *scandalum magnatum* against Cromwell: that Cromwell had hoped 'to live to see never a nobleman in England'.[44] Holles, who had played such a major role in the cabals

40. Cotton, 'Cromwell and the Self-Denying Ordinance', p. 216.
41. Mount Stuart, Rothesay, Isle of Bute, Bute MS 196 D.13/i (Whitelocke's diary), fo. 70r–v. (I am grateful to Miss Ruth Spalding for making available to me her transcription of this diary.) Such meetings on Sundays at Essex House, for the coordination of policy in the coming week, became a regular aspect of Essex's political practice: see B.L., Add. MS 37344 (Whitelocke's Annals), fos 29, 31v. Cf. H.L.R.O., Willcocks MS 1: Essex to [Manchester], 23 Mar. 1645 (formerly Kimbolton castle, Manchester MS 573).
42. Kenneth Spencer Research Library, University of Kansas, MS P539:2, fos 1–6v (MS formerly at Kimbolton castle). Another version is in B.L., Loan MS 29/123/31, unfoliated. Manchester had first responded to Cromwell's charges in a speech presented to the Lords on 28 Nov. Cf. P.R.O., SP 21/8 (Committee of Both Kingdoms, Day Book), p. 20 (2 Dec. 1644).
43. Kenneth Spencer Research Library, University of Kansas, MS P 539:1, fos 1–3; (printed, with a number of errors of transcription in John Bruce [ed.], *The Quarrel between the Earl of Manchester and Oliver Cromwell*, Camden Soc. 1875, p. 97); formerly Kimbolton castle MS 556.
44. S.R. Gardiner (ed.), 'A Letter from the Earl of Manchester to the House of

at Essex House the previous evening, relayed Manchester's charges to the House of Commons.[45]

Against this background, Saye and his allies found the best form of defence to be attack, and began their campaign, in Saye's words, 'to new model the army, and put the command into other hands'.[46] Manchester's presentation of charges through Holles was declared a breach of the Commons' privileges[47] – a device which produced stalemate between the two houses. Manchester could proceed no further against Cromwell; Cromwell's assault on the earl was similarly checked; but, as the Commons' decision to declare Manchester's counter-charges a breach of privilege demonstrated, the dispute had strengthened Cromwell's standing in the lower house.[48] With his stock in the ascendant, the parliamentary group centred on Saye, Cromwell and Vane, launched their bold strategy intended '[to] put command into other hands'.[49] On Monday, 9 December, exactly a week after Manchester's counter-attack on Cromwell had been thwarted in the Commons, Cromwell proposed a resolution for 'self-denial': for all members of both houses to give up civil and military offices conferred by the parliament. While Cromwell was proposing the resolution in the lower house, Saye was moving the same resolution in the House of Lords – where it was immediately thrown out.[50] In the Commons, where the resolution was adopted, the proposal's seconder was Sir Henry Vane, whose collaboration with Saye in the previous February had vested management of the war in the Committee of Both Kingdoms.

Lords', *Camden Miscellany*, VIII (Camden Soc., 1883), 1–3 (printing Bodl. Lib., MS Tanner 61, fo. 205); Cotton, 'Cromwell and the Self-Denying Ordinance', p. 222.

45. Cotton, 'Cromwell and the Self-Denying Ordinance', pp. 222–3; *C.J.*, III, 713; B.L., Harl. MS 483 (D'Ewes's Latin diary), fo. 120; Abbott, II, 313.
46. [Saye], *Vindiciae Veritatis*, p. 52; Saye was writing in 1646.
47. B.L., Harl. MS 483 (D'Ewes's Latin diary), fo. 120.
48. Mount Stuart, Bute MS 196 D.13/i (Whitelocke's diary), fo. 70v. The decision not to risk impeaching Cromwell at the beginning of December reveals the extent to which Cromwell's standing in the lower house had improved since mid-November. Dr Cotton's contention ('Cromwell and the Self-Denying Ordinance', pp. 222–3), that Cromwell's position in the Commons remained extremely vulnerable throughout December and January is incompatible with Cromwell's successful sponsorship of legislation – particularly that for the appointment of Sir Thomas Fairfax as the Lord General to succeed Essex – and the lack of success which met Manchester's attempts to revive the charges against him.
49. [Saye], *Vindiciae Veritatis*, p. 52.
50. H.L.R.O., MS Minutes, XI (22 June 1644–3 Mar. 1645), unfol. [Saye], *Vindiciae Veritatis*, pp. 40–1, 53; John Vicars, *Magnalia Dei Anglicana. Or Englands Parliamentary-Chronicle* (1646), pp. 74–5, 130. P.R.O., SP 16/503, fos 140–82.

Over the winter, this same group successfully effected a parliamentary coup: in the division on the question to appoint Fairfax as Lord General in place of Essex, Cromwell and Sir John Evelyn were tellers for the ayes; it was Saye who secured the appointment in the upper house. The pattern of collaboration was repeated in the bi-cameral manoeuvres to establish the New Model Army and to pass, in a revised form, an ordinance for 'self-denial' which was acceptable to a majority in both houses. By such means, the absolute victory which would secure the cause – so Cromwell and his allies hoped – could now, at last, be obtained.

If the resolution for 'self-denial' was an advance for the cause, for Cromwell it also risked the end of his military career. As an MP, he would also be obliged to relinquish his commission as lieutenant-general of the Eastern Association. It was a risk, but perhaps a calculated one. If Cromwell and his allies lacked the parliamentary strength to push the self-denial legislation through the houses, the question of Cromwell's resignation need not necessarily arise. If, however, they commanded the necessary majorities in the two houses to gain acceptance for self-denial and the accompanying military reforms, then there was at least a strong possibility that a resolution, exempting Cromwell from the obligation to resign his commission, could also be passed. From the moment the self-denial resolution was introduced as legislation, on 14 December 1644, the question of exceptions was openly canvassed.

If Cromwell did hope to secure his exemption from the bill,[51] it is not difficult to see why the bill's managers did not attempt such a strategy at this point. A motion to exempt the earl of Essex – thereby leaving the supreme command of the armies unchanged – was defeated by Cromwell's allies only by a margin of seven votes at the end of a debate that had lasted an entire day.[52] To have included a clause exempting Cromwell in the body of the Self-Denying Ordinance would have left its proponents open to the charge of hypocrisy and self-interest, fatally undermining support for the bill.

---

51. The question has been much canvassed: S. C. Lomas (ed.), *The Letters and Speeches of Oliver Cromwell: with elucidations by Thomas Carlyle* (3 vols, 1904), I, 191, 196–7. Gardiner, *Civil War*, II, 91–2; III, 223n; R. S. Paul, *The Lord Protector: Religion and Politics in the Life of Oliver Cromwell* (Grand Rapids, Michigan, 1955), pp. 94–6; Cotton, 'Cromwell and the Self-Denying Ordinance'; Christopher Hill, *God's Englishman: Oliver Cromwell and the English Revolution* (Harmondsworth, 1972), p. 72. Cf. Abbott, II, 302–20.
52. B.L., Add. MS 31116 (Whitaker's diary), fos 113v, 180; *C.J.*, III, 726. The tellers against the motion were Cromwell's allies, the younger Vane and Sir John Evelyn.

Prudence dictated that any exemption should be deferred until the acrimony of the winter had subsided, and until it had been seen whether the legislation for 'new modelling' the army would pass the two houses – an outcome which was still far from certain in December 1644.

What is certain is that immediately before Cromwell's commission would have lapsed under the terms of the Self-Denying Ordinance, his allies attempted to secure him a permanent exemption from its provisions.[53] Commissions were only to remain valid for forty days after the date the bill passed the two houses – 3 April 1645. While Essex and Manchester had laid down their commissions as soon as passage of the bill became inevitable, Cromwell retained his commission, which – under the terms of the ordinance – remained valid until 12 May; moreover, during that period, he appears to have made no attempt to relinquish it.[54] Immediately before it was due to expire, his allies moved that he be continued 'in the imploym[en]t he is now in', without any time-limitation.[55] The proposal proved how controversial the question of exemption from the ordinance remained. By the time it passed the Commons, the proposal for a permanent exemption had been whittled down to a temporary ex-

---

53. H.L.R.O., MP 10/5/45, fo. 96.
54. The frequently repeated story that the reason for Cromwell's visit to Fairfax at Windsor on 22 April 1645 was to deliver up his commission seems to have no foundation in fact. The story that Cromwell 'thought of nothing less in the world' than remaining in military employment at this time first surfaces in 1647 in the highly partisan (and pro-Cromwellian) account of the New Model by Joshua Sprigge, *Anglia Rediviva* (1647), p. 10; cf. Paul, *The Lord Protector*, pp. 94–6; Hill, *God's Englishman*, p. 72. Sprigge was writing with a polemical purpose, to vindicate the New Model and its commanders – in particular, to counter the accusation that Cromwell's appointment was a breach of the Self-Denying Ordinance which had been planned in advance. Sprigge was, moreover, closely associated with Saye's political interest. He had been attached to Saye's household at Broughton castle during his youth, where his father was Saye's steward. Indeed, Sprigge's *Anglia Rediviva* was explicitly commended by Saye in a section (written in 1648) of his *Vindiciae Veritatis* (published in 1654). The passage of *Anglia Rediviva* in question mentions nothing of Cromwell's commission, but merely states that Cromwell had gone to Fairfax to 'kiss the General's hand and to take his leave of him' (ibid., p. 10). It is highly unlikely, had Cromwell intended to deliver up his commission, that he would have gone to Fairfax to present it; far more likely recipients would have been Manchester (by whom it had been granted), or the Army Committee chaired by Robert Scawen, which was administering the transition from Essex's to Fairfax's command. For Sprigge, see [Joshua Sprigge], *The Ancient Bounds. Or Liberty of Conscience* (1645), (incorrectly ascribed in Wing to Francis Rous: Wing R 2011); *D.N.B.*; for William, P.R.O., SP 28/261/1, fo. 3v; SP 28/264, fo. 227; WARDS 9/556, p. 766; P.R.O. (Kew), WO 55/1937; and Bodl. Lib., MS Rawlinson D892, fo. 332.
55. H.L.R.O., MP 10/5/45, fo. 96r.

emption valid only 'for forty days longer'[56] – subject to the review of both houses.[57] For the remainder of the Civil War, Cromwell never secured a permanent grant of leave of absence from the parliament. When his first period of exemption was due to expire in June, his friend Sir John Evelyn again moved that he be exempted without time limit, and that he be appointed lieutenant-general 'during the pleasure of both houses'.[58] Only Cromwell's status as a popular hero after Naseby (14 June),[59] forced Essex's group in the Lords to accept a further temporary extension for three months, from 18 June.[60] Further short-term extensions followed: on 12 August, for four months[61]; on 22 October (before the August grant had expired), for four months[62]; and on 26 January, for a further six months, a grant which covered Cromwell's tenure of military service until he returned to regular attendance in the Commons in July 1646.[63]

Thus Cromwell never received an unequivocal exemption from the provisions of the Self-Denying Ordinance. Fairfax was permitted to commission him as Lieutenant-General of the Horse – the New Model's second-in-command – after his spectacular success at Naseby; but he was only permitted to execute that commission 'so long as his attendance upon the House of Commons may be dispensed with' by the two houses.[64] Even after Naseby, the continuance of his position in the army hung by a thread; all was contingent on the parliamentary strength and factional fortunes of his allies at Westminster.

This had two major effects on Cromwell's relations with parliament. His political vulnerability effectively silenced his parliamentary voice for the remainder of the First Civil War. Second, it made him still further dependent on the 'honest party' at Westminster – upon Saye and Wharton in the Lords, and Vane, St John and Evelyn in

56. H.L.R.O., MP 10/5/45, fo. 96; the phrase is interlined in the original bill.
57. H.L.R.O., MP 10/5/45, fo. 96; *C.J.*, IV, 138; *L.J.*, VII, 364.
58. *C.J.*, IV, 176.
59. B.L., Add. MS 18780 (Yonge's diary), fos 38, 40.
60. *C.J.*, IV, 169–70, 176; *L.J.*, VII, 433; Gardiner, *Civil War*, II, 238. The Commons had earlier voted for Cromwell to be Lieutenant-General of the Horse 'during the pleasure of this house': B.L., Add. MS 18780 (Yonge's diary), fo. 40; Charles Hoover, 'Cromwell's Status and Pay in 1646–7', *H.J.*, XXIII (1980), 705.
61. H.L.R.O., MP 12/8/45, fos 84–5. *L.J.*, VII, 535.
62. H.L.R.O., MP 22/10/45, fos 150–1. The bill had originated in the Commons on 17 October, two days before the former extension was due to expire. *C.J.*, IV, 312.
63. H.L.R.O., MP 26/1/46, fo. 175. *L.J.*, VIII, 127. The measure had passed the Commons on the 23rd.
64. H.L.R.O., MP 8/5/45, fo. 34. Cf. *L.J.*, VII, 433.

the Commons – for the parliamentary measures that would advance the cause. Indeed, what Gardiner first noticed as Cromwell's extraordinary 'silence on [the] subject of liberty of conscience' throughout the first half of 1645[65] – and the infrequency of, and hostile response to, his public statements on the subject throughout 1645 and 1646 – testify to the precariousness of his political position.

For the protection of 'liberty of conscience' in the impending Church settlement, as for the changes in the management of the war, Cromwell had to rely on his like-minded brethren at Westminster. Moments of military success regularly provided Cromwell with the occasion for reminding parliament of its duty to 'tender consciences' – those 'godly' protestants who could not conform to a presbyterian settlement in the Church. Appeals were addressed to parliament after Marston Moor, after Naseby, and after the relief of Bristol in September 1645. In the Commons, these exhortations fell on stony ground. Such support as these appeals attracted was mustered in parliament by the select band of the aristocratic godly led by Saye, Wharton, St John and Vane.

Capitalizing on his prestige after Marston Moor, in September 1644 Cromwell had launched his proposal for 'accommodation' for Independents within the Presbyterian Church. As Robert Baillie noted to his chagrin, Cromwell's principal supporters were, again, Vane and St John in the Commons; Saye and Wharton were equally active in the Lords. Committees were appointed; plans for 'accommodation' were conceived; but Cromwell's presbyterian opponents saw to it that his 1644 proposal was still-born.[66]

In 1645, the House of Commons was scarcely better disposed to Cromwell's ecumenical zeal. But for his constituency of support in the House of Lords, Cromwell's renewed plea for 'liberty of conscience' in his letter to parliament after Naseby would have met with a similar fate. When, in June 1645, the Commons printed Cromwell's letter,[67] all references to the request for liberty of conscience were deliberately excised. In retaliation, his allies in the Lords (almost certainly alerted by Saye and Wharton), ordered a new printing of the letter in which Cromwell's plea for 'the people of God'

65. Gardiner, *Civil War*, II, 252.
66. Bodl. Lib., MS Carte 80 (Wharton papers), fos 178, 196. *C.J.*, III, 626. Baillie, *Letters and Journals*, II, 230. For the Commons' recognition of Cromwell as 'a special instrument in obtaining that great victory', see *C.J.*, III, 626–7.
67. Abbott, I, 359–60n: Cromwell to Lenthall, 14 June 1645.

(formerly deleted in the Commons' printing) was restored to the text.[68] Lest there be any doubt over the matter, a copy of this uncensored version of Cromwell's letter was bound into the manuscript Lords Journal as a permanent record.[69]

Censorship by the Commons, protection by the Lords: the pattern was repeated after Cromwell's only other public attempt during the course of the Civil War to influence the form of the Church settlement, in September 1645. Writing from Bristol after the city's recapture, he concluded his letter with a homiletic entreaty for unity among protestants, and for parliament to retain its supreme authority over the Church.

> Presbyterians, Independents, all had here the same spirit of faith and prayer; . . . pity it is it should be otherwise anywhere . . . In other things, God hath put the sword into the parliament's hands for the terror of evil-doers and the praise of them that do well. If any plead exemption from it, he knows not the Gospel. If any would wring it out of your hands, or steal it from you under what pretence soever, I hope they shall do it without effect. That God may maintain it in your hands, and direct you in the use thereof, is the prayer of . . . Oliver Cromwell.[70]

In the Commons, this prayer went unanswered. The House repeated its response to the Naseby letter. Again, the entire paragraph (quoted above) was excised in the printing authorized by the House of Commons.[71] It is perhaps an illustration of Cromwell's vulnerability – his awareness that his leave to remain with the army

---

68. *An Ordinance of Parliament . . . together with . . . Lieutenant Generall Cromwell to the Speaker* (printed for Edward Husband, 16 June 1645), B.L., E288/26. Cf. *C.J.*, IV, 175. For the printing, see Sheila Lambert (ed.), *Printing for Parliament, 1641–1700* (List and Index Soc., special series, XX, 1984), p. 99. At the same time, it was the Saye group which foiled attempts in June to call into question the validity of Cromwell's appointment as General Officer of the Horse. *L.J.*, VII, 433; cf. Hoover, 'Cromwell's Status and Pay in 1646–47', p. 705.

69. H.L.R.O., MS Lords Journal, 16 June 1645.

70. Abbott, I, 377–8 and n: Cromwell to Speaker Lenthall, 14 Sept. 1645. The language of the whole paragraph is inspired by, and alludes to, the Epistle to the Ephesians (see esp. IV, 3–6; VI, 17).

71. For the Commons' (expurgated) priiting of the letter, by Edward Husband, see *Lieut: Generall Cromwells Letter to the House of Commons, of . . . taking of the City of Bristoll* (14 Sept. 1645), B.L., E301/18. Gardiner (*Civil War*, II, 320n) notes that the passage was later printed in October in *Strong Motives or Loving and Modest Advice unto the Petitioners for Presbiterian Government* (10 Oct. 1645), pp. 7–8 (B.L., E304/15); but it had first appeared on 22 Sept. as *The Conclusion of Lieuten: Generall Cromwells letter to the House of Commons concerning the taking of Bristoll: which was . . . omitted in the printed Copy* ([22 Sept.] 1645). The B.L. copy

could be revoked at any point – that he registered no protest. Nor did he attempt to influence further the legislation on the Church that occupied the houses throughout the first six months of 1646.

The response to Cromwell's appeal from Bristol was otherwise among his allies in the House of Lords. In Lord Saye, Cromwell's exhortation struck a common chord. He took steps to ensure the publication of the paragraph which the Commons had excised, and composed a small treatise defending his co-religionist from presbyterian detractors.[72] What linked their private piety and their concern for the public authority of the legislature was an Erastian conviction that parliament alone was the source of secular *and clerical* jurisdiction. Only if that principle was maintained could 'liberty of conscience' (and the liberty of Independent congregations) be preserved within a presbyterian national Church. 'God hath put the [ecclesiastical] sword into the parliament's hands,' Cromwell had declared; 'if any plead exemption from it, he knows not the Gospel.' It was a doctrine Saye wholeheartedly affirmed. 'Oh well spoken, with all my soul,' he wrote in Cromwell's defence in 1646. 'Here is the sum and substance of all contained in this piece of the letter . . . and what could be more Christianly desired, . . . what more consonant to the doctrine of the Apostles – witness *Romans* 13, and many other scriptures.'[73] There could have been no clearer demonstration of the common ecclesiology and spirituality which underpinned Cromwell's allegiance to the parliamentary defenders of God's cause.

This ecclesiology – and the unanimity between Cromwell and his allies it engendered – found its most concrete expression in the Toleration Bill of 1647. Here, at last, 'liberty of conscience' was to

(pressmark 669 f. 10/38) bears a MS note by Thomason, dated 22 Sept., that it had been printed by the 'Independents' and scattered in the streets the previous night – 'but expressly omitted by order of the house'. That Saye did not attempt on this occasion to issue it under the Lords' *imprimatur* is a reflection of Essex's factional dominance in the house from the autumn of 1645. Cf. *C.J.*, IV, 277.

72. [Saye], *Vindiciae Veritatis*, pp. 145–56; the treatise, intended for publication in April 1646, may be securely dated on internal evidence shortly after the City petition to the Lords against lay commissioners (March 1646), and before the City's remonstrance (of May 1646). Saye engages in a point by point rebuttal of criticism levelled at Cromwell's letter by David Buchanan in his anonymously published *Truth its Manifest, or a Short and True Relation* ([11 Nov.] 1645), B.L., E1175/5. It is significant that Cromwell had never been pro-Scottish, even in November 1640. (I am grateful to Professor the Earl Russell for this last point.)

73. [Saye], *Vindiciae Veritatis*, p. 147. Henry Burton's *Vindiciae Veritatis: Truth Vindicated*, whose title Saye borrowed for his own work, appeared on the same day as the unexpurgated text of Cromwell's letter from Bristol (B.L., pressmark 669 f. 10/38).

be permanently enshrined. Prepared in October 1647, when a final settlement with the king appeared imminent, the list of its sponsors reveals a familiar cast. Like the Committee of Both Kingdoms Bill of 1644, it began life in the Lords under the guidance of Saye; and it found its advocates in the Commons with Cromwell, Evelyn and Sir Henry Vane.[74] Elizabethan statutes enforcing Sunday church attendance were effectively repealed; doctrinal orthodoxy was defined by the first fifteen Articles of Religion – a relatively unexacting test with which most major protestant sects could comply; penalties for absence from parish services were abolished for those 'present to hear the word of God preached or expounded . . . elsewhere'[75]; reforms in the payment of tithes were attempted.[76] Such was the legislative embodiment of Cromwell's ideal of 'liberty of conscience' – an ideal in which parliament, not the clergy, was the custodian of that liberty, and in which 'toleration' was not a licence for heresy.[77] In 1647, the king abandoned this projected settlement, and the bill — on which Cromwell and what Liburne termed his 'lordly interest' had lavished such care – never reached the statute book. Yet, during the years of the Rump Parliament, long after that 'lordly interest'[78] had been scattered to the winds by the storms of 1648, the bill of 1647 formed the model for the celebrated Toleration Act, passed in the wake of Cromwell's victory at Dunbar in September 1650.[79]

---

74. H.L.R.O., MP 15/10/47, fos 162–3; the text was not entered in the Journals of either house. For contemporary reactions to the bill see *Mercurius Pragmaticus*, no. 8 (2–9 Nov. 1647), p. 58 (B. L., E413/8); *A Perfect Diurnall*, no. 220 (11–18 Oct. 1647), sig. 10 O[1v] (B.L., E518/45). For the background to the proposals and their relationship to the *Heads of the Proposals* of July 1647, see J. S. A. Adamson, 'The English Nobility and the Projected Settlement of 1647', *H.J.*, XXX (1987), 567–602.

75. Cf. the 1650 Toleration Act's insistence that every person 'upon every Lord's day, . . . diligently resort to some public place where the service and worship of God is exercised, or shall be present at some other place in the practice of some religious duty, either of prayer, preaching, reading or expounding the scriptures': Gardiner, *Constitutional Documents*, p. 394.

76. In this respect, the 1647 Bill was even more radical than the Toleration Act of 1650. No longer were tithes to be paid only to the parish clergy. Where the minister and the majority of the parish agreed, part of the tithes could be used to support a 'minister' of their choice — clerical or lay, Independent or presbyterian: H.L.R.O., MP 15/10/47, fo. 163. Adamson, 'The Projected Settlement of 1647', pp. 588–91.

77. For the limits of Cromwell's attitude to toleration, see Blair Worden, 'Toleration and the Cromwellian Protectorate', in W. J. Sheils (ed.), *Studies in Church History* (1984), pp. 199–233.

78. Lilburne to Henry Marten, 15 Sept. 1647: printed in John Lilburne, *Two Letters . . . to Col. Henry Martin* (1647), pp. 4–5.

79. 'The Act repealing several clauses in statutes imposing penalties for not coming

But before the deluge, in the years before the Second Civil War, it was with this 'lordly interest' in the two houses that Cromwell found his loyalist allies, the men whom he regarded as most devoted to 'the cause'. Their influence also afforded Cromwell a modest portion of the fruits of patronage and preferment. Lord Wharton found a seat in parliament, in 1645, for Cromwell's friend and future son-in-law, Henry Ireton.[80] Saye's stalwart supporter, Lord Howard of Escrick (the powerful chairman of the Committee for the Advance of Money), provided the means by which Cromwell tried to obtain a clerkship for a deserving friend of his youth.[81] Patronage and favour witnessed to ideology's bonds.

This ideology found its clearest expression in the proposals for an agreement with the king jointly formulated by Saye's group at Westminster, and Cromwell and Ireton in the army, over the summer of 1647 – the grand plan for a settlement that was finally published as the *Heads of the Proposals*.[82] It was an ambitious and comprehensive programme of reform; the basis, so its authors hoped, for a lasting peace. It presented, in a detailed form, the objectives which its sponsors had pursued in general throughout the war: regular (biennial) parliaments, a redistribution of constituencies to make the Commons more representative of the populous counties at the expense of the boroughs; parliamentary control of the militia, and of the right to nominate the great officers of state; leniency to the defeated royalists; and toleration of tender consciences.[83] Ambitious as these proposals were, they did not languish on the drawing-board. Each of the sixteen 'heads' was transformed into legislation during October 1647. Predictably, the major promoters of the bills in parliament were Wharton and Viscount Saye.[84]

to church', 27 Sept. 1650: Gardiner, *Constitutional Documents*, pp. 391–4. For a discussion of its frosty reception, Worden, *Rump Parliament*, pp. 238–40.

80. [John Musgrave], *A Fourth Word to the Wise* ([8 June] 1647), p. 2 (B.L., E391/9); David Underdown, 'Party Management in the Recruiter Elections, 1645–48', *E.H.R.*, LXXXIII (1968), 243. For Musgrave, see also B.L., Add. MS 18780 (Yonge's diary), fo. 57.

81. Abbott, I, 431: Cromwell to Lord Howard of Escrick, 23 Mar. 1647 (P.R.O., SP 19/106, fo. 36).

82. Adamson, 'The Projected Settlement of 1647', pp. 567–84.

83. Gardiner, *Constitutional Documents*, pp. 316–26. Bodl. Lib., MS Dep. c. 168, fos 36–42v (recension of the proposals dating from the last week of July 1647); cf. H.L.R.O., MP 21/9/47, fos 40–43.

84. *L.J.*, IX, 481–4; H.L.R.O., MP 15/10/47, fos 160, 161, 162–3; *The Moderate Intelligencer*, no. 134 (7–14 Oct. 1647), pp. 1319–20; *The Perfect Diurnall* (11–18 Oct. 1647), sig. 10 O[1v] (B.L., E518/45); *The Kingdomes Weekly Intelligencer*, no. 230 (12–19 Oct. 1647), p. 694 (B.L., E411/11).

Such proposals have an obvious importance as a summary of the political objectives of Cromwell and his parliamentary allies – as a detailed statement of what they understood 'the cause' to be. But their significance goes beyond that fact. For they continued to form Cromwell's political agenda well after the parliamentary alliance which created them had collapsed under the pressures of the Second Civil War. The relationship between the 1647 proposal for religious 'accommodation' and the Toleration Act of 1650 has already been noticed. Yet that was not the only part of the constitutional programme of 1647 to be revived during the years of the Rump (1649–53), and to survive into the years of the Protectorate.[85]

Indeed, one of the principal causes of Cromwell's growing disenchantment with the Rump during 1651–53 was parliament's reluctance (at times, its hostility) to implement these objectives which had first been clearly defined in 1647. Apart from the deficiencies in the Toleration Act of 1650, the hundreds of exceptions to the Rump's Act of Oblivion made a mockery of the principle of leniency to royalists adumbrated in 1647. And, most conspicuously of all, the Rump of the Long Parliament proved notoriously averse to naming a day for its dissolution, and providing for the election of its successor. When, in November 1651, the Lord General's arm-twisting finally forced the Rump to name a deadline for its dissolution (while legislation was prepared, in the interim, for the election of its successor), Cromwell was giving effect to a principle which had been first mooted in October 1647. Then, a bill had been sent down from the Lords to the Commons 'concerning the period [i.e. end] of this parliament and [the] sitting of those future'; its proposer was Cromwell's collaborator in the formulation of the *Heads of the Proposals,* Lord Wharton.[86]

The success of Cromwell's collaborations with this group of like-minded peers and MPs in advancing the cause profoundly affected

85. A. Woolrych, *Commonwealth to Protectorate* (Oxford, 1982), pp. 23–4; much of the *Heads* was incorporated into the 'Instrument of Government' of 1653: Gardiner, *Constitutional Documents*, pp. 405–17; Gardiner, *C.&P.*, II, 331–36, H. R. Trevor-Roper, 'Oliver Cromwell and his Parliaments, in *Religion, the Reformation and Social Change* (2nd edn. 1972), pp. 371, 374n. Cromwell's pursuit of West Indian colonization during 1650s perpetuated the puritan programme of colonization of Saye's and Brooke's Providence Island Company of the 1630s; for the continuities between the two schemes, see Karen Ordahl Kupperman, 'Errand to the Indies: Puritan Colonization from Providence Island through the Western Design', *William and Mary Quarterly*, 3rd ser. XLV (1988), 88–98.
86. Worden, *Rump*, pp. 284–5; *C.J.*, V, 338; *L. J.*, IX, 482; *Perfect Diurnall*, no. 221 (18–25 Oct. 1647), p. 1774 (B.L., E518/47).

his attitude to parliament. For in Cromwell's providential understanding of the working of politics, this parliamentary group was no less 'God's instruments' than were the soldiers he commanded in the field. Their *parliamentary* victories – the Committee of Both Kingdoms, the creation of the New Model, the vote to forbid further addresses to the king in 1648 – were no less God's 'providences' than were the military victories at Marston Moor, Naseby or Preston. 'A mighty providence to this poor kingdom and to us all' was the meaning he read into the votes in the parliament on 3 January 1648, at the end of an abortive series of negotiations with the king. Significantly, the parliamentary leadership whose success in these votes he regarded as so 'providential' was the same group with whom his fortunes had been intimately associated since the winter of 1643–44. In January 1648, it was Saye and Wharton who once again supported Cromwell's motion to suspend further negotiation with the king. Moreover, among the votes constituting this 'mighty providence' was one to re-establish 'the members of both houses who were of the Committee of Both Kingdoms' in 'all that power' which they formerly had – that is, to return to an executive dominated by Saye's parliamentary interest. The Derby House Committee – the executive highjacked by Denzell Holles and the opponents of the army during 1647 – was thereby superseded.[87] Furthermore, Saye's influence on the revived executive was to be increased by the addition of Sir John Evelyn and Nathaniel Fiennes to its number. These two appointments highlight the continuity and cohesiveness of Cromwell's parliamentary group. Evelyn, a long-standing parliamentary ally, had acted as teller with Cromwell in the vote to supplant Essex as commander-in-chief with Sir Thomas Fairfax back in 1645. Nathaniel Fiennes was the son of Viscount Saye, the architect of the original Committee of Both Kingdoms, in 1644.

What was providential to Cromwell was not only the success of this parliamentary group in 1648, but the consistency with which the members at its centre – Cromwell, Vane, St John, Nathaniel Fiennes, Saye and Wharton – had advanced 'this cause' since Cromwell 'first began to appear to the world' in the autumn of 1643.[88] It was his faith in these fellow godly members in the two houses – and in their commitment to a settlement with the king which guaranteed the ends for which they had fought – that sustained his faith in the Long Parliament through all the tribulations of the Civil War.

87. Abbott, I, 577–8: Cromwell to Hammond, 3 Jan. 1648.
88. Whitelocke, *Memorials*, I, 209.

If the political agenda of 'the cause', as defined in 1647, may have survived into the 1650s, the alliance which had been its proponents was neither as durable nor as long-lived. The group who had been Cromwell's intimates for much of the 1640s was broken permanently by the crisis of 1648. After the revolution of the winter of 1648–49, Saye and Wharton were conspicuously *not* among the peers who sought election to the Rump (unlike their colleagues, Pembroke, Salisbury and Howard of Escrick), and refused Cromwell's attempts to bring them into government again in 1657. Of the 'royal Independent' group that had been his closest allies in the Commons during the 1640s, only St John and Sir Henry Vane sat in the Rump after the Purge of 1648.[89] Former allies such as Nathaniel Fiennes, John Crewe, Sir John Evelyn, William Pierrepont and Samuel Browne would have nothing to do with the purged House of Commons, and clearly disapproved of Cromwell's part in the regicide; yet the bonds of godly fellowship remained strong on both sides, and, with most, the estrangement was never irremediable or complete. Vane, however, was to break with Cromwell permanently after the dissolution of the Rump.[90]

We have examined in some detail the influence which these allies at Westminster exerted on Cromwell's career during the 1640s, and on his attitudes to parliament and the cause. Yet why did Cromwell alienate, and become alienated from, the men upon whose parliamentary support his political and military careers had been founded? How had his attitude to parliament changed in the process? To answer these questions we must investigate two other major influences on Cromwell's conduct during the Long Parliament: his relationship with the army; and his relationship with God.

IV

Few prospects terrified Cromwell so completely as a kingdom with no visible authority but the sword. Veneration for parliament was deeply ingrained. Godly zeal would ultimately compel him to violence against it, but could never completely erase his conviction that the

---

89. Society of Antiquaries of London, MS 138 (Cromwell letters), fo. 22: William Rowe to Cromwell, 30 Aug. 1650. Vane served as Cromwell's principal informant of parliamentary news during the campaigns of 1648–51; cf. ibid., fo. 27: Vane to Cromwell, 10 Sept. 1650.
90. Worden, *Rump Parliament*, pp. 178–9; V. A. Rowe, *Sir Henry Vane the ·Younger: A Study in Political and Administrative History* (1970), pp. 202–3. V. Pearl, 'The "Royal Independents" in the English Civil War', *T.R.H.S.*, 5th ser., XVIII (1967), 69–96.

best guarantee of the liberty of the subject was parliaments in general, nor obliterate his respect for the achievements of the Long Parliament in particular. Cromwell believed there were men in parliament who read the auguries of providence as he did, and who would fight with him to preserve 'this glorious cause'. For the moment, harmony prevailed between the imperatives of respect for parliament, and conformity with the will of God. Parliament and the cause were as one.

Thus throughout the army disbandment crises of 1647, Cromwell used his influence within Fairfax's Council of War, and in the General Council of the Army, to prevent an open breach between parliament and the New Model. Parliament's authority was maintained. The House of Lords was defended. When proposals for disbandment were advanced in March 1647, Cromwell assured the Commons that the army would lay down its arms when commanded to by parliament.[91] For disbandment of the New Model was the necessary prelude to the formation of a new expeditionary force to quell the Irish rebellion, an enterprise which Cromwell ardently supported. It was only after April, when plans for the new force were announced by Holles – the MP who had suggested Cromwell's impeachment in 1644 – that he, and the army, came to resist disbandment and enlistment for Ireland on the terms then proposed.[92] Disbandment on these terms, Cromwell feared, would have placed the bulk of the New Model's forces under commanders of questionable loyalty in Ireland, and opened up the prospect of a royalist-Presbyterian coup in England.

His allies in the Lords were of like mind. Although they were in the minority during the spring of 1647, they fought a vigorous rearguard action – well noticed by the army – to oppose the disbandment scheme, and to vest command of the Irish expeditionary force in officers in whom the army could confide.[93]

91. J. Lilburne, *Ionahs Cry out of the Whales Belly* (1647), p. 3 (B.L., 400/4). Austin Woolrych, *Soldiers and Statesmen: the General Council of the Army and its Debates 1647–48* (Oxford, 1987), p. 31. Gardiner argued this was 'Cromwell's parliamentary defeat' and that Cromwell was on the verge of leaving England for service in Germany under the command of the Elector Palatine. Gardiner's evidence for this is uncharacteristically slight and unconvincing. His case rests on an unnecessary redating of a passage in Ludlow's *Memoirs* (to establish Cromwell's 'depression'); and an undated rumour, reported only (and then at second hand) in Bellièvre's dispatches, of the Elector's 'grandes conférences avec Cromwell'. Gardiner offers no firm, or even dated, evidence for this assertion: Gardiner, *Civil War*, III, 222–3 and n.

92. These events are discussed in detail in Woolrych, *Soldiers and Statesmen*, ch. 2–5; and M. A. Kishlansky, *The Rise of the New Model Army* (Cambridge, 1979); ch. 5–6.

93. *L.J.*, IX, 207–8; Worcester College, Oxford, Clarke MS XLI, fo. 137v; William

Confidence that God's instruments in the parliament were still a powerful, if narrowly outvoted, minority in the two houses was the mainstay of Cromwell's efforts, throughout 1647, to resist pressure within the army for the direct use of force against the two houses. Army pressure could be used to compel corrections of course at Westminster; but Cromwell still baulked at the demands of radical officers for a purge. Only if parliament's authority was upheld could the constitutional and moral integrity of 'the cause' be maintained. 'Work in them [the New Model's rank and file] a good opinion of that authority', Cromwell advised the delegates of the regiments in May 1647, for 'if that authority falls to nothing, nothing can follow but confusion.'[94] The following month, Cromwell was closely involved in the army's preparation of impeachment proceedings against 'the eleven members' – the ring-leaders of Holles's disbandment campaign.

What is striking about this initiative is the army's reliance on *parliamentary* procedures to achieve its ends. For in impeachment proceedings it was the Commons who presented the charges and evidence against the accused; the Lords who were to judge of the offence.[95] To those who argued at Putney in the autumn that it was the army, not parliament, which was now the repository of authority Cromwell offered the blunt rejoinder: 'Either they are a parliament or no parliament. If they be no parliament, they are nothing – and we are nothing likewise.'[96]

Underlying all these affirmations of the inviolability of parliament was Cromwell's practical sense of assurance that, given time, he and his allies could reach an agreement – and, moreover, an agreement which did not compromise their political objectives – with the king. Hence Cromwell's labours on the *Heads of the Proposals* over the sum-

---

Prynne, *Vindication of the XI Members* (1647); p. 8; Archivo General de Simancas, Estado consulta 2566: Alonso de Cárdenas to Philip IV, 31 May 1647.

94. C. H. Firth (ed.), *Selections from the Papers of Sir William Clarke* (4 vols, Camden Soc., 1891–1901), I, 73; speech in Saffron Walden Church, 16 May 1647; also printed in Abbott, I, 445–6, and Carlyle, III, 330–1. Cf. the report of Cromwell's speech in the Commons on his return from the army, 21 May 1647: Bodl. Lib., MS Clarendon 29, fo. 227.

95. B.L., Egerton MS 1048 (Parliamentary papers), fos 51–81 (6 July 1647): original of the articles presented against the eleven members, headed 'A particular charge or impeachment in the name of his Excellencie Sir Thomas Farefax and the Army under his command'. As Professor Woolrych has pointed out, 'the selection of the members to be impeached must have lain very much with Cromwell', advised by the other officer-MPs, Ireton, Harrison and Fleetwood: Woolrych, *Soldiers and Statesmen*, pp. 138–9.

96. *Clarke Papers*, I, 369 (1 Nov. 1647).

mer of 1647. He supported the redrafting of the *Heads* as bills to be sent to the king in the autumn. And early the following year, he and Saye breached the Vote of No Addresses – and risked the censure of the army[97] – to attempt a personal approach to the king at Carisbrooke on the Isle of Wight.[98] Yet by April 1648, all of their labours had come to naught. Cromwell left Westminster in that month to fight the Second Civil War. When he returned in December, the army had purged the parliament, the trial of the king was imminent, and the alliance of godly men with whom he had advanced the cause over almost a decade had been irrecoverably dispersed.

What led Cromwell, the professed servant of parliament, the principal defender of its authority in the army in 1647, to countenance the use of force against the sovereign power? What brought him to so politically revolutionary a course over the winter of 1648–49, and, in April 1653, 'to do that, the contemplation of the issue whereof made his hair to stand on end'[99] – forcibly to dissolve the Rump? What impelled Cromwell on so hair-raising a course of action, destroying first the king, and finally the Long Parliament itself?

V

The year 1648, 'the most memorable year . . . that ever this nation saw',[100] also saw a seismic shift in the bedrock of Cromwell's attitude to the legislative power. Cromwell had had, as we have seen, kindred spirits in the circle of Saye, Wharton, St John and their Commons allies, throughout the civil war. Assured of their fidelity to the cause, and heartened by their providential successes in parliament – the creation of the Committee of Both Kingdoms, of the New Model, the passing of the Self-Denying Ordinance, the acceptance of the *Heads* as a basis for a settlement by the parliament – Cromwell had risked the censure of radicals in the army during 1647, had defied

97. Bodl. Lib., MS Clarendon 31, fo. 7: letter of intelligence, 23 March 1648; see also, B.L., Add. MS 37344 (Whitelocke's Annals), fo. 142v; S.R. Gardiner (ed.), *The Hamilton Papers* (Camden Soc., 1880), p. 174: anonymous letter to the earl of Lanark, 4 April 1648; C. H. Firth (ed.), 'Narratives illustrating the duke of Hamilton's expedition', *Scottish Historical Society Miscellany*, II (1904), 295; for Saye's reported approaches to the king in July, Clement Walker, *Anarchia Anglicana* (1648), pp. 112–13.
98. Christ Church Muniment Room, Oxford, Browne Letters (Evelyn coll.), Box A–C: Lord Cottington to Sir Richard Browne, 19 April 1648.
99. Worden, *Rump*, p. 321.
100. Abbott, III, 54; cited in Worden, 'Oliver Cromwell and the Sin of Achan', p. 131.

accusations of being a 'creature' of the Court, had maintained at all costs the authority of legislature, and with it, the authority of his allies – 'God's instruments' – whom Providence had ordained to triumph in the parliamentary cause. Parliament was the means by which the political objectives of the cause – and liberty of conscience for 'God's people' – would be legally established and maintained. But what if parliament, 'after so many evidences of Divine Presence . . . prospering a righteous cause', should imperil that cause? Or should come to abandon it? What if parliament itself was now 'apostatized'?[101]

The first premonitory tremors of a shift in Cromwell's attitude to parliament were heard on 3 January 1648, in his speech to the Commons on the Vote of No Addresses.[102] 'Look on the people you represent, and break not your trust,' Cromwell warned, 'and expose not the honest party of the kingdom, who have bled for you, and suffer not misery to fall upon them, for want of courage and resolution in you – else the honest people may take such courses as nature dictates to them.'[103] The warning was clear: if parliament remained willing to treat with a king who was even then negotiating underhandedly for the intervention of a Scottish army on his behalf, with a king who had just rejected parliament's minimum terms (presented in the Four Bills of 1647), then it was obviously willing to contemplate an agreement with Charles so lenient that it abandoned the very principles for which the 'honest party' had fought. Parliament would have abandoned its trust.

It was against this background that the Commons' acceptance of the Vote of No Addresses appeared as the 'mighty providence' of which Cromwell spoke in his letter to Hammond at the end of that same day. Its providential significance lay not in foreclosing the possibility of further negotiation with Charles I, but as an unambiguous signal to a king who had just rejected parliament's minimum conditions (the Four Bills of December 1647), that there were certain terms below which the parliament would not go. However obstinate the king might prove to be, the 'honest party' could trust that parliament would not betray the cause. In the course of 1648, however, that was a trust Cromwell found increasingly difficult to sustain.

---

101. Cf. Abbott, I, 621: Cromwell to Lenthall, 11 July 1648.
102. Abbott, I, 577–8.
103. David Underdown (ed.), 'The Parliamentary Diary of John Boys', *Bull. Inst. Hist. Res.*, XXXIX (1966), 156; entry for 3 Jan. 1648. There is an inferior report of the same speech in *Mercurius Pragmaticus* (4–11 Jan. 1648), printed in Abbott, I, 576.

A critical turning point for Cromwell was the failure, in April 1648, of his and Saye's mission to the Isle of Wight to dissuade the king from his alliance with the Scots. Lord Cottington, writing on 19 April, noted 'Cromwell's return from the King, without having prevailed in the persuasions he carried'.[104] Cromwell had inevitably staked his personal prestige on the venture (a clear breach of the Vote of No Addresses), for despite efforts to keep it secret, the mission was known to royalist agents, and was almost certainly known at Westminster and in the army.[105] In Scotland, the efforts of Cromwell's emissary, the MP William Ashhurst,[106] had proved equally fruitless: a new civil war, and the invasion of the royalist army from Scotland, now appeared inevitable. Was not this reversal of their fortunes a singular providence? Was not the king now 'like unto Ahab' whose heart God had hardened? Consider 'our actions as an army', Cromwell urged his brother officers at the great prayer meeting at Windsor in the last days of April 1648, 'to see if any iniquity could be found in them, and what it was; that if possible we might find it out, and so remove the cause of such sad rebukes as were upon us by reason of our iniquities'.[107]

Yet Cromwell's decision to 'turn at God's reproof' was not a complete *volte-face*. Throughout the campaigns of the summer and autumn of 1648, he 'wrestled with God'; sought providential meaning in the army's triumphs and the parliament's tergiversations; and came to an almost mystical certitude of the immanence of God in the New Model, the instrument of His victories. Cromwell reserved

104. Christ Church Muniment Room, Oxford, Browne Letters (Evelyn coll.), Box A–C: Lord Cottington to Sir Richard Browne, 19 April 1648.
105. Bodl. Lib., MS Clarendon 31, fo. 7: letter of intelligence, 23 March 1648; see also, B.L., Add. MS 37344 (Whitelocke's Annals), fo. 142r–v; S.R. Gardiner (ed.), *The Hamilton Papers* (Camden Soc., 1880), p. 174: anonymous letter to the earl of Lanark, 4 April 1648; C. H. Firth (ed.), 'Narratives illustrating the duke of Hamilton's expedition', *Scottish Historical Society Miscellany*, II (1904), 295.
106. *Westminster Projects, or the Mysterie of Darby House Discovered* (1648), pp. 1, 7 (B.L., E433/15). Bodl. Lib., MS Tanner 58, fo. 783: Ashhurst to Lenthall, [1647]. See also, John Rylands Lib., University of Manchester, Eng. MS 296/206 (Pink papers); P. R. O., SP 28/269/2 (Cttee of Revenue warr.), fo. 176v. Broughton Castle, Oxon., Saye MS II/87.
107. Willian Allen, *A Faithful Memorial of that remarkable Meeting of many Officers of the Army* ([27 April] 1659), reprinted in Walter Scott (ed.), *Somers Tracts* (2nd edn, 13 vols, 1809–15), VI, 500. There are inconsistencies in Allen's account (see Woolrych, *Soldiers and Statesmen*, p. 333); but the version of Cromwell's words here appears to be substantially accurate. For the idea of reproof, cf. Worden, 'Oliver Cromwell and the Sin of Achan', p. 131.

his judgment on the Newport Treaty – parliament's last attempt to come to terms with the king; but his letters to his friends at Westminster, though still cordial, repeat his injunction to parliament first articulated in his speech on the Vote of No Addresses: fail not to maintain the cause.

It is not fit for me to give advice [he wrote after Preston, in August 1648], . . . more than to pray you, and all that acknowledge God, that they would exalt Him, and not hate His people, . . . for whom even Kings are reproved; and that you would take courage to do the work of the Lord, in fulfilling the end of your magistracy . . .[108]

'Courage to do the work of the Lord' was the one quality which the parliament – then considering the restoration of episcopacy as the price of settlement with the king – most conspicuously lacked.

Throughout the autumn, Cromwell's sense of loyalty to parliament was eroded and attenuated by the same providences which seemed to affirm his sense of confidence in the army's claim to be 'a lawful power', a power called by God to complete His work in Israel.[109] In September 1648, as the New Model rolled on to victory in the Second Civil War, Oliver St John could not but have been disquieted by the verses of Isaiah which Cromwell commended to him: 'The Lord spake thus unto me with a strong hand, and instructed me that I should not walk in the way of this people . . . And he shall be . . . for a stone of stumbling . . . and for a snare to the inhabitants of Jerusalem.'[110] Parliament was 'stumbling' in its reckless pursuit of the treaty; and 'the inhabitants of Jerusalem', St John, Saye, Wharton, Vane – the most trusted of his allies at Westminster – were caught in the same 'snare'.[111] '[You] have helped one another to stumble at the dispensations of God, and to reason yourselves out of His service,' Cromwell admonished Lord Wharton

108. Abbott, I, 638: Cromwell to Lenthall, 20 Aug. 1648.
109. Abbott, I, 634–8, 641–2, 644–5, 650–1, 653–4, 696–9.
110. Abbott, I, 644–5; Isaiah, VIII, 10, 14. Cromwell followed his recommendation with the injunction to 'read all the chapter'; Cromwell to St John, 1 Sept. 1648. Cromwell's letter of 28 June also alluded to this same section of Isaiah (God's punishment of Judah for its infidelity); see his references to 'the day of Midian': cf. Isaiah, IX, 4–5. It is possible that Cromwell's information of the progress of the treaty came from his doctor, Mr Simpcutt, if the figure of the same name granted a special pass by the House of Lords to go into the Isle of Wight in September 1648 may be identified with the Cromwellian physician. The identification must, however, remain highly speculative. H.L.R.O., MP 26/9/48, fo. 53; *L.J.*, X, 512; Sir Philip Warwick, *Memoires* (1701), p. 249.
111. Abbott, I, 644–5; Cromwell reiterated this image in his letter to Wharton after Dunbar, 4 Sept. 1650: ibid., II, 328.

in 1651, alluding to the same verse he had commended to St John in the fateful autumn of 1648.[112]

The Newport Treaty became parliament's 'rock of offence'.[113] In stumbling, it had betrayed the political and religious objectives for which, in Cromwell's view, the war had been fought. In negotiating with an 'accursed thing' it had betrayed the cause. Was not 'the whole fruit of the war like to be frustrated' by the treaty, Cromwell asked Colonel Robert Hammond, 'and all most like to turn to what it was, and worse? And this contrary to engagements, declarations, implicit covenants with those who ventured their lives . . .?'[114]Trust had been broken; parliament had thereby forfeited its authority. The workings of factions had 'made the parliament null'. Moreover, Cromwell believed, the two houses intended to 'call a new [parliament] and to do this by force', thereby all but guaranteeing that the new parliament was to be dominated by presbyterian or crypto-royalist interests hostile to the cause.[115] This was a fear which was to resurface in 1652–53. It was decisively to influence Cromwell's decision to expel the Rump.

Parliament and 'the cause' now represented antitheses. With parliament having failed to fulfil 'the end of [its] magistracy',[116] had not God revealed His 'presence' in the army, entrusting it with authority to prevent His cause from falling to the ground? Consider, Cromwell asked Hammond in the week before Pride's Purge, 'whether this army be not a lawful power, called by God to oppose and fight against the king upon some stated grounds, and being in power to such ends, may not oppose one name of authority, for those ends, as well as another, the outward authority that called them'.[117] Cromwell had engaged in the war believing that maintaining the authority of parliament had been synonymous with the cause for which he fought. Now he was convinced that this same authority of parliament had become a threat endangering the very existence of a cause the central element of which he had come to see as the religious liberty of the Saints.[118] The army's use of force to resist parliament's authority was now legitimate. On 7 December – after Pride's Purge had begun – Cromwell made his first appearance in the Commons

112. Abbott, II, 453: Cromwell to Wharton, 27 Aug. 1651.
113. Abbott, I, 644; Isaiah, VIII, 14.
114. Abbott, I, 697: Cromwell to Hammond, 25 Nov. 1648.
115. Abbott, I, 678: Cromwell to Hammond, 6 Nov. 1648.
116. Abbott, I, 638.
117. Abbott, I, 697.
118. For this process of redefinition, cf. Abbott, III, 585–7.

since the outbreak of the Second Civil War.[119] The delay of his arrival in London until after the purge was almost certainly deliberate. It is possible that he still 'baulked at the use of force against constitutional authority'.[120] But it is also possible that he wholly approved of the army's actions, yet saw a political advantage in distancing himself from direct involvement in the Purge in the hope of reviving his role as mediator between the army and moderates at Westminster (including his former allies in the House of Lords). Their support, in the long term, would be essential to the stability of the new regime. It was precisely this policy that Cromwell adopted during the months after the purge. Whatever his reservations, the revolution had now begun.

VI

In its wake, that revolution of the winter of 1648–49 left a parliament radically transformed. From representing three estates, parliament now represented less than one. Monarchy was abolished. Against Cromwell's protests that the Commons were 'mad to incense all the peers of the whole kingdom against them', so was the House of Lords.[121] The purged, truncated House of Commons, reduced to less than half its former membership, remained the sole repository of 'the authority of parliament': the body which was later to be known derogatively as the Rump. To Cromwell – who was later to censure the Rump for 'assuming to itself the authority of the three estates that were before'[122] – the reign of the purged House of Commons was never more than a temporary expedient.[123] In June 1649, shortly before his departure for the Irish campaign, Cromwell prevented the Rump from holding 'recruiter elections' to fill the vacancies left in the house by the purge. As soon as the royalist threat had been extinguished – in the long series of campaigns which occupied him

---

119. For Cromwell's behaviour during this period, see Underdown, *Pride's Purge*, pp. 148–50. Cf. *Mercurius Pragmaticus*, no. 194 (30 Nov.–7 Dec. 1648), B.L., E475/26; Bodl. Lib., MS Clarendon 34, fo. 73v.
120. Underdown, *Pride's Purge*, p. 150.
121. Bodl. Lib., MS Clarendon 34, fo. 73v; cf. Bedfordshire R. O., MS AD/3342; printed as H. G. Tibbutt (ed.), 'The Tower of London Letter-Book of Sir Lewis Dyve', *Publ. Beds. Hist. Rec. Soc.*, XXXVIII (1958), p. 84; *The Antient Land-Mark, Skreen or Bank betwixt the Prince or Supreame Magistrate and the People of England* ([2 Mar.] 1658[9]), p. 12; Ann, countess of Pembroke to Christopher Marsh, 15 July 1650: Cumbria R. O. (Kendal), Hothfield MS, WD/H, Box 44, unfol.
122. Abbott, IV, 487–8.
123. Worden, *Rump*, p. 200.

between July 1649 and October 1651 – it was the creation of a 'new representative' which became Cromwell's foremost political concern, the construction of a new legislature worthily claiming the authority of a parliament, yet one which did not jeopardize the objectives of the cause.

This was not, however, a political concern that the Rump could be persuaded to share. In November 1651, with the laurels of his triumph at Worcester still fresh upon him, Cromwell and St John finally prevailed upon the house to agree to its dissolution at a date not later than 3 November 1654: the fourteenth anniversary of the meeting of the parliament.[124] But thereafter Cromwell's attempts to raise the question of the new representative met with a succession of evasions, filibusters and procrastinations. Only the sound of sabre-rattling in the army, and millenarian rhetoric in the pulpits, jolted the house into a semblance of interest in the subject in the August of 1652. And, as relations between parliament and army deteriorated steadily over the autumn and winter of 1652, Cromwell repeated his role in the crisis of 1647: the authority of the purged parliament – for all its depleted numbers, once again loyal to the cause – was maintained; threats by radicals in the army to dissolve parliament by force were neutralized and resisted.[125] When, in March 1653, the Council of Officers came to the brink of resolving to expel the Rump immediately and call a parliament in the name of the army, it was Cromwell who quelled the storm, asserting, 'Then the parliament is not the supreme power, but this is the supreme power that calls it'.[126]

Cromwell did not simply want a new parliament. He wanted a parliamentary apostolic succession. Only the Rump – derided and tainted with self-interest though it was – could confer constitutional legitimacy, and continuity with the great cause of 1642, upon its *legal* successor. Desperate to avoid a breach in that succession by the army, Cromwell convened a series of some 'ten or twelve' conferences between October 1652 and 19 April 1653 (the eve of the Long Parliament's expulsion), between leading MPs and representatives of the army's Council of Officers. The contents of the bill for the new representative which formed the subject of these conferences, and

---

124. Worden, *Rump*, pp. 277, 307.
125. Bodl. Lib., MS Clarendon 45, fo. 204.
126. C. H. Firth, 'Cromwell and the Expulsion of the Long Parliament in 1653', *E.H.R.*, VIII (1893), 527–8. For Colonel John Disbrowe, P. R. O., SP 16/503/56, fo. 170; and Disbrowe to Cromwell, 30 Sept. 1650: Society of Antiquaries, MS 138 (Cromwell letters), fo. 54.

Cromwell's role in its drafting, have been brilliantly unravelled by Dr Worden.[127] What is now clear is that at the last of the conferences, on 19 April, a compromise agreement had been reached. The military and parliamentary representatives were apparently agreed as to what the contents of the bill for the new representatives should be.

It was Cromwell's belief that this agreement was subsequently betrayed by parliament's actions on the following day which provoked him to bring the Rump to its unceremonious end. That story has been ably told by Dr Worden and Professor Woolrych. The question which bears directly on our understanding of Cromwell's attitude to parliament is this: what was it about the bill for the new representative that impelled Cromwell to his impetuous and precipitate dissolution of the Rump? What moved Cromwell to destroy the authority of 'those [whom] God hath set over me'?[128]

From the beginning of the conferences on the legislation for the new representative, the aspect of the bill which most exercised the Lord General was the question of the qualification of members for the new assembly. This had been the central clause in the army's petition to parliament of 13 August 1652, a clause almost certainly of Cromwell's authorship: 'That for public satisfaction of the good people of this nation, speedy consideration may be had of such qualifications, for future and successive parliaments, as tend to the election only of such as are pious and faithful to the interest of the commonwealth to sit and serve as members in the said parliament'.[129] 'Qualifications' were the device by which Cromwell hoped to square the circle: to have a parliament genuinely representative of the political nation, elected after a redistribution of seats; yet also to impose restrictions on the eligibility of candidates severe enough to exclude any former royalists or 'neuters'.

The compromise agreed on 19 April 1653 seemed to have satisfied all parties. A bill for the new representative would now pass. The Long Parliament would dissolve itself, and transfer power to a temporary council of some forty officers and MPs, exercising authority during the interim, and empowered to prepare for new elections. Constituencies were to be redrawn. Candidates would be adequately tested for their piety and fidelity to the fledgling commonwealth

---

127. Worden, *Rump*, ch. 14–16.
128. Abbott, II, 235: Cromwell to Lenthall, 2 April 1650.
129. *To the Supreme Authority the Parliament . . . The Humble Petition of the Officers of the Army* (12 Aug. 1652); the petition is discussed in detail in Woolrych, *Commonwealth to Protectorate*, pp. 40–3.

regime.[130] Legal continuity would thus be maintained. And this successor parliament could be trusted to be faithful to the godly cause. So much had been decided at the final conference at Cromwell's lodgings.

Yet what happened the next day destroyed this agreement and sealed the Long Parliament's fate. It is now clear that the Rump threw out Cromwell's proposal for an interim council, resolving instead on immediate elections. Whether or not they dropped such qualifications as were formerly in the bill, the decision to reject the interim council and press ahead with immediate elections was almost certain to produce a new parliament scarcely sympathetic to even the moderate programme of godly reformation Cromwell and his army allies espoused. One of the questions Cromwell had put to those attending the conference on 19 April was 'Whether the next parliament were not like to consist of all Presbyters? Whether those qualifications would hinder them? Or Neuters?'[131] Gilbert Mabbott was almost certainly echoing Cromwell's fears when he wrote that the bill for the new representative, thwarted by Cromwell's expulsion of the Rump, would have filled parliament 'with such as probably would be disaffected'.[132]

To Cromwell, the Rump's offence in April 1653 was a repetition of the Long Parliament's offence of December 1648. Once again the cause was threatened by a 'new parliament'. As during December 1648, parliament had forfeited its authority in betraying the cause of 'God's people', the cause of the Saints-in-arms whose religious liberty was certain to be imperilled by the arrival of a new band of 'Presbyters and Neuters' at Westminster. 1648 had come again: in that year, Cromwell had first comprehended the dictate of his proprietary God that 'the poor godly people of this Kingdom' should not 'still be made the object of wrath and anger, nor that *our* God would have

---

130. B.L., Add. MS 37354 (Whitelocke's Annals), fo. 270; Firth, 'Cromwell and the Expulsion of the Long Parliament', pp. 528–9; Woolrych, *Commonwealth to Protectorate*, p. 63. In the absence of the text of the bill, how the disqualifications would have been imposed remains obscure; the principal difficulty would have been, as Dr Worden notes, in keeping out political Presbyterians with unblemished records of allegiance to parliament during the war who were nevertheless crypto-royalist, or hostile even to the socially conservative programme of secular reform and religious liberty that Cromwell espoused.
131. *The Lord General Cromwel's Speech* (1654), p. 15; *C.J.*, VII, 805.
132. Worcester College, Oxford, Clarke MS XXV, fo. 12; printed in *Clarke Papers*, III, 1; see also Woolrych, *Commonwealth to Protectorate*, p. 81; Worden, *Rump*, p. 351. Mabbott assumed, probably erroneously, that the bill was a recruitment bill rather than a bill for fresh elections.

our necks under a yoke of bondage'.[133] In 1653, the yoke of bondage threatened once again. 'The dissolution of this parliament', Cromwell told the Nominated Assembly in July 1653, 'was as necessary to be done as the preservation of this cause.'[134]

VII

Cromwell's parliamentary career to 1648 had met with intermittent success. From 1648 until his death, it was dogged by consistent failure. As Lord Protector he succeeded in managing the three kingdoms, but never the two houses. He looked to a source other than parliament for the validation of his actions. From the summer of 1648, Cromwell's letters and speeches are suffused with scriptural allusions to the millennium, and a sense of the 'power' that God had given to 'His people, now called Saints'[135] – a power evinced in the great chain of providences revealed in the army's succession of victories in the field. The 'wonderful works of God' had been revealed in June 1648 'as in the day of Midian', when God broke 'the rod of the oppressor'.[136] The biblical context of these allusions imbued them with millenarian significance. For the victory in the 'day of Midian' portended not only the emancipation of the Saints, but the imminent coming of Christ. The two verses Cromwell quotes (Isaiah IX, 4–5), introduce the great prophecy of the coming of the messiah: 'For unto us a child is born, . . . and the government shall be upon his shoulder' (Isaiah IX, 6). 'His appearances [are] patiently to be waited for', Cromwell reminded St John after Preston, in September 1648.[137]

From these tentative references of 1648, to his great homily on the power of the Saints to the Nominated Assembly – the 'Parliament of Saints' – in July 1653, millenarian allusions form a consistent thread running through Cromwell's spiritual reflections on politics and providence. They profoundly influenced his attitude to parliament and the institutions of secular power – what he termed 'outward authority'.[138] In moments of crisis, it was to afford him the

133. Abbott, I, 619: Cromwell to Fairfax, 28 June 1648.
134. *The Lord General Cromwell's Speech* (1654), sig. C2; Abbott, III, 60: speech to Barebone's Parliament, 4 July 1653.
135. Abbott, I, 697, 699; II, 328.
136. Abbott, I, 619: Cromwell to Fairfax, 28 June 1648.
137. Abbott, I, 644. For St John's own millenarianism, see his letter to Cromwell, 26 Sept. 1650: Society of Antiquaries, MS 138 (Cromwell letters), fos 52v–3.
138. Abbott, I, 697.

mainstay of his actions – as it did in 1648, in 1653, and in his refusal of the Crown in 1657.[139]

This thread is most clearly to be discerned in Cromwell's references to 'power' – a word which always resounded in Cromwell's vocabulary with biblical overtones of the power of God in his Saints.[140] Was not 'this army' a 'lawful power, called by God', Cromwell had asked on the eve of Pride's Purge; 'and being in power' may 'oppose one name of authority', in order to thwart the 'swollen malice against God's people'.[141] Urging Lord Wharton to rejoin the cause of 'God's people', in January 1650, Cromwell contrasted the 'formal' authority which parliament had had until the purge (when Wharton had abandoned Westminster) with 'the power' it now possessed as the custodian of the interests of the Saints. 'You were with us in the Form of things,' Cromwell demanded, 'why not in the Power?'[142] The leniency shown to the rebel garrison at Kilkenny was because 'God hath brought [them] to a sense of . . . the Power to which He hath subjected them'.[143] Again, after the 'eminent mercies' of his victory at Dunbar in 1650, Cromwell reminded parliament that 'God puts it more into your hands . . . to improve your power and His blessings' by 'own[ing] His people more and more, for they are the chariots and horsemen of Israel. Disown yourselves; but own your authority.'[144] In this Dunbar letter of September 1650, the injunctions to parliament to 'own God's people' and to 'own your authority' were almost synonymous.[145] Parliament's authority arose as custodian of the power of the Saints.[146] That parliamentary authority had been confirmed by the victory at Dunbar, the Independent minister Peter Sterry assured Cromwell, for 'the Providence and Power were of God'.[147]

139. Worden, 'Oliver Cromwell and the Sin of Achan', pp. 141–5.
140. Abbott, I, 697; II,190, 226, 325; Carlyle, II, 279 (ll. 6–7). Cf. Ps., CX, 3; I Cor., I, 18; IV, 20; IX, 12; XVI, 43: Eph., I, 19; I Pet., I, 5; II Pet., I, 16.
141. Abbott, I, 697.
142. Abbott, II, 190: Cromwell to Wharton, 1 Jan. 1650. The probable reference is to Psalm CX, 3: 'Thy people shall be willing in the day of His power' – a verse which Cromwell was to expound to Barebone's in July 1653.
143. Abbott, II, 226: Cromwell to the mayor of Kilkenny, 26 Mar. 1650.
144. Abbott, II, 325: Cromwell to Lenthall, 4 Sept. 1650; the allusion is to II Chronicles, I, 14.
145. Abbott, II, 325.
146. Cf. Abbott, III, 55 (ll. 44–5). Underdown (ed.), 'The Parliamentary Diary of John Boys', p. 156.
147. Society of Antiquaries, MS 138 (Cromwell letters), fo. 25: Sterry to Cromwell, 9 Sept. 1650. Sterry was another of the pre-civil war circle of Saye and Brooke who, like his friend Vane, looked to Cromwell as the continuator of their godly objectives during the 1650s. For Sterry's influence with Vane, see William Rowe to Cromwell, 28 Dec. 1650: ibid., fo. 79v.

Suffused with millenarian rhetoric though it was, Cromwell's fiduciary concept of parliament's relationship with the Saints marked a substantive difference between himself and the Fifth Monarchist enthusiasms of Colonel Thomas Harrison – Cromwell's nearest rival for the mantle of patron of the radical sects.[148] Harrison hoped to see a hagiarchic parliament – government by rule of the Saints; and he seemed to have exerted a considerable influence over Cromwell during the winter of 1652, and during 1653. But for all Cromwell's millenarian biblicism, his ideas about the relationship between legislature and 'the Saints' were never rooted in the principles of hagiarchy that Harrison and his adherents espoused. In describing the relationship between parliament and the Saints, Cromwell tempered the hagiarchic implications of his rhetoric with the familiar common law principle of the trust – the enfeoffment to uses, a device for vesting the administration of property in trustees without relinquishing the owner's rights of propriety. The trust, moreover, was conditional and could be revoked. Indeed, between 1648 and 1653, Cromwell regularly speaks of the relationship between the Saints' and parliament's authority in fiduciary terms. It is as if the members of the Commons were the 'feoffees' of the power of the Saints – an analogy which occurred naturally to a man who had been employed professionally to oversee leases, trusts, and enfeoffments on the estates of the dean and chapter of Ely during the late 1630s.[149]

With parliament, this fiduciary relationship was overlaid with a biblical imperative to ensure the trust was not betrayed. The Rump broke that trust when it attempted to convey this power to a new representative, a parliament of 'neuters' and 'presbyters' who seemed certain to be unworthy trustees. Expulsion of the Rump, Cromwell later claimed, was a biblical imperative, the fruit of his meditation on the prophecy of Daniel, to maintain the power of the Saints. 'Some of us thought that it was our duty,' Cromwell explained to Barebone's, '. . . not vainly to look at the prophecy in Daniel, "And the kingdom shall not be delivered to another people" '[150]; they could not 'passively wait' as the kingdom was handed over to the

---

148. Society of Antiquaries, MS 138 (Cromwell letters), fos 10v–11: Harrison to Cromwell, 3 July 1650.
149. Ideally, this meant that the parliament should be representative not only of the 'people of God', but also of 'the people'; and Cromwell seems to have hoped that 'the people' might in time be so educated in godliness as to remove the threat to the godly from enemies of liberty of conscience – a process which he looked, in vain, to Barebone's to commence. (I am grateful to Dr Blair Worden for his suggestions on this point.)
150. Abbott, III, 64; cf. I, 697 (ll. 32–3).

new representative.[151] Glossing this verse to the newly assembled members of Barebone's in July 1653, Cromwell rephrased its meaning in terms of hagiarchic power strikingly reminiscent of his reflections of November 1648. God had 'bless[ed] the military power', he claimed, and 'set it upon our hearts to deliver over the power to another people'.

'Outward' legal authority had of course been violated; Cromwell had been disappointed of his hopes that the Rump could effect the *translatio imperii* to its successor. But what were these legalistic objections beside the preservation of the power of God's people? 'He makes this one of the greatest mercies – next to His own Son – to have His people called to the supreme authority.'[152] Cromwell's exposition of Psalm 110 at the opening of Barebone's Parliament marks the apogee of his millenarian rhetoric of power.

Give me leave to begin thus . . . Jesus Christ is owned this day by your call . . . And you manifest this to be a day of the power of Christ. I know you will remember that scripture, in Psalm cx. 3: 'He makes His people willing in the day of His power.' God manifests it to be the day of the power of Christ, having, through so much blood and so much trial as hath been upon this nation, made this to be one of the great issues thereof . . . . I confess I never looked to have seen such a day.[153]

To Cromwell, who had entered upon the war thinking the cause of the godly and the authority of parliament were one and the same, such a day was indeed unthinkable. He had gone to war in the sanguine belief that military success, the 'absolute victory' over the king, would confirm parliament as the instrument by which the objectives of the godly could be achieved. Legalist devotion to the sanctity of parliaments had been in harmony (at least until the crisis of mid-1648) with puritan devotion to the cause of God's people, the cause of religious liberty he so passionately espoused. Until that date, confidence in parliament's commitment to that cause had been underpinned by his confidence in the godly principles – and brilliant powers of parliamentary management – of the circle centred upon St John, Wharton and Viscount Saye and Sele. Estrangement from this circle over the months from April to November 1648 – when even

151. Carlyle, II, 298–9; cf. Daniel, II, 44. The context of the verse makes clear the millenarian overtones of Cromwell's remark. The passage comes from Daniel's interpretation of Nebuchadnezzar's dream: 'And in the days of these kings shall the God of heaven set up a kingdom, which shall never be destroyed: and the kingdom shall not be left to other people, but it shall break in pieces and consume all these kingdoms, and it shall stand for ever' (Daniel, II, 44).
152. Carlyle, II, 295 (the text given by Carlyle differs from, and is superior to, that given in Abbott, III, 63).
153. Carlyle, II, 295; cf. Abbott, III, 63.

the godly Saye was seen in the army as an apostate, 'a pretended puritan', 'a professed babe of Court'[154] – brought him reluctantly to the conclusion that maintaining the legal proprieties of parliamentary authority was no longer compatible with preserving the interests of his long-suffering godly brethren.

The catalyst of this change of heart had been the parliament's treaty negotiations with the king at Newport over the autumn of 1648. The effect of the treaty, Cromwell had feared, would be a return to episcopal rule, and the election of 'a new parliament', one in which the religious liberty for which he had fought would be swept permanently away. April 1653 witnessed the recrudescence of that threat: parliament's intentions for the new legislature and his own responsibility for 'the whole weight of this cause'[155] were forces straining in diametrically opposite directions.

Cromwell's insistence during the 1650s on the slogans and catchphrases of 1642 – in particular his frequent references to 'the cause' – alerts the reader to the manner in which that rhetoric had been reappropriated, and its meaning radically redefined, by the godly minority who found their haven and protection in the London separatist congregations and among the religious zealots of the army's officer corps. In 1642, preservation of *parliament's* authority had been at the heart of 'the cause'. Military intimidation which threatened that authority – as witnessed in the Army Plots, or in the king's abortive attempt to arrest Mandeville and the Five Members – was an integral part of the justification of the war. Godly reformation had of course also been an aspect of the cause. But few in 1642, however, would have recognized the broad claim to 'liberty of conscience' (which had become so central an aspect of Cromwell's perception of the cause), as anything more tha.ı a peripheral and highly negotiable element. What had been central was the authority of parliament, so conspicuously violated by Char'es I. The profoundly ironical aspect of Cromwell's expulsion of th Long Parliament in 1653 was that in order to preserve the religiʲus extremities of the 'Good Old Cause' of 1642 he was forced to destroy its parliamentary heart.

Like Charles I, Cromwell needed to make the three kingdoms safe for a radical re-interpretation of English protestantism. The First Civil War had ended in 1646 with a parliamentary reaction against the growth of heresy and schism at least as severe as the reaction

---

154. *Vox Militaris*, no. 5 (14–21 Nov. 1648), p. 35 (B.L., E473/8).
155. Carlyle, II, 280 (speech of 4 July 1653).

against the perceived growth of popery and Arminianism during the 1630s. Against such a reaction, Cromwell's version of godly protestantism (like Charles's version of Laudian protestantism in Scotland) could only be secured, at least in the short term, by force: with the backing of military strength. During the years from 1647 to 1653, there was a steady increment in the amount of force required to defend the godly brethren from the forces of presbyterian and royalist reaction: impeachments of eleven members, and the threat of a purge in 1647; the execution of a purge in 1648; wholesale dissolution in 1653.

This escalation of violence against the parliament serves not so much as an index of rising radicalism among the army's officer corps, but rather as a measure of the extent to which Cromwell's interpretation of 'the cause' – the constitutional priorities and 'liberty of conscience' demanded during the civil war – had become alienated from the concerns and desires of an ever growing proportion of the English political nation. Freeing England from the burdens of autocratic county committees, extortionate taxation, free-quartering soldiers, socially disruptive preachers: all these were far more pressing objectives for most of Cromwell's countrymen than quieting the troubled spirits of the separatists.

In posing as the champion of the radical sects, Cromwell was forced to adapt and modify the parliamentary ideology of the cause: he played down the importance of parliament's role as the representative of the estates as the foundation of its authority, founding its authority instead on a fiduciary relationship with the Saints, its duty to protect 'God's people'. From 1648, the test now became: did parliament 'fulfill the end of its magistracy'?[156]

The autocratic expulsion of a parliament was not the only aspect of the British civil wars to suggest parallels with the reign of Charles I. Cromwell still wanted a government that was based on consent; but in 1648 and in 1653, Cromwell (like Charles I) could not tolerate a parliament that was 'truly representative of the people' without abandoning to their parliamentary enemies the religious minority he countenanced and favoured. Richard Salwey withdrew from Cromwell's interim council in May 1653 when it became apparent that Cromwell could not be 'persuaded that the power of the nation

---

156. Abbott, I, 638; Underdown (ed.), 'The parliamentary diary of John Boys', p. 156.
157. Abbott, III, 16; cited in Worden, *Rump*, p. 339. Significantly, Salwey had been a member of Wharton's interest during the 1640s. He owed his election at Ap-

is in the good people of England, as formerly it was'.[157] 'The liberties of the people of God and the nation,' Cromwell later claimed, could not be trusted to 'a bare representative of the people'.[158]

It is hardly coincidental that Cromwell's gradual rejection of parliament's representative claims to authority – a point on which the purged House of Commons was in any case particularly vulnerable – developed in tandem with his first intimations that he might have a divinely appointed and quasi-monarchical role in the State. The almost miraculous success of his campaigns in 1650–51 had exerted a powerful influence on the formation of his prophetic self-image. 'Our heavenly Father hath raised me out of the dust to what I am', Cromwell wrote in the summer on 1651; and the second half of that scriptural verse perhaps gives a clue to what Cromwell meant by the words 'to what I am'. For the verse which Cromwell had in mind continues, '[He raiseth up the poor out of the dust] to set them among the princes, and make them inherit the throne of glory'.[159]

Did Cromwell think he was to be 'set . . . among the princes' in the summer of 1651? Certainly Hugh Peter, the New Model chaplain, thought he did. Around this time, Peter noticed so great a change in Cromwell's demeanour that on returning to London he confidently told Ludlow that he believed Cromwell was on the point of making himself king.[160] Again in November 1652, as the crisis between parliament and army deepened, Whitelocke reported that Cromwell posed the question: 'What if a man should take upon him to be king'?[161] Although Cromwell's attitude to the kingship remained profoundly ambivalent,[162] he was nevertheless certain of his own vocation, at the behest of Providence, to an exalted role in the fulfilment of God's plan for Israel – a vocation which endowed him with at least quasi-monarchical powers. In April 1653 he exercised that most monarchical of prerogatives, the power to dissolve a parliament. 'If Mr Pym were alive again', Dorothy Osborne reflected a few days after the dissolution, 'I wonder what he would think of

pleby to Wharton in 1645; cf. Thomas Gape to Richard Herbert, 11 July 1648: P. R. O., PRO 30/53/7 (Herbert corr.), fo. 73. [John Musgrave], *A Fourth Word to the Wise* ([8 June] 1647), p. 2 (B.L., E391/9).
158. Abbott, IV, 488.
159. I Samuel, II, 8.
160. Ludlow, *Memoirs*, I, 344; II, 9.
161. Abbott, II, 587–92; *The Parliamentary or Constitutional History of England* (24 vols, 1751–62), XX, 104–12.
162. Worden, 'Oliver Cromwell and the Sin of Achan', pp. 141–5.

these proceedings, and whether this would appear as great a breach of the privilege of parliament as the demanding the five members.'[163]

The ending of the parliament of 1640–53, like the ending of the series of parliaments of 1621–29, marked the beginning of a period of 'personal rule'. Despite the brief and ill-fated intermissions in which Cromwell attempted to govern with the consent of parliaments – in 1654, 1656 and 1658 – the period from 1653 until his death in 1658 was the period of the Personal Rule of Oliver Cromwell scarcely less than the years between 1629 and 1640 had been a period of personal rule for Charles I. Both regimes founded their authority on an ideology of divine right. The typology of Charles as King David and of Cromwell as Moses, the custodian of the authority of the Saints, stood on intellectual foundations which were disconcertingly similar. Likewise, millenarian puritanism, no less than Laudian ritualism, found a common enemy in 'the representative of the estates'.

'This revolution of affairs' was hailed by Cromwell in 1653 as the blessing of God. To those who could remember 1629 and 1642, *that* English 'revolution' must have seemed a profoundly ironic accomplishment.

163. G. C. Moore Smith (ed.), *The Letters of Dorothy Osborne to William Temple* (Oxford, 1928), p. 39 (23 April 1653); Abbott, II, 654; Cf. Worden, *Rump Parliament*, p. 304.

CHAPTER FOUR

Cromwell as a soldier
Austin Woolrych

The most remarkable fact about Cromwell's military career is that he was forty-three years old and nearly three-quarters of the way through his life before it began. He had no experience of soldiering in 1642 — not even of the recent Bishops' Wars, no doubt to his relief. Nearly all the officers on both sides in the civil wars who commanded any force larger than a regiment had seen some action in the continental warfare that had been raging since 1618, whether as professionals or as gentlemen volunteers. A few magnates without any such experience did command regional forces in the earlier stages, such as the earl of Manchester on the parliament's side and the earl of Derby and the marquis of Newcastle on the king's, but before the end of 1644 their day was past; all too plainly, it took more than blue blood to win battles. James Graham, marquis of Montrose, was a brilliant unschooled soldier who, like Cromwell, learned how to fight as he went along, but his talents lay in a very special kind of warfare. Sir William Brereton, Sir Thomas Myddelton and Henry Ireton achieved general rank without previous military experience, but as soldiers they hardly rate with Cromwell.

Only a strongly committed minority of MPs actually fought in the civil war, but it was a sizeable minority. At least fifty-five took up arms for the parliament, though many only briefly, or in a purely local and defensive role.[1] Cromwell was not exceptional in having reached what was then reckoned to be middle age, for at least a dozen of the more serious warriors among them were older than he – in

---

1. A rough count, based mainly on the *Dictionary of National Biography* and M. F. Keeler, *The Long Parliament, 1640–1641* (Philadelphia, 1954), and doubtless incomplete.

Myddelton's case thirteen years older – and several more were over forty. But with a few local or temporary exceptions their military careers all ended in 1645 after the passing of the Self-Denying Ordinance, whereas the most important part of Cromwell's still lay ahead.

His began inconspicuously. Just before Charles I raised his standard at Nottingham in August 1642, Cromwell like many another member hurried down to his constituency to activate the local authorities in support of parliament and to counter the efforts of local royalists. He found the town of Cambridge cooperative but the university predictably hostile. Many of the colleges had already packed their plate to send to the king, but by manning the castle, posting musketeers on the road northward and arresting several heads of houses, Cromwell prevented more than a small part of it from getting away.[2] His men at this stage were hastily assembled local levies, but he was soon back in his native Huntingdon and raising a troop of horse of his own. By 7 September it had sixty men, and within a week the Committee of Safety ordered him to stand by to join the parliament's main army under the earl of Essex.

Accounts differ as to whether he led his troop into action in the bloody and indecisive battle of Edgehill on 23 October; the probability is that he brought it to the field after the fighting had started, but that he played no conspicuous part in it. He saw enough, however, to convince him that something urgent needed to be done if the parliamentarian cavalry were to stand up to the king's, and he told John Hampden so soon afterwards, in a conversation that he recalled many years later:

> Your troopers, said I, are most of them old decayed serving men and tapsters, and such kind of fellows, and, said I, their troopers are gentlemen's sons, younger sons, persons of quality: do you think that the spirits of such base and mean fellows will ever be able to encounter gentlemen that have honour, courage and resolution in them? . . . You must get men of a spirit . . . that is like to go as far as a gentleman will go, or else I am sure you will be beaten still.[3]

That is what he himself proceeded to do when he returned to Cambridge in mid-January 1643. From then on he was engaged in

---

2. Clive Holmes, *The Eastern Association in the English Civil War* (Cambridge, 1974), p. 54; Abbott, I, 190.
3. Abbott, IV, 471. This conversation occurred before Cromwell and Hampden went their separate ways in January 1643, for they did not meet again before Hampden was killed in action in June. On whether Cromwell was at Edgehill see Abbott, I, 202–4.

raising a whole regiment, and he was accordingly promoted from captain to colonel. He selected his officers, and through them his troopers, most carefully. 'I raised such men as had the fear of God before them, and made some conscience of what they did,' he boasted later.[4] By March he had five troops, by September ten, each probably of at least eighty men, and from an early stage they had a reputation for godliness and discipline. 'I have a lovely company,' he wrote to Oliver St John on 11 September; 'they are no Anabaptists, they are honest, sober Christians: they expect to be used as men.'[5] When some 'bachelors and maids' offered to raise a company of foot he responded warmly, but wrote that a troop of horse would help the cause more than two or three foot companies, 'especially if your men be honest godly men. . . . Pray raise honest godly men, and I will have them of my regiment.' This he did, and they were to be known as the Maiden Troop.[6]

Like other commanders, Cromwell had his tussles with the county committees who had to furnish his soldiers' pay, and who therefore expected a say in the choice of their officers. The Suffolk committee objected when Ralph Margery raised a troop of horse, on the grounds that he was not a gentleman. Cromwell took them gently to task:

If you choose godly honest men to be captains of horse, honest men will follow them, and they will be careful to mount such . . . . I had rather have a plain russet-coated captain that knows what he fights for, and loves what he knows, than that which you call a gentleman and is nothing else. I honour a gentleman that is so indeed.[7]

When the committee continued to cavil, Cromwell took Captain Margery and his troop into his own regiment — the thirteenth of the fourteen troops that came to compose the double regiment famous as the Ironsides. Margery did in fact rank among the minor gentry (and incidentally he was already fifty-two years old).[8] Cromwell's original troop captains covered a wide social spectrum. His cousin Edward Whalley, his nephew Valentine Walton, his future

---

4. Abbott, IV, 471.
5. Abbott, I, 258. Most of this and the next two paragraphs are based on C. H. Firth and G. Davies, *The Regimental History of Cromwell's Army* (Oxford, 1940), ch. 1: 'The raising of the Ironsides'.
6. Abbott, I, 248.
7. Ibid., 256; cf. 262.
8. Raymond and Jean Lock, 'Captain Raphe Margery, a Suffolk Ironside', *Cromwelliana* (1987), 5–17. Margery fought as a troop commander right through to Worcester and the subsequent capture of Jersey; he left the service only when mortally ill in 1653.

son-in-law Henry Ireton and his own son Oliver were undoubtedly gentlemen, but his brother-in-law John Disbrowe had trained as an attorney and lived as a farmer, while James Berry had been a clerk in a Shropshire ironworks. Several others ranked among 'the middling sort'. Four — Whalley, Disbrowe, Berry and Ireton — were to attain general rank, and five met their deaths on active service.

As long as his officers had what he called the root of the matter in them, Cromwell was as indifferent to the precise form of religion that they professed as he was to their social rank. Margery was an Independent; Captain Christopher Bethell and his lieutenant, John Pitchford, were sectaries, and filled their troop with men of like mind. Berry and Adam Lawrence, on the other hand, were close friends of the very orthodox Richard Baxter, and Whalley was reckoned a Presbyterian until at least 1647.[9] There seems to have been a brief phase in the second half of 1644 when the aggressive intolerance of rigid Presbyterians like Lawrence Crawford, major-general of the infantry in the Eastern Association army, made Cromwell do his best to get rid of such officers and promote Independents and sectaries in their places.[10] But it was over before he took up his command in the New Model Army. He spoke his true feelings in his dispatch after the storming of Bristol in September 1645, an action that tested the courage of officers and men to the limit: 'Presbyterians, Independents, all had here the same spirit of faith and prayer; the same presence and answer; they all agree here, know no names of difference: pity it is it should be otherwise anywhere.' The whole passage was a passionate plea for the religious liberty of 'these gallant men', whose joy it was 'that they are instruments to God's glory, and their country's good'.[11] Parliament excised all this when it printed his letter, as it had excised a similar appeal in his dispatch after the battle of Naseby, which ended thus:

Honest men served you faithfully in this action. Sir, they are trusty; I beseech you in the name of God, not to discourage them. . . . He that ventures his life for the liberty of his country, I wish he trust God for the liberty of his conscience, and you for the liberty he fights for.[12]

One of Cromwell's greatest strengths was his power to communicate to his officers and men his own utter certainty that they were the

9. A. Woolrych, *Soldiers and Statesmen* (Oxford, 1987), p. 41. Thomas Edwards singled Whalley out for praise in *Gangraena*.
10. Holmes, *Eastern Association*, pp. 199–205.
11. Abbott, I, 377.
12. Ibid., 360.

instruments of a divine plan in which England had a special part to play, as an elect nation; they were the shock-troops of the people of God. He upheld their right to worship and pray — and to preach too, if they were so moved — as their consciences directed them. But he also cared deeply for their material needs, as well as for their dignity and susceptibilities as human beings; 'they expect to be treated as men' was a very characteristic utterance. Twice in the autumn of 1643 he openly wept when no money was forthcoming for their pay, or for remedying their 'great want of clothes and other necessaries'.[13] 'Truly I count not myself worthy to be employed by God,' he wrote to his cousin Sir Thomas Barrington, a man of power in Essex, 'but for my poor men, help them what you can, for they are faithful.'[14]

From the first, Cromwell's Ironsides formed part of the forces of the Eastern Association, which comprised Norfolk, Suffolk, Essex, Hertfordshire, Cambridgeshire, Huntingdonshire and (from September 1643) Lincolnshire. It was one of a number of regional associations that parliament set up early in the war, primarily for local defence, and it was never clear how far they were subject to direct orders from the earl of Essex, the Lord General, or whether their forces could be called upon to operate for more than short periods outside their own territories. Financial provision for them depended heavily on their constituent county committees, and it was seriously inadequate. Lord Grey of Warke was the Eastern Association's first commander, and in February 1643 he was ordered to march all his forces to the Thames valley, to reinforce Essex's army. He took more than 5000 horse and foot with him, to the considerable dismay of his county committees, but Cromwell was left behind to defend the northerly flanks of the Association against the strong and aggressive royalist forces centred on Newark. Consequently Cromwell had the command of sundry local levies of infantry and dragoons, as well as his own Ironsides. With them he carried out various small-scale operations, including the siege and capture of Crowland.

It was not only such modest military exploits that earned him a growing reputation, but the energy and urgency with which he spurred the county committees, the deputy lieutenants and other local authorities into supporting and supplying his troops. His total and imperative commitment bursts from the page across three and a

13. Holmes, *Eastern Association*, p. 98.
14. Abbott, I, 264.

half centuries. 'This is not a time to pick and choose for pleasure,' he wrote to the commissioners of the Association at Cambridge when a self-important knight was being dilatory in sending up his regiment. 'Service must be done. Command you, and be obeyed! . . . The Lord give you, and us, zeal.' 'It's no longer disputing, but out instantly all you can,' he adjured them in August, when he had no infantry fit to withstand a threatened attack: 'Raise all your bands; send them to Huntingdon; get up what volunteers you can; hasten your horses. . . . You must act lively; do it without distraction.' 'Is this the way to save a Kingdom?,' he asked the Essex deputy lieutenants, when their reluctant conscripts had made off home almost as soon as they joined him. And on behalf of his own trusted soldiers, he wrote reproachfully to the commissioners at Cambridge: 'Gentlemen, take them able to live and subsist that are willing to spend their blood for you.'[15] Because he relied on impassioned persuasion rather than recrimination, he got much more response from these essential sources of support than Lord Grey of Groby did in the adjacent Midland Association, or even the more capable Sir William Waller in the South-Eastern.

The actions that he fought in 1643 — that at Grantham on 13 May, the storming of Burleigh House followed by the fight near Gainsborough on 28 July, and the cavalry battle at Winceby on 11 October — have been dwelt on lovingly by his biographers, searching for portents of his later achievements, but they were relatively minor affairs. Gainsborough is significant, not only because the Ironsides engaged a royalist cavalry force head on and won, but because they already displayed the discipline that was to win much bigger battles later. Cromwell was able to recall several troops that had been pursuing the beaten cavaliers and to launch them in a surprise attack on the one enemy regiment that had stood firm.[16] Winceby was the first engagement in which he fought alongside Sir Thomas Fairfax, who led the cavalry in the small army that his father, Ferdinando Lord Fairfax, had raised in Yorkshire. Fairfax senior had been besieged in Hull by the marquis of Newcastle's much larger army for over a month, and the rout of the royalist horse at Winceby led not only to the raising of the siege of Hull but to the surrender of Lincoln to the earl of Manchester. Leading the charge of the first line of cavalry, Cromwell took a heavy fall when his horse was shot dead, and

15. Ibid., 236, 251, 253.
16. Ibid., 240–6; P. Young and R. Holmes, *The English Civil War: a military history of the three Civil Wars 1642–1651* (1974), pp. 151–3.

he was knocked to the ground again almost as soon as he found his feet. He eventually got back into the fight on a trooper's borrowed mount, but Fairfax led the charge that clinched the victory. Yet however the honours were shared, it was the beginning of a memorable comradeship in arms.[17]

Meanwhile the continuing threat of Newcastle's army had led parliament to transform the status and size of that of the Eastern Association. In August the ineffectual and doubtfully loyal Grey of Warke had been replaced as its major-general by the earl of Manchester, who was empowered to recruit up to 20,000 men for it. That was far more than Manchester could raise, for the foot soldiers impressed by the associated counties were all too prone to mutiny or desert, but his personal standing among the puritan gentry in the region was very high, and he was as keen as Cromwell to fill his army with godly officers. Consequently it attracted a number of radical officers from Essex's army and the other provincial forces; John Lilburne, the future Leveller leader, was one of them. Time would eventually reveal a sharp divergence between Manchester's and Cromwell's notions of what constituted a godly reformation and what the parliament's war aims should be, but for the first year or so their relationship seems to have been good.

They certainly shared a common frustration over two things that hindered them from taking the war to the enemy and following up such promising successes as Winceby and Lincoln. One was the utter inadequacy of the monthly assessments that parliament imposed on the associated counties for the upkeep of their army, and the counties' chronic failure to meet even their modest quotas. The other was Essex's continuing assumption that he could dispose of the Eastern Association forces without reference to Manchester, whom he treated simply as a subordinate; on 26 August, for instance, he tried to order Cromwell and all the Association's cavalry to join his own army for the relief of Gloucester, just when a royalist revolt was simmering in King's Lynn. Such difficulties and conflicts could be resolved only by parliament, and the settling of them involved a contest between those peers and MPs who hoped, like Essex, to end the war by a negotiated peace and those who, like Cromwell, saw no prospect of an outcome worthy of the cause save through total victory.

The result was a verdict on Essex's feeble military performance

---

17. Gardiner, *Civil War*, I, 240–4; Abbott, I, 265–6; Young and Holmes, pp. 154–8.

and his qualified commitment to the war. An ordinance passed on 20 January 1644 placed the Eastern Association on a much stronger and more independent footing. Its nominal strength was set at 14,000; its financial provision was raised by half; its fiscal and military administrations were centralized, and Manchester was empowered to supervise the spending of its revenues, in place of the constituent county committees.[18] Essex's military establishment was actually reduced soon afterwards to 7,500 foot and 3,000 horse, to his bitter indignation.[19] Cromwell was promoted to lieutenant-general, making him second-in-command to Manchester, and (under him) commander of all the cavalry.[20] At least as important was his appointment, along with Manchester's, to the Committee of Both Kingdoms, the new central executive body which was to direct the war effort of both England and Scotland. It was dominated neither by Essex's faction nor by the extreme war party but by men of the middle group, Cromwell's natural political allies, who were continuing Pym's policies after his tragic death in December – men such as Viscount Saye and Sele and the earl of Northumberland in the Lords and Oliver St John, the two Sir Henry Vanes and William Pierrepont in the Commons. Cromwell was always as much a politician as a soldier, and although the enlargement of the Eastern Association and its role enhanced his military status it was not clear which function was going to occupy him most.

The military scene was transformed in January 1644 by the arrival of a Scottish army of 21,000 men under the earl of Leven, and when they and the Fairfaxes' northerners besieged the marquis of Newcastle's forces in York they brought on the biggest battle of the civil wars. Prince Rupert brought a composite force to relieve the city, and the Eastern Association army hastened north to support the besiegers. The combined armies faced each other on Marston Moor on 2 July, infantry in the centre and cavalry on either flank, with the parliamentarian allies facing north and numbering nearly 28,000 against Rupert's and Newcastle's 18,000. Manchester had only about 8,000 men on the field, but nearly half of them were Cromwell's cavalry, and he commanded the western wing, with about 800 Scot-

---

18. Holmes, *Eastern Association*, ch. 5; C. H. Firth and R. S. Rait (eds), *Acts and Ordinances of the Interregnum* (3 vols, 1911), I, 368.
19. Ibid., p. 398; L. J., VI, 505.
20. Abbott, I, 272. He was styled 'lieutenant-general of horse and foot' in the army's accounts, but the convention was that his rank carried the responsibility for the horse and that of major- general (which was and is junior to lieutenant-general) the responsibility for the foot.

tish horse under David Leslie in faithful support. It was Cromwell's
first experience of a full-scale battle, involving infantry as well as
cavalry, apart from his peripheral involvement at Edgehill as a mere
troop commander, and more than any other one engagement it made
his military reputation. While Sir Thomas Fairfax's northern horse
on the eastern wing were suffering a near-disaster, Cromwell's regiments broke and routed their royalist opponents; and their discipline
was such that instead of letting them loose on the wild pursuit that
always tempted victorious horsemen, Cromwell was able to re-form
them, lead them round the moor behind the royalist infantry and
then attack the cavalry that had defeated Fairfax's regiments. He not
only beat them soundly, but with the aid of the Eastern Association
foot under Major-General Crawford he arrested a serious collapse of
the allied infantry on the right; Leven, Manchester and Lord Fairfax
were already in flight. His cavalry turned imminent defeat into overwhelming victory, though credit is also due to Leslie's and
Crawford's supporting roles.[21]

The story of how the fruits of Marston Moor were thrown away
belongs as much to political as to military history. If the victors had
combined with Essex to bring the king's main army to battle, Charles could have been totally defeated within months — but that was
just the trouble: the very prospect dismayed Manchester, as it had
long dismayed Essex. They had dreadful visions of the ancient constitution being subverted, of the social hierarchy undermined, and of
sober puritan orthodoxy going down before a swarm of heretical
sectaries, if the 'fiery spirits' marched on to total victory. They
wanted to induce Charles to treat for peace and they closed their eyes
to the signs that he had no serious intentions of accepting any terms
that parliament might set. So Essex marched off to conquer the
south-west and met disaster at Lostwithiel, the Scots settled down
to the siege of Newcastle, and Manchester avoided further military
action as far as he could. Cromwell's relations with his general wor-
sened rapidly, especially after the combined forces of the Eastern
Association and Sir William Waller bungled the second battle of
Newbury on 27 October and let the king's army, which they greatly
outnumbered, get clean away.

21. Previous accounts are superseded by Peter Newman, *The Battle of Marston Moor
1644* (Chichester, 1981), though some topographical details may still be controversial. Newman deals faithfully with those detractors who tried to belittle
Cromwell's role, and concludes: 'Cromwell had won the battle of Marston
Moor' (p. 103).

Four weeks later Cromwell and Waller took the drastic step of accusing Manchester before the House of Commons, and Cromwell exposed in detail his 'backwardness to all action' since July. It was Cromwell the politician who chose, in concert with his political allies, just when to drop the personal charges and promote instead the positive remedies: a Self-Denying Ordinance and the recasting of the several battered field forces into a New Model Army. The interesting question is whether he was prepared to terminate his own military career as well as that of the peace party generals, and the indications are that he was. The ordinance that he supported totally debarred members of either house from holding army military command, and it was very unlikely that he could expect parliament to exempt him personally from it (even if that was in his mind), when he and his allies would not hear of exempting Essex. He was not to foresee that a revised version, eventually passed on 3 April 1645, would leave it open for a member to be reappointed after he had resigned his command. Nor was it clear where he was most needed. John Lilburne, to whom he was still a hero, met the objection that 'This [the ordinance] will fetch that gallant man Cromwell from the Army, which will be a mighty loss to the kingdom', with the answer: 'But if he come into the House of Commons (that proper seat whereunto he was chosen) and do them ten times more service there, than he doth, or can do in the Army, what loss hath the commonwealth then? . . . Oh for self-denying Cromwell home again!'[22]

Nevertheless parliament left the post of lieutenant-general in the New Model unfilled, and found itself unable to dispense with his military services in the somewhat precarious circumstances of the spring of 1645. Extending his commission for forty days at a time, it employed him very actively, with various detachments of horse, and mostly in connection with a projected siege of Oxford. But Rupert's fearful sack of Leicester on 30 May thrust such plans aside; the Committee of Both Kingdoms ordered the New Model to take the field and bring the king's main army to battle. Fairfax still had no lieutenant-general to take the overall command of the cavalry under him. At Stony Stratford on 8 June, with a major battle clearly imminent, he put it to a council of war that parliament should be urgently requested to appoint Cromwell to the vacancy. His officers warmly and unanimously agreed; the Commons voted the appoint-

---

22. J. Lilburne, *England's Birth-Right Justified* (1645), p. 31; partly reprinted in G. E. Aylmer (ed.), *The Levellers in the English Revolution* (1975), pp. 59–60. For a further discussion of the Self-Denying Ordinance, see above, pp. 60–5. .

ment at once, but the Lords, still smarting under the Self-Denying Ordinance's affront to their order, did not. Fairfax did not wait, and when Cromwell in response to his summons rode into the army's quarters at 6 a.m. on the 13th he was welcomed 'with a mighty shout'.

The battle of Naseby was fought the very next day, but Cromwell did not need to get to know his regiments and their commanders, since his Eastern Association cavalry had been incorporated in the New Model almost intact. He and they contributed as much to the crucial victory at Naseby as they had at Marston Moor. There were indeed certain broad similarities. His cavalry were as successful on one wing (the eastern, this time) as Rupert was against Commissary-General Henry Ireton on the other, while in the centre the king's infantry, though outnumbered, drove back the raw New Model foot. But whereas Rupert squandered his success in a pursuit that took him to the outskirts of Naseby village, Cromwell halted the main body of his horse as soon they had driven the opposing royalist squadrons off the field, and wheeled them round behind the king's reserve to attack the royalist infantry on their western flank, which Rupert should have been protecting. Rupert got back to the scene of the fighting too late, and though both he and Charles risked their lives in trying to make their men stand, the rout was complete. Cromwell's troopers did execution on the fleeing enemy for a dozen miles.[23]

A month after Naseby, the New Model engaged and destroyed Lord Goring's western royalist army at Langport. The success of the action hinged on an initial cavalry charge across a ford so narrow that only two or three men could ride abreast, in full face of the enemy horse drawn up to engage them. Fairfax entrusted the operation to Cromwell, and it was performed with tremendous dash by six troops that had once formed part of his own regiment of Ironsides.[24] Langport was the last considerable battle in the First Civil War, but many royalist strongholds remained to be reduced, and the greatest of them was Bristol. Rupert, who had stormed the city in 1643, was himself in command of the defenders. The question now was whether to assault the city or reduce it by a long siege.

23. For general accounts of the battle see Barry Denton, *Naseby Fight* (Leigh-on-Sea, 1988) and A. Woolrych, *Battles of the English Civil War* (1961), ch. 6. Peter Young, *Naseby 1645* (1985) is unsatisfactory on the battle but prints generous extracts from the contemporary sources.
24. Abbott, I, 364–6; Gardiner, *Civil War, II, 271–4; Young and Holmes, pp. 254–7.*

Cromwell's exceptionally long and eloquent dispatch to the Speaker describes the pros and cons, and tells how the decision was taken.[25] Storming a city whose fortifications could (in parts) barely be scaled with thirty-rung ladders could be a bloodier and more daunting business than a pitched battle, and depended particularly on the resolution of the infantry. At Fairfax's first council of war the difficulties seemed so great that opinion was against it, but at a second council a few days later all objections were overcome and a day and hour were fixed for the storm. The determination with which it was carried out showed how greatly the New Model foot had improved since Naseby, and when the key forts had been taken Rupert surrendered the city on terms – though not before setting fire to it. The evidence of Bristol (and of many other actions) also shows how much consultation preceded military decisions in Fairfax's army, and later in Cromwell's, and how much more collective they were than in most modern armies, with their hierarchical and specialized command structures.

The rest of the war was mainly a matter of reducing lesser strongholds, and for this Fairfax and Cromwell split up. Cromwell alone was in charge of the operations against Devizes, Winchester and Basing House, but when hostilities ended with the surrender of Oxford in June 1646 he had still never had the overall command of an army in a battle. It is worth pausing to consider what had given him his already formidable military reputation, and where that reputation would stand today if (as almost everyone hoped) parliament's victory had led to a firm and lasting peace.

His great strengths lay in his ability to raise and train cavalry regiments of superb courage and discipline, to fire them with his own high sense that they were fighting the Lord's battles, and to lead them in the field with a keen eye that told him where their striking power was most needed and would be most effective. In campaigns that were fought so largely by amateurs on both sides, moral qualities counted for more in commanders than high professional skill, and Cromwell's moral authority over his officers and men was potent. The English civil wars were quite different from the wars that Tilly and Wallenstein and Gustavus Adolphus had waged on the continent, where officers and soldiers alike were professionals and might fight together for decades, with time outside the campaigning seasons to teach recruits their elaborate drills. England by contrast had never had a standing army to provide cadres, so most of

25. Abbott, I, 374–8.

Cromwell's officers and nearly all his men had to learn their trade in very little time before they went into action. That being so, their strength lay in their discipline, their commitment and their total mutual confidence, rather than in exceptional skills in manoeuvre or horsemanship. Cromwell was not an innovator in tactics. In some early actions, Essex's cavalry had tried to practise the so-called Dutch drill, trotting forward at least five ranks deep, halting close to the enemy, and then each rank firing its pistols in turn and wheeling to the rear after doing so. But Cromwell, like Rupert, followed Gustavus Adolphus's practice, ranging each troop in only three ranks, charging smartly, sword in hand, and charging home. It was a method that relied on cold steel and sheer impact rather than on fire-power, though Cromwell's horsemen used their pistols in the mêlée as opportunity offered. They probably rode into action less hard than Rupert's, at a fast trot rather than a gallop, and in close order, with the riders almost knee to knee.[26] It was a tactic well matched to the order and solidarity in which they excelled, and their successes would have earned Cromwell a niche among cavalry commanders even if he had hung up his arms in 1646. His main achievements as a general, however, still lay ahead.

For almost the first year of uneasy peace his military career was so much in abeyance that it has been questioned whether he was in the army at all. The last of the special ordinances whereby parliament extended his appointment as lieutenant-general expired in July 1646, but Fairfax went on signing warrants for his pay from time to time, and when the New Model was threatened with imminent disbandment late in May 1647 he collected his arrears right down to that date.[27] The French ambassador Bellièvre transmitted an extraordinary report that earlier in the spring Cromwell had been in frequent conference with the Elector Palatine with a view to taking service under him in Germany, with as many of his old soldiers as he could enlist. This is profoundly improbable. Cromwell did not need the money, for parliament had conferred on him an estate worth over £2,000 a year, and there is no other evidence that he was ever interested in fighting for any cause but that to which he believed providence had called him in England.[28]

26. C. H. Firth, *Cromwell's Army* (1902), ch. 5, esp. pp. 142–4.
27. G. E. Aylmer, 'Was Oliver Cromwell a member of the army in 1646–7 or not?', *History*, LVI (1971), 183–8; Charles Hoover, 'Cromwell's status and pay in 1646–47', *H. J.* XXIII, 3 (1980), 703–15. See also above, pp. 64–6.
28. Gardiner, *Civil War*, III, 147 and 222. It is quite likely that Cromwell did discuss

When the army defied the parliament's attempt to disband it, the presbyterian politicians assumed that Cromwell was encouraging it, and they threatened to impeach him. They probably suspected him falsely. His only contact with the army during its mounting discontent was in a mediatory role, as a commissioner of parliament.[29] When he left Westminster to join the army at its general rendezvous early in June, it was not because he feared impeachment, which the Presbyterians could never have brought off, nor because he preferred a military to a parliamentary career, since he cannot have supposed that any further fighting would be needed, except in Ireland. It was not primarily a personal choice, and he probably did not see it as a choice at all. To have acquiesced in the destruction of the New Model would have opened the way to a peace settlement without adequate safeguards and to the entrenchment of the presbyterian leaders in power – besides flying in the face of Fairfax, the great majority of his fellow-officers and almost all his old soldiers.[30] As he saw it, the only way to bring the king to accept a settlement that would secure the civil and religious liberties for which they had fought was to support the claims and policies advanced in the army's *Solemn Engagement* and in its *Declaration* (or *Representation*) of 14 June.[31]

Not that he believed that the army had a right to impose its own terms on the country by force. In the new General Council of the Army, which included two officers and two soldiers ('agitators') elected by each regiment, he consistently opposed the pressure to march on London and present its demands at sword's point. 'Really, really,' he said in July, 'have what you will, that [which] you have by force I look upon it as nothing.'[32] From then until late in the year, when Charles deliberately abandoned the path of negotiation by fleeing from the army's custody and signing his fatal Engagement

with the Elector Palatine the terms on which English soldiers might take service in Germany when the threatened disbandment took place, and that Bellievre (an unreliable informant) jumped to the conclusion that he meant to go with them.

29. Woolrych, *Soldiers and Statesmen*, ch. 4, where Cromwell's dealings with Cornet Joyce over the abduction of the king are discussed.

30. See ibid., pp. 133–6, for some evidence that Mark A. Kishlansky overstated the proportion of officers who left the army at this stage in *The Rise of the New Model Army* (Cambridge, 1979), pp. 219–21. More detailed evidence will be presented in the forthcoming work on the army by Ian Gentles.

31. The essential parts of both documents are reprinted in A. S. P. Woodhouse (ed.), *Puritanism and Liberty* (1938), pp. 401–9. For a valuable concise account of the army's grievances see J. S. Morrill, 'The army revolt of 1647', in A. C. Duke and C. A. Tamse (eds), *Britain and the Netherlands* (1977), pp. 54–78.

32. Woodhouse, p. 418, and pp. 409–21 *passim*.

with the Scots, Cromwell gave all his support to a set of peace terms known as the Heads of the Proposals, which Ireton drafted in concert with Viscount Saye and Sele, Lord Wharton and probably some other moderate Independent politicians.[33]

Cromwell took the chair in the General Council's great debates at Putney in late October and early November, in which representatives of the Levellers and a small group of new agents or agitators, whom the Levellers sponsored and manipulated, sought to promote *An Agreement of the People*. This would have based the settlement of the kingdom not on a treaty between king and parliament, or even on the enactment of parliament alone, but on the direct assent of all its free citizens (though there was no intention that this should include women or royalists). There were points in the *Agreement* (few of them new) to which Cromwell could readily agree: biennial parliaments with rationalized constituencies, a very wide liberty of conscience and worship, and a radical reform of the law. But he was not yet ready to contemplate its implied denial of any authority whatever to either the Crown or the House of Lords, and he was deeply opposed to separating the right to vote in parliamentary elections from the possession of property. The Leveller programme could only have been implemented by force, and it was fundamentally inconsistent with the manifestos and declarations that the army had been publishing since June. Cromwell still believed that a durable settlement must come through parliament, and that the Heads of the Proposals offered the best way forward. So throughout the first day's debate he strove to focus discussion not on the merits of the *Agreement* but on how far it was compatible with the army's previous declarations and pledges.

The next day, at a meeting which was not a formal session of the General Council (nor incidentally held in Putney church), the Leveller representatives succeeded in getting the text of the *Agreement* discussed. Ireton committed the tactical error of focusing the debate on the question of manhood suffrage, which the *Agreement* did not expressly demand. In long exchanges with Colonel Rainborowe and the civilian Leveller John Wildman he found himself increasingly isolated, though Cromwell supported him; it was very clear that many officers as well as soldiers, who did not necessarily share the Levellers' desire to purge or dissolve the parliament by force, accepted the proposition that by the law of nature every man had a

33. J. S. A. Adamson, 'The English nobility and the projected settlement of 1647', *H. J.*, XXX, 3(1987), 567–602.

right to vote for the people's representatives unless he had somehow forfeited it.

By the time the General Council met again on 1 November, the generals knew that the Levellers and their creature agents (though only a handful of the original, genuinely elected agitators joined with them in this) were inciting the soldiery to disobey their officers and to forgather in an unauthorized general rendezvous. Cromwell, who had so far shown an impartial courtesy and patience towards all speakers, regardless of rank, found it necessary to assert his authority:

> I have a commission from the General, and I understand that I am to do by it. I shall conform to him according to the rules and discipline of war, and . . . I conceive it is not in the power of any particular men to call a rendezvous of a troop or regiment, or in [the] least to disoblige the army from those commands of the General.[34]

During the next week or two the unity and discipline of the army were under increasing strain, not only from the Leveller agents' subversive activities but from the divisive debates over the franchise question and that of whether they should support any further negotiation with the king. There was widespread feeling in the regiments themselves that the army should close its ranks, and Fairfax certainly thought so. Cromwell reluctantly gave up his and Ireton's long attempt to gain the General Council's acceptance of a version of the Heads of the Proposals that a united army could join with its allies in both houses in pressing upon both king and parliament. Fairfax presided over a General Council on 8 November and gave his tacit support to a motion by Cromwell, which was passed without demur, that the agitators – officers as well as soldiers – should return to their regiments until the general summoned them again. He never did.[35]

The move was well timed. The king made his escape just three days later, and four days after that the Leveller agents attempted a mutiny by bringing two regiments, with the *Agreement* stuck in the soldiers' hats, to a rendezvous near Ware – the first of three rendezvous arranged by Fairfax, but not the one to which they had been summoned. Cromwell's bold and furious reaction was largely instrumental in cowing them into submission,[36] and within a week the army's discipline and solidarity were triumphantly restored.

34. Woodhouse, p. 98.
35. The matter in this and the previous two paragraphs are discussed and documented in *Soldiers and Statesmen*, chs 9 and 10.
36 For two very different accounts of this episode see M. A. Kishlansky, 'What happened at Ware?', *H. J.*, XXV, 4(1982), 827–39, and Woolrych, *Soldiers and*

Charles's Engagement with the Scots promised him a Scottish army in 1648, but long before it was ready to march the Second Civil War broke out untidily with risings in Wales and south-east England in which royalism was only one element. Fairfax took on the insurgents in Kent and Essex, and soon settled to a long siege of Colchester; Cromwell set off for south Wales in May with about 6,500 horse and foot, but the back of the rising was broken before he got there by Colonel Thomas Horton's fine victory at St Fagans. Pembroke, however, held out until 11 July, thanks to the doggedness of its defenders and sundry misfortunes that delayed the arrival of the necessary siege guns. By that time the duke of Hamilton and his Scottish army were in Carlisle, and Sir Marmaduke Langdale had joined him with over 3,000 northern royalists; Major-General Lambert was shadowing them with a small northern force. Cromwell lost no further time in advancing northward to engage them, though he had to make a wide detour to collect shoes from Northampton and stockings from Coventry for his ill-shod men, and to take in contingents of local forces from Leicestershire, Nottinghamshire and Derbyshire. Despite execrably cold, wet and windy weather, which turned roads into quagmires and made many rivers unfordable, his army marched about 350 miles within a month in order to join up with Lambert near Knaresborough on 12 August. In the same period Hamilton had advanced less than seventy miles, to Hornby in Lancashire. Cromwell then crossed the Pennines with 8.600 men in all, and at Preston he fell upon fully twice that number almost before they were aware of his proximity. Very boldly, he chose to interpose his army between the Scots and their line of retreat, rather than simply to block their route south. The first phase of the battle, on 17 August, was a long, hard slog, in which the terrain allowed very limited use of cavalry, but by nightfall the Scots had been driven out of Preston and over the Ribble. For the next two days they were in desperate retreat southward, trying vainly to make a stand. By the time they reached Warrington they had only 2,600 foot left in a body to surrender, and all their cavalry were in flight. Cromwell reckoned he had lost less than a hundred men killed.[37] In speed, seizure of

---

Statesmen, pp. 280–4, where it is argued that the traditional version is essentially true.

37. Abbott, I, 630–42; Woolrych, *Battles*, ch. 8; Peter Gaunt, *The Cromwellian Gazetteer* (Gloucester, 1987), pp. 226, 232. My estimate of Hamilton's strength at Preston includes Langdale's men, but not Monro's 3,000 Scots and about a further 1,500 northerners who were far in his rear.

opportunities and iron determination, his whole conduct of the Preston campaign displayed generalship of a high order.

His subsequent advance to Edinburgh was more of a political than a military exercise, but after that he seems for a while to have taken refuge in his role as a soldier from a part that he was not yet ready to play as a politician. A small royalist garrison still held out in Pontefract, and throughout most of November he conducted the siege in person. He could easily have left it to Lambert. He detested the parliament's current negotiation with the king at Newport – 'this ruining hypocritical agreement' – but he could not yet go all the way with Ireton, who was busy aligning the Council of Officers behind a demand that Charles should be tried for his life. His letters to his cousin Robert Hammond, the king's reluctant gaoler, seem to be wrestling with his own conscience as well as trying to guide Hammond's.[38] Summoned by Fairfax, he arrived back in London on the evening after Pride's Purge had taken place, and he gave it his approval. By January, after vainly seeking an alternative solution, he had become as convinced a regicide as any, and since Fairfax would have no part in the king's trial and was not a member of parliament, Cromwell probably had a crucial say in who should represent the army on the High Court of Justice. Only the general officers and the commanders of regiments (with the puzzling exceptions of Charles Fleetwood and Nathaniel Rich) were nominated as commissioners, and most (though not all) took part in sentencing the king.[39]

Six weeks after the king's execution, Cromwell was the Rump's natural choice as commander of the force that was to reduce Ireland, but not unnaturally he hesitated for a fortnight before accepting. It was bound to be an arduous campaign, though Colonel Michael Jones's splendid victory at Rathmines on 2 August, shortly before Cromwell landed his 12,000 men, saved him from having to fight

38. Abbott, I, 676–8, 696–9; David Underdown, *Pride's Purge* (Oxford, 1971), pp. 116–27, 148–50.
39. The two officers below full colonel who were appointed commissioners, Goffe and Disbrowe, were the *de facto* commanders of Fairfax's own regiments of foot and horse respectively. Lieutenant-General Thomas Hammond and Colonel Tomlinson must be accounted regicides, even though they did not sign the king's death warrant, because they were in court when he was sentenced and gave their express assent: see A. W. McIntosh, 'The numbers of the English regicides', *History*, LXVII, (1982), 194–216, and the same author's *The Death Warrant of King Charles I* (House of Lords RO, 1981). The only officers who were commissioners but not regicides were Fairfax, Skippon, Disbrowe, Lambert and Overton; but Lambert was on duty before Pontefract and Overton in Hull. Abbott (I, 728–9) lists attendances at the High Court, but fails (as elsewhere) to distinguish between serving officers and men still accorded a military title by virtue of past service.

another pitched battle. Nevertheless the risk of getting bogged down (literally) in endless sieges amid a bitterly hostile population probably hardened an attitude made harsh enough already by his typical Englishman's belief that the Irish were barbarous by nature, corrupted by popish superstition, and (even less justly) collectively responsible for the massacre of protestant settlers in 1641. He certainly fought his Irish campaign in a spirit different from any of his other ones.

Drogheda was the first town he attacked, and after a week's siege his guns blew a large breach in its walls. By the rules of war, which Wellington was still justifying in 1820, a garrison that rejected a summons to surrender after a breach had been made, as Drogheda's governor Sir Arthur Aston did, was not entitled to quarter; but elsewhere Cromwell was wont to temper the rules of war with humanity. Here, the storming of the breach proving costly, he gave orders 'in the heat of action' (his own words) that Aston and his attendant officers should be put to the sword and that none who was still in arms within the walls should be spared. He reckoned that about 2,000 were slaughtered that night, including all the friars in the town, and they were not the only non-combatants to perish. Blind prejudice against the Irish does not fully explain his severity, for Aston and many of the defenders were English. Next day he gave limited quarter to the soldiers in two forts who surrendered, and those who were not decimated were shipped to Barbados. His long dispatch to the Speaker contained a hint of compunction, particularly in his claim that Drogheda's agony 'will tend to prevent the effusion of blood for the future, which are the satisfactory grounds to such actions, which otherwise cannot but work remorse and regret'.[40] That, in his mind, was probably the heart of the matter.

His next action, the reduction of Wexford, was a more confused affair, and harder to judge. The governor, Colonel Synnott, entered into a treaty with him, under cover of which he admitted 1,500 more defenders and then broke it off. But when the bombardment of the castle (the key to the defences) began in devastating earnest, Synnott sent an offer of surrender, though on unrealistically favourable terms. Cromwell nevertheless prepared a counter-offer that would have

---

40. Abbott, II, 125–8; Gardiner, *C & P*, I, 112–24. 'Decimated' is here used in a strict, classical sense. Every tenth man was shot. For a balanced account of Cromwell's campaign from an Irish standpoint see Chapter 13 by Patrick J. Corish in T. W. Moody, F. X. Martin and F. J. Byrne (eds), *A New History of Ireland*, vol. III (Oxford, 1976), and for a defence of Cromwell, Maurice Ashley, *The Greatness of Oliver Cromwell* (1957), pp. 230–3.

spared the lives of the garrison and the property of the citizens; but before it could be sent one of Synnott's captains surrendered the castle to its besiegers, and they, probably unaware of the treaty in progress, took immediate advantage of their now commanding position over the town. The threatened defenders abandoned the walls; some sought to escape across the river, in which about 300 were drowned, while others tried to make a stand behind improvised barricades in the marketplace, along with many townsfolk. Cromwell's soldiers slaughtered them indiscriminately, and again priests and friars were butchered. His dispatch makes unpleasant reading, with its invocation of God's righteous justice and just judgment upon the defenders. The question is whether he *could* have called off his enraged forces, once the wild fight within the town had taken fire; but if he had tried to do so he would probably have reported it, and he did not.[41]

Viewed in the context of the German wars that had just ended after thirty years' fighting, the massacres at Drogheda and Wexford shrink to typical casualties of seventeenth-century warfare. Cromwell's qualified justification of them, invocations of providence apart, was that the fear that they engendered reduced the casualties that his men would otherwise have suffered in the campaign; but though many places did fall more easily to him because of it, that fear did not prevent Duncannon and Waterford from repulsing him in November, or save him from heavy losses when Clonmel withstood his storm in May 1650. The arguments in mitigation are not ones that his admirers can use with much comfort, but in purely military terms Cromwell's Irish campaign displayed all his typical energy and determination. Irish resistance had almost disintegrated by the time he was called home in May 1650.

By then the young Charles II was preparing to use Scotland instead of Ireland as a springboard for the invasion of England, and Fairfax was unwilling to lead the pre-emptive strike on which the Rump had decided. Fairfax indeed had been out of sympathy with the regicide commonwealth from its inception, and he took this opportunity to resign his command. Inevitably, Cromwell succeeded him as Lord General, and so became commander-in-chief at last, less than fifteen months before his last battle.

For nearly six weeks after entering Scotland on 22 July, Cromwell's army suffered severe discomfort, much sickness and not a little danger. David Leslie, once his comrade at Marston Moor,

41. Abbott, II, 140–3, and authorities cited in n. 40.

was a shrewd, strong-nerved opponent, and constantly denied him the battle that he sought, except on ground that put him at a crippling disadvantage. Leslie was in just such a position on Doon Hill above Dunbar on 2 September, with more than 22,000 men and with his flank blocking the road south. Dysentery and fever had reduced Cromwell's force to 11,000; they had their backs to the sea and the rain-swollen Broxburn flowing across their front. In Cromwell's council of war that evening some advised evacuating the army by sea, and that is what Leslie assumed to be his intention; but Lambert argued for attacking the Scots, and one cannot imagine Cromwell accepting any other decision. He 'rid all the night . . . through the several regiments by torchlight upon a little Scots nag, biting his lips till the blood ran down his chin without his perceiving it'.[42] His men were spending their second wet and windy night in the open. He launched Lambert's cavalry attack before first light, and had both them and a large part of his infantry across the Broxburn before the Scots knew what was upon them. He then launched his main assault where his own cavalry regiments and Pride's splendid infantry could use the ground best. The Scots were still hopelessly unprepared to withstand it, and when he saw their ranks break he 'was carried on with a divine impulse: he did laugh so excessively as if he had been drunk, and his eyes sparkled with spirits'.[43] The Scottish losses – about 3,000 killed and 10,000 prisoners – exceeded his own total force, which by his reckoning lost only about forty killed.

'I assure thee, I grow an old man, and feel infirmities of age marvellously stealing upon me,' wrote Cromwell to his wife the day after Dunbar. Scotland was not conquered yet, and the strain of a hard campaign caught up with him in February. From then until late in June 1651 he was sick with a recurrent fever. By the time he recovered, Charles II was his own master and Leslie had a sizeable army again. Failing in his attempts to bring it to battle in Scotland, Cromwell deliberately left the way open for it to march into England, and Charles took the bait. Lambert shadowed the invaders as closely as he had in 1648, and Cromwell followed not far behind. So few Englishmen joined the king that he abandoned his plan for a swift strike at London and holed up in Worcester, hoping for time to build up his army in old royalist territory. But Cromwell arrived

---

42. Abbott, II, 317, from *Memoirs of the Life of Mr Ambrose Barnes*.
43. Abbott, II, 319, from Aubrey's *Miscellanies*. See ibid., pp. 321–5, for Cromwell's own account of the battle, and for the fullest modern narrative C. H. Firth, 'The battle of Dunbar', *T.R.H.S.* XIV (1900), 19–52.

there only a week after Charles, and with greatly superior forces. He took his time in preparing his assault upon the well fortified city, and threw bridges of boats across both the Severn and the Teme. He launched his attack on 3 September, the anniversary of Dunbar, with his forces divided into three bodies; it was a more complex operation than most of his earlier battles. The Scots fought hard in the fields south of Worcester, but at the end of the day the city had fallen and all that was left of Leslie's army were prisoners, fugitives or corpses. Cromwell lost less than two hundred men killed. As at Preston, large numbers of local levies fought as willingly and bravely for him as his seasoned regiments.[44]

Worcester was his last battle, but he remained Lord General until his death. Inevitably, his military status and reputation affected his conduct as a politician. He shared his officers' mounting dissatisfaction with the Rump, but he never encouraged them to defy the civil authority. As late as 11 March 1653, when the Council of Officers was pressing to dissolve it by force, he and Disbrowe checked them. He asked 'if they destroyed the parliament what they should call themselves, a state they could not be; they answered that they would call a new parliament; then, says the General, the parliament is not the supreme power, but that is the supreme power that calls it.'[45] When he did expel the Rump on 20 April it was not a planned military *coup* but a precipitate act, to whose consequences neither he nor most of his officers had given any clear thought. Exactly why he did it may never be known with certainty,[46] but he certainly believed that the Rump's 'bill for a new representative' contained no adequate safeguard against the imminent possibility of a new parliament being elected with a majority in favour of negotiating the restoration of the king, and that the hazardous transition from the Rump to its successor required a degree of partnership with the army, in common defence of their common cause.

If he had had any interest in a personal or military dictatorship, it was in his grasp during the short interregnum that followed. He and the Council of Officers decided, however, to entrust the supreme authority to an assembly nominated by themselves - a kind of sur-rogate parliament, empowered for a limited period in the hope that

44. Abbott, II, 458–63, 467; Gardiner, *C & P*, I, 282–97
45. C. H. Firth, 'Cromwell and the expulsion of the Long Parliament in 1653', *E.H.R.*, VIII (1893), 527–8.
46. For somewhat different interpretations see Blair Worden, *The Rump Parliament 1648–1653* (Cambridge, 1974), Part VI, and A. Woolrych, *Commonwealth to Protectorate* (Oxford, 1982), ch. 3.

the nation would soon become sufficiently settled to elect the real thing again. Cromwell probably initiated the decision not to nominate serving officers, so anxious was he that the army should not be seen as seeking power for itself, and when Barebone's Parliament (as it came to be called) co-opted him and several other leading officers to membership he declined to take his seat.[47] When Barebone's resigned its authority to him after five months and he became Lord Protector, the Instrument of Government (to his express approval) subjected his control of the armed forces to the consent of parliament when it was sitting and to that of the council when it was not. Of the twenty councillors who shared the executive authority with him at one time or another, only Lambert, Fleetwood, Disbrowe, Skippon and Montagu had fought with him in the New Model Army, and Montagu had left it back in 1645. When he was installed as Protector, and again when he opened his first elected parliament, he wore a plain black suit and cloak, and throughout his rule he never appeared in military dress on civil occasions. For a while after Penruddock's Rising in 1655, the extent of the royalist conspiracy that it revealed gave his military advisers an influence out of proportion to their numbers, and the result was the so-called regime of the major-generals. But this ran out of steam months before parliament virtually killed it off in January 1657, and the process of shifting the Protectorate from a military to a civil and constitutional basis was resumed.[48]

As Protector, Cromwell continuously reduced the size of the army. Four months before he expelled the Rump, it probably totalled not far short of 60,000 officers and men, of whom about 15,400 were stationed in England; the Second Civil War and the conquests of Ireland and Scotland had led to a great expansion. By December 1654 the total strength was just over 53,000, with slightly more than 11,000 in England. Two and a half years later there were about 13,500 in England, but thanks to more settled conditions in Scotland and Ireland the total was down to about 41,350, and it was still falling.[49] For comparison, James II had at least three times as many men

47. Ibid., chs 4 and 5.
48. I develop these arguments in a forthcoming article on 'The Cromwellian Protectorate: a military dictatorship?'; and see the chapters by David Underdown and myself in G. E Aylmer (ed.), *The Interregnum: the quest for settlement 1646–1660* (1972).
49. For these figures I am indebted to the valuable table in H. M. Reece, 'The Military Presence in England, 1649–1660' (unpublished D. Phil. thesis, Oxford, 1981), p. 287.

under arms in England in 1688 as Cromwell ever did during the Protectorate, and Cromwell never concentrated any large proportion of them close to London, as James did.[50]

Despite the reductions, there was strong continuity in the officer corps throughout Cromwell's years as Lord General. Among the rank-and-file, however, there was a much larger turnover, especially after the years of fighting were over; indeed an exodus began after the breaking of the second and more serious wave of Leveller mutinies in 1649. One result of this was that whereas between 1647 and 1649 political agitation, when it arose in the army, affected all ranks, dissension and opposition during the Protectorate were virtually confined to the officers. *They* remained as politically minded and independent of spirit as ever, and those who threatened disobedience to the Protector's government got short shrift: Harrison, Rich, Okey, Saunders, Alured and Overton in 1654, Ludlow in 1655, Lambert in 1657, and Packer and five other troop commanders in Cromwell's own cavalry regiment in 1658. But although Cromwell was adamant in requiring the army's obedience to the civil authority, he continued to honour its achievements, to plead with parliament for its needs,[51] and to uphold the broad ideals of religious and civil liberty for which it had fought. When parliament in 1657 pressed him to assume the Crown, it was not the hostility of the ambitious military grandees that made him refuse it but rather a deep reluctance to offend the plain russet-coated captains and the honest God-fearing troopers who believed that they had fought the Lord's battles with him. 'I cannot think that God would bless me', he told the parliament-men, 'in the undertaking of anything that would justly and with cause grieve them.'[52]

Each Monday he dined at Whitehall with any officers above the rank of captain who were in town.[53] Occasionally he made speeches to representative groups of officers, sometimes to inform them of current affairs or alert them to dangers, but once, in February 1657, to chide them sharply for interfering in the political process when they were agitating against parliament's offer of the Crown. [54] The last speech he ever made was at a banquet that he gave at Whitehall

50. J. Childs, *The Army, James II and the Glorious Revolution* (Manchester, 1980), pp. 2–4, 184.
51. Abbott, III, 478, 593; IV, 491, 497, 500, 576, 717–18.
52. Abbott, IV, 471–2.
53. Roy Sherwood, *The Court of Oliver Cromwell* (1977), p. 147; Reece, 'Military Presence', pp. 63ff.
54. Abbott, IV, 248, 417–19.

to two hundred officers on 6 February 1658, two days after his stormy dissolution of his last parliament. Many toasts were drunk and many bottles of wine emptied that evening, which apparently succeeded in restoring for his brief remaining lifetime the loyalty that the republican politicians had been striving to undermine.[55] But tensions remained; many junior officers looked askance at the increasingly regal trappings of the Protector's court, and resented the wealth and privilege of the army grandees who frequented it, while the grandees themselves chafed at Cromwell's increasing preference for the advice of conservative civilians, inside and outside the council. While he lived, he kept a sort of balance between the old comrades in arms (or most of them) who had raised him to the Protectorship and the newer party of civilian, constitutionalist Cromwellians, though he increasingly leaned towards the latter. He did not live long enough, however, to save his son Richard from a heavy backlash from the frustrated army officers, both high and low.

The main difficulty in appraising Cromwell as a soldier lies in finding any appropriate standard of comparison. The nature of the campaigns that he fought makes it meaningless to compare him with men like Gustavus or Marlborough, let alone Napoleon or Wellington, all of whom commanded vastly larger armies – armies with at least a strong professional core – over much longer spans of time. George Washington comes nearer to a comparable figure, though his military career was much longer than Cromwell's, and the scale of his major campaigns much greater. Dunbar and Worcester were the only battles in which Cromwell commanded more than 10,000 men. At the end of the First Civil War he stood out as an inspired and inspiring leader of cavalry, whose regiment's discipline and dedication had been the decisive factor in winning the crucial battles. He had yet to prove himself as the director of entire campaigns; but from his hunting down of Hamilton's Scots at Preston through the rigours of his Irish and Scottish campaigns to the 'crowning mercy' at Worcester, the boldness and sweep of his conceptions, his shrewdness of anticipation and his ability to coordinate quite complex manoeuvres suggest that he was a natural soldier, who could have distinguished himself in any type or scale of warfare. His authority over his officers and men in the field was truly charismatic, and he had a deep care for their needs. He seems to have been totally without physical fear, and his iron determination was unshaken by setbacks. He also had

55. Ibid., 736–7.

the born soldier's sheer zest for the thrill of battle; his almost wild exaltation at Dunbar had been prefigured at Naseby and elsewhere.

Yet war as such had no appeal for him outside the particular call to which he responded from 1642 onward. He saw England's civil wars as an unhappy necessity, and he was keenly aware of the suffering that they imposed on his fellow-Englishmen.[56] He was at heart a country gentleman who took to soldiering in middle age because a specific cause seemed to demand all he could give; the ardour with which he fought and the confidence that he radiated to his soldiers are inseparable from his conviction that he and they were the humble instruments of God's purpose. He could not return to the plough after his last battle because the cause as he understood it still needed his army's support, but he could only think of his office as Protector as that of 'a good constable, to keep the peace of the parish'. A constable was, of course, a civil officer, chosen from among his neighbours to enforce the law of the land. The self-descriptions of men of power are not necessarily to be taken at face value, but Cromwell's ideal conception of his role as Head of State was about as far from that of a military dictator as could be.

56. Abbott, I, 314, 344.

CHAPTER FIVE

The Lord Protector, 1653–1658

Derek Hirst

I

Oliver Cromwell dominated the political life of England throughout the 1650s, and wielded more raw power than any English ruler before or, perhaps, since.[1] He commanded an army and a navy which earned the respect, even the fear, of his European neighbours, and which succeeded in crushing all overt resistance in England, Scotland and Ireland. In face of the swords of his army the three nations were for the first time united. His constitutional position some found equally threatening. As conservative members of his second parliament reminded him anxiously when urging him to take the Crown, his office of Lord Protector was an anomaly in English history; so anomalous was it, they contended, that it was not clear whether he could be bound by laws and customs inherited from ages which assumed government by kings.[2] Not surprisingly, the fears were matched by the hopes of others. At the end of the Protector's first year in office Andrew Marvell saw in him limitless potential. Although unsure whether Oliver's mission was secular or prophetic, the poet wrote confidently of a new order, even of a potentially millennial future.[3]

1. I am indebted to Steven Zwicker for reading and commenting on an early draft of this essay.
2. Abbott, IV 459–60.
3. Andrew Marvell, *The First Anniversary of the Government under O.C.*. Such high expectations were not the peculiarity of poets. Writing in January 1654 to Bulstrode Whitelocke, England's ambassador to Sweden, Marvell's friend the journalist Marchamont Nedham heralded 'a new world framed (like the old) out of chaos'. Longleat, Whitelocke MSS, vol. 15, fo. 1. See below, Chapter 10, for a fuller consideration of contemporary perceptions of Cromwell.

The fate of that power forms the central paradox of the decade. Historians have long noted that in its broad constitutional outlines the England of the 1660s seems much like the England of the 1620s and 1630s. In recent years many have argued that the 'real' revolution of the seventeenth century in fact occurred in 1688–89 rather than at mid-century.[4] There is ready warrant, in the statutory denial after the Restoration of all measures enacted between 1641 and 1660,[5] for those who would call into question the achievements, even the impact, of those years. But the doubts did not originate then. Even at the time of Oliver's death, when the Protectorate seemed unchallengeable, the most acute minds found it nearly impossible to unfold his significance. There is something more than a little suggestive in the absence of any funeral sermon for that assertively godly man. Even more palpable, and more eloquent, are the uncertainty and sense of dislocation that mark the elegies for the dead Protector.

Marvell once again provides the measure. No longer could he suggest, as he had in both the *Horatian Ode* and the *First Anniversary*, that Cromwell might shape a new age. Though undeniably greater than others, Oliver had proved the captive rather than conqueror of time. The only promise for Marvell in the winter of 1658–59 was of an uncertain future – Oliver at least had, in his son Richard, a successor. Marvell's perplexity as he wrote the *Poem upon the death of O.C.* is nowhere more obvious than in his bathos, remarkable for this most controlled of poets: 'Oh human glory, vain, Oh death, oh wings,/ Oh worthless world oh transitory things!' [ll. 255–6]. Nor was John Dryden, Marvell's colleague in the republic's service, more certain. A young man on the make might have much to gain from singing the praise of those in power; yet Dryden found it as difficult as did Marvell to comprehend Cromwell's character and career once the obvious tribute had been paid to military greatness. After casting the dead protector as alchemist and magus,[6] Dryden could hardly have found a more veiled conclusion to his *Heroique Stanza*'s:

His ashes in a peaceful urn shall rest,
His name a great example stands to show
How strangely high endeavours may be blest,
Where piety and valour jointly go.

4. J. P. Kenyon's recent verdict that the Restoration restored the *status quo ante bellum*' [The Stuart Constitution (2nd edn, Cambridge, 1986), p 2] may be taken as representative of the one position, and A. McInnes, 'When was the English revolution?', *History*, LXVII (1982), 377–92, of the other.
5. 13 Car., II, c. 1.
6. Stanzas 25 and 26; see also stanza 19.

It was not merely the critical intelligence of poets which struggled to grasp the meaning of Cromwell and the course of recent history. Their confusion paralleled heart-searchings at the centre. Oliver's chief legal officer, Nathaniel Fiennes, opening the last session of Oliver's last parliament less than nine months before his master's death, made in the course of one speech the baffling interpretive journey which had taken Marvell four years. At first he celebrated the Protectorate as a new Creation, a prospect of Eden; but by the end of what was very much a public-relations presentation Fiennes was reduced to offering the Protectorate for approval as an exercise in the second-best. Talking of the difficulties that beset England, Fiennes regretted

the apprehension of novelty in this constitution, because it is not in every point agreeable to what was before. For removal hereof, let us consider, that neither is the condition of the nation at present, as it was before; and it may be, it is not good it should be so, or at least, that it is not God's will it should be so . . . it is no wonder if every one cannot have what he thinks best in his judgment to be done, but ought rather to content himself with what he may think next best.[7]

On one level, that of constitutional form of which Fiennes was thinking, the difficulty in finding the right terms with which to interpret and celebrate Cromwell is easily explained. The very office of Protector was ambiguous.[8] The army officers who drew up the Instrument of Government in 1653 – in a process from which Oliver very deliberately distanced himself – sought to shroud its novelty by drawing on precedents from the tutelage of the child-kings Henry VI and Edward VI in order to give Cromwell the vaguely familiar title of Lord Protector.[9] And though his office was manifestly not regal, Oliver in the course of his rule took upon himself more of the trappings of regality: a quasi-royal seal in 1655, an orb and sceptre and royal robe for the re-installation of the Protector under his second constitution, the Humble Petition and Advice, in 1657. And the court which surrounded him became ever more stately.[10] Yet,

7. *C.J.*, VII, 583, 586.
8. And hence the uncertainties of the early celebrations of his rule: see D. Hirst, ' "That sober liberty": Marvell's Cromwell in 1654', in J. M. Wallace (ed.), *The Golden and the Brazen World* (Berkeley, 1985), pp. 17–52.
9. The title probably unwittingly hinted at another, and discordant, theme of rule, that of the Hobbesian sovereign-as-protector; that figure had been in debate since the crisis of the new republic which had spawned *The Leviathan* in 1651. For the establishment of the protectorate, see A. Woolrych, *Commonwealth and Protectorate* (Oxford, 1982), pp. 352–90.
10. Abbott, III 624 and n.; the regalia for the 1657 installation had, however, been

while he was powerfully drawn to kingship as a guarantor of the political stability that he sought throughout his rule, after prolonged and public reflection he rejected the Crown when it was offered in 1657. Even so, the 1658 patent for one of the two peerages Oliver created listed the conferment of honours among the chief prerogatives of 'the imperial crown of these nations'. And in that last weary year of his life he once again found himself at the centre of renewed expectations and rumours.[11] Uncertainty as to the note to sound at his death was understandable, all the more so once the fragility of the position of his son and successor, Richard, became evident.

Had that uncertainty been reducible to matters of constitutional categories or political prognostication the task of those who sought to comprehend would have been simple. But their doubts went deeper. Central to any assessment of Oliver Cromwell as Lord Protector must be an enquiry into the causes of their diffidence; into why Dryden, for example, found him such an enigma. Our enquiry must ask the questions the elegists and still more the preachers avoided: What did the rule of Oliver Cromwell mean to others and, more poignantly, to himself? What was his relationship to the faltering revolution which had begun and almost stopped in the winter of 1648–49? Why did all that power, both of the sword and also of Oliver's personality, fail to achieve more? But though in some respects they maintained an awkward silence, the elegists did have tribute to pay too. It must be our business as well to determine whether such tribute was merely conventional hyperbole – to determine, in short, the nature of Oliver's claims to greatness.

II

The Protector himself certainly had some answers, and these cast light on the difficulties of those who would interpret. With defensive regularity the Lord Protector reverted to the objectives, and merits, of his rule. Perhaps he sought to persuade himself; he certainly aimed to persuade a wider audience of the divine providence of his own history.[12] Sometimes the claims were tangible enough – the securing of a protestant, and English, interest in Ireland; restraints on feudalism, and the protection of the 'meaner sort' and 'middle sort'

chosen by parliament: *Burton*, II, 303, 309; for the court, see R. Sherwood, *The Court of Oliver Cromwell* (1977).
11. Abbott, IV 790; C. H. Firth, 'Cromwell and the crown', E.H.R., XVII (1902), 429–42, and XVIII (1903), 52–80.
12. For discussions of his understanding and use of the idea of 'providence', see below, pp. 141–2, 186–90, 199–202, 249–53.

in Scotland; and, more important by far, the formation of a godly ministry by means of the committee of Triers established in 1654 to vet the qualifications of those seeking a parish living. 'There hath not been such a service to England' as the last 'since the Christian religion was professed in England,' he insisted. Cromwell felt entitled to conclude with some pride in 1658, 'We hope we may say we have arrived at what we aimed at, if not at that which is much beyond our expectations.'[13] But at this point what he had in mind was rather more nebulous, a matter now of liberty of conscience and of peace.

He could still descant on the subject of religious liberty – 'Who would have forethought, when we were plunged into the midst of our troubles, that ever the people of God should have had liberty to worship God without fear of enemies?' – just as he had so often in the past; but what he saw in it had changed. In practice he allowed considerable latitude to all; but a decade of radical upheaval had narrowed Cromwell's sense of what was fit to be tolerated, especially among radical protestants. He gave eager praise to the provisions for liberty of conscience in the second written constitution, the Humble Petition and Advice which parliament drew up for him in 1657: 'The things that are provided for in this Instrument have the liberty of the people of God so as they have never had it' – though those provisions were rather more restrictive than the parallel clauses of the 1653 Instrument of Government. That he was not simply seeking to impress a parliamentary audience is clear from his private judgment in 1656 on New England persecutors of radical enthusiasts: 'They acted like wise men, and God had broken the designs of evil instruments.'[14]

More remarkable than the shrinkage in Cromwellian tolerance was the direction from which the Lord Protector saw the threat to liberty of conscience coming. His dictum that in the end the civil wars had been about liberty of conscience – 'religion was not at first the thing contested for, but God brought it to that issue at last . . . and at last it proved to be that which was most dear to us' – is famous. It stemmed from his disgust at the conservative presbyterian campaign in his first parliament of 1654 against Baptists and others, to 'put their finger upon their brethren's consciences, to pinch them there.' But in a very few weeks a more radical audience, of enthusiastic Fifth-Monarchists, drew from Cromwell the warning that conserva-

13. Abbott, IV, 718–19, 495, 707.
14. Abbott, IV, 705–6, 490, 345; for a compelling discussion of the extent of Cromwell's tolerance, see B. Worden, 'Toleration and the protectorate', in W. J. Sheils (ed.), *Studies in Church History*, XXI (1984), 199–233.

tives were not alone in endangering liberty. His 'work', he told them, was 'to preserve [the churches] from destroying one another . . . to keep all the godly of several judgments in peace, because like men falling out in the street [they] would run their heads one against another'. It was in this meeting that he first used his most famous characterization of his position: 'a constable to part them, and keep them in peace.'[15] At least part of the Protector's sense of his mission arose from the need to police the radical forces that he himself had helped to generate. Such ambiguous self-justification yielded little to those who sought to interpret his life and death.

Cromwell had not much else to offer. Some of his most heart-felt protestations were of his commitment to 'the interest of those that have an interest in a better world', as he defiantly told parliament when dissolving it in January 1655: 'It is my glory that I know a cause, which yet we have not lost, but do hope we shall take a little pleasure rather to lose our lives than lose.'[16] Yet what had he done for 'God's people' other than test the credentials of the public ministry and – more important, and within certain limits – protect godly consciences? Time and again the answer he gave amounted to a paraphrase of St Paul, extolling the embrace of righteousness and peace.[17] Anyone considering his defiant motto, '*Pax queritur in bello*' [peace is sought in war], the war with Spain he initiated in the West Indies in 1655, the loan of troops to France for an attack on Spanish Flanders in 1657–58, let alone the enormous fiscal cost of – and the constant threats to – the domestic peace, would have had doubts about the latter claim. Of righteousness in action he dreamt intently; 'that God would give rulers as at the first, and judges as at the beginning', he told his first parliament, quoting the prophet Isaiah.[18] While that dream certainly, as he acknowledged, precluded hereditary rule[19] it did not provide a programme, a blueprint for action – the Old Testament judge was moral arbiter, not builder or

15. Ibid., 586, 607. As so often, Marvell saw the point when he noted, 'What prudence more than human did he need/ To keep so dear, so diff'ring minds agreed', *Poem on the Death of O.C.*, ll. 217–18. It was an effort not without its costs. As Cromwell observed to his son-in-law, General Fleetwood, in 1655, 'The wretched jealousies that are amongst us, and the spirit of calumny, turns all into gall and wormwood. My heart is for the people of God: that the Lord knows, and I trust will in due time manifest; yet thence are my wounds', Abbott, III, 756, and see also IV, 471.

16. Ibid., III, 583.

17. Ibid., III, 435, 579–80, 707, 760–1, and IV, 716.

18. Ibid., III, 589.

19. That dream also precluded self-help and self-aggrandizement. Without some reference to this conception of rule we cannot fully understand Cromwell's hostility

even reformer of institutions. As his son-in-law General Fleetwood reminisced in 1656, 'when they talked of his policy, his answer was, that his policy lay in this, to witness against, and punish wicked men and to encourage . . . as many good men as he could'.[20]

The advancement of the virtuous and the punishment of the vicious: on both of these topics Cromwell had much to say. He prided himself, for example, that, in his law courts, 'the laws did proceed with as much freedom and justice, with less private solicitation', as in the 'halcyon days' of Queen Elizabeth and King James; equally, as he told his second parliament, 'you have now a godly ministry . . . such a one as, without vanity be it spoken, the world has not [the like]'.[21] Milton accordingly spoke the mind of his master when in 1654 he trumpeted the prominence of virtuous men in its councils as the prime achievement of the republic.[22]

But others doubted whether virtuous counsel fulfilled the engagements of headier days. It was not simply that the mountain had laboured and brought forth a mouse; the whole purpose of the Civil War was involved. As he came to realize this in the winter of 1654–55 the radical Colonel Eyres burst out, appalled, that if this was all, 'they could not clear themselves from [the charge of being] king-murderers.'[23] The undertow of army dissidence throughout the Protectorate stemmed as much from inchoate dissatisfaction with what the regime had delivered as it did from doctrinaire republican impatience with Oliver's apparent drift towards kingship. There was something emblematic in the position of the officers of his own regiment whom Oliver angrily dismissed for their defiance in February 1658. They would, they declared, 'follow his highness upon the grounds of the old cause, but would not express what they meant by the old cause'[24]: perhaps they could not, though they were confident Oliver had done too little to put it into effect.

to 'self-ends', his repeated denials of his own ambition, and the apparent reluctance with which he advanced his sons. On the last point, see ibid., III, 280, 756; C. H. Firth (ed.), *Selections from the Papers of William Clarke* (4 vols. Camden Society, 1891–1901), III, XXIV–XXV; *T.S.P.*, VI, 774.

Abbott, III, 589; *T.S.P.*, V. 548; cf. below, pp. 127–8.

21. Abbott, IV, 469, 707, 494.
22. In his *Second Defence of the English People*.
23. *T.S.P.*, III, 126.
24. *Clarke Papers*, III, 140; D. Underdown, 'Cromwell and the officers, February 1658', *E.H.R.*, LXXXIII (1968), 106. Oliver's forceful son Henry Cromwell may have caught the right note when he saw amidst the army radicals in 1658 not reasoned argument but gut conviction: refering then to the formative army rendezvous of 1647 he sneered at the 'Triploe-heath-habit of their affections', *T.S.P.*, VII, 107.

But the Protector too had indicated that he looked for more than he was finally able to give. In 1654 secretary Thurloe repeatedly informed England's ambassador to Sweden, Bulstrode Whitelocke, that 'the reformation of the law and the ministry' was Cromwell's chief concern. The Protector underlined this in his opening speech to his second parliament. Exhorting his audience to the work of reform he insisted, 'there is one general grievance in the nation. It is, the law.' This was not simply pious rhetoric.[25] In 1654 he took the unusual step of postponing the Easter law term while he and various committees pursued reform; at the same time he promoted England's leading advocate of law reform, William Sheppard, into his own service and commissioned reform schemes from him.[26] The Protector's continuing commitment to law reform cannot be doubted[27]; yet the silence of the eulogists, of Oliver himself, on this score at the end suggests how little had been achieved.

Some suspected the location of the cause. Shortly before the 1654 parliament Fleetwood wrote in alarm to Thurloe, 'It is much to be wondered at that the regulation of the law goes on so slowly . . . the eyes of all are upon my lord.'[28] The reasons for the lack of progress go to the heart of Oliver's rule. Certainly there was opposition within his parliaments and the legal and clerical professions to major reform, and most MPs thought removing the army a much more urgent priority; but the effectiveness of his own commitment is in question. As always, he was torn between his desire for godly reform and his desire to preserve the ranks and ordering of society. Most revealing of his commitment to hierarchy – 'A nobleman, a gentleman, a yeoman . . . That is a good interest of the nation and a great one' – is the vehemence of his attack in January 1655 on the Leveller threat: 'so is it some satisfaction if a commonwealth must perish, that it perish by men, and not by the hands of persons dif-

---

25. Longleat, Whitelocke MSS., XV, fos. 27v, 135v; Abbott, IV, 274.
26. Several of these schemes found their way as draft bills into the 1656 parliament, while some 45 of the ordinances issued before the first parliament met in September 1654 dealt with legal matters, albeit mostly details. For Sheppard's career, see Nancy L. Matthews, *William Sheppard, Cromwell's Law Reformer* (Cambridge, 1984).
27. See below, pp. 144–5.
28. *T.S.P.*, II, 445. Fleetwood also questioned the lack of progress on the abolition of tithes – compulsory payments towards the support of parish ministers – to whose replacement Oliver had once committed himself; but it is clear that the latter had been drawing back from that commitment as the republic exhausted the confiscated Church revenues which might have supported an alternative and as parliament demonstrated its reluctance to fund any other means.

fering little from beasts; that if it must needs suffer, it should rather suffer from rich men than from poor men, who, as Solomon says, when they oppress, they leave nothing behind them, but are as a sweeping rain.'[29] It should come as no surprise, therefore, to learn that at the same time as Thurloe was assuring Whitelocke of their master's quest for reform he was also insisting that the people would be 'governed by the good old laws'. And when Oliver the reformer came to appoint committees to look to the law Oliver the conservative staffed them with lawyers, 'being resolved', reported Thurloe, 'to give the learned gentlemen of the robe the honour of reforming their own profession'. The unlikelihood of such an outcome seems not to have occurred to Cromwell, despite his long experience of lawyers in politics. The hesitant nature of the lawyers' proposals for the equity court of chancery eventually so exasperated him that the council rejected them and, with Sheppard's help, drew up their own, still limp, ordinance – which lawyer opposition soon blocked; meanwhile, the lawyers' half-hearted gestures at reform in the common-law courts were allowed to stand.[30]

The slow pace of reform cannot, however, simply be attributed to Oliver's conservative impulses. This godly Independent had, in his confidence of further revelation of God's purposes through His providences in the world, declared in 1647 that forms of government were 'but . . . dross and dung in comparison of Christ'.[31] Like so many of his co-religionists, Oliver was less interested in institutions than in the spirit, in morality: 'The mind is the man. If that be kept pure, a man signifies somewhat; if not, I would very fain see what difference there is betwixt him and a beast. He hath only some activity to do some more mischief.'[32] What mattered was virtue not constitutional forms: that conviction, which the Protector shared with Milton, underlay their satisfaction with the promotion of the virtuous. Good men would do God's work whatever the office in which they found themselves. So, as Cromwell insisted to parliament when explaining his reluctance to take the Crown in 1657, the name

29. Abbott, III, 435, 584.
30. Longleat, Whitelocke MSS., XV, fos 27v, 117, 136; see also fos 6, 138v. See Matthews, *Sheppard*, pp. 36–41, for a brief account of the chancery ordinance; for reform in the common-law courts, see D. Veall, *The Popular Movement for Law Reform 1640–1660* (Oxford, 1970), *passim*, and S. Black, 'Coram protectore: the judges of Westminster Hall under the protectorate', *American Journal of Legal History*, XX (1976), 32–64; also M. Cotterell, 'Interregnum law reform: the Hale commission of 1652', E.H.R., LXXXIII (1968), 689–704.
31. Abbott, I, 540.
32. Ibid, IV 273–4.

of king was less important than good government and godliness.[33] And so too he believed that he could cope with the ills and vested interests of local government by sending major-generals, with no formal institutional role, to act as exemplars and scourges in the counties.[34]

Innate conservatism, a belief in the paramount importance of good men: both factors help explain Cromwell's reliance on such a universally respected lawyer as Matthew Hale not only as judge but also, futilely, as reformer. But there was an important element of calculation too in Oliver's capitulation to the gown-men. Marvell caught a central feature of Cromwell's political practice when he observed that in his career up to 1650 his tendency had been 'to inclose . . . more than to oppose' his adversaries.[35] The legend of Cromwell the consummate Machiavellian is contemporary, and charges abounded that his every move was calculated.[36] His appointment of respectable senior lawyers to the bench, and his willingness to bend to them in the matter of reform, might therefore – indeed, should – be seen as in part his tribute to the danger they represented. But Oliver, certainly a skilful politician, had also throughout his public life been deeply committed to the principle of unity among the godly. Such unity both registered the conformity of the godly with God's purposes, and flowed inexorably from Christian charity.[37] His commitment was duly reinforced when he took power and set him-

33. Ibid, IV, 469. Compare the advice of another independent, the law reformer Sheppard: 'Let able and fit men be chosen to and kept in . . . offices. And truly . . . herein lieth almost the whole work of reformation in church and commonwealth, to make and keep the officers thereof good . . .', quoted in Matthews, *Sheppard*, p. 72.
34. That he did see the rule of the major-generals in such terms is clear in his opening speech to the 1656 parliament: 'It hath been more effectual towards the discountenancing of vice and settling religion, than anything done these fifty years.' Yet he saw their rule as the rule of men, and urged support in those terms: thus, Major-General Goffe was ' a gracious man if I know one', and deserved to be backed if 'a reformation of wickedness be part [of] the return we owe to God': Abbott, IV, 274, 25.
35. *An Horation Ode upon Cromwell's Return from Ireland,* II, 19–20.
36. The most graphic example comes from the Leveller pamphlet, *The Hunting of the Foxes,* quoted in G. E. Aylmer, *The Levellers and the English Revolution* (1975), p. 149. The great royalist historian Edward Hyde, earl of Carendon, thought Oliver 'the greatest dissembler living', *History of the Rebellion,* W. D. Macray (ed.), (6 vols, Oxford, 1888), IV, 305.
37. For the former, see above all Cromwell's speech at Putney in 1647, Abbott, I, 544; more generally, see the 20 March 1654 declaration of a day of fasting and humiliation, *ibid.* III, 225–9. 'Throughout the Protectorate, calls for fast-days repeatedly lamented the disunity of nation and godly alike.

self the task of 'healing and settling' the nation.[38] Thus in November 1655 he urged his son Henry, governing Ireland, to show forbearance towards opponents in terms which smack of a sense of Christian mission.[39] The Protector's gestures towards the lawyers, though they might impede the drive towards reform, were therefore essential not simply to the achievement of unity but also to true godliness. His politically unfortunate selection of the ineffectual Sir Thomas Widdrington as Speaker of both his parliaments could be seen in such a light: it was certainly conventional for a senior lawyer to sit in the chair, the lawyers needed to be placated, but, equally, they had to be included. So did royalists, to whom as individuals he repeatedly showed favour, particularly by mitigating 'decimation' (ten per cent income) taxes imposed on them in 1655–56, though his major-generals commanding in the provinces despaired.[40]

Cromwell's reluctance to commit himself unequivocally may indeed be read as that opportunist inconsistency for which he was notorious. Coherent reform stood little chance under a Janus figure. But the even-handedness he displayed in a discussion with some very divided Scots in 1657 suggests something more. The Protector

did speak his sense of what he had heard the last day, yet so as that no expression passed him which should bear the determination of his judgment to either of us. I observe that all along in his discourses to us, that when he does speak that which may seem favourable to the protesters (as he often doth to gratify them by a pleasing expression), he adds somewhat in favour of us, so to guard his expression towards them, as I may not apprehend his alienation from us more than from them.[41]

If the effort to balance was as instinctual as this account suggests, then personal choice as much as political necessity impelled Cromwell 'to inclose'. The Protector did indeed placate his critics, protect his rear, just as he always had whenever he had been on the point of departing on campaign. Thus, he met with Fifth Monarchists in the winter of 1654–55 when army discontent assumed dangerous dimensions.[42] Moreover, given the importance of religious radicalism in the army throughout the decade, Oliver's willingness to debate with such an extreme figure as the Quaker George Fox virtually

---

38. Ibid., III, 435.
39. Ibid., IV, 26.
40. T.S.P., IV, 294, 359, 434, 545; ibid. V, 9. His success with such gestures became a matter of royalist comment early in his rule: ibid., III, 208.
41. Abbott, IV, 416. The narrator was the future archbishop and 'martyr', James Sharp.
42. Abbott, III, 546–47.

whenever the latter wanted might be deemed politically motivated.[43] Other religious leaders enjoyed almost equal access, and his councillors evidently relied on the Protector's ability to speak the language of faith: thus, amidst fears of a royalist uprising late in 1657 the council advised him to confer with two London anglican leaders.[44] Yet Oliver enjoyed such activity. In the midst of political crisis and disarray in the spring of 1658 he found time to break off for a long discussion with a minor New England cleric, to whom 'he spoke very experimentally . . . of the work of God's grace, and . . . exhorted . . . to perseverance . . .'.[45] The Protector sought instinctively to make personal contact with men of all persuasions, however confusing such gestures proved to partisans and their programmes, however much he opened himself to allegations of bad faith, and however much he sank into a morass of business.[46]

Reform foundered on Oliver's very ambivalence, but it foundered too under the sheer pressure of time. No early-modern government had anything like a modern bureaucracy capable of devolving business into orderly channels. All rulers and their councils, though they might dream of policies and programmes, responded primarily to petitions from interested parties.[47] Revolutionary regimes, unable to count on unthinking habits of obedience, and perhaps with more consciously formulated objectives, depended more than did others on the initiative and intervention of the central authority. But those very conditions made the revolutionary regime the hope of petitioners, who saw at the centre the real locus of power and source of redress – still more so as Oliver did so little to establish new institutions and procedures. Still more so too since the formal provisions of a written constitution precluded that easy exercise of executive authority by the council alone which had in routine matters characterized the pre-war monarchy: the Protector had to sign letters and warrants of all kinds, and spent long hours doing so. The council, and Oliver above all, were thus deluged with minutiae which would have been wearisomely familiar to their predecessors. The records of the regime

43. Ibid., III, 639 and IV, 309, 440, 867–8; another Quaker with strikingly easy access to the Protector was Anthony Pearson: ibid., III, 372–3, 504, 734n.
44. *Cal. St. Pap. Dom., 1657–1658*, p. 226.
45. Abbott, IV, 776.
46. See also below, pp. 134–6.
47. See M. Hawkins, 'Central government: its role and aims', in C. Russell (ed.), *The Origins of the English Civil War* (1973), pp. 35–65, and D. Hirst, 'The privy council and problems of enforcement in the 1620s', *Journal of British Studies*, XVIII (1978), 44–66.

are full of the Protector's personal queries, recommendations, orders, in matters trivial as well as great. The result can be seen in the report of the Venetian ambassador in mid-1656: 'They are indeed so fully occupied that they do not know which way to turn, and the protector has not a moment to call his own.' Indeed, there were times when Oliver was too busy to eat, holding audiences in the afternoon when he had been in council all morning.[48] Small wonder that weariness helped to kill him, just as it helped to kill reform.

III

If public life meant to Oliver something much more complicated than merely reforming zeal or conservative yearning, or even a combination of the two, what did he mean to the government and the cause of which he was such a prominent part? The most unambiguous testimonial to the Protector is of course the collapse of the protectorate soon after his death. However much the political gossips of the 1650s liked to talk of Oliver's periodic withdrawals from the council chamber to his sick-bed, or of the ambitions and capabilities of General John Lambert, they recognized that through Oliver flowed the republic's life-blood. His son Henry only put into pugnacious words what all recognized when he asked secretary Thurloe two months before the Protector's death, 'Have you any settlement? Does not your peace depend upon his highness['s] life, and upon his peculiar skill, and faculty, and personal interest in the army? . . . there is no other reason why we are not in blood at this day.'[49] That strange combination of godly zeal and military sympathy, personal approachability and reflexive conservatism which both shaped and doomed the drive for reform during the Protectorate also held the regime together. It was an impossible act to follow.

Oliver proved a subtle and often successful politician. True, the edifice of his rule soon crumbled, and his twin goals of 'healing and settling' and toleration, uniting 'the interest of the nation' and of 'the people of God', eluded him. Parliament alone could bring settlement; yet the army alone could – in that intolerant age – guarantee toleration, and for that reason above all Oliver regarded the army as akin

---

48. *Cal. St. Pap Ven., 1655–1656*, pp. 221, and 213, 216; M. Roberts, 'Cromwell and the Baltic', *E.H.R.*, LXXVI (1961) 410, 412; Cromwell protested his preference for private life in his defensive second speech to the 1654 parliament, and Marvell duly picked up the theme: Abbott, III, 452; Marvell, *First Anniversary*, ll. 221–4; cf. also *Horatian Ode*, ll. 29–32.
49. *T.S.P. VII, 218.*

to a fourth estate in the commonwealth.[50] But, as Henry Cromwell recognized, only Oliver's person could bridge parliament and army. To that end the Protector brought considerable skills. His long service had taught him when to use the carrot and when the stick, and just how much of the latter, with the army. His punitive response to dangerous expressions of republicanism among senior officers late in 1654 was a model of delicacy; he knew how in 1657 to reassure officers, disgruntled by the moves towards kingship, of 'his constant regard to his army, and the ancient cause of the honest people under his government'; and he moved swiftly to head off gathering discontent in the army in February 1658 by giving 'a great feast', and a two-hour speech, to two hundred of their comrades.[51]

Not only did he speak the same language as the godly, but he was adept in the art of dividing and ruling, using the testimonials of fellow-saints against each other.[52] He was skilled, too, in purveying a different message – one that came equally naturally to this ambivalent man – to a different audience, attesting to parliament his hatred of levelling and to the magistrates of London his loathing for Quakers.[53] His language in fact provides the best evidence of his chameleon-like qualities, and thus of the grounds of his success. The complaint of the Fifth-Monarchist leader John Rogers that everyone who went to see Oliver came away persuaded that they were in agreement[54] finds its vindication in a letter the Protector wrote to the poet Edmund Waller in 1655. Waller, in the country, had presented a panegyric, and Oliver urged in reply,

Let it not trouble you that, by so unhappy a mistake, you are, as I hear, at Northampton. Indeed I am passionately affected with it.

I have no guilt upon me unless it be to be avenged for you so willingly mistaking me in your verses. This action will put you to redeem me from yourself, as you have already from the world. Ashamed, I am, your friend and servant, Oliver P.

Such stately affectations are far from the protestations of godly authenticity which resound in, for example, his insistence to Fleetwood a few days later that 'indeed my heart is plain to thee as thy

50. Abbott, III, 588.
51. *Cal. St. Pap Dom.*, *1653–1654*, pp. 303–4; B. Taft, 'The Humble Petition of the Officers, 1654', *Huntington Library Quaterly*, XLII (1978), 33–4, 37–8; *Clarke Papers*, III, 95–6; *T.S.P.*, IV, 736. In the last instance it should be noted that his efforts were not wholly successful: Underdown, 'Cromwell and the officers', pp. 101–7.
52. For example, Folger Library, MS. Add. 667; *T.S.P.*, IV, 629.
53. See, for example, Abbott, III, 435–7, and IV, 761n.
54. Ibid., III, 639.

heart can well desire: let nothing shake thee in this . . . this I say as from a simple and sincere heart'. The switch to the intimate 'thou' form is particularly revealing.[55]

The Venetian ambassador, with some reason,[56] likened the Protector's oratory more to the preacher than the prince, but to pass such a verdict is not to ridicule Oliver's language. Oliver himself, undoubtedly a trifle disingenuously, disclaimed any interest in the speaker's art: 'Rhetoricians, to whom I do not pretend, neither to them nor the things they use to speak: Words. Truly our business is to speak Things; the dispensations of God that are upon us do require it.'[57] And his speeches were certainly idiosyncratic enough, in their length, in their repetitive emphases and in their use of the first person pronoun as he strove to convey sincerity of heart.[58] They grew impenetrable in the latter stages of the kingship crisis of 1657, as he sought both the correct course and, perhaps, improved terms, and, by the end of his life, their prolixity and emotion had become by-words.[59] But they could move some audiences, and their deliverer, to tears as they dwelt on God's mercies to His people. They could also be surprisingly logical in their structure,[60] as might befit an orator who found relaxation – and this is one of the few glimpses we have of the private Oliver – in the composition of extem-

---

55. Ibid., III, 748–9, 756.
56. See, for example, the remarkable psalmic crescendo to his opening speech to the 1656 parliament: *Ibid.*, IV, 227–8.
57. *Cal. St. Pap Ven., 1657–1659*, p. 41; Abbott, IV, 260; see also his protestation in 1657, 'I do profess it, I am not a man scrupulous about words or names or such things, I am not: . . . I have the Word of God . . . for my information': ibid. IV, 472, III, 451, 580, and IV, 267, 276, 712, 719, 722, 736.
58. An egregious example of his multiplication of emphases came in his denunciation of Spain in his opening speech to the 1656 parliament: 'Why, truly, your great enemy is the Spaniard. He is. He is a natural enemy, he is naturally so. He is naturally so throughout, as I said before': ibid., IV, 261. His speeches were not, however, always as extemporaneous as he claimed: ibid., IV, 712, 713, 722.
59. Ibid., IV, 453, 459, 480–3; Underdown, 'Cromwell and the officers', pp 105, 106.
60. This assertion rests on the assumption, admittedly a large one, that the speeches which Abbott prints in *Writings and Speeches* come down to us more or less as they were delivered, and not as tidied up for publication. In this connection, it is suggestive that someone at the time seems to have decided not to publish those of Cromwell's major speeches which strike us as the most rambling and least coherent, such as that opening the 1656 parliament, or the second speech to the 1658 session; until discovered by modern editors, these existed only in manuscript copies: Abbott, IV, 260–79, 712–20. Futhermore, the speeches which most puzzled contemporaries, notably those on the question of kingship in 1657, are those which strike us as most opaque.

poraneous verse.[61] If what Marvell lamented as 'that powerful language'[62] was not quite such an all-conquering weapon as was Oliver's sword, each instrument had its querulous victims.

The Protectorate depended as much on Oliver's aptitude for business as it did on his tongue. It is hard to think of another English ruler – except perhaps Henry VII – who so immersed himself in both the outline and the details of administration. Intermittent though his attendance at recorded council meetings may have been, it was scarcely negligent, since meetings averaged around two a week.[63] His Calvinist sense of the need to 'up and be doing',[64] and of Christian stewardship, had not left him. It is clear that there were many secret council meetings, not recorded in the council's order book and dealing with far more sensitive matters than did the often mundane regular sessions; at these the Protector was presumably often present. Like any other ruler, the Protector also took advice outside his official council, mixing business with pleasure. Bulstrode Whitelocke reported that Oliver frequently met with a group of intimates, councillors and non-councillors alike but all of them no friends of the army: 'laying aside his greatness', the Protector 'would be exceeding familiar with us . . . he commonly called for tobacco, pipes, and a candle, and would now and then take tobacco himself; then he would fall again to his serious and great business, and advise with us in those affairs'.[65] More detailed is the evidence of Oliver's deep involvement in foreign affairs. Britain's military strength in the 1650s, and Oliver's sense of how that ought to be used – 'God has not brought us hither where we are but to consider the work that we may do in the world as well as at home'[66] – ensured that Whitehall bustled with foreign ambassadors and emissaries from the first year of the Protectorate to the last. The diplomats' reports home testify to the

---

61. See, for example, the coherent organization of the Protector's long first and second speeches to his first parliament: ibid., III, 434–43, 451–62; for Oliver the versifier, see B. Whitelocke, *Memorials of the English Affairs* (1732), p. 656.
62. Marvell, *Poem upon the death of O. C.,*. l. 237.
63. The totals of attendance at council meetings are given in the prefaces to the nineteenth-century collections, the *Cals. St. Pap. Dom.* for these years. edited by M.A.E. Green.
64. Abbott, I, 245.
65. Whitelocke, *Memorials,* p. 656. Whitelocke went on to claim that the Protector usually took their advice. During the heated debate of the summer of 1658 over whether to call another parliament Oliver once again looked outside the council for guidance: T.S.P., VII, 192.
66. *Clarke Papers,* III, 207. Cromwell also of course had very real material hopes of an active foreign policy: see below, pp. 145–7.

Protector's close involvement with every step in negotiations and to their lengthy discussions with him: and only rarely did an envoy complain that Oliver had not been well briefed.[67] But the measure of his rule is better provided by the very informality of his activity. A Scottish churchman involved in discussions at Whitehall with some English councillors at the time of the kingship crisis in 1657 reported that the Protector 'looks in on a sudden at the door, and viewing us all, said, "Gentlemen it were good we had a council to night. I see there are but 5 of you there. I will send for the president [of the council, Henry Lawrence]"'. Here was a man who himself responded to emergencies, who bustled about his business. A future archbishop of Canterbury, John Tillotson, attending the Protector about college matters in 1656, wrote home that he 'could not speak to him though I was a great while in the room where he was . . . busy with the marquess of Dorchester and my Lord Fiennes'[68]

In part, such a preoccupation with business, like so much else, was forced on him, not just by the provisions of the Instrument but also by the precariousness of the Protectorate. Constant vigilance was essential, and the intelligence provided by Thurloe through control over the mails and a necessarily stinted payment of bribes was not enough: the Protector himself participated in the examination of most suspected conspirators brought up to Whitehall. And most of all it behoved him to look to the army, since there was no escaping the fact that ultimately all rested on that body – 'What hinders this nation from being made an Aceldama [or field of blood], if this do not?' he demanded of an unsympathetic parliament in 1658.[69] Accordingly, Thurloe confided to Henry Cromwell, Oliver himself 'weighed every officer with all possible care and exactness,[70] and spake with

---

67. See the report of Schlezer, the envoy from Brandenburg, in 1655, who found Oliver unsure of the causes of the dispute between Brandenburg and Sweden; but then, Schlezer noted, the protector could scarcely be blamed, for England was very distant and 'had no intercourse with these countries. The interests, rights and privileges were somewhat complicated and not very well known here'. Nevertheless, Oliver did ask the ambassador to brief him, which the latter duly did: Abbott, IV, 74, and see too ibid., IV, 106; but cf. ibid., IV 625–6, and *Cal. St. Pap Ven., 1657–1659*, pp. 136–8. Since this essay was completed, much new material on Cromwell's diplomatic dealings has become available in M. Roberts (ed.), *Swedish diplomats at Cromwell's court* (Camden Soc., 4th ser., vol. XXXVI, 1988).
68. Abbott, IV, 429, 363–4; though compare *Cal. St. Pap. Dom., 1653–1654*, p. 419.
69. Abbott, IV., 717.
70. Whether as a result of his age and illness or increasing instability in the army, Oliver may in the spring of 1658 have been contemplating handing over some of this responsibility by at last establishing a more orderly chain of command,

the most of them himself' before appointing them, having 'the opinion . . . of knowing men better than any other man'.[71] Cromwell was by no means as infallible as he sometimes thought. His appointments of Venables and Penn, and of the adjutant-general, Jackson, to the command of the 'Western Design' against Hispaniola in 1655 were as ill-judged as the expedition was ill-supplied; his first choice as personal secretary was dismissed for corruption; and the godliness he sought in candidates provided no guarantee of dynamism, as the cases of his son-in-law Fleetwood and his too-reticent southern major-general, Goffe, showed. But his administration was as a whole, and as he claimed, comparatively free of corruption and incompetence[72]; and of course his army and navy not only showed by European standards considerable efficiency and élan but also remained overwhelmingly loyal to him to the end. In that sense, the plaudits he gave himself were warranted.

Cromwell kept busy; but was the administration really his? The Instrument of Government, the written constitution for the Protectorate established on 16 December 1653, carefully sought to distribute power. Instead of looking to the three modern branches, executive, legislature and judiciary, the Instrument attempted to divide power between the Protector,[73] a strong council and parliament, when a parliament should be called. Since Charles I had ruled so much under the tutelage of 'evil counsellors' instead of his sworn councillors, Cromwell should not. The Instrument therefore bound the Protector to act only 'with the major part of his council' in almost everything; moreover, he was not to have a free hand in determining the composition of that council, for appointments required parliamentary approval.[74] The Protector clearly resented such

with the institution of a lieutenant-general of horse and a major-general of foot; nothing came of this, however: *Cal. St. Pap Dom., 1657–1658*, p. 348; *T.S.P.*, VII, 115, 500; *Cal. St. Pap Dom.*, *1658–1659*, pp. 89–90.

71. *T.S.P.*, V, 504 and VI, 609; Oliver's enemy, Clarendon, agreed with him in this at least, judging that he had a 'wonderful understanding in the natures and humours of men': *History of the Rebellion*, VI, 91.

72. G. E. Aylmer, *The State's Servants* (1973), pp. 141–3, 263–5, 342.

73. Or 'single person' as he was called by those who sought to fit that unmonarchical figure into the Aristotelian categories of monarchy, aristocracy and democracy.

74. For the text of the Instrument, see S. R. Gardiner, *Constitutional documents of the Puritan Revolution* (3rd edn, Oxford, 1906), pp. 405–17. The purposiveness of the distribution of power is reflected in the tributes to it in the early apologies: see, for example, *Perfect Occurrences*, 20–27 Feb. 1653–54; Marchamont Nedham's *Case of the Commonwealth Truly Stated* (1654) contains a fuller elaboration of this argument.

arrangements.[75] When his second parliament in 1657 set about the construction of a second constitution, the Humble Petition and Advice, Oliver protested that he had been tied as by 'swaddling bands' under the Instrument.[76]

Evidence does survive of the Protector's having been overborne by his council under the Instrument.[77] In the early days at least he claimed to have acted only in conjunction with it in matters of foreign policy.[78] And so, too, in ecclesiastical business: when a Fifth-Monarchist in December 1654 charged that he had not kept his earlier promise to abolish compulsory tithe-payments, Oliver insisted on his own powerlessness, claiming that 'for his part, he could not do it, for he was but one, and his council allege it not fit to take them away'.[79] Although he clearly had an interest on that occasion in directing the blame elsewhere, other evidence is less self-serving. In 1655 Oliver sought formally to readmit the Jews to England, whence they had been expelled by Edward I. His motives were various – hope of access to Jewish capital, belief that the Jews of Europe constituted a potential intelligence network, conviction that the conversion of the Jews was necessary to the fulfilment of the millennium, and perhaps humanitarianism as well. But the Protector encountered opposition within and without the council: what can only be called antisemitism, stirred by the lawyer and self-appointed custodian of the conservative conscience William Prynne, blended raw prejudice, the commercial fears of London merchants and clerical apprehensions of the erosion of Christian orthodoxy in an age already heterodox enough. Thwarted in the council, Oliver took the unprecedented step of opening its proceedings to the public, only to be

---

75. Whatever else they did do, the Instrument's provisions did not guarantee clarity. In the peace negotiations of the spring of 1654 the Dutch were justly uncertain of who at Whitehall had responsibility for what: *Thurloe*, II, 143, 193, 194–5; 208.
76. Abbott, IV, 488.
77. And perhaps under the Humble Petition too: see below, n.90. In his helpful survey of the council, 'The councils of the protectorate' (unpublished Ph.D. thesis, Exeter University, 1983), P.G.I. Gaunt provides some further discussion of its relations with the Protector.
78. Roberts, 'Cromwell and the Baltic', p. 409.
79. He also denied that there had been a promise: *Clarke Papers*, II, xxxiv–xxxvii. To a different, and parliamentary, audience some time later the Protector predictably sounded a more conservative note: 'I should think I were very treacherous if I should take away tithes, till I see the legislative power to settle maintenance to [ministers] another way . . . whoever they be that shall contend to destroy them, that doth as really cut their throats . . .': Abbott, IV, 272; and see above, n.28.

defeated again since the public which crowded into the council chamber was already swayed by Prynne. He had, finally, to content himself with tacit rather than formal readmission.[80]

In the most sensitive areas of policy, too, the Protector seems to have been unable to assert his will as a monarch might have done. We have only one detailed account of debate in council, the debate of July 1654 over Spanish policy, but this indicates a freer discussion of the making of war than could be imagined occurring under any of Oliver's royal predecessors.[81] Granted, the Protector seems finally to have won that argument. Yet it is tempting to read divisions into the evidence of long policy debates in the council during the political crisis after the parliament of 1654–55 had failed to ratify the Instrument of Government,[82] and the following spring as financial crisis threatened the rule of the major-generals.[83] Moreover, during the debates over kingship in 1657 Oliver repeatedly maintained that he had been overborne in the 1656 arguments. Confronted by alarmed senior officers in February 1657, the Protector pointed out in exasperation that they themselves had in 1656 urged him to assemble the 'kinglings' in parliament and then, not content with interfering in the elections, had purged the House. 'What would you have me do? Are not they of your own garbling? Did not you admit whom you pleased and keep out whom you pleased? And now do you complain to me? Did I meddle with it?'[84]. Four days later, to a larger assembly of officers, Oliver ranged wider in his allegations of responsibility. He claimed that the army, and by implication its allies and spokesmen on the council, had pushed him into every major decision – the expulsion of the Rump, the constitutional experiments of the summer of 1653, the formulation of the Instrument, the dissolution of the first parliament ('it was against his mind'), the summoning of the second parliament ('it was against my judgment, but I could have no quietness till it was done'), and then the purging of the members. All had been their work. He returned to the theme a year later, reminding the officers after he had finally dissolved the parliament that its calling was 'advised by his council, [to which] he yielded,

---

80. Abbott, IV, 51–55; for a full modern account, see David S. Katz, *Philosemitism and the Readmission of the Jews to England 1603–1655* (Oxford, 1982), pp. 190–231.
81. *Clarke Papers*, III, 207–8.
82. *T.S.P.*, III, 135, and, for example, *Mercurius Politicus*, weeks of 18–25 Jan., 25 Jan.–1 Feb.and 1–8 Feb. 1654/5, and 19–26 July 1655.
83. The lengthy discussions of the instructions for the major-generals during the late summer and autumn of 1655 may also indicate major differences.
84. Abbott, IV, 414.

though he professed it, in his own judgment, no way seasonable'.[85] Some of his assertions, such as his denial of responsibility for the expulsion of the Rump, must be discounted. Similarly, his sarcastic plaint, 'You might have given me a kick on the breech and turne[d] me going', is surely rhetorical overkill. Yet the major-generals had been hopeful about elections and the prospects for a parliament, and had been called up to the council for consultations in the summer.[86] Cromwell's account may also have a more general plausibility. There is nowhere any hint that either then or later any of the officers – some of whom spoke out on other occasions – disputed his claims. This point is all the more important in that the speech contained some specifics which, if untrue, would have merited rebuttal. 'Who bid you go to the house with a bill and there receive a foil?' he thrust at Major-General Disbrowe, whose provocative attempt to confirm the system of major-generals had ushered in the kingship proposal.[87] The army officers certainly helped persuade Oliver in 1657 to reject the Crown; they may have made their voice felt at other times.

But there remains a certain implausibility to the image of a passive Oliver, or Oliver the plaything. Too many of the council were his creations for him to have stood subordinate – his former fenland landlord Lawrence, the youthful former royalist Wolseley, his son Richard's father-in-law, Maijor. Even the army leaders, Disbrowe and Fleetwood, his brother-in-law and son-in-law respectively, were viewed by contemporaries as secondary figures – Oliver's famous rebuff to the 'milksop' Fleetwood at the time of the 1658 dissolution is justly famous, though Disbrowe was no mean parliamentary speaker or administrator. True, almost all were highly conscientious in attendance, in committee work, in government generally. But there was only one, Lambert, who ranks as an independent political figure in his own right, thanks both to his personality and to his following in the army. This brilliant commander, drafter of the Instrument and vitally important in the early years of the Protectorate, was widely suspected of ambitions to replace the Protector.[88] Yet

---

85. Ibid., IV, 417–19, 736.
86. Ibid., IV, 418; for the events of 1653, see B. Worden, *The Rump Parliament* (Cambridge, 1974), pp. 317–41, and A. Woolrych, *Commonwealth and Protectorate* (Oxford, 1982), pp. 25–102. For the context of the summoning of parliament in 1656, and of the elections, see P. J. Pinckney, 'A Cromwellian parliament' (Vanderbilt Univ. Ph.D. thesis, 1956).
87. Abbott, IV, 417.
88. The royalist report of mid-1654, that 'Lambert doth with the protector, as the protector did with Fairfax', is fairly typical: *T.S.P.*, II, 414. For Lambert's career, see W. H. Dawson, *Cromwell's Understudy* (1942).

even he could not stand alone, and there was no sign of resentment among officers or rank-and-file when Oliver finally dismissed him in 1657 for his opposition over the Humble Petition and Advice.[89] The councillors, therefore, may not have been quite the check that the constitution professed, all the more so after the Humble Petition and Advice elevated the position of the Protector.[90]

Oliver may have allowed himself to be persuaded into courses about which he had reservations. But he certainly could not be taken for granted, and his capacity for mercurial action on occasion dumbfounded those around him. His gathering impatience with the Rump in 1653, which finally propelled him into furious action, is neatly paralleled by his dissolution of his second parliament in February 1658. Then, ostentatiously consulting none of his council, commandeering 'the nearest coach', and with only a handful of attendants, he hurried to Westminster, where he brushed aside Lord Commissioner Fiennes and the hapless Fleetwood, angrily invoking 'the living God' against councillors and parliament.[91] He was capable of calmer initiatives too. The forthright denunciation of toleration by Philip Skippon, a councillor as well as an MP, during the angry parliamentary debates in 1656 on the flamboyant Quaker, James Nayler, suggests a policy originating with the Protector: several councillors, as the debates show, were extremely unsympathetic to its consequences.[92] More generally, the preoccupation of a great deal of council time, primarily on days that Oliver was present, with matters relating to the adjustment of parish boundaries and the rationalization of parochial provision argues the Protector's own responsibility for the shaping of religious policy as a whole.[93] And most important of all, on the question of the Crown Oliver at the last made his own decision.[94]

89. *T.S.P.*, VI, 425, 427.
90. In contrast to the Instrument, the Humble Petition was silent on the role of the council: for the text, see Gardiner, *Constitutional Documents*, pp. 447–59. It also required of councillors an oath of personal loyalty to the protector: Abbott, IV, 565. The new council was not, however, impotent, particularly when Oliver himself had doubts – thus in December 1657 it voted down his recommendation that the cavalier duke of Buckingham should be released: *Clarke Papers*, III, 129, and *T.S.P.*, VI, 617.
91. Ibid., IV, 727–32.
92. *Burton*, I, 271, 50; see also Gaunt, 'Councils of the protectorate', pp. 200–2. The debates on Nayler extend through November and December 1656, and much of the first volume of *Burton* is given over to them.
93. Orders concerning parishes abound in the council's order books summarized in the various *Cal. St. Pap. Dom.* for the last years of Oliver's life.
94. Although written after the fact, the verdict of the Protector's physician, George

In such crucial fields as investigations into plots, moves against parliaments, the war against Spain, the shape of religious policy, and the matter of republic as against monarchy, the Protector played a definite and usually decisive role. How is this record to be reconciled with his complaints of army and conciliar pressure. Much of the answer lies in Oliver's conscience, in his conviction of the guiding role of God's providence in human affairs.[95] Many have been the charges of sheer opportunism levelled against him, and the reasons are clear. Providence to Oliver looked unconscionably close to necessity – when action seemed necessary he took it, and deemed it providential that God had put him in the position where such an action was necessary. Indeed, he had almost as much to say when in power on the subject of necessity as he did on the providence – rather than the ambition – that had put him where he was: and on that last matter he must have wearied many listeners.[96] Not surprisingly, given the number of extraordinary actions he had to defend to his parliaments, necessity became his watchword: as he told his first parliament defiantly,

Necessity hath no law. Feigned necessities, imaginary necessities, are the greatest cozenage that men can put upon the providence of God, and make pretences to break known rules by. But it is as legal and as carnal and as stupid, to think that there are no necessities that are manifest necessities, because necessities may be abused or feigned.[97]

Crises that forced themselves on him he would meet readily. But when it came to policy choices, to *initiatives* where neither scripture

Bate, that all his would-be advisers were 'alike dubious and ignorant of his real intention', sums up the evident uncertainty of every observer; see too the suggestive reports of Oliver's new-found tranquillity once the decision was taken: Abbott, IV, 448; C. H. Firth, 'Cromwell and the crown', *E.H.R.*, XVIII (1903), 73, 73n. 96.

95. It has been well said that for Oliver, as he made clear when contesting Quaker claims to be guided by the light within, God's spirit as manifested in external events complemented scripture as authority in human affairs: W. A. Cole, 'The Quakers and politics, 1652–1660' (unpublished Cambridge Ph.D. thesis, 1955), 53.

96. His second speech to the 1654 parliament, on 12 September, is almost entirely preoccupied with providence, though he reverted to it in most of his parliamentary speeches. His odd response to congratulations from the small town of Guildford in 1654 suggests his sensitivity: 'what you there express touching my taking of the government upon me, you say what is truth; I did not desire it, nor have I (I am sure) told you so. I believe God put it into your hearts': Abbott, III, 451–62, 254.

97. Ibid., III, 460; cf. also ibid., 590–2, and IV, 261, 274–5, 293. My necessities are divine providences, yours are not only fictions but blasphemous (because all true necessities come from God): it was not a very cogent argument, but he fervently believed it.

– as in the plain requirements for moral reformation and liberty of godly worship – nor necessity (or providence) was compelling, Oliver was as always much more hesitant. His ostentatious detachment from the council's purge of a handful of disreputable or dissident members returned to the 1654 parliament provides an important clue.[98] It may have been an attempt to keep his hands clean; but it could also have signalled the unease of Oliver the providentialist when a political initiative was to be undertaken. If it did – and it would certainly fit well with his absence from that other, much larger, purge in December 1648 – then the officers' shaping of policy in the summer of 1656 must be seen in a different light. Rather than being overborne, Oliver may simply have stepped back, uncertain, when a new departure was mooted.[99] In similar fashion he played no part in the preparation of the Instrument late in 1653,[100] although when the officers put their new constitution before him he acquiesced to installation as Protector. As he showed time and again, he could accept the initiatives of others, if not his own, as providential.

Cromwell's predicament in mid–December 1653 was more straightforward than some. The constitutional vacuum left by the expulsion of the Rump and, by then, the abdication of the Nominated Assembly plainly had to be filled; to make the point clearer, and to force the occasion into Christian providentialist categories, he insisted repeatedly and at length on the 'call' of various kinds that he had received at that time.[101] The Crown was another matter. There was no similar providential necessity for kingship, since government under protectorship, as he proudly pointed out to a supplicant parliament in the spring of 1657, had been good.[102] And if there was no manifest call from God, neither was there from the people, from the city of London, from the army; instead, when the silence of a largely passive nation did break, the noise heard – from gathered churches, from groups of army officers – was hostile.[103] He

---

98. P. G. I. Gaunt, 'Cromwell's purge? Exclusions and the first protectorate parliament', *Parliamentary History*, VI (1987), 17–18.

99. See his distrust in 1647 of extraordinary political initiatives, Abbott, I, 545–6.

100. See Woolrych, *Commonwealth and Protectorate*, pp. 352–90. He did of course make a virtue of this self-effacement when he came before his first parliament in September 1654 to disclaim ambition.

101. See especially Abbott., III, 452–6.

102. Ibid., IV, 469.

103. For examples of the voices of the godly, see J. Nickolls, *Original Letters and papers of State* (1748), pp. 139–40; *Clarke Papers*, III, 91–2. It was doubtless for similar reasons that he had refused the Crown when the officers had sought to include it in the Instrument they were drafting in late 1653: Abbott, IV, 417.

was therefore left a prey, throughout that spring, to the promptings of those more self-confident, or more 'wedded and glued' to specific forms of government. He vacillated accordingly, and his speeches became steadily more impenetrable as he cast around for some sure sign.[104]

Oliver would of course have judged his indecision in 1657 the appropriate 'waiting posture', providence as yet remaining inscrutable. But that he lay open to the charge of vacillation the following year seems incontestable. Oliver then faced the need to construct a new path into the political and constitutional future. As his bitter dissolution of parliament on 4 February 1658 and his incoherent breach with his subordinates in his own regiment in the following week showed all too clearly, the old one was crumbling away.[105] The Protector's characteristic response to the inability of his divided council to point the path forward was to appoint an advisory committee of councillors and non-councillors which was almost exactly balanced between hard-liners and conciliators – and then to rage at it for its paralysis.[106] The ambivalence of this man, drawn simultaneously towards the godly party and the advocates of ancient ways, and always looking to God to tip the balance, had now assumed disastrous proportions. It may have averted further alienation, but it scarcely guaranteed the future.

Such reticence equipped him ill for one of his most important tasks. The Instrument of Government required the Protector periodically to share certain powers and responsibilities with parliaments. This requirement might be expected to entail the provision of guidance to the often deeply provincial gentry who filled the benches.[107] An unlikely enough outcome, perhaps; yet the most influential criticism levelled at him has not focused on his providentialism but has instead attributed his lack of managerial skills

104. There were of course many who insisted that Cromwell's apparent indecision, his 'waiting on the Lord', was simply hypocritical opportunism, a delay until circumstances were more propitious or until responsibility could be thrust onto others; and certainly, the net result of Oliver's delays and of his 'dark' speeches was a major improvement in the terms of the Humble Petition, particularly in the financial field. See *Cal. St. Pap. Ven., 1657–1659*, p. 36, for a typically cynical view.
105. Abbott, IV, 728–32; Underdown, 'Cromwell and the officers', pp. 101–7.
106. *T.S.P.*, VII, 38, 56, 153, 154–5, 176, 192, 269.
107. See C. Russell, *Parliaments and English Politics 1621–1629* (Oxford, 1979), for an account of early-modern parliament-men which still has some relevance when applied to a later generation.

to the fact that he was himself the quintessential back-bencher.[108] Such critics forget that not until the Restoration did parliaments become more-or-less permanent; only then had programmes and supporters to be carefully prepared. Until that point, king's servants trusted to luck and loyalty to get their business and their supply bills through. Conventions changed little in the Cromwellian republic; indeed, they may have been reinforced by Oliver's providentialist circumspection. And the Protector's opening speeches to his parliaments are certainly remarkable for their air of generality, and for their failure to give any clear lead.

Something may be said in extenuation of Oliver's less than forceful posture. His regime desperately needed to gain willing acceptance, to make itself worthy of something more than the most lukewarm acquiescence. The Protector's meditations, and the even odder and more ill-judged address by Lord Commissioner Fiennes in 1658, might therefore be seen as appeals to the heart. Furthermore, when finances were the most pressing problem facing the Protectorate throughout its short life, and as always the main concern of parliament, Oliver was not helped by his woeful ignorance in face of figures: 'here is somewhat that is exceedingly past my understanding, for I have as little skill in arithmetic as I have in the law. There are great sums; it is well if I can count them to you,' he told the house in 1657.[109] Such ignorance may explain the absence of a detailed statement of the regime's financial plight for the opening of the 1658 session, when it was tottering at or beyond the verge of bankruptcy.

There is, however, more to criticize in Oliver's stance in the 1656 parliament. Then his government did have a programme, and a programme, in Sheppard's detailed proposals for law reform, to which Oliver was deeply committed. Yet in his opening speech the Protector spoke only in the most general terms. Although he protested that he would 'cheerfully join' with parliament in the work of reform, he and his councillors in the house set too few priorities, allowing the house to lose itself in satisfying morass of petty bills. Oliver returned twice more to the theme that session, but to no

108. By H. R. Trevor–Roper, 'Oliver Cromwell and his parliaments', in his *Religion, the Reformation and Social Change*, (1967), pp. 345–91.
109. His ignorance did not, however, prevent him at the opening of the 1656 parliament indulging in a transparent attempt to minimize the scale of the debt – of a sort very familiar to those living in America in the 1980s – in order to convince his audience of the government's fiscal probity: Abbott, IV, 496, 275–6.

greater effect. His final remarks on the subject suggest the strangeness of his relationship to parliament:

> . . . surely the laws need to be regulated! And I must needs say, I think it is a sacrifice acceptable to God upon many accounts, and I am persuaded it is one thing that God looks for . . . I confess, if any man would ask me, Why, how would you have it done? I confess I do not know how. But I think verily at the least, the delays in suits and the excessiveness in fees, and the costliness of suits, and those various things, that I do not know what names they bear, – I have heard talk of 'demurrers' and such like things as I scarce know, – but I say certainly, that the people are greatly suffering in this respect; they are so.[110]

It is as though he had thrown up his hands in despair at the problems of reform and of guidance alike. But, of course, when necessity dictated action – as it did in April 1653 when the Rump seemed set to perpetuate its hold, in September 1654 when his first parliament sought to dismantle the Instrument of Government, or in February 1658 when radicals in parliament, London and the army tried to make common cause – then he could intervene decisively, full of righteous anger.

At first glance, Cromwell's foreign policy appears to present a more purposive, if outmoded, picture. After the Restoration, Slingsby Bethel, a former republican, derided Oliver for possessing too fixed a vision in foreign affairs. Bethel's charge, that his outlook had been warped by the Elizabethan experience, has stuck. Dominated by memories of the Armada, Oliver – so the story runs – saw a declining Spain, not the resurgent France of Louis XIV, as the national enemy. Catastrophically unconcerned with the balance of power, he allied with France against the Spanish position in Flanders; more generally, he saw the map of Europe in religious terms, and sought to build an anachronistic pan-protestant alliance against the Habsburgs in central Europe as well as in the western hemisphere, instead of confronting England's trading rivals, the Dutch.[111] Elements in the story cannot be denied. The protector did admire both the Elizabethan legend and the adventurer Charles X of

---

110. Ibid., IV, 274, 389, 493. For Sheppard's proposals and the 1656 parliament, see Matthews, *William Sheppard*, pp. 186–230.
111. Slingsby Bethel, *The World's Mistake in Oliver Cromwell* (1668); for a modern version, see M. Prestwich, 'Diplomacy and trade in the protectorate', *Journal of Modern History*, XXII (1950), 103–21. The essential analyses of Cromwellian policy are Roberts, 'Cromwell and the Baltic', pp. 402–46, and R. Crabtree, 'The idea of a protestant foreign policy', in I. Roots (ed.), *Cromwell* (1973), pp. 160–89, on which the following discussion is largely based.

Sweden, whom he mistook for a protestant hero. He talked expansively and often of the protestant cause in Europe;[112] and – apparently over the protests of a majority of his council – he committed England to the capture from Spain of Dunkirk, a toe-hold on the continent which was deemed expensive and irrelevant by many then and since.[113]

In other respects, the picture of Oliver the diplomat is both less purposive and more familiar. As in his domestic policy, so internationally, Oliver sought to reconcile the twin interests of the nation and of 'the people of God'. He was by no means blind to England's trading and strategic needs, and accordingly sent Admiral Blake on his impressive expedition against pirates in the Mediterranean in 1654. But he was always more comfortable when those needs coincided with the promptings of religion – as they did in the un-protestant world of the Mediterranean. Bethel was certainly correct in his claim that the cause of religion prompted a quarrel with a catholic power: thus, Oliver reminded the council in July 1654 of the 'work' to be done 'in the world' – and of the large fleet in being which had to be used or expensively laid up (and here providence and necessity once again merged). Yet as so often, though it might be clear to Oliver that *some* action was required, it might not be clear what. Accordingly, throughout 1654 he listened to the envoys of Spain and France as they bid against each other for the support of his powerful army and navy. And his eventual decision against Spain was not simply the fruit of inherited animosities or of myopia about France. It gave him hopes of empire and Spanish gold in the West Indies[114]; perhaps even more important, it gave political advantages

112. Foreign ambassadors in London were less sure of the Protector's pious unrealism, and tended to see his godly protestations as simply a cover for opportunism and materialism; for example, *Cal. St. Pap. Ven., 1655–1656*, p. 103; Abbott, IV, 73–4. The problem of hypocrisy at least is not too hard to resolve. Since, Oliver held, God's ways were visible in the world in material dispensations, the cause of religion and the course of history had to go hand-in-hand. That Oliver should seek to advance the interests of England while using godly rhetoric was not to be wondered at, since, as he never tired of pointing out, God's cause and God's providences had centred in England in the last, extraordinary, decade.
113. See, for example, ibid., III, 860, 879–91, IV, 261–3, 270, 383, 649; for Dunkirk and the council, see ibid., IV, 649.
114. The conquest of Dunkirk should be seen in similarly mixed terms – as a bridgehead in the unlikely event of a protestant crusade perhaps, but far more urgently as both a further guarantee against joint Cavalier – Spanish adventures and a blow against the Spanish privateers who preyed on British trade, as well as a check on the Dutch.

over Charles Stuart, against whom God had repeatedly witnessed.[115] Providence and partisanship[116] pushed him forwards.

If his attitude towards the catholic powers was considerably more purposive than was his policy towards parliaments – where the choices were necessarily less clear cut – that attitude was by no means simple-minded. Still less can we easily dismiss his policy towards the Baltic, an area in which he took the closest interest. The naval supplies of the Baltic were vital to England, but the region bordered on the Habsburg Emperor's sphere to the south, and that proximity drew from Oliver his most extravagant protestant rhetoric. Yet his religious instincts in this case would not square with divine dispensations – or the facts of life. For England depended on access to a sea which that protestant opponent of the Empire, Charles X, threatened to make into a Swedish lake. Oliver was forced into circumspection, almost passivity – a course whose outcome was the division of the Sound (the entry to the Baltic) between Denmark and Sweden, which survives today. For once, his policy can be deemed realistic.

Oliver's reputation in Europe stood justifiably high – higher than it did at home. The Protector's 'waiting posture' suited the stately tempo of pre-modern diplomacy more than it did the hard-pressed parliamentary time-table, where waiting had such unfortunate consequences. And whether as a result of his military background or of his godly determination to 'up and be doing', the Protector showed a novel and sophisticated recognition of the strategic use of force, in the Mediterranean and in North America too, where the 1650s saw encroachments on both French and Dutch possessions. While they might disdain the usurper, diplomats and their masters were used to disregarding breaches of 'ancient rights' and to dealing with the facts of life.[117]

For his devotion to the duties of his office, for his political

---

115. By driving Charles Stuart out of neighbouring France and into the arms of Spain, more distant and the anti-Christian enemy: see Oliver's opening speech to the 1656 parliament for the polemical use he made of this: ibid., IV, 260–79. In the same way, the 1654 peace with the Dutch – unpopular as it was with the Rumpers who had begun the war and with some mercantile interests – appealed to Oliver not simply because it seemed ungodly to pick a fight with fellow-protestants but still more because the Dutch were well-placed and ready to support Charles Stuart.
116. These were close to synonymous to Oliver, since his cause was God's.
117. The phrase is Marvell's comment in *An Horatian Ode*, at ll. 37–40. One royalist aptly summed up the diplomats' acceptance of the *status quo*: 'Good God! What damn'd lick-arses are here' (*T.S.P.*, II, 144).

acumen, for the scale of his vision and even for his achievements, Cromwell is one of England's most impressive rulers. Yet though the small remnant of his fellow-saints lamented the loss of their champion, his death was otherwise little regarded. One royalist observer of the hugely elaborate and expensive obsequies thought it 'the joyfullest funeral that [he] ever saw; for there was none that cried but dogs, which the soldiers hooted away with a barbarous noise, drinking and taking tobacco in the streets as they went'. An Essex clergyman, though more sympathetic, observed, 'Cromwell dead, the people not much minding it.'[118] The reasons for the discrepancy between the claims to greatness and the nation's response are obvious. Although the extent of devotion to the house of Stuart, even to monarchy, can be questioned,[119] the Protector's dependence on the army as a guarantee of toleration and as physical protection[120] necessitated a level of taxation that alienated almost everybody; the periodic excesses of the Saints, and the military extremes exemplified in the episode of the major-generals, only confirmed an impression already bad enough. It was no wonder the pride Cromwell sometimes expressed was mixed with bitter disillusionment, the dominant mood of his last months, and a mood best caught in his cry at the close of the 1658 session of parliament, 'I would have been glad . . . to have been living under a woodside, to have kept a flock of sheep, rather than to have undertaken such a place as this was.'[121] No wonder, too, that the eulogists, who had seen the failure of one parliamentary venture after another, who had pondered the Protector's failure to provide for the future, and who had experienced the oddly discordant funeral,[122] had such difficulty in summing it all up. Perhaps the crowning irony of Oliver's whole career is that the scale of the funeral procession left no time for a sermon. It was emblematic that none should have expounded the spiritual meaning of the life of a man who had insisted above all on the God-given nature of his mission.

118. *The Diary of John Evelyn*, E. S. De Beer (ed.), (6 vols, Oxford, 1955), III, 224; *The Diary of Ralph Josselin 1616–1683*, A. Macfarlane (ed.), (1976), p. 430.
119. See T. Harris, *London Crowds in the Reign of Charles II* (Cambridge, 1987), pp. 38–61.
120. It is arguable that the matter of toleration has primacy here, for had Oliver not been so committed to that cause he would have been able to throw himself more fully on the parliamentary gentry, thus obviating the need for such protection.
121. Abbott, IV, 705, 729.
122. Discordant too in its regal air, with its crown, sceptre and orb on the effigy of one who had refused kingship: *Mercurius Politicus*, 25 June–2 July and 18–25 November 1658; Sir John Prestwich, *Respublica* (1787), p. 188; but cf. *Burton*, II, 303, 309, and *C. J.*, VII, 575.

CHAPTER SIX

Cromwell, Scotland and Ireland

*David Stevenson**

When Britain collapsed into civil wars in the years around 1640 the crisis began in the periphery, first in Scotland and then in Ireland, and then spread to England as failure to crush revolts in these out-lying kingdoms discredited Charles I's regime. A decade later the process was reversed, the power of government centralized in London being first asserted in England, then applied to Ireland, and finally to Scotland where the breakdown of power had begun. And just as failure in the periphery had discredited Charles I, so the assertion of English power in it was central to the prestige of Oliver Cromwell.

In one respect Cromwell's basic attitude to the two outlying kingdoms was the same. They posed threats to England, not just in that they had overthrown control from London, but more actively in that they sought to impose their wills on the central kingdom. The security of England thus necessitated their conquest. Yet in other ways his attitudes to the two differed fundamentally. Whereas from 1641 onwards he can have had no doubt that Ireland would have to be reconquered, until late in the day he hoped it would not be necessary to conquer Scotland.

Where the Irish were concerned, doubtless Cromwell's starting point was the simple view of the Irish as barbarous papists who, through their religion, were potentially disloyal as well as being a standing reproach to the protestant Crown of England. In the later 1630s, however, Cromwell's perceptions of Ireland would have begun to change. The 'thorough' policies of Lord Wentworth as Lord

* I am grateful to John Morrill and Sarah Barber for their comments on a draft of this paper.

Deputy suggested that in the short term a threat from Ireland might not be presented by native Irish, but through Ireland being deliberately made into a bastion of arbitrary royal power, a test-bed for policies later to be introduced in England. Then, after the Scottish revolt of 1637 broke out, Ireland assumed a new threatening role, when a largely catholic army was raised for use against protestant Scots, a worrying precedent that might later have an application in England.

Yet of course when Ireland did suddenly become a major threat to English interest, it was in a traditional way – by the revolt of the native Irish in October 1641. This revolt, the real suffering inflicted on protestant settlers, and the vastly exaggerated rumours of catholic atrocities hardened and fixed attitudes to the Irish for most Englishmen, Cromwell among them. He took an active part in planning to restore English control of Ireland, and was a substantial subscriber under the 1642 Adventurers' Act, by which parliament raised money for a campaign there by promising repayment in land confiscated from the Irish.[1] But with the approach of civil war in England later in 1642 Cromwell's attention, like that of parliament as a whole, was diverted to problems closer to home: Ireland would have to wait until England's destiny had been decided.[2]

After the First Civil War was over parliament had resources free to devote to Ireland, and Cromwell's commitment to reconquest was emphasized by his offer in March 1647 to invest arrears of pay due to him plus up to £5,000 in the Irish venture.[3] In the event a major campaign in Ireland was delayed by the need to deal with the Scottish invasion and English royalist rebellions of 1648. But in 1649 attention swung back to Ireland. With rebellions defeated, Charles I executed and monarchy abolished, the new commonwealth regime was at last free to deal with the threats to its authority presented by Ireland. In all we know of Cromwell's attitude to Ireland and the Irish up to this point, there is no sign of any distinctive outlook, any special insights into the Irish problem. He simply shared the attitudes of most Englishmen. Ireland had to be reconquered, as historically subordinate to England, as a potential strategic threat, and as the home of barbarous papists whose crimes must be punished, whose religion must be suppressed.

1. See K. S. Bottigheimer, *English Money and Irish Land. The 'adventurers' in the Cromwellian settlement of Ireland* (Oxford, 1971).
2. See Abbott, I, 147–8, 160, 162, 172, 182.
3. Ibid., I, 588

By contrast, Cromwell's attitude to the Scots was – or became – more subtle, and he showed a readiness to modify stereotyped attitudes based on prevailing English prejudices. From an English viewpoint the Scots shared some of the characteristics of the Irish: they were poor and backward, even barbarous, and not to be trusted. On the other hand, they were protestants, and by the 1630s traditional perceptions of the Scots were being modified in the eyes of those who, like Cromwell, were worried by Charles I's policies in England, by sympathy for the Scots as a people suffering from the same misguided religious and other policies as Englishmen. Such an attitude would have been strengthened, in Cromwell as in so many other Englishmen, into positive respect and support for the Scots when their open resistance to royal policies demonstrated the brittleness of the king's power in and after 1637. It is said that Cromwell told some officers of the army the king was gathering against the Scots that he disliked the war.[4]

Yet once the Scottish covenanters had defeated the king, their ambitions for a peace settlement protecting their interests seemed to many Englishmen to amount to interference in English affairs. There is, however, no direct evidence of Cromwell's changing attitude to the Scots until after parliament negotiated the Solemn League and Covenant and a military treaty with the covenanters in the autumn of 1643. Like most parliamentarians Cromwell accepted the necessity for gaining Scottish military help against the king; but he also resented and feared the price the Scots demanded in return. Cromwell's attitude was indicated by his long delay in signing the new covenant,[5] and he quickly emerged as the leader of those parliamentarians opposed to Scottish pretensions on all fronts: in religion he opposed their demands for a religious monopoly for presbyterianism; in the conduct of the war he opposed their demands for a compromise, negotiated peace with the king; and in constitutional affairs he was opposed to what he saw as their attempt to determine England's future.

The hostility of Cromwell to Scottish pretensions came into the open after the battle of Marston Moor in July 1644. The Scots, who had fought alongside parliamentary armies in the battle, claimed the victory as largely a Scottish one, but they found that in London it was widely presented as a victory won above all by Cromwell. As the independents and other opponents of the Scots tried to exploit

4. Ibid., I, 107–8.
5. Gardiner, *Great Civil War*, I, 262, 310–11.

the victory for propaganda purposes, the embittered Scots found that 'their' victory had greatly increased the prestige of Cromwell and others determined to limit their influence.[6]

The Scots fought back, winning considerable English backing. They seized on evidence that Cromwell had 'spoken contumeliouslie of the Scots intention in coming to England to establish their Church-government, in which Cromwell said he would draw his sword against them' – as readily, indeed, as against any in the king's army.[7] The Scots therefore proposed in December 1644 that he should be impeached under the terms of the Solemn League and Covenant as 'an *incendiary*' who was kindling 'coals of contention and raises differences in the state to the public damage'. The attempt failed, but that it was made at all showed how Cromwell was by this time clearly recognized as the leader of opposition to their ambitions in England.[8]

As anti-Scots attitudes spread among parliamentarians, so Cromwell's prestige grew, he being regarded as 'the first to incense the people against the Scots' nation'.[9] The frustration of the Scots, betrayed (as they saw it) by their English parliamentarian allies, led them to sign the secret Engagement treaty with the imprisoned Charles I in December 1647. But the convenanters were now deeply divided. The dominant faction, the Engagers, was an alliance of moderate covenanters, with royalists, determined to help the king, while the more extreme covenanters, supported by most of the parish ministers, felt there was no justification for a war between the kingdoms.

The split among the Scots into Engagers and their opponents, soon to be known as the Kirk Party, was seen by Cromwell as corresponding to the dichotomy present in his own attitude to the Scots, and this dictated his conduct in the 1648 campaign against the Scots and its aftermath. He accepted that in the past decade the Scots had been essentially agents of God's work, and that in their theology, worship, Church organization at the local level, and generally sober and 'puritan' outlook they had much in common with him and his

---

6. D. Stevenson, *Revolution and Counter-Revolution in Scotland, 1644–51* (1977), p. 12; R. Baillie, *Letters and Journals* (3 vols, Bannatyne Club, Edinburgh, 1841–2), II, 203, 209.
7. Baillie, *Letters*, II, 245; Gardiner, *Civil War*, II, 23
8. Baillie, *Letters*, II, 245; Stevenson, *Revolution and Counter-Revolution*, p. 15; Gardiner, *Civil War*, II, 87–8.
9. E. Hyde, earl of Clarendon, *The History of the rebellion and Civil Wars in England*, ed. W. D. Macray (6 vols, Oxford, 1888), IV, 307.

English allies. Yet in their insistence on a strongly centralized system of Church government and in its complete separation from the state, and in their political ambitions, the Scots were enemies of both God and England. Now the Scots had split. The Engagers were clearly enemies of God and England, while the Kirk Party was revealing the essentially godly nature of its supporters by opposing the Engagement. Thus at this point there was no question of a war to conquer Scotland. The war was to defeat the Engagers and help godly Scots gain power in their own country. A new Kirk Party regime, once established in Scotland, would be bound in· firm friendship to whatever godly regime emerged in England, tied to it by gratitude (as English intervention had brought it to power), by political expediency (as it had shown that it had the power to make or break a regime in Scotland), and by common godliness. The Scots would recognize that Cromwell's victory was a demonstration that he was indeed an agent through whom God was revealing His intentions.

The Engagers' invasion of England was routed by Cromwell at the battle of Preston in August 1648, and he then advanced north, confident that the Scots would see his victory as overwhelming proof of whose side God was on, as 'The witness that God hath borne against your army'.[10] The Kirk Party now staged a *coup d'état*, and Cromwell believed that it was God's will that he treat the new Scottish regime not as representing an enemy nation, but as an ally with which he should cooperate. One of God's motives in allowing the Engagers and English royalists to rise in arms was to show the necessity for friendship between the kingdoms.[11] Enthusiastically he reported that 'I do think the affairs of Scotland are in a thriving posture, as to the interest of honest men.'[12] The godly now ruled the land, and he was eager to discuss the future with both politicians and ministers. One account survives of him trying to persuade godly Scots of his sincerity. At a meeting with some ministers he 'had a long discourse to them, with a fair flourish of words, and sometimes tears, taking God to be a witness of their sincerity and good intentions'. On leaving one minister was impressed: 'I am very glad to hear this man speak as he does'; but a harder-headed colleague retorted

---

10. Abbott, I, 650.
11. Ibid., I, 653.
12. Ibid., I, 669.

And do you believe him. If you knew him as well as I do, you would not believe one word he says. He is an egregious dissembler and a great liar. Away with him, he is a greeting [crying] devil.[13]

As this indicates, the success of Cromwell's 'hearts and minds' campaign in Edinburgh was in reality very limited. Godly though it might be in many respects, the Kirk Party remained implacably opposed to him on matters of Church government and toleration.

Nor was Cromwell's conduct popular in London. Instead of teaching the Scots a harsh lesson by following up victory at Preston with further military action, Cromwell had offered them friendship. Thus the man notorious for years as a hater of the Scots now came to be suspected of undue leniency to them. This provoked Cromwell into defending his attitude to the Scots. He had prayed and

waited for the day to see union and right understanding between the godly people (Scots, English, Jews, Gentiles, Presbyterians, Independents, Anabaptists, and all). Our brothers of Scotland (really Presbyterians) were our greatest enemies. God hath justified us in their sight; caused us to requite good for evil, causing them to acknowledge it publicly by acts of state, and privately, and the thing is true in the sight of the sun. It is an high conviction upon them. Was it not fit to be civil, to profess love, to deal with clearness with them for removing of prejudice, to ask them what they had against us, and to give them an honest answer? This we have done, and not more. And herein is a more glorious work in our eyes than if we had gotten the sacking and plunder of Edinburgh, the strong castles into our hands, and made conquest from the Tweed to the Orcades; and we can say, through God we have left by the grace of God such a witness amongst them, as if it work not yet there is that conviction upon them that will undoubtedly bear its fruit in due time.

Conquest 'was not very unfeasible, but I think not Christian' – and anyway parliament had not ordered a conquest. By requiting evil with good Cromwell hoped he had put the Scots under an unbreakable moral obligation to live in friendship with England.[14]

Just as the Scots were, Cromwell hoped, ready to learn from him, he was ready to learn from them. The Kirk Party (which only formed a minority in the Scottish parliament of 1648), had, after seizing power, disqualified the Engager majority from sitting in the 1649 and later sessions of parliaments. Cromwell was deeply impressed:

. . . a lesser party of a Parliament hath made it lawful to declare the greater part a faction, and made the Parliament null, and call a new one, and do this

---

13. T. M'Crie (ed.), *The Life of Mr Robert Blair, Minister of St Andrews, containing his autobiography* (Wodrow Society, Edinburgh, 1848) p. 210; Abbott, I, 665–60.
14. Abbott, I, 677–8.

by force . . . . Think of the example and of the consequences, and let others think of it too.[15]

A month later 'Pride's Purge' saw the army expel most of the members of the House of Commons. Cromwell claimed not to have known of the planned purge, but it is hard to believe he did not have a part in inspiring it, through drawing the attention of 'others' to a useful Scottish precedent.

Cromwell was soon disappointed by the Scots. The trial and execution of the king turned uneasy alliance between the revolutionary regimes of the two kingdoms into hostility. Again Cromwell argued with them, seeing their attitudes as tragically misguided rather than totally ungodly. He even, in an argument the irony of which must have been evident to all, cited the very article of the Solemn League and Covenant under which the Scots had once tried to impeach him as justification for acting against the king: Charles was an incendiary![16]

It was all to no avail. When Charles was executed the Scots immediately proclaimed his son Charles II as king – and king of England and Ireland as well as Scotland. Cromwell at last admitted that his policy of leniency towards the Scots had failed. In the new Council of State on 23 March 1649 he explained his understanding of the situation:

In the kingdom of Scotland, you cannot too well take notice of what is done nor of this; that there is a very angry, hateful spirit there against your army, as an army of sectaries, which you see all their papers do declare their quarrel to be against. And although God hath used us as instruments for their good, yet hitherto they are not sensible of it, but they are angry that God brought them His mercy at such an hand.

The ungrateful Scots had spurned England's proffered friendship, and the godly Kirk Party, like the ungodly Engagers before them, were seeking, through links with royalists, 'the ruin and destruction of those that God hath ordained to be instrumental for their good'.[17]

England having been lost to Charles II, it was obvious that any attempt to restore monarchy would come through Scotland or Ireland. He at first favoured Ireland as the base for an attempt to regain his thrones, and Cromwell told the Council that the Irish might soon be able to land their forces in England. Given the deep divisions in Ireland he probably exaggerated, but his statement showed where

15. Ibid., I, 678.
16. Ibid., I, 746.
17. Ibid., II, 37.

he believed England's priorities lay. An informal aside confirmed this:

I confess I have had these thoughts with myself, that perhaps may be carnal and foolish. I had rather be overrun with a Cavalierish interest than a Scotch interest; I had rather be overrun with a Scotch interest, than an Irish interest; and I think of all this is most dangerous.[18]

Ireland presented the most immediate threat, so action against Ireland was the first priority. Moreover the adventurers, with their claims to land in Ireland in return for their investments, were clamouring for action.

The political situation in Ireland was chaotic. Most of the Irish who had originally rebelled in 1641 had, by 1649, joined themselves to protestant royalists under the marquis of Ormonde, uniting in an uneasy alliance as this seemed to offer the only hope of resisting the attack which would clearly come from the armies of the English parliament – which indeed already held Dublin. But minorities of both protestants and catholics rejected such an alliance based on political expediency, so there also existed forces of Irish catholics which refused to work with royalists, and disaffected protestant royalist forces which were moving towards acceptance of the authority of the English parliament rather than ally with catholics. In Ulster the situation was further complicated by the presence of many thousands of Scots presbyterians whose political sympathies lay with Scotland rather than England.

Cromwell landed in Dublin on 15 August 1649. Just two weeks before parliament's commander there, Michael Jones, had won a remarkable victory at Rathmines over Ormonde's combined Irish and royalist army, a disaster to the Irish which was so complete and demoralizing that they never again dared face the English army in the field. Instead they concentrated on garrisoning towns and castles. Cromwell's campaign was therefore one in which the only large-scale fighting took place at the storming of such strongholds, though there was a good deal of mopping up of small bands of Irish to be done as their armies disintegrated.

Cromwell hailed Rathmines as 'an astonishing mercy; so great and seasonable as indeed we are like them that dreamed. What can we say! The Lord fill our souls with thankfulness.'[19] He told Dublin's inhabitants – mainly protestant – that he intended with divine aid to

18. Ibid., II, 38.
19. Ibid., II, 103.

restore them to their just liberty and property.[20] Thus some in Ireland were to be able to win the favour of the commonwealth: but the vast majority of the country's inhabitants were not offered such hopes. It was not just the catholic Irish (who were now taken to include the 'Old English' – catholics of English descent – as well as native Irish) who could expect no mercy. Protestant royalists who were now allied to the Irish were regarded as sharing in their crimes. Even among protestants who had not joined the Irish there were few who had not at some point in the chaotic events since 1641 collaborated with Irish or royalists, and the Scots in the north were suspect as collaborators with their misguided countrymen in Scotland. There was, therefore, no possibility of military action in Ireland giving way to a compromise settlement negotiated with some existing faction in the country, as had happened in Scotland the year before.

The Cromwellian conquest of Ireland is associated above all else with the names of Drogheda and Wexford. Brutal though the massacres in these towns are in the British context, in a wider context of European warfare they are not outstanding. Indeed they can be taken as examples of the two most common types of massacre after the fall of a stronghold. At Drogheda Cromwell summoned the governor to surrender, adding that 'If this be refused you will have no cause to blame me' for the consequences.[21] According to the accepted conventions of warfare (see page 111–2 above), if a garrison inflicted casualties on a besieging army after refusing a summons to surrender, and it was then taken by storm, the victors were justified in exacting retribution for the unnecessary losses they incurred. Cromwell applied this convention: it was his bitterness at the losses of his army in the storm of Drogheda that provoked him into sanctioning indiscriminate massacre. But though this provides an explanation, it does not provide an excuse: and undoubtedly the fact that his enemy was 'Irish', representing a people whose blood guilt was regarded as putting them almost beyond the bounds of humanity, contributed to his readiness to sanction the deed. In reality, most of the garrison was composed of English royalists, under an English commander, but in Cromwell's eyes as they had allied themselves to the Irish they shared the blood guilt of the latter.

Cromwell felt no need to excuse his conduct at Drogheda, but he did feel it needed explaining: 'And truely I believe this bitterness will save much effusion of blood, through the goodness of God', as it

20. Ibid., II, 107.
21. Ibid., II, 118.

would frighten other garrisons into surrendering without a fight. Thus it was 'a marvellous great mercy',[22] a 'righteous judgment of God on these barbarous wretches, who have imbrued their hands in so much innocent blood', and this and the hope of preventing later bloodshed 'are the satisfactory grounds to such actions, which otherwise cannot but work remorse and regret'.[23]

At Wexford Cromwell again summoned the town, but he agreed to negotiate terms for a surrender. The massacre took place in confused circumstances when the captain of Wexford castle suddenly surrendered while negotiations about the town's fate were still in progress, and parliamentary troops broke into the town from the castle and began killing and looting indiscriminately. Drogheda was an officially sanctioned massacre: Wexford was one which took place when a sudden and unexpected development led to soldiers acting outside the direct control of senior officers. Cromwell was probably being honest when he said he had wished to avoid the sack of the town. Yet his conduct at Drogheda had given his men a terrible example to follow, and Cromwell believed that at Wexford his intention to be merciful had been overruled by God's determination to impose justice instead. Cromwell had

intended better to this place than so great a ruin, hoping the town might be of more use to you and your army, yet God would not have it so; but, by an unexpected providence, in His righteous justice, brought a just judgment upon them.[24]

Cromwell's belief that the bloodbath at Drogheda would limit later bloodshed was probably correct; news of the massacre, and of that at Wexford, led to the rapid collapse of resistance, and town after town surrendered as Cromwell approached.

Not until May 1650, when the back of Irish resistance was clearly broken, did Cromwell return to England and turn his attention to the Scots, who were now replacing the Irish as the main threat to the Commonwealth. Ironically, the very fact that he had been successful in Ireland increased the threat from Scotland, for it had led Charles II to despair of help from Ireland, and this had driven him back to negotiations with the Kirk Party. By the end of April 1650 he had reached agreement with the Scots, and they invited him to Scotland. There could be little doubt that this would mean war with

22. Ibid., II, 124.
23. Ibid., II, 127.
24. Ibid., II, 142.

England, and by June 1650 the Council of State had resolved that a pre-emptive invasion of Scotland should be launched. Cromwell had no doubts as to the justice of this: the Scots had invaded in 1648 and were preparing to do so again. This being the case, it was obviously best from England's point of view that the war should be fought on Scottish rather than English soil, and that England should seek to strike before the Scots were fully prepared.[25] Yet Cromwell regretted having to fight the Scots. Once again godly – or potentially godly – Scots had been deluded into fighting for an ungodly cause. A declaration issued by his army on its march to Scotland in July spelled out his attitude. England hoped bloodshed could be avoided. She was willing to discuss religious and other differences, in attempting to reach agreement on the interpretation of the Word of God. The English had displayed Christian love to Scotland in 1648, and were willing to do so again.[26]

After the army had crossed into Scotland Cromwell maintained the pressure, though with increasing frustration at the lack of response. He wrote to the Church of Scotland expressing sadness at its attempts to prejudice those 'who do too much (in matters of conscience, wherein every soul is to answer for itself to God) depend upon you' against the English. He accused the Church's leaders of suppressing the English declarations offering love to the Scots, and invited them to send as many of their papers to his army as they liked: 'I fear them not.' Were they really sure they spoke infallibly for God? 'I beseech you, in the bowels of Christ, think it possible you may be mistaken.' To their repeated appeals to the covenants he replied 'there may be a Covenant made with death and hell. I will not say yours was so . . . .'.[27] But the bald reply of the Church showed a confidence of righteousness equal to his own: 'would yow have ws to be scepticks in our religion?'[28] Cromwell reported to parliament that 'Since we came in Scotland, it hath been our desire and longing to have avoided blood in this business, by reason that God hath a people fearing His name, though deceived':

We have been engaged on a service the fullest of trial ever poor creatures were upon. We made great professions of love, knowing we were to deal with many who were Godly, and pretended to be stumbled at our invasion; indeed, our bowels were pierced again and again; the Lord helped us to sweet

25. Ibid., II, 265–70.
26. Ibid., II, 283–8.
27. Ibid., II, 302–3.
28. Ibid., II, 305.

words, and in sincerity to mean them. We were rejected again and again, yet still we begged to be believed that we loved them as our own souls; they often returned evil for good.[29]

These expositions of Cromwell's attitude to the Scots were contained in dispatches announcing the turning point of the Scottish war. A decisive battle had been fought near Dunbar on 3 September. God had arisen and his enemies had been scattered. But even among those who had fought for the enemies of God there were many godly people, and it was his duty to try to reclaim them for the Lord. Thus when Edinburgh was occupied after the victory Cromwell redoubled his propaganda assault on the Scots.[30] Surely, now that God had shown His will so openly, they could not continue to shut their eyes to the truth?

The propaganda was indeed having an effect on the morale of the more 'godly' Scots, and this worked to Cromwell's advantage – but not quite in the way he had hoped, for only a tiny handful of Scots gave up the fight against him. Many of the more extreme supporters of the Kirk Party, however, concluded that they were suffering defeat because they were offending God: their offence lay not in fighting Cromwell, but in fighting him in the king's name. Remedying this became a matter of urgency after Dunbar, for defeat destroyed the already tottering Kirk Party regime, as worldly arguments convinced most Scots that all men, including royalists or Engagers, should be recruited to face the enemy. Even more clearly than in the past Scotland was fighting for an ungodly king. The godly extremists, concentrated in the western Lowlands, reacted by establishing what amounted to a separate administration and godly army under the name of the Western Association (its very name reflecting grudging admiration for Cromwell and his Eastern Association). In the event, however, God's mysterious failure to bring godly Scots victory continued, and the Remonstrants (so called from the Western Remonstrance in which they set out their attitudes to the war) devoted much of their energy to agonizing over precisely what they were fighting for. It became clear that some of them at least found it increasingly hard to justify fighting Cromwell, whose repeated appeals to them helped to sow dissention in their ranks. Thus though he was disappointed that he could not persuade the Remonstrants to submit peacefully, the speed with which their resis-

29. Ibid., II, 325, 327–8.
30. Ibid., II, 335–41.

tance collapsed after their defeat at the battle of Hamilton (1 December 1650) indicated the extent to which he had undermined their resolve. Yet Cromwell was sad they had had to be defeated in battle: 'Those religious people of Scotland that fall in this cause, we cannot but pity and mourn for them, and we pray that all good men may do so too.'[31]

Cromwell's efforts to conquer Scotland with words rather than bloodshed continued. Since the occupation of Edinburgh he had debated with ministers there. He visited Glasgow to persuade the godly of the west of his sincerity, hoping to win them over by his conduct and arguments.[32] But the majority of those he believed godly remained stubborn in adhering to their errors, and the main enemy, Charles II's army north of the Forth, would not succumb to his rhetoric. It took hard fighting to out-manoeuvre it, push it into a despairing invasion of England, and finally rout it at the battle of Worcester on 3 September 1651. Thereafter Scots resistance collapsed – and Cromwell could relax and admit something that he had not hinted at while the war was still to be won: of all the regime's actions, justifying the Scots war had caused him 'greatest difficulty', 'by reason we have had to do with some who were (I verily think) godly, but, through weakness and the subtlety of Satan involved in interests against the Lord and His people'. He had therefore proceeded carefully, making sure that his every action was fully justified: and as a result of this care, 'The Lord hath marvellously appeared even against them.'[33]

In 1649–51 Cromwell had conquered two kingdoms for the English commonwealth. But what was to be done with these prizes? How were they to be governed? Ireland presented few problems as to her status once conquered: she was an English dependency in which a great rebellion had been crushed. When the English parliament had abolished monarchy in England and established the republic, it had done the same in Ireland: the new commonwealth was that of England and Ireland. When Cromwell landed there in 1649 he held the traditional office of Lord Lieutenant as well as that of commander-in-chief. But his ambitions for Ireland's future were far from traditional, for he brought ideals as well as an army with him, and he believed that Ireland offered an unrivalled opportunity

31. Ibid., II, 365; D. Stevenson, *The Covenanters and the Western Association* (Ayrshire Archaeological and Natural History Society: Ayrshire Collections, 11, no. 1, 1982).
32. Abbott, II, 352–7, 360–72, 408; Stevenson, *Western Association*, pp. 160–3.
33. Abbott, II, 483.

for implementing these ideals. It had long been an irritation that in England even though power had been seized, introducing radical reform in such matters as law and religion was proving unexpectedly slow and difficult. The dead weight of tradition, of existing legal and administrative frameworks and of strongly entrenched vested interests was almost impossible to overcome. But in Ireland nearly a decade of chaos had virtually destroyed all previous frameworks. The structure of society and authority had collapsed. The opportunity to build a new godly society, and a legal system and government guaranteeing liberty and equality before the law, should not be missed. Thus the Cromwellians, like Wentworth back in the 1630s, saw Ireland as a test site for policies ultimately to be introduced in England.

Cromwell's vision of unlimited possibilities is explained in a letter written at the end of 1649. When his army had landed in Ireland

there was a dissolution of the whole frame of Government; there being no visible authority residing in persons entrusted to act according to the forms of law, except in two corporations [Dublin and Londonderry] under the Parliament's power, in this whole Land.

This vacuum provided immense opportunities. It would be possible to establish

a way of doing justice amongst these poor people, which, for the uprightness and cheapness of it, may exceedingly gain upon them, who have been accustomed to as much injustice, tyranny and oppression from their landlords, the great men, and those that should have done them right, as, I believe, any people in that which we call Christendom . . . . they having been inured thereto. Sir, if justice were freely and impartially administred here, the foregoing darkness and corruption would make it look so much the more glorious and beautiful; and draw more hearts after it.[34]

A few months later he talked of the exciting possibilities of Ireland to Edmund Ludlow. In England the law encouraged the rich to oppress the poor, but the strength of lawyers' vested interests and fears for social stability prevented reform. Ireland, by contrast was 'as a clean paper',

capable of being governed by such laws as should be found most agreeable to justice; which may be so impartially administered, as to be a good precedent even to England itself; where when they once perceive propriety preserved at an easy and cheap rate in Ireland, they will never permit themselves to be so cheated and abused as now they are.[35]

34. Ibid., II, 186–7.
35. Ibid., II, 273

That parliament shared at least some of this vision is indicated by the abolition of the office Lord Lieutenant (and the subordinate office of Lord Deputy) in May 1652: Ireland was to be governed instead by parliamentary commissioners.[36] The old offices, associated with monarchy and the old relationship between Ireland and England disappeared now that they formed a single commonwealth. But many questions remained unanswered. It was evidently intended from the first that the Irish parliament would be abolished, Ireland instead sending representatives to parliament at Westminster, but public confirmation of this did not come until March 1653, when the number of such representatives was fixed at thirty. Not until 1656 was a bill introduced in parliament for the union of England and Ireland – and though it was revived in 1656–57 it never completed its passage through parliament.[37]

In Scotland's case explicit definition of the country's place in the political system was required more urgently than Ireland, for here England had conquered an independent State, not re-asserted control over a dependency. But whereas in Ireland's case England had sought complete conquest and union into one commonwealth from the start of Cromwell's campaign, this was not so in Scotland. The aim of the Scottish war was to remove the threat the alliance of the covenanters with Charles II presented to the commonwealth: quite how this would be achieved was secondary, dependent on how the situation developed. Thus when Cromwell wrote to the Scots on 9 October 1650, all he said was needed to end the war was for the Scots to give the English 'satisfaction and security for their peaceable and quiet living by you'.[38] Only when it became clear that such satisfaction would not be forthcoming did conquest become the goal.

Not having planned to conquer Scotland, the English had no ready-made plans for what to do with their prize. At first the areas under English control were treated as conquered territory, and many felt that Scotland as a whole deserved no better. But more moderate counsels prevailed. England should offer Scotland union with England and Ireland to form one commonwealth.[39] Expediency suggested that generosity to the defeated would help to reconcile them

36. Ibid., II, 556–7; T. C. Barnard, *Cromwellian Ireland. English government and reform in Ireland, 1649–60* (Oxford, 1975), pp. 13–15, 18.
37. *C. J. VII*, 263, 415, 452–50 *passim*, 519; P. J. Corish, 'The Cromwellian regime, 1550–60', in T. W. Moody, F. X. Martin and F. J. Byrne (eds), *A New History of Ireland*, III, *Early Modern Ireland, 1534–1691* (Oxford, 1976), p. 354.
38. Abbott, II, 350.
39. F. D. Dow, *Cromwellian Scotland, 1651–60* (Edinburgh, 1979), pp. 30–1.

to the new order. Moreover, how could a regime which claimed to stand for liberty and justice justify ruling its neighbour by brute strength alone? In Cromwell's mind the Scots were already basically godly: treating them justly and removing the forces which had led them astray (king, feudal landlords and bigoted ministers) would convert them into active supporters of the commonwealth.

This policy was fully expounded in a declaration 'concerning the Settlement of Scotland' compiled in October 1651 though not published until February 1652. Parliamentary commissioners for the administration of Scotland were appointed (as they soon were to be for Ireland). Their first priority was to be the advancing of the word of God, protection being given to all who worshipped according to His revealed word. Such toleration would not only allow the spread of Independency in Scotland but would undermine the power over the people of the ministers of the kirk, whom Cromwell believed had misled them. Concerning the 'freedome to be established to the people there', and for future security, Scotland was to be incorporated into one commonwealth with England. To help pay for the wars of 1648 and 1650–51 the estates of all those involved in resistance to the English were to be confiscated (with exceptions for those who had submitted after Dunbar or who had served the commonwealth). Those not liable to punishment who, having at last discovered their true interests, agreed to cooperate with the commonwealth would be taken into parliament's protection and enjoy the liberties of the free people of the commonwealth of England. Vassals and tenants of the nobles and gentry 'the chief Actors in these invasions and wars against England', drawn into participation in the wars by their superiors, would be pardoned if they put themselves under parliament's protection, and would be freed from their former feudal dependences, becoming instead tenants of the State on such easy terms that they could live 'like a free People, delivered (through Gods goodnesse) from their former slaveries, vassalage, and oppressions'.[40]

Thus the English would bring to Scotland not just the sword, but godliness, liberty and prosperity. Apart from the upper classes virtually all stood to gain. Further, not only was Scotland offered all these benefits: she was to be allowed to choose whether she wanted

40. C. S. Terry (ed.), *The Cromwellian Union* (Scottish History Society, Edinburgh, 1902), pp. xix, xxi–xxiii; Dow, *Cromwellian Scotland*, pp. 31–2; L. M. Smith, 'Scotland and Cromwell. A study in early modern government' (unpublished D.Phil. dissertation, Univ. of Oxford, 1979), pp. 55–6.

them. A forcible union would be an unjust union, based on conquest. Thus after the commissioners for the administration of Scotland had issued the declaration of England's intentions, delegates of the shires and burghs were summoned to receive a 'tender' or offer of union. In reality, of course, the English were making an offer that could not be refused. It was made clear that the alternative to accepting the union was to be treated as a conquered people, and under English threats most of the delegates reluctantly declared their acceptance of the offer.[41] To maintain this stage-managed picture of two countries freely entering into union some of the delegates were then sent to London to negotiate details with parliament, but their presence was merely cosmetic. The process of consultation was a solemn farce, but it revealed the English ideal of what the union should be, insisted on in the face of almost universal hostility in Scotland. That the Scots remained stubbornly suspicious of Englishmen bearing gifts was ignored.[42]

The English sincerely saw themselves as acting generously: they were pressing on the Scots the inestimable gift of being treated as Englishmen. As Ludlow remarked, 'How great a condescension it was in the Parliament of England to permit a people they had conquered to have a part in the legislative power.'[43] Cromwell himself had taken no direct part in the moves towards a peace settlement in Scotland, but his approval of it may be assumed: it was entirely consistent with his attitude to the country in previous years. However, as a result of his quarrels with successive parliaments, it was a long time before the new union was formalized: in April 1654 Cromwell (by now Lord Protector) and his Council of State issued an Ordinance of Union, but a parliamentary act did not come until 1657. As in the case of Ireland, however, it was assumed from the first that union was in operation. Scots and Irish representatives were summoned to 'Barebone's Parliament' in 1653 and the Instrument of Government in December which created the Protectorate referred to the Commonwealth as being that of England, Scotland and Ireland, with Scotland (like Ireland) being represented by thirty members of parliament.[44]

41. Terry, *Cromwellian Union*, pp. xxvii–xxix; Dow, *Cromwellian Scotland*, pp. 38–41.
42. Dow, *Cromwellian Scotland*, pp. 46–51; Smith, 'Scotland and Cromwell', pp. 57–60.
43. Quoted in Terry, *Cromwellian Union*, p. xv.
44. Ibid., pp. xlvii, xlix–l, lxxiv; C. H. Firth and R. S. Rait (eds), *Acts and Ordinances of the Interregnum, 1642–60* (3 vols, 1911), II, 814, 818–19, 871–5.

Cromwell dreamed of an ideal new society in Ireland, but in reality there were major constraints on the freedom of action of the new regime there. What was the place of the catholic Irish in the new Ireland? Cromwell wrote as if 'the people' of Ireland would benefit from equality before law and good justice, but policies to which the commonwealth was already committed made it almost inevitable that the Irish themselves would be brushed aside as an irrelevance, if not indeed an impediment, to the new just society. Harsh punishment was what was planned for the Irish, and that this would include massive confiscations of land had been made clear by the 1642 Adventurers' Act and further legislation in 1643 and 1649 which provided for payment of the arrears due to soldiers in land in Ireland.[45]

Scotland at least was given a pretence of choice about joining the Commonwealth; Ireland was not consulted. The sorts of benefit and privilege that were offered to most Scots, were only promised in Ireland in vague and general terms, and restrictions and exceptions meant that few if any native Irish would benefit from commonwealth idealism. The October 1651 declaration concerning the settlement of Scotland had been mainly concerned with offering advantages; the 1652 Act for the settlement of Ireland was almost exclusively concerned with punishment. In Scotland the upper classes were to be swept aside to adapt existing society to new ideals; in Ireland almost an entire society was to be destroyed to build a new one, for the guilt of shedding innocent blood was believed to be almost universal. The act was a blueprint for the destruction of the nation – though the preamble of the act denied any design to extirpate 'the entire nation'. All those of rank and quality would be treated according to their 'respective demerits', a phrase which at once indicated that it was assumed that none had merits. Among these classes in society many individuals and categories were singled out for execution. Other landowners, somewhat less guilty, would forfeit their estates, but would receive land elsewhere worth one-third of their value, or in some cases two-thirds. Those whose only crime was that they had not been actively loyal would have one-third of their existing estates confiscated, but would retain the rest. To most of the 'inferior sort' pardon would be granted, sparing their lives and property.[46]

One estimate suggested that if the act had been fully implemented up to half the adult male population of Ireland would have been ex-

45. Corish, 'The Cromwellian regime', p. 360.
46. *Acts and Ordinances*, II, 598–603; Corish, 'The Cromwellian Regime', pp. 357–9.

ecuted. In the event no more than a few hundred were killed, and while this seeming 'leniency' can partly be explained by the fact that many of those liable to execution went into exile – there was an exodus of about 34 000 Irish soldiers and a further 10 000 or so Irish were transported to the West Indies – it also reflects both inefficiency and a gradual moderation of desire for revenge.[47]

The place of the former Irish landowners was to be taken by godly protestants, adventurers whose investments in 1642 had at last matured, and former soldiers. These, and other protestant colonists, would form the basis for the new Irish society. Quite what the fate of the Irish landowners was to be in practice was at first uncertain, with many differences of opinion as to how harshly they should be treated and whether any deserved a degree of mercy through only having been marginally or passively involved in the rebellion or through having shown signs of repentance. Eventually, in 1653, the views of those favouring indiscriminate punishment prevailed: catholic Irish landowners in general would have their estates confiscated, the partial compensation due to them being land in Connaught and County Clare.

The site for this vast Irish penal settlement was not chosen because of its lack of resources (Connaught was regarded as a richer province than Ulster) but for strategic reasons. Penned in between the sea and the River Shannon, with a belt several miles wide of protestant soldier-settlers along the coast and the line of the river surrounding them, in an area remote from the centres of commerce and government in the east, it could be ensured that never again would the Irish present a threat to protestant and English interests.[48]

The scheme to transplant the Irish was vastly ambitious. In addition, it was planned to break up the predominantly Scottish population of parts of Ulster, resettling landowners in other parts of Ireland intermingled with English proprietors, so they would no longer be a political threat.[49] Once Scotland was conquered the schemes for moving the Ulster Scots were shelved: but the transplantation of the Irish went ahead. It proved a major millstone round the

47. Corish, 'The Cromwellian regime', pp. 359–60, 362, 364; R. C. Simington (ed.), *The Transplantation to Connacht, 1654–8* (Irish Manuscripts Commission, Dublin, 1970), p. xxiv.
48. Corish, 'The Cromwellian regime, p. 364; Simington, *Transplantation* pp. vii, x; N. Canny, *From Reformation to Restoration: Ireland, 1534–1660* (Dublin: 1987). p. 220; Barnard, *Cromwellian Ireland*, pp. 10–11.
49 D. Stevenson, *Scottish Covenanters and Irish Confederates* (Belfast, 1981), pp. 285–90.

neck of the regime, for processing the claims of thousands of adventurers and soldiers to land, moving Irish landowners to Connaught, and allocating them land there, represented a huge and complicated administrative burden. Moreover, fundamental flaws and ambiguities in the transplantation and resettlement scheme soon emerged. First, there simply was not enough land available for all the adventurers and soldiers who had valid claims. As a result, much of the land originally assigned to transplanted Irish, including whole counties, was withdrawn from the scheme, while simultaneously the decision not to execute many held to deserve death swelled the numbers of Irish claimants, for those spared were regarded as entitled to land in Connaught. The basic sums for the resettlement of Ireland simply did not add up. As for the ambiguity of the scheme, were all Irish to be transplanted? Or only landlords and their families? The intention at first was probably that virtually all should go: when landlords left, the assumptions was that their tenants, dependants and followers would go with them. But in practice in the great majority of cases this did not happen. In time this was tacitly accepted. As the difficulties of resettling even landlords became clear, limiting the numbers transplanted became expedient. Another argument was even stronger: if the common people were transplanted to Connaught, who would work the land for the new protestant landlords? Hopes for large-scale immigration from England of farmers, farm workers and tradesmen soon faded, so the removal of the Irish labour force would have been a recipe for economic disaster. They were too useful to be uprooted. By the time of the 1657 Act for the attainder of rebels in Ireland it was accepted – though still only tacitly – that only landlords would be forcibly transplanted. But at least where Irish landlords were concerned the transplantation policy was (on its own terms) ultimately fairly successful. Before the troubles catholics had owned about 59 per cent of Irish land: by the 1660s they only owned 20 per cent largely in Connaught. But if concentrating and limiting Irish landownership was accomplished, the attempt to build a new protestant society in the rest of the country failed. Some 12 000 soldiers settled, but most of those entitled to land grants in Ireland, whether soldiers or adventurers, preferred to sell their rights rather than settle in Ireland.[50]

The contrast with Scotland is striking. There too it had originally been planned to disinherit many native landowners, though there had

50. Corish, 'The Cromwellian regime', pp. 360–2, 365, 368–70, 373; Simington, *Transplantation*, pp. xx–xxv; Barnard, *Cromwellian Ireland*, p. 11.

been no thought of uprooting whole populations. Virtually all the larger landlords had been involved in making war on England, and it was intended to destroy them – even more thoroughly, indeed, than their Irish counterparts, since there was no provision for compensation in some Scottish Connaught. And what was to happen to confiscated lands in Scotland? Talk of lands being leased on easy terms to those supporting the regime indicated an intention of keeping land in the hands of the State, but in 1651 parliament ordered land grants in Scotland to be made as rewards to senior army officers,[51] and the duke of Hamilton's estates passed into the hands of such officers for some years.[52] In 1654 trustees for confiscated estates were appointed,[53] but their significance was limited as most estates were either returned to their former owners (on payment of fines) or handed over to their creditors.

Confiscating the lands of most great landowners was supposed to secure the stability of the new regime in Scotland, by removing the powerful elements in society hostile to it. In practice the policy had the opposite effect, for it left such men nothing to lose. The result was the incoherent rebellion of 1653–55 known as Glencairn's rising, based on the Highlands and reducing much of northern and central Scotland to chaos.[54]

The rebellion was crushed, but it forced a rethink of policy, and this was reflected in the 1654 Act of Grace and Pardon. Instead of blanket disinheritance of all tainted with war guilt, it listed twenty-four individuals (mainly nobles) who were to lose their estates, and seventy-three other landlords who were only to retain their lands on payment of heavy fines. Other landlords (except any found to have supported the rebellion) were to retain their estates. Further, in the event those excepted from pardon were shown leniency. In the years that followed fines were often substituted for confiscation, and most of the fines were eventually reduced or cancelled altogether. Thus though at first virtual extinction of Scotland's greater landlords had been threatened, in the end they escaped with lighter punishment than English royalists.[55]

51. *C.J.* VII, 14.
52. R. K. Marshall, *The Days of Duchess Anne* (1973), p. 26; *Register of the Great Seal of Scotland, 1652–9* (1904), nos 188, 453, 568; *Register of the Privy Council of Scotland, 1665–9* (1909), pp. 27–8.
53. *Acts and Ordinances*, II, 885–8.
54. Dow, *Cromwellian Scotland*, pp. 42, 53, 57–8.
55. C. H. Firth (ed.), *Scotland and the Protectorate* (Scottish History Society, Edinburgh, 1899), pp. xxvii–xxxi; *Acts and Ordinances*, II, 875–83; Dow, *Cromwellian Scotland*, pp. 77, 112, 117, 122–3, 157.

Clearly the commonwealth had watered down its plans in Scotland. It had accepted that seeking to destroy the great landlords was more trouble than it was worth: it was expedient to try to reconcile them to the regime. This was all the more necessary as by the mid-1650s the regime had to admit that it had not won the support it had hoped for among the common people of Scotland. As the people had failed to respond with loyalty to offers of liberty, it made sense to attempt to recruit their former social superiors to influence and control them. There was no question of restoring the feudal powers and jurisdictions of the mighty, but there was an admission that the exercise of their traditional influence would help stabilize the regime.[56]

This change of emphasis was not, of course, an isolated phenomenon. In other aspects of policy in Scotland, and in England and Ireland as well, Cromwell was turning away from ambitions of radical change to concentrate on more immediate problems of maintaining stability and winning support for a regime which was deeply unpopular throughout Britain, back-peddling on some of the policies which alienated powerful interests. The acceptance of the title of Lord Protector by Cromwell at the end of 1653 was symptomatic of this change, and the change in form of government at the centre was soon reflected in Ireland and Scotland. In 1654 the office of Lord Deputy was revived, and a Council of State was established in Dublin.[57] Scotland did not receive a deputy – such an appointment would have been regarded in Scotland as implying subordination to England. But she received a Council of State, with a president who was Lord Deputy of Scotland in all but name, in 1655.[58] The establishment of two outlying councils, replacing former parliamentary commissioners in both cases, seemed to imply a degree both of decentralization and of recognition that more permanent and formal arrangements than in the past should be made for governing Ireland and Scotland separately from England. Further, just as executive power had been to some extent concentrated in the hands of one man at the centre, the Lord Protector, so such individuals, subordinate to him, should be established in the peripheral capitals.

With changes in policies and in machinery of government went changes in personnel. The majority of the parliamentary commissioners in Ireland, and after them the Lord Deputy (Charles

56. Dow, *Cromwellian Scotland*, pp. 159–60; Smith, 'Scotland and Cromwell', pp. 209–10.
57. Barnard, *Cromwellian Ireland*, pp. 19–20; Corish, 'The Cromwellian regime', p. 354
58. Dow, *Cromwellian Scotland*, p. 160; Smith, 'Scotland and Cromwell', pp. 77, 83.

Fleetwood) and his council, had been radical in their religious and political outlooks. Like Cromwell in 1649–50, they saw Ireland as a land where a new godly society could be built. So far as the future was concerned, the native Irish were brushed aside. Even Ireland's 'Old Protestants' – those there before the Cromwellian influx – were excluded from the new design, being suspect through their political actions in the past and for their episcopalian religious inclinations. Thus the 'Old Protestants' found their advice was not needed. The presbyterian Scots in the north were equally anathema to the sectaries who now prevailed in Dublin. But by the mid 1650s the excessive zeal of the Protectorate's representatives in Ireland was becoming an embarrassment to Cromwell in London, for it alienated many unnecessarily. As in Scotland, one of parliament's first priorities in Ireland was to cut costs so the massive subsidies provided by English tax-payers could be reduced. This meant that reconciling as many as possible to the regime so that the expensive armies of occupation could be reduced and encouraging the recovery of the economy so local tax revenue would increase were now given priority.

The anabaptists and other sectaries in power in Dublin in 1652–55, with their exclusive policies and insistence on pushing ahead with harsh transportation policies, seemed almost to be going out of their way to minimize support and maximize disruption. A lead in attacking such policies was taken by Cromwell's son Henry, who was appointed a member of the Irish Council of State in December 1654.[59] Fleetwood remained Lord Deputy in name until late 1657, when Henry replaced him, but Henry was in practice acting deputy from September 1655 as Fleetwood was then recalled to England, leaving Henry as the dominant force on the Irish council. With Henry's rise came more moderate policies. The still powerful Old Protestant interests increasingly found their advice listened to, their support sought. It was in part their arguments about the economic consequences of wholesale transportation of the common Irish to Connaught that led to the policy being tacitly abandoned. Willingness to show favour to presbyterian ministers in the north reconciled many to the regime.[60] Even catholics benefited: while there could be no question of official acceptance of the presence of priests in Ireland, the lessening of repression allowed their numbers to increase significantly in the later 1650s.[61]

---

59. Abbott, III, 558; Barnard, *Cromwellian Ireland*, pp. 20–1, 98, 102–5, 300, 302.
60. Barnard, *Cromwellian Ireland*, p. 14, 22, 52, 58.
61. Corish, 'The Cromwellian regime', p. 355.

In Scotland the same general process can be observed. The replacement of Robert Lilburne as commander-in-chief in Scotland by George Monck in 1654 substituted a presbyterian and former royalist for an independent, a gesture that was conciliatory – though in fact Lilburne had already begun to urge moderation. It went hand-in-hand with the move away from attempting to destroy the greater landlords and instead making it worth their while to accept the regime. The part played by Henry Cromwell in Ireland was shared in Scotland by Monck and Lord Broghill. The son of the earl of Cork, Broghill had played a prominent part in Irish affairs, helping win over his fellow Old Protestants to support the Commonwealth and seeking to persuade Cromwell that they should be treated better. His views finally prevailed in the mid-1650s, but though Old Protestants were increasingly favoured by the regime it was politically inexpedient to promote one of them to high office in Ireland, so reward for Broghill's services and abilities came through his appointment in 1656 to be president of the Council of State in Scotland. Experience gained in dealing with one outlying territory was thus applied in the other. Under the clear-headed and amiable Broghill, progress was made on two fronts: winning the acceptance, if not the active support, for the regime of the landowning classes; and at least partly solving the religious problems which plagued the regime. Broghill left Scotland in August 1656, but he had set the regime on the course it was to follow until after Cromwell's death.[62]

The number of Scots converted to sectarianism under English- imposed toleration was very limited, though handfuls of Anabaptists, Independents and Quakers can be traced.[63] But this was not seen as necessarily disastrous, for the Church of Scotland was regarded as providing a godly alternative. The problem, as before, was that though Cromwell would tolerate the Presbyterian Church, it would not tolerate him. In any case, the Church was deeply divided. The split which had emerged when the Remonstrants virtually disowned Charles II had spread and solidified. The Protester minority, successors to the Remonstrants, squabbled endlessly with the Resolutioner majority, which supported the exiled king. The split meant that the Church could not unite against the English, and this obviously was to their advantage in some respects, but continued disruption in the church was seen as interfering with the general settlement of the

62. Dow, *Cromwellian Scotland*, pp. 162, 210.
63. G. D. Henderson, 'Some early Scottish Independents', in *Religious life in Seventeenth-Century Scotland* (Cambridge, 1937), pp. 100–16.

country. At first the English favoured the Protesters: they had refused to fight for the king, so at least they were not tainted by royalist malignancy. The English hoped to win the Protesters' support by giving them control of the Church and helping them against the Resolutioners. In fact there was no real possibility of this: the Protesters would not accept the legitimacy of a regime which insisted on State supervision of the Church and on toleration.[64]

Broghill swiftly broke the religious deadlock. Seeing that the Resolutioners' hostility was partly a reaction to the regime's support for the Protesters, he decided to see what could be done by offering a share of favour to the Resolutioners. In return he did not ask for promises of loyalty to the Protectorate, but simply that ministers should live quietly under the regime and give up their public prayers for Charles II. It is a mark of Broghill's charm and skill as a negotiator that most Resolutioners accepted this tacit bargain in 1656.[65] But further hopes, of reconciling the two factions in the Kirk and winning their positive support for the regime, failed. Representatives of both parties debated the matter with Cromwell in London in 1657, but he found Scots ministers as reluctant as ever to accept his ideas, and threatened that if they could not reform themselves 'an extraordinary remedy' should be employed.[66] But in reality he knew that any attempt to impose unity on the Kirk would cause massive resentment which would be politically dangerous. He could defeat the Scots in war, but not in debate.

Nonetheless, at least a settled parish ministry preached godly doctrine throughout most of Scotland, and in this the country was in a much more satisfactory condition than Ireland. The organization and ministry of the Church of Ireland had been destroyed by the wars since 1641. The commonwealth sought to build a new Church, but there was never any official decision as to precisely what form it should take. At first the anabaptists prevailed, but the efforts of their officially sponsored sectarian preachers were concentrated on newcomers – English soldiers and administrators – with little attempt to cater even for other protestants. The best organized Protestant ministry in the country, that of presbyterian ministers in Ulster, was regarded as an alien Scots intrusion to be repressed. Many had expected that propagation of the Gospel in Ireland would mean

64. Abbott, IV, 399–400
65. Dow, *Cromwellian Scotland*, pp. 195–8, 206; J. Buckroyd, 'Lord Broghill and the Scottish church, 1655–6', *Journal of Ecclesiastical History*, XXVII (1976), 359–68.
66. Abbott, IV, 399–404, 618–19.

primarily an attempt to persuade the catholic Irish of the error of their ways, but this was neglected: at heart, it seems, the country's rulers believed trying to convert them was a waste of time. That many wanted transplantation to Connaught to involve Irish commons as well as landowners seemed to reflect such despairing attitudes to the redemption of the Irish, for such a policy would have created an entirely catholic population in much of the province. Those who came to argue against transplanting the commons added to economic arguments a religious one taking a more optimistic view of the potential of the Irish: if the commons were allowed to remain scattered through the country, where most would have protestant landlords and (hopefully) preachers and neighbours, there might be a real chance of converting them.[67]

However, though in the later 1650s a few gestures were made towards concern for the spiritual welfare of the Irish,[68] the emphasis remained on providing a ministry for existing protestants. Henry Cromwell, alarmed by the divisive and exclusive policies of the anabaptists, switched official favour to the independents instead. But they proved just as intolerant of rivals, trying to impose their own monopoly of influence, and eventually Henry swung round to supporting the presbyterians. In 1655 he reached an agreement with the dominant (as in Scotland) Resolutioner party among the presbyterian ministers, whereby they would receive government salaries without having to make any political commitment which would interfere with their loyalty to Charles II. The policy was unpopular both in England and with new protestants in Ireland, but it worked – and formed a precedent for the similar 1656 agreement with the Resolutioners in Scotland. The numbers of State-sponsored ministers rose from about 110 in 1655 to about 250 in 1658, but this was still a remarkably low total – and it was achieved largely by the inclusion of existing presbyterian ministers rather than by provision of new preachers. Overall the efforts of the regime to spread the Gospel in Ireland were a humiliating failure.[69] There was little more success in education. Many had hoped that encouragement of education would convert Irish children. But by 1659 there were only thirty-five State-supported parish schoolmasters – and they mainly served English garrisons.[70] If things were better in Scotland it was, again, because

---

67. Barnard, *Cromwellian Ireland*, pp. 12–13, 91–6, 102–21.
68. Ibid., pp. 135, 171–82, 297–8.
69. Ibid., pp. 122–9, 143, 146–7, 155–7, 168.
70. Ibid., pp. 97, 183, 186–8, 194, 206.

the existing established Church there had not been destroyed by war and continued to support schools and universities. As in Ireland, Cromwellian attempts to increase the resources devoted to education were welcome, but very limited.[71]

Propagation of the Gospel was almost invariably the first priority in commonwealth declarations and instructions to officials in both Scotland and Ireland. Good intentions were frustrated in Ireland by lack of money, indecision about what sort of religious settlement should be made, and despair about the unregenerate Irish. In Scotland they were frustrated by failure to establish a relationship based on mutual trust with either faction in the Church. Another high priority repeatedly stated by the commonwealth was the spread of justice and liberty. People must be treated equally by the law, whatever their social status. Justice should be impartial, cheap, and reasonably swift. But as in so many other spheres, early reforming zeal soon gave way to expediency. The judicial system had collapsed in Ireland, so there was an opportunity for a new start. But though the building of a largely new systems of courts began, it was soon abandoned. In 1655 the traditional Four Courts were revived, and soon the legal system became almost indistinguishable from that which had existed in 1641. Not only was reverting to old ways convenient, especially when there was much disagreement about what should replace them, but the speedy justice of those zealous for new ways had often turned out to be summary justice, making reverting to old procedures welcome.[72] In any case, as far as the great majority of the population was concerned, talk of liberty was a mockery, for justice as applied to them was a euphemism for punishment.

Scotland differed from Ireland in that instead of largely conforming to English law she had her own law and procedures.[73] The general assumption among Scotland's conquerors was that in law (as in many other matters) things English were superior to things Scots. Thus, paradoxically, while the existing legal system in England was under strong attack for its many defects, north of the border it was presented as a model for Scotland. There was, however, no attempt at immediate wholesale introduction of English law. The old feudal jurisdictions vanished along with the old central courts (the Court of Session and Court of Justiciary), which were replaced by commis-

---

71. Dow, *Cromwellian Scotland*, pp. 58–60; Abbott, III, 395, 874; IV, 794–5, 582–3, 825, 852–3.
72. Barnard, *Cromwellian Ireland*, pp. 249–61, 267–8, 274–7.
73. Ibid., p. 250.

sioners for civil and for criminal justice. But the new courts continued to work, with a few exceptions, in accordance with existing Scots law. Parliament's instructions in 1652 were that English law was to be introduced only 'as to matters of government', and even then only as far as 'the constitution and use of the people there' and circumstances permitted.[74]

The quality of justice provided by the Cromwellian regime in Scotland is often cited as a major achievement,[75] but the praise heaped on it appears to be exaggerated. Glowing tributes by Englishmen to their achievements among the benighted Scots should not be accepted uncritically, for obviously they are likely to be biased, and the one Scottish source supporting them is no more convincing. In his *Diary* John Nicoll writes enthusiastically of how fast and impartial English-administered justice was, and how delighted litigants were with it in comparison with old Scottish justice.[76] However, Nicoll requires to be used with great care, for he himself explained that what he wrote was not what he believed, but 'the reall wordis, deidis and actiones' of those in power at the time.[77] Thus the views he expressed changed according to what regime was in power, and he is not a reliable witness.

It would, however, be going too far to say English rule brought no benefits in the administration of justice in Scotland. It seems very likely that the English judges were more impartial than their predecessors, less influenced by vested interests and the power of great men. But above all what contributed to making the courts popular was the simple fact that they sat regularly and gave judgments at all. Scotland had experienced nearly fifteen years of turmoil, during which much had happened that tended to increase the amount of litigation, while the meetings of courts had frequently been interrupted. Thus for many, any settled system of justice which resolved cases was welcome. The commonwealth worked hard and honestly

74. Firth, *Scotland and the Protectorate*, p. 395. H. R. Trevor-Roper, 'Scotland and the Puritan Revolution', *Religion, the Reformation and Social Change* (1967), p. 420, erroneously cites this as a general attempt to introduce English law into Scotland.
75. Trevor-Roper, 'Scotland and the Puritan Revolution', pp. 418, 421; Dow, *Cromwellian Scotland*, 56; A. R. G. McMillan, 'The judicial system of the Commonwealth in Scotland', *Juridical Review* (1937), pp. 232–55, Smith, 'Scotland and Cromwell', pp. 120–1, 244.
76. J. Nicoll, *A diary of public transactions and other occurrences, chiefly in Scotland, from January 1650 to June 1667* (Bannatyne Club, Edinburgh, 1836), pp. 64, 66, 69, 104.
77. Ibid., pp. ix–x; D. Stevenson, 'The covenanters and the court of session, 1637–51', *Judicial Review* (1972), pp. 244–5.

to improve justice in Scotland, and the number of cases settled is impressive. But the evidence for this being perceived as a major benefit by Scots is unconvincing.[78]

The other main benefits that the Cromwellian regime sought to bring to the people of Scotland were freedom from feudal and clerical oppression. Again there is virtually no evidence of a positive response to this. The abolition of feudal jurisdictions and superiorities appears to have been greeted with indifference.[79] Moreover, the regime never even got round to the formal abolition of feudal tenure in Scotland,[80] and even some regality and baron courts seem to have continued to meet on a feudal basis (rather than in the guise of the new 'courts baron' introduced in 1654 to replace them).[81] In religion few Scots had a real chance to exercise their new liberties, for the intolerant Kirk remained dominant in most parishes. It is doubtful if the vast majority of Scots noticed that they had new liberties, civil or religious, and as the regime moved towards reconciliation with landlords and with the Resolutioner majority of ministers the possibility of such liberties meaning anything in the future declined.

By the time of Cromwell's death in September 1658 there was in Scotland a growing feeling of returning normalcy – or acceptance of a new normalcy for the time being as there seemed no immediate prospect of anything better. At least the regime was now trying to make itself attractive to powerful interests such as landowners and ministers. It still had to be based on an army of occupation, but its numbers were declining – from about 18,000 in 1654 to an establishment of about 10,500 in 1657.[82] Increasingly English civilians were taking over from soldiers in civil offices, though their numbers remained small. The numbers of Scots prepared to hold office or sit in parliament grew – though again progress was slow.[83] Relations

---

78. Smith, 'Scotland and Cromwell', pp. 106–21, 244; Dow, *Cromwellian Scotland*, p. 221.
79. Trevor-Roper, 'Scotland and the Puritan Revolution', p. 418, cites enthusiastic Scots in 1651 crying 'Free the poor commoners and make as little use as can be either of the great men or clergy'. But though the cry did come from Scotland the context makes it clear that it was in fact the cry of the English conquerors. See C. H. Firth, *Scotland and the Commonwealth* (Scottish History Society, Edinburgh, 1895), pp. 339.
80. See C. J. VII, 407, 427 for attempts to do so.
81. Smith, 'Scotland and Cromwell', pp. 205–7.
82. C. J. Firth, *The Last Years of the Protectorate* (2 vols, Oxford, 1900), II, 87–8.
83. Dow, *Cromwellian Scotland* pp. 149–50, 177, 179–81, 185–8, 221–2; P. J. Pinckney, 'The Scottish representation in the Cromwellian parliament of 1656', *Scottish Historical Review*, XLVI (1967), 95–114.

with English officers and officials were often good. Broghill in particular won a good reputation through both personality and policies, and Geneal Monck was respected.[84] Yet the repeated themes of Robert Baillie's summaries of the state of the country from 1654 to 1659 are negative – military occupation, deep poverty ('the English hes all the moneyes'), high taxes, nobility broken, commons oppressed.[85] Monck's reports were little more optimistic: things were 'well' in that Scotland was quiet, but at heart the Scots were still malignant.[86]. Cromwell himself, just months before his death, described Scotland as 'a very ruined nation'.[87] The mood seems one of desolation. If Cromwell had not quite made a desert, he had created something that Scots found hard to think of positively as peace.

That the great and idealistic ambitions of Oliver Cromwell for Scotland and Ireland were thwarted, that he remained conqueror rather than a liberator, is of course no surprise: the same is true in England, where his regime was endured rather than loved. Next to lack of positive support from the populations concerned, the most basic of all problems was money. Visions for reform often failed because they were expensive in themselves, or because they entailed alienating powerful interests – which in turn meant that increased military expenditure was necessary. Even after radical policies were abandoned Ireland and Scotland showed no prospect of becoming self-supporting. In 1659 Scotland's regime needed a subsidy from England of £164,000 – 53 per cent of total public expenditure.[88] Ireland at least covered 75 per cent of her own costs of government, but even here the expected deficit for 1658 to be met by England was anticipated as £96,000.[89] There was no realistic possibility of either nation being able to pay its own way until the armies of occupation were very greatly reduced in size – and there seemed little prospect in the near future of it being safe to do that.

Another major problem concerned the personnel of government. Who was to adjudicate and administer in Scotland and Ireland? There were three constraints that made this a problem. First was acceptability to the regime. In Ireland almost the whole population was disqualified from office, and the same was true of Scotland's ruling

84. Nicoll, *Diary*, p. 183; Baillie, *Letters*, III 315, 321.
85. Baillie, *Letters*, III, 249–50, 252, 287, 289, 317, 357, 387.
86. Dow, *Cromwellian Scotland*, p. 228.
87. Abbott, IV, 718.
88. Dow, *Cromwellian Scotland*, p. 219.
89. Barnard, *Cromwellian Ireland*, pp. 26–7.

élites at first. In the early years civil government was very much subordinate to military, and leading officers held civil offices, later being joined by English civilians. Soon, particularly in Scotland, office was opened to those inhabitants regarded as suitable, the plan being for offices to be divided between natives and Englishmen. But here the second constraint appeared: many to whom the privilege of office was offered declined it, not being willing to serve the regime. And the final constraint was that the number of Englishmen of ability willing to accept office in the outlying countries of the commonwealth was very limited. The results were continuing involvement of army officers in civil affairs – since they were qualified and on the spot – and that the small numbers of English civilian administrators often held several positions at once, leading to inefficiency. And though the loyalty of English administrators might be certain, their experience of the countries they were helping to rule often limited their effectiveness.[90]

Another problem lay in uncertainty as to where power in making decisions and appointments lay – in Dublin and Edinburgh, or in London? Frequently those unable to get their way in the sub-capitals of the Commonwealth by-passed them and got favourable decisions from Cromwell or parliament, thus undermining the authority of those struggling to rule in Edinburgh and Dublin.[91] Further, decisions based on ignorance of circumstances were often made in London which were difficult or impossible to implement in the peripheral nations of the commonwealth. Before the troubles Scotland and Ireland had suffered from being governed by a system of absentee monarchy. The 1650s experiments proved that absentee republican government could be just as blundering, ignorant and insensitive, with just as little time or priority for their concerns. That an act of union for Ireland was never passed; that Ireland was left without a civil government for two months in 1657 through delays in commissioning a new Lord Deputy, that Scotland was ordered to set up new courts baron based on 'manors' (which did not exist in Scottish land law) were all examples of the 'haphazard processes of the Cromwellian regime'.[92] In both countries news of Cromwell's death was greeted with apprehension, for it opened up worrying

90. Ibid., pp. 12–13, 19–20, 25, 284, 287; Dow, *Cromwellian Scotland*, pp. 162–4; Smith, 'Scotland and Cromwell', pp. 102, 134.
91. Barnard, *Cromwellian Ireland*, p. 25; Smith, 'Scotland and Cromwell', pp. 99, 101.
92. Barnard, *Cromwellian Ireland*, pp. 21–2, 98, 294; Smith, 'Scotland and Cromwell', p. 102; *Acts and Ordinances*, II, 883.

questions of what would follow, but in neither country was there much sorrow except among the members of the English armies and administrations of occupation. With the restoration of monarchy in 1660 the parliamentary unions with Scotland and Ireland were dissolved: not until 1801 were the three legislatures again to be united.

One final observation on Cromwell's attitude to the outlying kingdoms within the British Isles is called for. He conquered them and incorporated them into a single State. But it retained a tripartite name: the Commonwealth of England, Scotland and Ireland. Cromwell might rule the entire archipelago, but its periphery had only been conquered to protect England, and for 'God's Englishman' the name of England was sacrosanct, the concept of 'Britain' an unwelcome intrusion associated with the ambitions of the Stuarts and the covenanters which had threatened England's identity. He had dreams of just and godly futures for Ireland and Scotland – through making them little Englands; but England would remain England.

CHAPTER SEVEN

Cromwell's religion

*J. C. Davis**

'. . . wherever anything in this world is exalted or exalts itself, God will pull
it down, for this is the day wherein He alone will be exalted.'
    [Cromwell to William Lenthall after the battle of Preston, 20 August 1648]

'Whatsoever our profession were, that is that would do it, namely the power
of godliness.'
    [Cromwell speaking to ministers of the French Church, 5 January 1654]

If we take Oliver Cromwell's words at their face value, it has been
suggested, we should then see his religious attitudes and views as the
most important thing about him.[1] It is an appraisal of which we can
imagine him approving. We are obliged, even when adopting a healthy scepticism, to give full weight to the religious context which
shaped and gave force to his religious utterances. As it was not a
context of naive, banal or clichéd religious expression, we must allow
for a degree of sophistication in Cromwell's religious, if not
theological, thought and belief. Considerable importance should be
attached to the form and content of what he said in religious terms.

Yet, before the 1980s, surprisingly little, of a serious and direct
kind, had been written about Cromwell's religion. A biography
which saw religious faith as the crucial dimension of his life[2]; two
books purporting to be studies of his religion, only one of which

---

* I would like to acknowledge the assistance of the following, all of whom read
  an early version of this essay and made valuable comments on it: Glenn Burgess,
  Anthony Fletcher, John Morrill, Jonathan Scott and Blair Worden.
1. George Drake, 'The ideology of Oliver Cromwell', *Church History* XXXV
  (1966), 259.
2. Paul, *Lord Protector* (1955).

lived up to that promise[3]; and a handful of articles[4] make up a meagre yield, of specialized reconstructions of his beliefs and their context, from the rich harvest of Cromwell studies. Blair Worden's brilliant and, to a large extent, pioneering work of the 1980s – on Cromwellian toleration, providentialism and the political/spiritual crisis of the mid-1650s[5]– has refocused our attention in this direction and offered an enticing prospect of a freshly envisaged and recovered Oliver.

How are we to explain the previous neglect of a dimension so important to understanding the man? Partly because of the very confidence with which his religious identity was asserted, it was assumed that there was virtually nothing to explore. Oliver was a puritan, a Calvinist, an Independent, the darling – at least in his rise – of the sects. These assurances passed down the historiographical chain from one historian to the next. Between 1890 and 1914 our view of Cromwell's religion was confirmed and stabilized in the consensus of a remarkable series of biographies and related works.[6] When W. C. Abbott's apparently definitive edition of Cromwell's writings and speeches appeared between 1937 and 1947, his commentary did nothing to revise the perceived image of Cromwell's piety.[7] For want of disturbing evidence to the contrary, his assumed religious identity could remain unchallenged. But there are problems facing any historical account of Cromwell's religion which need to be confronted at the outset.

First, there are problems of evidence. Cromwell left no program-

---

3. Robert F. Horton, *Oliver Cromwell: a study in personal religion* (1897) which despite its subtitle this remains a conventional biography; H. F. Lovell Cocks, *The Religious Life of Oliver Cromwell* (1960).

4. Winthrop S. Hudson, 'Denominationalism as a basis for ecuminicity: a seventeenth century conception', *Church History*, XXIV (1955), 32–50; John F. H. New, 'Cromwell and the paradoxes of Puritanism', *Journal of British Studies*, V (1965), 53–59; Drake, 'Ideology', pp. 259–72; Sarah Gibbard Cook, 'The congregational independents and the Cromwellian constitutions', *Church History* XLVI (1977) 335–57.

5. Blair Worden, 'Toleration and the Cromwellian protectorate', in W. J. Sheils (ed.), *Persecution and Toleration: Studies in Church History*, 21 (Oxford, 1984), pp. 199–233; 'Providence and politics in Cromwellian England', *Past and Present*, CIX (1985), 55–99; 'Oliver Cromwell and the sin of Achan', in Derek Beales and Geoffrey Best (eds), *History, Society and the Churches* (Cambridge, 1985), pp. 125–45.

6. Frederic Harrison, *Oliver Cromwell* (1890); Samuel Rawson Gardiner, *Oliver Cromwell* (1899); John Morley, *Oliver Cromwell* (1900); C. H. Firth, *Oliver Cromwell and the Rule of the Puritans in England* (Oxford 1901). Also influential were: William A. Shaw, *A History of the English Church during the Civil Wars and under the Commonwealth 1640–1660* (2 vols, 1900); G. B. Tatham, *The Puritans in Power: a study in the history of the English church from 1640 to 1660* (Cambridge, 1913).

7. Abbott, for which see below, pp. 282–3.

matic statements, no credos on which we can base a description of his faith and its personal or social meaning. There are no verbatim records of the discussion by him of matters of spirituality which we may presume occupied the circles to which he belonged; no confessional records. Unlike many of his pious contemporaries, Cromwell left no journal, no diary revealing the nature of his spiritual self-examination. No record of his reading nor of the contents of his library survives. The only book which he recommended – apart from the Bible – was Raleigh's *History of the world*.[8] For all the sermons which he must have heard and their presumed importance to him, Cromwell never discusses or criticizes one in his extant utterances. What form of service did his worship take in 1630s, the 1640s and the 1650s? Did he lawfully adopt the Directory of Worship when its enforcement might have been thought realistically obligatory? How far was he personally prepared to participate in the services of the Book of Common Prayer by which, we assume, he himself was married, his children were baptized and at least one of his daughters was married?[9] If, and when, neither of these service books was endorsed by him, what form of worship did he observe? Our inability to answer any of these questions with precision exposes an ignorance of the religious practice of so public a figure which can only be regarded as remarkable.[10] It is with due caution then that we should approach the next vexed question of Cromwell's religious identity.

So conventional is his brief, almost cryptic, account of his conversion experience, down to castigating himself 'the chief of sinners' and lamenting his pre-conversion hatred of light, as to tell us almost nothing specific. What was he converted to: a church-puritanism compatible with his business associations with Ely cathedral in the later 1630s, or something closer to a quasi-separatism epitomized by the cause of John Lilburne for which he showed some zeal in 1640 and 1645?[11] Even confident assertions of Cromwell's religious identity have to be qualified. In an untypical piece of confusion, S. R. Gardiner could describe Oliver as 'the foremost Independent of the day', while acknowledging on the previous page that 'in the sectarian

8. Abbott, II, 236. Cromwell to Richard Cromwell, 2 April 1650. By the 1650s this was a conventional choice.
9. Ibid., IV, 664. Marriage of Mary Cromwell to Lord Fauconberg at Hampton Court on 18 November 1657.
10. Symbolic of the problem is the fact that, despite lavishly detailed accounts of Cromwell's funeral procession, we know next to nothing about the actual service.
11. Abbott I, 29. For Cromwell's support of Lilburne see ibid., I, 120, 363–4.

sense indeed, Cromwell never attached himself to the Independent or any other religious body.'[12] On the one hand, the evidence is lacking. As Christopher Hill concluded, 'Cromwell can be identified with no sect.'[13] On the other, our confidence in the old religious discriminators – puritan, Independent, Calvinist – is not what it was. 'Puritan' is a term which some historians would discard, others would confine to conformist, protestant zeal.[14] The study of the Independents, who in some sense disintegrated in 1648–49 under the pressure of a coup in which Cromwell played no small part,[15] is bedevilled by problems associated with the legacy of using the term in divergent political and religious senses, by a denominational hindsight which imposed too rigid a categorization too early, and by uncertainties as to precise membership and identity before some confessional coherence was established in 1658, the year of Cromwell's death.[16] Finally, by the mid-seventeenth century, 'Calvinism' was a category of such elasticity as, without qualification, to explain almost nothing in terms of specific individuals. Cromwell never showed the slightest interest in declaring himself an experimental predestinarian or an orthodox Calvinist predestinarian. His views, if he had any, on the pre-Laudian Church as a Calvinist consensus or otherwise, he wisely kept to himself.[17] Robert Paul has argued that an Independent identity for Cromwell can be based in his experience of a kind of congregational, gathered Church within the army and that this experience partly shaped his spirituality, religious policy and political

---

12. Gardiner, *Cromwell*, pp. 28–9. See also Paul, *Lord Protector*, p. 66; Geoffrey F. Nuttall, *Visible Saints: the Congregational way 1640–1660* (Oxford, 1957), p. 105.

13. Christopher Hill, 'Oliver Cromwell', in Hill, *Collected Essays*, III (Brighton, 1986), p. 75. This essay was first published as an Historical Association pamphlet in 1958. Cf. Hill, 'History and denominational history', in *Collected Essays*, II (Brighton, 1986), p. 7. 'Who knows what label to attach to Oliver Cromwell, John Milton, Major-General Fleetwood, John [sic] Ireton? . . . .'

14. C. H. George, 'Puritanism as history and historiography', *Past and Present*, XLI (1968), 77–104; R. T. Kendall, *Calvin and English Calvinism to 1649* (Oxford, 1979. Kendall avoids the term 'Puritan' as unhelpful. Patrick Collinson, *The Religion of Protestants: the Church in English society* (Oxford, 1982).

15. David Underdown, *Pride's Purge: politics in the Puritan revolution* (Oxford, 1971).

16. George Yule, *The Independent in the English Civil War* (Cambridge and Melbourne, 1958); Tai Lui, *Discord in Zion: the Puritan divines and the Puritan revolution 1640–1660.* (The Hague, 1973); Hudson, 'Denominationalism'. The most helpful studies in this field remain the works of Geoffrey F. Nuttall, esp. *Visible Saints*.

17. Kendall, *Calvin and English Calvinism*; Nicholas Tyacke, *Anti-Calvinists: the rise of English Arminianism c. 1590–1640* (Oxford, 1987); Peter White, 'The rise of Arminianism reconsidered', *Past and Present*, CI (1983), 34–54; William Lamont, 'The rise of Arminianism reconsidered', *Past and Present*, CVII (1985), 227–31; Peter Lake, *Moderate Puritans and the Elizabethan Church* (Cambridge, 1982).

attitudes.[18] However, while such experience was no doubt influential, it was too diffuse to be given specific denominational identity. In the seventeenth century sense of a covenanted Church, there is little upon which to base conferring congregational cohesion and identity to a diverse and soon to be conflicting cluster of associations which Cromwell enjoyed through his military career. Like a significant number of his contemporaries – Lambert, Ireton, Berry, Milton and many others – Cromwell is impossible to identify with any one Church, sect or 'way'.[19]

A third problem, compounding and illustrating that of his religious identity, arises from the evidence that we have of his relationship with other religious groups, the sects in particular. Richard Baxter saw Cromwell as a patron of the sects, gathering and favouring sectarians in his military commands.[20] There is no evidence that Cromwell ever saw things in these terms. He did seek godly men for his service but, in individuals, sectarian, or other, religious identity seems to have been a matter of indifference to him. Given that the heresiographers' trade of identifying and inventing sects flourished from the early 1640s, it is worth noting that the impact of the sectarian phenomenon on Cromwell's consciousness seems to have come relatively late.[21] Even in 1658, speaking to his last parliament, he was hesitant about the usefulness of the category.[22] Furthermore, once the phenomenon was accepted, and despite his willingness to persist in dialogue with the most recalcitrant of his sectarian opponents, Cromwell showed an antipathy to religious parties, sects and sectarianism amounting to aversion. The sects were associated in his mind with the 'scatterings, divisions and confusions' which he came to lament so ruefully. They lacked 'that spirit of kindness' that could encourage mutual toleration, that charity without which the forms of religion were as nothing. They were merciless, ready to 'cut the throats of one another, should not I keep the peace'. They were hypocritical in their demands for liberty, all

---

18. Paul, *Lord Protector*.
19. See also Geoffrey F. Nuttall, 'The Lord Protector: reflections on Dr. Paul's life of Cromwell', in Nuttall, *The Puritan Spirit: essays and addresses* (1967), ch. XIII. For some suggestive comments on process rather than organization as an approach to religious history in this period see Jonathan Scott, 'Radicalism and Restoration: the shape of the Stuart experience', *H. J.*, XXXI (1988), 455.
20. R. Sylvester (ed.), *Reliquiae Baxterianae* (1696), pp. 47–8, 50.
21. His first reference to the term 'sect' comes in October 1646 in a letter to his daughter, Bridget: Abbott, I, 415.
22. Abbott, IV, 716–17, 718; 'each sort of people, if I may call them sects', 'I speak not of sects in any ill sense, but the nation is hugely made up of them.'

too ready to deny to others what they insisted on for themselves. In them were 'Christ and the Spirit of God made the cloak of all villany and spurious apprehensions'. Their internecine squabbling prevented the achievement of any consensual basis for a post-monarchical regime. Indeed they were subversive to the point of intriguing with royalists. All Cromwell's efforts to talk them into some compliance with the regime in return for reasonable liberty seemed fruitless. In March 1654, the nation was called upon to fast and pray for an end to 'Faction' in 'Profession', to overcome the absence of 'Brotherly Love' and 'Healing Spirit'. Writing to Major-General Fleetwood a year later, Cromwell struggled with despair:

> The wretched jealousies that are amongst us, and the spirit of calumny, turns all into gall and wormwood. My heart is for the people of God: that the Lord knows, and I trust in due time will manifest; yet thence are my wounds; which though it grieves me, yet through the Grace of God doth not discourage me totally.[23]

So far was he from welcoming the sects and sectarianism that towards the end of his life he could only encourage himself and others with the thought that in the end God would wipe them all away.[24]

How important to Cromwell was religion and how sincere was he about it? These two related questions have been perennially posed since the post-Restoration vilification of him as a Machiavellian or Faustian figure. There can no longer be any doubt that Cromwell was saturated in the providentialism of his contemporaries. No event or facet of his life was untouched by God's presence and guiding will. That presence was not simply a piece of self-justifying, ego-boosting, self-deception. The news of the failure of the Hispaniola expedition, which arrived in July 1655, threw him into a crisis underlain by the sense that God's favour had come to an end. Perhaps he, like Achan,[25] had turned away from the path of the Lord and he,

---

23. Ibid., III, 461; III, 89, 92; IV, 278; III, 615; IV, 716–17; III, 459; III, 436; IV, 221, 267; III, 225–7, 756. For examples of Cromwell's attempts to conciliate the sects, see ibid., III, 119, 125–6, 176n, 116, 373.
24. Ibid., IV, 776–7: conversation with Mr Wheelwright, pastor of Hampton, Massachusetts. 'Mr. Wheelwright stand fast in the Lord, and you shall see that these notions will vanish into nothing.'
25. Achan was the man who brought the wrath of God down on the Israelites by taking plunder, 'the accursed thing', after their successful capture of Jericho. The Book of Joshua, 7. For a brilliant treatment of this theme see Worden, 'Cromwell and the Sin of Achan'. For a broader colonial context in which the providential rebuke at Hispaniola should be placed see Karen Ordahl Kupperman, 'Errand to the Indies: Puritan colonization from Providence Island through the Western Design', *William and Mary Quarterly*, XLV (1988), 70–99.

and his people, were being punished accordingly. The crisis of 1655–56 was a political, diplomatic and foreign policy crisis but it was also, as Blair Worden has shown, a spiritual trauma and a crisis of religious prestige. The notion of a self-deceiving manipulator of the language of religion, imperturbably confident in the 'Divine Right of Oliver' will no longer survive critical examination.[26] The high years of the protectorate – 1654 to 1656 – should be seen as years of profound religious/political crisis. The declaration, on 20 March 1654, of a day of national fasting and humiliation was a graphic indicator of anxiety that the bondage of Egyptian tyranny might only have been escaped for a loss of bearings in the wilderness. Oliver devoted his opening speech to the first protectoral parliament, in September 1654, to what might be called a crisis of spiritual enthusiasm. The nation, he urged, must progress out of the wilderness and not repine there forever. Only in a second speech, eight days later, did he turn to constitutional matters and, even then, the twin problems of sectarian disunity and sin loomed large. Into this context the Hispaniola defeat came like a hammer blow from the Lord. On 17 September 1656, speaking at the opening of his second parliament, Cromwell's theme was again 'the dispensations of God' in a world where His 'most peculiar interest' was beset by external enemies and torn by merciless dissension and a soul-killing lack of charity. Later, 'a great deal of experience of providence' prefigured his rejection of the Crown. 'I would not seek to set up that that providence hath destroyed and laid in the dust, and I would not build Jericho again.' He would not repeat the sin of Achan.[27] The Cromwellian regime has frequently been criticized for an absence of clear policy objectives and of management strategies for their realizations. But such criticism overlooks the fact that reliance on providence implied, in one sense, the absence of policy, the foregoing of trust in fleshly reasoning and its instruments and institutions. We will only fully understand if we accept the centrality and seriousness of religious concerns.

Cromwell's private religious thinking and devotion are sparsely documented. We are dealing almost entirely with public utterance; to a surprising degree with public, pastoral utterance. The language is of comfort, exhortation, rebuke, counsel.[28] Personal spirituality,

---

26. The phrase in Christopher Hill's. See Hill, 'Oliver Cromwell', pp. 75, 72–3.
27. Abbott, III, 225–8, 434–41, 451–61; IV, 260–78, 473.
28. For one example, among many, see Cromwell's letter to Blake and Montagu, 28 April 1656 (Abbott, IV, 148). The naval commanders are instructed to rely on providence and to follow the counsel of Solomon. See also Paul, *Lord Protector*, pp. 222, 273–80.

confessional definition, liturgical theory or practice cannot be the concern of an examination of Cromwell's religion which must be primarily an exercise in the uncovering of a public spirituality enunciated for essentially public purposes. At the heart of that public spirituality is an image of God presiding over the national destiny and pursuing it through varying, if chosen, agents. The context which Cromwell occupies here is not that of high theology nor that of popular *mentalité*. On the one hand, it is the landscape of the good constable or the godly magistrate; on the other, it is that of the divinely chosen and providentially endorsed instrument, leader, pastor and virtual prophet of God's peculiar interest at what might very well be an apocalyptic moment in the cosmic drama.

We can divide the record of Cromwell's religious experience into four broad phases or periods. The first two phases – his early religious experience and his commitment to reforming the Reformation in the root and branch campaign of 1640–42–are dealt with by John Morrill elsewhere in this volume. I deal here only with what, for Cromwell's religious sense, was the enormously formative experience of war and then the more chastening experience of government – phases which can be taken as running from 1642 to 1653, and from 1653 to 1658 respectively.

If it was religious feeling which mobilized the country outside Westminster for war in 1642–43, Cromwell stands as an archetypal figure of that process. The third phase of his religious experience from 1642 to 1653 is that of a man of action; in war, politics and things of the spirit prepared to follow God's leading in the wilderness, to stake his all on providence and its tutelage. However godly the man, this can have been no easy thing for a forty-three-year-old with no fitting experience, a family to provide for and a measure of material security only recently achieved. By 1646 Cromwell's already astonishing run of military successes left no room for doubt of the hand of the Lord. Time after time, his reports on military activities insisted that God was directly the author of all that parliament's forces had won. Indeed 'God', he complained to the Committee of Both Kingdoms in April 1645, 'is not owned enough.' Five months later he informed the Speaker of the House of Commons that the fall of Bristol was the work of God, warning that 'He must be a very Atheist that doth not acknowledge it'. God it was who would bring forth 'a glorious work for the happiness of this poor Kingdom' reconciling 'righteousness and peace'.[29]

29. Abbott, I, 341, 377, 387.

The best agents for God's work were 'honest men', 'godly, honest men', 'conscientious men'. Describing his troops to his cousin, Oliver St John, in September 1643, he denied that they were anabaptists, sectarians. They were 'honest, sober Christians' who expected to be used as men. Rather than deliberately recruiting sectarians, he seems to have looked through and beyond the formal religious affiliations of individuals in search of the qualities he prized and respected – earnest godliness and 'honesty'. Against Major-General Crawford's zealous presbyterian arrest of Packer, an anabaptist, Cromwell objected not by insisting on the rights of sectarians but on the wisdom of the State's choosing men who would serve it faithfully regardless of their opinions.[30] In part such pragmatism derived from a sense of the unfathomable nature of providence and its choice of instruments. When, on 13 September 1644, Cromwell argued in the Commons for due provisions for 'tender consciences' it was only on the stipulations that their doctrines were compatible with the 'Word of God', the public peace and, significantly, the advancement of business.[31] It may be more sensible to regard Cromwell in his military decade, not so much as a promoter or defender of the sects, as a man enamoured of godliness but indifferent to its forms, provided they fell within the limits of mainstream, evangelical, Trinitarian protestantism.

We have no record of Cromwell's attitude to the Westminster Assembly or the debates about forms of Church government which it engendered. But his attitude towards the prospect of a presbyterian settlement was relaxed, as we would expect of one to whom forms were secondary. He took the Covenant himself early in 1644 and was known to require it of others. In 1647 not only was he reported to be willing to accept a presbyterian system but on 13 October he acted as a teller for the ayes in the vote on a Commons proposal to establish presbyterianism for three years. As late as April 1649, he was, according to Walker, prepared to move a presbyterian settlement in parliament.[32] Cromwell then does not emerge as the anti-presbyterian champion of Independency. He was no more wedded and glued to forms of Church polity than he was to forms of civil government. The substance of God's will was not found in such forms but in the dynamic interplay of individual and corporate wills with a chain of mercies, a series of providential indicators which

---

30. Ibid., I, 256, 258, 277; Baxter, *Reliquiae*, pp. 50–1.
31. Abbott, I, 294.
32. Ibid., I, 275, 276–7, 460; II, 50, 52.

could in the end lead men, who had thought of no such things, to regicide and the overthrow of the old order.

At the expulsion of the Rump in April 1653, Cromwell's sympathizers saw him as a Moses who had shaken off the last vestiges of his people's bondage to Egypt. Before him, and the three nations he had united with the armies of the Lord, lay – variously interpreted – a godly mission of purification at home and apocalyptic imperialism abroad.[33] The snares in his path were, on the one hand, that he could stray after 'the accursed thing', into the sin of Achan, pursuing fleshly reward, heeding the carnal reasoning of policy; on the other hand, that, heeding the religious zealots who were all too quick to accuse him of apostacy, Cromwell could reduce the nation to ungovernability and become himself a 'man of blood'. It was a dilemma which was to haunt the last phase of Cromwell's religious experience and the tragic dimensions of it have already been outlined by Blair Worden.[34]

What briefly were Cromwell's religious objectives?[35] First, he wished to remain a servant of providence, guarded against 'unbelief, self-seeking, confidence in an arm of the flesh, and opinion of any instruments that they are other than as dry bones'. Secondly, he belonged to that evangelical, magisterial tradition that sought a 'reformation of manners' in society at large. God would, in fact, chastize any nation which did not purify itself. The English gentry and nobility, prized by Cromwell as by Harrington, could only be preserved by such a self-purification. Thirdly, he saw himself and his followers 'at the edge of the promises and prophecies',[36] obliged to weigh seriously the prospect of a coming millennium, the conversion of the Jews, and Christ returning to rule with his Saints: his own role as Godly Prince to prepare the nation for that happy consummation.[37] His fourth objective was to end the 'penal statutes that force the conscience of honest conscientious men', to create an environment of liberty of conscience for all those whom he bluffly

---

33. For Cromwell's depiction of this as early as 1650 *via* sustained commentary on Psalm 110 see *Ludlow*, I, 246.

34. Worden, 'Sin of Achan'.

35. These are discussed more fully by Anthony Fletcher below, 212–5.

36. Abbott, II, 127, 325, 215; II, 110–11; III, 845; IV, 273; III, 64. See also John F. Wilson, *Pulpit in Parliament: Puritanism during the English Civil Wars* (Princeton, 1969), esp. pp. 212–23.

37. See Bernard Capp, 'The political dimension of apocalyptic thought', in C. A. Patrides and Joseph Wittreich (eds), *The Apocalypse in English Renaissance Thought and Literature* (Manchester, 1984), pp. 113–16; Paul J. Korshin, 'Queueing and waiting: the apocalypse in England, 1660–1750', in ibid., p. 251.

regarded as 'honest', 'godly' or 'conscientious'.[38] They were those who pursued Christianity in substance and not merely for form's sake, and Cromwell's fifth objective was to promote a Christianity of substance, of the heart and spirit. We shall look at these fourth and fifth objectives more closely shortly, but Cromwell's final religious objective was clearly and understandably his own salvation. In the midst of all his 'mercies', it was his sense of the redeeming Christ within which gave assurance. It was this which he tried to convey to his son, Richard, that, indeed, Christ's kingdom and image came inwardly first.[39] In the light of these objectives, four themes are worth exploring further. They are: liberty of conscience and Cromwell's consistency in regard to it; his desire for religious unity; his providentialism; and what I shall call his antiformalism, his concern to raise the substance – as he saw it – of religion above its forms.

Cromwell and the Cromwellian regime have long been famous for the extent of religious toleration that they were prepared to embrace. We are again indebted to Blair Worden for sharpening our perception of what is at issue here.[40] He draws the distinction between toleration and liberty of conscience. The unacceptable danger of toleration was that, in permitting heresy, it could condemn those who espoused it to eternal damnation. Liberty of conscience, on the other hand, arose out of a concern not to impose human authority between God's grace and the soul. Underlying the Cromwellian attitude on liberty of conscience was the faith that truth lay in the spirit rather than the institution – in spiritual power rather than ecclesiastical, confessional or liturgical form. A religion of conscience, rather than ritual, could not bind pilgrims from their future judgments nor spiritual stewards from their obligations to God in the management of their own consciences. But central to Cromwell's motivation remained the desire for unity in diversity among the conscientious godly. Cromwell's definition of the latter was, in Worden's view, not wide-ranging. His fitful extensions of it owed more to diplomatic and political considerations than to the Lord Protector's own convictions. Cromwell, Worden concludes, 'neither wanted toleration nor

38. Abbott, II, 104.
39. Ibid., I, 646; II, 236; III, 226, 437.
40. Worden, 'Toleration and the Cromwellian protectorate'. Inevitably my synopsis simplifies Worden's argument. Also useful on this issue is Roger Howell, 'Cromwell and English liberty', in R. C. Richardson and G. M. Ridden (eds), *Freedom and the English Revolution: essays in history and literature* (Manchester, 1986), pp. 25–44.

provided it' but his entourage contained a group of rational, sceptical erasmians who did favour a 'wider liberty of belief' – Bulstrode Whitelocke, Matthew Hale and Sir Charles Wolseley. It is worth re-examining Cromwell's attitudes on liberty of conscience in the light of Dr Worden's reassessment.

God would work what He willed in the minds of men. In *A declaration of the army of England upon their march into Scotland* (July, 1650), the standard by which his apostasy was later to be judged,[41] Cromwell stated this as his motivation for defending liberty of conscience against a nation bent on defying providence to coerce consciences. No form of Church government should be imposed by force. True Christianity did not inhere in forms but in faith working by love.[42] Undoubtedly godly, Scottish protestantism presented a particularly illuminating case of Cromwell's response to religious coercion. The justification for a war, which Fairfax had blenched at, against erstwhile Scots allies, was that they had succumbed to sacerdotalism and religious violence. As Naseby had been fought for civil freedom, so Dunbar was a crucial contest over religious freedom. Writing to the governor of Edinburgh castle, in the aftermath of his providential victory at Dunbar, Cromwell pointed out that in England ministers had liberty to preach but not to rail, nor to overtop and debase the civil power. No man was molested for preaching the gospel, since neither force nor compulsion but the Word of God alone would accomplish what was necessary.[43]

In Ireland the lines were more sharply, but not simplistically, drawn. After the brutalities of Drogheda and Wexford, Cromwell called upon the defeated Irish to build on faith, not on the practice of 'mumbling over Matins'. 'Keeping ourselves in the love of God, not destroying men because they will not be of our Faith.' The majority of poor, lay people in Ireland were, he claimed, ignorant of the grounds of the Roman Catholic religion. Whereas the Scots were portrayed as enlightened but wrong-headed, the Irish were either papist barbarians or the poor deluded. Of the Irish, the former 'must expect what the Providence of God . . . will cast upon them'. The latter, as long as they behaved peaceably and honestly, would receive equal justice with the English.[44] Active, proselytizing papists

41. See, for example, 'A word for God' reprinted in *T. S. P.*, IV, 380–4 (also reprinted in [William Sedgewick] *Animadversions upon a letter and paper* (1656); report on a sermon by Christopher Feake on 5 January 1657, *T. S. P.*, V, 758.
42. Abbott, II, 285–6. See also Nuttall, *The Holy Spirit*, pp. 125–33.
43. Abbott, II, 335–6.
44. Ibid., II, 199–205.

– anti-Christians in Cromwell's terms – were beyond the limit of liberty of conscience. The rest would be afforded such liberty as the law – English law – allowed.

The liberty of the godly was the irreducible cause. To Cromwell's mind, in the Second Civil War, it appears to have become the dominant one. 'I rejoice much to hear of the blessing of God upon your Excellency's endeavours,' he wrote to Fairfax on 28 June 1648,

> I pray God to teach this nation, and those that are over us, and your Excellency and all us that are under you, what the mind of God may be in all this, and what our duty is. Surely it is not that the poor godly people of this Kingdom should still be made the object of wrath and anger, nor that our God would have our necks under a yoke of bondage; for these things that have lately come to pass have been the wonderful works of God; breaking the rod of the oppressor, as in the day of Midian, not with garments much rolled in blood, but by the terror of the Lord; who will yet save His people and confound His enemies as in that day.[45]

To Lenthall, after the battle of Preston, he urged that parliament exalt God 'and not hate His people who are the apple of His eye, and for whom even Kings shall be reproved'. Two weeks later, writing to his friend Lord Wharton, Cromwell identified himself with 'the poor godly people' and their weakness.

> When we think of our God, what are we. Oh, His mercy to the whole society of saints, despised, jeered saints! Let them mock on. Would we were all saints. The best of us are (God knows) poor weak saints, yet saints; if not sheep, yet lambs and must be fed. We have daily bread, and shall have it, in despite of all enemies.[46]

There were, however, two problems which came to haunt Cromwell and which were already implicit in his vision of unity in diversity amongst 'the poor godly people'. One was that the godly adamantly refused to recognize a mutuality of rights among themselves. The other was the problem of distinguishing between the liberty of 'the poor godly' and the licence of the impious.

At times Cromwell seemed genuinely bewildered by the propensity of those who had been granted a newly-won liberty of conscience, to deny the same right to others.[47] 'Every sect saith, Oh! Give me liberty. But give him it, and to his power he will not yield

---

45. Ibid., I, 619. For God's dealings with the Midianites see Numbers 21.
46. Abbott, I, 638, 646.
47. Cf. his comment at the Putney debates, Abbott, I, 534. For George Fox's insistence to Cromwell that his followers had a monopoly of godliness and providential favour see Wilson Armistead, Daniel Pickard and Norman Penny (eds), *The Journal of George Fox* (2 vols, 1901), I, 363.

it to anybody else. Where is our ingenuity? Truly that's a thing ought to be very reciprocal.' The ideal could readily be stated:

. . . a free and uninterrupted Passage of the Gospel running through the midst of us, and Liberty for all to hold forth and profess with sobriety, their Light and Knowledge therein, according as the Lord in his rich Grace and Wisdom hath dispensed to every man, and with the same freedom to practice and exercise the Faith of the Gospel, and to lead quiet and peaceable Lives in all Godliness and Honesty. without any Interruption from the Powers God hath set over this Commonwealth . . .

But this statement is itself drawn from a proclamation announcing policies designed to prevent the godly from disturbing one another in the professions of godliness.[48] The Protector came increasingly to see his task as that of keeping all the godly of several judgments in peace, striving for some reciprocity, mutuality. To restrain those who railed against others was immediately to be charged with persecuting the godly. 'I tell you there wants brotherly love, and the several sorts of forms would cut the throats of one another, should not I keep the peace.[49]

While Cromwell could bemoan the hypocrisy of those, freed from episcopal oppression, who could not resist putting 'their finger upon their brethren's consciences, to pinch them there', at the same time he pointed out that profanity, blasphemy, sedition, evil-speaking and loose conversation should be being disciplined by the magistrate but were not. The problem was to distinguish those 'who are sound in the Faith, only may perhaps be different in judgment in some lesser matters' from those who had run out of godliness into blasphemy and impiety.[50] What were the distinguishing characteristics of soundness in the faith? Various official attempts were made under the Protectorate to tackle this problem. The Instrument of Government offered toleration to all but Roman Catholics and the amorphous category of the 'licentious'. In the oath taken by the Protector, council and MPs under the Humble Petition and Advice it was 'the True, Reformed, Protestant, Christian, Religion' based in the scriptures of the Old and New Testaments which was to be maintained.[51] The Triers, appointed in 1654 to approve candidates for benefices or lectureships, were given slight criteria to operate with: evidence of grace, 'holy and unblameable conversation', 'knowledge and ut-

48. Abbott, III, 459, 626.
49. Ibid., III, 607–16.
50. Ibid., III, 586.
51. Ibid., III, 149; IV, 565–6.

terance fit to preach the Gospel'. No doctrinal tests were recommended. When it came to the complementary activity of removing scandalous incumbents the guidelines were explicit on moral failings, offering only blasphemous or atheistical opinions, and frequent use of the Prayer Book as doctrinal grounds for dismissal.[52] The debate on a statement of fundamental doctrine, adequate to the identification and disciplining of blasphemy and impiety, rumbled through the 1650s flaring up in the face of apparent provocations.[53]

Cromwell was clear that liberty of conscience was not to be stretched to the denial of the divinity of Christ, the socinian blasphemy, as he saw it, of the 'unitarian', John Biddle. But getting beyond the self-evident truths of a reformed protestant godliness was not an enterprise that appealed to his antiformalistic pragmatism. 'Whoever hath this faith, let his form be what it will.' The magistrate had, in Christian charity, a duty to punish outward abuses. He must react when there was a danger of disorderly confusion. But ideas could surely be let alone. 'Notions will hurt none but them that have them.' He could sympathize with one 'that having consulted everything' could hold to nothing – not 'Fifth Monarchy nor Presbytery, nor [Independency], nothing but at length concludes he was for nothing but an orderly confusion'.[54] The rub, of course, was in the chasm between order and disorder; a distinction which Oliver related to that between diversity within a framework of a common, Christian (preferably reformed, protestant) charity, and an internecine conflict in which brotherly love had withered and domination was all. The tragic side of this he brought out to parliament in January 1658, employing one of his most vivid metaphors. Not content with variety, he said, every sect sought to be uppermost, 'to be not only making wounds, but as if we should see one making wounds in a

---

52. *An ordinance appointing commissioners for approbation of public preachers: Monday March 20 1653* (i.e. 1654); *An ordinance for the ejecting of scandalous, ignorant and insufficient ministers and schoolmasters: Tuesday August 29 1654* (1654). Presumably infrequent use of the Prayer Book was acceptable. For a fuller treatment of these issues see Chapter 8, below .
53. For the 'fundamentals' exercises see Abbott, II, 520–37; III, 284, 834; 'Guibon Goddard's journal of a parliament 1654–5', in Burton, I, xvii–cxxx. For the attempt of a voluntary association to confront the same problem see H. W. P. Stevens, 'An ecclesiastical experiment in Cambridgeshire', *E. H. R.*, X, (1895), 744–53. Incidents like the publication of the Racovian catechism in 1652, parliament's censure of John Biddle in 1654, and outrage over James Nayler's activities in 1656, revived the quest for defining fundamentals.
54. Abbott, III, 834; IV, 272; III, 436–8; IV, 719.

man's side and would desire nothing more than to be groping and grovelling with his fingers in those wounds'.[55]

The sincerity of Cromwell's religious faith was seldom questioned by his contemporaries but many regarded his profession of concern for liberty of conscience as specious. Edmund Ludlow saw it as 'an engine by which Cromwell did most of his work', a device to gull those who would otherwise have opposed him or opposed him earlier.[56] Dr Worden rejects such cynical motivation. Cromwell was sincere but his puritan theological conservatism endowed him with a narrower concept of religious freedom than has often been allowed. His concern was unity, not toleration. God's peculiar interest was to be found almost exclusively among presbyterians, independents and baptists. Oliver remained unsympathetic to quakers, socinians, anglicans and Roman catholics. Such extensions of religious liberty as there were to these groups came under political/diplomatic pressures or the influence of the Christian stoics – Whitelocke, Hale and Wolseley. First, however, it is by no means clear that the last group exercised anything like the influence which Worden claims for them. Secondly, it is doubtful whether Cromwell's religious views can be traced to any one source of influence but others seem to have as good a claim, if not better, to having been taken seriously by the Lord Protector in religious policy formation. It is always difficult to disentangle public and private attitudes in the occupant of a quasi-monarchical position and the attempt may be suspected of anachronism. It is clear, nevertheless, that Cromwell's legal position under the protectorate constrained him, as it was intended to do. Allowing for this, his operation both within and outside those constraints remains strikingly untypical of his age and may suggest a broader tolerance of attitude than Dr Worden concedes.

Although John Biddle was, in Cromwell's eyes, rightly condemned for an intolerable heresy, Oliver provided, apparently out of his own pocket, a weekly allowance of ten shillings for the condemned man who was safely confined to the Scilly Isles.[57] Quakers were released by the personal intervention of Cromwell. Many of them had sufficient faith in 'that of God' remaining in the Protector to assume that he could be influenced on their behalf.[58] Anglicans

55. Ibid., IV, 717.
56. *Ludlow*, I, 378–9.
57. *T. S. P.*, VII, 288.
58. Cf. Geoffrey F. Nuttall, *Studies in Christian Enthusiasm: illustrated from early Quakerism* (Wallingford, Pennsylvania, 1948), pp. 29, 33. Worden seems to me to be right about Cromwell's lack of personal sympathy for Nayler. Cf. Abbott, IV, 350.

likewise could see some hope of toleration in Cromwell. Archbishop Ussher, John Gauden, Nicholas Bernard all had sufficient faith in Cromwell's sincerity to sustain the hope that he would deliver liberty of conscience and practice to them.[59] The Lord Protector's nominations of parochial incumbents included many who conformed to the Restoration and it was not unknown for royalist anglicans to be admitted by the Triers.[60] As John Morrill has argued, there may have been a good deal more continuity at the parish level than has been supposed[61] and given the apparatus at his disposal it is hard to imagine that Cromwell would have been unaware of this. His own admiration for James Ussher, archbishop of Armagh – payment for his funeral in Westminster Abbey and generosity towards his dependents – is well known.[62] In July 1649 Ireton and Cromwell had acted as tellers against a Commons ordinance to curb preaching against the new regime. Consistent with this, in December 1656, Cromwell was writing encouragingly to presbyterian ministers in north-eastern England.[63]

It may well be that some of Cromwell's discreet consideration towards Roman catholics had more to do with political prudence than with his own personal preferences. His assurances to cardinal Mazarin and his refusal to restrict admission to catholic services at the Venetian ambassador's residence may fall into that category. But, unless we make some allowance for a personal disposition towards a broader tolerance, other actions of his are not so easy to accommodate. His protest against the execution of a jesuit, John Southworth (or Southwell) appears genuinely disinterested.[64]

59. *T. S. .P.*, V, 597–600; J[ohn] G[auden], *A Petitionary Remonstrance* (1659); Abbott, III, 714; IV, 69, 102. Nicholas Bernard, chaplain to Cromwell in the 1650s, was chaplain to Ussher in 1627.
60. Much more work needs to be done on Cromwell's ecclesiastical patronage as Lord Protector but in Sussex, for example, of 33 nominations by him, five, of those for whose fate at the restoration we have evidence, conformed in 1660–61. E. H. W. Dunkin, 'Admissions to Sussex benefices . . . by the commissioners for the approbation of public preachers', *Sussex Archaeological Collections, XXXIII (1883), 213–24; R. W. Blencowe, 'Extracts from the journal and account book of the Rev. Giles Moore rector of Horstead Keynes from 1655–1679', *Sussex Archaeological Collections*, I (1848), 65–127.
61. John Morrill, 'The Church of England 1642–9', in J. S. Morrill (ed.), *Reactions to the English Civil War* (1982), pp. 89–114. For a regional example see Bryan Dale, 'Ministers of the parish church of Bradford and its three chapels during the puritan revolution', *The Bradford Antiquary*, n.s., II (1905), 124–34, 360–84.
62. *T. S. P.*, IV, 121–2; Nicholas Bernard, *The Life and Death of . . . Dr James Ussher* (1656); R.Buick Knox, *James Ussher, Archbishop of Armagh* (Cardiff, 1967); James Caulfield (ed.), *Cromwelliana* (Westminster, 1810), p. 156; *Mercurius Politicus*, 27 March–3 April 1658.
63. Abbott, II, 90; IV, 361–2.
64. Ibid., IV, 69; III, 321; *Cal. St. Pap. Ven. 1653–4*, pp. 253–4.

Friendships within the Cromwell family circle could extend to catholic ex-royalists.[65] Most extraordinary of all, the catholic Lord Baltimore was restored to his full proprietorial rights in the colony of Maryland. There was toleration for all trinitarians in the colony but governmental control remained firmly in catholic hands. The vindication of Baltimore's rights came after the second protectoral parliament attempted to tighten up the prosecution of papistry by the Act of 26 June 1657.[66]

Cromwell's tolerance may not have been quite so narrow nor so *politique* as Worden would have it. Religious unity was a priority *not* to be achieved by the coercion of the conscientious spirit. But the problem of interpretation is engendered at a deeper level. Onto the question of Cromwell's tolerance we impose a sectarian grid. Did Cromwell, we ask, extend liberty of conscience to anglicans, presbyterians, independents, baptists, roman catholics and the sects alike? The question is badly put, I would suggest, because the sectarian grid is inappropriate and I shall want to argue shortly that it is Cromwell's antiformalism which makes it so. It was only when unity had been abandoned as an unrealizeable goal that a sectarian or denominational response became appropriate, and this was not to be for Cromwell and others in the 1650s. Where Worden is absolutely correct is in linking the twin Cromwellian aspirations of unity and liberty of conscience. Paralleling Cromwell's fear of disintegration, wounding ourselves and others, is a deep desire for unity as not only healthy but God's will for us, a hatred of 'carnal divisions and contentions among Christians'. Liberty of conscience is in a sense the response of charity and faith in God's providence to a situation where unity is not yet possible. In this regard, Cromwell's aspiration, if not his optimism, remained constant.[67] In the autumn of 1644 Cromwell, Vane and St John initiated moves for an accommodation between presbyterians and independents with the proviso that, if this were not possible, there should be liberty for tender consciences.[68] Liberty

65. For the friendship of Elizabeth Claypole with Sir John Southcote see John Morris (ed.), *The Troubles of our Catholic Forefathers related by themselves* (1872), 1st ser., vol. 1, ch. VIII, esp. pp. 393–6.
66. James W. Vardaman, 'Lord Baltimore, parliament and Cromwell: a problem of church and state in seventeenth century England', *A Journal of Church and State*, IV (1962), 31–46. See also Dom Hugh Bower (ed.), *London Session Records 1605–85*, Publications of the Catholic Record Society, XXXV (1934), x1vi.
67. Abbott, III, 437. Cf. William Lamont, 'Pamphleteering, the protestant consensus and the English Revolution', in Richardson and Ridden (eds), *Freedom and the English Revolution*, pp. 72–92.
68. John Willcock, *Life of Sir Henry Vane the Younger: statesman and mystic 1613–1662* (1913), p. 145; Shaw, *English Church*, II, 35–48.

was a second best to unity. A year later Cromwell could rejoice in the unity of the godly in the army: 'Presbyterians, Independents, all had here the same spirit of faith and prayer; the same pretence and answer; they agree here, know no names of difference: pity is it should be otherwise anywhere'. 'I have waited', he wrote to Hammond in November 1648, 'for the day to see union and right understanding between the godly people (Scots, English, Jews, Gentiles, Presbyterians, Independents, Anabapists and all).' It was, of course, not to come. '. . . how hard and difficult a thing it was to get anything carried without making parties . . . .' Still it might be that, at least temporarily, God had a providential purpose in this diversity. So Oliver could pray: 'God help England to answer His minds.' Unity would come in the end out of diversity, out of the plurality of God's minds.

> . . . sure I am, when the Lord shall set up the glory of the Gospel Church, it shall be a gathering [of] people as out of deep waters, out of the multitude of waters: such are his people, drawn out of the multitudes of the nations and people of this world.[69]

Like William Erbery, Cromwell waited for the Spirit to make us one and take us out of Babylon.[70] Apparently, the waiting could not be endured without anxiety and nowhere is this better illustrated than in the tormented questions, about division, lack of brotherly love, and pride, accompanying the announcement in March 1654 of a day of national fasting and humiliation.[71] Given the perdurability of sin, providence, not human effort, seemed still to offer the best hope and it is to this theme that we now turn.

In what remains one of the better biographies of Cromwell, John Morley suggested that his religion was one, not so much of dogma, as of providential experience. The context of that providentialism and its importance has been magisterially laid out by Blair Worden and there is little to add to what he has said.[72] In the mid-seventeenth-century heyday of providentialism, God's constant intervention in human affairs, to admonish or encourage, reward or scourge, was assumed. Providences were not isolated, disconnected interventions but linked sequences expressive of God's will for men and nations. Defiance of providence, neglect of providential signals, failure to respond, could themselves provoke providential reaction. Cromwell

69. Abbott, I, 377, 677; III, 57; I, 639; III, 65.
70. *Clarke Papers* IV, 239. Cf. Abbott, IV, 776–7.
71. Abbott. III, 225–7.
72. Morley, *Cromwell*, p. 55; Worden, 'Providence and politics'.

was not only seen by many of his contemporaries as an agent or instrument of providence, he was almost archetypal in his immersion in providential ways of thinking. He affectionately compared himself to Vane, who made not enough of providences, while he himself perhaps made too much. In this scheme of things there was no room for blind fate, chance, *fortuna* perceived as a pagan concept. Ultimate unity was in the hands of providence but disunity would persist until:

we admire God and give Him glory, for what He has done. For all the rest of the world, ministers and profane persons, all rob God of all the glory and reckon that to be a thing of chance that has befallen them.[73]

Two things are worth emphasizing about Cromwell's providentialism. One is a marked distrust of the human agencies and institutions through which God mediately operates. Often, in fact, God's appearances were to be seen 'crossing and thwarting the purposes of men' even on the winning side. Only God's 'counsel shall stand, whatever the designs of men, and the fury of the people shall be'. Had human design engineered the death of the king it would have been an outrageous crime but providence had cast them on it. To the sceptical Wharton, Cromwell conceded that it was easy to condemn the 'glorious actings of God' if we only regarded his human instruments. Wharton paradoxically, as Oliver pointed out of him, ran the risk of setting his own human judgment up against providence. Success came not from human attributes – brains, courage, strength, which were as dry bones – but through following God and gathering 'what he scattereth'. We cannot, he admonished Blake and Montagu, turn away evil or attain good through our own efforts. Human endeavours and abilities were to be distrusted; all reliance placed in divine providence. Writing in 1652, Cromwell warned his daughter to beware of fear. Love casts itself on providence.[74] Cromwell himself was constantly reminded by others not to put faith in human institutions, resources, knowledge or policy.[75] As Hugh Peter had said, 'Outward strength & human

---

73. Abbott, I, 621, 687; II, 287; III, 572; I, 644; II, 38. In this context Worden's contention that Cromwell's quest for unity was at war with his providential zeal is too simplistic. Worden, 'Providence and politics', pp. 95–6. For a dismissal of the notion of the chance of war see Abbott, II, 205. Cf. C. H. Firth (ed.), *Memoirs of the Life of Colonel Hutchinson by his Widow Lucy* (2 vols, 1885), I, 1–2.
74. Abbott, III, 53–4; I, 421, 719; II, 189; II, 328, 453; II, 215, 235; IV, 148; II, 602.
75. For example: T. M., *Veni, vidi, vici* (1652); Arise Evans, *The Voice of Michael the Archangel* (1653); Colonel Edward Lane, *An Image of our Reforming Times*(1654).

policies are no sufficient Bulwark against Batteries from heaven
. . . .'[76]

The corollary of distrust in the human was, accordingly, total trust, whatever human prudence might suggest, in the divine. Nothing illustrates this better than Cromwell's attitude to the Irish expedition: 'It matters not who is our Commander-in-Chief if God be so; and if God be amongst us, and His presence with us, it matters not who is our Commander-in-Chief.' He repeatedly presented the Irish mission as one conducted under God's direct command.[77] Cromwell was by no means alone in these general attitudes. At the Whitehall debates in late 1648 much of the discussion was about the extent to which any constitutional provision usurped God's providential freedom of action and the necessity for faith. The only true agreement, or constitution, was from God and not from men.[78] Similarly pervasive was suspicion 'of men's inventions in God's worship'.[79] For many of his critics, the essence of Cromwell's apostasy lay in his reliance on men's inventions rather than on divine providence.[80] Such reliance was an invitation to divine chastisement. Vavasor Powell replied to an invitation to attend the Savoy conference in 1658 with the dour warning, 'if you go upon political or worldly accounts, or by a humane spirit, to work, you may expect God to blast the work'.[81] Even a 'cool rationalist' like Cromwell's neo-platonist chaplain, Peter Sterry, warned against trust in reason and human prudence.[82]

Distrust of human prudence, policy and invention and the injunction to total faith in God's sustaining and guiding providence led to one of the most important aspects of Cromwell's religious disposition, his antiformalism. Forms divided the godly. They were man's work, fleshly, not God's, divine. Led by their Lord, godly people would transcend forms and rediscover unity. Writing to Hammond on the eve of the regicide, Cromwell argued that, while authority is of God, its forms are of human institution and therefore may be law-

76. Hugh Peter, *Digitus Dei* (1631) – quoted in Raymond Phineas Stearns, *The Strenuous Puritan: Hugh Peter 1598–1660* (Urbana, Illinois, 1954), p. 63.
77. Abbott, II, 37, 39. For the general point about the Irish expedition see ibid., II, 107, 110, 127, 128, 142, 165, 205.
78. *Clarke Papers*, II, 76–100, 184–6.
79. Firth (ed.), *Memoirs of Hutchinson*, I, 3.
80. 'A word for God' in *T. S. P.*, IV, 381.
81. Geoffrey F. Nuttall, *The Welsh Saints 1640–1660* (Cardiff, 1957), pp. 50–1.
82. Peter Sterry, *The Spirits Conviction of Sinne* (1645), pp. 16–17; *The Clouds in which Christ Comes* (1648), pp. 40–2.

fully resisted.[83] John Owen, preaching at the opening of parliament in September 1656, warned against attaching any importance to debates over forms of Church worship and discipline. God would achieve what he willed with these things in his good time. Our wills and judgments must not be allowed to run before his. As part of our preparation, Owen recommended, we should eliminate 'formality'.[84] A more extreme version of the same message is William Erbery's reported assertion that Christ 'would confound all forms'.[85]

Cromwell, in this regard, is best seen as a 'meere Catholic', putting substance above form, the spirit above the letter. It is this which leads him to regard the clerical/lay distinction as anti–Christian. The only ministry of true descent, he informed the Nominated Assembly, was through the spirit.[86] Distrust of forms helps to explain Cromwell's lack of interest in a Church establishment alternative to the abortive presbyterianism of the Westminster Assembly. His faith, as an actor of rich, providential experience, was that God would provide and that His custom was not to work through forms, institutions and rituals but inwardly through the hearts of men. According to Mr Bacon at Whitehall, magisterial power was one of outward forms and coercion but 'all matters relating to the Kingdome of God and purely and altogether spiritual'.[87] God moved spiritually through the world, His providential substance subverting the shells of form that were irrelevant to it.[88]

While both the Irish and Scots wars could be seen as providential exercises, the Scots campaign was specifically against formalism, its divisive violence, against Scots faith in coercion which, in turn, betokened a lack of trust in providence and its spiritual efficacy. Providence had been slighted by the Scots in 1650 when they chose to follow human instruments, platforms, 'your form's sake', rather than the will of God. They had preferred forms to love and accordingly had found that God would not do their will.[89] Peter Sterry, in a dramatic sermon which argued that England's delivery from Scots presbyterianism was a greater mercy than its delivery from the Roman papacy – a sermon published in both Scotland and England – acknowledged that presbyterianism might be one of the purest

83. Abbott, I, 377; II, 173; III, 51–65; I, 697.
84. John Owen, *Gods Work in Founding Zion* (Oxford, 1656), pp. 30–1, 36–8, 41, 43.
85. *Clarke Papers*, II, 234, 236–7.
86. Abbott, II, 197; III, 63.
87. *Clarke Papers*, II, 108.
88. Abbott, II, 199, 285.
89. Ibid., II, 340; II, 286, 325, 340.

forms. 'Yet there is a more excellent way which is that of Love'. Outward forms should not divide. The marriage between the saviour and the soul was spiritual. 'No union with any form makes this marriage . . . .' The endeavour of both papistry and Scots presbyterianism was the 'Annexing the Spirit to outward Formalities', 'Legall Dispensation' and 'Carnall Administration'.[90]

Cromwell's antiformalism may have strengthened as his assurance of providence grew. At Putney in 1647 he insisted on the obligation to honour prior engagements or covenants. Three years later, in the wake of the Scots campaign, covenants could be regarded as formalistic contrivances, inessential to the progress of providence and therefore disposable. In his post–Dunbar letter to the governor of Edinburgh castle, Oliver asked, 'Whether the Lord's controversy be not both against the ministers in Scotland and in England, for their wresting, straining, and improving the Covenant against the Godly and Saints in England (of the same faith with them in every fundamental) even to a bitter persecution.' Ministers, the engineers of formalism, had brought men of a faith united in substance to a conflict over forms. In the process providence had been slighted, forms preferred to brotherly love.[91] The watchwords of the two armies at Dunbar – 'The Covenant' for the Scots; 'The Lord of Hosts' for the English – were held to symbolize this struggle between forms and substance. The Lord of battle had decided accordingly.[92]

However dramatic God's demonstrations in the field, men perversely reinsinuated preoccupation with form rather than spirit into public life. Opening the Nominated Assembly, Cromwell complained, 'How God hath been compassed about by fastings and thanksgivings and other exercises and transactions I think we have all cause to lament.' In the aftermath of that assembly's failure, both he and John Rogers could argue against each other that they represented the claims of substance over form. To the ministers of the French congregations in London, Cromwell stressed the importance of 'the power of godliness' over the formalities of profession. Toleration should be extended to all who live in the love which is in Jesus Christ.[93] Conversely, intolerance of spirit betokened a raising of

---

90. Peter Sterry, *England's Deliverance form the Northern Presbytery compared with its deliverance from the Roman Papacy* (Leith, 1652), pp. 6, 7, 18, 43.
91. Abbott, II, 340.
92. See, for example, John Canne, *Emanuel, or, God with us* (1650), p. 19 and *passim*.
93. Abbott, III, 61, 157. For the exchanges between Cromwell and John Rogers see Hur Horton & c., *The Faithful Narrative* (1654), p. 37.

forms above substance, an unwarranted trust in fleshly instruments and a lack of faith in divine providence. The declaration of a day of national fasting and humiliation in March 1654 was also an invitation to consider whether preoccupation with forms was shattering unity, undermining brotherly love and engendering a many-sided conflict of reciprocal intolerance. A series of questions directed attention to these points.

iv. Is Brotherly Love, and a Healing Spirit of that force and value amongst us that it ought? v. Do we own one another more for the grace of God and for the Spiritual Regeneration, and for the Image of Christ in each other, or for our agreement with each other in this or that form, or opinion? . . . viii. Are there not too many amongst us that cry up the Spirit, with a neglect of Love, Joy, Peace, Meekness, Patience, Goodness, Temperance, Longsuffering, Forbearance, Brotherly Kindness, Charity, which are the fruits of the Spirit . . . x. Do not some of us affirm ourselves to be the only true Ministry and true Churches of Christ, and only to have the Ordinances in purity, excluding our Brethren, though of equal gifts and having as large a seal of their Ministry, and desiring with as much fervour and zeal to enjoy the ordinances in their utmost purity?

Beyond these causes of 'Faction' in 'Profession' the godly were asked to consider whether they remembered primitive simplicity – self-denial, mercy to the poor, uprightness and justice – and whether in these aspects of practical christianity they were not put to shame by the anti-christian and the carnal.[94]

It was this yearning to get beyond forms, and the ugly strife which preoccupation with them engendered, to the unity which he believed lay in the substance of faith, that enabled Cromwell to maintain an extraordinary range of religious contacts and counsellors through the 1640s and 1650s.

Whosoever hath this faith, let his form be what it will . . . Give me leave to tell you, those that are called to this work, it will not depend upon formalities, nor notions , nor speeches [but upon] . . . men of honest hearts, engaged to God, strengthened by providence, enlightened in his works to know his word, to which he hath set his seal, sealed with the blood of his Son in the blood of his servants.[95]

Such people were found by Cromwell in a surprising diversity of situations. From Sir Henry Vane with his 'withdrawing from all forms'[96]; to Archbishop Ussher's combination of deep hostility to

---

94. Abbott, III, 225–7. The significant texts of Jude 4 and 2 Peter 2:1, warning against false prophets and a general apostasy, were invoked.
95. Abbott, IV, 272, 277–8, 965.
96. Willock, *Vane*, p. 254. The comment is Burnet's. See also Vane's final advice to his children, ibid., pp. 336–7.

Roman catholicism with temperate pragmatism about protestant forms and great personal piety[97]; to Walter Cradock, of the Welsh saints, with his insistence on the simplicity of the gospel, the priority of the spirit to the form, Cromwell found 'fellowe citizens of the commonwealth of Israell' whatever the formal barriers.[98] As early as 1643, Charles Herle had warned against taking differences over presbyterian and independent church politics too seriously. 'Our difference 'tis such as doth at most but ruffle a little the fringe, not any way rend the garment of Christ'.[99] Jeremiah Burroughes in *Irenicum* (1646) had explained that differences between saints arose because of human weakness. No faith therefore should be placed in them but rather in God's unifying providence. In the same year, in an atmosphere of rising disillusion with religious fragmentation, John Goodwin urged faith in this providence and less confidence in human formalities and institutions:

> . . . reformation according to the Word of God must give leave to the wind to blow where it listeth and give liberty to the Spirit of God to do with his own what he pleaseth; to make what discovery of truth he pleaseth and to what persons and when and where he pleaseth; and must not confine him to his market or compel him to traffic only with councils and synods for his heavenly commodities.[100]

Mention of Goodwin, the republican critic of the Cromwellian church settlement brings us to Cromwell's own spiritual spokesmen and defenders,. his chaplains, a subject worth further investigation for, amongst other things, the degree of antiformalism amongst them. John Owen, one of the most famous of them, was clear that to place form before substance in religion was to enter 'the confines of self-righteousness, if not hypocrisy'. No form of church government was immune to degeneration. His own recommendation for church reform was to be relaxed about institutional issues and to give priority to pastoral care.[101] Peter Sterry insisted that 'to be subject to . . . the Church in the outward forme for the outward forme's sake is a bondage'. In an important sermon delivered to the House of Commons in October 1647, Sterry likened reliance on human

---

97. Knox, *Ussher*.
98. Nuttall, *Welsh Saints*, pp. 25, 28. The phrase is Cradock's, see ibid., p. 3.
99. Charles Herle, *The Independency on Scriptures of the Independency of the Churches* (1643). Cradock also used the ruffling of the fringe metaphor.
100. John Goodwin, *Twelve Considerable Serious Cautions* (1646). See also Hudson, 'Denominationalism', pp. 36–42.
101. John Owen, *Complete Collection of Sermons* (1721), pp. 73, 221–2, 562–5.

prudence to the Israelites' worship of the golden calf. Glossing Colossians 2:20, he asked,

If Christ be Risen from the dead, why do you subject him to Ordinances? . . . Formes are sweet Helps, but too severe Lords over our Faith . . . When we Consecrate, or converse with any Ordinance or Peculiar way of Worship; let us then remember, that our Object is the Person of Jesus Christ, that Wisdome of God, whose way is more untrac'd than the Eagle, whose extent is wider than the Earth. The Heaven of Heavens cannot take in All of Him, to containe or Confine Him, much lesse any One Ordinance in this World, or Fleshly Fashion . . . Tis in vain to attempt to shut up Christ in any Thing.[102]

Sixteen months later, in February 1649, Sterry was appointed preacher to the republican Council of State as he was Cromwell's personal chaplain throughout the Protectorate. Such men formed what might be called the hard core of Cromwell's spiritual entourage when he was at the height of his power. At a superficial level they may be seen as denominationally diverse.[103] At a deeper level they shared a common antiformalism. These are the men with whom and through whom Cromwell worked for religious harmony without uniformity, for unity in diversity.[104] Their greatest achievement, which now has to be seen as an intentional one borne out by Oliver's personal interest, was the Cromwellian Church settlement which avoided liturgical and ecclesiological formalism while trying to guarantee substantial and decent Christian provision throughout the nation.[105]

In his own day, Cromwell's antiformalism fed the charges of hypocrisy and apostasy against him. In his search for the substance which united, he frequently appeared willing to agree with his last interviewee, if not everyone. To those – Levellers, Fifth Monarchists or others – committed to forms of government he seemed to have a slippery way with forms, civil or ecclesiastical, apparently holding that 'it is lawful to pass through any Forms of Government for the accomplishing his Ends'.[106] Perhaps especially to radicals, liberating themselves from established forms, Cromwell's antiformalism gave the appearance of freedom to act and to transform. The faith of radi-

---

102. Tai Lui, *Discord*, p. 49; Sterry, *The Clouds*, pp. 40–1, 46, 47–8.
103. Examples of 'presbyterians' in the group are John Howe and Thomas Manton.
104. See, for example, the preaching of William Strong in June 1653 and the initiative of Cromwell and the ministers reported in the autumn of that year. *Several proceedings of state affaires, 27 October–3 November 1653*, p. 3391.
105. A much fuller treatment of this theme is to be found in Chapter 8, below. See also, Claire Cross, 'The church in England 1646–1660', in G. E. Aylmer (ed.), *The Interregnum: the quest for settlement 1646–1660 (1972)*, pp. 99–120.
106. Abbott, I, 627.

cals in Oliver is certainly remarkable. Fifth Monarchists, Republicans, Levellers, Winstanley, Harrington, even anglican, royalist, millennialists like Arise Evans, Elinor Chanel, Walter Gostelow and John Saunders, were prepared, temporarily perhaps but in many cases with surprising persistence, to put their faith in him. Once we look at his religion out of the strapping of a denominational grid, the connections and shared contexts can be surprising. Aspects of his emphasis on the sovereignty of conscience look like William Walwyn; his providential warrants for action combined with his belief in Christian liberty remind one of the Christian republicanism of Milton, Vane or Ludlow; his hints of an imminent millennium and the urgency of moral reformation recall fifth monarchism; his emphasis on the second coming of Christ as an inward, spiritual process bring to mind Winstanley; and it may be more than fanciful to suggest that there are parallels between Cromwell's antiformalism and Abiezer Coppe's.[107] The desire to get beyond forms to substance, to get beyond words to things,[108] to cast aside fleshly considerations, to hold fast to the spirit and ride the rollercoaster of providence are all common radical dispositions of the period and Cromwell, too, is imbued with them.

What, it has been asked, held Cromwell back, from the full revolutionary potential of the providentialist,[109] from being the Robespierre of the English Revolution, a role which he almost seemed to envisage when contemplating the *tabula rasa* of post-conquest Ireland?[110] A first answer must be found within his religious attitudes. He is caught and restrained within a cycle. While his antiformalism liberates him for radical potential, it is intimately connected with a providentialism which inculcates distrust of human agency and total reliance on the divine, and so pushes him back to an antiformalist quest for the substance of a simple reliance on the spirit, a primitive piety and a practical Christianity. The qualifiers, or modifiers, of Cromwell's antiformalist providentialism are the word of scripture, the spirit of charitable meekness, and reason.[111]

---

107. For Coppe's antiformalism see J. C. Davis, *Fear, Myth and History: the Ranters and the historians* (Cambridge, 1986), pp. 48–57. See also Abbott, II, 325 for Cromwell's view that the exploitation of the poor by the rich did not suit a commonwealth.
108. For Cromwell on words and things see Abbott, III, 609; IV, 260, 716–17.
109. Cf. Worden's discussion of this in 'Providence and politics', pp. 88–97.
110. For Cromwell on Ireland: Abbott, II, 93, 110, 186–7, 273, 327; *T. S. P.*, III, 715; *Ludlow*, I, 246, 254.
111. Abbott, I, 542–6; III, 373; IV, 309, 471–3.

We might perhaps trace a growing insistence on their cautions in the face of an anarchy of formal providentialisms and a mutual harrowing of the saints, but, in a fundamental sense, Cromwell retained an antiformalist faith in providence to the end. It is his distrust of the human which holds Cromwell back from an incipient religious radicalism and allows other, more socially conservative elements in his temperament to dominate. Man, the agent of the divine will operating mediately, must be tolerated but is not to be trusted.

It may be better to drop the search for Oliver Cromwell's religious identity, at least in the traditional terms, not simply because good evidence is hard to find but because it is a counterproductive quest whose terms of reference obscure – even invert – the true situation. The denominational grid – of independent, presbyterian, anabaptist and the rest – is indeed a perverse instrument by which to measure the religious faith and sincerity of a man who struggled to free himself and the godly in his society from formalistic declensions and paradigms. Cromwell's success was as an arm of providence, a servant of the God who made him strong in battles. He did not see himself called upon to formalize the flow of providence in new Church ordinances, politics and confessions. To do so in the civil sphere was apostasy enough for those among the Saints who became his enemies. Liberty of conscience – also anathema to the formalists – flowered briefly while Cromwell' s antiformalism held the stage. Of its very nature it was hard to conceive of its institutionalization and time was denied for its consolidation. Nevertheless, it might be held to represent a greater and more sincere Christian achievement that any for which he has hitherto been credited.

CHAPTER EIGHT

Oliver Cromwell and the godly nation

Anthony Fletcher[*]

I

Oliver Cromwell's speeches to his parliaments tell us more than any other source about his practical Christianity and his yearning to work with the godly for a spiritual regeneration of the whole English nation. They explain what he hoped for both in terms of evangelization and of moral reforms. This chapter offers an account of how he attempted to realize this programme and attempts – within the limitations imposed by the current state of knowledge – to assess the extent of his achievement and the obstacles he failed to overcome.

Cromwell talked frequently of, and clearly thought incessantly about, God's people. A brief analysis of the theme and message of his celebrated speech to the Barebone's Assembly will show how they fitted into his scheme of things. He began on 4 July 1653 with an account and interpretation of the happenings of the thirteen years since the meeting of the Short Parliament in 1640. The Self-Denying Ordinance, Pride's Purge, the execution of the king, the abolition of the House of Lords, the creation of the commonwealth, the conquest of Ireland and Scotland, the 'marvellous salvation' at Worcester in 1651: this was the 'series of providences wherein the Lord hath appeared, dispensing wonderful things to these nations from the beginning of our troubles to this very day'. The victors were, he declared, 'a poor and contemptible company of men' who owned 'a principle of godliness and religion, which so soon as it came to be owned and the

* I am grateful to Russell Hart, Ann Hughes and Sarah Jones for their helpful comments on a draft of this essay.

209

state of affairs put upon the foot of that account, how God blessed them, furthering all undertakings'. The army's desire since 1651, Cromwell explained, had been to see the nation 'reap the fruit of all blood and treasure that had been spent in this cause'. The dissolution of the Rump in April 1653 arose from their frustration in this respect. What precisely was 'this cause'? Cromwell's words make it clear that he saw the army as the militants at the core of those who were God's people. There was no illusion in his mind that the godly were in a majority. Indeed he reckoned that God now looked directly to a small minority to evangelize and reform the rest of the nation. The Rump had to go because God's people, the chosen evangelizers, had been ignored: 'the interest of his people was grown cheap . . . the cause of the people of God was a despised thing.' As he went on that hot July day in 1653, Cromwell became increasingly explicit about the mission which the men crowded around him in the Council Chamber at Whitehall were called upon to undertake. They were nominated as well-affected men who were given the task, in conjunction with the puritan clergy and magistracy, of creating the godly nation. Cromwell's role, in handing over all civil power, was simply to 'lay down some charge how to employ it', but he offered no specific guidance on religious matters. In the final section of the speech, where he sought to drive home his argument with references from scripture, Cromwell became deeply emotional, almost ecstatic: 'Jesus Christ is owned this day by you all, and you own him by your willingness in appearing here, and you manifest this, as far as poor creatures can, to be a day of the power of Christ by your willingness.'[1]

In an important passage of this speech Cromwell set out his view of who God's people were. They included, he declared, all who were serious seekers after religious truth and faith however poor, however mistaken at times as they stumbled on their spiritual path. He did not at this stage speak directly about the issue of liberty of conscience, which was to become such a bone of contention in the following years, but his meaning is as clear as in later utterances. When he insisted that 'if any shall desire but to lead a life of godliness and honesty let him be protected', he referred once more to those with the root of the matter in them.[2] At the opening of the second Protectorate parliament three years later, Cromwell gave the closest

---

1. Abbott, III, 1, 53–65. For discussion of this much cited passage see A. Woolrych, *Commonwealth to Proctectorate* (Oxford, 1982), p. 148.
2. Abbott, III, 1, 62.

definition he ever offered of what this root of the matter was. He described 'the peculiar interest all this while contended for': 'that men that believe in Jesus Christ . . . men that believe the remission of sins through the blood of Christ and free justification by the blood of Christ and live upon the grace of God, that those men that are certain they are so, are members of Jesus Christ and are to him as the apple of his eye.' The godly, it became apparent from his words, were, by and large, presbyterians, independents and baptists: both the rest of the sects, on the one hand, and anglicans and Roman catholics, on the other, would in the end if they remained recalcitrant have no place in God's peculiar.[3] Cromwell's religion was firmly biblical and Christocentric. His imagination, Blair Worden has noted, 'could not enter the world of the Ranters· and Quakers and Socinians'.[4]

So Cromwell mixed a limited conception of the further truth that was to be discovered from the radical tendencies of the splintered puritan movement of the 1640s and 1650s with a belief in the necessity of gentleness and sensitivity towards those who had strayed or continued to do so. In July 1653 his patience remained considerable. They should be 'very much touched with the infirmities of the saints', he told his audience, 'that we may have a respect unto all and be pitiful and tender towards all though of different judgments'. The challenges to this regime by Fifth Monarchists and Quakers in the period that followed tried his patience to the uttermost. But Cromwell's devotion to the principle of religious unity never wavered. He declared it to Barebone's with the cry 'have a care of the whole flock'.[5] Five years previously, he had written to Robert Hammond, 'I have waited for the day to see union and right understanding between the godly people.'[6] In 1655 he commissioned a pamphlet which looked forward to 'a glorious union of the people of God, made to be of one spirit'.[7] It was this commitment which led Cromwell to give himself unstintingly to disputation with leading sectarian opponents of the Protectorate.[8] It also inspired the conference which he sponsored at Whitehall in December 1655 to discuss the readmission of the Jews to England. He had no engagement to

3. Abbott, IV, 271–2.
4. A. B. Worden, 'Toleration and the Cromwellian Protectorate', in W. J. Sheils (ed.), *Persecution and Toleration*: Studies in Church History, 21 (1984), pp. 211–12.
5. Abbott, III, 1, 62.
6. Abbott, I, 677.
7. Cited by Worden in *Persecution and Toleration*, p. 211.
8. For example, Abbott, III, 1, 372–3; II, 2, 606–16.
9. Abbott, III, 1, 65; IV, 51–5; D. S. Katz, *Philo-Semitism and the Readmission of the Jews to England 1603–1655* (Oxford, 1982), pp. 190–231.

the Jews but what the Bible held forth, the Protector told some merchants who feared that their admission would simply enrich foreigners: 'since there was a promise of their conversion means must be used to that end.' Conversion could only come about by preaching and this could not begin until the Jews were in England to hear sermons.

The godly nation then would be a nation bound together by the unity of its believers. These believers would no longer be a despised minority, as the puritans had been when, Cromwell recalled, the term was one of abuse. Instead they would become the majority, setting a standard of righteousness for all to emulate.[10] This was the mission announced by Oliver Cromwell on 4 July 1653, to an expectant assembly of men gathered from the shires and aware of the political uncertainty which the country faced. Some constitutional thinking of sorts had been going on. But this was secondary.[11] All Cromwell's other aims and objectives, both social and political, were ways and means to a higher religious mission. This was founded directly on his reading of the Old Testament. His providentialism is fundamental to an understanding of this mind: he believed that, just as God had delivered the Israelites from slavery in Egypt and Babylon, so now God had chosen him to lead a new chosen people towards a new Jerusalem. In this sense his regime, from first to last, was bound to be intensely ideological. Yet Cromwell's providentialism was always tempered by a sense of circumstances. It enabled him to pursue long-term goals but adapt to short-term exigencies. The dynamic of his regime was provided by the constantly shifting relationship between his personal spiritual ponderings and the unfolding of the political process. The speeches show how politically instrumental the Protector made his providentialist thinking. If his view became darker and more troubled after the news of the reverse at Hispaniola, his basic vision of a godly nation undisturbed by jarring sects remained intact.[12]

A brief review of a series of incidents between 1653 and 1658 will illustrate the consistency of Cromwell's religious objectives. In a short speech when he took the oath as Lord Protector on 16 December 1653, he declared 'that he desired to rule and govern the three

10. Abbott, IV, 273.
11. Woolrych, *Commonwealth to Protectorate*, p. 150.
12. J. S. Morrill, 'Cromwell', in *Late Great Britons* (1988), p. 24; B. Worden, 'Oliver Cromwell and the Sin of Achan' in D. Beales and G. Best (eds.) *History, Society and the Churches* (Cambridge, 1985), p. 140.

nations no longer than it might have a perfect dependency on the great work of the Lord; that so the gospel might flourish in its full splendour and purity and the people enjoy their just rights and propriety'. Writing intimately to his son-in-law Charles Fleetwood in June 1655, he confessed that he felt sorely tried by the 'wretched jealousies' which hindered spiritual growth and renewal but that the grace of God enabled him to persist.[13] He enthused about the 1656 parliament's careful provision for defining fundamentals, a task in fact never completed, and for the protection of liberty of conscience on this basis. In their concern for men professing godliness 'under a variety of forms amongst us', he told a committee during the negotiations on the Humble Petition and Advice, 'you have done that which was never done before and I pray God it may not fall upon the people of God, or any sort of them, as a fault if they do not put such a value upon what is done as never was put upon anything since Christ's time for such a catholic interest for the people of God'.[14] A few months previously, the ministers of Durham and Northumberland had reported the progress of their voluntary association in healing breaches among the puritans of the north-east and building a union which could act as a bulwark for the growth of religion and reformation. The Protector promised every encouragement, 'there being nothing more upon our heart'. In conversation with Lord Wariston in July 1657, he waxed enthusiastic about planting churches and purging abuses in Scotland, especially in the Highlands and Isles. They talked about new schools and about sending selected poor scholars to the university college at Durham, the founding of which was then much in Cromwell's mind, where they might be 'put to trades and callings and then sent home again'.[15] Opening the new session of parliament in January 1658 Cromwell's mood, despite the ill health which shortened his speech, was optimistic once more. Reminding the members of his earlier references to Psalm 85 with its story of God's favours to his land, he insisted that they now, as the Hebrews then, were a redeemed people. He claimed achievements for the Cromwellian Church. 'We have peace and the gospel,' he declared: this represented 'the greatest mercy of God'.[16]

13. Abbott, III, 1, 138, 2, 756.
14. Abbott, IV, p. 445; Worden in *Persecution and Toleration*, pp. 218–19, 227.
15. Abbott, IV, 361–2, 580–1.
16. Abbott, IV, 705–8.

II

Oliver Cromwell grew up in a protestant country. But what do we mean by stating this? Queen Elizabeth's protestant settlement was forty years old when he was born in 1599, yet recent scholarship has emphasized the slowness with which the Reformation was actually achieved in England. The reasons for this have been set out: the inadequacy of the clergy, the accompanying problems of pluralism and non-residence, the peculiarities of a parochial structure which provided a dense network in much of south-eastern England but enormous parishes in such areas as the Weald and the northern dales. In these circumstances it is not surprising that the progress of evangelization was both gradual and uneven between the accession of Elizabeth and the civil war.[17] Calvinist predestinarianism, in any case, was not the stuff of which popular religion was easily made. The doctrine of God's providence, so irresistible for Cromwell in his triumphant progress from Marston Moor to Worcester, so appealing for some who had the chance to better themselves, must have appeared a gloomy philosophy to many in the normal conditions of early modern society. 'The poor man', as one contemporary reflected, 'lies under a great temptation to doubt of God's providence and care.'[18] Groups and cliques of the godly rather than whole communities came into being. So Cromwell was enunciating nothing new in harping upon the people of God as a minority and as some kind of separate estate.

Patrick Collinson and Eamon Duffy have perceptively explored the concepts of the godly and the multitude in Elizabethan and Stuart England, drawing upon the works of partisan commentators like Robert Bolton, Arthur Dent and George Gifford. Such men Cromwell himself very likely read in his youth. He would have understood what John Field had meant when he avowed that if the queen and parliament failed 'the multitude and people' would bring about further reformation. It is evident Field was thinking of a special multitude not of the mass of the people, of a spiritual élite in fact, the enlightened, responsible, dynamic people of God. We can compare this usage with the puritan writers' denunciations of the ignorant and profane multitude who resisted and defied the gospel. This multitude, the godly like Bolton, Dent and Gifford were quite clear, was not on their side. But the scathing tone of their dismissals of the

---

17. K. Wrightson, *English Society 1580–1680* (1982), pp. 206–8; P. Collinson, *The Birthpangs of Protestant England* (1988).
18. Cited in K. V. Thomas, *Religion and the Decline of Magic* (1971), p. 112.

ungodly reflects the deep seriousness with which the preachers and writers viewed their urgent task. Many puritans, Eamon Duffy has reminded us, emphasized the duty of compassion and love for the multitude. The hallmark of the puritan movement was a fervent desire to reach the poor, the ignorant and the apathetic.[19]

This commitment to mission is the essence of the tradition in which Cromwell was nurtured. Richard Baxter, who came from the same tradition, described in his autobiography how he and his family stayed indoors reading the Bible on Sundays in the 1620s while his neighbours, spending the day dancing under a maypole close to his father's door, derided them as puritans.[20] Cromwell's upbringing and youth in Huntingdonshire may have done slightly less to inculcate a sense of social isolation than Baxter's in Shropshire, but the knowledge of belonging to a godly minority who were looked upon askance by many must have been similar. The puritan way was so demanding and so rigorous, both spiritually and morally, that it was bound to produce the dramatized view of society which dominates Cromwell's speeches in his middle age. For what puritanism was about was the transcending of any merely conventional piety or attendance on religious duty. The exacting standards the godly set for themselves in their own circles were the standards, through the achievement of mission, that they set for the nation. But for this very reason we should be careful not to take at face value their diagnosis of the spiritual state of the nation. There is a good deal of evidence that the puritan picture of a nation divided down the middle between the people of God and the irreligious is a seriously distorted one.

To understand the actual situation in the decades of Cromwell's youth it is necessary to read between the lines of the comments made by men who were bent on the destruction of popular superstition and traditional culture and were therefore hardly disinterested reporters.[21] Two of the most celebrated puritan ministers of the period provide relevant commentaries. Ralph Josselin distinguished three groups at his Essex village of Earls Colne: 'our society' were the committed godly; 'my sleepy hearers' were the deferential majority; those that 'seldom hear' were the more fully recalcitrant.[22]

19. P. Collinson, *The Religion of Protestants* (Oxford, 1982), pp. 191–241; E. Duffy, 'The godly and the multitude in Stuart England', *The Seventeenth Century*, I (1986), 31–55.
20. N. H. Keeble (ed.), *The autobiography of Richard Baxter* (London, 1974), p. 6
21. Collinson, *Religion of Protestant*, p. 203.
22. Cited in Wrightson, *England Society*, p. 218.

Richard Baxter's breakdown of the 1800 or so adults in the large Worcestershire parish of Kidderminster in the 1640s is much more detailed. About 500 he rated 'serious professors of religion . . . such as the vulgar call precise'. Then there were three categories of people he regarded as more or less within the fold: some of 'competent knowledge and exterior performance', some more who were 'tractable' but lacked knowledge of the essentials of faith, some others who were of 'competent understanding' but disowned his ministry out of loyalty to episcopacy and the prayer book. The further groups he listed included public attenders whom he believed were in fact insincere, willing listeners who 'confess that we must mend our lives and serve God' but had a Pelagian reliance on good works and people of 'tolerable knowledge' who mixed too much with the idle and unruly of the parish.[23] The complexity of the situation and the spectrum of religious commitment is well illustrated by Baxter's account. It also warns against any simple view of the godly and ungodly in terms of the gentry and middling sort versus the poor.[24]

In a series of sermons in 1638, John Angier complained about the spiritual unpreparedness of the people. 'They see no good in preaching, prayer, sacraments,' he declared; 'they have too low thoughts of God's worship as if it were outward and did only deserve the worst part, the presence of the body'.[25] Much of the puritan burden of complaint is not about irreligion as such but about this low level of commitment. It is perfectly compatible with Keith Wrightson's claim that by the 1630s 'the English could be regarded as fairly thoroughly protestantized'.[26] The state of the ministry had by then been vastly improved and the Church courts had done much to improve standards of religious devotion and observance.[27] At one level the Reformation had been achieved. The fact is that, by the time the Long Parliament met in 1640, the English prayer book had become part of the fabric of people's lives. 'Is not this your religion?' was the question Richard Kilby had put to 'the common people' in James I's reign: 'I mean, to say your prayers to hear service without any special stirring of your heart.'[28] The depth of popular attachment to

23. Cited in Duffy, 'The godly and the multitude', 39–40.
24. Collinson, *Religion of Protestants*, pp. 216–18, 239–41; M. Spufford, *Contrasting Communities* (Cambridge, 1974), *pp. 319–44*; M. Ingram, *Church Courts, Sex and Marriage in England, 1570–1640* (Cambridge, 1987), pp. 92–8.
25. Cited in Wrightson, *English Society*, p. 213.
26. Wrightson, *English Society*, p. 212.
27. R. O'Day, *The English Clergy 1560–1640* (Leicester, 1979); Ingram, *Church Courts, Sex and Marriage*, p. 366.
28. Cited in Collinson, *Religion of Protestants*, p. 191.

the forms and institutions of the Elizabethan Church settlement became evident in 1641 and 1642 when there was a wave of county petitioning in defence of episcopacy and the liturgy. What is important about these petitions is that they show how a very positive alternative view of the Church from the puritan one, stressing its corporate nature without William Laud's ritualistic emphases, was held by substantial numbers of people.[29] This makes sense in view of what we know about the parochial situation in the years before the civil war. It also supports John Morrill's argument that the most striking feature of the Church in England during the 1640s was grass-roots loyalty to prayer-book anglicanism.[30]

But all this was something Oliver Cromwell could never come to terms with. There are hints that, in the uneasy period between the end of hostilities and his assumption of power in 1653, he did contemplate trying to bring at least some leading anglicans into the victors' fold. There were discussions in January 1652 with the moderate bishop of Exeter, Ralph Brownrigg. Brownrigg told William Sancroft afterwards that he had been asked to wait 'till some greater affairs may be transacted and some differences composed'.[31] Political manoeuvring apparently precluded a return to this negotiation and it came to nothing. Yet there is no question that some of those who felt an attachment to the liturgy which had been abolished in the 1640s at the same time shared with varying degrees of understanding the basic faith – the sense of 'free justification by the blood of Christ' – which was to Cromwell the root of the matter. This was where the ideological protagonists of the puritan cause paid the price of their own zeal and of their loyalty to each other as the deliverers of the nation from popish bondage. When Cromwell was swept of power by the army the political exigencies came first. The comprehensiveness of the religious settlement in the Instrument of Government was for this reason hopelessly flawed. Liberty of conscience, the new constitution of December 1653 flatly stated, was not 'extended to popery or prelacy'.[32] This was the crucial linkage. The cause was a struggle against catholicism but in the emotional politics of the years when it was created episcopacy and the anglican liturgy had become fatally identified with the Pope and the idolatry of the mass. Those, like Cromwell, who went forward into the war with

---

29. See my *The Outbreak of the English Civil War* (1981), pp. 284–90.
30. J. S. Morrill (ed.), *Reactions to the English Civil War 1642–1649* (1982), pp. 89–114.
31. R. S. Bosher, *The Making of the Restoration Settlement* (1951), pp. 9–10.
32. J. P. Kenyon, *The Stuart Constitution* (Cambridge, 1986), p. 313.

John Pym were those who, having destroyed Arminianism, were still obsessed with a popish plot that carried the ecclesiastical hierarchy in its wake.[33] In the 1650s the prayer book remained a symbol of political allegiance. Publicly at least, there was no way that the godly, having triumphed over popery and prelacy, could treat erstwhile opponents who were insistent upon using it as capable of salvation.[34] Thus the ordinance establishing the Ejectors in 1654 allowed for the removal from their cures of ministers who had 'publicly and frequently read or used the common prayer book since the first of January last or shall at any time hereafter do the same'.[35]

Throughout the Protectorate, anglicanism was officially outlawed. Some however had begun to hold prayer-book services in conditions of rural seclusion before 1653. As it became apparent that Cromwell's regime was much more preoccupied with sectarian challenges to its authority than anglican ones, there was a more widespread resumption of the old liturgy. A 1653 newsletter spoke of frequent 'conventicles for common prayer' in London. St Peter's. Paul's Wharf, St Benet's, St Mary Magdalen, Milk Street and St Gregory's were among the parishes in the city which more or less openly returned to the prayer book.[36] John Evelyn went to anglican services at intervals when he was in London throughout the Protectorate. It seems to have been fairly generally believed that Cromwell knew about and connived in all this. 'The news is very current in town', wrote a correspondent of the staunch royalist Sir Justinian Isham, 'that the Protector expresses thus much that the ministry would discreetly use the common prayer. I hear this from persons of great credit.'[37] There is no specific evidence which would confirm or deny this gossip. But it would not be surprising if Cromwell did have some sense of the dilemma he was placed in with regard to prayer-book worshippers, whose spiritual lives were as blameless as his own and who morally could claim to be treated with the same love and understanding as those Cromwell had no difficulty about including within God's peculiar. He may also have been influenced in the long run by the shift in the public mood from anti-papist paranoia of the early 1640s to the anti-sectarianism of the late 1650s. If so, his policy of quiet acceptance was politically circumspect.

33. See my *The Outbreak of the English Civil War*, pp. 408–12; J. S. Morrill, 'The religious context of the English Civil War', *T.R.H.S.*, XXXIV (1984), 165–78.
34. Worden in *Persecution and Toleration*, p. 213.
35. Kenyon, *Stuart Constitution*, p. 315.
36. Bosher, *Making of the Restoration Settlement*, pp. 11–12.
37. C. Cross, 'The church in England 1646–1660', in G. E. Aylmer (ed.), *The Interregnum* (1972), p. 114.

Cromwell was probably more compassionate towards anglicans in fact than he felt able to be publicly, when making declarations which his closest associates would be watching with care.

III

Cromwell's thinking about the pattern of Church life in the nation he found himself called to lead began with his deep sense of man's sinfulness and unworthiness. Everyone's greatest need, in his view, was spiritual and moral regeneration. Life was a quest for assurance based upon a lively faith and strict personal standards. The means to this end lay with the ministrations of a godly clergy, responsible heads of households and reforming local governors. There were no directions from the centre in Cromwell's Church about ordination, administration of the sacraments, liturgy and ceremonial. Colin Davis has emphasized his antiformalism. His assumption about his rule was that should provide for a loose framework of organization that protected the parochial structure and enhanced its potential effectiveness. Hence his fierce support for tithes. This was not a matter of principle, he explained in a passage on the subject in a speech to his second parliament. Moreover he would welcome an alternative form of State provision for the livelihood of ministers. Meanwhile, though, tithes were essential 'for the keeping of the church and people of God and professors in their several forms of liberty'. Tithes, which Cromwell knew all about from his experience before the civil war, were 'the root of visible profession'.[38]

Cromwell was in no doubt that there had to be doctrinal limits drawn and enforced: the Instrument of Government and the Humble Petition and Advice both grappled with this contentious issue, though neither solved it to the general satisfaction of Protector and parliament.[39] He was also ready to legislate about the ministry in order to secure its quality. But beyond these measures the essence of his Church polity was a negative rather that a positive principle. His clearest explanation of this comes in his somewhat heated denunciation of his first parliament on 12 September 1654, when he came back to Westminster to insist that they must accept his rule and the fundamentals of the constitution under which he had been appointed. In his account of why liberty of conscience must be regarded as one of these fundamentals we can detect the historical experience which made him unwilling to erect a centralized ecclesiastical structure. He

---

38. Abbott, IV, 272–3; Kenyon, *Stuart Constitution*, p. 302.
39. Worden in *Persecution and Toleration*, pp. 215–27.

recalled those who had abandoned 'estates and inheritances here where they lived plentifully and comfortably' and had journeyed to 'a vast howling wilderness in New England' rather than live under the repressive Laudian regime. He had nothing favourable to say about Scottish presbyterianism, which he saw as having threatened repression in a new guise. He was no happier with the prospects that had been opened by the English version of presbyterianism, formulated by the Westminster Assembly in the 1640s. He found this 'sharp and rigid' and made it clear he was thankful it had not been fully enforced.[40] The negative principle on which he intended to build was the principle of defending the right of presbyterians, independents and baptists to worship in their own manner. At the same time, he believed, they should work together to create the peace and harmony between men professing several forms of godliness which was at the core of his notion of a godly nation.

Irritated by the clericalism of the Scottish Kirk, Cromwell spoke his mind on how he saw entry to the ministry of the gospel in a letter to the governor of Edinburgh castle in 1650. Ordination, he insisted, was 'an act of conveniency in respect of order, not of necessity to give faculty to preach the gospel'. 'Your pretended fear lest error should step in', he continued with feint mockery, 'is like the man who would keep all the wine out of the country lest men should be drunk.'[41] Probably half the parish pulpits, it has been suggested, were filled in the 1650s by men who had been ordained by the bishops before 1642.[42] Many had continued to get themselves ordained during the 1640s. But by 1653 there were nevertheless plenty of vacancies following the purges of the various parliamentarian regimes.[43] Cromwell's solution to this problem was the Triers, a commission established by ordinance in March 1654 'for approbation of public preachers'. All who were presented to or chosen for benefices in future, and all lecturers as well, had to go forward with their seal of approval. Applicants would be assessed in terms of their spirituality, conduct, knowledge and ability to preach. Ordination, the ordinance made quite clear, did not come into it; the objective was to ensure that where maintenance was available proper persons

---

40. Abbott, III, 1, 459.
41. Abbott, II, 335–6.
42. D. Hirst, *Authority and Conflict* (1986), p. 322.
43. For these purges see I. Green, 'The persecution of scandalous and malignant parish clergy during the English Civil War', *E.H.R.*, XLIV (1979), 507–31; Morrill (ed.), *Reactions to the English Civil War*, pp. 100–3.

should labour in the work of the gospel. The commission of thirty-eight men given this task carefully balanced presbyterians, independents and baptists.[44] Poor documentation makes it hard to assess how well the Triers did their work but Cromwell himself was convinced about their achievement. Through their efforts, he told parliament in January 1658, 'you have a knowing ministry. . . Men knowing the things of God and able to search into the things of God.'[45] Richard Baxter later recalled the 1650s, in this sense, as a halcyon period. The Triers, he declared, 'did abundance of good to the church . . . many thousands of souls blessed God for the faithful ministers whom they let in and grieved when the prelatists afterward cast them out again'.[46] This judgment is obviously coloured by the partisanship of an aging nonconformist. Yet it does seem probable that the service of his Triers was something Cromwell could reasonably boast about and that their contribution to religious teaching and to stability within the Protectorate constitution was considerable.

The Ejectors scheme – the second prong of the Cromwellian framework for ministry – was potentially more radical and far reaching since it posited the notion of removal of large numbers of those currently holding benefices on account of their 'ignorance, insufficiency, scandal in their lives and conversations or negligence in their respective callings and places'. The ordinance establishing the ejectors, which was passed on 28 August 1654, was detailed and specific in spelling out what this meant. Ignorance included contravention of the 1650 Blasphemy Act and holding popish opinions; scandal included, besides swearing, fornication, adultery and drunkenness, playing cards or dice and countenancing breach of the sabbath or 'licentious practices' such as wakes, morris dancing and stage plays. The parochial ministry, in other words, was to be judged on the basis of its support for the full programme of puritan demolition of the traditional and festive culture of rural England. The mechanics of the scheme were decentralized. Modifying provision of removing scandalous ministers in the 1650 acts for the propagation of the gospel in Wales and the northern counties, the ordinance nominated commissioners in each county. The number of them varied and certain counties in the north and midlands were grouped together under

44. Kenyon, *Stuart Constitution*, pp. 313–14.
45. Abbott, IV, 707, see also p. 495.
46. Cited in C. Cross, *Church and People 1450–1660* (1976), p. 215.

a single committee; Wales was divided into two groups of counties north and south.[47]

There was plenty of scope in the Ejectors scheme for radical cliques to attempt purges, for factionalism and divisiveness. Nothing in fact seems to have happened at all in most counties during the rest of 1654 and the first nine months of 1655. The exception, where ejection did get off the ground, was Berkshire. Here a small group within the commission – the ordinance set a quorum of five – were causing considerable dissension in early 1655, it appears, by their partisanship. John Owen, in a letter to John Thurloe, described them as 'men of mean quality and condition, rash, heady, enemies of tithes'. He was shocked to find that they had removed several very worthy men on 'slight and trivial pretences', including a professor of Hebrew and Arabic at Oxford University 'of repute for learning throughout the world'.[48]

The instructions to the major-generals in October 1655 included the implementation of the 1654 Ejectors ordinance. The council was no doubt well aware that it had so far been virtually a dead letter.[49] Early reports from Edward Whalley and Charles Worsley in the midlands and north confirm that this was so. They sought to overcome the inertia of the commissioners and summoned them to meetings. Worsley reported from Preston on 30 November that the Lancashire committee had chosen a clerk and had sent warrants for notification of complaints with detailed articles in terms of the ordinance. Three weeks later, he gave an account of a further meeting which was taking up numerous cases, having sent out summonses, both for the ministers concerned and for witnesses, to appear. Worsley also got things going in Cheshire and Staffordshire.[50] Whalley concentrated first on Lincolnshire, reporting in mid-November that the business of ejection was proceeding well there. At the end of the month he attended a two-day sitting of the Ejectors at Leicester.[51] Another of the major-generals who was very energetic in this matter was Hezekiah Haynes. He summoned a meeting of all the ministers, lecturers, curates and schoolmasters in the whole of Essex at Chelmsford on 20 February 1656. They were to certify how they

---

47. Kenyon, *Stuart Constitution*, pp. 315–16; W. A. Shaw, *A History of the English Church during the Civil Wars and under the Commonwealth* (2 vols, 1900), II, 244–7; D. Underdown, *Revel, Riot and Rebellion* (Oxford, 1985), pp. 239–70.
48. *T.S.P.*, III, 281.
49. Kenyon, *Stuart Constitution*, p. 323.
50. *T.S.P.* IV, 187, 189, 267, 300, 333.
51. *T.S.P.*, IV, 211, 272.

held their livings and for how long they had done so. This tactic, which was also used by Whalley in May 1656 in Nottinghamshire, had the merit of bringing a large crowd of men under the immediate eye of the county's commissioners. Ralph Josselin, who thought the proceeding rigorous, went to Chelmsford, recording in his diary that the roads were 'wonderful dirty but it rained not'. The meeting included a sermon from a local preacher commending and encouraging the commissioners. Josselin declared he 'saw no beauty in the day', though he was probably the last of the throng attending that was likely to be faulted. It is interesting that he, Cromwell's model puritan minister if ever there was one, felt oppressed by the central interference that actual enforcement of the ordinance involved: he did not 'joy to see ministers put under the lay power'.[52] Both the unfortunate proceedings in Berkshire and this hint of tension in Essex exemplify the practical problems for the Protector of improving the ministerial foundations of evangelization.

Cromwell's personal interest in the local ministry and in the improvement of provincial educational opportunity deserves fuller investigation so that we can assess the extent of his involvement in establishing his kind of evangelizing ministry at the grass roots. His enthusiasm for the project of a university or college at Durham undoubtedly lay behind the issue of letters patent for its founding in 1657 following a series of petitions from the county.[53] The record of his patronage shows that he was regularly involved in the minutiae of recommendation and presentation. In November 1653, for example, he wrote to a Surrey gentleman about the settlement of Mr Draper at Speldhurst in Kent, a man, he had been told, 'well approved of by most of the good ministers thereabout and much desired by the honest people who are in a religious association in those parts'.[54] In September 1657, he presented to a Chichester living in Sussex and wrote to the Triers about their approbation of the man he was nominating to the rectory of Gawsworth in Cheshire. The following month he found a living in Sussex for Nehemiah Beaton, one of the leading puritan ministers of the county, after Francis Cheynell had petitioned on behalf of 'this precious man'.[55]

52. A. C. Wood, *Nottinghamshire in the Civil War* (Oxford, 1937), p. 202; A. Macfarlane (ed.), *The Diary of Ralph Josselin* (1976), pp. 362–3.
53. Abbott, IV, 522–8; R. Howell, *Newcastle-upon-Tyne and the Puritan Revolution* (Oxford, 1967), pp. 330–4.
54. Abbott, III, 1, 120–1.
55. Abbott, IV, 627–8, 658; A. J. Fletcher, *A Country Community in Peace and War: Sussex 1600–1660* (1975), pp. 109–23

There was probably no project closer to Cromwell's heart than the scheme for propagating the gospel in Wales, which had taken several strides forward in the three years following the establishment of the itinerant preachers there in 1650.[56] 'God did kindle a seed there indeed hardly to be paralleled since the primitive times', declared Oliver to the Barebone's Assembly. He was bitter about the Rump's failure to give the scheme whole-hearted support and about its rejection on 1 April 1653 of a bill for continuing the propagators. One of the first things he did after his dissolution of the Rump was to write to the commissioners named in the 1650 act advising them 'to go on cheerfully in the work as formerly'. 'In so doing', he promised, 'the Lord will be with you and you shall have all fitting assistance and encouragement therein from myself until those placed in the supreme power shall take further order.'[57] Unfortunately they never did take further order. The momentum of orthodox evangelization in Wales was lost: the sectarian churches, Christopher Hill has noted, took over where the propagators left off.[58]

The achievement of the 1640s and 1650s with regard to the reform of parochial finance has begun to be addressed in the research of Ann Hughes and Rosemary O'Day on Derbyshire and Warwickshire. Cromwell's Trustees for the Maintenance of Ministers appear in their account as the heirs of the Committee for Plundered Ministers, doing the same job rather more effectively but on a more limited basis than the previous body.[59] The new Trustees were established by an ordinance of 1654 which gave them responsibility for authorizing and paying all augmentations, where appropriate on the basis of union or division of parishes.[60] On paper, 63 of the 200 Warwickshire livings received some augmentation before 1654 but much of the money may never have reached the parishes. The Trustees favoured only 23 of these 63 livings together with 5 new ones. But some £940 in all was definitely being paid to these 28 benefices in the later 1650s.[61] The Trustees were certainly a more highly organized body

56. C. Hill, *Change and Continuity in Seventeenth Century England* (1974), pp. 32–44.
57. Abbott, III, 1, 13, 57.
58. Hill, Change and Continuity, p. 45.
59. R. O'Day and A. Hughes, 'Augmentation and amalgamation: was there a systematic approach to the reform of parochial finance 1640–1660?', in R. O'Day and F. Heal (eds), *Princes and Paupers in the English Church 1500–1800* (Leicester, 1981), pp. 167–93.
60. C. H. Firth and R. Rait (eds), *Acts and Ordinances of the Interregnum* (3 vols, 1911), II, 1000–6; for the Trustees report to the Protector and Council in 1655 see Shaw, *English Church*, II, pp. 496–513.
61. A. Hughes, *Politics, society and Civil War in Warwickshire 1620–1660* (Cambridge, 1987), p. 307.

than the Committee had been, having their own bureaucracy and treasury. They benefited from Cromwell's insistence that they should have proper access to information about the character of ministers, the value of livings and the revenue available. Both the 1650 survey of the ministry and the papers of the Triers were helpful to them. They did make a serious effort to augment the clergy's maintenance and to match parish provision more closely to the distribution of the population. Ann Hughes and Rosemary O'Day conclude by remarking that the Trustees, through trial and error, made maintenance of ministers more equitable, while taking account of the sensitivities of lay patrons and impropriators.[62] Many of their amalgamations were sensible rationalizations. At Chichester in Sussex, for example, the St Antholin's lecturer William Martin, persecuted by William Laud in the 1630s, emerged as the well supported minister of one of two new parishes after an amalgamation of the eight previous parishes in the city. At least nine other amalgamations were carried out in Sussex between 1656 and 1658.[63] At York twenty-five parishes were reorganized according to a plan which reduced them to eight: each of these was then provided with a godly and learned minister.[64] Here then is an area where the achievement owed much to the Protector himself and was not negligible. But what overall can be said about the direct results of ecclesiastical policy implemented from the centre between 1653 and 1658? Cromwell's chief preoccupation, we have seen, was the quality and effectiveness of the ministry. His ideals in this respect were pure and noble. But, given the problems of enforcement that he faced, it must be said that what he could do from Whitehall was exceedingly limited.

IV

This view from the centre however is no substitute for an account of the spiritual life of the Cromwellian Church in the parishes. This is a story that cannot be told in full here. Yet it is worth briefly exchanging the central perspective for some local ones in order to sketch the realities of this final stage of the abortive puritan reformation of England. It has been argued above that neither the godly nor the ungodly predominated in the parishes. What had been created through the efforts of the puritan preachers were islands of godliness

---

62. O'Day and Heal (eds), *Princes and Paupers*, p. 190.
63. Fletcher, *A County Community*, pp. 109–10; P. S. Seaver, *The Puritan Lectureships* (Stamford, 1970), pp. 163, 252.
64. Cross, *Church and People*, p. 215.

in a sea of more or less apathetic orthodoxy. One of these islands in the 1650s was Rye, led by John Allin, a Suffolk man who had emigrated to New England to escape the persecution of Bishop Wren in the 1630s and had then returned in 1643 to hold a London lectureship. This Sussex town, celebrated among puritans as a 'city set on a hill', was ordered by a strict corporation which set the .constables on the watch for any who danced, sang, drank or loitered on Sundays. Three lads there who profaned the sabbath in 1654 by going out to slide on the ice found themselves in court before the mayor.[65] John Evelyn, visiting Rye in 1653 to meet his wife off the Channel boat, was shocked at the plain Calvinistic form of worship in the parish church. He wished he had not gone 'having hitherto kept my ears incontaminate from their new fangled service'.[66] Another of these islands was York where Edmund Bowles, Lord Fairfax's chaplain in the 1640s, worked closely with the aldermen to ensure compulsory church attendance throughout the city.[67] Another again was the Essex village of Terling, which from 1632 to 1662 enjoyed the ministrations to the pious and dedicated John Stalham. In his *Vindiciae Redemptionis* Stalham recalled how during the civil war the godly of the parish joined with him in 'casting out of ceremonies and service book as a menstruous cloth' and established 'a true church here in being'.[68]

The partnership of magistracy and ministry, described by Patrick Collinson with examples from the Elizabethan and early Stuart periods, was still the foundation of rural puritan reform in the 1650s.[69] Ketton in Suffolk is one famous example, led by Sir Thomas Barnardiston, heir to the great patriarch Sir Nathaniel Barnardiston. He exhibited such blatant attachment to the regime of Major-General Haynes that the county gentry dropped him from top in 1654 to bottom in 1656 of the successful candidates in Suffolk's Protectorate elections.[70] Brampton Bryan in Herefordshire is another example. There the end of an era came on 6 November 1656 with the death of Sir Robert Harley. In his funeral sermon, Thomas Froysell

65. Fletcher, *A County Community*, pp. 111–13.
66. E. S. De Beer (ed.) *The Diary of John Evelyn* (Oxford, 1965), III, 67.
67. Cross, *Church and People*, p. 206.
68. K. Wrightson and D. Levine, *Poverty and Piety in an English Village: Terling 1525–1700* (1979), pp. 160–2.
69. Collinson, *Religion of Protestants*, pp. 141–88.
70. P. J. Pinckney, 'The Suffolk elections to the Protectorate parliaments', in C. Jones, M. Newitt and S. Roberts (eds), *Politics and People in Revolutionary England* (Oxford, 1986), pp. 205–24.

described Harley as the pattern of a puritan leader in the local community:

He was a copy for all great men to transcribe in all descending ages. . . . He was the first that brought the gospel into these parts. This country lay under a veil of darkness till he began to shine. . . . His planting of godly ministers and then backing them with his authority made religion famous in this little corner of the world. . . . He was a man of fixed principles: religion and solid reformation was all the white he shot at . . . his compass without trepidation or variation stood constantly right to the pole, the good of his country and gospel, which he kept ever in his eye.[71]

Harley was of Cromwell's generation; indeed he was a close acquaintance. The Protector cannot have heard that inspiring eulogy in the little Herefordshire village. But he must have appreciated the significance of Harley's passing and the need for others to build on his work. For in debate with a parliamentary committee about the reduction of garrisons two years previously, Cromwell referred to the district around Hereford as a 'mountainous country' with 'mountainous qualities and for religion and other things not so well qualified as would be desired'.[72]

The diaries and autobiographies of some of the most energetic and devoted puritan ministers are our best entry to the clerical life of this period. Henry Newcome's autobiography, for example, provides a moving account of his emotional reaction to the move he made from Gawsworth in Cheshire to Manchester in 1657. This section of his account, detailing his sense of loyalty to the congregation he was leaving and his fears of reproach for doing so, is followed by notes on some of the incidents of his first months in his new parish. He had an early opportunity to preach on the ways of God's providence when a 'drunken wretch' called John Rawlinson died after breaking his neck 'over the churchyard wall': 'I preached on Ecclesiastes VII, 17 and did what I could to show the danger of the gross wickedness that abounded in some.' Newcome found the most godly of his Manchester parishioners critical of his love of shuffleboard. This bothered him sufficiently for him to decide to set an example by avoiding the recreation altogether, 'unless I had been alone at serious business all day'. When he was in company and enjoying the fun and laughter of others, which Newcome 'was afraid of taking too great a latitude in', he regarded it as his duty 'to let some savoury things

71. T. Froysell, *The Beloved Disciple*. I am grateful to Jacqueline Levy for this reference.
72. Abbott, III, 1, 511.

fall where I had spoken merrily'.[73] Newcome's autobiography provides illuminating information on his evangelization of the Manchester district and of his little victories, like the 'private day' kept at Broughton in July 1658, 'the first ever kept in that house and as some thought in that township'.[74]

More generally, however, the diaries are a record of ministers on the defensive, tackling but unable to resolve satisfactorily two major challenges to their evangelistic effort: the challenges of sectarianism and of popular ignorance and apathy. There were numerous ministers in many parts of England who thought the civil war had been fought to establish orthodox religious reform. But those who had apparently been their closest allies often fell away from them after the war as radical doctrines took hold. Samuel Clarke recounted how many of the youth of Alcester to whom he had preached went to Warwick during the war, 'where falling into the company of anabaptists and other sectaries they were leavened with their errors'. Coming home they 'set up private meetings to the neglect of the public and many young men whom I looked upon before as children begotten by my ministry to lead were turned preachers'.[75] This was how the situation, from the viewpoint of the Calvinist orthodox, had got out of hand all over England by the 1650s. The essence of sectarianism was the rejection of a State Church and of an educated professional clergy, the violation in other words of the cherished ideal of parochial unity. The theological reaction which underpinned it was the reaction against biblical Calvinist predestinarianism. The authority of Church and scripture was replaced by the authority of the inner light.[76] By the 1650s, Ann Hughes has stressed on the basis of her investigation into the religious life of Warwickshire, the crucial division did not lie between Presbyterians and Independents but between those who accepted some form of national Church organization and those who did not.[77]

The irretrievable weakness of Cromwell's loose ecclesiastical framework was its lack of coercive powers. Nothing had replaced the Church courts. Ministers in the 1650s could not enforce attendance; they had no punitive authority against the immoral or those

73. R. Parkinson (ed.), *The Autobiography of Henry Newcome* (Chetham Society, XXVI, 1852), pp. 67–76, 80.
74. Parkinson (ed.), *Newcome*, p. 94.
75. Cited in Hughes, *Warwickshire*, p. 314.
76. See generally J. F. McGregor and B. Reay (eds), *Radical Religion in the English Revolution* (Oxford, 1984).
77. Hughes, *Warwickshire*, p. 310.

who scoffed. They had nothing besides the force of their own personalities and their learning with which to face the sectarian onslaught. One of the many who found their monopoly of spiritual guidance broken was John Stalham at Terling. He went into print in 1647 to refute the message of the wandering baptist Samuel Oates who had preached at a private house in the village without Stalham's consent, announcing 'an universal redemption by the death of Christ for all'. As an orthodox Calvinist, Stalham felt bound to reiterate his position that 'Christ died but for some' and that 'most men will lose their souls', but this was hardly the kind of news that his more wayward parishioners wanted to hear. In 1657 he returned to the fray when Quaker ideas took hold in Terling, this time patiently answering George Fox, James Nayler and others with arguments which showed his careful reading of their teachings. Stalham implored his flock to beware 'an itching desire of novelty or of knowing any new way to Christ and Heaven' but, as Keith Wrightson and David Levine have pointed out, he was simply trying to shut the stable door in Terling after the horse had bolted.[78]

The 1650s was a decade of incipient religious plurality. There was virtually nothing the Protector could do about this from his palace at Whitehall. There was little the orthodox clergy could do about it in the localities. They did attempt two solutions. The first was the association movement. In at least seventeen counties ministerial associations were formed to provide in the absence of a fully fledged presbyterian system for ordination, to coordinate policy on admission to communion as an instrument of discipline and to combat popular heresies, especially attacks on the divinity of Christ and on puritan notions of sin.[79] Richard Baxter's Worcestershire association was the model. He later described in his autobiography how he found eagerness for cooperation among his local colleagues, 'a company of honest, godly, serious, humble ministers' untainted by denominationalism. Henry Newcome describes the founding of the Cheshire Association in the autumn of 1653, 'in the darkest time' when it was feared that Barebone's Parliament might vote down the national ministry all together. These associations did much to boost the morale of the orthodox clergy as they struggled to stem the sectarian tide. They also did something, especially where as in

---

78. Wrightson and Levine, *Poverty and Piety*, pp. 163–4.
79. D. Hirst, *Authority and Conflict* (London, 1986), p. 324; Shaw, *History of the English Church*, II, 440–56; C. Hill, *The World Turned Upside Down* (1972), pp. 121–260.

Kidderminster ministers met regularly with local JPs and substantial godly householders, to support spiritual teaching and the enforcement of moral discipline.[80] But this was the more particular objective of the second attempted solution: parochial catechizing. This, the puritan clergy at last fully realized in the 1640s and 1650s, was the only way to teach religion at the congregation's own level and to inculcate the minimum standard of godliness among the uneducated that would provide the semblance of a godly nation. Before the civil war catechizing had largely been confined to the household.[81] The new catechisms that appeared after it were more precisely an adjunct to or even substitute for the pulpit. Thus John Stalham published in 1644 his *Catechism for Children in Years and Children in Understanding*, an abridged version of a series of sermons which he had first preached and then circulated around the parish of Terling in manuscript.[82] Adam Martindale, faced with a huge and struggling parish to cope with, took up preaching 'a catechistical lecture' at Rostherne each Sunday 'in as plain a manner as I could possibly devise for the information of the ignorant' there. He subsequently repeated this for the townships of Leigh and Tabley later in the week. But Martindale's general observations on the catechizing movement provide a gloomy verdict. The clergy, he recorded in his autobiography, 'met with great discouragements through the unwillingness of people (especially the old ignoramuses) to have their extreme defects in knowledge searched out and the backwardness of the prophane to have the smart plaster of admonition applied (though lovingly) to their sores'.[83] The fact was that catechizing had come too late. As Martindale and his like struggled to drive basic protestant doctrine home, the puritan movement was shattering about his ears. It was a sobering experience for such men to realize that Reformation as they understood it had still not been accomplished. Peter Ince at Donhead St Mary in Wiltshire faced this when he attempted to make some basic instruction of their parents a condition of the baptism of children. 'I did not think rational creatures subject to so gross and affected ignorance,' he wrote to Richard Baxter; 'they seem to be afraid of knowledge lest it should force them upon holiness and unless I will

80. Shaw, *History of the English Church*, II, 154–5; Parkinson (ed.), *Newcome, p. 46*.
81. Hirst, *Authority and Conflict*, pp. 324–5. Dr Ian Green is preparing a full study of catechizing in the early seventeenth century.
82. Wrightson and Levine, *Poverty and Piety*, p. 162
83. R. Parkinson (ed.), *The Life of Adam Martindale* (Chetham Society, IV, 1845), pp. 122–3.

baptize them in all haste away they run to some idle drunken fellows and think all well.'[84]

Cromwell's objective was to create a godly nation yet he placed his faith in a Church structure that was wholly non-didactic and non-directive. This is the paradox at the heart of his ecclesiastical policy. All he provided was the preservation of parish maintenance and a system, which was highly fallible, of checks on the ministry. There were no stormtroopers, there was no national strategy for teaching the people more effectively the foundations of the protestant faith. This was a Church without evangelistic momentum. Nothing was done to fill the vacuum in terms of preaching, teaching and discipline left by the collapse of the Church courts in 1641. Into that vacuum marched the sects. How they did so is a process which requires much fuller investigation but Margaret Spufford's account of Cambridgeshire is a model for further studies. She shows how the main period of baptist evangelization by Henry Denne's gathered church at Fenstanton was in the early 1650s. In 1654, since there were many villages in the district that had 'no teachers' he went on a recruiting tour through Kingston, Toft, Harston and Shelford into Essex, returning by way of Royston and Melbourn. Persecutions of ministers for going to meetings and public testifying show that Quakerism had taken root by 1656 in both the south and the north-west of the county. Francis Holcroft's Congregational Church at Bassingbourn, founded when he replaced one who had 'grown old and worn and hath not a good delivery' in 1655, was based on a covenant which bound the members together. It was attended, we are told, by 'a great many people of other parishes, as well as of his own, besides several of both town and gown from Cambridge'.[85] Developments of this kind, which were occurring in many parts of England while Cromwell ruled as Protector, were a powerful solvent of parochial unity. They foreshadowed the religious pluralism of the Restoration period and the whole subsequent history of religion in England. In district after district the orthodox ministry was put on the defensive, forcing it to grapple with controversy and debate and distracting it from the business of Calvinist evangelization.

Prayer-book anglicanism, which was to emerge so triumphantly as the bedrock of an incipient class society in the 1660s and succeeding decades, was an even more serious obstacle to the creation of

---

84. Cited in G. F. Nuttall, *Visible Saints* (Oxford, 1957), p. 136.
85. M. Spufford, *Contrasting Communities* (Cambridge, 1974), pp. 272–89.

Cromwell's godly nation. For, if they failed to meet the challenge of the sects, he even more strikingly failed to lift the mass of the people out of their unlettered, comfortable piety based upon attendance at the saying of the liturgy and upon the ministrations of the clergy at the critical points of the individual's life cycle. David Underdown has documented the continuation of the puritan struggle to uproot the traditional culture of ales, revels and festivity in the years following the civil war and has demonstrated its failure. A Wiltshire man commenting upon rumours of religious changes which threatened the customary rhythms of rural life in 1646 declared that if the parliament 'did take away common prayer we were good to go to plough upon the Sundays'.[86] His remark reminds us of the need communities felt for communal gatherings, for the weekly demonstration of order and accord which was represented by church attendance which made matters of pews and seating so crucial and often so contentious.[87] In this sense there was widespread and sincere acceptance of English protestantism. In this sense there was widespread and sincere acceptance of English protestantism. But at the same time there was very general rejection of the much more rigid pattern of godliness offered by men like Richard Baxter, Ralph Josselin and Adam Martindale. What people wanted was an undemanding religion compatible with fellowship and fun on the day of rest. George Herbert's country parson had been 'a lover of old customs, if they be good and harmless and the rather because country people are much addicted to them so that to favour them therein is to win their hearts and to oppose them therein is to deject them'.[88]

Why was all this, we may ask finally, not evident to Oliver Cromwell? In the first place there was no reason why he should recognize that a turning point in the long history of religion in England had arrived and that religious plurality had come to stay. Everything pointed, for a man brought up in the last years of Elizabeth and the first of James I, to the opposite conclusion: that religious unity might and could be restored. Cromwell saw himself as in the mainstream of the protestant reformation. He understood how the puritan slur had been used by those who wanted to direct the course of that reformation into new paths. Secondly, Cromwell had no time to obtain an objective view. Driven on and at the same time sustained by his

---

86. Cited in Underdown, *Revel, Riot and Rebellion*, p. 256.
87. S. Amussen, *An Ordered Society* (Oxford, 1988), pp. 137–44
88. Cited in Duffy 'The godly and the multitude', p. 42.

providentialism, he reacted to each emergency with the flexibility and agility of the skilful politician that by the 1650s he had become. Though there was tiredness and disillusion by 1657 and 1658, the Protector never lost sight of his vision of a nation united in godliness. What he could not face or recognize was that the cause he led was becoming more blatantly simply the preservation of the army and of his own regime. The country gentry, meanwhile, were waiting and hoping for a political future that would better suit their needs. The army of God doing God's work no longer dominated the national scene in 1658 as it had done in 1648. In so far as the people of God flourished in the provinces they did so largely without the army's support and despite its existence. In this sense the army and the godly had moved apart. Oliver's sincere attachment to liberty of conscience, as it turned out, was paving the way for the religious plurality and the denominationalism of the modern State.

CHAPTER NINE

Oliver Cromwell and English political thought

Johann Sommerville

I

Oliver Cromwell was a man of action and not a deep philosopher.[1]
Yet thoughts underlie actions, and to understand what Cromwell did
it is well worth investigating his ideas – even if these turn out not
to be very subtle or sophisticated. It has become fashionable of late
to examine the writings of the great thinkers in the context of their
times – and in particular against the background of political events.
The same method works equally well in reverse; that is to say, in
order to understand the actions of great statesmen and politicians it
is useful to grasp the intellectual context in which they acted. Yet
political historians in recent years have shied away from questions of
ideology or principle. Very little has been written about Oliver
Cromwell's political thinking.[2] The purpose of this chapter is to
describe Cromwell's thinking, and to set it in its ideological context.

II

What, then, was the political thought of Oliver Cromwell, and what
were its ideological roots? There were, of course, a number of such
roots, and not just one. Among the most important were a group
of ideas about God's Providence, which deeply affected Cromwell's
attitudes towards history, and towards politics. At times, too, he

---

1. Dates in this chapter are old style but the year is taken to begin on 1 January,
   except that in bibliographical references the dates are as given on the title page.
   Spelling and punctuation have been modernized except in the titles of seventeenth-century books.
2. Perhaps the most accessible account of Cromwell's political ideas is the brief
   survey in G. P. Gooch and H. Laski, *The History of English Democratic Ideas in the
   Seventeenth Century* (Cambridge, 1927), pp. 192–204.

came close to endorsing the antinomian and millenarian notions that the godly should govern, despite the fact that no one had elected them – though he turned against this position after 1653. But the most important context for his thought – and, indeed, for Civil War political thought in general – is provided by a set of doctrines which we might call natural law contractualism – and which were characteristic as much of Roman catholics as of protestants. This theory emphasized the importance of popular consent in validating political arrangements – and Cromwell too stressed consent. However, other aspects of his outlook pulled him in different directions. He held the religious liberties of the godly in high esteem, and he also took seriously his own providential role. These various elements existed in dynamic and creative tension within Cromwell's mind, and they explain much about his actions. Let us begin with natural law contractualism.

During the Middle Ages and early modern period it was widely maintained that God ruled the universe through laws, of which some (the laws of nature) had been promulgated to all mankind – and not just to Christians. The laws of nature informed people of their political rights and obligations, but gave only limited information on religious duties. It was from the law of grace or revelation, set out in the Bible, that people derived their knowledge of the Christian message. Most thinkers claimed that Christian faith was *not* a necessary qualification for any ruler. They rejected the idea that the saints – the elect – had the right to govern, and that anyone who turned out not to be one of the elect automatically forfeited political authority. The notion that a king need not be obeyed unless he was one of the elect, they said, confused the realms of grace and nature, and also led to dangerous, anarchic consequences, since it was often difficult to establish whether a particular ruler was or was not elect – and therefore whether or not he should be obeyed. The doctrine that only the saints can rule was condemned by the Council of Constance in 1415. Catholics claimed that 'dominion is founded not in grace but in nature', and the great majority of protestants endorsed this position.[3] As we shall see, Cromwell himself gave unusual stress to the political rights of the elect, but he too abided by the conventional

---

3. Cardinal Robert Bellarmine, *De membris ecclesiae*, book 3 (De laicis), ch. 8, in *Disputationum* (4 vols, Venice, 1602–3), II, col. 468 ('dominii fundamentum non est gratia, sed natura'. Protestant examples include Thomas Jackson, *Works* (12 vols, Oxford, 1844), XII, p. 193; John Davenant, *Determinationes quaestionum quorundam theologicorum* (Cambridge, 1634), p. 136: 'Dominium temporale non fundatur in gratia.'

wisdom. One of the virtues of the Instrument of Government, he told parliament in 1655, was that it did not 'found *dominium in gratia*'.[4]

It is possible that Cromwell was directly influenced by catholic political thinking, especially on the question of resistance to tyrants. According to Gilbert Burnet, Cromwell on one occasion 'entered into a long discourse on the nature of the regal power, according to the principles of Mariana and Buchanan.[5] Certainly, some parliamentarians did draw on the notorious Jesuit defender of tyrannicide, Mariana, and on other papists. Moreover, their Calvinist sources – such as Buchanan – themselves owed much to catholics. But of course there were areas in which parliamentarians – like other protestants – diverged sharply from catholic thinking on politics. This is especially true on questions of Church–State relations. Protestants extended the idea that government is not founded in grace to rebut catholic arguments that the Church – which *was* founded in grace (since it had been instituted by Christ in the Bible) – had political power over Christian rulers. All protestants opposed the catholic idea that clerics could depose civil rulers, but some went further and argued that it was wrong for ministers of religion to exercise any form of political power, even if it was delegated from the temporal ruler. One of the main criticisms levelled at the bishops on the eve of the civil war was that they combined secular with spiritual functions. Later, presbyterians were accused of imitating the bishops in attempting to establish a clerical tyranny over men's bodies and consciences. Cromwell opposed all such clerical claims to power. But on the issue of the nature and origins of *civil* (as opposed to ecclesiastical) power, Cromwell and many other parliamentarians shared the views of catholics. This point deserves to be emphasized.

Civil government, it was commonly said, was founded in the law of nature – a law that told everyone that government was necessary if mankind was to fulfil its objectives on earth. Virtually any government was better than none at all. As Cromwell put it, 'misrule is better than no rule, and an ill government, a bad one, is better than none'.[6] This did not necessarily mean that the people were without remedy against misrule. For though the law of nature stipulated that people ought to live in political societies, and under governments, it did not give governing power to any specific individual or group. Some royalists, of whom Filmer is the best known, argued that

4. Abbott, III, p. 587.
5. Gilbert Burnet, *Bishop Burnet's History of his Own Time* (1857), p. 26.
6. Abbott, IV, 717.

political power had at first been held by fathers, from whom it descended to their successors. Virtually everyone agreed that a father's authority over his family was natural – that is to say, it was built in to human nature, and was not a consequence of any transference of power to the father by his children. But parliamentarians were more or less unanimous in rejecting the idea that the power of Adam had been kingly. Fatherly power, they said, was domestic (or 'economical') but not kingly or political. Political power came into existence only when a number of families voluntarily joined together in a larger group. Since by nature no member of this group had political authority over his fellows, it followed that at first such authority was held by the people as a whole. Whether the group could itself exercise this power, or had to transfer it to a smaller number, was disputed both during the Civil War and earlier. But even those who believed that direct democracy was possible denied that it was convenient. The recommended move for the people was to transfer authority to one or a few magistrates. In doing this, it was open to the people to impose contractual limitations upon the magistrate(s), and to reserve some powers to themselves. If the magistrate broke the conditions on which power had been granted to him, he could be called to account by the people.

Cromwell subscribed to these views. At Putney in 1647 he declared that 'the king is king by contract'.[7] 'Authorities', he wrote to Hammond in 1648,

and powers are the ordinance of God. This or that species is of human institution, and limited, some with larger, others with stricter bands, each one according to its constitution. I do not therefore think the authorities may do anything, and yet . . . obedience [be] due, but all agree that there are cases in which it is lawful to resist.[8]

Of course, not all *did* agree that resistance was lawful, for royalists repeatedly denied that the king could be resisted. Even among parliamentarians it took some time for the idea to gain ground that it could be lawful to resist the king's *person*. But from the beginning of the Civil War propagandists on parliament's side regularly argued that the king's power was derived from the consent of the people, and limited by whatever conditions they had chosen to stipulate. In July 1642 Henry Parker, one of the most famous of the parliamentarian pamphleteers, declared that '[p]ower is originally inherent in

7. Abbott, I, 539.
8. Abbott, I, 697.

the people', and that when the people transferred power to a king it could 'ordain what conditions, and prefix what bounds it pleases', Indeed, said Parker, however much power the people might generously have chosen to grant their ruler, it was necessarily the case that they reserved certain rights; for no people could grant its prince power to destroy them, or give up the right to defend themselves against destruction.[9]

'That there be in all societies of men a government', said Charles Herle in 1642, 'is out of question God's institution', 'but that this government be so or so moulded, qualified and limited is as questionless from the paction or consent of the society to be governed.'[10] 'Though power abstractively considered, be originally from God himself', said William Bridge in 1643, 'yet he hath communicated that power to the people'. It followed that 'the first subject seat and receptacle of ruling civil power . . . is the whole people or body politic', and that 'the prince hath no more power than what is communicated from the community'. Since the people 'cannot give away from themselves the power of self-preservation', they could always resist a ruler whose actions threatened their destruction.[11] 'God and nature,' declared John Cook, 'for the good of mankind, not only commanded but commended a government', but except in the extraordinary cases of such Old Testament figures as Saul and David God did not directly empower governors: 'all just power is now derived from the people.'[12]

In 1643 Jeremiah Burroughes argued similarly. 'That there should be civil government', he said, 'God hath appointed: but that it should be thus or thus, all in one, or divided into many, that is left to humane prudence.'[13] So the king's power was derived 'from election or covenant.'[14] Burroughes claimed that resistance to the king himself was sometimes justified, and cited the Jacobean divine Andrew Willet to confirm his opinion.[15] But in the early days of the Civil

9. Henry Parker, *Observations upon some of his Majesties late Answers and Expresses* (1642), pp. 1, 2, 8, 20.
10. Charles Herle, *A Fuller Answer to a Treatise written by Doctor Ferne* (1642), p. 6.
11. William Bridge, *The Truth of the Times Vindicated* (1643), pp. 4–5, 14; cf. *The Wounded Conscience Cured* (1642), pp. 4–6.
12. John Cook, *Redintegratio Amoris* (1647), pp. 4, 5.
13. Jeremiah Burroughes, *The Glorious Name of God* (1643), p. 35.
14. Ibid., p. 121.
15. Ibid., p. 120. A different interpretation of Burroughes may be found in Julian H. Franklin, *John Locke and the Theory of Sovereignty* (Cambridge, 1978), pp. 33–9. Edward Harrison, *Plain Dealing: or, the Countreymans Doleful Complaint and Faithful Watchword* (1649), p. 6 also cites Willet (in turn citing Paraeus) on resistance.

War people were more willing to talk about self-defence against the king's wicked advisers than about resistance to the king (though the practical difference was of course slight[16]). One reason for this was that moderates were more likely to join the parliamentarians if they portrayed themselves as dutiful subjects of King Charles. Another, and equally important reason was that Tudor and early Stuart propaganda had repeatedly and effectively rammed home the point that it was papists who advocated resistance to kings. In 1642 John Goodwin justified fighting against the Cavaliers, but left the defence of 'offering violence to the person of a king, or attempting to take away his life' 'to those profound disputers the Jesuits'.[17] A few years later, Goodwin himself penned apologies for Pride's Purge and for the execution of the king.

The idea that government in the abstract is the institution of God, but that the form of a particular government depends on the wishes of people, was commonly expressed by catholics, including Cardinal Bellarmine, whose version of the case was singled out for special criticism by Sir Robert Filmer.[18] It also featured in the notorious *Conference about the next succession to the crown of England* of the Elizabethan Jesuit Parsons. 'Government', said Parsons, is 'of nature', but 'the particular form or manner of this or that government, in this or that fashion' is 'ordained by particular positive laws of every country'. Clearly, these ideas closely resemble those which Cromwell expressed in his letter to Hammond. Parsons' book was reprinted as parliamentarian propaganda in 1648 since (as the title page suggested) it could be read as a vindication of 'the power of parliament to proceed against their king for misgovernment'. 'There can be no doubt', wrote Parsons, 'but that the commonwealth hath power to choose their own fashion of government, as also to change

---

16. Franklin, *John Locke and the Theory of Sovereignty*, p. 20, argues that the parliamentarian case was inconsistent since its proponents claimed that parliament could do all that was necessary in order to secure the public safety and yet held back from permitting the deposition of the king (though such action might have helped to secure the public). However, many believed that God would punish sin by inflicting calamity upon its perpetrators, and so that public safety could not be achieved by deposing a monarch. Moreover, since the parliamentarian theory permitted the coercion of everyone except the king it was arguably adequate as it stood to secure the people – for the entire population could be coerced into disobeying a wicked monarch.
17. John Goodwin, *Anti-Cavalierisme* (1642), p. 10.
18. Bellarmine, *Disputationum*, II, col. 463. Sir Robert Filmer, *Patriarcha and Other Political Works*, Peter Laslett (ed.) (Oxford 1949), p. 56. A typical protestant discussion, essentially the same as Bellarmine's, is Edward Gee, *The Divine Right and Original of the Civil Magistrate* (1658), pp. 33–5.

the same upon reasonable causes.' He held that 'Princes are subject to law and order, and that the common-wealth which gave them their authority for the common good of all, may also restrain or take the same away again, it they abuse it to the common evil.' In Parsons' theory, the commonwealth remained superior to the king even after it granted him power.[19] The same idea was expressed by Henry Parker, Samuel Rutherford and others. Peter Bland and John Warr both cited John Foxe's *Acts and monuments* to confirm the notion. They drew on Foxe's account of the Council of Basle, and William Prynne used the proceedings at Basle to similar effect – testimony to the origins of the theory in catholic conciliarism.[20]

So far, we have seen that many of parliament's most eminent publicists argued that the king's power was derived from the people, and limited by conditions which they had imposed upon him. We have also seen that such ideas were familiar to catholic theorists of the medieval and early modern periods. These points deserve to be stressed, for several reasons. One is that it is sometimes mistakenly suggested that the civil war lacked an ideological dimension, or that if it possessed such a dimension it was overridingly religious and not political or constitutional in character.[21] In fact royalists generally claimed that the king's power was derived from God alone, while parliamentarians usually sought its origins in an act of transference by the people. There is, therefore, at least one clear formal difference in the political theories put forward by the two sides.

A second reason for emphasizing the early and frequent use made by parliamentarians of natural law contractualism is that in much recent writing on seventeenth-century English political thought this tradition is given short shrift, particularly by comparison with the common lawyer's notion of an ancient constitution – which famously

---

19. Robert Parsons, *A Conference about the Next Succession to the Crown of England* (1594), reissued as *Severall Speeches Delivered at a Conference Concerning the Power of Parliament, to Proceed against their King for Misgovernment*, (1648), pp. 1–2, 6, 26.

20. Parker, *Observations*, p. 2. Samuel Rutherford, *Lex, Rex, or the Law and the Prince* (1644, reprinted Edinburgh, 1843), p. 69. Peter Bland, *A Royal Position* (1642), p. 8. John Warr, *The Priviledges of the People* (1649), p. 11. William Prynne is discussed in Brian Tierney, *Religion, Law, and the Growth of Constitutional Thought 1150–1650* (Cambridge 1982), p. 60.

21. According to J. P. Kenyon, *Stuart England* (Harmondsworth, 1985), p. 158, the civil war was 'no bitter ideological struggle'. The religious element is emphasized in John Morrill, 'The religious context of the English Civil War', in *T.R.H.S.*, 5th ser., XXXIV (1984), 155–178, and in Conrad Russell's forthcoming Ford Lectures for 1988.

featured in the writings of that great oracle of the law, Sir Edward
Coke. Coke argued that the rights and duties of king and subject
could be deduced from the ancient customary laws of the land. These
laws had demonstrated their excellence by surviving, and they were
a better guide to the subject's liberties and the prince's prerogatives
than any airy philosophical speculations. If a question arose about
some royal power, it could be answered not by abstract reasoning –
which was an uncertain and fallible tool – but by consulting the laws,
and their interpreters the lawyers, who would point out deviations
from ancient custom, and so facilitate a restoration of the *status quo*.

This attitude was not well suited to a period of rapid political
change such as the 1640s. In those years, both sides flouted known
law. The two houses found it necessary to exercise emergency
powers which clearly contravened old custom. In 1628, parliament
had condemned the actions of Charles I since he had (at least in their
opinion) infringed liberties enshrined in Magna Carta – the grand
repository of the subject's freedoms. The fact that he claimed to have
been acting in accordance with the public good or safety (*salus populi*)
cut little ice with them. But in the 1640s parliament itself began to
claim the authority to ignore old customs where *salus populi* required
such a course. In 1648 *salus populi* was invoked by Cromwell against
parliament and on behalf of the army.[22] The doctrine of the ancient
constitution was useful in criticizing royal policies before 1640. But
after 1642 it could equally easily be used to criticize the two Houses.
So their propagandists abandoned appeals to Magna Carta, and instead spoke of contract and popular consent. Cromwell himself
mentioned Magna Carta only very rarely. In 1655, indeed, he
declared that 'in every government there must be somewhat fundamental, somewhat like a *Magna Charta*'. Cromwell was here
defending the Instrument of Government as fundamental, and his
words can be read as implying that Magna Carta itself was no longer
in force.[23] Certainly, there is little evidence that Cromwell ever subscribed to the Cokeian theory of the ancient constitution. Rather, his
thinking centred on the notion of Providence, and on ideas derived
from the tradition of natural law contractualism. In the mid-1640s
some writers extended natural law ideas in a radically democratic
direction. Cromwell, as we shall see, was reluctant to follow them.

22. Abbott, I, 697.
23. Abbott, III, 459.

III

As the Civil War progressed, some parliamentarians began to voice increasingly radical ideas – and radicalism was not confined to the lunatic fringe. The country gentleman Sir Cheney Culpeper was an acquaintance of Cromwell – and a leading member of Samuel Hartlib's famous and influential circle of reformist intellectuals – who in his private letters to Hartlib put forward quite startling suggestions for political change in England at an early date. He proposed amalgamating the two houses of parliament in 1644, and hoped that England's nobility would die out. In 1645 he claimed that the only function of successive monarchs was to act as figure-heads. Culpeper disliked the House of Lords and what he took to be its spiritual equivalent – Presbyterianism (or 'Scottish aristocracy'). Against them both he opposed the true English interest – which he called 'our democratical interest'. But Culpeper was no full-blown democrat. In particular, he denied the people could call to account their representatives in the House of Commons as long as parliament was sitting. The idea they could ever refuse 'active or passive obedience' to the house while it sat was, he said, 'a most pestilent doctrine'.[24] One of the major developments of English political thinking during the 1640s was precisely that this 'pestilent doctrine' acquired increasing support. Levellers and army polemicists came to argue that the people could call parliament to account. In 1648 Cromwell himself turned his sword against the houses in Pride's Purge.

We saw earlier that contractualists divided on the question of whether the people had originally been empowered to govern themselves directly. Some (like the great catholic thinker Francisco Suarez) argued that they could, while others (the catholics Bellarmine and Molina are examples) took the opposite point of view. Practical implications followed from each position. If the people had to transfer their power, then it followed that they were not now wielding sovereign authority – though they might still retain vestigial rights to defend themselves against the misuse of power by their ruler. Debate on this point ran parallel to a dispute on Church government which divided puritans throughout the 1640s: did sovereign power in a congregation reside in the minister and elders, or in the whole body? The relationship between ideas on secular and ecclesiastical government was close, and deserves fuller investigation than it has yet received.

24. Sheffield University, Hartlib Papers 13/50b, 99b, 90a, 127b. The Papers are cited by kind permission of Lord Delamere.

Government, said parliamentarians, rests on the consent of the governed, and they went on to argue that the king is accountable to the people represented in the two houses. But as royalist pamphleteers were fond of pointing out, the claim could easily be extended in a radically democratic direction – for it could be argued that parliament was itself accountable to the people at large – and therefore that gentlemen were subject to their social inferiors. To rebut this suggestion, such parliamentarian pamphleteers as Parker and Herle declared that the people had no rights against their elected representatives.[25] Soon, however, more radical writers argued that if parliament became corrupt it could indeed be resisted by the people. The idea that sovereignty inheres in the people as a whole and that they can call parliament to account if they find its actions wanting was expressed in the first two years of the war by Jeremiah Burroughes and others. From 1645, the theory acquired increasing practical importance as it gained adherents in the army – and as the army gained importance in politics.[26]

The notion that sovereignty inheres in the people – and not in their representatives – was often combined with calls for a widening of the franchise. Levellers held that since the people were sovereign they could alter constitutional arrangements which they found unsatisfactory. They also argued for extending the right to elect members of parliament. Though Cromwell believed that government was founded in consent, he rejected Leveller thinking on the franchise, and it was only reluctantly that he came to accept the need for drastic constitutional change in England. By 1647 those who supported natural law resistance theory had split into two camps – one conservative, the other radical. In the Putney debates of the autumn of 1647 Cromwell took the conservative side.

At Putney Oliver rejected Leveller calls for reform. Like everyone else, he admitted that 'the good of the people' is 'the supreme good' under God. He was not, he said, 'wedded and glued to forms of government'.[27] Henry Marten had claimed that Cromwell was 'King-ridden',[28] and at Putney Oliver was certainly anxious to

---

25. Parker, *Jus Populi* (1644), p. 18. Herle, *A Fuller Answer*, p. 25.
26. Burroughes, *The Glorious Name of God*, p. 134. *A Discourse upon the Questions in Debate between the King and Parliament*, n.p., n.d. [1642], p. 13. *Maximes Unfolded*, n.p., n.d. [March 1643], p. 74. David Wootton (ed.), *Divine Right and Democracy* (Harmondsworth, 1986), pp. 45–51, contains an interesting relevant discussion. Wootton dates the first appearance in England of the radical argument to 1645.
27. Abbott, I, 527.
28. Henry Cary (ed.), *Memorials of the Great Civil War, 1642–1652* (2 vols, 1842), I, pp. 354–5.

rebut the notion that he was an inflexible devotee of kingship or of the House of Lords. He was not yet convinced, he said, that the public good did indeed require the destruction of monarchy or lords.

In Cromwell's view, the Leveller *Agreement of the People* was far from representing the true opinions of Englishmen. He doubted that the *Agreement* would accord with 'the spirits and temper of the people'.[29] Moreover, he argued that anarchic implications underlay the notion that we should adopt constitutional suggestions put forward by such groups as the Levellers. Perhaps the Leveller constitution would succeed in improving on current arrangements. But what if other groups formulated equally excellent proposals? 'Would it not be confusion?', he asked rhetorically, 'Would it not be utter confusion?' Different localities might adopt different constitutions, and England could fragment into Swiss-style cantons.[30]

In the debates at Putney Cromwell pointed out that the adoption of the Leveller *Agreement* would conflict with the army's earlier undertakings. It would be wrong, he argued, for us to break old promises whenever we found it convenient to do so. We were justified in failing to abide by our engagements only if they were unrighteous or destructive. The army's engagements were neither unrighteous nor destructive, and therefore continued to bind. Cromwell argued that the preservation of the kingdom did not require the abolition of monarchy or lords. He also opposed radical reform of the franchise though he was willing to compromise by granting the suffrage to at least some copyholders by inheritance. Oliver's ideas on the franchise lacked the theoretical subtlety of those put forward by his son-in-law Henry Ireton. But the two men were agreed in opposing major change.[31]

The events of the year after Putney led Cromwell and Ireton to conclude that the destruction of monarchy was indeed necessary – and that parliament had therefore to be purged of those who stood in the way of what had to be done. Cromwell argued that all powers could be resisted. If parliament were not resisted in November 1648, he wrote to Hammond, the 'whole fruit of the war' was likely to be frustrated.[32] Cromwell now advocated a major alteration in England's constitution – and forcibly carried through the Purge and the execution of the king. But these events do not indicate any sig-

29. Abbott, I, 518.
30. Abbott, I, 518.
31. Abbott, I, 522, 527, 532–3, 544–5.
32. Abbott, I, 697.

nificant shift in Oliver's political thought. He had not become a committed democrat or republican. Rather, he regarded himself as bowing to necessity, and Providence.

Pride's Purge flouted the principle that government must rest on the consent of the governed. But in later years Cromwell continued to invoke the concept of consent, and hoped to restore a freely elected parliament. In 1653 he told the Barebone's Parliament that its meeting was justified because of extraordinary circumstances, and he declared his hope that God would soon make the people fit to elect their own representatives: 'none can desire it more that I'.[33] In the following year he told the members of his first elected parliament that the free elections which had brought them there were 'that which . . . I have desired above my life'.[34] Government, he told them later, rests on 'the acceptation and consent of the people'.[35] It was 'by the voice of the people', he declared in 1656, that he had become 'the supreme magistrate'.[36] In 1657 he once more spoke on the same theme, arguing that government at first arose from the 'consent of the whole', and that consent could still effect constitutional change.[37] Looking back on some of his earlier actions, he claimed that necessity had justified them but that consent was normally required.[38]

Cromwell's continued appeals to the idea of consent bear witness to the strength of natural law contractualism. But such revolutionary measures as the destruction of the monarchy in 1649 and the establishment of Barebone's Parliament in 1653 patently lacked popular consent. How were they to be justified? One line of approach was to suggest that in extraordinary circumstances God might grant special powers to groups (such as the army), or individuals (such as the Old Testament figure Phineas – who though no magistrate greatly pleased the Lord by enforcing His will). This attitude was often connected with the ideas that the soldiers were saints in arms and that their victories testified to their providential mission. At times, those who expressed such views strayed across the thin line which separated much conventional puritan thought from antinomianism and argued that the saints had a right to rule. A second means of

33. Abbott, III, 60, 64.
34. Abbott, III, 440.
35. Abbott, III, 588.
36. Abbott, IV, 277.
37. Abbott, IV, 469.
38. Abbott, IV, 481–2.

justifying the Revolution of 1649 (though in practice it frequently blended with providentialism) was to claim that the army had conquered, and that its commanders now ruled by right of conquest. Much was heard of both these kinds of argument in the controversy over the Engagement of 1650.

IV

On 2 January 1650 the Rump Parliament passed an act requiring all males aged more than eighteen to take an 'Engagement' promising to 'be true and faithful to the commonwealth of England as it is now established, without a king or House of Lords'.[39] Many people had previously sworn allegiance to the Stuart kings. A pamphlet controversy resulted, in which some said that these earlier agreements (and in particular the Solemn League and Covenant, and the oaths of supremacy and allegiance) rendered the Engagement unlawful. Others claimed that the old agreements had ceased to apply, and that the Engagement could therefore be taken. One argument used to show that people no longer owed allegiance to the Stuarts was that they were not protecting the people. Many of those who justified taking the Engagement contended that protection and obedience were linked. A government had rights to obedience only from those whom it was in fact protecting. In 1650 Charles Stuart was manifestly providing the English with no protection. On the other hand, the new govenment of the commonwealth *was* protecting the people by enforcing law at home and by defending the country from foreign attack. So the commonwealth did have a right to the subject's obedience.

The debate over the Engagement has received much attention from recent writers. It led, says one, to 'a number of important conceptual breakthroughs',[40] while according to another it first drove Englishmen 'to confront what government was and what its claims were, questions the avowed conservatism of both sides in the civil war had enabled them to avoid'.[41] Perhaps the main reason why the debate has been given so much scrutiny is that an eloquent argument has been mounted to show that Hobbes's *Leviathan* – probably the

39. J. P. Kenyon, *The Stuart Constitution: Documents and Commentary* (Cambridge, 1966), p. 341.
40. J. G. A. Pocock, 'Political thought in the Cromwellian Interregnum', in G. A. Wood and P. S. O' Connor, *W. P. Morrell: a Tribute* (Dunedin, 1973), pp. 21–36, at 28.
41. Derek Hirst, *Authority and Conflict: England 1603–1658* (1986), p. 297.

greatest political treatise in the English language – was a contribution to it.[42]

The controversy over the Engagement did stimulate some exciting political thought. But most of the arguments used by the debaters were variations on themes that were already well known. The problem of whether individuals should obey a usurping government was not new in English history, and a complex casuistry on usurpation had been developed by Elizabethan catholics long before the Engagement. Attempts to show that the controversy marked a watershed between a medieval past – when people viewed politics primarily in religious terms – and a more secular present, are difficult to sustain, because most of the participants in the dispute combined religious with secular opinions.[43] Nor would it be correct to suppose that the idea of a link between subjection and obedience was first invented by defenders of the Engagement.[44] In fact, the idea of a mutual or reciprocal connection between subjection and obedience was commonplace long before 1650. That Hobbes employs the idea in his *Leviathan* therefore provides little evidence for concluding that he was influenced by writings on the Engagement.

In 1642 the pamphleteer John March wrote that 'protection and legiance are relatives, and have a necessary and reciprocal dependence the one upon the other'. 'Reason', he said, 'will arm every man thus far, as to conclude, that the cause and ground of his obedience, is his sovereign's protection, and therefore if his sovereign withdraw the one, he may deny the other.'[45] The two houses of parliament themselves declared in March 1642 that protection and allegiance were 'the mutual bands and supports of government and subjection.'[46] Propagandists repeated the claim throughout the 1640s, using it to show that it was lawful to disobey the king – or parliament. 'It is an axiom political,' said William Ball in 1645, 'where there is no protection [*ubi nulla protectio*], there is no subjection [*ibi nulla subjectio*].'[47] Thomas Chaloner took a similar line in 1646, declaring that

---

42. Quentin Skinner, 'Conquest and consent: Thomas Hobbes and the Engagement controversy', in G. E. Aylmer (ed.) *The Interregnum: the Quest for Settlement 1646–1660* (1972), pp. 79–98.
43. This point is well made in G. Burgess, 'Usurpation, obligation and obedience in the thought of the Engagement controversy', in *H. J.*, XXIX (1986), 515–36. See also S. A. State's stimulating article, 'Text and context: Skinner, Hobbes and theistic natural law', in *H.J.*, XXVIII (1985), 27–50, esp. at p. 34.
44. Skinner, 'Conquest and consent', pp. 88, 92.
45. John March, *An Argument or, Debate in Law* (1642), p. 3.
46. John Rushworth (ed.), *Historical Collections* (7 vols, 1659–1701), IV, p. 530.
47. William Ball, *Tractatus de jure regnandi et regni (1645)*, pp. 13–14.

'[n]o man can be said to bee protected, that is not withal thereby subjected'.[48] Thinkers as different as Ireton[49] and Richard Overton[50] adopted the same point of view.

So the idea of a mutual connection between protection and obedience was well known before 1650. In the 1640s it had been employed to show that the king, or the two Houses, had forfeited their claims to the people's allegiance by failing adequately to protect them. After 1650 it was used to prove that people had a duty of allegiance to the Rump, since it *was* protecting them. But the shift was relatively slight, and involved no conceptual revolution. Another argument which was used to justify the Rump's powers, and which also drew on ideas current earlier, was that conquest had taken place in England – and that conquest conferred rights of rulership upon the conqueror – in this case, the Rump. During the 1640s (and indeed long before) some writers had argued that the Stuart kings governed as absolute monarchs in virtue of their descent from William the Conqueror.

The notion that conquest – at least in a just war – gave political authority to the conqueror was accepted by many early seventeenth-century thinkers. In the 1650s Marchamont Nedham and others adapted the old idea to novel circumstances by arguing that England's new governors ruled by right of conquest.[51] A major problem with this line of argument was that it contradicted earlier parliamentary propaganda. For when royalists had derived the king's rights from conquest, their parliamentarian opponents had rejected the claim by arguing that only consent could make a conqueror a king. It was 'some compact, covenant or agreement' and not mere force which originated government, said Burroughes in 1643, while Parker and Bridge both argued similarly, as did John Cook.[52]

Cromwell adopted the same attitude. 'That [which] you have by force', he declared during the army debates at Reading in July 1647, 'I count upon it as nothing.'[53] It is possible that Cromwell came to

---

48. Thomas Chaloner, *An Answer to the Scotch Papers* (1646), p. 6.
49. Ireton in A. S. P. Woodhouse (ed.), *Puritanism and Liberty* (1938), p. 66.
50. Richard Overton, *An Appeale from the Degenerate Representative Body of the Commons* (1647), sig. C1b.
51. Marchamont Nedham, *The Case of the Common-wealth of England Stated* (1650), 22. Cf. Skinner, 'Conquest and consent', *passim*.
52. Burroughes, *Glorious Name of God*, p. 39, cf. p. 125. Parker, *Jus populi*, p. 53. Bridge, *The Wounded Consciense Cured*, pp. 27–8; *The Truth of the Times Vindicated*, p. 17. Cook, *Redintegratio Amoris*, pp. 5–6, 20; *King Charls his Case*, 1649, pp. 8, 21–2.
53. Woodhouse, (ed.), *Puritanism and Liberty*, p. 418.

think that individuals should quietly submit to the rule of a usurper. In 1650 he praised early Christian Church leaders for meekly acquiescing in the government of usurping Roman emperors. But his point may only have been that *churchmen* had no authority to lead resistance to usurpers – and not that they were irresistible.[54] Certainly Cromwell never grounded his own powers upon the rights of usurpation. When Hobbes's friend Thomas White 'maintained that possession was the only right to power', it has been said , 'Cromwell expressed the utmost abhorrence for the doctrine and ordered the book to be burned'.[55] In Cromwell's view, mere success did nothing to justify a government or a cause. But a series of successes, by contrast, might be a sign of special divine favour, particularly if those who won them were godly folk who appealed to the Lord by fasting and prayer before each critical turning point along the road to triumph. Next to consent, the most important concept in Cromwell's political thinking was Providence.

V

When he wrote to Hammond in November 1648 to justify resistance against parliament, Cromwell claimed that the army's cause was just, and that it possessed lawful power. To thrust home the message of these 'fleshly' reasonings, he drew attention to the whole tenor of recent history – in which he believed it possible to discern God's purposes for the English: 'let us look into providences; surely they mean somewhat. They hang so together; have been so constant, so clear and unclouded.'[56] God's mercies, he told his daughter Dorothy in August 1649, indicated that 'the Lord is very near', and he instanced recent events in Ireland.[57] A few months later he wrote to Speaker Lenthall, arguing that his Irish victories were 'the seals of God's approbation of your great change of government, which indeed was no more yours than these victories and successes are ours'. It was time, he concluded, for the contending religious groups in England to acknowledge the Lord's handiwork and to unite in support of the regime.[58]

The victory at Dunbar was yet another of God's 'marvellous dispensations'. The Scots erred in claiming that it was a mere 'event', of no use in discerning the divine will, for both sides had prayed to

54. Abbott, II, 338.
55. Gooch and Laski, *English Democratic Ideas in the Seventeenth Century*, p. 201.
56. Abbott, I, 697.
57. Abbott, II, 103–4.
58. Abbott, II, 173–4.

God before the battle, thus inviting His providential intervention. Moreover, the outcome at Dunbar was of a piece with recent English history, confirming the lessons which Providence had already been teaching.[59] From 1642 onwards, he told the Barebone's Assembly a series of political incidents had foreshadowed the great changes in government. Taken together, these incidents were manifestly connected, and contained so evident a 'print of Providence' 'that he who runs may read it'.[60] 'God . . . most providentially' put power 'into my hand' Cromwell told parliament in September 1654.[61]

The idea that historical events reflect divine purposes was utterly conventional among both protestants and catholics. Such works as George Carleton's frequently reprinted *Thankfull remembrance of God's mercy* had long accustomed the English to seeing their own history in providentialist terms. Nor was there anything novel about the idea that God could intervene in human affairs by changing the form of government or the person(s) of the ruler(s). In 1606 the Church's canons recognized that Providence could set up new regimes, and in his *Patriarcha* Sir Robert Filmer made the same admission. God, said the canons, might make use of such evil human actions as rebellion to effect His purposes, and once 'throughly settled' a rebellious regime could become legitimate. But this did not mean that success retrospectively justifies evil acts. Rebellion remained sinful even if the rebel leader made himself king.[62]

Cromwell and army propagandists denied that they had rebelled. In time of war it was the army above all which was entrusted with the people's safety, said a pamphleteer in 1653[63], and as we have seen Cromwell regarded the army's actions as legitimate resistance, not rebellion. He never claimed that Providence could justify evil deeds. But he and others argued that it had validated the use of extraordinary powers in times of necessity. The Bible demonstrated that on occasion the Lord had granted special commissions permitting private individuals to do things for which public authority would ordinarily have been required. The New Model army's success showed that it had been given a similar commission.

In 1649 Samuel Richardson asserted that the army's proceedings were 'justified by the word of God'. He cited the example of Phineas,

59. Abbott, II, 339.
60. Abbott, III, 54.
61. Abbott, III, 454.
62. *Bishop Overall's Convocation-Book, MDCVI* (1690), p. 59. Filmer, *Patriarcha and Other Political Works*, p. 62.
63. *The army no usurpers, or the late Parliament not almighty and everlasting* (1653), p. 9.

who by slaying some idolators had averted the Lord's wrath from Israel. Phineas 'was no magistrate', but his deed was 'an act of judicature', and the people he killed 'were his superiors, for they were Princes'. The Bible manifestly approved of Phineas's conduct: 'God doth in express words commend it, and reward it.'[64] A year later Cromwell argued in much the same way in a letter to Philip Lord Wharton, suggesting that God sanctioned the actions of those who had destroyed the Stuart monarchy just as much as he had Phineas's. Mere human reason would have condemned Phineas, but the Lord was wiser, and Cromwell ended with a warning against 'mistaken reasonings' which contradicted God's approbation witnessed in the hearts of saints and in 'signal outward acts.'[65]

The notion that the soldiers were saints in arms possessing a divine commission to reform the land was commonplace among apologists for the army from 1647. They 'were instruments of God's own choosing', said William Dell in that year, and he declared that 'I have seen more of the presence of God in that Army, than amongst any people that ever I conversed with in my life.'[66] They were 'by Divine Providence modelled into a body', said a pamphleteer in January of the same year, and their father was 'God himself' who had brought them into being 'not only without but against the contrivences of human policy'. Indeed, '[m]any of the members thereof' were 'able by an eye of faith to behold him, who is the king of saints, walking in the midst of them.'[67] The power of God, said another writer in November, was 'absolutely the supreme power' even if it resided 'in a company of mean men'. God had set up and maintained the New Model army and it was there that His power was now to be found. So the troops need not worry if their actions lacked parliamentary authorization.[68]

Those who saw the soldiers as saints in arms were divided on the wider significance of this idea. Some regarded the army's power as only temporary and believed that it existed solely because there was an emergency in which the public safety was at stake. Usually, argued John Goodwin in 1649, it was the people as a whole who held ultimate power, but in an emergency authority might come to reside

---

64. Samuel Richardson, *An Answer to the London Ministers Letter* (1649), p. 3. The biblical reference is to Numbers chapter 25.
65. Abbott, II, 189–90.
66. William Dell, *The Building and Glory of the Truely Christian and Spirituall Church* (1647), sig. A4b, a1b.
67. W. G., *A Just Apologie for an Abused Armie* (1646), pp. 2–3.
68. *A Little Eye-salve for the Kingdome and Armie* n.p., n.d., [1647], pp. 4, 6, 7.

in 'such a part of it as shall be spirited and strengthened by God', and he clearly had the army in mind. In his view, *everyone* was empowered to act for the 'preservation and benefit' of the commonwealth though it happened that the army was particularly well placed to do so. Once normality had been restored, power would return into the hands of the people and their representatives.[69] Others, by contrast, maintained that the army and the saints in general should continue their rule. 'When we began the war there was this in our minds,' said William Sedgwick in 1649, 'that we were the saints', and that 'the saints are to have the high places in the earth.' Though initially sceptical, Sedgwick came to recognize that the troops were in fact the saints. ''Tis now clear', he informed them, that God will 'set up an everlasting kingdom for the saints that shall never be destroyed: And all must own you and confess you to be the holy people.'[70] Some regarded the events of the later 1640s as a consequence of necessity, possessing only fleeting importance. But Fifth Monarchists believed that they augured the approach of the rule of the saints on earth.[71]

Appeals to Providence by Cromwell and others failed to persuade everyone, and probably contributed to the growth of doubts about the whole enterprise of discovering God's purposes in events. Filmer came to abandon the idea that Providence could alter the royal succession. When some grounded Cromwell's powers upon Providence in the parliament of 1654, others observed that 'the providences of God are like a two-edged sword', and that if success proved divine approval 'a thief may make as good a title to every purse which he takes by the highways'.[72] Providence was too liable to misconstruction to serve as a trustworthy guide to action, declared Nathaniel Ward in 1650, and God had in any case told us only to abide by His will revealed in Scripture, not by what we imagined to be providences. Whether particular circumstances constituted a case of necessity was something that should be judged by a public assembly, and not by individual soldiers.[73]

69. John Goodwin, *The Obstructors of Justice* (1649), p. 32; *Right and Might Well Met* (1648), p. 5.
70. William Sedgwick, *Justice upon the Armie Remonstrance* (1649), pp. 23; *A Second View of the Army Remonstrance* (1649), pp. 33–4.
71. The Fifth Monarchists are discussed in Bernard Capp, *The Fifth Monarchy Men* (1972), and their political ideas are briefly surveyed in Perez Zagorin, *A History of Political Thought in the English Revolution* (1954), 96–105.
72. Burton, I, xxx
73. Nathaniel Ward, *Discollominium* (1650), p. 18. Cromwell's talk about Providence

Cromwell himself toned down his views on Providence towards the end of his life. At the time of the Barebone's Parliament his attitudes inclined towards those of the Fifth Monarchists. 'God doth manifest it be a day of the power of Christ', he told them at the beginning of the assembly, 'having, through . . . so much trial . . . made this to be one of the great issues thereof, to have a people called to the supreme authority upon an avowed account.'[74] But he soon became disillusioned with the meeting's radicalism, and turned against the Fifth Monarchists. His first speech to the parliament of 1654–55 denounced 'the mistaken notion of the Fifth Monarchy', rejecting the claims of the group unless they could 'give clear manifestations of God's presence with them', and he reverted to the same theme in 1657, criticizing his former friend Thomas Harrison and others.[75] Though he still appealed to Providence and necessity (for instance, to justify war with Spain, and the rule of the major-generals) Cromwell made it plain that deductions drawn from Providence were useless 'without or against the word' of God, and in his final years he arguably placed less emphasis upon the concept.[76]

The providentialist and millenarian notions which helped to lead him to destroy the traditional constitution may have receded in his later years, but the belief that all legitimate government must stem from the people's will remained, and he hoped to restore freely elected parliaments. One practical reason why he found this difficult was that such parliaments would have tried to reduce the burden of taxation by disbanding the army – a prospect which the soldiers naturally feared. Other more theoretical reasons were connected with Cromwell's views on the purposes of government, for he suspected that a free parliament would subvert these aims, not least by persecuting the godly.

almost certainly underlay Gee's rather sceptical attitude towards the subject: Gee, *The Divine Right*, pp. 61–96, esp. p. 66.
74. Abbott, III, 63.
75. Abbott, III, p. 437; IV, p. 489.
76. Abbott, IV, pp. 261, 274–5, 473; cf. III, p. 592. The fullest recent discussion of the ideas of Providence of Cromwell and his contemporaries is Blair Worden, 'Providence and politics in Cromwellian England', *Past and Present*, CIX (1985), 55–99. See also Worden's 'Oliver Cromwell and the Sin of Achan' in Derek Beales and Geoffrey Best (eds), *History Society and the Churches: essays in honour of Owen Chadwick* (Cambridge, 1985), pp. 125–45, and Karl H. Metz, ' "Providence" und politisches Handeln in der englischen Revolution (1640–1660). Eine Studie zu einer Wurzel moderner Politick, dargestellt am politischen Denken Oliver Cromwells', in *Zeitschrift für Historische Forschung*, XII (1985), 43–84.

VI

Cromwell thought that the forms of government were indifferent and could vary, but that its goals or ends remained unchanging.[77] If *salus populi* – the public good or safety – demanded a change in forms then such change was fully justified. People had preferences among the possible varieties of government, but few were so wedded to their chosen model that they thought it altogether indispensable. Amongst believers in the Divine Right of Kings most held that such republican governments as those of Venice and the United Provinces were acceptable if inferior regimes. The Jacobean catholic William Barret was a rare exception in claiming that monarchy was the sole valid kind of government, and it was only late in life that Filmer reached the same conclusion.[78] Harringtonian republicans argued that the distribution of wealth in England made a restoration of monarchy impossible, but their importance should not be exaggerated though their opinions were vigorously expressed in Richard Cromwell's parliament. The common view was that several forms of government were possible; which was best depended upon circumstances. In 1651 Cromwell claimed that 'a settlement with somewhat of monarchical power in it would be very effectual' in England,[79] and most doubtless agreed with him.

Cromwell held that the purpose of government was to promote the public good. Like Charles I, he believed that the people's safety justified breaches of settled law: 'if nothing should be done but what is according to law, the throat of the nation may be cut', he said when defending the rule of the major-generals.[80] The Civil War, he claimed in 1658, had been fought to maintain 'the liberty of these nations; our civil liberties as men, our spiritual liberties as Christians'.[81] He stressed the role of churchmen in the conspiracy to subvert these liberties.[82] 'Arbitrary power,' he said in 1650, 'men begin to be weary of, in kings and churchmen; their juggle between them mutually to uphold civil and ecclesiastical tyranny begins to be transparent.'[83]

---

77. Abbott, I, 697; cf. III, 591.
78. William Barret, *Ius Regis* (1612), pp. 8–9. Filmer, *Patriarcha and Other Political Works*, 231–5.
79. Abbott, II, 507.
80. Abbott, IV, 275.
81. Abbott, IV, 705; cf. 720.
82. Abbott, IV, 705.
83. Abbott, II, 200.

Arbitrary, unlimited power was objectionable because it enabled its possessor(s) to invade liberties – particularly the religious liberties of the godly. These were the liberties about which Cromwell cared most. The aim of government, he said in 1657, was to promote 'the interest of the people of God in the first place',[84] and he declared that one of the great virtues of the Humble Petition and Advice was that its provisions secured the liberty of the people of God 'so as they have never had it'.[85] He insisted that the civil authorities were empowered to punish blasphemers and other profane persons,[86] but saw himself as a champion of liberty of conscience for orthodox Calvinists, whatever their views on Church government. The protection of the rights of independent congregations was, he said in 1656, 'one of the main ends for which God hath planted me in the station I am in'.[87] 'Liberty of conscience', said Cromwell, 'is a natural right'.[88]

Cromwell believed that the 'great fundamentals' were 'civil rights and liberties' and 'liberty of conscience'.[89] Of these, the second was more important than the first. In order to secure these fundamentals, it was necessary to prevent any man or group from acquiring arbitrary power. In his own opinion, Cromwell himself had held arbitrary power after the dissolution of the Rump, and again after the dissolution of Barebone's. On both occasions he had been anxious to give up the power as soon as possible.[90] He praised the Instrument of Government because it limited his power, and asked that the Humble Petition and Advice be revised to make the Protector financially accountable to parliament.[91] Earlier, he argued, the Rump had wielded equally unlimited power, and any parliament which sat perpetually could do the same. If parliament controlled the army it would be in an excellent position to perpetuate itself and to impose whatever religion and form of government it chose.[92]

It followed that parliaments should sit for only a limited period and that they should not have sole control over the armed forces.

---

84. Abbott, IV, 481.
85. Abbott, IV, 490.
86. Abbott, III, 586.
87. Abbott, IV, 360. The best recent discussion of the views on toleration of Cromwell and his contemporaries is Blair Worden, 'Toleration and the Cromwellian Protectorate', in W. J. Sheils (ed.), *Persecution and Toleration: Studies in Church History*, 21 (1984), 199–233.
88. Abbott, III, 459.
89. Abbott, IV, 513.
90. Abbott, III, 454–5.
91. Abbott, III, 455; IV, 492–3.
92. Abbott, III, 588; IV, 486.

Cromwell also held that as a safeguard of fundamental liberties the executive powers of government should be separated from the legislative and the judicial.[93] Though he argued that government should rest upon consent, he refused to grant full sovereignty to the people represented in parliament, claiming that essential rights would not be adequately safeguarded without a written constitution incorporating a variety of checks and balances. The ideas of the separation of powers and of constitutional checks and balances first gained common currency in England in the later 1640s and 1650s – because many felt that both king and parliament had abused their authority. 'The more checks, the better the constitution', said one member in 1659.[94]

Cromwell argued that in every government there must be some fundamentals, which could not be questioned even by parliament itself. The Instrument of Government, he believed, incorporated a number of fundamentals, including 'government by a single person and a parliament', and the provision that parliament sit for only a limited term.[95] The powers of Protector and parliament were to be 'co-ordinate', and neither was to have sovereignty over the other.[96] Without some such conditions arbitrary government could too easily develop. Like the Instrument, the Humble Petition and Advice was intended to guard against arbitrary power. The resurrection of a second parliamentary chamber, for example, introduced what one member termed 'a balance, a medium between the House and the single person'[97].

Cromwell's belief in fundamentals prevented him from handing full sovereignty to parliament. But it did not harmonize with the idea that government stems from consent. For what right had he, rather than the people's elected representatives, to declare certain principles to be fundamental? In both of his parliaments this point proved a major bone of contention between members and the Protector. The sovereign power of the people in parliament continued to be asserted – not least by such republicans as Haselrig and Scot (who had themselves flouted parliament's privileges in 1648).[98] In their opinion it was parliament alone which could introduce constitutional change.

---

93. Abbott, IV, 487–8.
94. Burton, III, 157.
95. Abbott, III, 458–9.
96. The history of the concept of coordination is discussed in C. C. Weston, 'Coordination – a radicalizing principle in Stuart politics', in Margaret Jacob and James Jacob, (eds), *Origins of Anglo-American Radicalism* (1984), pp. 85–104.
97. Burton, II, 22.
98. Burton, I, xxv; cf. II, 380, 389–90, 440–1.

Others held that there was no need for such change. In 1654 Goddard mocked his fellow members, who talked as though 'each man had liberty to propose his own *Utopia*, and to frame commonwealths according to his own fancy' as if England were now being instituted – and were not already a long-established State.[99]

Disagreements on what the constitution was, or should be, created practical difficulties. For example, it was unclear whether the unicameral parliament of 1656 had inherited the rights of the old House of Lords, and this made it hard to know what powers they had in Naylor's case. The famous trial of the Quaker James Nayler for blasphemy highlighted divisions of attitude among members and raised important constitutional issues. Traditionally it was the Lords who passed sentence on malefactors, and it was doubtful whether the assembly of 1656 had any authority to punish Nayler. Calls for the restoration of the old constitution were as much a response to such practicalities as a consequence of deep veneration for the past. There would be no rest until the return of 'that old constitution of King, Lords, and Commons', said one member of the Lower House in 1658, while another declared that 'to bring us to stability is to have recourse to the ancient constitution'.[100]

This belief in the virtues of the old constitution underlay parliament's offer of the kingship to Cromwell in 1657. Cromwell's wide powers were already quasi-monarchical, but unlike the powers of a king they were ill-defined at law: Broghill observed that an act of the reign of Henry VII validated obedience to usurping kings – but not to usurping Protectors.[101] Speaker Widdrington told Oliver that for him to accept the kingship would be 'a change of name only'.[102] Cromwell already exercised such traditional kingly powers as minting coins with his head and inscription, and his style of life had become increasingly monarchical. Crucially, Widdrington observed that the powers of English monarchs were specified by the law: 'The King's prerogative is part of the law'.[103] This was the main point of the offer of kingship. The activities of the major-generals had persuaded many that the time had come to restore traditional ways. 'They are so highly incensed against the arbitrary actings of the

---

99. Burton, I, xxxi–ii.
100. Burton, II, 412, 414.
101. Abbott, IV, 460.
102. Burton, I, 398.
103. Burton, I, 403.

major-generals', said one commentator, 'that they are greedy of any powers that will be ruled and limited by law'.[104]

In the end, Cromwell refused the title of king. Considerations of expediency certainly influenced his decision. But typically he justified his action by appealing to Providence and to conscience. Providence, he said, had 'blasted the title' of king – and he 'would not seek to set up that that Providence hath destroyed and laid in the dust'.[105] Oliver declared that if he accepted the Crown 'I should do it doubtingly'. But 'whatever is not of faith' 'is sin to him that doth it.[106] So conscience demanded that Cromwell refuse the kingship.

The old constitution was finally restored only with the return of the old dynasty. Those who believed that power stemmed from the people could claim that the Restoration took its force from popular consent. The return of Charles II did not mean the victory of Coke's theory of the ancient constitution, nor the demise of notions of contract and of legitimate resistance, which lived on in Whig theory. Cromwell's doctrines of the separation of powers, of coordination among the different ruling elements in the constitution, and of the need for written fundamentals were also destined to a long future, on both sides of the Atlantic. Of course, the fact that Cromwell adopted these positions had little to do with their later survival. His association with appeals to Providence, by contrast, may well have aided the demise of the doctrine – for after the Restoration few statesman claimed that divine Providence gave them the power to flout the law or the constitution.

104. Quoted in C. H. Firth, *The Last Years of the Protectorate* (2 vol, Oxford, 1900), I, p. 126.
105. Abbott, IV, 473.
106. Abbott, IV, 513.

CHAPTER TEN

Cromwell and his contemporaries

John Morrill

I

The dominant voice in most of the preceding chapters has been Oliver Cromwell's. So many of his letters and accounts of so many of his speeches have come down to us and are readily available to us in nineteenth- and twentieth-century editions, that he has proved one of the most accessible and open of Englishmen. In seeking to make sense of him, the essays in this volume have quite properly allowed him to speak for himself. They have not been insouciant or uncritical; but they have presented a picture of a man very close to the image he projected of himself.

There was another Cromwell, the man presented to us by his contemporaries. It is a rather different image, of a man consumed by personal ambition, a man whose religious enthusiasm was in part fraudulent, a man of little loyalty to friends, colleagues or the causes he espoused. This image does derive in part from writings committed to paper in his lifetime – Leveller accounts of him, for example[1]; but it derives rather more, and rather too much, from the reflections of contemporaries written down much later, through the distorting glass of the Restoration, when both experience and prudence prevented accurate recollection. Without accusing Edmund Ludlow, Richard Baxter, Bulstrode Whitelocke and Edward, earl of Clarendon of deliberate distortion,[2] it is unsafe to depend upon their

1. See below, pp. 262–5.
2. C. H. Firth (ed.), *The Memoirs of Edmund Ludlow* (2 vols, Oxford, 1894), esp. I, pp. 318–20, 347–59, 366–72, 398–72, 398–411, 432–5; II, pp. 10–15, 20–9 (but see A. B. Worden (ed.), 'A Voyce from the Watchtower', *Camden Society*, 4th ser., XXI (1978), pp. 1–10, 55–80 for discussions of the authenticity of the text); N.

memoirs as the best guide to how Cromwell was viewed in his own lifetime.

This chapter has then a dual purpose: it seeks to clarify how those who encountered Cromwell at first hand recorded their impressions *at the time*; and it attempts thereby to confirm and to qualify what modern historians perceive to be his character, precepts and practice. The picture that comes down to us from the 1640s and 1650s proves to be less black-and-white, less stereotyped, than that to be found in the memoirs of those who wrote to blame him for the Restoration. In the uncertainties, hesitancies and grudging acknowledgments of those who wrote before 1660, we can gain a better sense of the ambiguities, and the price, of that achievement.

II

Oliver Cromwell was the subject of well over two hundred tracts and broadsheets in his own lifetime.[3] All aspects of his career – as soldier, statesman, and servant of God – were the subject of discussion in a variety of genres: from execrable poems via playlets and spoof speeches to serious and weighty political analyses. The latter attracted equally long and serious defences of his conduct by his friends. We shall consider examples of all these genres. At his death, sermons were preached to memorialize his character and achievement, and three serious biographical sketches were published,[4] all, it would seem, journalistic ventures directed at the market rather than as part of a State-managed cult of personality. Indeed, one of the striking things about the eighteen months after his death was the lack of controversy about his memory and about his personal achievement.

In what follows we shall consider the unfolding debate about Cromwell in chronological sections. We shall find, as one would expect, that the volume of reference to him fluctuates over time. His local military exploits apart, he was little referred to in print until his very public row with the earl of Manchester in the autumn of

---

Keeble (ed.). *The Autobiography of Richard Baxter* (Harmondsworth, 1974), esp. pp. 45–55, 60–72, 85–9; E. Hyde, earl of Clarendon, *History of the Great Rebellion* (6 vols. 1887), bk IX §5, bk X §§125, 132, 136, 168–9, bk XV §§147–56; B. Whitelocke, *Memorials* (Oxford, 1847), *passim* – most references to Cromwell abstracted and printed in Abbott, II and III

3. This chapter is based on a reading of items identified by a trawl through G. Fortescue, *Catalogue of the Pamphlets . . . of George Thomason* (2 vols, 1908), and the entry for 'Cromwell' in D. G. Wing, *Short Title Catalogue . . . 1641–1700* (3 vols, 1945–52) and items encountered serendipitously.

4. See below, pp. 275–82.

1644, and then not again, his national military exploits apart, until the late summer of 1647. From then until mid-1649 he was the subject of intense criticism from several directions, charges of personal ambition being constantly to the fore. Between 1649 and the middle of 1654, the volume of criticism dropped away. A new peak was reached in the following eighteen months down to the end of 1655, before declining again over the last three years of the Protectorate, not returning to 1648 or 1655 levels even at the height of the kingship crisis in 1657. This finding is itself rather surprising. But much more surprising was the absence of any campaign of vilification in the eighteen months after his death. As we shall see, the publications of that period are often cautious in their praise, and none is uncritical. But with the exception of a sermon preached before the Lord Mayor and Aldermen of London two days after his death,[5] there were few attacks on him until after the Restoration.

III

Cromwell first became a public person in the winter of 1644/5. Fenland fogs obscured him until the age of forty; and his intemperate interventions in the debates of the Long Parliament gave him a notoriety within the House of Commons that did not extend far beyond its walls. He was not one of the five members accused of treason by the king at the turn of 1641/2, nor one of the dozen commoners charged with treason in *His Majesty's Declaration to all his loving subjects concerning the proceedings of this present Parliament* of 12 August 1642. His seizure of the Cambridge plate gave him a brief notoriety, but in the welter of events that summer, his name would have been quickly forgotten by most people. His exploits as a cavalry commander in East Anglia and especially his controversial role at the battle of Marston Moor were widely reported[6] and would have given him a high profile at Westminster and throughout the counties of East Anglia, and his religious radicalism was well publicized (even though the House of Commons chose to censor the versions of his letters that they ordered to be printed in order to remove some of his fiery puritan rhetoric).[7] But it was his outbursts against his commanding officer, the second earl of Manchester, conducted through

---

5. T. Cartwright, *God's Arraignment of Adam* (1658), discussed below, pp. 276–7.
6. C. H. Firth, 'Marston Moor', *T. R. H. S.*, n. s., VI (1899), *passim*; P. R. Newman, *The Battle of Marston Moor* (Chichester, 1984), *passim*.
7. See above, pp. 66–7.

the presses as well as in parliament,[8] culminating in his appointment as lieutenant-general of the New Model in the spring of 1645, that finally established him as a figure of lasting national renown. Even so, he was listed thirteenth in a list of 'warlike worthies' drawn up in 1646,[9] being listed after regional commanders such as Brereton, Massie and Sir William Fairfax. More striking is the description of him in an early (military) history of the achievements of the New Model, written in 1647 by one of its chaplains, Joshua Sprigge. This began with an account of Sir Thomas Fairfax that emphasized his personal honour and professionalism. Of Cromwell, it said:

. . . long famous for godliness and zeal in his country, of great note for his service in the House; accepted of a commission at the very beginning of the war; wherein he served his country faithfully and it was observed God was with him and he began to be renowned; insomuch that men found that the narrow room whereunto his first employment had confined their thoughts must be enlarged to an expectation of greater things and higher employments whereunto divine providence had designed him for the good of this kingdom.[10]

The myth of the man peculiarly singled out by Providence was clearly already well established.

In late 1647 a sustained assault on him was launched by the Levellers, and especially by John Lilburne. There is no doubt that the latter felt deeply and personally betrayed. Cromwell had launched the campaign to have him released from prison in 1640 and to have his sentence quashed, and had been an ally in the bitter in-fighting within the armies of the Eastern Association in 1643–44.[11] But whatever the secrets of the dealings of the two men in the late summer of 1647, Lilburne clearly felt that he had been duped and betrayed by the lieutenant-general. Cromwell, it was alleged, had called upon the Leveller leaders to join with him in a campaign to get rid of a corrupt parliament and to bring round the devious king to a package deal that would promote civil liberties and religious freedom. In the event, once Cromwell had secured their support in

8. J. Bruce and D. Masson (eds), 'Documents relating to the quarrel between the Earl of Manchester and Oliver Cromwell', Camden Society (1975), passim.
9. J. Vicars, *Magnalia Dei Anglicana* (1646), preface. This is a four-part military history of the whole civil war. Vicars' potted biographies of the parliamentarian generals (*England Worthies* [1647]) lists him as involved in only seven engagements.
10. J. Sprigge, *Anglia Rediviva* (1647), pp. 10–11.
11. C. Holmes, 'Colonel King and Lincolnshire Politics' *H. J.*, XVI (1973), 462–471; M. A. Gibb, *John Lilburne the Leveller* (1948), pp. 94–102.

uniting the army and in purging the parliament, he had cast the
Levellers aside and had put peace proposals to the king that had been
secretly drawn up in meetings between senior army officers and his
patrons in the House of Lords. The events of the weeks after the
Putney debates were repeatedly retold over the next eighteen
months, as were the events in the weeks before and after Pride's
Purge and the regicide.[12] The allegations were constant, in essence
that a feigned love of civil liberties masked a brutal ambition for
personal power. Time and again the names of Cromwell and Ireton
were linked. Fairfax was their stooge, the other officers their
lackeys.[13] The form of that ambition was never quite clear: at times
Cromwell was portrayed as being obsessed with baubles of honour –
the earldom of Essex, for example[14] – or more generally as a man
who had set himself above the people – one who sought 'to make
himself able, like Cardinal Wolsey, to say "I and my king" '[15]; at
times he is said to have had a desire to exercise absolute power himself. He had used the House of Lords, it was said, to break the power
of the Levellers, but

hath since been the principal instrument to pluck up the House of Lords by
the roots, as usurpers and encroachers, because they would not join with
him to cut off the king's head . . . that he might be absolute king himself,
as now he is, and more than ever the king was in his life.[16]

His means to these vainglorious ends were seen as strictly machiavellian. One of the most interesting discussions of this was simply called

---

12. For a cross-section, see B. L., Thomason Tracts (=T. T.), E421(19), J. Wildman,
    Putney Projects (1647); T. T., E409(22), J. Lilburne, *The Juglers Discovered* (1647);
    T. T., E421(20), *A Word to Lieutenant General Cromwell and two words for the set-
    tling of the King Parliament and Kingdom* (Dec. 1647); T. T., E422(12), *Machivilian*
    [sic] *Cromwell* (Jan. 1648); T. T., E568(20), J. Lilburne, *An Impeachment of High
    Treason against Oliver Cromwell and his Son in Law Henry Ireton* (1664); *The Hunt-
    ing of the Foxes* (1649) in D. M. Wolfe (ed.), *Leveller Manifestoes of the Puritan
    Revolution* (New York, 1944), pp. 355–83; and *Legal Fundamental Liberties* (1649)
    in W. Haller and G. Davies (eds.), *Leveller Tracts* (New York, 1944), pp. 399–
    449. The replies published on Cromwell's behalf make the same point: e.g.
    T. T., E431(7), *A Vindication of Lieutenant General Cromwell and Commissary
    General Ireton* (March 1648), *passim*.
13. E568(20), pp. 29–33, 53–61 [this tract is miscatalogued by Fortescue as E508(20)];
    Wolfe, *Manifestoes*, *passim*; E409(22), *passim*; E421(19), pp. 5–7.
14. Cromwell's family had changed their name from Williams to that of Cromwell
    in the days of Thomas Cromwell, who became earl of Essex shortly before his
    fall in 1539/40 (they were connected in the female line). Cromwell's wife,
    Elizabeth Bourchier, was also descended from fifteenth-century earls of Essex.
15. E568(20), p. 4.
16. Haller and Davies, *Tracts*, p. 413.

The Machiavilian Cromwell, and the subtitle of *The Juglers Discovered* included the following: 'discovering the turncoat Machiavell practices and under-hand dealings of Lieut.-Gen. Cromwell and his son-in-law, Commissary General Ireton and the rest of the hocus-pocus faction.' Several pamphlets offer a detailed narrative of Cromwell's machiavellian deceptions. One attributed all his acts to four 'principles':

1. that every single man is judge of just and right, as to the good and ill of a kingdom.
2. that the interest of honest men is the interest of the kingdom, and those only are deemed honest men by him that are conformable to his judgment and practice . . .
3. that it is lawful to pass through any form of Government for the accomplishing of his ends and therefore either to purge the Houses, and support the remaining party by force everlastingly; or to put a period to them by force, is very lawfull, and suitable to the interest of honest men.
4. that it is lawful to play the knave with a knave.

Lilburne added this marginal gloss:

He holds it lawful for a man to commit any manner of wickedness and baseness whatsoever that can be named under the sun for the accomplishment of a man's proposed end, whether in itself it be wicked or righteous . . . the people's lives really and truly being of no more value to him than so many dead dogs.[17]

This charge of constitutional antinomianism was one that was to stick. It is far and away the most persistent accusation that Cromwell had to face for the rest of his life. He was rarely to be accused of hypocrisy in his religion. His sincerity as a believer and as a promoter of godly reformation and of moral rearmament was rarely challenged. But his political judgment, his personal integrity in political dealings, his manipulation and abandonment of those who thought him their friend, these were charges that were brought again and again.

The Levellers were the first to create a reasoned assault on his reputation; but their charges were quickly taken up and crudely developed in a sequence of poems, lampoons, and play-form dialogues. They were mainly produced by royalist hacks out to make trouble and a few quid from cheap belly-laughs. Examples include a play *Crafty Cromwell or Oliver ordering our new state wherein is discovered the traiterous undertakings and proceedings of the said Nol and his levelling crew;* a spoof constitution entitled *A New Magna Carta*

17. E568(20), p. 60 (from a section entitled, 'sundry reasons inducing Major Huntingdon to lay down his commission').

Enacted and Confirmed by the High and Mighty States, the Remainder of Lords and Commons now sitting at Westminister in empty Parliament under the command and wardship of Sir Thomas Fairfax, Lieutenant Generall Cromwell (our present king) . . . *and Prince Ireton*; and a spoof speech, claiming to be Oliver's words as he lay dying at Chepstow, *Lieutenant General Cromwell's Last Will and Testament* (July 1648). One striking thing about these satires from 1647 to 1649 was the straightforward way they assert that Cromwell was striving for the Crown, as the title of *A New Magna Carta* makes clear, or, as *The Last Will and Testament* puts it, 'yet he must confess withall that there were some rising thoughts of personal sovereignty in him'.[18]

By far the most sophisticated and weighty of the early satires was one published in June 1649 and entitled *A Most learned, conscientious, and devout exercise, held forth the last Lord's Day*. This was in the form of a sermon alleged to have been preached by Cromwell to a gathered congregation at Sir Peter Temple's lodgings in Lincoln's Inn Fields.[19] The text of the sermon was the classic defence of obedience to constituted authority in Romans XIII, 'let every soul be subject unto the higher powers; for there is no power but of God. The powers that be are ordained of God.' The tract is full of knockabout stuff. For example,

my very face and nose are weekly maligned and scandalized by those scribbling Mercuries . . . it's true I have a hot liver, and that's the cause my nose is red; for my valour lies in my liver not in my heart[20];

and there is an extraordinary passage proving that women as well as men have souls, and that although most godly women are very plain (the wife of Major-General Lambert, for example, whom he calls 'something foggy and sunburnt . . . what nature had denied her as ornament without, I found she had within her') there are a few women both godly and comely, for instance his landlady at the siege of Pembroke.[21] But the bulk of the pamphlet is very sophisticated, combining a highly sympathetic account of the need to obey the new regime with a cleverly portrayed vanity in Cromwell himself. Whoever wrote this pamphlet was an Independent who wanted to portray Cromwell as a man whose personal ambition was destroying the good cause he had been in large part responsible for establishing.

18. B. L., T. T., E426(17), Feb.1648; E427(15), Feb.1648; E454(13), quote at p.2.
19. B. L., T. T., E561(10) by (?) Aaron Guerden.
20. Ibid., p. 1.
21. Ibid., pp. 3–5.

Dear brethren and sisters, I speake not in ostentation, but with thankfulness and glory to him who made me so useful an instrument in this blessed work of reformation. For (beloved) it was I that juggled the late king into the Isle of Wight, it was I dissolved the treaty, it was I that seized upon and hurried him to Hurst Castle, it was I that set petitions on foot throughout the kingdom against the personal treaty and for bringing the king, and other capital offenders, to justice, it was I that continued with the help of my son Ireton the large Remonstrance of the Army. It was I that prescribed the erecting of the High Court of Justice, and which brought the King to his trial. In a word it was I that cut off his head, and with it all the shackles and fetters of the Norman slavery and bondage . . . It was I that surprised the Levellers at Burford and in Northamptonshire, it was I that broke their design and appeased the rest, and which have healed up the late distempers in the army, whereby the land is now restored to this blessed peace, tranquillity and plenty.[22]

The pamphlet also contains a highly sophisticated diagnosis of the Irish situation and of the possibilities of dividing and ruling the anti-parliamentarian factions there.[23] Its most remarkable passage describes how on the eve of the king's execution a group of moderates had drawn up a petition to Sir Thomas Fairfax begging him to use his authority as head of the army to prevent the regicide. This petition was allegedly taken to him by Obadiah Sedgwick, one of Warwick's chaplains. Cromwell and Ireton, hearing of it, are said to have gone to Fairfax's quarters in Queen's Street to reason with him, and to have taken two troops of horse to detain him in case reason failed. Fairfax ('fitter far to be passive than active in the affairs of state; he is fitter for a charge than a council; and the truth is . . . he wants brains to do anything of moment . . . willing always to submit to better judgments than his own') was readily convinced not to heed the petition.[24] In a pamphlet that for the most part put un-flattering glosses on actual events, the account of this episode deserves further study. This is far longer, more complex and more sophisticated than any other satire produced before the mid 1650s, and it is just possible that it is a hostile account of a speech that Cromwell actually made.[25] It is in form very similar to his known addresses. It could have been an attempt on his part, on the eve of

22. Ibid., pp. 6–7.
23. Ibid., pp. 9–12.
24. Ibid., pp. 7–8.
25. Sir Peter Temple, at whose house the meeting is supposed to have been held, was an ally of Saye's in the Long Parliament who, like him, deplored the regicide. It is just possible that 'Aaron Guerden', the author, was related to John Gurdon, another member of the independent alliance who refused to go along with the regicide.

his departure for Ireland, to rally the old Independent alliance which had been sundered by the regicide.[26] If so, it backfired, and was published in this carefully rewritten version. It certainly sums up the criticisms of Cromwell made in the years 1647–49: no attack on his military record or the sincerity of his religious beliefs; deep suspicion of his constitutional pragmatism as masking personal ambition and a ruthless disregard for the rule of law.

IV

Agitation against Oliver died out (with the Levellers) after June 1649. From then until 1654 little was written directly for or against him beyond glowing accounts of his military victories in Ireland and Scotland. The episodes which have caused most controversy in the last century or so – his massacres of the inhabitants of Drogheda and Wexford – were not the subject of debate or denunciation at the time (or in any of the writings about him before the Restoration). The most important discussion of him in these years came in Andrew Marvell's *An Horation Ode Upon Cromwell's Return from Ireland*. Previous accounts of him had been unambiguous: but, as Blair Worden says of the *Ode*, 'it is not merely that there is ambiguity in the poem. There is layer upon layer of it.' As he goes on to show, at its core is both deep regret that monarchy and the political morality of the age had been brutally destroyed, and a recognition that 'the future belongs to Cromwell, who has razed cavalier culture, and after Cromwell to [those] who will inherit the world Cromwell will have built', a dark and doubtful, but an inevitable world. Destiny had to be their choice as well as his.[27]

The events of 1653 – though the establishment of the Protectorate in December far more than the dissolution of the Rump in April or the establishment of the Nominated Assembly – created a second wave of criticisms and personal attack. There was some criticism in 1653, such as the broadside entitled *A Charge of High Treason exhibited against Oliver Cromwell esquire*, which George Thomason noted to have been 'scattered about the street the 14 of August 1653'.[28] This attack concentrated on the summoning of the Nominated Assembly

---

26. D. Underdown, *Pride's Purge* (Oxford, 1971), ch. 4 and J. S. A. Adamson, 'The Peerage in Politics, 1645–9', Univ. of Cambridge Ph. D. thesis (1986), chs 5 and 6, for the collapse of the Independent alliance.
27. A. B. Worden, 'Andrew Marvell, Oliver Cromwell and the Horation Ode', in K. Sharpe and S. Zwicker (eds.), *Politics of Discourse* (Princeton, 1987), pp. 147–180. The Ode is helpfully reprinted on pp. 147–50.
28. B. L., T. T., 669 f. 17, no.54.

in July and accused Oliver of ignoring the rights of 'the Lords the people of England' to elect their own representatives. It called upon all men to appear armed in self-defence at their county towns on 16 October to elect knights and burgesses to attend a free parliament. Characteristically it said little about the dissolution of the Rump. As Blair Worden and Austin Woolrych have pointed out, not the least puzzle about that episode was the failure of those who witnessed this military putsch to put their accounts of it, and Cromwell's part in it, into print.[29]

From his assumption of the Protectorate, Cromwell was subjected to a steady flow (though not a flood) of criticism. It came from all sides: from the royalists and religious presbyterians on the one side, from disillusioned Independents and sectaries on the other. The former stressed his tyranny in overthrowing established authority and in setting himself up at the point of the sword. His rule was characterized as lacking legitimation and as a brutal exercise of will at the expense of the rule of law. Typical was the broadsheet *A Declaration of the Freeborn People of England now in arms against the tyranny and oppression of Oliver Cromwell* which called for an end to 'all assumed and usurped power', for the due bounds of all magistracy to be observed, ancient liberties (such as those enshrined in Magna Carta and the Petition of Right) to be restored, no man imprisoned without cause shown, and for freely elected parliaments on a regular basis.[30] The same charges occur in *A picture of a new courtier drawn in a conference between Mr Timeserver and Mr Plainheart*, a typical socratic dialogue in which Plainheart is made to say that Oliver as Protector had the faults of kings only more so.

The difference lyeth only in this, that his little finger is thicker than the king's loins, as will appear by these considerations: first his imprisoning of men contrary to law, at his own will and pleasure, yea many of the Commonwealth's best friends . . . the King chastiseth us with whips, but Cromwell chastiseth us with scorpions.[31]

Plainheart rammed home his point with an attack on unparliamentary taxation, on Protectoral interference with free parliaments, and with an unfavourable comparison between Charles I's failure before La Rochelle and Cromwell's at Hispaniola.

29. A. B. Worden, *The Rump Parliament* (Cambridge, 1974), pp. 364–76; A. M. Woolrych, *Commonwealth to Protectorate* (1982), pp. 68–102.
30. B. L., T. T., 669 f. 17, no.70 (March 1655).
31. B. L., T. T., E875(6), p. 11 (April 1656).

As in 1647–49, Cromwell's ruthlessness and political deviousness was portrayed as being grounded in personal vanity and ambition, as in the pamphlet *The Protector so-called in part unveiled . . . the abominable apostacy, backsliding, and underhand dealing of the man above-mentioned who [has] usurped power over the nation.*[32] Many former friends now began to see him as a good man corrupted by power. As Colonel Robert Duckenfield, a religious Independent and governor of Chester castle under the Rump, put it in a letter to Cromwell, 'I believe the root and tree of piety is alive in your Lordship, though the leaves thereof, through abundance of temptations and flatteries, seem to me to be withered much of late.'[33]

One of the interesting developments of the mid-1650s was the emergence of a genre of pamphlets that attempted an even-handed review of the Protector and of his government, combining praise and criticism. Such 'balanced' writing is harder to find before 1653 except, and perhaps importantly, in Marvell, but thereafter we move on from his hesitant, grudging, fatalistic admiration of a man who had come to bestride his times, to much less coy and more frank evaluations. Let us consider one lengthy example, William Sedgwick's[34] *Animadversions upon a letter and paper first sent to His Highness by certain gentlemen out of Wales.* The 'letter and paper' had been published as *A Word for God*, a bitter attack on the Protectorate for its backsliding, 'inasmuch as many Barnabases are carried away with their dissimulations,[35] and as well ministers as military men'.[36] It had gone on to rehearse the godly work of the 1640s and the new modelling of Church and State, and to recall the millenarian hopes expressed (under Cromwell's signature) in the army's *Declaration from Musselburgh*[37] on its way to invade Scotland. It concluded with a fierce denunciation of the current régime for forgetting the great deliverances worked by God through them, for abandoning the great task of extirpating popery in all its forms and for restoring 'old abominable and damnable impieties', for chopping and changing

32. B. L., T. T., E857(1) (Oct. 1655).
33. *T. S. P.*, III, 294.
34. Sedgwick had been town preacher at Ely since 1644 and therefore may have been well known to Cromwell.
35. A reference to Galatians 2 v. 13. Barnabas had refused to join St Paul in eating with the Gentiles, and generally opposed his evangelical strategy.
36. Sedgwick, *Animadversions*, p. 3.
37. Printed in A. S. P. Woodhouse, *Puritanism and Liberty* (1938), pp. 474–8.

constitutions without warrant, for imposing illegal taxes, and for imprisoning gentlemen, ministers and soldiers without showing cause.[38]

These were the stock criticisms from royalists and sectaries alike. Sedgwick's reply was a long and reasoned analysis of the needs of the times, rich in biblical parallels and injunctions. But at its heart was a consideration of Oliver himself. He was a 'great man risen from a very low and afflicted condition', whose eminency rested upon his religious faith, especially 'as to the active and practical part' of it. He was said to have a natural talent for public work, he was not easily discouraged but had 'a singular spirit of brightness, cleanness, largeness and self-denial'. Above all he had 'an honesty, an integrity, a nobleness in him, which did attract and unite honest men to him'. Guided by the word of the Lord in his great undertakings, he had not flinched to break civil and worldly powers where God's work demanded it. Yet there was another side, Sedgwick admitted: 'I must prefer Cromwell *in querpo*[39] (with the stamp of God upon him) before Oliver Protector, and his train of greatness.' His reputation was damaged by 'the dirt and malice cast upon him and the pollution contracted from the nature of the work', but also by more personal failings: 'rash promises, sudden engaging for and as sudden turning from things, which shows want of foresight, incontinency and inconstancy of mind. . . .'[40] Here we encounter that central paradox of his nature: his providentialism and his impulsiveness, his appeal to a purposeful God and his constant chopping and changing of governmental forms. The well-disposed Sedgwick can endorse the integrity of intention without disguising the irresolution that others took for serpentine self-advancement.

Once again, it is instructive to see which of Cromwell's actions provoked most controversy. The dissolution of the Rump did not lead to much of an attack on Cromwell personally; nor did the establishment of the Nominated Assembly. It was the Instrument of Government, and the proclamation of Cromwell as Head of State which provoked a rather delayed but then intense burst of criticism from both conservative and republican sources. Thereafter grumbling persisted, but neither the establishment of the major-generals nor the

---

38. Sedgwick, *Animadervasions*, p. 5.
39. No such word in my dictionary. Probably *'en cuerpo'* = Spanish for 'in a close-fitting dress: without cloak or coat: in one's short sleeves'. I owe this rendering to Andrew MacLennan.
40. Sedgwick, *Animadversions*, pp. 19–25.

debate on the kingship provoked as much dissent as had the events of 1647–49 or the establishment of the Protectorate. It is noticeable that defences of Cromwell used royal language and metaphor far more freely from mid-1656 on (before the formal offer of the Crown by parliament in February 1657).

John Moore in November 1655 defended the Protectorate on religious and providentialist grounds. God by his 'secret decree has brought Oliver to power over three kingdoms' so that the godly 'may without fear of any penal, bloody, persecuting law, worship Him in the administration of the Gospel with freedom and liberty, without confines of time or space'; it is a form of rule that 'comes closest to Christ'. But he also drew freely on the language of biblical kingship: 'God's main desire for his people on earth is, that the powers below touch not his anointed . . .'[41] A pamphlet of September 1656 praised Cromwell for his 'vigour of mind, undaunted courage of spirit, true bravery of his resolutions and unparallelled design . . . his zeal for the true protestant religion'. These kinglike qualities were summed up in the title of the pamphlet: *The Unparallelled Monarch, the Portraiture of a Matchless Prince.*[42]

One other point about the pro-Cromwellian writing is even more striking: the constant analogy drawn between the careers of Cromwell and Moses. It was an analogy Cromwell himself was fond of drawing. He never hailed himself as Moses, but he constantly compared the English people's experiences as being those of the Exodus: of deliverance from Egyptian (= Stuart) tyranny; of a crossing of the Rea Sea (=Regicide); of being led by the pillar of Fire (= God's Providences on the battlefield); and of being in the desert for many years unable to reach the Promised Land because of a lack of submissiveness to the will of God.[43] In such a schema, Cromwell himself had to be a type with Moses.[44] Others made this explicit. Hugh Peter was the first man known to me to draw the parallel in a sermon in Westminster Palace Yard on 17 December 1648.[45] More startling was Gerrard Winstanley's preface to *The Law of Freedom in a Platform* (November 1651), which addressed Cromwell thus: 'God hath

41. B. L., T. T., E860(5), pp. 2,5,*passim*.
42. B. L., T. T., E1675(1) (Sept. 1656)
43. For an example of Cromwell's reliance on the Exodus story, see, e.g. Abbott, III, 442.
44. For the general theme of puritan typologies and the way events in the Old Testament were genuinely believed to prefigure and to be the basis for modern choices, see J. F. Wilson, *Pulpit in Parliament* (Princeton, 1965), pp. 197–207.
45. Underdown, *Pride's Purge*, p. 164.

honoured you with the brightest honour of any man since Moses' time, to be the head of a people who have cast out an oppressing Pharaoh.'[46] The first lengthy working out of the parallels was attempted by John Spittlehouse, in Cromwell's honeymoon period with the Fifth Monarchists between the dissolution of the Rump and the meeting of the Nominated Assembly. He summarized the criticisms of Cromwell he had heard from the Cavaliers and from 'demi-royalists' (viz. presbyterians) and from other sectaries:

I shall oppose [to their views] the story of Israel's deliverance from their Egyptian bondage; in which simile, I shall compare our present General to Moses . . . [He has] taken us from the power of our Egyptian Pharaoh, and from the iron furnace of tyranny, and from the brick kilns of Papacy, Prelacy and Presbytery, these three days journey to serve the Lord in our present wilderness condition; he it is that hath brought destruction upon our Pharaoh and all his host and that hath led us through the Red Sea of a bloody war which we have by providence passed and in which our aforesaid Pharaoh and all his host have been destroyed.[47]

Similar passages can be found in several tracts in 1655,[48] but the most remarkable example came rather later, in 1659, in a 309 page tract, aptly subtitled *The 24 Heads of the Ascents wherein his late Highness our Lord Protector stands parallel with the great Patriarch Moses.*[49]

Throughout Oliver's period as Lord Protector, other biblical typologies were employed, principally by his supporters: David, Joshua and Gideon were perhaps the most common.[50] But none was used as frequently, or developed as fully, as that of Moses. After his death, however, a second biblical figure was brought forward as being a type for Cromwell. Two sermons preached at memorial services for Oliver were later published. One was preached by George Lawrence in London in mid-October 1658, and the other was preached by Thomas Harrison in Dublin cathedral in February 1659. Both drew parallels between Cromwell and Josiah, king of Judah

---

46. C. Hill, *Gerrard Winstanley, The Law of Freedom and Other Writings* (Harmondsworth, 1972), p. 275
47. B. L., T. T., E697(11), J. Spittlehouse, *A Warning Piece Discharged* (May, 1653), pp. 6,10.
48. For another excellent example, see B. L., T. T., E729(4), 'E. M.', *Protection Persuading Obedience or a Word of Peace to the Well Affected, A Caveat to the Contentious and a Rod for the Rebellious* (Feb. 1654),pp. 2–3,17.
49. B. L., T. T., E1799(2), H. Dawbeny, *History and Policie Reviewed in the Heroic Transactions of His Most Serene Highness, Oliver the Lord Protector* (1659).
50. E. g., B. L., T. T., E1675(1) p. 9; E729(4), pp.16–18; T. T., 669 f. 21(8), Robert Row[land], *Upon the Much Lamented Departure of the High and Mighty Prince, Oliver.*

from B.C. 640 to BC. 609, noted for his purging of all heathen altars and superstitious objects from the Temple – for his reconsecration of the Temple, and for his defeat by Assyrian and Egyptian forces. Neither preacher spared his congregation a sense of doom. They praised Cromwell's achievements in purifying and strengthening the true protestant religion; his justice and valour; his restoration of order and discipline. But both recalled Josiah's end'. Harrison fuses two images:

. . . after all this, when Josiah had prepared the Temple, then Necho King of Egypt comes and cuts him off, when the Church had most need of him; for Israel to lose a Moses when they are yet in the wilderness (which is the case at this day), this is lamentable.

But he concludes that if the people stick by God's ordinances, God will this time not expose them to a new Necho.[51] Lawrence was gloomier. His exegesis of the story of Josiah is more nuanced. But after listing Josiah's (=Cromwell's) achievements –

. . . his zeal against a proud, cruel and lofty person . . . his assistance to confederates . . . his justice, commutative and distributive, punishing few and rewarding many . . . his religion, being a man mighty in scripture, enjoying a praying spirit, a spirit of communion with God, love to all saints, and living by faith . . .

– he goes on to list Josiah's weaknesses, such as over–confidence and pride. The preacher's conclusion, however, is bleaker still: 'consider our miseries which we deserve, even the miseries that befell Judah and Jerusalem after Josiah's death . . . a captivity stricter and longer than a Babylonian.[52]

These biblical analogues are not matched in the pro–Cromwellian literature by any parallels from classical or modern times: Cromwell is not likened to Scipio, Augustus, Constantine or Gustavus Adolphus. Nor did his opponents develop unflattering typologies of Old Testament, classical or modern tyrants, except occasionally and in passing. Thus the anonymous author of a tract late in 1655 said that it was 'very unworthy of him, having begun in the spirit, to go down to Egypt and to be building again the things which He [God] hath destroyed'.[53]

51. T. Harrison, *Threni Hybernici of Ireland Sympathising with England and Scotland in a sad Lamentation for loss of their Josiah* (1659), p. 9.
52. B. L., T. T., E959(4) (incorrectly listed in Fortescue as E549[4]), G. Lawrence, *Peplum Olivarii, or a Good Prince Bewailed by a Good People* (1658), pp. 3–4, 24–33.
53. B. L., T. T., E857(1) *The Protector so-called in Part Revealed* (Oct. 1655), p. 19.

By the time of his death, therefore, a pattern had been set. Cromwell was recognized as a man sincere in his faith, driven by what he believed, rightly or wrongly, to be the will of God. His enemies railed against his personal ambition and disregard for civil liberties. But his claims to godliness of intent were not seriously challenged. For his supporters his willingness to subordinate means to ends, his political pragmatism, was justified because of the justness of those ends; for his detractors his arbitrariness with forms revealed the weakness and folly of his attempts to read the mind of God. His enemies saw him as dangerously self-deluding; his defenders as the only hope of salvation for a nation bewildered, divided and without a sense of direction:

If the people are the end of Government, that which most aims at the good of the people, comes nearest that end, and since the people, in regard of the variety of humours, can neither well determine, nor consent about the circumstances of their own safety, he certainly doth a very laudable action that turns doubtful emergencies and dangerous junctures of time into their advantage . . . tis the physician, that is to say, the wise man in power, that must be the judge, not the patient, that is to say the multitude in danger.[54]

V

His death served only to reinforce these public images. It did not produce a great flood of writing. Perhaps the low-key nature of State mourning helps to explain the lack of response. There was little to challenge. Cromwell's corpse, incompetently embalmed and stinking, was privately interred within three weeks of his death. An effigy made from a cast of the corpse lay in state for three months, in a manner modelled on the precedent of James I, initially on its back invested in purple, later upright and wearing an imperial Crown. The State funeral took place on a bleak late November day, and it took the hearse and the long crocodile of dignitaries seven hours to wend their way around central London to Westminster Abbey. The event was poorly reported, and when the procession finally reached the Abbey there was no ceremony of any kind: the effigy was bundled into a grave and everyone departed. Amazingly there was no formal funeral oration. Cromwell never had what was expected by and for all good puritans: a funeral sermon which apotheosized his witness and drew out the marks and signs of a saving faith. The State also missed the opportunity to rehearse (and to publish) a full account

---

54. B. L., T. T., E715(5) [anon.], *Sedition Scourged or a View of that rascally paper entitled a Charge of High Treason Exhibited against Oliver Cromwell*, p. 4.

and memorial of the benefits of the Revolution.[55] It is something which defies explanation. As we have seen, there were two sermons printed in the following months at memorial services for the departed Protector.[56] But other eulogies were few and far between. Even the versifiers were uninspired, Edmund Waller and John Dryden being distinctly below their best. Thomas Sprat produced the one telling image:

> Thy wars, as rivers·raised by a shower
> Which welcome clouds do pour;
> Though they at first may seem
> To carry all away, with an enraged stream,
> Yet did not happen, that they might destroy
> Or the better parts annoy;
> But all the filth and mud to scour
> And leave behind a richer slime,
> To give a birth to a more happy power
> And make new fruits arrive, in their appointed time.[57]

In this dross is one pearl: 'a richer slime'. It nicely captures the ambiguities of Cromwell's perceived achievement.

Against this conventional praise, we can set some continuing criticism. It is limited in scope and volume. Neither his death, nor (perhaps more surprisingly) the removal of his son, led to any outpouring of criticism. There was some, typified by the Fifth Monarchist Christopher Feake's *A Beam of Light Shining in the Midst of Much Darkness and Corruption*, a long and thorough history of England cataloguing the oppressions of the 1630s, the liberations of the 1640s, and 'the abominations that made desolate and laid in the dust the most honourable interest under Heaven' in the 1650s.[58] The hinge of the Revolution, the moment of betrayal, came in December 1653, when

> that General, those great commanders, those under-officers and soldiers which had publicly owned and submitted unto the Lord Jesus, by word and writing . . . do now lift up the idol into the throne of supreme authority in

---

55. The fullest account is in 'L. S.', *The Perfect Politician or a full view of the Actions (military and civil) of Oliver Cromwell* (1660), pp. 339–345. Even press coverage at the time was sketchy. See M. J. Seymour, 'Public relations in Interregnum England', Univ. of Cambridge Ph. D. thesis (1986), ch. 6.
56. See above, pp. 272–3.
57. *Three Poems upon the Death of His Late Highnesse Oliver, Lord Protector of England, Scotland and Ireland* (1959), p. 20.
58. B. L., T. T., E980(5), p. 51

these nations and relinquish the cause, the interest and service of Him that was their Saviour and Lord Protector.[59]

The most remarkable attack on Cromwell in the eighteen months between his death and the Restoration was also an oblique one. It came in a sermon preached before the Lord Mayor and Aldermen of London on 5 September 1658, two days after his death. That date and the unusual plea in the preface to the published version of the sermon requesting the sheriff of London's protection from those who would resent his plain words, alert us to the sermon having a subtext. Thomas Cartwright's theme was *God's Arraignment of Adam*. Cartwright argued that the greater the authority one held in this world, the greater the punishment for sins both committed and permitted. Adam had responsibility for Eve and therefore as 'a superior shall be called to account not only for his own but likewise for the offences of those that are under him'. He continued:

a magistrate is as it were the physician of his subjects, upon whose prescription their lives and safeties do depend. If therefore he either administer things that are prejudicial to them or by his ill example or silence seem to countenance them, their blood may justly be required at his hands . . . As in the body natural so likewise in the politick, those diseases are most dangerous which seize first upon the head.[60]

This evocation of the head/body image was beloved of James and Charles I, of course, as a metaphor for king and people, and it seems probable that the 'head' Cartwright had in mind was Oliver. To make this clearer, he drew on even more familiar images: 'if Moses, the prince of God's people, sin, how can he expect to enter the Promised Land?'[61] He then levelled some specific charges:

If you who should be like Constantine and Theodosius . . . shall butcher them . . . those Christian people that are committed to your charge . . . if you, who are as it were fingers of that hand with which God does rule this part of the world, shall favour some, fear others, and so not judge uprightly, God will certainly sweep you away as He did Nebuchadnezzar, with the besom destruction.[62]

He later rails against magistrates 'crumbling His Zion into factions'.[63] The later parts of the sermon drift into a discussion of the faults of the City Fathers, but was the besom of destruction directed

59. Ibid.
60. T. Cartwright, *God's Arraignment of Adam* (1659), pp. 5–6.
61. Ibid., p. 7.
62. Ibid., p. 8.
63. Ibid., pp. 21.

at them or at the corpse lying at that very moment on the embalmers' table only a mile or so away? Had the City Fathers failed to tackle the abuses of the soldiery, perverted the course of justice, allowed Zion to crumble? It was a harsh judgment, and one might have expected others to spit on the grave of the dead Protector. In fact Cartwright's charges were barely heard again until after Charles II was sitting on the throne.

VI

Those eighteen months between the death of Oliver and the arrival of Charles yielded three short biographies of the late Protector: one by Samuel Carrington, one by Richard Flecknoe and the third by an anonymous author.

Of these, Richard Flecknoe's *The Idea of His Highness, Oliver Lord Protector*, dedicated to his son Richard, was the earliest and shortest (just 68 pages). It gave a glowing account of his military career, stressing that 'he never entered battle but by the port of prayer',[64] and glosses over the controversies of the 1640s (the Self-Denying Ordinance, the events of May–November 1647, etc). The Rump is brusquely dismissed as 'imperious' 'immoderate' and as 'five hundred kings instead of one'.[65] Cromwell's achievement is portrayed as a paradoxical one: at once to heal and settle and to permit a broad liberty of conscience. Thus:

If we count it so great a happiness when bones are broke and splintered, to light on such an excellent surgeon as could set them right again, and apt every splinter to its proper place; how much more happiness must it need be for states, when all disjointed and out of frame, to light on so excellent a statesman as he, who could without maim or scar set all things right again. Now if we examine what had so disjointed it, we shall find it chiefly to have been this reformation they talk so magnificently of.[66]

And

. . . [the people], none talking liberty, nor understanding it, less than they . . . above all most tenacious in their liberty of conscience, rather to follow every new fangled opinion, then remain constant to the old. This considered, he framed a militia, more to quiet then molest or trouble them, warlike in appearance, but peaceable in behaviour, nowhere entrenching on their liberties, but where they entrenched upon the privileges of government, allowing them their dear liberty (or license rather) of their tongues and for their

---

64. R. Flecknoe, *The Idea of His Highness, Oliver, Lord Protector* (1659), p. 24.
65. Ibid., p., 38.
66. Ibid., p. 54.

chiefest darling of all, the liberty to err in their opinions; he permitted them to follow and embrace what sect they pleased so they all concurred in obedience to civil government.[67]

This sounds like damning with faint praise: but there was more to be said for Oliver than he had yet said:

This point of policy many have wondered at, not knowing, it seems, or not remembering that parable in the Gospel of the good corn and tares; and but weak politicians, not to understand that who intends any great reformation, must not amuse themselves with lesser things till that performed once, then the greater of those, which in comparison seemed less before, becomes the object of their Reformation, and so by degrees, till they have reformed all. For want of which method, the ignorant and rash bring all things to ruin and confusion, by plucking down more than they can build up again; and vainly imagining the best way of reforming any part to be the total destruction of the whole. . . [whereas he] Atlas-like, could support the whole, could support so mighty a frame and machine, all composed of so many different and disjointed pieces and hinder them from slipping and falling all in pieces, which he did, riveting them so fast together, and making them all so firm cohere amongst themselves, as so many pieces of soft wax, melted and moulded all in one, could not cleave faster in one ball or sphere.[68]

Flecknoe's tract, written from the stance of a Cromwellian conservative, is the most polemical and the least critical. It sees the period 1647–53 as a time of darkness and chaos from which Cromwell had rescued the nation, restoring as much as creating. Charles I had been a tyrant, but the anarchy which civil war had produced was worse. A stern, militarized pragmatism was as much as England deserved.

Samuel Carrington's history is much fuller (272 pages).[69] It gives the most detailed and accurate account of Cromwell's campaigns at home, and of British expeditions abroad. Like Flecknoe, he brushes past the events of the winter of 1644/5, the second half of 1647, and the winter of 1648/9 and again justifies the dissolution of the Rump because of its failure to 'give the people the harvest of all their labour, blood and treasure, and to settle a due liberty in reference to civil and spiritual things'.[70] In comparison with his vagueness on the political crises of the 1640s, he gives a full account of the calling of the Nominated Assembly and of Cromwell's opening address to it, and of the 'confusion in their counsels, contrariety in their opinions,

67. Ibid., p. 58–9.
68. Ibid., pp. 59–61.
69. B. L., T. T., E1787(1), S.Carrington, *The History of the Life and Death of his most serene Highness, Oliver, Late Lord Protector* (1659). It too was dedicated to Richard Cromwell.
70. Ibid., p. 141.

dissonancy in their actings and disparity in their aims and projections' which caused it to surrender power back into his hands.[71] The establishment of the Protectorate is justified by a favourable account of the Instrument of Government and by careful attention to the various authorities who had recognized its validity.[72] There follows a narrative of the Protectorate strongest on foreign triumphs (largely silent on the major-generals and the debates in the first session of the second parliament), and a conventional character sketch. Beyond praising Cromwell's 'especial care to have piety and godliness in his armies',[73] Carrington pays little attention to religion. His technique is simply to describe the chaos and disintegration which constantly threatened and which Cromwell constantly prevented. There is no endorsement of his providentialism, nor does Carrington seek to justify the means he used to maintain order. It is a bleak but effective defence of *de facto*-ism. Thus the title of Lord Protector was:

a very fit appelation, in regard of the infantine, and as yet growing state of England, which the several factions and divisions, as also the different opinions in religion, would have exposed to a numberless kind of unavoidable miseries, had not a powerful genius, armed with Force and Judgment, protected it from ripping up its entrails and bowels by its own hands . . . .[74]

The most interesting of these three early lives is that by L. S., published in February 1660.[75] It is the longest of the three, clearly borrows from the others[76] and is at least as accurate and informed. It covers the period up to Naseby very briskly and then gives a slow, circumspect, rather coy account of both the campaigning and the politics of the years 1645–49. This covers the first 50 of the 360 pages. The next 160 pages cover Cromwell's campaigns in Scotland and Ireland. Again the tone is neutral or cautiously approbatory. The remainder reviews the Protectorate in an increasingly sour tone. The peace with the Dutch (who are likened to the Carthaginians, such natural enemies to Rome that one or the other had ultimately to be destroyed) is sharply criticized[77]; but for the most part the comments

71. Ibid., p. 163.
72. Ibid., pp. 166–72; this section is a paraphrase of Cromwell's own defence of the Instrument in his speech of 12 September 1654 (Abbott, III, 456–7).
73. Carrington, *History*, p. 344.
74. Ibid., p. 166.
75. B. L., T. T., E1869(1), 'L. S.', *The Perfect Politician or a full view of the life and actions (military and civil) of Oliver Cromwell* (Feb. 1660).
76. A simple example: the phrase 'he studies men more than books' (p. 349) is borrowed from Carrington, *History*, p. 244.
77. 'L. S.', *Perfect Politician*, pp. 254–60, and cf. 213.

are tart rather than forthright. Thus Cromwell's removal of more than a hundred members from the first Protectorate Parliament by making them swear to uphold the Instrument of Government was described as 'a laxative composition wrapped up in a Recognition, . . . a dose [which] purged some Members out of the House [whilst] others against swallowed it without any reluctance'[78]; and Cromwell is said to have set up the major-generals (his 'Viceroys') to force the royalists to pay for 'the sins of their youth', but then to have ended their power 'fearing they might in time eclipse his own greatness'.[79] This edginess is sometimes tinged with irony:

> Nothing could satisfy Caesar's ambition but a perpetual dictatorship, nor Alexander's but to have more worlds to conquer, and why should our Cromwell having the same aspiration (and inspiration above them) be satisfied with less than a perpetual Protectorship.[80]

The concluding character sketch is a masterpiece of indecision, of frustrated admiration.

> We find in the beginning of England's distractions a most active instrument to carry on the cause for King and Parliament; this pretence holding water, and proving prosperous, he then became the main stickler for liberty of conscience without any limitation. This toleration became his masterpiece in politics; for it procured him a party that stuck close in all cases of necessity. . . . After he had made use of all that could augment his interest, then humility condescended to look through his fingers at a crown, but still waiving the airy title of King, he rather chose to accept the substantial power of Protector. . . . In his governing of England, Scotland and Ireland, it is obvious to all, he studied men more than books. . . . His speeches were for the most part ambiguous, especially in public meetings, wherein he left others to pick out the meaning then did it himself. But when offenders came under his own examination, then would he speak plain English and declare his power unto them in a ranting style. They that go about to diminish his valour, do little less than rob him of his right; for in the camp his armour depressed fear, and made him stand in defiance of all guns under a demi-canon. . . . The pride and ambition which some say he was guilty of, may be easily excused as an original sin inherent in nature. . . . To conclude, he carried his design clear and hit the mark he aimed at, notwithstanding the Parliament, Triploe Heath[81] and Dunbar's engagements[82] which shows that policy and piety may both lie in a bed and not touch one another. . . . His religion must not pass my pen. In this he was zealous, not altogether like

78. Ibid., p. 272.
79. Ibid., pp. 286–9.
80. Ibid., p. 252–3.
81. The site of the rendezvous in June 1647 where the Council of the Army (officers and agitators) first met.
82. Probably a reference to the near disaster occasioned by Cromwell's poor strategic sense in late summer 1650. It led to an overwhelming victory against the odds.

the Pharisee that prayed in the Temple[83]; but really often would he mourn in secret and many times his eyes in public distil tears at the Nation's stubbornness.[84]

This is not only a marvellously ambiguous and grudging tribute to Cromwell's flawed achievement. It set a seal on a decade of public debate that centred around an acknowledgment of Cromwell's achievements as a soldier and as a convinced protestant, but which could not come to terms with an anti-formalism[85] not only over religious forms but over constitutional forms. He was unable to settle for what he had already achieved, a world made safe for the gentry and the propertied, a prudent measure of religious pluralism, an effective English imperialism, especially within Britain. He insisted on going beyond freeing the godly into liberating the ungodly, seeking to turn them from the things of the flesh to those of the spirit, from carnal reasonings to the responsibilities of Christian freedom, to recognizing and obeying the Will of God. He could not settle for a vanguard State in which an enlightened minority representing the various forms of godliness in the nation governed for the unregenerate majority. He wanted the godly to be the leaven in the lump. He wanted to find a constitutional form that would either frogmarch (Barebones/the major-generals) or wheedle (the 'healing and settling episodes') God's new elect nation, the English, to the new Promised Land. He had a vision of building a more just and a less sinful society. A man more willing to relax with his achievements, to settle for settlement, could probably have handed on a constitutional monarchy, liberal in its political and religious values, to a new royal house. But a man with a less fierce vision, with a more compromising spirit, with less certainty of God's special call to him and to England,[86] would never have risen from being a failed Huntingdon businessman and fenland farmer to be Head of State and Lord Protector of a united England, Scotland and Ireland. The nature of his achievement divided his contemporaries as it divides historians. 'L.S.' loved and hated him; respected and feared him; could see the dynamism and the wilfulness. He bears testimony to the fact that Cromwell was from the moment of his death one of the best-known and least easily understood of all the great men of history.

---

83. Whom Jesus denounced for praising God that he was better than other men.
84. L. S., *Perfect Politician*, pp. 346–50.
85. I am now using the term as Colin Davis does above, pp. 201–4.
86. In this paragraph I am using 'English' advisedly: I do not believe that Cromwell had a sense of God's election of the British.

Suggestions for further reading

CHAPTER 1: INTRODUCTION
(AND GENERAL READING)

There is a vast literature on the life and achievement of Oliver Cromwell. W. .C. Abbott, *Bibliography of Oliver Cromwell: a list of printed materials* (Cambridge, Mass., 1929), already itemized more than 3,000 works! It has been supplemented by an appendix in volume IV of his edition of Cromwell's Writings and Speeches (below), and by an essay by Paul Hardacre in *J. Mod. Hist.*, 33 (1961).

There are two separate collections of Cromwell's own words. The earlier and more readily available was compiled by Thomas Carlyle and first published as *Oliver Cromwell's Letters and Speeches, with elucidations* (2 vols, 1845). This was reprinted in many editions throughout the nineteenth century and a particularly attractive edition, complete with an excellent introduction by C. H. Firth, and notes by S. C. Lomas (3 vols) was published in 1904. This was, or is widely assumed to have been, superseded by the edition by W. C. Abbott, *The Writings and Speeches of Oliver Cromwell* (4 vols, Cambridge, Mass., 1937–47). This contained far more Cromwell material, especially in relation to foreign affairs in the 1650s, and it had far more editorial matter. It also lacked the extraordinary asides and rhetorical comments with which Carlyle enjoyably but distractingly littered his edition. The authors of the essays in this collection have always cited Abbott as being the standard work of reference. But it should be stressed that for everyone up to and including final year undergraduate level the Carlyle/Lomas edition is more convenient to use, easier to come by and contains almost everything of importance. Abbott has an appearance of scholarly solidity which disguises hundreds of factual errors, some very poor and uncritical editing and some unreliable texts. Most disappointing is his failure to explain his editorial policy in regard to the often widely discrepant original texts for the speeches. The texts printed in the (rare) collection edited by C. L. Stainer, *Speeches of Oliver Cromwell* (Oxford, 1901), are generally to be preferred. The 26 most important speeches have been published, largely from the Stainer edition, but without the notes, just as this book goes to press, by Ivan Roots (ed.), *Speeches of Oliver Cromwell* (London, 1989).

Any serious study of the period has to begin with a thorough reading of S. R. Gardiner, *History of England from the accession of King James I to the outbreak of the civil war* (10 vols, 1882), *History of the Great Civil War* (4 vols, 1893), *History of the Commonwealth and Protectorate* (4 vols, 1903), completed after Gardiner's death by C. H. Firth, *The Last Years of the Protectorate* (2 vols, Oxford, 1909). Among recent surveys, G. Aylmer, *Rebellion or Revolution?* (Oxford, 1987), is a clear account; Derek Hirst, *Authority and Conflict 1603–58* (1985), is especially recommended on both the 1640s and 1650s; and both T. Barnard, *The English Republic* (Harlow, 1982), and A. Woolrych, *England without a King* (Lancaster, 1983), are excellent introductions to the 1650s.

There are legion biographies of Cromwell, and the authors of each chapter have referred below to those most pertinent to their theme. A cross-section of recommendable ones is given here, but this does not imply that others are worthless.

J. Morley, *Oliver Cromwell* (1900).

C. H. Firth, *Oliver Cromwell and the Rule of the Puritans* (Oxford, 1900).

S. R. Gardiner, *Oliver Cromwell* (1909).

J. Buchan, *Oliver Cromwell* (1934).

R. S. Paul, *The Lord Protector* (1955).

M. P. Ashley, *The Greatness of Oliver Cromwell* (1957).

C. Hill, *God's Englishman* (Harmondsworth, 1970).

A. Fraser, *Cromwell, Our Chief of Men* (1973).

R. Howell, *Cromwell* (1977).

If only three of these can be chosen for their contrasting views, then the editor's personal recommendation is that a good sense of the man be gained from reading the lives by Firth, Paul and Hill.

In addition to the eighteen volumes of his *History*, and his biographical essay, S. R. Gardiner wrote *Cromwell's Place in History* (1898), a stimulating set of six lectures. One collection of essays stands out as of particular importance: I. Roots (ed.), *Cromwell, A Profile*, (1973), with especially influential essays by Roger Crabtree on foreign policy and Hugh Trevor-Roper on Cromwell and his parliaments. The most important recent work on Cromwell has undoubtedly been that of Blair Worden, who is writing what is certain to be the outstanding biography of him written this century: thus far, four important essays have appeared: three are listed at the head of the reading for Chapter 7; the fourth on Marvell's Horation Ode on Cromwell's return from Ireland was first published in *H.J.*, XXVII (1984) and subsequently reprinted in a slightly amended version in K. Sharpe and S. Zwicker (eds), *Politics of Discourse* (Princeton, 1987).

CHAPTER 2: THE MAKING OF OLIVER CROMWELL

The purpose of the essay in this volume is to offer the most comprehensive guide to Cromwell's early life. Almost all existing accounts rely on the same small number of documents, all printed in Abbott, *Writings and Speeches*, vol. I. The fullest account has been J. L. Sanford, 'The Early Life of Oliver Cromwell' in his book *Studies and Illustrations of the Great Rebellion* (1858). Mark Noble, *Studies in the Protectoral House of Cromwell* (1787), and J. L. Weyman, 'Oliver Cromwell's Kinsfolk', *E.H.R.*, VI (1891), fill out his social context. Robert Paul, *The Lord Protector*, (1955), covers the early life better than any other biography.

CHAPTER 3: OLIVER CROMWELL AND THE LONG PARLIAMENT

Cromwell's mercurial personality has defeated all his biographers to date, and none can be recommended without serious reservations. The best account of his career during the Long Parliament remains that presented by S. R. Gardiner in his *History of the Great Civil War 1642–9* (4 vols, 1893; rep. 1987). The greatest recent advances in the study of Cromwell have been achieved by Dr Blair Worden, whose study of *The Rump Parliament 1648–53* (Cambridge, 1974), and subsequent articles on aspects of Cromwell's career, have presented the most subtle and convincing account to date of the paradoxes and apparent contradictions of his extraordinary personality. Of central importance are Worden's articles, 'Cromwell and Toleration', in W. Sheils (ed.), *Studies in Church History* (1984), and 'Oliver Cromwell and the Sin of Achan', in D. Beales and G. Best (eds), *History, Society and the Churches: essays in honour of Owen Chadwick* (Cambridge, 1985).

Cromwell's early parliamentary contributions may be gleaned

from the parliamentary diary of Sir Simonds D'Ewes, portions of which are published as *The Journal of Sir Simonds D'Ewes* edited by W. Notestein (New Haven, Conn., 1923), and W. H. Coates (New Haven, Conn., 1942); and in the Yale edition of the *Private Journals of the Long Parliament*, edited by W. H. Coates, A. S. Young and V. F. Snow (New Haven and London, 1982–). Important aspects of Cromwell's role in the Long Parliament are examined in Clive Holmes, 'Colonel King and Lincolnshire Politics, 1642–1646', *H.J.* XVI (1973), 451–484; while his activities in the localities are discussed in Holmes' *The Eastern Association in the English Civil War* (Cambridge, 1974). Differing interpretations of the background to the Self-Denying Ordinance are presented in A. N. B. Cotton, 'Cromwell and the Self-Denying Ordinance', *History*, LXII (1977), 211–231; M. A. Kishlansky's fine study of *The Rise of the New Model Army* (Cambridge, 1979); and in J. S. A. Adamson, 'The Baronial Context of the English Civil War', *T.R.H.S.*, 5th ser., XL (1990).

Major surveys of the relationship between the army and politics at Westminster, including substantial material on Cromwell's role, are presented in David Underdown, *Pride's Purge: Politics in the Puritan Revolution* (Oxford, 1971); Worden's study of the Rump Parliament (cited above); Austin Woolrych, *Soldiers and Statesmen: the General Council of the Army and its Debates 1647–48* (Oxford, 1987); and in Woolrych, *Commonwealth to Protectorate* (Oxford, 1982), covering the period between the dissolution of the Rump and the emergence of the protectoral régime after the failure of Barebone's Parliament. Important evidence relating to the end of the Rump is presented in C. H. Firth, 'Cromwell and the Expulsion of the Long Parliament in 1653', *E. H. R.*, VIII (1893).

Cromwell's relations with the nobility are discussed in J. S. A. Adamson, 'The English Nobility and the Projected Settlement of 1647', *H. J.*, XXX (1987), 567–602, and in Adamson, *The Nobility and the English Revolution* (Oxford University Press, forthcoming).

The best account of Cromwell's later parliaments remains H. R. Trevor-Roper, 'Oliver Cromwell and his Parliaments', in *Religion, the Reformation and Social Change* (1967), reprinted in I. Roots (ed.), *Cromwell: A Profile* (1973).

CHAPTER 4: CROMWELL AS A SOLDIÉR

C. H. Firth, *Cromwell's Army* (1902; 3rd edn, 1921), is unsurpassed as a general account of the parliamentary armies of the civil wars and is judicious about Cromwell's qualities as a commander. Though needing correction in detail, C. H. Firth and G. Davies, *The*

Regimental History of Cromwell's Army (2 vols, Oxford, 1940: reprint imminent), is indispensable to the military historian. Gardiner's *Great Civil War* and *Commonwealth and Protectorate* maintain a high level of accuracy and authority with regard to the campaigns and battles that Cromwell fought. The best of the several strictly military histories by professional soldiers is P. Young and R. Holmes, *The English Civil War: a military history of the three Civil Wars 1642–51* (1974). A. Woolrych, *Battles of the English Civil War* (1961), focuses mainly on Marston Moor, Naseby and Preston. The biography that deals most fully and vividly with Cromwell's campaigns and battles is John Buchan, *Cromwell* (1934). The army's political activities between the First and Second Civil War, and Cromwell's part in them, are dealt with by A. Woolrych, *Soldiers and Statesmen* (Oxford, 1987). H. M. Reece is preparing a book on the subject-matter of his valuable D.Phil. thesis, 'The military presence in England 1649–60' (Univ. of Oxford, 1981), and Ian Gentles' large work on the army in society from 1645 to 1653 is at an advanced stage of preparation.

CHAPTER 5: THE LORD PROTECTOR, 1653–1658

The scholarly literature on Cromwell as Protector is thin. It consists chiefly of two fine essays by Blair Worden on Cromwell's religious politics, 'The sin of Achan', in D. Beales and G. Best (eds), *History, Society and the Churches* (Cambridge, 1985), and 'Cromwell and toleration', in W. Sheils (ed.), *Studies in Church History*, XXI (Cambridge, 1984); and H. R. Trevor-Roper, 'Oliver Cromwell and his parliaments', in I. Roots (ed.), *Cromwell: a Profile* (London, 1973) and elsewhere, a provocative essay which is helpfully modified by P. Gaunt, 'Law-making in the first protectorate parliament', in C. Jones, M. Newitt and S. Roberts (eds), *Politics and People in Revolutionary England* (Oxford, 1986). Additionally, D. Hirst, 'Marvell's Cromwell in 1654', in J. M. Wallace (ed.), *The Golden and the Brazen World* (Cambridge, Mass., 1985), discusses early attitudes to the protector. Until the forthcoming study by Blair Worden appears, in general the Protector has to be approached through studies of the Protectorate. R. Sherwood, *The Court of Oliver Cromwell* (1977), gives a nuts-and-bolts account of Cromwellian house-keeping, while G. E. Aylmer, *The State's Servants* (1973), provides invaluable information on the personnel of Cromwellian government. Three unpublished Ph.D. theses, by P. G. I. Gaunt (Exeter, 1983) on the council, by D. Massarella (York, 1978), on the politics of the army, and by H. Reece (Oxford, 1981) on the army's role, are important; Massarella summarizes part of his argument in an essay in I. Roots

(ed.), *Into Another Mould* (1981). That collection also contains a valuable examination of local government reform by S. Roberts. Roots
himself discusses 'Cromwell's ordinances' in G. E. Aylmer (ed.),
The Interregnum (1972), while M. Ashley, *Financial and Commercial
Policy under the Commonwealth and Protectorate* (2nd edn, Oxford,
1962), is still the best treatment of its themes. On politics rather than
policy, A. Woolrych, *Commonwealth and Protectorate* (Oxford, 1982),
and 'Last quests for settlement', in Aylmer, *Interregnum*, analyses
both the beginning and the end. In the latter volume, C. Cross, 'The
church in England 1646–1660', and D. Underdown, 'Settlement in
the counties', discuss local ecclesiastical and political developments.
Religious preoccupations are also illuminated by W. Lamont, *Godly
Rule 1603–1660* (1969), while Roots, 'Swordsmen and decimators –
Cromwell's major-generals', in R. H. Parry (ed.), *The English Civil
War and After* (1970), introduces those disturbers of the local scene.
Lastly, a study of another man, W. H. Dawson, *Cromwell's Under-
study* (1942), on Lambert, calls the Protector himself into question.

CHAPTER 6: CROMWELL, SCOTLAND AND IRELAND

Books

T. C. Barnard, *Cromwellian Ireland. English government and reform in
Ireland, 1649–1660* (Oxford, 1975).

G. Donaldson, *Scotland: James V to James VII* (Edinburgh, 1965),
ch. 18.

F. D. Dow, *Cromwellian Scotland, 1651–1660* (Edinburgh, 1979).

R. Dunlop, *Ireland under the Commonwealth* (2 vols, Manchester,
1913).

W. Ferguson, *Scotland relations with England. A survey to 1707* (Edinburgh, 1977), ch. 7.

C. H. Firth, (ed.), *Scotland and the Commonwealth* (Scottish History
Society, 1895)

C. H. Firth, (ed.), *Scotland and the Protectorate* (Scottish History
Society, 1899)

C. S. Terry, (ed.), *The Cromwellian Union* (Scottish History Society,
1902).

Thesis

L. M. Smith, 'Scotland and Cromwell. A study in early modern
government' (Univ. of Oxford, D.Phil. thesis, 1979).

Articles and Essays

T. C. Barnard, 'Planters and policies in Cromwellian Ireland', *Past
and Present*, (1973).

P. J. Corish, 'The Cromwellian conquest, 1649–53', in T. W. Moody, F. X. Martin and F. J. Byrne (eds), *A New History of Ireland*, III, *Early Modern Ireland, 1534–1691* (Oxford, 1976), pp. 336–52.

P. J. Corish, 'The Cromwellian regime, 1650–60', ibid., pp. 353–86.

T. M. Devine, 'The Cromwellian Union and the Scottish burghs: the case of Aberdeen and Glasgow, 1652–60', J. Butt and J. T., Ward (eds), *Scottish Themes. Essays in Honour of Professor S. G. E. Lythe* (Edinburgh, 1976), 1–16.

E. D. Goldwater, 'The Scottish franchise: lobbying during the Cromwellian protectorate', *H.J.*, XXI (1978), 27–42.

P. J. Pinckney, 'The Scottish representation in the Cromwellian parliament of 1656', *Scottish Historical Review* XLVI (1967), 95–114.

I. Roots, 'Union and disunion in the British Isles, 1637–60', I. Roots (ed.), *'Into another Mould'. Aspects of the Interregnum* (1981), pp. 5–23.

H. R. Trevor-Roper, 'Scotland and the Puritan Revolution', *Religion, the Reformation, and Social Change* (1967).

Excellent modern surveys and analyses of the Cromwellian regime in Scotland and Ireland are provided by Dow, Smith and Barnard. Corish provides a full account of both the conquest and the activities of the conquerors in Ireland. Briefer surveys of Scotland in the same years are to be found in Donaldson and Ferguson. Goldwater and Pinckney study some aspects of politics in Scotland in the 1650s, while Devine makes a preliminary investigation of the country's economic performance. Trevor-Roper's over-view of England's ambitions in Scotland and the latter's reactions is highly stimulating but very one-sided. Important collections of source material (relating to Scotland) are provided by Firth and Terry, and (relating to Ireland) by Dunlop.

CHAPTER 7: CROMWELL'S RELIGION

A. Blair Worden, 'Toleration and the Cromwellian Protectorate', in W. J. Sheils (ed.), *Persecution and Toleration: studies in church history* xxi (Oxford, 1984), 199–233.

Blair Worden, 'Providence and politics in Cromwellian England', *Past and Present* CIX (1985), 55–99.

Blair Worden, 'Oliver Cromwell and the sin of Achan', in Derek Beales and Geoffrey Best (eds), *History, society and the churches* (Cambridge, 1985), 125–45.

B. Geoffrey F. Nuttall, *The Holy Spirit in Puritan Faith and Experience* (Oxford, 1946).

Geoffrey F. Nuttall, *Visible Saints: the congregational way 1640–1660* (Oxford, 1957).

Geoffrey F. Nuttall, *The Puritan Spirit: essays and addresses* (1967).

Alan Macfarlane (ed.), *The Diary of Ralph Josselin 1616–1683* (1976).

Paul S. Seaver, *Wallington's World: a puritan artisan in seventeenth century London* (1985).

The point needs to be made that the serious literature on Cromwell's religious thinking and its context has been surprisingly thin. Students should now begin with Blair Worden's work (listed under A) which is indispensable. For background Nuttall remains the surest guide. Students may find it rewarding to compare Cromwell's religious sense with those of Ralph Josselin and Nehemiah Wallington.

CHAPTER 8: OLIVER CROMWELL AND THE GODLY NATION

The best entry to Oliver Cromwell's religious thinking and religious policies is through his speeches, now available in a new edition edited by Ivan Roots, *Speeches of Oliver Cromwell*. Three important articles by Blair Worden illuminate aspects of the protector's mind and activities: 'Toleration and the Cromwellian Protectorate', in W. J. Sheils, (ed.) *Persecution and Toleration* (Studies in Church History, 21, 1984); 'Oliver Cromwell and the Sin of Adam', in D. Beales and G. Best, (eds) *History, society and the churches* (Cambridge, 1985) and 'Providence and Politics in Cromwellian England', *Past and Present* CIX (1985). Protestantism in early Stuart England is best approached by way of Patrick Collinson's *The Religion of Protestants* (Oxford, 1982) and his *The Birthpangs of Protestant England* (London, 1988). E. Duffy 'The godly and the multitude in Stuart England', *The Seventeenth Century* I (1986) is a seminal article. Claire Cross opened up important issues with regard to the Cromwellian church in 'The church in England 1647–1660', in G. E. Aylmer (ed.), *The Interregnum* (London, 1972) but, apart from some work on particular localities, her lead has been little followed. John Morrill's, 'The Church of England 1642–1649', in his *Reactions to the English Civil War* (London, 1982) establishes useful lines of thought about the religious developments of the period which need to be more fully pursued in relation to the 1650s. W. A. Shaw, *A history of the English church during the civil wars and under the Commonwealth* (London, 1900) remains valuable for reference.

CHAPTER 9: OLIVER CROMWELL AND ENGLISH POLITICAL THOUGHT

The only volume to cover this period in any depth in a general survey is Perez Zagorin, *History of Political Thought in the English Revolution* (1954). For the particular themes of this chapter, the following are useful: J. Franklin, *John Locke and the Theory of Sovereignty* (Cambridge, 1978); Richard Tuck, *Natural Rights Theories* (Cambridge, 1979); J. Daly, *Sir Robert Filmer* (Toronto, 1979) – to be used with caution; *Complete Prose Works of John Milton*, 8 vols. (eds. D. M. Wolfe, E. Sirluck *et al.*) (New Haven, 1959–1982); especially vols I, III and IV; G. P. Gooch and H. Laski, *English Democratic Thought in the seventeenth century* (Cambridge, 1927); J. Wallace, *Destiny His Choice* (Cambridge, 1968); B. Capp, *The Fifth Monarchy Men*, (1972). There are some important articles in G. Aylmer (ed.), *The Interregnum* (1972) – above all the one by Skinner; and C. H. Firth, 'Cromwell and the Crown', *E.H.R.*, XVII (1902), 429–40 and XVIII (1903), 52–80, remains the fullest on that episode. Anthologies include D. Wootton, *Divine Right and Democracy* (Harmondsworth, 1986), A. Sharp, *Political ideas in the English civil wars* (Harlow, 1983) and A. S. P. Woodhouse, *Puritanism and Liberty* (1983) for the period 1647–49 and especially the Putney Debates. None of the biographies does justice to this subject.

CHAPTER 10: CROMWELL AND HIS CONTEMPORARIES

The only advice that can be given here is an encouragement to seek out the tracts and others like them that are referred to in the footnotes.

Notes on contributors

J. S. A. Adamson is a Fellow of Peterhouse, Cambridge, where he is currently Director of Studies in History. He is the author of a number of articles on seventeenth-century English history; and in 1989 was awarded the University of Cambridge's Seeley Medal for his forthcoming book, *The Nobility and the English Revolution* (Oxford University Press). In 1990 he was a Visiting Fellow at Yale University.

J. C. Davis is Professor of History at Massey University, Palmerston North, New Zealand. Colin Davis has published *Utopia and the Ideal Society* (Cambridge, 1981) and *Fear, Myth and History: the Ranters and the Historians* (Cambridge, 1986) as well as a number of articles on early modern political thought.

Anthony Fletcher is Professor of Modern History at the University of Durham, Professor Fletcher's publications include *Tudor Rebellions, A County Community in Peace and War, The Outbreak of the English Civil War* and *Reform in the Provinces*. He is a co-editor of Cambridge Studies in Early Modern British History.

Derek Hirst was educated and taught for some years at Cambridge University before moving to Washington University in St Louis, where he is currently Professor of History. His publications include *The Representative of the People? Voters and Voting in England under the Early Stuarts* (1975) and *Authority and Conflict: England 1603–1658*.

John Morrill is Fellow, Senior Tutor and Director of Studies in History at Selwyn College, and a Lecturer in History at the University of Cambridge, whither he migrated from Oxford via the University of Stirling in 1975. He has written several books, notably *The Revolt of the Provinces* (Longman edn, 1980), *Reactions to the English Civil War* (1982) and most recently (with Christopher Daniels) he has edited a collection of documents for class and seminar use on *Charles I* (C.U.P., 1988). He is the President of the Cromwell Association.

Johann Sommerville is Assistant Professor of British History at the University of Wisconsin. He took his M.A. and Ph.D. at Cambridge, and was for four years a Research Fellow at St John's College, Cambridge. He taught at Cambridge, London and Birmingham Universities before taking up his current position. He is the author of *Politics and Ideology in England 1603–42* (Longman, 1986) and of many articles.

David Stevenson is a Reader in Scottish History and the Director of the Centre for Scottish Studies at the University of Aberdeen, where he has worked since graduating from the Universities of Dublin and Glasgow. He has published a number of books on Scottish history in the seventeenth century, including *The Scottish Revolution, 1637–44* (1973), *Revolution and Counter-Revolution in Scotland, 1644–51* (1977), *The Origins of Freemasonry* (1988) and *The First Freemasons* (1988). His interest in the relationships between the three kingdoms in the British Isles led to his *Scottish Covenanters and Irish Confederates, Scottish–Irish Relations in the mid seventeenth century* (1981).

Austin Woolrych came nearest to an experience of mounted warfare when he commanded a troop of tanks at the battle of El Alamein. Since then he has been much happier as a freshman at Oxford at the age of 28, an assistant lecturer at Leeds University three years later, and first Professor of History at Lancaster University from 1964 to his retirement (more or less) in 1985. His publications include *Battles of the English Civil War* (1961), a book-length introduction to Milton's later political tracts in volume VII of the Yale edition of the *Complete Prose Works, Commonwealth to Protectorate* (Oxford, 1982), and *Soldiers and Statesmen: The General Council of the Army and its Debates* (Oxford, 1987).

Index

THE ART OF
DROWNING

FRANCES FYFIELD

SPHERE

First published in Great Britain in 2006 by Little, Brown
This paperback edition published by Sphere in 2007

Copyright © Frances Fyfield 2006

The moral right of the author has been asserted.

A CIP catalogue record for this book
is available from the British Library.

ISBN 978-0-7515-3620-1

Papers used by Sphere are natural recyclable products made
from wood grown in sustainable forests and certified in accordance
with the rules of the Forest Stewardship Council

Typeset in Plantin by M Rules
Printed and bound in Great Britain by
Clays Ltd, St Ives plc
Paper supplied by Hellefoss AS, Norway

Sphere
An imprint of
Little, Brown Book Group
100 Victoria Embankment
London EC4Y 0DY

An Hachette Livre UK Company

www.littlebrown.co.uk

For Robert Acton

With thanks to Ken, for showing me a farm quite different from the one of my childhood, and the one in this book. All mistakes are my own.

PROLOGUE

Someone wants to kill me.

It was the first time he had got this far, and he toyed with it in a thoughtful way, because he had reached this conclusion logically. Carl was always thoughtful. He only wrote something down when it was true. *SOMEONE WANTS TO KILL ME.*

He looked at the words he had typed on the screen, typed instead, *SOMEONE WISHES I WAS DEAD.* This did not have the same impact. *Wish* was different to *want.* Wishes were easier to misplace; they could be substituted by instance, by another wish, like saying to a child, you cannot have that sweet, but you can have this piece of chocolate instead. The more assertive words still sounded louder in the silence of his room. He made a correction.

SOMEBODY wants to kill me.

He shivered, typed in, *How do you know?* And then his own answer, *Perfectly obvious.* Then, *Why?* He sat back.

Because he could feel it. Because someone had invaded his

sacrosanct office space two miles from the safety of here, accessed his computer to send him the image which sat on his desk now in printed form. A black-and-white drawing of a hanged man on a gibbet, suspended over water with his feet kicking and his hands clawing at the rope round his neck, embellished with a crudely written caption, *Even the judge is judged.*

He knew someone wished him dead, because of that, because of the car and the rubbish. Because of the violence which was out there all the time, the formless desire to kill. None of that, not even the image, was nearly enough to threaten the composure of someone who lived as he did in an apartment overlooking the Thames at Canary Wharf. It defied logic to be afraid. He did not have enough money to attract pointless murder, or a sufficiently great profile to woo his own terrorist, no known affiliations to any cause or religion which excited extremes, nor enough power to excite envy. He was no more or less than an Englishman of mixed heritage who had done rather well. Not popular, yes, but that went with his territory. The weekly threats of the present and the recent past were all merely verbal and spontaneous, as harmless as shaking a fist at a passing train.

Somebody wants to kill me

He looked at the image of the hanged man, questioned it as if it could speak. Why do you want me dead, since there is nothing to survive me which is of any use to you? I have nothing to treasure except the son who does not resemble me, and once he is older, he will be free. Someone will profit from my premature death, but no one who would do this, and surely him least of all. Who wants me to feel this malice, creeping up from the river like a mist? I am not worth kidnap, let alone murder.

Who am I? he typed in, along with his own answer, *It doesn't matter.* And alongside that, *So, it's only a feeling that someone wishes you were dead? Only a feeling?*

Feelings are ephemeral. There are only passions. No one tried to push you under the train; it was crowded; we all pushed one another. There are thousands of blonde women in this city. You did not see her. Someone is playing jokes on you and your boy. You are maudlin and overimaginative because today is the tenth anniversary of your disgrace, and you are dreaming of what she would be like now.

Anniversaries have that effect.

So that was that, then. The past was past, the future what it would be, and the screen was full of the gobbledegook of legal text. He closed it down, and found the photographs long since scanned into the memory of the machine, etched into his own. He needed to dwell on them to gain perspective, to honour the dead, consult his conscience and be made humble. Mourn.

Ten years ago, and it felt like yesterday. Vivid snapshots, glowing with summer. The first one showed an aerial overview of the landscape, crisscrossed with narrow roads leading to distant huddles of buildings, which looked insignificant against the rest. There was one such huddle in the foreground, nearest to the pale patch which was the lake. The buildings seemed small and colourless against the vast expanse of gold-and-green fields, and the broad, dark bands of trees which littered the scene into the distance, the real landmarks. The lake was shrouded by trees on one side. A track led into these woods. The view encompassed miles, to where the land petered out into a blue line of sea at the top of the picture.

He went on to the next. This featured the lake itself, looking larger once in focus, the vehicles parked by the edge like tiny toys. A large piece of still water, reflecting the sun from a slate-grey surface, showing a spit of brown land protruding into the grey and another track leading away from it. The next shot was earthbound, taken from the edge of the lake, as if the camera had closed in. A lyrical picture of a hot summer day, with the trees on the far side reflecting vivid greens into the mirror of the water, through which four majestic swans – two adults followed by two cygnets – swam in a military line, leaving an elegant ripple in their combined wake. Grey summer willows encroached in the water, and a paler object drifted beneath, attached to the bank, blurred by sunlight and reflection.

The camera changed tack for the next shot, taken from behind the posse of men standing around the object, but leaving a clear view of the white body, sprawled on the bank, feet still in the water. Then a shot of the head and neck of a yellow-haired girl, beautiful in sleep, half-profile, with sandy eyebrows and soft down on her cheek, the calm loveliness of her marred only by the livid patches of red on her chin, the watery blood which had seeped from her nose into her mouth, staining her lips a deeper red, and the mark on her neck. Death by drowning had not otherwise disfigured her. She was still his daughter, before the brutality of a postmortem changed her.

He had wanted to see how that was done, indeed, had wanted at the time to supervise it. He had wanted no one to touch his daughter's body but himself. If she was to be brutalised by the scalpel of some forensic surgeon, he wanted to be there, guiding his hand, making sure they did not play her false. But there is no property in a body; it belongs to no one.

He had no rights, and in the end he was glad he had not seen. Better not to know what was done. They had mended her nicely for her cremation and arranged her golden hair to hide the missing portion of skin they had excised from her neck. He had asked for this to be returned to him. Reluctantly, they had done so. He never told anyone about that. He kept it, like others keep a relic, a small piece of skin desiccated into hard brown leather, in a box, somewhere.

Carl played back the photographs to the beginning, pausing at the one of the swans in their regal progress, ignoring the body they sailed past. They were all dead now. Ten years ago he had been a good shot, even with such an old rifle. He turned away from the screen and wiped his eyes.

Then had nothing to do with *now* and anyone wanting him dead *now*, except to inflame his imagination and make him worry about the boy. The death of his ten-year-old daughter had been nothing but a freakish accident. The lake was not deep; she could move like an eel; the water had been her natural element as soon as she had learned to swim in the sea with her mother. Water babes, both of them. The problem had been that Cassie loved the water so much she would not come out, and her father could not make her obey orders from the bank. Nor could he have fetched her out, or even threatened it, because, to his deep and abiding chagrin, he could not swim.

The thought of this ridiculous omission in his otherwise comprehensive education made him ashamed, even now. Athletic on land, unable to swim, like any child of his striving back-street background, where any such knowledge was redundant. He had learned only to study, plus the other skills acquired on those summer days, such as the handling of a gun and the making of hay. There was something self-indulgent about immersing the body in water without any particular purpose. No one passed exams that way. But in the end it was this knack with the water and the love of it which gave them the power. It was the one thing she could do which he could not, and she flaunted it.

He looked out of the window, thinking what a terrible irony it was that he lived with this urban view of the water, and wondered why he had done it. Because it was desirable, good for the boy and therefore valuable. If someone wants me dead, all they would have to do is push me into deep water. I would sink like a stone and die. Maybe Cassie would want to watch me drown, as I watched her, poor brave child. Maybe it would be better to believe she had not died, but simply turned into another creature instead. That was what her mother believed.

The tyres of his car had been deflated whilst it had been parked in the underground car park overnight. Nothing stolen. There were empty, grubby envelopes bearing his address in his post box; the beggar outside in the street stuck out his dirty foot to trip him as he passed; he had been jostled by an old woman who glared at him as he pushed his way into the Tube; someone had searched through his rubbish and spread it on the floor. City life, that was all, not enough to amount to this sense of menace. Someone had yelled in his courtroom, 'You're dead, mate,' and he had merely smiled, because it was true. Death was an ongoing process, part of him dying with his first child, needing to live for the other.

And yet it was true. Somebody wanted him dead, or if not dead, suffering. His bones ached; that was how he knew. He could feel the eyes on him all the time, and that was how he knew. He could feel the knife in his chest, in his back, and the water closing over his head. That was how he knew.

There was a timid knock at the door of his apartment. He moved towards it without hurry, pausing to comb back his hair with his fingers. Then stopped abruptly. There was no reason to knock; there was a video screen to reveal any legitimate visitor, provided they pressed the bell, alienating security that he detested. Who the hell . . . The cleaner, the caretaker, the man about the car? There was a spyhole in the door; he was not going to stoop to looking through spyholes, so he opened the door, yelling '*Yes!*'

There was a pitter-patter of distant footsteps along the laminate floor of Level Five. The footsteps were light as mice and then grew silent.

A dead rat lay on the floor, so freshly dead there was bright blood in its nostrils.

He laughed with sheer relief.

He was not squeamish. He picked it up, as it was, shut the door behind him, marched across the floor, flung open the balcony door and hurled the rat overarm into the river beyond.

Judge not, he told himself, that you may not be judged.

He would have to do something, for the sake of his son, but the relief was enormous. He knew now who it was *not*.

Ivy would never, ever go anywhere near a rat.

His name was Joe, aged twenty-six. Worked in IT.

He had not really wanted to go for a drive to the sea, and had not even imagined the prospect of a swim in the dark after an evening in the pub, but the whole project was infectious. He was, after all, well and truly chilled out, buoyed up by night after night of good, loud company, and still illuminated by the entirely novel experience of five days in a farmhouse. Yup, that was him, city slicker living on a fucking *farm* for a week; wait till he told *them* at work. You bastards go snorkelling and deep-sea diving, he would tell them. I had a ball. Before this, he could scarcely manage a short cut across a park. Now he could walk for ever. The whole experience had worked better than he could ever have imagined. It had healed one of the rifts in his broken heart, and the ongoing welcome, the seductive sense of belonging, culminated in the last night. He really felt as if he belonged in that house, in the front room of this pub, with that family, and the girl who had walked out on him, cancelling the holiday for which this had been a last-minute substitution, would be jealous of that. Nothing like country air, and nothing as good as a real country pub. For a start, it was the men who ruled it. You could squeeze a girl's tit and put your hand up her skirt, no one minded and everyone laughed.

Joe's bags were packed, ready for the early start home in the morning. He was like that, considered a trifle anal about his clothes and personal possessions, always prepared, but for now he was no longer a man who merely read magazines about how to spend money, but an amusing devil, sitting in a pub with his new friends, drinking another, sneaking a spliff, and then someone suggested they drive to the sea for a swim. The sea was two horizons away, even if it was only a matter of miles. It had not featured in this glorious valley, and suddenly it seemed a great idea to include it. One last experience, hey? Another first, appropriate for this freak-ishly hot, humid early summer evening, a suddenly good adventure to cap all the others. The simplest things were best. He could not remember which of the group had made the suggestion, only that the word went round faster than a virus. Yeah, yeah, yeah, great: only take fifteen minutes on deserted back roads. And while he had been a wimp when confronted with horses and cows this week, as well as a bit of a weakling over a ten-mile walk, he knew he was a good swimmer, and this might be his chance to excel. He could do forty lengths in the pool near the office. All nannyish thoughts about swimming when pissed got shoved to the back of his mind. They'd helped him home before, these lads, earlier in the week, and anyway, he wasn't drunk, he was intoxicated on atmosphere, with the cosy, hot pub room and the pressure of that arm alongside his on the table and the smoky air full of other perfumes and laughter. He had walked the ten miles and his blisters had healed; he had ridden a horse and the ache of that humiliation had faded. The one thing he had not done was swim. The one thing he was any good at.

It seemed like a real crowd in the bar, full of sweaty armpits. Hot. Shiny, smiling faces. *Horses sweat, men perspire and ladies glow,* someone said. It was him who said it, and it made them laugh. Over the week he had certainly developed a talent to amuse. They didn't laugh at him; no way, only with him. He had been mothered and brothered and loved.

So, whoopee, transformed from an ordinary computer nerd into an amusing flirt and Action Man by the simple fact of a holiday, he found himself in a car, bumping down a track, with his companion giggling beside him and driving the thing at the same time. Never been skinny-dipping, my lovely, well, there's nothing like it. You said you were a good swimmer, didn't you? That I have to see. Yes, I could probably do a mile. And fast. All those things he used to do, and would do again, after this. Joe could see the headlights of the car behind theirs, good that the mob were tagging along, feeling utterly safe with this crowd. Yokels he would call them when he got back to London. He would poke fun at their thick, Kentish accents when he returned home and told the tales. The person at the wheel had strong brown arms, with light hair, tanned by the sun.

The bay was as promised, lit by moonlight, calmer than the lake he had merely glimpsed, and far more inviting. The warmth of the night and the calm of the sea were ripped by banshee yelling as the posse alighted and ran down on to the sand. He was not sure it was actually sand; it felt harsher than that, like ground shingle, but sweetly cool on the feet.

First one to the Point! See that bunch of rocks? Race you. See what kind of swimmer you are. Last one buys the drinks. First one gets a shag, later. You waiting for something, or do you want to give me a start?

He was waiting. He was suddenly scared, focusing on the rocks, spot-lit by the moon, listening to the smooth hiss of little waves, nibbling. A final shuffling-off of clothes, the lithe form next to him naked, the yelling of support, and all doubts vanished. He was going to be at the rocks first, he would, he would, he *would*. Someone overtook him on the way across the beach and crashed into the water first. Joe ran, following the track of foam-kicking heels. He would show them.

It was shockingly cold, until after a few strokes the memory of the first exhilaration of learning to swim came back with a force of delirious warmth and wonderful weight-lessness. He was plump, but in here he was slim and forceful. He spat out the first, involuntary gulp of water, developed his best crawl stroke, deviated to the side of those teasing heels, revelling in the bracing salt, and swam furi-ously. It was not long before he had overtaken the first swimmer; in his mind's eye he could hear the amazement of all who followed that he had gone so far, so fast. Forty strokes crawl, forty breaststroke, forty on the side, keep the rocks in sight, he would win, and when he came back they would all know he was the winner.

When he looked up, the rocks had moved. Everyone else was far behind.

The lone figure moving out of the gentle waves, back on the sand, paused for a little while to view his progress. Then picked up Joe's clothes and went back to the car. The only car.

Oh Lord, look at him now, still ploughing out to those rocks. Only the current will have really and truly got him now, because it isn't a bay, it's a treacherous piece of coast, and you can swim for the Olympics and not have a chance of beating that, and the cold gets you sooner when you're pissed, and you were waiting for me to catch up. Only I didn't, having more sense than to go out of my depth here. So I'm going to drive your car back, with your bags already inside it, and tomorrow or the next day, since you told me so much about yourself, I reckon I've got time to put it outside your house in London.

You were a gift, Joe, an absolute gift. A sad git who was never going to be happy. A waste of space.

Murder by persuasion. You were the perfect practice, but I need more.

Rachel Doe's personal file, kept in her pocket organiser

I look back at myself and the person I was and I can't believe it. I was a vacuum, and nature abhors such a thing. I don't know how I evolved like that. Perhaps I'd had a slight breakdown, I just don't know. I don't know, either, how I evolved into what I was. I had tunnel vision, you see. If I succeeded in a conventional way, by which I mean being someone with a status in life approved of by the majority of the population; if I became, in other words, a professional woman of whom it could be said, 'She's done well,' and provided I achieved that through work, rather than cheating, I thought I would be proud of myself, and others of me. But it's all compromise. I never believed I could have it all; only those with a sense of entitlement can have that. To anyone else, the prospect is simply too bewildering. So it never occurred to me that I could have love and contentment as well as hard graft, to say nothing of fun. I was a drone from fifteen to thirty-one. I was my father's Thatcherite baby.

I had a partner of course, in my twenties, de rigueur. I fell in with him, and he with me, same ambitious attitudes, same ambitious firm, and we locked ourselves away together, he with his mortgage and me with mine, never quite trusting one another, never committing, too busy, just needing to keep the rest of you at bay. Couples don't need friends; couples don't necessarily know one another either. I never noticed how much he criticised me (I was used to that), or how prudish and shy he considered me, but I did notice when he upped the ante of his ambitions and started to steal. I blew the whistle on him, and then it was as if a bomb went off, and the fall-out came down like a nuclear cloud. At the end of that, I realised I was hardly anyone's most popular person, and also as ignorant of any world outside my own as if I had never glimpsed it; a philistine, a number-cruncher, living on an island of my own making. A stranger to real cruelty, suffering, privation or even lack of self-control. A person without a talent or inclination for self-analysis, a very shallow creature who had avoided all the lows, as well as the highs. A two-dimensional creature. Even my hormones had never bothered me. I knew my rights, and had always been granted them; I had never wanted for anything, since I had never really considered what I might want because I was too busy doing it. I had never looked sideways, or shied away from decisions which were clearly *right*, contemptuous of time-wasters, and now I had to look up, or down into an abyss. I had to learn to *look*. Timid and obstinate, he said. A bitch. Only one of these descriptions is true.

All my life I've been chivvied and criticised. I have a Pavlovian attitude to it, and, as I found, a completely over-the-top reaction of unutterable delight and gasping gratitude to its opposite. Protection and criticism were my parents' way of making me do better; criticism was my partner's way of making me look better and my employer's cultural method of making me achieve more. It was only as far as I was useful that I deserved to exist. No one had ever been curious about what else I might be good at, least of all myself, apart from doing sums and earning a living. I had no other skills to offer, no talents, and worst of all, in comparison to others, all my tragedies were pathetically small. More than anything, I was ashamed of that. I was never, ever going to betray anyone ever again. All my life I have knocked on the door of belonging, and found it locked.

I was unlocked by praise. I was knocked sideways by acceptance. I wanted to be passionate about the suffering of others, to understand it, to grow.

Wait a minute, I'm telling lies. I was naïve for my years; I wanted mother, sister, friend to fill the gap. I needed to *give*. I needed a mission to be not useful, but indispensable. I wanted to make life better for somebody. I wanted to be loved and trusted, and when I found it, it went straight to my head.

Love, the universal need, the most selfish ingredient in the mix. If only it had been lust, so much less complicated. At least with lust you think you know what you want. It's a poor imitation of the real, grateful thing.

I was wide, wide open. They could have spread my legs in the air and tickled my tummy, raped me alive or dead, and I still would have loved them.

Still do.

CHAPTER ONE

'It's lovely to be here,' Rachel said, sounding lame and rather overpolite to her own ears. It was a feature of herself, among many others, which she did not like. Her social awkwardness, which she reminded herself was hardly surprising in the circumstances, and she should not make it worse by dwelling on it. Or on any of her so-called faults for that matter. There was nothing wrong with her, except desperately wanting to make a good impression.

'It's so marvellous that you could come,' Grace Wiseman said. 'The pleasure's all ours. And you brought the fine weather with you. We're well and truly blessed.'

It was a formal welcome speech, but delivered at such breakneck speed and with such warmth that the sincerity was obvious. It occurred to Rachel to wonder what she should call Ivy's mother. Surely not Mrs Wiseman? Grace? Definitely Grace. Grace addressed most people as 'darling' and meant it. Grace was a name which suited her. Warm and gracious.

Grace Wiseman had been outrageously pleased to see them both, actually quivering with excitement and pleasure, beaming with joy and holding out her arms. Hugging Rachel into an embrace which smelled of baking and lavender, soap and polish, overlaid with pipe smoke, somehow exactly the mix of aromas belonging to a comfortable farmer's wife straight out of the pages of fiction. She was not apple-cheeked; she was as brown as a plump, sun-dried raisin. The embrace was strong; Grace looked far younger than her sixty-five years, possessed the strength of a man of fifty. She had grannyish spectacles parked on her head and a vigorous amount of bulk. There was precious little resemblance to her daughter, who seemed, when they stood together, a whole foot taller, cool and willowy, even in her trademark T-shirt, jeans and trainers. The smell of Grace, the scent of a provider, nurturer, cook and cleaner, went with the confident physique. She could just as easily have smelled of diesel fuel and emerged in dungarees with a spanner in one hand. Her bare brown arms were both soft and muscled. Then there were the other surprises, adding another dimension. Her cotton shift was brilliant green, her abundant hair was a startling shade of purple, and her wrists rattled with bracelets.

'She's every inch the farmer's wife and landlady,' Ivy had explained on the way from London. 'Only she never quite got over the hippy stage. Probably peaked in the 1960s just before I was born, and I wouldn't put it past her to dance naked in the moonlight, even now, but you'd certainly know if she did. If you want my mother, follow the noise.'

Rachel loved her. She thought she would have killed to have a mother like this. A housewife who baked bread and biscuits, washed and ironed, thrilled to visitors and the drudgery of cooking, and in the meantime tended a garden of flowers, vegetables and herbs whilst oozing sympathy and wisdom. Watch out for homilies and homemade wine, Ivy warned. They're her specialities.

'They have to augment the farm income,' she said. 'Ma thought of that long before anyone else. Long before Common Agricultural Policies, BSE and foot and mouth. She said, if you've got a big house, use it. Bed and breakfast, with ambience. Only she can change the ambience at a whim. It's been an artists' retreat, writers' retreat, partygoers' paradise. Actually, it's all her. She has to turn them away.'

'Won't I be taking a room that someone might have paid for?' Rachel asked.

'Don't be daft. Rooms are something we have, and she does insist on having weeks off, even in the height of summer.'

Hers was a pretty room under the eaves, adjacent to Ivy's and separated by a shared bathroom. It had a mellow wooden floor, a white rug for feet getting out of the warmth of the high bed, which was covered with a blue-and-white patchwork quilt. Fresh white towels on the iron frame of the bed, flowers in a vase and a jug of water on a folding table next to the bed.

'She's got the knack,' Ivy had said. 'She loves it.'

'And your father?' Rachel had asked anxiously.

'Couldn't give a shit. As long as he doesn't have to part with his animals or his privacy, he's as happy as one of his pigs. Turn right at the next junction.'

Ivy had chattered like a sparrow throughout the journey, surprising Rachel with the knowledge that she was actually nervous on both their accounts, anxious that Rachel should like what she would find at the other end, and that she, in turn, would make a good impression. As if Rachel's opinion was vital. It touched her. As the car lurched down the narrow track towards the farm, Rachel ceased to listen and lost herself in the novelty, finding it all as beautiful as it was mysterious. Hawthorne branches flicked against the windows, making her flinch; it was like going into a tunnel marking the boundary between one country and another, but then she had felt like this in the months of utter loneliness, last year, living in a dark tunnel, bursting into sunlight only after she had met Ivy, and now this glorious fuss and juvenile excitement of being *wanted*. No wonder she did not quite know how to behave. It was all too much, like a surfeit of love and caring.

Grace hugged her again, those big brown arms like delicate pillows. Rachel looked towards the attic window and the blur of sunshine and wanted to turn her head from the light.

'It's all too much, isn't it?' Grace said. 'We're all too much. I'm so sorry. You mustn't let us overwhelm you. But Ivy's talked about you so much, I really was, literally, dying to meet you. You've done her so much good. You're so welcome, you've no idea.'

Rachel stood, smiling idiotically.

Grace scrutinised the room and then made for the door. 'Come down for tea or whatever, whenever you're ready. I'd better get my big flat feet out of here and leave you to it. You can orientate yourself from this window, not like the paying guests. They never get beyond ground level.'

She came back and tweaked the curtain. 'Ivy'll be having her scout round the territory, like she will later as well, I expect. She's like a cat. She does that whenever she comes home, even if it's only for a couple of days. We can sometimes pin her down for a week at a time in the summer, when she stays on to help. She always has to check that things are the same. Fortunately, or unfortunately, they usually are. Right, I'm off to brew tea. Whenever you need me, just listen out. I'll be somewhere around, you'll always be able to hear where I am.'

She paused at the door and grinned. 'Do you know, there's one thing Ivy failed to mention about you, although she's told us an awful lot. Can't stop talking about you when she phones. She never said quite how beautiful you are. Sorry, that's rude of me, people must tell you that all the time.'

Then she was gone, in a jangle of bracelets.

Rachel could feel the lump in her throat. It was so *nice* to be here. An understated description of a feeling of intense pleasure to which she hoped she would never become accustomed. Exhausting. She tried to control it by analysing why she felt as high as a kite. You are so suspicious of happiness, John used to say. You even treat contentment with contempt. Like someone with a healthy flowering plant who keeps digging it up to see if the roots are still OK. What's wrong with you? You can't accept the good things in life. You don't even think they exist. She had believed everything he said, and it was only much later that she realised how little he had ever wanted to know her at all, and how small a person he had made her. And no, he had never told her she was beautiful to look at. He had simply implied there was good enough raw material to justify a makeover, and she must not blame him. It was she herself who made life so small.

It was *nice* to be here, she analysed, because it was a good place to be in which she would learn a little of a way of life so different from her own she may as well have travelled to Mars for the experience; and also, and more importantly, because no one had been so wonderfully pleased to see her since the second time she had met Ivy on her own, by prearrangement, outside of the classroom. On that occasion Ivy's face had lit with such pleasure and relief that Rachel had felt as if her own mere presence was a miracle. Oh, you've got here, Ivy had announced, with a sigh of rapturous relief. I can't tell you how good it is to see you. I was worried about you. I've been thinking about you.

Worried about me? Thinking about ME? No one had done that in a long time. It had been like music to the ears, as well as ironic. She was not the sort of person people worried about. Capable thirty-two-year-old accountants did not excite worry; if anyone in her civilised city world deserved worrying about, it was footloose, scatty, penniless, unstable and riotous Ivy, who was way too old at thirty-nine to live the squalid way she did. The other *nice* thing about being here, from Rachel's point of view, was to see that her anxious concern for Ivy might have been misguided. It was a little as if she had discovered that a seemingly poor friend was really rich. Ivy might have lived like a hobo in London, but she had to be as stable as a rock, because this was her parents' home, and she was rooted here.

In this house it was if the roots had risen to the surface and extended themselves, haphazardly, to form a shelter. The kitchen, once Rachel found it again, was a joy. A film-set kitchen, with an Aga, a huge, well-scrubbed pine table, flowers on one window ledge, an orderly row of herbs in pots on the other and a real ham hanging on a hook. All it lacked for theatrical perfection was an old dog to greet strangers with a wagging tail, and a cat curled in a basket by the stove. The heartbeat of the house, on a second look not quite so old-world conventional. There was plenty of stainless steel, too, and the walls, which might have been whitewashed, were tinted bright yellow. Homely, yet vivid also, like Grace herself.

'The thing is,' Grace was explaining while pouring tea from a surprisingly elegant china pot, 'the buildings on this so-called farm are the only blasted things about it which are really organic. It was all based round the needs of the animals, you see. Human beings took second place. So the first permanent things were animal shelters. The house comes second. First a house, then bits added to a house. I think we've redressed the balance towards human priorities, but I'm never quite sure. I doubt if the paying guests realise they live in the old pigsties.'

Rachel realised it would take her a while to get the measure of it, and then thought it didn't really matter if she did or she didn't. She must stop trying to control her environment by pinning it down into a map in her head. She just wanted to *be*. Happy. Ivy's descriptions had always concentrated on the land, rather than the house. Rachel felt it a disgrace in herself that she had never set foot on a real farm, except once to ask directions to somewhere else. Farming and the countryside was the stuff of myths and politics. It revealed her ignorance and innocence. She was secretly rather afraid of animals larger than a cat.

'Will you look at yourself, Ivy!' Grace bellowed as Ivy came ambling in through the open door. 'You're five minutes out of doors and you've already got mud on your shoes. Don't know how you find it. It hasn't rained in days.' She turned to Rachel. 'She was always like that, you know.'

Ivy grinned and bent to unlace her undoubtedly muddy shoes. Rachel could not remember ever seeing her wear anything else other than a variation on jeans and T-shirts, except for the first time they had met, when Ivy was wearing nothing at all. Even then her bare feet had been black with dust.

Ivy nudged the soiled training shoes away from the door and into an alcove next to it, containing a washing machine of industrial size and other footwear on the floor.

'Everything goes in there,' Grace mourned. 'Shoes, the lot. My darling husband thinks the washer's omnipotent, reckons it can clean boots too. He puts his in there, next to it, in hope. Where is he, by the way, Ivy? Did you find him?'

'With the piggies,' Ivy said. 'Says he's too shy to come in while he smells. And doesn't want me giving Rachel the tour of his fiefdom. He wants to do it himself, when all's clear and fresh in the morning, he says. What a spoilsport. He says it's his privilege.'

They are vying for my attention, Rachel thought. I like it. Grace pushed a plate of biscuits towards her. Somehow she had expected scones, but these were small and delicate almond wafers, perfect with strong tea. The bubble of happiness remained intact.

'So that's where you throw your clothes,' Grace said, nodding in the direction of the alcove. 'Some of the paying guests have such a strange notion of what people wear in the country. They bring the whole caboodle of waxed coats and things and don't seem to realise that all you need is a lot of old rags and a washing machine, since everything's dirty or wet most of the time. Ivy, love, if your dad's earmarked the livestock tour, why don't you show Rachel the rest while the sun's still out? Supper'll be a couple of hours. You could take a bottle of wine to the lake.'

'Sure. It's mad to stay indoors.'

'What lake?'

'It's a pond, really,' Grace said.

A look passed between mother and daughter which Rachel could not decipher. She looked down at her own feet, and noted with satisfaction that her old, worn sandals had certainly not been bought for the occasion.

'You just want us out of the way,' Ivy said.

'I just want you out of the kitchen,' Grace said. 'It's far too soon for Rachel to see what goes into the food.'

'You didn't tell me about a lake,' Rachel said, as they walked down the hill. 'Can you swim in it?'

'Ah, yes. Your exercise of choice.'

It had seemed like an endless day, which was always on the point of beginning a new episode.

'Here, hold this, would you? Thanks.'

Ivy handed over the bottle of wine with cork perched precariously on the rim of the neck, making it look as if it was already tipsy itself, a creature with an undersized head held at an angle. She rummaged in her canvas bag for her cigarettes, lit one and then took back command of the bottle, with another, murmured thanks. It was what they both did, Rachel realised, Ivy and Grace. Never a demand, always a request. Would you? Could you possibly? And then, thanks: a recognition that whatever you had done was not taken for granted. The charm of that was infectious.

Ivy stopped at the curve of the track, and took a deep breath. She had her carpet bag of many colours over her shoulder, the bottle of homemade wine held between two fingers of her left hand, and was using her right to puff on the cigarette.

'I don't usually come down here,' she said. 'Grace must have wanted you to see. She's so manipulative. She hates things to be hidden.'

She had walked ahead by then, round the turn of the track, which seemed to Rachel to lead to nothing but trees, and then, on another turn, the water stretched below them, gleaming in the evening sun, a great, even stretch of lake, the shore they were approaching littered with shrubs, the far side flanked by dense woods. It shimmered calmly with reflected colour, the foliage mirrored in the water in shades of gold to olive to dense, hungry green against the further bank. It took Rachel's breath away. She simply followed Ivy's expert steps down the side of the overgrown track, right to the edge of the water. They were not entirely alone. Two skinny kids were stuffing towels into a bag, shivering as they left on foot. A swimming place should have attracted far more than these on a hot evening, but they were all.

'It's usually deserted,' Ivy said. 'There's no road to it, only a path.'

Rachel sat down suddenly. It felt like her own decision, but Ivy had sat first. Big bunches of hay grass, natural resting places close to the edge.

'Oh, Ivy,' Rachel whispered. 'Why would you keep quiet about this? This is heaven. I'd have come for this alone. Water magics me. Even a bath.'

'Like I said, I don't come here so much myself,' Ivy said.

She pulled out the cork from the bottle, produced the two glasses which had clinked together in her bag all the way here, balanced them on the tufty ground and poured. It was elderflower, described earlier by Grace as a thin thing with a mean punch, delicious if you wanted to drink the flavour of hay. Rachel sipped. From the woodland side of the lake four swans appeared, as if they had been waiting: two portentous adults, followed by two cygnets, sauntering across the lake, mirrored in it, in a regal procession.

'According to Irish legend, there was a king whose second wife was so jealous of his daughters that she used her powers to turn the girls into swans,' Ivy said. 'The spell was incomplete, as all spells are, so they were left with the ability to sing, and sing they did. The song enticed suitors and friends, and in the end the stepmother was killed, for her sins. I like that story. Only fucking swans don't sing. Not ever.'

She pulled on another cigarette, pointed again.

'See that one, over there? That's my girl. The most beautiful of the tribe. She can sing if she wants, I bet. I don't believe much, but I do believe that a girl can be turned into a swan. Like the daughters of Lir. I always wanted to be turned into a swan when I was a child. Shame it never happened.'

'There's nothing I wouldn't believe in a place like this,' Rachel said. She shuffled to sit close to Ivy. Their thighs touched, companionably. Shared warmth. From doubtful beginnings the wine grew better by the mouthful. The grass tickled her calves. Rachel felt as if she was floating free, suspended between the water and the sky.

'I suppose you shouldn't believe in myths and legends, except when tempted,' Ivy said. 'And you know me and temptation. Always give in.'

'Is that why you don't come here first when you come home? In case you succumb to the lure of legend? Big old bruiser like you?'

Ivy shook her head, violently. She had tough blonde hair which looked as if it had been hacked with scissors rather than styled. Hair which had been bleached and tinted, permed and ignored, and finally left to grow into a thatch.

'No. I don't avoid that. I leave it until last, because . . .'

'Because what?'

Rachel watched the white swans fading into the darkness of shadow. Ivy lit another of the hand-rolled cigarettes she kept in a battered tin.

'Because this was where my daughter drowned.'

The sun was sinking lower in the sky; the outline of the woods was blurred. Nothing was as silent as it seemed. There was a myriad of noises, the sound of water, the calling of birds over the trees, the slight, audible movement of the long grass. Rachel did not know if it was the beauty of the place, the sounds or the announcement which made her want to cry. She felt an absurd sense of disappointment, and hated herself for her own selfishness. Ivy plucked a grass and chewed the end.

'Sorry for springing that one on you. I know I told you about it. Child, *children,* marriage, death and breakdown. I just didn't tell you where it happened.'

'I thought she drowned in the sea.'

Ivy shook her head. 'No. Here. Yards from home. Don't let it poison the lake for you. You must come here and swim whenever you want. It's wonderfully safe now.' She touched Rachel's hand. 'I didn't tell you the details,' she went on, lightly, 'because, first of all, it's a lot to burden anyone with, and I thought I'd burdened you with enough.'

'You don't burden me,' Rachel said, equally lightly. 'You've brought colour and meaning into my otherwise monochrome existence and I want to know everything about you. I've told you everything about me. Knowing stuff isn't a burden, it's a privilege.'

'Do people ever tell one another everything?' Ivy said. '*Especially* if they love one another.'

Then, suddenly, she was laughing. 'There, I've said it. I love you. What an utterly scandalous state of affairs. What a fucking admission. Two straight women, crazy about one another. But seriously, dear, I didn't tell you all about Cassie, and how and where she died, because I can't trust myself to tell you the truth. I no longer know it, you see. So, if you really want to know, ask my mother.'

Rachel nodded.

'And then you can ask my father about the lake. There's quite a history. He'd love to tell it. They both love to talk. But for serious swimming, dearest, we get in your car and go to the sea.'

The swans disappeared into the deep shadow of the woods. Rachel wanted them to come back.

'They were so different, my two kids,' Ivy said. 'Cassie loved it here. My son hated it, probably in self-defence, but then he hated everything except his father, poor mite.'

'Was he here too? How did he react, oh, poor boy . . .'

'React? With the indifference of childhood, I hope. I really don't know for sure. I was absolutely out of it. Incapable of motherhood. Post-heroin fucked up for years, and then it was all too late.'

Her tone was still light. The air was still warm.

'All for the best, probably,' Ivy said, without rancour. 'He was better off without me. I don't much like men, especially young ones. Shall we amble home? I could eat a horse.'

She was always hungry. Rachel was torn between two tempting prospects, moving towards food with a belly so empty it wanted to crawl, and staying where they were. Hearing more, not wanting to ask, waiting to be led.

'Do we have to?'

Ivy was smiling. 'How many times do I have to tell you, Rachel Doe? You have to learn to do whatever you like and not hesitate about it. But I must warn you, my father likes to talk and can be a bit of a bore.'

'Wait,' Rachel said, 'until you meet mine.'

CHAPTER TWO

Ernest Wiseman should have been a teacher. A long, lean, stooped but nimble old man, waiting to start his lecture. Younger than Grace, but looking older, in his owlish way, with his half-glasses perched on his nose. There was something about those two which made Rachel think they were still lovers. The way they touched, perhaps, or more aptly, the way Grace touched him in passing behind his back to the stove, quickly pressing his shoulder as if to let him know he was never forgotten, making him smile in acknowledgement. Maybe it was merely a code, an affectionate giving of signals, or just an expression of some sort of delight in one another. Maybe it was just the joy of the feeder and the being fed. The food, should Rachel have noticed it, was casually excellent. The outside light seemed to die, leaving them sweetly marooned around the anchor of the candlelit wooden table, full and contented, too lazy to move. It was quite appropriate for Farmer Wiseman to be called Ernest. He was, rather. There were just the three of them sitting round the table at the end of the meal, completely at ease. Ivy had gone to the pub: the invitation had been extended, but nobody else wanted to go.

'Ah, the lake,' Ernest said, squinting at Rachel with his sweet smile. 'You wanted to know about the lake. Well, when you and Ivy find a hilltop and look down, you'll see a landscape which looks as old as time. But it isn't that old. What you see is only what's emerged in this decade, never mind this century. Much further back than that, you'd have seen an estate, this farm and the next farm all serving a big house, with a river landscaped into a series of lakes as part of the grounds. No more house, only one farm, and a single lake in limbo. Recent history, too. My lifetime, anyway. It was the war changed it more than anything else, far more than the decay of a dynasty. There are half the trees there were.'

He crumbled a piece of cheese, picked up the crumbs with his forefinger and swallowed delicately. The cheese lay, waiting to be picked at, an invitation to linger where they were. It was a part of their hospitality, Rachel thought, not to rush food away from the table, but always to leave something there to nibble.

'Towards the end of the war,' Ernest said, 'there were more Germans here than English. Prisoners, you see. A camp built round the big house, which had been used as an army billet and came to serve as HQ for a prison settlement. You wouldn't have recognised the landscape then. Nissen huts and wire, although they hardly needed that. Where were they to go, poor sods? Not that people round here thought of them with pity. I was told when I was five that they were better fed than we were, and what with rationing, I could believe it. But then my father, who farmed this farm, got to like them. One or two, anyway, because they worked the land. We got more free labour then than ever since. And that was when you realised that while they weren't actually starving, they were always hungry. Well, the ones who worked here were.'

Grace coughed, and touched his arm. 'Rachel was asking about the lake.'

His hand hovered over the cheese, and took an apple instead. 'Oh, yes. Not much choice then. At the start of the war, before the family in the house gave it over to the army, or were forced to, the lake was a place for swans. All swans were once registered to the Crown you know. Preserved for beauty and for eating, latterly only for decoration. Fat chance of that in wartime. People roasted crows, for God's sake. So the swans went, German prisoners always suspect, but they didn't have guns, so it probably wasn't them. So the lake was empty, got fouled up and polluted. You need birds to keep a pond clean. Birds and fish. Both dead. And the water level rose.'

'Rose?' Rachel asked.

'Soldiers. Soldiers and guards, going into town – well, not much of a town, and only a village without a shop now, but a town with three pubs and *girls* then. As well as the sea for swimming. On the way back they'd pinch every bicycle in sight and dump it in the pond. A car, once, and God bless us, even a tractor, and both of those things like gold dust, as well as petrol. The river silted up. The thing became a stagnant pond.'

He bit into the apple.

'My father told me that farmers like him came to reckon they were better off with German prisoners of war than bloody soldiers. They did a deal less damage. And some of them really felt for the land. My dad said we were lucky to have them. Well, we were lucky with Carl, and he reckoned he was lucky with us.'

'Humph,' Grace snorted.

He touched her hand. 'That was later, sweetheart,' he said. 'That was Carl the younger. We weren't so lucky with him. Where was I? Oh, yes.'

He seemed to tire suddenly, then brightened. Rachel loved the way Grace listened to him so intently, when she must have heard this dozens of times before. This family had the habit of listening. Ivy listened as if every word counted; Rachel listened now.

'Carl was a German, from Berlin. It took a while after peace broke out before all these Germans could be got back, and Carl, who seemed old to me – I was only ten, but he was scarce more than twenty – found out that his whole family had died in the bombing. He was at home with us, billeted in the outhouse. We needed him; he stayed. And he made a start on the pond. He loved to work, that one.'

He finished the apple, including the core.

'I found him there one day, dragging a bike out. We made that lake a project, him and I. My dad used to say, fancy him caring, but he did. Said he wanted to see swans on it again. So there's the history of the lake. We owe its survival to a prisoner of war who left when he finished, fifty-five years ago. Shows you can honour what you don't own.'

'Did he ever come back? This . . . Carl?'

Grace stiffened. Then she moved and began to clear the table, surreptitiously. The place where Ivy had sat was comfortably empty, her absence as natural as her presence. They were well-mannered, without strict rules. Each evening would vary. Rachel hugged the thought that there would be more evenings like this, this time and the next. She knew there would be a next time.

'Oh yes, he came back. I don't think he ever wanted to go.

I know I didn't want him to: he was a sort of big brother to me, but I don't suppose there was any money or future for him here. He went to London, worked his balls off, married, had a son, and came back, in the summer usually, year after year. Haymaking, he loved making hay. Then he brought his son. We were his family, you see, or as close as it got. Summer holidays . . . it was always hot, wasn't it Grace?'

'When we were first married,' Grace said, 'child bride that I was, sharing a house with my in-laws, I used to resent this big, silent bloke and his son pitching up for two weeks at a time, and every other weekend. Especially the little boy. I resented the fact that my husband adored him, and they spoke a language all of their own. One does, at that age.'

'He wanted his son to know about things other than smog,' Ernest said. 'He wanted him to know about the land.'

'God knows what they wanted,' Grace said sharply.

She had been moving deftly between sink, stove and fridge, putting away, wiping down and organising with an almost deferential quietness. Rachel realised that she was not always noisy. Even with the bracelets, she could be as quiet as a fox. Ernest's head drooped.

Grace stood behind him, kneading his shoulders. 'To be continued,' she said, kissing the top of his head. 'Tomorrow is *always* another day.'

'Boring you, am I?' Ernest asked.

'No, no, quite the opposite,' Rachel said, truthfully.

'He doesn't need much encouragement really,' Grace said. 'You'll have much more of it in the morning. Time for bed, I think.'

He nodded agreement, rose, flexed his knees before leaving the room, his mellow voice drifting back. 'Good night, sleep tight . . . a good night.'

There was a comfortable silence after he left. Grace took his seat and sighed happily. 'Bugger me,' she said. 'There's a bit of wine left. That won't do, will it? We can't go to bed sober in case Ivy comes home pissed. Here . . .'

Bottles had appeared, wine had been drunk. Rachel did not know how much; she felt mellow. It crossed her mind to wonder if she was being nicely manipulated. No, that was the wrong word: manoeuvred, so that she was left without Ivy in the company of Ivy's parents together, and then her mother alone. If there had been an element of calculation about it, she certainly didn't mind. She was utterly charmed by both of them; she wanted to listen for hours. She was being trusted, that was all. Ivy really wanted her to know them, and it was a very flattering thought. It felt like midnight and was only half past ten. She wanted to be here on the longest day of the year and every day before it. She was excited by the thought of the morning.

'Well,' Grace said. 'This is nice. Not that I don't like the pub, but I'd rather have a person to myself. Must be my age. A little bit of deafness. I can only hear one person at a time. Ernest says it's deliberate. He says I must have deafened myself.'

In this light, she was pink and flushed. Definitely apple-cheeked in the way of a russet apple. Her strong fingers stroked the stem of her glass affectionately. A bottle a day keeps the doctor away, she had said earlier. Plus an apple.

'Do you talk to the paying guests?' Rachel asked impulsively. She thought it was a rude question. It sounded possessive, jealous, as if wanting to know if others were as welcome and as trusted as she felt herself.

'Oh yes, if they want. We only have one or two at a time. Some of them love to talk. Some of them want company, book dinner every night. Some of them are lonely and silly, and . . . oh, never mind. Some need introducing to the pub. Some want mothering. Talking at them makes them relax. It's the only way to get them to talk. If they don't like it, they can always run away. You can too, you know.'

Another question hung in the air, like a light shadow of the first. It said, are you a true friend of my wayward daughter? Can I trust you?

Rachel laughed. 'I love people who talk,' she said. 'And anyway, you don't fool me. You talk to make people talk. You got the whole story of my life out of me while we were making the salad. Ivy's the same. She could get blood out of a clam, and she talks nineteen to the dozen without ever missing a single thing anyone else says. I suppose it's an inherited talent.'

Grace grinned. 'You've rumbled us. Nope. It's entirely accidental. The result of curiosity. I'm not clever enough for anything else. I'm not like you. Not educated, apart from reading. Ivy'll mislead you. She blows my trumpet for me. She thinks I had commercial foresight to do what I did with this house and the old pigsties. It was nothing like that. I just wanted Ernest to go on doing what he does, and to have a home for Ivy.'

Rachel pushed away her wine. She wanted a clear head for the morning, but she did not want to move, either.

'Tell me about Carl the younger. And how Cassie drowned in the lake.'

'Whoah,' Grace said. 'Did Ivy give permission for this?'

'Yes. She's told me some of it.'

Grace lit a cigarette from the burning stump of a candle. The multicoloured wax clinging to the sides of the old Chianti bottle which held it bore tribute to the dozens of candles this one had supplanted. Grace breathed smoke through her nostrils like a dragon. Rachel was absolutely sure this was not what she talked about to the paying guests.

'Of course she must have told you. Carl the younger, son of Carl the pond-maker, was the man Ivy married. At seventeen, I ask you. He and his father came here first when he was a mite, and Ivy not even a twinkle in the eye. And then, in another twinkle of the eye, he was a teenage boy, and she was a little girl who adored him. And then, in another fucking twinkle of an eye he was a man a decade older than her, the bastard, coming back to lay claim. I wanted so much for her. She was destined for art school.'

'She got there in the end,' Rachel said.

Grace sat back, letting out an indignant whoomph. Then sat forward, bracelets jangling, noisy again.

'I wanted a wild child who wanted to experiment, like I did. You know, go native, take to art and everything. Not get bogged down far sooner than me, even. Not a pregnant teenager, with a child begotten behind a haystack by a man ten years older, and just as much of a control freak as his fucking father. I ask you. You still had to get married in those days. There's a hell of a difference between then and now. Anyway, he wanted it. That was what it was all about. It was part of his master plan. He was always clear about what he wanted. Establish a career; get a wife, in that order. Preferably one with a lineage he could prove. That's the German in him.'

She was holding the stem of her glass as if she wanted to crush it.

'And then they came back, with *their* children. He wanting for them what he had had as a child, and Ivy a mother of two before she was even twenty. Unbearable. But lovely for me, as well.'

Grace put out her cigarette in the spluttering wax, and looked at it critically.

'The boy and the girl, fifteen months apart. Chalk and cheese as they grew. Ivy, always wanting to bring them back, because she never really left. She wasn't grown up enough to leave. Never settled there. They fought like cat and dog, Ivy and Carl, over everything. Cassie was part of the game. Every inch her mother's wayward child. Ivy threw her in the sea when she was four. She simply started swimming.'

'She's certainly a city person now,' Rachel said.

Grace released the stem of her glass and waved her hand at the smoke.

'Oh, you are a lovely creature, for wanting to know.'

'She told me to ask you. I do want to know.'

'Tomorrow, if you still want. My sweet child, you're dead on your feet. We won't wait up for Ivy. You know what she's like.'

'Yes, I do. Night-owl Ivy. Works and plays all hours. Has to be independent and not questioned. Free agent. Blithe spirit.'

'Can you cope with that when she moves into your flat? All those jobs, all those funny hours?'

'No problem. I'll love it. We aren't in each other's pockets. She's taken some persuading, though.'

'You are the most wonderful girl,' Grace said. 'The most beautiful thing on the planet.'

She really wants them to know me, and me to know them, Rachel thought wonderingly as she splashed water on her face. I've never been treated like this. She would not have let her own contemporaries near her father. Tucked into her high bed, she thought of her London flat, as she might have done of some distant, grubby planet, to be congratulated for being so far away. I shall tell *them*, she told herself, thinking of the office where she worked, that I slept beneath the eaves and below the stars, and they will not believe me. I am mended by knowing Ivy and her kind.

Now, it really was silent. There was the selective deafness created by food and wine and then there was her own, delightful exhaustion from the doing of nothing much really, other than driving, being loved and cared for and the lake, and listening, and everything. And then a deafening sound from the tiny bathroom which was between her room and Ivy's room on the top floor. Water, gurgling away with a sound, in that silence, like the end of the world. *Whirrrup, bang shcush, gargle gargle spit*.

She got out of bed, lifted the latch on her bedroom door, and moved sideways over the half-landing. The door to the shared bathroom was open. Ivy was there, as Rachel had first seen her, naked as stone, bent from her slender waist over the basin. The taps gushed, noisily. The pipes gurgled, without rhythm. The room was whiter than white, the tiles white, the paint white, the bath white, white white, and the water flowing into the basin from Ivy's big, capable hands ran pink as she washed. The tufty blonde hair stood up in spikes. The face in the mirror was deathly pale. Ivy had seen her, gave a fleeting smile.

'Oh Christ. I forgot what a noise the plumbing makes. Sorry I'm so late. You been OK with Mother?'

'Your hands. You're bleeding.'

Ivy looked at her hands, then stretched towards the also white towels and began to wipe them dry, shaking her head.

'Me?' she said. 'No, it's not me. I'm not bleeding, just a bit bloody. Some car on the road hit a bird, and left it thrashing. Had to finish it off.'

She finished drying her hands. The towel remained white.

'Country life, honey. Road kill. Mercy killing. Had to be done. Sorry I woke you. Go back to bed.'

Rachel did as she was told, sleepy and reassured, leaving the door ajar. The latch was cold to the touch. She did not know how much later it was when she woke again into shivering consciousness. Footsteps on the stairs, the abrupt ending of screams, which dwindled away into muffled noises. Almost silence. Rachel did not know from where it had come, outside or inside, animal or human, only knew city sounds, stood by the door of her room, shivering and indecisive, listening to noises now minimal and human. She slipped round the open door and stood on the landing.

Light streamed from the room which was Ivy's. Through the half-open door, Rachel could see the shape of Grace, with her back turned, leaning over the bed in which Ivy was huddled and mumbling. Grace made hushing, soothing sounds with skilful ease. It was something they had done before.

'Only road kill, darling. You mustn't let it upset you.'

'No, Mummy, no. Mustn't.'

'There, there.'

'Can't do it. We've got to get him here. *Here.*'

'Yes, darling, yes, yes. Shhh.'

'Gotta get him here. So he can see. He's got to come here.'

'Bogey man dead, bang, bang,' Grace's voice teased softly. 'There, there.'

Rachel withdrew, as quietly as she could. The instinct for diplomatic self-effacement was always there. Eavesdropping was contemptible, her own father had told her. She was half in love with them all, and she wanted to belong; she knew nothing and wanted to know what it was like to be them. Silence fell, as if there had never been noise. All Rachel knew was that Ivy should not live alone.

You are coming to share my empty space, Ivy. I don't want to be your keeper. I just want to give you a base. I want to make things better for somebody, the way I never have.

Grace would like that. They were already allies.

The boy stood looking at the London river before going indoors. He was either a boy or a man, depending on the eye of the beholder. So what if the wing of the other car got smashed when he parked downstairs? The wall had come up and hit it; underground car parks confused him; it was a crap car. Not his; his father's. Everything was his father's. The damage to the other car would not be noticed for days – the owner rarely used it – but his father would notice because his father always did, and would, if necessary, own up on his behalf, like the bloody bully he was.

There were rats in the car park. He would say he was distracted by a rat. They came out at night, he would say, to and from the river at low tide.

He went back into the underground space, kicked some of the broken glass under the front wheel of the other car, then went up, via the steps, and stood by the door of home, feeling as if he was going back into prison. Sam. Nineteen. Scared of his dad, sneaking into his own home as if he was a thief. Well, that was how his dad made him feel. Own room, everything a student could want, DVD, mobile, laptop, so it made economic sense to live with Dad at Canary Wharf, even if it meant living with a tyrant. Key in the door, reminding himself to be up early enough to get to the post before his father, post never arrived now before ten, good, no problem, plenty of time to get rid of anything he didn't want him to see. The credit card bill, another of those whingeing letters . . . Why should he want to see her? She was the one who left.

Tiptoeing through the apartment to his own room, he could recall the last sodding lecture, word for word, *na na nanana . . .* Dad by the window, him by the door. *We're different generations, Sam, stands to reason we get on one another's nerves. Time you moved out, broke your own things and learned the value of them, instead of this ridiculously privileged and private way of life which exposes you to nothing.*

He mimicked himself in the bathroom mirror. There are rats in the underground garage, Dad, isn't that real enough? I'm not going anywhere, and *don't* give me that old lecture again. That old aren't-you-lucky theme. Brought up in peace and plenty, as if I'm supposed to do penance for that. Remember again that I can't take anything for granted, because you couldn't and your father couldn't. Why not, Dad? Why can't I take it for granted? Other people do. Isn't that progress? Why do I have to be so grateful all the time? For fuck's sake, you even expect me to be grateful for the generation I was born into. Well, I'm not. I didn't choose it, and I think it sucks. And I'm not moving out. Or do you just want me to go so you won't be blamed for something I've done? You want me to leave for my own safety? Get lost, that really is stupid.

He would turn his back so he could not see the expression on his father's face. The expression, or lack of it, anger, sadness or nothing, his best blank face, the face of an inscrutable judge, talking the way he talked in court, the old hypocrite. An echo of his dead grandfather's verdict, *Er ist richtiger Junge*. Or face him to hear him say, We all have issues, Sam. Don't you think it would help if you would . . .

No, he would say. No. Leave me alone. Why should I? Just all of you, leave me alone.

It's your fault I'm scared to go it alone. You've done too much.

Fuck you, Dad.

And then, getting into bed, Are you awake, Dad? I didn't mean it, Dad. I just go into one when I'm ashamed of myself – and scared.

We both need a bit of looking after sometimes, don't we, Dad?

Oh, and I heard this really good joke, I've got to tell you in the morning. Don't let me forget, you'll love it.

I wish you were awake.

I need to talk. You're not so bad when you laugh.

Chapter Three

Ivy Wiseman (her maiden name; Schneider when married) had three or four jobs on the go at any given time. She was also a very part-time student at the art college on a foundation course which had so far lasted five years. That's what saved me, she told Rachel. Going back to the beginning of something, that, and work. Who cares about the hours? There's still plenty left, and I don't want anyone else's money. I pay my own rent.

Somewhere in between a day shift, a modelling session and a night shift, Ivy arrived with her refugee bundle of belongings at Rachel's flat. She was not a stranger to it; she had stayed overnight, but this felt permanent. She had a single, but huge, bulging gingham bag of clothes and shoes, a folio case in pink plastic, a mobile phone, and that was all. Not much to show for my years, she laughed

On Tuesday evening Rachel faced her own father, who disapproved, as he would. He was a small, grey widower who came up once a month to check his daughter was all right.

Unless he could do something practical and useful, he liked to keep these visits brief, in case it looked as if he was interfering in her life. He was proud of his daughter, but constantly worried about her financial security, especially since she had changed her job. He suspected extravagance and held debt in horror. After two redundancies, prudence was his own personal God and anxiety his constant companion, which all served to make him awkward when sitting in her London flat, perched on the edge of the armchair as if afraid to sit back into it. Rachel's father never looked as if he belonged, and always seemed anxious to leave, as if the distance between himself and his own home, a mere commuter train ride away, was really a thousand miles and he needed to get back before his retreat into safety became impossible.

Rachel was still tingling from the sensations of the weekend before, anchored in her mind as being mainly sunshine, laughter, fascination and a longing to go back there as soon as possible, to somewhere which already felt like home. She had daydreamed through Monday, almost forgotten the meeting with her father and knew it showed. It was wrong to compare parents with other parents, but she could not avoid it. Ivy's were glamorous; her own was not.

'Everything all right, Dad?'

'Yes, yes, perfectly all right.'

'All right' was the height of his ambition. Anything better than 'OK' would alarm him. She could not admit to either happiness or sadness with him, nor he with her. Whenever Rachel met her father, she felt as if she was letting him down by failing to give him something to do. And failing to understand him. She loved him helplessly, worried for him, always expected it to be different, but it never was. He would never allow himself to be spoiled. Shall we go to a show, Dad? Eat Italian?

What for?

He would never ask for anything. He despised spongers, believed you should work yourself out of your own messes, never borrowing, lending or begging. His wife had been the centre of his universe, and their tiny house in Luton was a temple to the art of do-it-yourself, through which all love was expressed. The children of parents in love are often orphans. Rachel hated every brick of it.

They talked on parallel lines, the way they always did, with nothing much to say. She could hear Grace's full-bellied laughter echo in her mind, and wished that she and her father could hug one another like that.

'How are you really, Dad?'

'Mustn't complain.'

'What've you been doing?'

'Not a lot. What about you?'

The joys of London life left him cold; the wonders of Sky TV and shopping on eBay had a similar effect on her. Not much to say, really. At least, this time, she could tell him about the farm. That way they could postpone irritating each other, if it was not already too late. She looked at her watch. Time for class. He would respect that.

'I don't like you sharing this place,' he said. 'But I suppose it'll help with the mortgage. You don't want a freeloader.'

In his eyes, the world was full of freeloading thieves. People who promised security, and then took it away.

'No, Dad, it won't help with the mortgage. She's no money. Anyway, I was telling you about this brilliant weekend with her parents. They've got a farm, with a lake . . . well, the lake's not theirs, but it's there.'

'Oh good, they must be worth a bob or two then.'

Rachel gritted her teeth. 'Doesn't follow, Dad. Only if they sold it. Not otherwise.'

'Can't see you on a farm. Did they get you milking cows?'

'They get milked by machine.'

There was a glimmer of interest in that. He forgot to look at the time and finger the train timetable in his pocket along with his medications.

'Oh, do they now?'

'Yes. And it's all on computer. They each have a number round their neck. There was one that was blind, poor thing. They're probably going to have to get rid of that, because it won't calve. They all plod into this milking parlour, like they're on autopilot, and when you see how much milk they've got to get rid of, you can see why they're pleased to be there. The weight of it! Then they're plugged in. Three hours a time, it takes, every drop measured. Then they plod out, and go and eat more hay. Silage, mixed with stuff. Molasses. It smells wonderful. I couldn't believe how *technical* it is. The milking side of it, I mean. The rest is sweated labour. Moving tons of straw and food. They seem to eat their own weight, every day.'

Rachel did not mention that standing in the well of the milking parlour with the penned beasts surrounding her had almost made her sick. They stood level with her head, while Ernest demonstrated how the suckers he fixed to the teats of those enormous udders actually worked. They don't pull, or suck, see? They just exert a little pressure. He had made her put her finger into one; it squeezed, slightly. The atmosphere was thick with the smell of milk, shit and, most of all, the sweet, fetid breath of the beasts themselves as they looked at her with intense curiosity, and she tried not to shrink from their monstrous size.

They were huge, soft machines themselves, with sharp spines and helpless faces. They trod in their own faeces. They needed a barn as big as a church. They tried to ride each other when they were in heat. They were that stupid. And strangely, vulnerably lovely.

'I didn't see the pigs. I'll see them next time. I saw the fields. He grows grass for the cows, and he's giving up on growing wheat. Except it's useful if the hay runs out. He can cut the wheat when it's green, and add it to the silage.'

Too much information. Rachel's father adored technicalities; details of the construction of the barn and what it was made of would have kept him there, but enough was enough. He looked at his watch.

'I'd best be off. And you to your evening class, isn't it?'

'Oh, yes.'

'I've heard farms are dangerous places,' he said. 'You don't want to be going back.'

Don't rise to it. Rachel helped him into his coat. Always a coat, even in a heat wave. Always wearing too many clothes. The coat was the equivalent of a handbag, but he would never have carried a bag. His pockets jangled with his inhaler for chronic, controlled asthma, his tranquillisers, the acid stabilisers he took like sweets for his suspect ulcer; he had the illnesses of a worrier, the stoop of a labourer and a whole raft of prejudices. She looked round her flat as they left. What a colourless place it was. A good buy; he had approved of it. Her father turned at the door.

'You want to be careful about sharing this place, you know. It's difficult to get people out. You don't want to risk it.'

She felt an overwhelming rush of irritation then. Enough to make her want to shout at him. She wanted to scream because she could not make him happy, but all the same, like every other time, when she waved him goodbye and watched him descend into the bowels of the underground, she wanted to cry. He looked so small, so free of any enchantment.

I want to meet your friend, he said. You should have kept that man of yours, you need someone to look after you.

No, Rachel thought. It's the other way round. I am your child, a child of the Thatcher era, bred to succeed, to own property, to wed myself to a career and not look left or right. Exactly as my untrained, factory-working father, traumatised by two redundancies, wanted for me. The pride of prosperity, the solidity of a good, professional job, and the safety of a qualification. Master, not servant. And now he worries in case he got it all wrong. He's not the only one.

She was walking fast, aware that her step was light, and her face was turned to the sun. After the weekend at Midwinter Farm, she was always looking towards the sun, dreaming of it. The farm, and the promise of the farm, was only the last of a long line of gifts from Ivy.

London was sweaty inside, dry out. Looking out of the dusty window as the bus lumbered down Oxford Street, she reflected, not for the first time, that the London she inhabited was so very different from the one Ivy knew. Rachel's was high-rise, glass-fronted buildings, computer screens, takeover bids, carpeted floors, civilised meals out and microwaved meals indoors. She was highly focused, driven, the city just a place to work, admired from a taxi. Ivy's was sleazy bars for cheap booze, a series of more or less dirty jobs to fund survival and an art course which had run on for years, with her cash payments never quite enough, her homes a series of squats rising to the tiny basement room she had just relinquished, her employment status that of a reformed heroin addict, and her instincts those of the streetwise, homeless beggar she had also been. Ivy knew hostels for the dispossessed and the temperature of cold pavements. Washed up at thirty, that had been Ivy. Once upon a time, Rachel would have walked round her and left her there, if she had even noticed her.

Rachel walked into the Institute and nodded a greeting to the man on the door. She loved the contrast this place made with the tidiness of the rest of her existence. There were no uniforms, such as suits, no social code, no rules, no pretensions; you were whatever you wanted to be. No one noticed or cared; no one remembered your name or questioned why you were there, but simply accepted you were. She went down the corridor, through the swing doors which bore the scuff marks of a thousand kicking feet, into the alleyway, left past the lockers and into the studio where the life drawing class was held. Strange how quickly this anarchic place, so unlike a sanitised office, had become part of her life. It was gloriously scruffy, like her first, beloved primary school, and Rachel had always loved school. Perhaps that was why she breathed the musty air with pleasure and blinked in the bright, artificial light. It was hotter than a hospital ward, hotter than outside. Models without clothes needed heat. This was where Rachel had met Ivy.

'Hi. Warm in here, isn't it? Who do you think we'll get today?'

Somebody else was early, putting out chairs, teacher's pet. The only awkward student, the Plonker. Norman. The only one with a less than intellectual interest in the unclothed female form. You get them, Ivy said cheerfully. One weird man per dozen.

Rachel had gone to the life drawing class originally because it was available, because she had needed something radically different to do, and because she wanted to learn how to *look*. She had known she had been naïve; she wanted to learn how to observe. It was more than an attempt to fill a gap; it had a purpose. At the time she had been assiduous, organised, and utterly hollow. Her mother was three years dead, her lover of a decade had gone. She was an earmarked stranger in a new job where she was suspected, but no nervous breakdowns were allowed. You filled blank time and cried in private, that was what you did. You distracted your awful, inconvenient conscience by doing something which demanded total concentration, especially if it offered a warm room filled with other people on a cold winter night and the chance to learn something missing from a streamlined education. Besides, it was essentially pointless in career terms, and that, too, was deliberate. Every other course had *led* somewhere; this didn't and no one would judge her success or failure. It was a private process. She could justify the time by saying there were terrible gaps in her cultural knowledge; observation had never been a strong point. And then, after lesson three, she was hooked. Something about the science of drawing began to make sense. You had to learn with your eyes. The hand from wrist to fingertip is usually the same length as the face from chin to hairline. Only a small part of the head is the face, leave space for the rest. You must get the essentials on the page, otherwise you run out of space. LOOK. Measure, if you will. Feet are enormous, beautiful things, and hands are obscure; everything is curves and angles, nothing is straight. Her own hand began to move against her will. The models fascinated her, made her understand how much personality a human being could express without saying a word. How much we give away, express or withhold while simply staying still, without the disguise of clothes or speech.

The room was shrouded in a cloak of dust, with a paint-stained podium in the centre and a mess of plastic chairs and easels lying against the walls. The hum of bus traffic permeated through the frosted windows. The room bore the paint splashes and charcoal residues of countless experiments. There was a sink and a waste bin and a row of hooks, the accumulated rubbish of old work. The life model had a cubicle in the corner in which to change. From it, Ivy had emerged in all her glory. Week six, that was. Bolder than brass, fluid as water. Giving and grinning. A lined face, a thatch of hair, a long, lean body with pendulous breasts, giving off a great big heady cloud of life and the soles of her enormous feet already grey with dust from stepping across the room.

Four short poses, two long poses, and then there was an interval after an hour. Most models rested, sat in dressing gowns and chewed. Not Ivy. Ivy perambulated in a raggy T-shirt. Rachel was always anxious about the models. Were they warm enough? Were they treated with respect? Who would do this for a pittance an hour? It beats the shit out of waitressing, Ivy told her later, it helps pay for the course. It's not as good a rate as cleaning on the night shifts, though, but it's OK, it's fine.

Ivy used the interval time to swig tea and talk. So what do I look like, then? she said. You tell me, I don't know. She laughed with them, teased them, created chatter in a normally silent, serious group. Rachel had seen her out of the corner of her eye, pulling up alongside, stopping like a bus when someone has flagged it down. She had stood, and stared.

51

'Good God,' she said. 'I could be looking in a mirror. You've got me. You've really got me.'

I had, too, Rachel thought. I was having a good day and Ivy inspired me. I forgot my passion for detail, went for the broader strokes, made quick decisions. I was freed by *her*. Ivy had been standing in a classic pose half turned towards where Rachel sat, looking over her shoulder, one arm clasping her waist. Rachel had drawn a long, lithe animal, pausing before flight or fight. She had even sketched in the suggestion of a tail.

Ivy laughed, a gorgeous sound in the dusty room more used to murmurs and the forgotten hum of the road outside. Then she took Rachel's pencil and sketched in a pair of ears for herself.

'Could be a cat,' she said. 'Or a skunk. Anyway, it's me.' She bent towards Rachel, and whispered in her ear.

'Better than that idiot over there. Pity I was facing him. He goes to other classes too, and never gets further than my tits.'

Today, Rachel glanced across the room where the dust dazed and settled, and sharpened her pencils and thought of the moment when she had felt so flattered by a sense of achievement and Ivy's praise.

'I think you're the one person in the room who ought to persist,' Ivy said. 'You've really got me. No one else has. That means you've got a piece of me, for ever.'

At the end of the session Ivy waited, Rachel waited. They went out for a drink which turned into many. Laughed themselves sick. Arranged to meet again, and the rest was history. Rachel adjusted the sketchbook, propped it on the plastic easel, and opened it, turning the page back carefully. She could not resist being careful with paper, although in the intervening months she had become relatively careless with everything else. She was breaking the habits of a lifetime.

Waiting for the model to take the stand, Rachel found her-self wondering what her father would have done if he had found himself with a daughter like Ivy. What it must have been like for Ivy's parents to stand by and watch while she drove her own life over a cliff, and then clawed her way back. They were proud of her. They had learned not to be overtly protective. They were right to be proud; Ivy had done braver things in her life than Rachel ever had. Dispelled demons Rachel had never had to acknowledge.

Emerged like sunshine on a rainy day. Generous and strong, still fighting.

'It was me who screwed up,' Ivy had said. 'And me who had to unscrew it. If I'd taken help, it wouldn't be the same. And I did have help. I always knew I could go home. Now I can. I'm thirty-nine. I'll get to the end of this blasted course, and then maybe even my son will want to know me.'

Five years on a foundation course which should have taken two. Ivy was an art school fixture, who haunted the place. Ivy was a cleaner. She cleaned offices and shops and theatres and clubs.

She did not look thirty-nine. She looked eighteen, apart from her older, wiser, watchful, mischievous face.

There would be no Ivy in this week's life drawing class, although she was a regular round several venues. The models varied in sex and age; they needed to see different bodies, different proportions in order to learn, but all the same, there had come to be a sense of communal disappointment when it was someone else's, because Ivy's spirit lifted them all. The man Rachel and Ivy called the Plonker, the one who attempted to confine his drawing to bosoms and genitals whenever the teacher was not watching, drew his chair nearer to Rachel's, so that she could almost smell his breath. There was always someone who wanted to be too close.

'I wish we could have Ivy all the time,' he whispered to her. 'She grows on you, you know. I do the Saturday class too. She followed me halfway home, you know. Think I'm in with a chance?'

Rachel ignored him and the peppermint smell of his breath, bent to the task. She was all fingers and thumbs today. Would Ivy be home later?

'We'll begin as usual with the quick poses. Three minutes only. Remember, get down the essentials.'

Today's model had coffee skin and a black scrotum, a yoga-honed body and a sense of mischief, using modelling as a form of exercise. Ivy could have trained him in attitude. You have to have a degree of confidence to do this, Ivy said. You have to *give* something. And you can play tricks when you're bored.

Slowly and deliberately, the model stood on his head, cradling his skull in his hands, everything pointing down, and held the position.

The class collapsed into giggles and then into howls of laughter.

I must tell Ivy, Rachel thought, Ivy would *love* this. Ivy would be home soon.

There were a fleet of them who descended on the building at eight o'clock. They gathered in the foyer, some arriving on foot, some waiting, some disgorged from a van with the supervisor who counted them in and counted them out and showed the newcomers where things were. All doors were

open to them, all secrets revealed if they knew where to look.
The aim was to be in and out as fast as possible and on to the
next. There was the six-to-eight shift, the eight-to-ten, and
the morning shifts. Most did either/or; some did all of them,
committing themselves to a rolling timetable the week before.
No show, no pay. There was an endless supply of them.
There was the minimum opportunity for theft, and not much
for camaraderie. Three people to each floor and a strict
timetable. They advanced like tired foot soldiers. More like a
herd of cattle, slow-footed and obedient.

The night cleaners had arrived.

They spread around the place like busy ants, fetching and
carrying after the supervisor unlocked the cupboard doors.
Machinery was released, rubber gloves donned. A large, griz-
zled black man joshed a bigger, broader Nigerian woman,
under the gaze of an inscrutable Albanian. They were not a
team, but they could behave as if they were. Jokes made the
dirty business easier. A little revenge upon the inconsiderate
was permitted, if not permissible. Curiosity about their environment was not a virtue and there was no time for it.

Most of them knew the building and went on to automatic
pilot. They liked it for being relatively easy. Nothing old,
nothing wooden, no areas which did not permit the ruthless
application of short-cut chemicals, all done with a wipe. No
hierarchy among them, no pecking order. Everyone had to
do lavatories.

The woman with the scarf tied over her hair always
hummed as she worked, inaudible over the whir of Hoovers
and polishers. Polish on the shiny floors by the lifts could be
an excuse for sabotage to anyone so inclined. Left half-done,
someone might slip and break an ankle when he came out of
the lift in the morning. Some of the people who worked here

were no better than pigs. One of them littered the floor round his desk with the detritus of what he ate during the day. Chicken bones, soup, sticky crumbs, and his high-smelling spare shoes under the desk. Another left grubby gym kit over the back of his chair. The men who used the washrooms on this floor had very poor aim. Someone had wanked at his desk last week and dropped the tissues in the bin. Amazing what could be done in an open-plan office.

The floor spread, with its islands of desks, each accompanied by a pedestal drawer stand, easily shifted, for the tools of their trade and personal possessions. They could lock their little drawer in accordance with office policy, and they mostly did, but they could still leave traces of personality hanging like a cloud around their own little bit of space. The expression of a personality in its absence.

Here was a desk which deserved extra care. A nice tidy desk, with photos of children pinned to the barrier wall which separated it from the next, a well-watered flowering plant, and a box of sweets. No litter in the desk-side bin; a considerate desk. The cleaner cleaned the surfaces, and looked at the children. This woman had a top drawer full of household bills and divorce papers, poor cow.

The cleaner was on the wrong floor today. The next floor was off limits.

What did they do, all these punished people who worked in this silent place? A shelf of books at one end. Advertising, insurance, buying and selling, accounting, something, and who cared anyway? There was plenty of time for a quick worker to explore, but by eight thirty-five it was time to speed up. The supervisor was on his way upstairs, the lift whining, someone waiting to explain the bits they could not reach, the need for more equipment. Or things which needed special attention, such as a washroom flood. Not their problem.

The only problem on this floor was the man asleep at the last desk in the far corner, on the left. Out for the count. A big, fat, ugly brute, with a belly distending his shirt as he sprawled on a swivel chair, trousers mercifully zipped, head lolled into stillness, one arm resting on the desk, with his fingers next to a pint glass of water. Gone out for a drink or seven at five, slipped back into the building. Fallen asleep. His desk was sticky; he had fetched the water while he could stand, been sick in the bin, would wake with a raging thirst. All that was predictable.

The cleaner held the plastic container of clear bleach in one hand. It was the unnamed brand they used in the lavatories, more powerful than the milder antiseptic spray used for other surfaces. What they used on the stained porcelain was not available in the supermarket. Pure poison was quicker.

Pour out the water in the full glass, top it up with bleach, swirl it around a bit, and leave it for him. Easy. He was a loser. Revenge of a sort, could not be easier. Three minutes to go.

Then she saw that his cheeks, lined into grooves of exhaustion, were still wet with tears. Salt crusted his eyelids.

She drew back.

Not even for practice. No matter how miserable he was. It was too much like killing a dumb animal.

Do it anyway.

At eight thirty, the klaxon sounded in the Institute which housed the evening life class, and the model stepped down off the podium with relief. Reprimanded for the headstand joke, he had become subdued.

Unlike Norman, who sat next to Rachel. A sad-looking man, when she troubled to notice, always seeking attention. A fidget, when the model was male.

'Fancy a drink?' he asked her.

There were ten women and fifteen men in this class. Rachel reckoned the Plonker had probably asked the same question of all the women and certainly some of the models. He had the contagion of loneliness. She was sure her response was the same as all the others.

'No time, thanks. Got to rush.'

Then she was sorry for him. She knew about rejection. The sorrow had faded to anger by the time she reached the top of the road and waited to cross. It was still bright summer light, the evening crowds waning, settling in to their entertainments. She wanted to be home, and there he was behind, following her, waving. Then he was not pitiable; he was a nuisance. A lone figure in the playground of central London. Rachel began to run.

Her flat seemed ultra-quiet, as well as bland, when she reached it. On the bus she had longed for the sensation of going home and finding someone there. Once indoors, she went to the phone and called Ivy. Ivy wore her mobile in a pouch on a leather necklace at all times. Even when she stripped to model, it was the last thing she took off.

'Hi! Are you coming home?'

'In a while. Mopping up here. How was the class?'

'He stood on his head!'

'Good,' Ivy said, laughing with Grace's laugh. 'Good boy. Good, good, good. We're going to learn how to do that.'

CHAPTER FOUR

This was a complete waste of time, but never mind. No one knew quite what to do with him anyway. In his own view, the police service had always been excellent in the mismanagement of its human resources when it came to the proper use of age and experience. He was used to it and entirely resigned. It was years since he had wanted to be at the sharp end of anything, even a pin. Lost his bottle, see? Known for it, especially to himself. Detective Sergeant Donald Cousins, enthusiastic historian, was the perfect officer to manage paperwork rather than a riot. The pen-pushing man of non-action who liked a quiet life. He had the advantage of being unfazed by the officialdom which scared most of his contemporaries far more than a straight fight, and he was the ideal diplomatic candidate for something pointless going nowhere. Nursemaiding a judge, not even a quality judge elevated to the red robe and the trials of terrorists or murderers, simply a crown court judge who dealt with a daily diet of theft burglary and bodily harm. If the said Judge

Schneider thought he was going to qualify for protection, he had another think coming.

What irked Donald Cousins, albeit slightly, was the fact that if the judge had been anyone else, his nebulous complaints would receive no attention at all. It was simply not fair, but at least the judge did himself a favour by being embarrassed. The first thing he did was apologise.

'I'm sorry,' he was saying. 'I wouldn't have said anything on the basis of this kind of evidence, except that my son lives with me. Not an ideal state of affairs, but I worry about him. Do you have children, Mr Cousins?'

'Call me Donald, please, sir. Yes, two daughters. As grown up as they ever are. It does go on for a long time, my wife says.'

They both nodded, agreeing with each other. Parenthood was a great leveller.

'Not long enough, in my case,' the judge said.

Men could usually bond, or unbend a little, by mentioning their children, Donald thought, but there was no answering invitation from Judge Carl Schneider to use his Christian name. Cousins liked that: he did not mind what he was called, and preferred the anonymity of sir as a method of address to any member of the public, especially one who wore a wig. The term could easily be divorced from either endearment or respect.

'Sam's nineteen,' Judge Carl said. 'Not a particularly mature nineteen, I have to say. Public school since he was ten; now he's a student, living with me, and he doesn't know much about the real world. He's clever and lazy, and vulnerable. His mother left when he was small and I've overprotected him. Do we ever know if we're doing the right thing by our children? I don't.'

The judge was nervous, talking too much. Wanting to have

something in common. It established a working balance of power Donald liked. The man needed him and his approval, much more than the other way round.

'We do the best we know how at the time,' he said. 'That's all we can do. The awful thing is wanting to give them everything and not getting it right.'

Carl bent his head in acknowledgement. In the sunlight streaming through the window, Donald noticed how his hair was blond, laced with grey, in a cruelly selective process of ageing which made it look as if he had paid for streaks. Dark-haired, sallow-skinned himself, he found it slightly repellent. A woman would kill for hair like that.

There was no hurry to get on with the matter in hand; nor was this a bad place in which to waste time. They were in the judge's office, which surprised DS Cousins with its sheer, modern austerity. Minimalist. Where he would have expected old-fashioned tradition, plenty of old wood and leatherbound volumes, here were laminate floors and furniture contrived from pale wood and black metal. The reference library was behind the flat screen of the computer, rather than in venerable books. Cousins was disappointed by the lack of the wood-panelled tradition he had associated with the chambers of a barrister. There was no sense of history, or even comfort, a single framed photograph on the wall which looked as if it had been there for a long time, forgotten, rather than chosen. The man's home, from where he had collected him, was even worse. Not Cousins' taste, but then he knew, with his passion for history, that his own preferences were on the old-fashioned side. His daughters said so. His wife always teased him about it. The judge had caught his not so subtle examination of the scenery. It was a small room.

'I'm lucky to have this, since I went to the Bench. Space is at a premium. These days chambers have to be high tech. We look like any other office in the City. We could be peddling soap. Instead, we are merely people, peddling ourselves and our forensic skills. This room's my refuge, from court and home.'

'And the trouble started here?'

He tried to inject sympathy into his voice. So far he felt little.

'No. It was the slashed tyres at home, in the car park, which may have nothing to do with anything. The post going missing, the rubbish bags taken apart and examined. Perhaps I have it the wrong way round, now I come to think of it. There was some . . . interference here, which seems to have been confined to my room. I thought at first it was . . . internal. One of my colleagues, looking for something. Not theft, as such, simply interference; we don't lock doors. Someone wanting a bit of space. The use of a computer. Then I got the e-mails. A bit too erudite to ignore.'

Such a dry wit the judge had. He was drier than old bone, with his yellow-streaked hair. It was that and his expressionless face which made Cousins think not only of a hairdresser, but of someone who had been at the Botox, to redeem or improve his middle forties. As though he was so pampered with treatment, he could not afford to smile. The features of a sphinx, but then it would not do to have a judge who giggled. Maybe it was entirely natural: the youngest of Cousins' daughters, the beautician, would know more than he could guess. He himself knew only that in previous centuries the place in which he now was had been a stew of prostitutes who preserved their blonde locks by dyeing their hair in their own piss.

'I forwarded you the e-mails, didn't I?'

'Yes,' Cousins said. 'A mixed blessing, e-mails. I only know enough not to open any if I don't know who sent them, let alone open anything attached. You can't risk porn, viruses, that kind of thing. You surprise me. I would have thought . . .'

'But I *did* know who sent the first. The first was sent from *me* to *me*. As if to prove that whoever had done it could. I have this computer and the laptop at home, you see. Sometimes I work here after court; sometimes I work there. I e-mail unfinished business to myself. So I opened it.'

Cousins was appalled.

'But even supposing the sender of the first e-mail had got into your office here, how on earth could he log on to your computer? Don't you have passwords? Doesn't it turn itself off if you leave it at night? Surely there's a firewall?'

The judge looked shamefaced.

'Hmm, yes, there's *supposed* to be, but I'm not very good at that stuff. I forget the password and things, so I leave a note of it here,' he pointed to a worn Post-it, stuck to the desk, 'telling me how to do it. How to get in and out, my password, my e-mail address in case I don't remember.'

He seemed rather proud of the care he had taken.

'I see, *sir*,' Cousins said heavily. 'You leave yourself and anyone else a clear set of instructions which a child could understand, telling them how to access your confidential information and bypass the security system. Amazing. Isn't it a bit like leaving your house unlocked?'

He was enjoying a sense of superiority. Carl looked even more ashamed.

'It's simpler, you see,' he said. 'We lawyers aren't necessarily clever like that.'

You lawyers are stupid, Cousins thought, but didn't say.

Wait till he told them back in his own office what idiots barristers were. His supply of sympathy shrank even further, but telling others would be fun.

'What did the e-mail say, *sir*?'

'You know. *Please see attached.* The same as what I say to myself when I e-mail myself with, say, a judgment. It was a drawing, of a hanged man.' He swallowed. 'The next was of a man drowning. About to drown. He's tied up and being pushed over the side of a boat.'

'And the next?'

'A boy, drowning. And the next was a girl, chained by the neck, laid on a slab, overlaid with wooden planks and big stones. They were not from me, to me. I don't know where they came from.'

'Messages?'

'Nothing specific. *I want justice. You must die.* Then, *You will die.* Almost as if I had failed to co-operate. Or the sender was puzzled. Very crude drawings.'

Cousins coughed. 'You think so, sir? Do you know what they are?'

'Crude little drawings.'

Cousins did not know why he was suddenly so disappointed. Had the man, a judge, for God's sake, never studied the history of his own profession? Or looked at the illustrations of his forebears?

'I think you'll find, sir, that they are all illustrations of the Inquisition, I believe. Or maybe even trial by ordeal. The precursors of the modern trial. You can get such things out of a book or on a website. They were a matter of record, then, sir. This one,' he pointed to the third, 'is a woodcut, produced all over Europe.' He coughed politely. 'From Germany, I believe. A favourite method of the Inquisitors, in

64

order to extract the truth, was to weight a body down with stones until it literally burst. Little, yes. Crude, no. They were the record of what the Inquisitors did, in secret. Protests. They regarded the confession as the last word in truth, however it was obtained. Some say the modern method of trial is no better.'

A hint of mutual dislike was percolating between them now; no way to know how far it would go, until the judge smiled.

'Tell me,' he said. 'My fascination with the law began with my father's fascination with Nuremberg. Didn't trial by ordeal pre-date the inquisitorial method? Even less reliable, but still avoiding the inconvenience of the jury, invented, or at least established I think, by the English?'

Donald noticed that the picture on the wall was of swans. An old, tired photograph. 'Someone is sending you old illustrations, sir. A well-wisher, perhaps.'

When he came to think of it, Carl looked more like a farmer than a scholar. A man who lived in a series of solid bubbles, moving from courtroom to chambers to apartment without his feet ever touching the ground. He would be very difficult to get at.

'I suppose, with the messages, it amounts to threats to kill, although they're usually more specific. I'm looking ahead, sir, to the matter of proof. Of intent. Have any of your colleagues received any of these?'

'I presume not. They would have complained if they had, and they haven't as far as I know.'

'And they stopped when you changed your e-mail address?'

'I didn't change it. It's far too much of a nuisance. Besides, I want to know what's being sent. I haven't received one for a week.'

Give me patience, Cousins sighed. 'Who do you think dislikes you enough to do this?'

'I don't know. Judges aren't popular people.'

'Anyone you're afraid of?'

Carl paused to straighten the framed photo on the wall, spoke in a judge's voice, which reminded Donald of a lecturing priest.

'Mr Cousins, we all have people we would prefer not to meet. People who dislike us for what we are, or for real or imagined injuries. Especially a judge in a court of law, and also, if I may suggest it, a policeman. In a court, some might imagine it is I who convict them, whereas it is not. It's the jury. Others might also blame the judge for the failure to convict, which leaves them without redress or revenge. I do know a little history, although not as much as you. I know, for instance, that the word *miasma* once referred to the vapour exuded by murderers, but which also attaches itself to the one who fails to avenge the death, and poisons his life for ever. It exists, today, that obligation, in cultures older than ours, and it certainly still exists with us. So I am quite sure I am blamed and disliked for appearing to fail to punish, for failing to be that instrument of revenge in the event of acquittal. The defendant who goes to prison from my court, on the other hand, is usually prepared and ready. Since I've never had the onerous privilege of sentencing anyone to death, I suspect the real anger comes from the first category.'

Donald forced himself back into pragmatic police mode. Abandon *miasma*, although he did like the word. Only investigate the obvious. He could not investigate the obscure, however long he wanted this job to last. So, those disgruntled by a negative result were an impossible line of enquiry, unless they had announced themselves first. What he could and would do was waste time going through the records to find any of the judge's old defendants who had made known their displeasure at their treatment and check them out. Isolating those still aggrieved, still aggressive, taking it personally, and who also had historical illustrations to hand as well as the means to send them, should keep the number small. Forget the slashed tyres. Look at the son, obfuscate the report to invite conspiracies, avoid the conclusion that the judge had colleagues who played tricks on him. He could make it last weeks. Good.

'What worries me,' the judge said, 'is the order of things. Someone invaded this room here, and thus found out where I live. This room is more important than home. I keep my private life here, albeit very carelessly, as you've pointed out.'

At least he admitted it. Donald wanted to say he was criminally careless, but refrained.

'Any personal enemies, sir? Family, perhaps?'

Carl shook his head. 'There are none of those left, Donald. Few enough to begin with. My parents were both orphans of war, no uncles or aunts. There's only my son, who studies economics, so he knows it's hardly in his interests to do me harm.'

Cold, but interesting. Give him the usual spiel. 'You should vary your route to work, sir. How do you usually go?'

The judge was surprised. 'I walk. How else do I see the world?'

Oh, shit. He was beginning to like the bloke. There were worse ways to waste time.

Must get a look at the son.

Ivy had the chance of weekend work. Good money. Well-paid life modelling on Saturday, followed by a theatre shift.

Look, I can't go home this weekend. Got to settle in, got sixteen hours' paid work, can't do it. Got to work, got to pay for myself, got to study. Go yourself. Mother will love it, Ivy said. Mother phoned, and Mother did. Rachel could not resist.

So there she was, proceeding down the dappled lane to the house she already loved better than the farm. There would be paying guests in the pigsties, she had been told, the private kind who stay in their rooms and go to the pub to eat. Dead easy. Walkers, twitchers. I'll have time. Ernest will have time to show you the pigs. How lovely to have you back, by yourself. We'll go shopping. We'll go to the sea.

It was ridiculous, Rachel thought, to be so happy with all three of them. I don't care if it doesn't last.

The air was musky. It was nine in the evening, still light at that time of the year when light seemed endless and summer was going to last for ever. Rachel shivered. She detoured up a side road, in pursuit of a view. This time last year she would never have detoured at all. She would have gone straight to her destination, criticising her own navigation. Following her instincts, she found Pointed Hill, a mile away from the farm, with a view of the flatter land. From the top, where the wind gusted warm and strong, she orientated herself and looked. There was the valley; there was the narrow road going through it, meandering to the village, which was nothing but a smattering of houses, a church and the pub; there was the other, shaded track which led to the farm, and there was the faint glimmer of the lake shrouded in trees. A bright red car chugged towards the village, as if seeking the company of other, parked cars. Instead of looking down, she looked across, and was surprised to spy, in the distance, separated by further dips and hollows and fields of wheat, the sea, stretched in a blue line. A full stop, where the land ran out. It only surprised her because, from the shelter of the valley, the land seemed endless and limitless. In the middle distance she could see a deserted air strip, unattached by any road, and closer to the edge of the valley, a site of low, derelict buildings, surrounded by green. How different this would have been, sixty years ago, populated by soldiers and strangers, bicycles and horses, rather than cars.

Grace was in saffron yellow, with endearing grey roots to her plum-coloured hair, bellowing welcome and rattling with different silver bracelets. 'They're all out! Isn't that marvellous! You must be starving.'

Rachel was.

It was cooler in that room she already thought of as her own. A breeze through the window, the next-door room and the shared bathroom vacant.

Cold chicken. Roasted potatoes with rosemary and a crust of salt. Earthy spinach. You don't think I grow all this, do you? Grace said. What on earth is the point of a supermarket if I did?

Darkness fell, and the kitchen exerted its charm.

'I've had an excellent week,' Grace said. 'A couple staying, been before. Walkers. Out all day, even when it rains. Don't want more than breakfast, and a meal midweek. Don't want conversation, either. They spend the evening in the pub and walk home singing. You might hear them later. Would you like to try this cheese?'

'No thanks. Tell me something: if the paying guests stay in the pigsties, where do the pigs live?'

'Oh, I forgot, you never got round to that last time. Pigs live in barns these days. Like cows, but not like cows. The pigsties, sorry guest rooms, were stables before. Once used for horses, then pigs. They make nice little single rooms, or two adjoining. Rather dark, of course. Ernest put windows in the back walls, long before you needed planning permission for that kind of thing, of course.'

'Were is he?'

'Milking. Cowman's day off, so he has to do both milkings. Which leaves us more wine. I do love this one you brought. It tastes expensive. The only time I get to drink good wine is when people bring it.'

'I'll remember that,' Rachel said.

The now familiar sloth was stealing across her, the same laziness which had turned the weekend before into little more than half a tour of the farm and a lot of sitting around in the garden while Grace fed them senseless. Without Ivy, she would behave more like a tourist, who explored and asked questions.

'I can't tell you how pleased I am that Ivy's moved in with you,' Grace said in a rush, anxious to say it, but postponing it until now. 'Pleased and grateful. What did she do to deserve you? What has she done to deserve someone who sweetly and sensitively trusts her to get used to her new abode in private? Aren't you worried she'll trash it?'

'No. She's the tidiest person I know. And it wouldn't matter if she did.'

Grace nibbled a breadstick.

'If I were your mother,' she announced, 'I'd go after that man who left you, and cut his balls off. He must have been out of his mind.'

'Oh, I think he was totally in command of his mind. I just wish he hadn't lasted so long. My mother would have said it was all my own fault, but I don't have a mother any more.'

'Yes you do,' Grace said airily. 'You've got me. Thirty-two

is way too young to be without one, and I've always needed more children, so count me in. I'll kill him for you.'

Rachel laced her fingers together on the warm wood of the table, looked down at them.

'Did you feel that way about Carl? Carl the younger?'

Grace touched her fingers. The touch was rougher than the wood. 'Do you really want to know?'

'Yes. If you're going to be my mother too, of course I really want to know.'

Grace plucked a daisy from the jug of flowers on the table. A tiny little blue jug, like the jug full of lavender Rachel had noticed in her room. Small enough to be significant.

'Kill him? Nothing as mild as that. Getting her pregnant was forgivable, I could see he was crazy about her. Marrying her, well, who wouldn't? You should have seen her then. I don't think anyone could have resisted her. The passion was mutual. It was after that. He wanted to tame her, make her a respectable wife and mother. Understandable, also. She longed for city lights, that kind of life; she wanted to be what he wanted her to be. And he wasn't bad, as husbands go. Let her enrol on the arts course, paid for it. Then, when she wanted to come back and give her children what she'd had, he didn't like that. I could see it was threatening. I tried to understand him. I never knew what a cold monster he was.'

She put the daisy back in the jug before she could damage it in her twisting fingers, selected a piece of fern.

'No, not then. I didn't know him then. Ivy wasn't going to tell me. As you'll notice, she has her pride. I only began to detest him for his refusal to admit things. Cassie's death was his fault. He was supposed to be looking after them both, down by the lake, on his own, for once. He always had more time for the boy. Sam was acting up, so Carl brought him home. He left her to drown. OK, an accident. It was what he did after, and has done ever since. Closed down and shut Ivy out, hugged the boy close to him for comfort. And when Ivy wailed and screamed, he hit her . . .'

'No,' Rachel said, sharply.

Grace shook her head.

'Oh, to be fair, she was impossible. Crazy with grief and guilt, sure, but she was already into the drugs. Living the sort of student life she'd missed, only worse, because he gave her money. Drink and drugs. Didn't go home to the nice town house to be hit again. She ran away from them. Came back. He locked the door on her. The worst thing he did was not tell us. Until she cracked and disappeared. Then he told me. I got used to tramping those London streets, I tell you. I found her in Centrepoint. It took a year. The worst year of my life.'

'I somehow can't see you in London, Grace.'

Grace laughed. 'Can't you now? I know it well. I used to go to every exhibition, but I know the less salubrious bits better. Hostels and hospitals. Of course she wouldn't co-operate. She was shacked up with some druggie. Panhandling for dope and food. Told me to fuck off. Then she got arrested for the last time, and got shoved on a reha-bilitation scheme. That, or prison. The first one didn't work, the second did. She began to see the light. God, those people were patient, but then Ivy never lost her charm. She got better. Not a linear progress, I can tell you. And she did it all by herself. Got better. That's when Carl did his very worst.'

'Could he do worse?'

Grace nodded. 'Yes, he could. To her, and to us. Much worse. He kept her from seeing her son. And his son from seeing us. He still does. Which is why,' she added with a watery smile, 'I have such a dearth of children. Do you know, you're the first person Ivy has ever brought home?'

The kitchen door opened quietly. The sound of scraping. Grace turned towards it. 'Oh, Ernest love, you late-night stop-out, you. Do you want a cup of tea?'

Ernest Wiseman came in, and struggled with his boots. He kicked them into the washing machine alcove, came into the circle of light around the table, leaving the door open. His blue eyes widened and his face opened into a smile of guile-less pleasure as he looked first at Grace, then at Rachel.

'Now here's a sight for sore eyes,' he said. 'Hope you've brought boots for tomorrow, girl. You're going to need them.'

From the open door they could hear singing, and the soft sound of rain. The paying guests were home.

Never was the early morning so wonderful as after rain. Ernest and Rachel, in her borrowed boots and socks, walked over the field to the cow barn. Next to it was a barren little office which housed desk, chair, filing cabinet, and the dirti-est computer screen she had ever seen. It was a civilised hour of the morning, post-breakfast, if only nine o'clock. Milking still in progress, half done. A long process, even for forty cows, with some of them back in the barn. Ernest walked her through them. They ranged free in the hugeness of the barn, and yet converged on her with wide eyes.

'Just curious,' Ernest said. 'All newcomers get that. Come here every day and there's never a flicker. Unless one's got a calf, and you were to come in here, newer than paint, with a dog. Then she might have a go at you. Not otherwise. They'd only ever knock you over by mistake. The pigs are over there. OK to walk?'

Despite the reassurance, Rachel did not think she could bring herself to trust the cows. Stupidity, weight, and the feelings she could not doubt they had unnerved her. It was better out in the field, away from the dirty backsides of the ten-ton beasts.

'Pigs are much cleaner,' Farmer Wiseman said. 'They won't lie in their own shit, they hate it, but all the same they smell worse, whatever we feed them. I shall have to phase out the cows, never the pigs. I love 'em. P'raps because they're not lovable at all, except sometimes.'

Certainly he loved the pigs, and gave her every detail. The pig barn was a one-storey unit with a pit beneath, with a raised wooden floor made of slats. The pigs seemed to demand little to lie on except these slats, through which faeces fell to the level beneath. Ernest explained all this. Rachel could only think of who would clear away what fell between the slats into the pit, grateful it was not her, worried that she might one day be asked to do it. In the barn there were fifteen stalls, the first two occupied by enormous sows-in-waiting. The next stalls were sows with newborn, suckling pigs; then sows with older piglets. She could see how they doubled their weight in a week. She hated them and shrank away from them, keeping to the middle of the central aisle which ran between the pens, not touching anything and hoping he would not notice.

'You can wean these in days,' Ernest said, pointing at a crop of almost shockingly pink piglets draining mummy dry. Mummy lay on her side, held in position by bars.

'But only if you give them the right food,' he added. 'Which is very expensive. So leaving them with mum is best. Greedy little buggers, aren't they? Don't worry, she can always roll on to her tummy and deny them. The bars only stop her rolling over and squashing them to death. I can open the pens from the outside when they go to market. Then they try and bash down the doors.'

The somnolent sows with their sniffling, squealing feeders raised heads and slumped back. Like the cows, it was the sheer enormity of them which disturbed her. In one stall, an undersized thing, as pink as a flamingo and the size of a small cat, crawled away from brethren three times its size and lurked in a corner.

'He won't last,' Ernest said.

The last pens were young pigs, squealing for food.

'They'll eat anything,' Ernest said with evident admiration. 'Problem is, we can't feed them it.'

'How do you clean them out?' Rachel asked, itching to get out.

'Sweep out the straw down the middle, let it drop through into the pit. Empty the pit every now and then. Grace won't let me in the house after I've done that, not until she's hosed me down. You don't like them, do you?'

'No, they scare me, to be honest.'

He laughed. 'I won't tell.'

He pushed a lever, which sent pellets of food into the dishes by every stall in a clatter of sound. Silence fell.

The smell: she knew the stench of them would scent her clothes. A feral, animal, acid smell which permeated everything. *Eau de Cochon.*

'I love them because they haven't any inhibitions. No manners either. When a boar mounts a sow, there's no pleasure like it, really. His eyes roll and his feet tap, and he makes noises like I never heard, while she vibrates like a violin. They know how to have fun. They take pleasure in everything.'

Rachel found the stench made her dizzy. She was

remembering a murder story, with a body fed to the pigs. They'd eat anything. Outside, she gulped for air. There were steps down from the door; Ernest stumbled and put his hand on her shoulder for support, briefly, then stood upright.

'I'm getting old,' he said. 'They're too much for me, really. Pigs and cows and fields to feed me. Makes nothing. There you go. Got a friend in Normandy makes a living out of fourteen cattle. Not here. Come on, love, I'll show you the hay barn where me and Carl used to hide.'

It was as if she was part of a story, and he assumed she knew the rest. Ivy was like that too, but Ivy had none of the occasional vagueness she noticed in Ernest, the long-term memory so much better than the short.

The barn was vaulted beauty, the beams as old and bent as time, the roof littered with holes.

'I've no duty to this,' he said, 'except to preserve it for ever. These days, I'm paid to preserve buildings and hedgerows, not to grow food. There's nothing for sons and grandsons. I still keep hoping he'll come back, though.'

She did not know what he meant. Didn't want to know.

'Last week,' she said, 'I saw the little blind cow who could not calve. Is she still here?'

'For a while,' he said. 'I can't kill her. I've got to call for the knacker. I can't just kill a beast unless she's running wild, then I get a man with a rifle to do it. No rifles on this farm; well, none anyone knows about except me. I kept Dad's hidden. We've only got handguns. A handgun does, from three feet away. I can't do it, myself, have to wait for Ivy or Grace. I'm not allowed to kill my own cattle and give them a decent burial, oh no. Not since BSE. You have to have your cattle killed for you. Different for pigs.'

She was relieved to be further away from the pigs. The

stench clung to her clothes. She was glad she would never have to clean out that pit. The mud of the yard squelched beneath her feet. She could see the virtue of rubber boots. Ernest looked at hers, and his own heavy suede boots.

'I get through a pair of these every six months,' he said. 'They rot. Then they can go in the incinerator. Here it is. Fired it up, especially for you. Too expensive for every day.'

They had walked away from the barn. In the yard on the other side, nearer the pigs, was a small bunker. It reminded her of an old pill box she had seen in the field, a war relic too heavy to shift. Nearer, the bunker hummed. Ernest fiddled with a thermostat on the side, and then opened the door on the front.

There was a blaze of heat and light from inside. A roar of flame. A cupboard of fire, the size of a large wardrobe. Propped at the back was the remnants of a smouldering form, and at the front the still identifiable forms of three piglets, surrounded by ash. It smelt clean. Ernest leant down, plucked something white from the front, and closed the door.

He handed it to her, beaming. 'There you are,' he said.

She took it gingerly. It was like a small piece of crumbling chalk.

'Just a bit of bone. Everything in there will be pure ash by tomorrow. Magic, isn't it?'

He looked at her pale face. 'Time for a cup of coffee, I think. Grace wants to take you to the sea. I think that's what she said.'

On the way back, downhill across the field, she felt she had been churlish, should have asked more questions. She pointed to a mound by the side of the path. A funny thing, looking like nothing, except for the huge manhole cover on top.

'What's that?'

'Oh, that's the pit. Goes down like a well shaft. Don't know who made it. That's where we used to put dead animals. They rot down nicely, except sheep. Can't use it now, in case it does something to the water table. Bollocks, it never did before. Locked shut. You should be allowed to kill your own, only way to show respect. You shouldn't be forced to send them away to die. Animals have souls. They should die at home.'

He swiped at the long grass by the side of the path with a filthy hand. 'I wish he'd come back. Then I could cope.'

Then he patted her shoulder.

'Sorry, lass. Shouldn't go on, should I? Especially when I've lost my place. Only we've got this grief, see? Such grief. All of us. We're just like those swans.'

CHAPTER FIVE

Rachel paused at the kitchen door, listening to the sound of it. The birds sang in the garden, and someone wept within. Ernest went in ahead of her, as if she did not exist. She waited on the threshold.

'Don't be silly,' he was saying. 'There, there, don't carry on so.'

'Another letter sent back! I can't bear it. He reads what I write, puts it back in the envelope and sends it back. Second-class post, I ask you. Insult on injury. Oh, the bastard.'

'You mustn't upset yourself.'

'Oh, mustn't I? Why the hell not? Why not, why not?' Her voice was rising. The bracelets on her wrists jangled. Then she saw Rachel at the door and stopped moving.

Rachel's eyes were blinded by sunlight, the kitchen was dark; there was an adjustment to be made. Grace was embarrassed. Rachel was glad she could scarcely see, until Grace began to wipe her face with a dishtowel. There was a slight smell of bacon, the residue of the paying guests' breakfast. The dishwasher hummed.

'Ernest, make the coffee, there's a darling. Sorry, Rachel dear. I'm being tragedy queen this morning. It's my turn.'

'For what? What happened?'

Again she caught the glance between them: Grace looking to Ernest for some sort of approval, not getting it. He had turned his back and stood nursing the kettle. Grace blew her nose on the dishtowel and sat up straight. She made a quick recovery. Then she crumpled again. It was unbearable to see her cry. Rachel put an arm round her shoulder, clumsily. She welcomed gestures of affection herself, but was slow to learn how to make them. She was always waiting for the other person to withdraw. Grace leaned against her. It was extraordinarily satisfying to give someone strength and have them take it.

'Can you tell me?'

'No,' Ernest said. 'Don't. It isn't fair.'

'Please,' Rachel said. 'I want to help.'

Grace had massive shoulders, but the flesh on her bare arms was damp and feverish.

'Ernest darling,' Grace said. 'Ivy's living in Rachel's home now. I think perhaps she ought to know. Even though it isn't fair she should.'

She turned towards Rachel with a tremulous smile which touched Rachel's heart. Grace and Ivy; Ivy and Grace: they were both in her bloodstream now. In months she had learned the necessity and privilege conferred by trust and she was going to honour it. She could feel the small piece of bone she had taken from Ernest beginning to crumble in the pocket of her shorts. Life was short. Now that her eyes had adjusted, Rachel could see the morning's post scattered over the table. A few unopened envelopes, which looked like bills, circulars, adverts, and a couple of sheets of hand-written paper.

'Why does he scrunch them up?' Grace said. 'I always write so carefully. Why mess up my writing, stuff it into an envelope and send it back? Why not reply? Or ignore me?'

Ernest left the room.

'It's that bastard Carl,' Grace said. 'Look, I don't know quite what Ivy's told you. About her son.'

Rachel hesitated.

'Very little. Except that she has no contact with him, and that's probably the best thing for them both.'

'Huh. So she might say. It simply isn't true. It's *torture* for her, and what about me? Once she got better, she wanted to see him. I'd always kept in touch with Carl. Ernest always kept in touch with Carl the elder, until he died. Not long after Cassie. He was the voice of reason, I tell you.'

'Hang on. Ivy told me she'd tried to establish contact with her husband in order to keep contact with her son, once she surfaced from the mire, but he – Carl, I mean – thought it was a bad idea. She only really resurfaced when Sam was in his teens. She agreed. She doesn't seem bitter about it. How old is he now? Eighteen? Nineteen?'

'What Ivy doesn't know,' Grace snapped, 'is that *I* have always kept in contact with Carl. I wanted to know what happened to my grandson, even when that bastard got an injunction taken out against her. Barring her from the house. He was good at first, I must admit. He sent me progress reports. He told me, not in so many words, of course, never specific, where he went to school, how he was doing, all that. Turning into a little public school prick of a product, probably. I told Carl that Sam should meet his mother. Then he wrote, after a whole fucking year, saying, sorry, Sam's doing exams, et cetera. I held off. Then I wrote again, and this is what happens. Five times now. Bastard.'

She dabbed at her eyes. 'And never mind *me*. What about Ernest? Carl the elder was the big brother he never had, Carl the younger was the son he never had, and he dreams of his grandson. Oh, shit.'

'Does Ivy know this?'

'No. Of course not,' Grace said, quickly. 'She was beyond receiving any information of any kind for years. And there was this injunction forbidding contact. Even I don't know where they live. The letters always go to his solicitor, who forwards them. That was the only way Carl would consent to keep in contact at all. I can't tell my daughter that I've been going behind her back, can I? And I know my child. I know she'll never be right until she sees her son. Whatever she says.'

For the first time, Rachel felt the burden of information. She did not want such secrets.

'Ivy doesn't know her arse from her elbow,' Ernest said, coming back into the room.

'Who are you talking to?' Grace yelled. 'She could shoot handguns when she was five, drive when she was ten, paint when she was fourteen, procreate at seventeen, and Rachel knows her better than you do. Get out of here. No, not you, petal. You need coffee. Come back, darling, please. Please.'

Ernest left, quietly. Rachel sat down again.

'Ah, fuck it,' Grace said. 'Men. Forget I spoke. He's right, I'm not being fair. Let's go to the sea. That's what we were going to do, wasn't it?'

Grace drove with the same verve with which she did everything. The car was the oldest Rachel had ever seen, so old she could hardly discern its make. A third-hand Volvo of ancient shape, built like a tank.

'Good for absolutely everything,' Grace yelled. 'Except when it comes to getting it out of a ditch. Did you bring your swimming things?'

'No.'

'No worries. There's some in the back. Not that you have to. You don't have to do anything. Oh God, what a glorious day.'

It was the height of a green, wet summer, before the rot set in. The car rattled down the lanes on to the main road, where the presence of other traffic seemed almost impertinent. They passed the pub at the crossroads and the hamlet surrounding it, charged downhill, then uphill, past fields of wheat, then on to the flat, where Grace surprised her by slowing down to a sedate pace in deference to bigger vehicles.

'That's better,' she said. 'Sometimes I just need to get out of there. A trip to the supermarket doesn't do it. Sometimes I feel trapped. There's that push–pull effect of loving things and hating them at the same time. Do you feel that way about work? Is it worse when it's high-powered and responsible?'

'Don't know about that,' Rachel shouted above the rattle of the engine. 'Sometimes I can't wait to get to work. Other times, I'd do anything not to go.'

She watched the road ahead, thought about what she was saying. 'But then, I work purely for money. It never occurred to me there could ever be any other motive. I check and balance other people's money. I sort out companies in danger from the tax man. I advise on due process. I'm a cog in a wheel. I never once imagined there might be a chance to do something enjoyable *and* be well paid for it. I'm not vocational. I definitely went for the money. And that's what I get.'

'It must be strange,' Grace said, slowing down for a junction, 'to do something where you never quite see the end result. Strikes me you're always sorting out cock-ups. No wonder you like drawing.'

The dark mood was gone and Rachel had reached a decision. Which was not to resist being dragged into the lives of this family. If they needed her, she was theirs, dark moods and all.

The first sight of the sea always made her want to clap her hands in applause. Any stretch of water had the same effect on her. Calm or stormy, it spoke of freedom. There had been dutiful, hygienic trips to the coast when she was a child, when she was allowed to paddle, before her feet were dried and put back into solid sandals, in case of glass, prickles, turds and germs. Later, there had been package holidays to Spain, full of complaints about the heat and the food, where, lathered in Factor 50, Rachel learned to swim in the safety of a small hotel pool, stinking of chlorine. She wished she had learned in the sea.

The place where Grace slewed the tank to a halt in a scrubby car park was not an idyllic piece of coastline. It was a flat, untidy shore, full of thistles and stones, but the sea and the sky were there.

'When I was a kid,' Grace said, 'all these beaches and bays would be crowded out in summer. Now they get in aeroplanes and go somewhere else, thank God. Be careful here, won't you? You're safe by the shore, but further out, the current's stronger.'

Rachel could see why this particular bay did not attract families. It had a clandestine air of neglect and the beach was littered with the detritus of bonfires and picnics, adult frolics, bottles and cans. Sea-lovers did not notice. None of that mattered, if it kept the others away and left them with a whole expanse of water to themselves. They stood by the boot of the car, stripped quickly and unselfconsciously. Rachel tugged on an old swimsuit which both covered her and hung off. They were both laughing like children. She had never done this with her own mother. Hand in hand, they tiptoed to the water. It was twinkling cold; they screamed. A few minutes splashing in the waves was enough. It was the act of immersion which gave the sense of triumph; distance and duration were unimportant. Rachel had always found the desire to be in water difficult to describe. Grace understood it instinctively. It simply made everything better.

'Is the lake warmer?' Rachel asked through curses and chattering teeth.

'Oh, yes. Much. Warm and shallow.'

Grace stood back and looked at her while she towelled her hair dry with a thin towel.

'Rachel, you've got to get yourself an itsy-bitsy teeny-weeny bikini,' she said. 'You're drop-dead gorgeous, you know. Even with blue skin. Clothes are bloody wasted on you.'

Rachel looked out to sea and laughed. It was the remark; it was Grace's own beauty, as she stood towel-clad, like a magnificent, gnarled tree trunk restored to strength by sacred immersion in cold water. Baptised, redeemed.

'That's exactly what I said to your daughter, madam. The day I met her. She threatened to test the point by leaving class without her clothes, but it was rather cold.'

'She would have done, you know. Never dare Ivy to do anything. It's as good as done,' Grace said, shivering. 'I first started to worry about her when she was twelve,' she went on. 'She had a school report which said, *This girl is a bad influence*. I congratulated her, of course. Maybe they were right. What was your mother telling you, at that age?'

They were huddled back into clothes before Rachel replied.

'That I'd better lose weight, work harder, stop eating so much, and stop complaining about the braces on my teeth. Otherwise she'd be stuck with me for ever. I paraphrase, but that's the gist. She was right, too. She always was. She wanted her ugly duckling to become a swan and sail away.'

'A swan?' Grace said, faintly.

'Anything that could fly,' Rachel said.

'Bit of a bum deal, being a swan. A bird that can't sing.'

Rachel laughed again, twisted her hair into a knot, and sat down on the shingle, tingling warm. Ivy was the one, the only one who had ever suggested she was good enough as she was. She felt disloyal talking about her own, strict mother, whose ambitions for her daughter were translated into constant criticism.

'She may have had in mind a beautiful creature mating for life, without singing or dancing either. The way she did with my father. She loved me, and she meant for the best, but the fact was that she loved my father more.'

Grace nodded, understanding. 'I think I know what you mean. There are parents like that. It's tough on a child when the parents stay in love. Send baby to bed or to study, so they can be alone.'

'I was very lucky,' Rachel said.

'So was your mother,' Grace said. 'Christ, look at the time. You ate scarcely any breakfast, you must be starving.'

'You're at it again.' Rachel laughed – it was natural to laugh with Grace – and the sea glittered. 'Do you ever *stop* being a mother?'

Grace shuddered. 'No,' she said fervently, 'never. There's always room for more. Should have had a brood. Shame it didn't happen. God knows, I tried hard enough.'

Seagulls wheeled overhead, joining in the chorus of laughter with their piteous, cunning cries. Talking in code to one another. Rachel loved that sound.

'I'm guessing,' she said, 'that you're the kind of parent a million miles from mine. The sort who believes the child can do no wrong.'

'Absolutely definitely. In Ivy's case, and now in yours, dear. You'll always be right. Fuck the rest, they're wrong. Anyway, in Ivy's case, she never did wrong. She had it done to her.'

'I don't think she thinks that.'

'Well,' Grace smiled, 'mothers know best. And it's only because I now love you both that I'll have to tell you a little more about husband Carl. So that you'll know what kind of a destructive freak she married. And I know it isn't fair, but she's living in your flat, and she still has nightmares. Better to know why. You both need space to grow. And, by the way, Ivy will be nesting in your house. She does that, but not like a cuckoo, I promise.'

It was lovely to be here. There was nothing better than being welcomed into a home, told to treat it as your own nest, even a corner of it.

Ivy was nesting in the small, second bedroom of Rachel's flat, wondering from time to time what her best friend and her mother were doing, but not thinking about it that much. There was no point in thinking about anything much. It interfered with the contentment of the day. Plans had to form in a vacuum, of their own accord.

She must pull her weight here, Grace said. It had to work. First she rearranged the room, and found a place to hide the portfolio of drawings. Rachel would want to see those; Rachel always wanted to see her work, but she couldn't. For this arrangement to work, it had to be equal. She would not be a taker. Love of whatever kind depended on each giving what the other needed. Rachel was giving her a home and a base: that was an awful lot. Ivy felt light in the balance and she was drawing up her own list of what had been given and received. She drew it on a sheet of paper in a series of scribbles and symbols which were her own shorthand, checked the time. She was the model in the second half of a one-day life drawing course, due in an hour. Better paid on Saturdays. Easy work.

What did Rachel need? Acceptance, praise, fun, less inhibition. She drew a mouse. Ivy had supplied plenty of that. Encouraged Rachel to let down that long blonde hair and reveal the beauty. Dress in colours. On a shallower level, taught her to drink without having a conscience, listen to music and look at paintings without feeling self-indulgent, nurture a talent, find new routes, eat heartily, be late for work, and occasionally answer back. Made her explore her own city. Ivy had even made her dance. Rachel could dance, a natural rhythm, deeply suppressed. What else had she given? She had given her own mother, gift-wrapped. The best therapist under the sun. A gift of love, both ways round, that is. Grace always needed another daughter as well as me. Yes, they were pegging equal, as if they were sisters.

Ivy looked in the mirror. There was, after all, a superficial resemblance. A pair of gorgeous blondes. Teutonic-looking, her ex-husband's type. She covered her thatch with a cap. She owned three. A hat and a naked body worked wonders in drawing class. Rachel was two inches shorter. Rachel should learn to wear heels.

Time to go. Life modelling for amateur students and beginners, Saturday afternoon four till eight at the Institute. Strictly clean work at weekends. No offices to polish. It would be so good to come back to a convenient flat, instead of trailing out to the boondocks on the grubby Central Line train.

She could do murals on the walls in this flat, here. Perhaps. Only if Rachel wanted, but a different colour scheme at least. What she could do before Rachel came home was fill it with flowers. It would be sparkling clean and full of bloom. Give her ideas.

She would take a hat to class, make them laugh, lower their inhibitions.

The phone rang. Not the mobile she wore round her neck on a leather thong, retrieved, warm from contact, from the inside of her bra. The other one. Rachel's landline. She had forgotten there were people left who still depended on these. She picked it up.

'Hallo.'

'Is that you, Rache? It's your dad. Look . . .'

'It's not Rachel. She's away.'

'She never goes away,' he said petulantly.

'She does now,' Ivy said cheerfully. 'She's staying with my mother at the minute. Getting a bit of fresh air. How are you, Mr Doe? I'm the new flatmate.'

'Oh.'

There was a full beat of silence, redolent with mistrust.

'We were hoping you might come up to town for supper one day next week, Mr Doe. I know you're worried about my existence, but I am paying rent and everything. Would love to meet you. Can you do it? Wednesday and Friday are best for us. I can cook.'

Another, longer beat of silence.

'Wednesday,' he said.

'Fine. Look forward. About six thirty? Rache says you like to eat early, so you can get back.'

'OK.'

She was only trying to do more to equal the balance and please Rachel, but he sounded suspicious and confused. Fine. She put the phone down, distastefully. Anything larger than a mobile felt like an intrusion in the hand. She scribbled the date on a piece of paper, thought of phoning them. Should I ring? No. She might be down by the lake with Grace, and anyway, it was time to go to work.

Norman, the Plonker, would be at the weekend class; he went to them all. The one with the blond hair, who had frightened her darling Rachel a few days ago. There was way too much of the wrong kind of love all round. Some of it a person could do without. If Norman asked her out for a drink this time, she would go, because she felt like it and Saturday night made her restless to prowl. She wanted to be out, to see what would happen. Maybe he would buy her something to eat. He would be the sort of company she could ignore, use, shed like a cloak, possibly an ally. She thought no further than that, and missed her other friends from the good old, bad old days, where someone might really know who she was.

She was dressed in neat dark blue jeans, matching top, almost official. She looked more like Rachel dressed for the office, before Rachel discovered colour, except for the cap. She could merge with the darkness, coming home. It would be light for hours yet. She could feel the energy of the street waiting for her.

Later. Sticky, hot Saturday night. There was a running fight in Leicester Square, where the last, paralysed spectators ebbed away with the first sirens and the arrival of police and ambulance. There had been a stabbing, there were blood and teeth on the ground, injuries, a flashpoint reached so quickly that no one rightly saw, even less knew why the carnage had happened. There was confusion for the paramedics and the shirt-sleeved uniforms, struggling to establish priorities. Who to chase, who to treat, who to question or rescue first.

A couple, still looking for an open bar, paused on the corner, not sure what to do. They needed to get across, to that side road over there, but waited, huddled in the doorway of the cinema. An ambulance was parked in the pedestrian zone, with the doors open. They had a view straight into the brightly lit interior, where a man lay on the gurney, mask on face, unattended. Two paramedics and the driver were twenty-five yards away, tending to another youth, who lay on the ground, screaming.

'Come away,' the man said nervously, pulling at his friend in the doorway of the cinema. 'Let's go. This is awful. Why did you want to come here?'

'*You* go. Go on, just go. That's the best way. Run down there, I'll follow. Quick. There'll be police around. We don't want to get caught up in it.'

He looked to the left and ran, skirting round the square. Stopped, uncertainly, looked back. No sign of his friend. The light from the ambulance illuminated the nearest piece of ground. The orange street lights threw shadows through the trees. He blinked. There were two figures in the island of white light which was the ambulance.

Two. The one on the gurney, and another one, standing over it.

A police car edged into the square.

He ran.

The second figure sprinted from the ambulance, running like a greyhound, something utterly gleeful and carefree in the stride.

The morning light was kind in the country. It seeped into the room, rather than intruding, as it did in London. It invited her out, rather than reminding her that she must get up. This Sunday, with the idea of departing already looming like a threat, Rachel joined the paying guests for breakfast. They were dressed for a day's serious walking, anxious to be off while eating whatever Grace served and looking out to the perfect morning seen through the open door. There were no leftovers for nonexistent pets. Midwinter Farm did not run to pets.

'Where were we?' Grace asked, after the guests departed in a chorus of thanks. 'Oh, that's where we were.'

She settled herself.

'In all fairness,' Grace said, 'Ivy wasn't fit to look after Sam after Cassie drowned. She was sedated with legal drugs and sedated herself with the other kind. Carl wouldn't let me take the boy, even for a while. Who could blame her? She blamed herself for not being there, for encouraging Cassie to fight with her father. And I think she blamed Sam for not going to the rescue. We all expect too much of men, even little ones. Carl had already brought him home.'

Grace snorted into her tea.

'Carl exaggerated, of course. He's such a convincing liar, believes his own lies. Said the boy was terrified of her, but really he was terrified of seeing his mother being beaten up. Better keep them apart, he said. She ricocheted between

London and here. To begin with, she was delusional. She convinced herself that Cassie wasn't really dead. She kept saying Cassie had been turned into a swan, not dead, simply transformed. It was the drugs talking, but she believed it. I let her. Anything for comfort. Then . . . something else happened. She went back home to London, but he locked her out, and then she disappeared.'

'Didn't he try to find her?'

'Not for long. He sent me money to do that. And divorce papers. All she had to do was sign.'

'But, rights of access, alimony, all that kind of thing. Grandparents' rights. There's law, isn't there? You've got rights.'

'You've got rights if you want to pursue them,' Grace said bitterly. 'You've got rights if you've got *money* to pursue them. You've got rights if you're not in the middle of nowhere with no idea of what to do. You've got rights if you've got qualifications, know someone who has. We didn't, we don't. We had to keep a farm going. We didn't have a bean, still don't. Not much sophistication, either. I wouldn't have a clue where to start exerting rights. Pay a detective? With what? What chance, anyway, against a lawyer? All he ever had to do was stay still, and hide. Tear up letters and send them back. He knows we're helpless. Ivy knows it too. I wouldn't even know how to begin to find him. Nor would she.'

'She could, couldn't she? She could look him up if she wanted.'

'Sweetheart, don't you realise Ivy can scarcely read the small print? She sees shapes rather than letters. Our fault, undiagnosed dyslexia. Carl despised her for that too, she told me. She hides it; she learns everything by practice, off by heart. He was ashamed of her. Doesn't do, does it, lawyer with semi-literate wife? How could she defend herself?'

Grace was crying again. Rachel wanted to cry too, out of shared frustration and rage, pity for what she had not known.

'And you know the worst thing about him? The one thing I do know, because I saw it in a newspaper someone left. You know what that bastard does for a living now? Why he would never want to know us? He's a judge. A fucking judge. Therefore untouchable.'

'Does Ivy know that?'

'Yes. That's all I told her.'

'Oh.'

There was so much Ivy omitted. Ivy despised pity, and therefore deserved it.

You might not be able to find him, Rachel thought. But I could.

CHAPTER SIX

Donald Cousins waited at the back of the court of His
Honour Judge Schneider on Tuesday morning, watching and
only half listening while a witness blundered through evidence. It had been difficult to force himself inside, out of the
sun, but in here the cool was welcome. Middlesex Crown
Court, facing the Houses of Parliament, was once poetry in
carved oak and Donald mourned it. Now, Court Five, where
the judge sat, was a white-walled box full of power points and
laptop screens, as anonymous as any other, although an
incongruous throne-like chair had been preserved for the
use of the judge. The shield and coat of arms above it, bearing the old legend *Honi soit qui mal y pense*: *Evil to him who
evil thinks,* was painted in bright blues, reds and golds, and
looked like a garish warning sign. The insecurities of the
English, Donald thought. The language of the law was Latin,
the courtroom mottos were ancient French, and in this case
the judge had a Teutonic name. Schneider. Next door's court
was presided over by a diminutive Goan, whose brown skin

was peculiarly suited to his white wig. The witness in this court was a resident Scandinavian, who had seen a man savagely attacked by a group of other men, one of whom was in the dock. She was being cross-examined by African counsel. Donald Cousins felt his chest swell with pride in being English. Nowhere else was the law quite so colourful. He attempted to concentrate.

The trial in progress was rehearsing the story of an outdoor fight on a dark night, witnessed by strangers, six months before. A man had been disfigured for the simple crime of being in the wrong place at the wrong time. The witness currently on the stand was distressed by the reliving of it. He said something, yes; then he hit him, then the other one went to hit him back, and then they were fighting, then one went to the ground. Three of them kicked him.

Can you identify the man in the dock as one of those men?

Yes. He was the one who went on longest. The others stopped.

Yes, but can you identify my client?

To Donald Cousins, it was all no more than proof that fists, feet and knives still prevailed as the favourite inner-city weapons. On Saturday nights, high days and holidays, post-football, the west end of central London reverted to historic type. Strong drink was the recreation of choice long before Victoria ruled and gin was a penny a pint; brawling followed and still did. In the same central areas, on Saturday nights, a drunken swathe, lured by bright lights, music, cheap drink and each other, were left marooned with no means of getting home and no sense of direction either. Donald blamed the 1960s, for the kick-starting of a new wave of no inhibitions. Carnaby Street, all that. Silly clothes and drugs, new money. Protest marches sponsoring the right to violence. He had first really lost his nerve much later, in the vicious poll tax riots, buried it for good on future demos, and kissed it good-bye on a New Year's Eve celebration policing gig in Trafalgar Square. *Honi soit* . . . The love of life which went with New Year's Eve rapidly turned rancid in the early hours of the new year itself. There were endless opportunities for casual murder. Currently the action was in the environs of Leicester Square, haven of bars, cheap eats, cinemas, where pubs and clubs disgorged their fun-loving thousands after the night buses became scarce, leaving them to wander aimlessly, fight indiscriminately and abandon one another. Even a prime minister's son. And nothing united a celebratory or protesting mob better than the presence of the police, who rapidly became the common enemy. It was on these battle lines, these unpredictable Saturday nights, that a man in uniform, surrounded by historic monuments, learned to hate, fear and hold in contempt the pitiful, pitiless public. Sometimes that particular iron never left the soul.

He listened. The witness stuttered. Of course it was him. He was wearing a baseball cap. He had stripes on his shoes. He was kicking the man on the ground, long after he was still. It made me feel sick. He was the worst, he aimed for his head. It was as if he never wanted to stop.

How blind are you, Miss Gunstrom? Were you wearing your spectacles that night? I note you wear them now. You couldn't really see, could you?

Donald groaned. Cheap tricks from defence counsel, questioning the witness like that.

'Many of us wear spectacles, Mr Peal,' the judge said, adjusting his own. 'They don't nullify sight, and can, indeed, enhance it. That's what they're for. And you must not bully the witness. I think we should adjourn here. Back at two thirty.'

Judge Schneider wasn't bad at this, Donald conceded. He kept his interruptions minimal and took care of the witness. Cold and careful and surprisingly sensitive. He had recently begun to suppose that the same iron which entered a policeman's soul might also infect that of a judge, only later, rather than sooner, since the judge was better rewarded, never had to handle the bodies or touch the blood, regarded the evidence of carnage from a distance, at third hand. But the verbal and visual repetition of man's inhumanity to man would always be wearing in the end, however sanitised it became in the telling, especially when it was as pointless and stupidly wicked as this. As for punishment, the judge could never deliver an eye for an eye and a tooth for a tooth. He had no such privilege. He would sentence by formula, while the hungry eyes in the public gallery lusted for revenge.

It was an apposite case for this particular Tuesday morning, when the *Evening Standard* headlined a variation on Saturday-night brutality. A stabbed man had been left alone in an ambulance in Leicester Square, safe at last, until someone joined him there and finished off what wasn't even half done. Throttled him, like a chicken, with a wire garrotte, while a phalanx of preoccupied police officers stood yards away. Someone with plenty of malice aforethought, getting into an ambulance and killing an injured man. Donald did not know which shocked him more, the cruelty, or the nerve.

On the Monday he had spent hours with the judge's clerk, going through records, and realised during the process that Carl couldn't be all bad, because his twelve-stone, big-bosomed, no-nonsense Jamaican clerk, shared with three others, actually seemed to like him. She was very helpful with the facts, had a memory like Methuselah, and was interesting. He gets racial abuse all the time, she said, 'cos of his name. Only from thick whites, I ask you. I keep telling him to change it to Smith. If he calls himself Dolores Smith, I tell him, and puts on some jewels, then he'll get promoted. He's a nice warm man.

What about his personal life? Donald asked. She shook her head, and said if she knew she wouldn't tell him.

Nice? Warm?

He was like an iceberg when he came into the tiny retiring room, smiled so briefly it was like watching a light bulb turned on and then off, in the same second. He nodded towards Donald, acknowledging the appointment.

'Can we go out?' he said. 'If that's all right with you. I prefer to go out.'

'Certainly, sir.'

'You're the only one round here calls him sir,' the clerk chipped in. 'The rest of us call him God. Don't we, Carly baby?'

He smiled at her then, and the real smile was a revelation. He led the way down the labyrinth of corridors which led from the back rooms of the courts, and out of a side entrance. Once out in the street he took the lead, walking away from the building with what seemed to Cousins to be unnecessary speed.

'We can walk down the river to my chambers,' he said. 'Or sit in Parliament Square with Winston Churchill. That's what I tend to do on a day like this. Anything to avoid other lawyers.'

His yellow-grey hair was flattened by wearing the wig for a morning. It was a mystery to Donald why courtroom lawyers failed to rebel against that bizarre and unflattering piece of uniform. Anyone sane would resent wearing horsehair on their head on a day like this, but perhaps it made them concentrate and forget what they looked like. Wig, gown and white wing collar made all equally anonymous. Carl simply looked smaller without them.

To reach the square from the court, they had to sprint across the road, avoiding three lanes of traffic. The judge seemed used to it. The square was not the ideal place for conversation, because of the pigeons and the noise, but the traffic isolated it into an island which few people chose to risk, even for a better view of the Mother of Parliaments and the smiling face of Big Ben. Carl sat on the stone surround of a flowerbed facing the massive back of the statue of Winston Churchill, who was dressed in his old overcoat and glowering at the world. Donald had no option but to sit alongside. The stone was nicely cool. Donald could imagine the judge sitting here even when it was covered in ice. He did not seem a man who revelled in creature comforts. Carl patted the stone with a large, capable hand.

'Winston was my father's hero,' he said, as if explaining his choice. 'Since my father was a German prisoner of war, I never quite understood why. He said we needed to be vanquished.'

It was a remark which did not seem to demand a reply. Carl sat, expectantly, with his hands in his lap. Donald, who had looked up the judge's history for the scant detail available, simply nodded to indicate he knew about that, and then asked a question, because he wanted to know. They sat close together, the better to hear above the traffic which circled around them and became a neutral hum of sound.

'You were born in the late fifties, weren't you? Not so long after the war. How did your father being German affect you?'

'I'm honestly not sure. Maybe simply that I had a different childhood from other people, although it didn't seem so. If he was discriminated against, he didn't say. He was simply very pro-British. I was brought up to be grateful for being alive and to venerate all things British, with a certain Germanic discipline, of course. The difference was later.' He smiled apologetically. 'By the time I was a teenager, and my mother had died, it was puzzling to see my English contemporaries pouring scorn on tradition and hating the establishments I was taught to revere, as I still do, although perhaps a bit more selectively. I was always slightly at odds, I suppose. Ultra-conservative, with a small c. Nothing more than that. Do you have any news for me? Again, I'm so sorry to be such a nuisance.'

Donald cleared his throat. He was yearning for a nice warm pint. 'I've isolated a few possibles,' he said. 'The good news is that the list isn't long; the bad news is that they're difficult to trace. And I have no means of making any one of them answer questions when and if I do find them.'

'How on earth do you select?'

'By using a few basic principles, which even in themselves take a lot for granted. First, I've been looking for any person who has expressed a grievance against you, i.e, the widest category. There are plenty of those. Angry young men, mainly, customers who shout out threats as they go down to the cells en route to prison . . . Those who were free before.'

'I told you . . .' Carl interrupted.

'That they're usually prepared and resigned, yes,' Donald said impatiently. 'As people are, theoretically, for deaths and smaller tragedies which have been looming for a time. We may have been warned, but nothing prepares us for what we feel when it actually happens. We're still angered and insulted by it. As I said, the widest category of threateners are those who publicly blamed you for them going to prison. Hatred is so often the displacement of blame, especially blame of one-self.'

Carl was silent.

'So,' Donald continued. 'the widest category is the *I'll see you dead, you bastard* brigade. Those who actually shouted, because they were humiliated by the sentence. Especially those within that category who already had a propensity for violence. I mean, those you sentenced for violent crimes, as opposed to any other kind.'

'That's very scientific,' Carl said. 'But those people aren't the most cunning. Fraudsters are worse. They ruin lives without a shred of violence. They almost make thugs look admirable.'

This felt like an attempt to change the subject.

Donald went on. 'I've also ignored the other category you mentioned. Those who may loathe you for what, in their eyes, you *failed* to do. Such as not imposing a sufficiently vengeful sentence on someone who hurt their child. Or over-seeing an acquittal which seemed unfair. Those deprived of a fitting revenge – the old *miasma*-ridden we were talking about – because of a technicality which got someone off. I can't possibly track down those, unless they expressed them-selves publicly. I have to stick with the obvious, which is the violent, verbal ones who shouted, and I've broken down this little grouping into those with the necessary skills. And endurance.'

Carl leaned forward to rest his hands on his knees. He looked up towards the sky, enjoying the warmth on his face, like a cat reacting to the sun, stretching his neck. His profile was harmless, with a stubby nose, broad forehead and round, non-aggressive chin above a thick neck, but his hands were enormous, as if meant for toil. The hands of a surgeon were like that. Donald had the uncomfortable feeling that for all that the judge was older than himself, he would not like to be on the wrong side of him in a dark alley at night. His was a solid body.

'What exactly do you mean by endurance? Is this new police jargon?'

Donald had the feeling that the man was laughing at him; that he knew in advance that the investigation was useless and all this was playing with words. He raised his voice and slowed down.

'I mean the capability, and the willpower, to carry through. To go on wanting to do something. To harbour revenge, to plan it and hone the plan, to have an aim and sustain it, over months, years if necessary. I'm only looking at the last two years. I'm also only looking at men. Women don't do this stuff, and anyway, you've only ever sent a handful of the fairer sex to jail.'

'The jury convict,' Carl began. 'I don't.' He was being obtuse.

'Or fail to convict,' Donald said, suddenly furious. 'The stupid jury may convict, they carry the can, but it's you who actually send the bastards to jail, and it's you they'll remember, not the twelve grey people.'

'I never think the jury stupid,' Carl said. He *was* trying to change the subject. 'They've been bullied for centuries, first as hired witnesses, then dummies, ordered to do nothing but convict. No heat, food or water until they did. Then they rebelled with the trial of William Penn, the Quaker: 1670, wasn't it? Trumped-up charges about a prayer meeting. Not a million miles from here. The jury wouldn't convict. They were starved and imprisoned, and still they wouldn't. They resent it when the state creates bogeymen and expects them to hang them. The jury won, in the end. Penn took the jury trial system to America. Now look what they've done with it. What was it William Blackstone said? *The judgement of twelve men, indifferently chosen and superior to all suspicion . . .*'

'*. . . is the sacred bulwark of the nation's liberties,*' Donald finished.

The judge looked at his watch. 'That's all I have to preserve. The jury's right not to be bamboozled. So that *they* can judge. I do wish defendants could see that. I digress. You were saying?'

The crafty bastard, pretending he knew nothing of history, Donald thought. In other circumstances he might enjoy this man. He wanted to argue that the William Penn jury were hardly unbiased, since the leader was a diehard Quaker himself. And what about the fate of the poor deluded imbecile who was hanged for starting the Fire of London? That was a jury too. They could go on, he sensed, for a long time, and the judge was trying to distract him. He wondered why, and could only guess.

'The man who sends you threatening images, sir, and who maybe got into your room in chambers, is certainly dangerous, potentially at least, because he's calculating, and he has to have two qualifications. The last three images, by the way, came from two sources: one from a college with a bank of computers open to everyone in the place, two from an internet café. Maybe our man is capable of untraceable trespass, but he's got to be computer literate. Capable of accessing or scanning a picture, using a machine.'

'Isn't everyone, these days?' Carl said airily.

He did live in an ivory tower, after all.

'Not the unemployed riff-raff who pass through your court, yelling threats, unless, of course, they go to prison, where they may learn how. They do learn computers in prison.'

'I'd be glad if they learned anything,' Carl said, 'apart from a drug habit. So you think the person who is threatening me is an ex-con, still holding a grievance *after* he's free? Having learned the necessary skills?'

'A computer-literate ex-con, capable of breaking into your chambers. Multi-skilled, perhaps with a history of harassment and planning. I doubt if he cares if you live or die, but he does want you to be uncomfortable.'

'Anyone obvious on your little list?'

Donald sensed he was trying to keep the sarcasm out of his voice. He could risk being offended, because he was waiting to play his trump card. Produce the jack of spades which justified keeping him going on with this cushy number as long as he liked. Unless, of course, the murder of the man in the ambulance turned into a spate of murders. Then they would all be called in.

'Yes, there is, as it happens. Remember a man called Blaker? Recidivist, drop-out? Leniency because of age, even though he's spiteful? Convicted for robbery. He mugged women for handbags, sold on the credit cards, kept the cash. Then, just when they were beginning to recover, he contacted the women. Told them he knew where they lived, watch out. Scared them for no particular purpose except his own enjoyment. When he was arrested, which he was because he only had one patch and always went back to the same places – he can't operate or feel at home in any place other than Soho, that one – he had a fine old collection of keys. Hadn't tried to use them, but still, must have had it in mind. You've sentenced him twice, and he didn't like it either time. Released in April. Crazy but articulate.'

Carl sat up. He seemed to be enormously relieved.

'Ah, yes. Blaker. Unpleasant, to say the least. Yes. He did shout, didn't he? Said he was framed and I was part of an endless conspiracy against him. He should still be inside. Where is he now?'

Big Ben chimed two. The sonorous notes cut through all other noises and echoed around them. Donald waited for the sound to roll away.

'Don't know where he is,' he said. 'Early release, courtesy of the parole board. There's an address where he isn't, so I either walk the streets where I know he might be, or wait for him to call on his parole officer. In the meantime, I have to talk to your son. I've called his mobile, like you said. He doesn't get back to me.'

A stiffening of the judge's shoulders showed Donald he had been right, and that this was one of the subjects His Honour wanted to avoid. Carl seemed deafened by the chimes of the clock, shifted uncomfortably. Then he rallied, shook his head. 'I do apologise for his rudeness. I've had to tell him, of course. He says I'm paranoid.'

'When's the best time to catch him?'

Donald wanted to call him Carly baby, if only to provoke. Carl sighed, rose from the bench, and looked back at Winston, as if for inspiration.

'He's a student,' he said. 'Of economics, I think I told you. So it makes sound sense for him to live with his father and sleep all morning. That's where you'll find him in the early part of the day. I'll tell him to expect you, shall I? By now, on a day like this, he'll be sitting outside college holding court with his friends. He might conceivably be attending a lecture, but I doubt it. You've got the photo I gave you?'

'Yes.'

He had photos of both, as a matter of course. Donald wondered how anyone who had formed a grievance against the judge whilst he was wearing his wig would ever recognise him without it. Maybe that was what it was for.

'The photo of Sam may not be very helpful,' Carl said. 'They change very quickly at that age. My son in particular.'

'Funny, that. My wife says that about the daughters.'

They began to walk back towards the courthouse together. There was this strange moment when Donald did not want to leave him. Wanted, instead, to say, let's go for a pint and find out what you really know about history. Discuss the ignorance of children. How they know bugger-all about it. He was momentarily grateful to Carl. After all, the judge was facing the next few hours effectively locked up with scumbags, lawyers and jurors, while he himself could roam free.

'Do you think your jury'll convict the bloke in the dock?' he asked, as they waited to cross the road back towards the court. The traffic seemed endless and angry, racing against time, as if wanting to be far away before the monstrous clock struck the time again.

'Oh yes. The evidence is all there, for once. It was like the witness said, *it was as if he couldn't stop*. He didn't stop kicking, our man in the dock, until he was hauled off, with blood on his striped shoes. A frenzy. I don't understand it, do you? Repeated kicks to the body and head, ruptured spleen. Where does that kind of hatred come from? They didn't even know each other.'

They were on the other side of the road, breathless.

'Does that make it better or worse, Carly baby?' Donald asked, panting.

Carl stopped in his tracks and considered. It was as if the question was all that mattered and all questions had to be answered. He spread his big hands, honestly bewildered. 'I just don't know. I wish I did. Only the victim could tell you that. It's violence without any purpose that I can't understand. I can understand planning it, for money, retribution, whatever you like, but not for *nothing*. I can understand running and hiding and lying. Sensible people take aim and fire once, don't they, Don? I can't understand the kind of anger which doesn't fizzle out.'

'Oh, I can,' Donald said, smiling. 'I can understand that. Did Your Honour ever learn to shoot? You have to go on until you stop missing.'

'Don't be hard on my son,' Carl said. 'He's very . . . young.'

He inclined his head, left him abruptly. Donald stood on the lonely pavement, with no priorities for the afternoon, except how he would later justify the time spent. A little creative reporting. He was lured by the thought of a walk by the river, any vain mission which involved staying out of doors, so he may as well try and track down the student. There was something satisfying about looking for needles in haystacks in a way that could be regarded as important, at least on paper. The rude little bastard who did not respond to phone calls could also be a prime suspect, and both he and the judge knew it.

He walked. Westminster to the Temple was not far along the side of the river. The son's college was uphill from the Embankment, not far from the Aldwych. Stone buildings were the order of the day everywhere after the Great Fire in 1666, all of them built and rebuilt beyond recognition, changed by wars, fashion, money. He was taking a bet that a spoiled student had no idea how lucky he was to be where he was, in an age of extraordinary peace and prosperity lasting longer than almost any in centuries. His own daughters were just the same.

It was hot. Eighty degrees, humid, London hot. He turned away from the river with regret, uphill to the Aldwych and the pale buildings of the London School of Economics. The kids sat outside in their dozens. The crowds, as he went uphill, seemed to move downhill, thicker as he moved. He hated not being able to walk in a straight line; it was like being inside a swarm of flies. He surveyed the milling groups of students with profound distaste, and turned back. Even with a photo of the boy, he would never find him here. Instead he found a pub and a place to sit outside with a pint, pulled out his time sheet and scribbled on it.

Mr Terry Blaker, loony tunes of no fixed abode except a hostel address, did exist, of course. The judge remembered him better than he was letting on. Blaker's valedictory message as he was led screaming from the dock was unusually biblical, according to the court notes. Judgement will be upon you, he had yelled. Your own sins will find you out. You murderer! It would be nice to know what all that was about. Donald began to be convinced by his own argument, his own categorisation of the various degrees of potential culprit for the heinous crime of giving the good judge sleepless nights. The more he thought about it, the more he convinced himself that Blaker could be good for this, because Blaker might consider himself vindicated by the parole board, an innocent, bent on revenge. Donald found to his surprise that it was all, also, beginning to matter, just a bit. He would rather it was Blaker than the judge's son, because he liked the judge. He liked his men served dry, when they knew about history. He liked it when they tried to protect their children. It did not follow that there was any urgency. He was perfectly sure that the judge was safer than most people who risked crossing the road, and that meant tomorrow would do.

It rained in the late afternoon of the Tuesday, overdue rain released in a rush after the muggy heat of the day. Rachel thought differently about rain these days. In the city it was simply a nuisance, even if it cleansed the air and brightened the trees, it did not have any obvious purpose. Now she thought of Farmer Wiseman and his hay. They needed rain, he had said, proper rain, not like the drizzle of Saturday. The more the better. A week's worth would be nice. She no longer resented the rain, except for the fact that it made people behave badly. A downpour after drought had the same effect as a snowfall in the city, creating bad temper and amazement, as if it had never happened before. It was an excuse to be late and for trains to stop. The model for the life drawing class failed to turn up. Everyone else did, and no one believed the excuse.

It happens, the teacher said. They aren't all reliable. Sorry, folks, we have to rely on ourselves. Regard it as an opportunity. Today we do heads. Our heads. Any volunteers? You? May as well start with a pretty one. Five minutes, please.

Rachel followed his instructions, sat on the dusty plastic chair on the podium in the middle of the room and made herself comfortable, as she had watched other models do, trying to find a position she could maintain. It was more difficult than she had imagined. There were precious few times in the day when anyone kept entirely still for any length of time, except when asleep, and not even then. She stared at the far wall, and immediately wanted to move. The room was silent apart from the swish of traffic in rain outside. It was a sound as soothing as the sea. She did not find the sensation of being scrutinised uncomfortable; keeping still, gazing in the same direction, she let her mind roam free. It was a great time for dreaming and planning, Ivy had told her.

'You rarely see a smiling portrait,' the teacher was saying. 'Not in pencil or charcoal, anyway. Not drawn straight from life. No one can keep up a smile for long. Not even a politician. Remember the way it seems fixed on their faces? It starts to hurt after a while. Solemnity's the natural repose for the face.'

What a short memory you have, Rachel thought. Ivy could keep up a smile for ten minutes. She had once done it here, but the teacher was right. It had been slightly disconcerting.

'Those of you who've only got a view of the back of the head,' the teacher said, 'don't worry. It's just as revealing as the front. Especially when you can see the angle of the neck. Necks are like stalks, always bending.'

Rachel's hair was severely knotted on the top of her head as usual. Lately, she was always longing to let it hang free. Now she felt she was being obliging.

'Thank you. Now you, Norman.'

A male head, by way of contrast. The one they called the Plonker took the hot seat. It reminded her of a medical examination in front of an audience. He was facing her, chose to stare at her beseechingly, rather than at the wall. Not a bad face, once she looked at it directly, gauging the distance between hairline and eyes, nose and mouth, the narrow chin. Nothing unkind about it. Any slight frisson of dislike and embarrassment he had caused disappeared completely. He was simply a face. No one else noticed that he was staring at her, willing her attention with his pleading eyes. He twitched; he was limited to three minutes. She decided that heads were less revealing than bodies. On his way back to his seat on the other side of the room, he paused by her easel.

'Listen,' he whispered urgently, taking advantage of the shuffling round as a new head took up position, pages turned to a fresh sheet of paper. 'Listen, I've got to talk to you. You flat-share with Ivy, don't you? I've got to tell you . . .'

'No you don't.'

'I was with her on Saturday night,' he said, his voice growing louder as the shuffling ceased.

'In your dreams,' Rachel muttered.

'Five minutes, please.'

He went back to his seat.

'When drawing the head,' the teacher intoned wearily, glaring at Norman, 'always remember to leave room for the brain.'

Rachel got out first at the end of the class, leaving someone else to stack her easel and chair. Ivy would be at home and her flat was full of flowers. It was still raining, and it was lovely to be going home.

In the pocket of her jacket she found the piece of bone Farmer Wiseman had handed to her out of the incinerator. A souvenir of another country. She and Ivy would go back there soon. This was the summer of her happiness, and her achievement.

She *could* find him. It was only a question of whether she should.

CHAPTER SEVEN

Rachel was proud of her flat. More aptly, she was proud of owning it. Owning anything was an achievement. Your own place, with your own door, that was the goal. It was the promised land, her father swore, the only honourable debt, the passport to safety, but then, the repossession of his own had been a nightmare never forgotten, not even when they struggled back into the gentler waters of being able to manage in a place improved within an inch of its life. They never thought it was a false dream to aspire to a lifetime of debt, or that there were others worth pursuing. Their daughter would do better. Their daughter did. Ivy didn't get it at all.

'I think he might be envious of me sometimes,' Rachel explained to Ivy. 'As well as terrified that someone will take it away. First flat at twenty-five? Beyond his dreams. His generation began with rationing, saved up to get married. Then he saved up to have me. Couldn't afford another.'

'What a pity,' Ivy said. 'There should have been more of

us. Mine tried and couldn't. I suppose I couldn't give a toss about owning anything because it was always *there*. Dad's farm was Dad's farm and his dad's farm; our house was our house, never a landlord's. It didn't make them free, because they're bound by it. They've had to fight tooth and nail to keep it, no question they could ever leave it. Dad's in debt to his ears, but he couldn't do anything else. There's never been a bean to spend and they could no more sell it than fly to the moon. It owns *them*.'

They were curled in armchairs, as comfortable as cats, barefoot and warm. The window was open to the sound of rain.

'Who's going to take over when they get too old?'

'No one.'

'You could.'

Ivy shook her head. 'No, I'd never be strong enough for that. It's not in my blood, and he couldn't bear it. It's just not the natural order of things, you see. It simply has to go to a man. He doesn't talk about it, but I know what he dreams of. A son to take over, or a grandson now. Or if not to take over, at least to admire, understand, appreciate. To *see*. To share, or mourn, something like. Poor man. I've let him down.'

Rachel focused on her glass. 'You never know. Maybe Sam's out there, yearning for real country life. Wanting a grandfather.'

Ivy laughed. 'Wouldn't that be nice? Carl would have to be dead before Sam would ever be allowed to go back there, even just to see.'

'You don't know that.'

Rachel was uncomfortable. It was the wrong time for the conversation. Ivy thought so too.

'Yes I do. Believe me, I do. He'd do anything to prevent it.

Where does this wine come from? It's a lovely piss-coloured yellow. I'd rather talk about that than talk about parents. Why do we always do it?'

'Because you invited my father to supper, and we were talking about him. Because we're attached to them by that blasted umbilical cord no one ever severs. They have their hypodermics into our veins. We want them happy; they want us happy. They're the only people who remain the subject of mutual fascination. Oh God, look at the time. Again. What time are you starting in the morning?'

'It is the morning. I start at five. I'll have plenty of time to go to Berwick Street after I've finished the shift. It's my old stomping ground. There's a bit of this lovely stuff left.'

'Wish you didn't work such crazy hours,' Rachel grumbled. 'Don't know how you do it. Three hours' sleep and you're raring to go.'

She was drowsy. Well past midnight. They could talk for hours; it was easier than breathing; they were pleasantly, indolently drunk. She had come home to home-cooked food: Ivy could cook like her mother. The flat was still full of flowers, smelled of herbs and perfume and coffee and home, like a lived-in lair. Ivy had that knack, without changing a thing. It was a strange talent for someone who also relished homelessness.

'I'll do better with the grub when you father comes. What time did you say that was?'

'Tomorrow. About six thirty. He won't have anything with garlic. How much did you use? Oh, I shall be sweet in the morning. Mustn't breathe on anyone.' Rachel burped, discreetly.

'Will he be safe to get home if we give him wine like this?' Ivy asked.

'Oh yes. He'll go like a homing pigeon, soon as he can. He's only sixty-eight. One stroke, plenty of anxiety, bit of arthritis, asthma, controlled as long as he's got his inhaler and his calming pills. He's short of breath and timid. Doesn't like the dark. Lonely and refuses to admit it. God know what he's inhaled from DIY. More than the forty fags a day which were mandatory in his youth, he says. Gave them up when they got pricey, mourned them ever since. I never know where real illness ends and hypochondria begins, he won't tell me. And he won't drink wine unless I tell him it's cheap. The cheaper the better.'

'Speaking as one weaned on the homemade variety,' Ivy said, 'I think anything else is wonderful.'

The flat was on the fringes of the City, where Gray's Inn Road met Theobald's Road in a welter of multipurpose streets. It had been bought for investment, rather than beauty. Rachel had not cared. She could walk or bus to work.

Not a thing of beauty in its own right, a series of four featureless rooms in an old house, with no hint of what it might have been. The advent of Ivy, the presence of the flowers and the contrast of Midwinter Farm made Rachel notice how bland her own home was. That was going to change too. There was a single wall in her bedroom she had begun to paint and never finished. She was going to be late for work tomorrow, again, and she didn't care.

'I swear there's an old fireplace behind that wall,' Ivy said, pointing vaguely. 'Should be, anyway. We could make this place really cool, you know. Don't ever ask Grace to visit. She'd rip the wall down as soon as look at it. Forgot to ask. How was the life class? Did you miss me?'

'We certainly did. Absentee model. We did heads. The Plonker was there, asking after you.'

'Was he now? He was at my Saturday class too. I reckon he goes to them all. It's me next week, I think. I'll certainly turn up.'

It was so easy, being with Ivy, having Ivy there and a bottle of wine between them. A full stomach. No need for the conversation to make much sense. No need to be clever, or witty, or even talk in a straight line. Nothing to prove.

'My father will ask you lots of questions,' Rachel said. 'He's like that. Critical and suspicious.'

''S only natural. Wants you safe and well with suitable friends, preferably male. No debts or debtors, get the picture. No probs. That's a parent for you. Oh God, we should be asleep. Honestly, what are we like? I'm bad for you.'

'No you aren't. You're good for me.'

Rachel stood up, uncertainly, sat down again. Surely there was no real urgency about going to bed. It was nicer here.

'Did you hear about that man who got murdered in the ambulance? They said it was done by garrotte. Who the hell goes round with a garrotte in his pocket?'

'Oh, I dunno,' Ivy said. 'People who sell cheese.'

It seemed, at the time, inordinately funny. The best thing about Ivy was the giggling.

The fourth image had been sent to the judge the evening before. He had e-mailed it on, as instructed. A printed copy was folded into Donald's pocket.

Another old woodcut, from a book maybe. It showed Eve being banished from the Garden of Eden. God stood by an apple tree, waving a sword, with his foot upon the head of a serpent, directing Eve from the safety of the wood towards a wilderness containing nothing but water. She covered her face with her hands, begging for mercy. Even with the large foot of God standing on its head, the conquered serpent he trod into the ground squirmed with delight at its own success. Donald thought it was amazing how many messages could be shown in a few lines.

It was embellished with the legend, *The worm has turned. You will die soon.*

Donald loved a good misty morning. Especially if it obscured traffic in the mean end of the city, round about City Road, Whitechapel, Commercial Road, where all was ugliness. He could concede the hinterland was rich in exotic markets, sweat shops, Asian and African endeavours, but all he could think of was the solid identity and history it had lost, and he could not love it. The high rise of the City, the gherkin tower and all the landmarks were behind, while in front was early-morning, heavy-duty traffic on the way to the Blackwall Tunnel, that sinister, curving, underground conduit which snuck under the river Thames and connected the east of London to the east of Kent on the other side, without ever affording a view of either. Slower by car than by water. It would have been better to take the monorail train which sailed above and over, and made the sweating developments and distinctly old-fashioned poverty beneath look glamorous in sunlight, even better in mist. You could live by the river on the south side and commute into the centre without your feet ever touching the ground, without ever seeing how all those who crowded on and off came to reach their point. It was the same, less picturesque, but equally removed experience by car. Eyes straight ahead, looking for the chance to overtake, avoiding the humiliating prospect of getting lost.

He found the complex, got rid of the car, and cursed the fact that he would, at some point, possibly sooner rather than later, have to come back and find it and do the route back all over again. Never mind, it clocked up the hours. No one ever could ever deny or disbelieve the amount of time it might take to get to anywhere in London.

The judge's apartment was part of a complex, where residents parked cars underground and visitors reported to a gate for instructions from a man in a booth, who looked as if he was rooted to the spot, in command of two syllables, yes and no. The man in the booth seemed to be dealing with another man, both of them debating methods of pest control. Twenty apartments here, all turned outwards, so nobody faced the hinterland, only the water. He found his way.

It was always a gamble to imagine a nineteen-year-old would keep an appointment, or return a phone call, but less of a one to calculate that a student would still be asleep at ten in the morning, even in his father's house. Donald kept his finger on the buzzer, and turned his harmless profile to the small screen which would show his face inside. Video entry. Localised to this flat. Appropriate for a judge, perhaps. Not, as far as he knew, for a student of the wider world.

He was right in his assumption, based on his own experience, that Sam would not have left the house; Donald's wife would have said the same, and both of them would be wrong in assuming he would be asleep. The boy who flung open the door, without giving himself time to look at the screen within, was wide awake, as if waiting to present himself and knowing he was a pleasure to behold, as if dressed in new clothes he wanted to show. His face fell, then he lifted his shoulders in exaggerated acceptance as he glanced at the ID card.

'Oh, shit. I thought you were the man about the rats. Or my friend.'

'I'm everyone's friend,' Donald said. 'Can I come in?'

Sam turned from the door, leaving Donald to close it behind him and follow him into the living room he recognised from before, with a balcony facing the river, easy seating, comfortable enough, unnaturally, office-like tidy and as much dominated by a desk as another kind of room would be by an overlarge piano. Donald was grateful to turn his back on the boy in order to compose his face for the second view. The judge was right: the photo of the teenage child did not help. This was a vision of loveliness, moving like a dancer interrupted in the middle of a rehearsal, midway between a change of scene and certainly a change of clothes, possibly awaiting a second opinion. The outfit for Scene Two included voluminous white trousers, spilling over bare brown feet, a sleeveless top of orange linen, a small row of delicate beads round a slender neck, and studs for ear and nose which, in the light of the room, flashed purple, discordant with the red streak in his short, dark, spiked hair.

'Do you like it?' he said, rubbing one hand through. 'It takes *ages*.'

'Prefer long hair on a bloke myself,' Donald said. 'Hate this short stuff. I love a good curly perm myself. Least you don't have a buzz cut, like all the gays. Is that you, by the way? Or are you just camp?'

Sam shrugged.

'Both,' he said. 'Been this way since twelve. Coffee or tea? You must be the copper dealing with Dad's bugbears, right? OK, OK. I'll own up. I did it. 'Twas I brought in the rat. On my coat tails. So to speak.'

'Oh? Why was that?'

'There's a woman lives downstairs, keeps her precious car in the basement. Afraid I scratched it, parking ours. I forgot to mention it. She might have left the rat as a message.

There's always a problem with rats. Tee hee hee. Terrible people live here.'

'Coffee, please,' Donald said.

The peacock son disappeared, with waggling hips. The trousers did not fit. Thinking as a father, Donald hoped they had not cost a lot of money. Not for the first time, he was grateful for the experience of being a parent, had a fleeting memory of trying to control his own sense of shock and outrage the first time one of his daughters had appeared with a belly button stud. If this father's son thought he had the capacity to shock with his peacock display, he had chosen the wrong type of person, although Donald did have to admit to surprise. A judge's son? Dressed like that and as camp as a tent? Why not? Look how judges had to dress, for God's sake. Red robes and ermine for special occasions. Maybe it was catching. From the sad vantage point of impending middle age, Donald wished he had once had the nerve to dress like that.

He followed the boy's flowing progress into the kitchen. The room was small and spotless, utterly functional, devoid of any decorative touch. There were no residual cooking smells. The kitchen was not the heart of the house in this place; it did not seem to have any heart. Framed by the window, the sun striking though the thin fabric of his shirt to reveal a thin body as he filled the kettle from the tap, Sam looked suddenly vulnerable. He was just another kid, with kid's problems and a hell of a lot more thrown in, poor sod. No wonder his father wanted to protect him. He had a lifetime of trouble ahead already. What a boy like that needed was a mother. Donald was more at home with a boy he could think of as a girl than he would have been with some sporty, macho, more typical public school youth. He perched himself on a high stool, next to the kitchen counter. There was another stool on the far side, which would leave a comfortable gap between them.

'Your dad tells me you're studying economics. Shouldn't it be fashion design?'

Sam spoke over his shoulder, spooning ground coffee into a cafetiere. No simple instant here.

'Politics *and* economics. No, I find it fascinating. Sometimes. Besides, it's a safer option, and whatever my father thinks, I do want to earn a living some day. Milk?'

'Please. Isn't it a bit restricting, living with your father? Wouldn't you be better off in digs or something?'

Especially if you crash cars and go out dressed like a tart.

'For the good of my soul, yes. For the good of my pocket, no. I don't study economics for nothing. He's always trying to get me to go, especially now. Says all this is too overprivileged for words, unsuitable for my age, blah blah blah, but why should I? Why should I rough it in some dump when I can smooth it here?'

His voice was shrill with almost childish indignation.

'He's always going on about it. How a generation of peace and prosperity has spoiled us. Why not? Isn't that progress? Why should I have to live in squalor and work every hour just because he did as his father did? Honestly. He wants me to go back to his ghastly roots. No way.'

'His German roots?'

'No, the other ones.'

Donald found all this slightly amusing and kept quiet until the coffee was poured. Sam sat across from him, challenging him to say something. Donald was wondering if the tan was fake, then sighed and shook himself. He found the young desperately fascinating, but there was the matter in hand.

'You know why I'm here. Someone's threatening your dad. It happens with judges. They aren't popular people.'

Sam snorted. 'I think it's all bollocks. I think he's exaggerating. He's trying to get me to leave . . .'

Think of him as a daughter. Make yourself at home. Risk having an argument.

'Oh, come on. You really think he'd tell lies, just to make you go? Draw attention to himself like this? He could just put your stuff in the street and change the locks, if that's what he wanted.'

He wants to protect you. I can quite see why.

Sam slumped. Then he shrugged and smiled. It was a great relief to find a kid without an in-built attitude problem to the filth. Maybe it was just his own face. Maybe the boy was lonely.

'No, to be honest. But he wouldn't actually throw me out either. He can't make things up, he's too literal. But he might want to make me feel sorry for him, so I'll do what he wants. You know, poor me, someone's after me, just do this little thing to please me, like, leave. He's always going on at me...'

Probably frightened of leaving. Donald sighed.

'Parents do that, Sam. That's what we're paid for. What I wanted to know from you was whether you had any idea of who might be doing it. Such as, was it yourself? Or might this little campaign have been aimed at you, rather than him?'

He waited for an explosion of offence at the very outrageous suggestion, but there was none. Sam seemed mildly amused, even flattered, fluttered his eyelashes and placed his hand over his heart.

'Me? What a thought. Some poor broken-hearted rejected, spiteful boyfriend of mine? Puleese! No, Mr Cousins sweetie, despite what I say, I'm quite fond of the old bugger, except when he nags me and bangs on about the past. I don't want to leave him alone, and I don't want him dead until I'm ready to inherit. He hasn't done too badly by me, really, and I haven't made it easy. At least he didn't drag me in front of a shrink when I showed all the signs and got expelled from the first school. But he isn't consistent. First he keeps me away from my mother, now he wants me to get in touch with her. He nags and nags.'

The self-absorption was fascinating, but children were irritating when they whined. How many times had he told his own it was the worst thing they could ever do, especially when they wanted their own way. Hysteria was more effective. Donald did not need family confidences; he simply wanted to be seen to be thorough. Of course he had to interview the son, but he did not really need adolescent angst, even if he was interested. It wasn't as if a missing mother/wife could come into this equation. She and the judge had parted years ago, amicably, the judge said. There was a daughter who had died in a drowning accident. The marriage never recovered; they went their separate ways, and he brought up the boy. Donald had not, so far, investigated mummy at all, except to see, from her sheet, that she was a bit of a raver. He wished the records would show who had paid her fines, but they didn't. Odd that she wanted no contact with her boy, but then maybe he wasn't her type. Not everyone would cherish a son like this. What he really needed to ask was had sonny boy seen anyone hanging around, in a real or metaphorical sense? Did Carly baby have a jealous girlfriend, was there another, obvious suspect?

He had already put aside the notion that Sammy was either the target or the perpetrator. He was far too ineffectual for that, and there was something about the boy which shrieked of virginity. Not literally, perhaps, no one ever knew about that, but he did seem to have an innocence of subterfuge. Too innocent by far, too self-absorbed for any criminal enterprise, way too concerned about what had been done to *him*. There was always the circuitous route to information, such as let them blather on and pick up a clue. Make them think they were witty and wise beyond their years. Really, he had learned more about interviewing technique from being a father than he had from any other training course. His wife said so.

'I expect your mother's worried about you,' he said. 'They never stop, you know. Worrying.'

The result of these remarks was dramatic, as if he had placed a syringe into a major vein, or given the kid an electric shock. Sam picked up the empty cafetiere and flung it against the wall of stainless steel units to his left. It thumped, intact, fell to the floor, and smashed into pieces. The result was a mess of coffee on the pristine floor, and a shower of black liquid over Donald's trousers, below knee level. They were dark blue jeans; he didn't care and stayed still, aware the boy was watching him.

'My mother,' Sam said dramatically, 'did not give a shit about me. OK, so she was fucked up when my sister died. I can get that. She was *awful*. She pinched me, she tormented me, she was fucking *dangerous,* and then she went. When I was a kid, I was dragged to this farm, chucked in the sea, dunked in a pond, because that's what my sister wanted. I hated that stuff. My mother hated me because I hated that stuff. *I hate her.* So when my grandmother writes, I get to the letters first and send them back. Dad doesn't know. Why the hell should I ever have to go back to that awful place? Why should I *ever* see her? *He* thinks I should. Oh, fuck.'

He got up, and with scrupulous, speedy care wiped up the mess with a wodge of paper towels, using a fistful to clutch at the glass remnants. He ignored the impact on Donald's ankles, blue denim not worth preserving. Donald stayed fairly still, merely extending his ankle to survey the damage. It would look as if he had been wading in liquid shit. In pursuit of rats on a riverbank. Never mind.

'Go through many of those, do you? Like, one a day, or what?'

There was a rattle from the area round a corner as Sam tipped the rubbish into a bin. He came back, visibly refreshed; sat on the opposite stool.

'Only when you mention my mother. You won't tell Dad about the letters? I mean, they're written to him, from my grandmother, but I see them first 'cos I'm always here when the post comes. Then I send them back. And it would be nice if he were to know about the rat from someone else. I can't tell him.'

'When I was a boy,' Donald said, 'you got a man with a ferret in to deal with rats.'

'So did they, on the farm,' Sam said dreamily. 'My father is always reminding me that his father was a farm labourer. He thinks that's part of my heritage, and he thinks I ought to rediscover it. They want to drag me back there. Into that lake. My mother would drown me. She tried hard enough. Why should I want to know her?'

This really was getting off the point. Or maybe not. The lad smelt clean, no dope, just kind of volatile. Donald cleared his throat.

'We might have found someone with the right kind of grudge against your father,' he said. 'Someone he sent to prison. Can you think of anyone else who might hate him? After all, you know him best.'

Sam was making more coffee. Donald reflected that it was his own, desperate ordinariness which was the talent most overlooked by his employers. People told him things because he was indistinguishable from the man who came to read the gas meter. And because, after all, he looked like everyone's dad. Not everyone's dad, to be fair. Sam continued the process of making the coffee.

'Know him? I doubt if anyone does. He's a hard bastard who drives himself hard and thinks everyone else should do the same. Work, work, work. He doesn't need anyone threatening to kill him to make him miserable. He can't even get himself a woman. Wish he would.'

There was a quick grin in Donald's direction.

'He moans at me, you know? Like you all do, right? Other days, I tell you, he's a laugh a minute, a fucking gem. He needs a bit of teasing, know what I mean? It's just sometimes I wish I wasn't the only one loves the silly sod. He deserves better than me, really. A real woman. Have you ever seen him laugh? It's a treat, I tell you.'

No.

'Has he ever done anything he's ashamed of? As far as you know?'

Sam shook his head, then reconsidered.

'No. I very much doubt it. Unless you include shooting the swans.'

There were great advantages to a big, blank face.

'Oh, he can shoot, can he?'

Sam poured water into the new jug, releasing the coffee smell to which Donald remained addicted, even when he shook with caffeine shock.

Sam's hands were steady. Donald admired anyone who could move from temper tantrum to calm as if cleansed by it.

'My father can bring in the harvest, pick apples, climb trees and shoot,' Sam said proudly, counting off these talents by clapping his hands together in slow applause. 'Which gifts he would like me to share. But . . .' He moved across to the countertop, depositing the coffee before going back to wash his hands beneath the tap. No way this boy ever handled a dead rat. 'That was a long time ago. He was taught by his father, *liebling,* and his father was a soldier. So, copper, don't go looking for guns around here. All that was down on that bloody farm. Where Mummy came from. I can hardly blame my father for learning about murder. Animal farming's all about killing things. And shooting the swans was a terrible thing, because his father had done the same. Blah, blah, blah.'

'Do you think,' Donald said, 'we could go back to the beginning?'

Grace took the gun in both hands and shot into the wall. The sound always surprised her. The blind cow which was never going to have a calf skittered at the sound of the shot, but without spirit. They were in the far barn, away from the others. The cow, which was smaller than the rest, was teth-ered to the wall with a rope halter, and it was not the rope which steadied her. She knew. Grace was talking to her. Your daddy bought you without a passport, silly sod, because he thought he could see promise in you. Do you wonder no one ever gave him the money to buy a racehorse? And you have to go, because the others shun you. They know you're never going to come on heat. You are causing ripples of discontent. Cows have feelings; they are capable of bearing grudges, fearing for the future, knowing one of them is under a death sentence and wanting it to be over.

There was something horribly moving about an unseeing head, swaying, ears twitching away flies, tongue working, digestion rumbling, all of that muscle supporting that flesh and mammoth quantity of weight, even her shrivelled udders. This one was so small, she was no bigger than three large men welded together. She allowed herself to be led. She would not eat, she would not grow, she would not reproduce. Her infertility rendered her undesirable even to those dumb females, herded together, mounting the one in heat in order to satisfy some primeval itch, mimicking the bull. No heat, no insemination, no pregnancy, no calf, no milk. That was that. If only she did not look so ashamed. She reeked of the sweet, bad breath of unproductivity. At least she was blind.

Grace raised the gun, steadied it. The shot made less sound than the practice shot which had hit the wall. Guns like these were only useful at close range, about three feet. Better this way, darling, than being herded on to the lorry with everyone else. So much more distinctive, and quick.

Grace was angry with Ernest. Ernest should be doing this. Ernest had agonised about the beast, as Ernest did, and she was sick of it. Ernest could not kill anything. He had bought the animal out of sentiment, and he could not even kill her. They could buy cattle and raise them, but not kill them, unless they had slipped the bureaucratic net, as she had. They could nurture but they could not kill humanely; they must pinion a bovine beast in terror and make it wait its turn for transport and ignominy. They could not kill, or bury decently, their own stock, raised on their own hay, on their own land. Piglets, yes, cattle, no.

The cow had buckled, gracefully, like a performer taking a drunken bow, collapsing on stage with a little elegance and scarcely a tremor. Grace eyed the size of her. Too big for the incinerator. Too much for the freezer.

She wandered off for a minute, smoked a cigarette; leave it a minute or two, let the blood settle. Tried not to get cross with Ernest for leaving her to do this. It was always her, or Ivy. Woman's work. Ernest could use the guns to scare rooks from trees, was all. He could use his knife to slit the twine on bales. Grace stubbed out her cigarette, grinding the stub into the mud.

She found the axe and swung it down. If she could take off that great big head, and sever the legs at the knees, the torso would fit, although it would take a long time to burn the bone. Hack it and make it manageable. He could do the rest. He was the butcher. Once a thing was dead, Ernest ceased to mourn. He could not kill, but he could pick up pieces. He was still as strong as the ox he would refuse to slaughter, with the memory of the elephants he had never seen in reality. If ever he watched TV, it was wildlife programmes.

She had stood to one side to sever the head with the long-handled axe, and still got splattered. It took practice. You could not kill things without practice; it was a skill, slow in the learning.

She put the head inside the incinerator, temperature at max, left the rest for him, and took the tether she had rescued first back to the house.

They knew: the cattle knew, the Polish herdsman knew what she had done. Beasts and humans. They were all in there, straight after milking. Looking at her as she went into the barn under the scrutiny of all those bovine eyes. Huge eyes, above slow-moving, chewing mandibles, staring as if fixated with accusation. Instead of ignoring her, letting her walk through, they turned on her and moved towards her, as they did with someone new, frightening in their fresh, accusatory curiosity. A hundred tons of flesh and bone, barring her path. She shouted at them: they stood back a step, and then came forward. Grace ignored them.

She peeled off the oversized, splattered overall outside the kitchen door, carried it in with her at arm's length and stuffed it into the washing machine in the alcove. Licence to kill meant licence to wash. Kill, wash, kill, wash. She hummed over the preparation of the late breakfast. Omelettes today; toast; cereal. No bacon, although, as she thought, she had never had the least sentiment about pigs. She hummed as she worked.

My young love said to me, your mother won't mind.
And my father won't mind you for your lack of kind,
And she stepped away from me, and this did she say,
It will not be long, love, till our wedding day . . .

Ernest came in, shyly.

'You've got to cut her up,' Grace said gently. 'You should have cleaned the gun. Oh darling, what are we going to do?'

'Wait for Ivy,' he said, then corrected himself, in the face of her stare.

'Wait for him?'

His eyes were still the same, pellucid, far-seeing blue. Paler now.

The guests trooped in for breakfast.

Ernest told them about the lake. He had told them about the lake yesterday.

They looked around for the cat and the dog they considered mandatory in a farmhouse kitchen.

Grace missed them too. And the chickens they had had when Ivy was small.

CHAPTER EIGHT

Pets were an indulgence, Grace explained. They did not need a dog to round up sheep, since there were no sheep. They did not need a cat to catch mice; chemical poisons did the trick.

What about rats? one of them said. You must get rats, on a farm. Grace opened her mouth to deny it. After harvest or haymaking, surely? the guest asked, with the wise look of one who knows such things from years of walking across other people's fields. She guessed he must have seen one: the next step would be to ask for a reduction in the bill. There was often a method behind the most artless of questions.

Ernest shook his head. For those you get in the rat man, he said. With his ferret. That's his job. Have you seen any ferrets? There's lots around here. You only see them at night. Beautiful things. Now that's what I'd call a worthwhile pet.

She had been aware of the rat in the house for the last three days. Their appearance was a mystery at certain times of year, although she was sure there was a logical explanation. *I can't stand the rats,* Ivy would say. Can't kill them either. She missed her daughter with a sudden, sharp pain.

As they scraped back their chairs, thanking her for omelettes and toast and fruit compote, an extra figure loomed in the doorway. Ed did not deserve the sobriquet of village policeman, although he looked as though he could audition for the role because he was fat, wore an unseasonal uniform and played the part of a weary paterfamilias. He usually arrived to check licences or the occasional stolen car left abandoned in a field, and Grace regarded him as simply another lazy bureaucrat with an alien accent. He smiled at the paying guests like a time-worn uncle, wished them a nice day, and wasn't it a good one.

It was, if she had time to notice. Bright and warm, but not too warm, just right for walking about in shirtsleeves. A good day, following rain, with more rain promised in the afternoon. Obliging weather for the hay.

'Make it quick, Ed,' she said, handing him a mug of coffee and banging about behind his back. 'Because I've got a lot to do. Like go out for a walk with my husband. You can't have come to check gun licences. You know we haven't had a rifle here for years.'

Ed sat down heavily, with the right ponderous manner for a serious errand.

'Not even an old one, I'll bet. No, Mrs Wiseman. It's about one of your B and B people. Do you recall a bloke who stayed here for a week, earlier on? Middle of May or thereabouts? Young man from London? He came on his own. They remember him in the pub.'

'I remember them all, but none of them in particular. Why?'

'Only it seems he went missing, back in London, or so they thought. Took a couple of weeks after he left here for anyone to notice. Then this body turned up, off the coast, six miles down from Wethering. Taken them all this time to put the two together.'

Grace was clearing the table. Ernest sat quietly.

'What's that got to do with us?' she said.

'Don't rightly know, but it looks like his last night staying with you was the last time anyone saw him. There was a party at the pub.'

'There's always a party at the pub, if someone's willing to buy the drinks,' Grace said crossly.

'He was in the pub most nights, they say.'

Her face cleared, she nodded and sat down.

'Oh yes, *that* one. I do remember him. Jack something. Jack the lad . . . No, it was Joe. Having a holiday because he'd split up from a girl or something. Remember him, Ernest? He was the only one I've ever had who wanted a quiet, healthy week in the country for the express purpose of getting drunk every night. Poor soul. What happened?'

'Don't know. He drove back to London, for sure. Put his suitcase inside his house, and that's all he did. They say in the pub that Ivy was in that last night.'

Grace nodded, trying to remember. 'So? Yes. I've got it now. She was home that week, wasn't she, Ernest? We were *both* in the pub that night. I'm allowed out sometimes, you know. They give me free drinks, for all the people I send there. We're good for trade.'

'That's nice.'

'He was a bit obnoxious, to be honest,' Grace said. 'My God, he was even flirting with *me*. I'd mothered him a bit. Now I remember. It was that little heat wave we had, like we sometimes do in May. I got him back here, he went to bed. He was packed and ready, wanted to go early in the morning, to miss the traffic. And he did. Not so much as a thank-you. I thought that was funny, since he'd really enjoyed himself. Made friends, he said.'

Ed got up. 'Is that all? You've no idea why he might have come back to the coast?'

'You want to ask them in the pub. They'd have known him best. We've no idea. He said he'd definitely book for next year. I don't know, I just don't know.'

They all bowed heads in silent sympathy.

'Ah well,' Ed said. 'I was asked to ask. I'll let you get out for your walk. Lucky for some. How are you keeping, Mr Wiseman?' he shouted, as if Ernest was deaf, the way he did with anyone old.

'Fine.'

It was not true.

It was an old habit, walking round the farm, or further afield. The courtship of Ernest and Grace had taken the form of walking, getting away from scrutinising eyes. What could not be done in a house could be done in a field or a copse. He could buy her a drink in a pub, once borrowed his dad's car for a drive somewhere else. The permissive, expensive hedonism of the 1960s had simply not applied here, only the same old rituals. The first time he had ever seen her semi-naked was by the lake. Grace in a swimsuit had taken his breath away; Grace being the better swimmer had alarmed him. She had been born by the sea a few miles away; she loved the sea. He had offered her the lake of which he was so proud, as if he had created it for her pleasure, presented it to her as a substitute for the sea. I made this with Carl, he told her. Carl was with me.

Ivy swam here, every summer day, only after Grace taught her first in the sea. It was easier to learn in the buoyant salt water. Even after the enormous expanse of the sea, the lake seemed romantically large to a child, from a child's height. In reality it was a hundred yards long at most, dwindling to the point where it became river, then stream, with a narrow breadth between the bank and the woods on the far side, where the swans nested. A swimmer could treat it as a pool and do laps. It was safe and sheltered, and semi-secret, because it was so far from a road, there was no official foot-path, and people were lazy. Locals knew; kids with bikes knew, but it never featured on a map. It was supposed to have died. There was no toilet, no coffee shop, and no games to play except sitting and eating picnics. There were occasional campers, who asked at the house first. There was no easy access to the water, which was muddy near the edge, and the place had a reputation for contamination and danger. The Wiseman family did not own the water, although everyone assumed they did because it was Ernest who picked up the litter. But it was his. It was their starting point and their nemesis.

Grace had fallen in love with the idea of a pond on the doorstep far sooner than she had fallen in love with Ernest. Carl was always there, then and now.

The habit was to walk, and sit, anywhere, including here, to talk about what was important, or not. Sometimes the point was not to talk at all, and then whatever it was which was festing cured itself and could be dealt with later. Or never, because it had ceased to matter. The presence of the lake was indeed his gift to her. Grace had sat in the field above, paused at the curve in the track, sat on the bank, swum herself into exhaustion, and chewed the cud here, and in the process had submerged all her greatest resentments without actually burying them. The fact that it had turned against her, and that the place itself, as well as its reigning swans, had delivered up to her the corpse of her grandchild, was a temporary aberration, a defection and betrayal held deep, but usually forgiven. The impact of that event went far beyond. She wondered now, as they sat on the bank in high summer, if Ernest saw what she saw, or if she could see what he did through his dark glass, and how long ago it was since they had lost the knack of telling one another the truth, or at what point she had decided he could not stand it, any more than she could. Or quite when it was he had begun to fade. All she knew was that when they looked at the lake, he had memories longer than hers, different visions of happiness and horror. And that he had never once had an ounce of her cunning or her acumen, or her passion, for which she thanked what passed for God, and loved him more, because he was still beautiful and he could always surprise her. As long as he would do as he was told.

'Why did you lie?' he said to her, absently, as they lounged in the grass.

'About what?'

'About who brought who back from the pub. That poor, silly boy. What a pain in the neck he was.'

'I didn't lie. That's what I remembered.'

'You lie all the time, lovely. Thank you for dealing with the cow. You were singing in the kitchen. Can you do it again? You might bring them out.'

Grace hummed.

She stepped away from me, and she moved through the fair.
And fondly I watched her move here and move there,
And she made her way homeward with one star awake,
As the swan in the evening moves over the lake.

'There they go,' he said. 'Not waiting for evening.'

The swans came into view on the wooded side of the lake, the cygnets, two months old, big enough to fend for themselves, preening each other. The bulky nest was hidden away. Ernest knew what went into the nest, every single ingredient; he followed its progress. Grace never had. The nest was built in March and April, favouring an isolated shoreline. Made of vegetation, rushes, short-stemmed grasses, hidden but clumsy. Defended aggressively. They moulted on nesting, to feather the heap, could not fly away for seven weeks after and could only defend their citadel from the water. The babies were downy brown, half adult weight, but without their dignified serenity.

'Took them a while, didn't it?' he said. 'I mean, they're getting on, aren't they? They can start nesting at three, and these buggers were that old when I got 'em. How long ago was that, Grace? Five years? I know they can go on doing it, and it takes 'em a while to settle, and they'll maybe live until a swan song at twenty-one years, but isn't it great? They're eight years apiece, that mother and father, and aren't they proud? I am. It changes the view.'

She knew what he was seeing. He was not talking about *these* swans; he was talking about the other swans which had swum here a decade ago. The May swans, with their babies, blasted over the lake. May blossom from the hawthorn scattering the surface. Greasy blood on the rippling water, like an oil slick, white feathers dancing in the draught of a breeze, the reverberation of rifle shots, echoing. The real death. He could see it now, and Grace knew he could see it. He could see it behind the relatively new swans; he could see the old carnage. Ernest remembered a succession of swans, some more than others, Nina and Hans most of all.

'Oh Lord, how I hated him,' Ernest said. 'Old Carl and I, we got those swans, can't remember how. That pair we had ten years ago, we called them Nina and Hans, after his own siblings. They were already old, six if they were a day. I'd given up hope of them ever doing it. They built nests for three years, but it was only going through the motions, poor sods. No cygnets until that year, and then, hey presto, there they were. The darlings, they did it. No wonder Hans was so stroppy. It was probably his last chance. No one should swim here in May. And then he shot them all, even the cygnets. I hated him then.'

'So does our daughter.'

He did not seem to hear. She knew what he could see, and if she had not loved him for what he was, she would have hated him for the nature of his regret. Always Carl and the swans. It was as if he cared more about the death of the swans than the death of a child, as if the memory of the swans was superimposed on the image of that other, less interesting, less damaged, almost bloodless corpse.

'He came back in the evening. He got one of the rifles and blasted them out of the water.'

'I don't hate him for killing the swans,' Grace said. 'That's the one thing I could understand. I might have done it myself.'

'And I don't hate him any more, Carl the younger. Why should we? Nina and Hans came back. I want *him* to come back. And bring his son, like old Carl did.'

There were pockets of fluffy clouds moving across the blue sky, casting shadows on the water, turning it dull, then bright as they moved away. The swans were bright white one moment, dull white the next, with the orange beaks of the cob and his mate glowing as they appeared to confer. She could remember the other scene, the May assassination, when the feathers scattered over the water were confused with drifting blossom; saw the birds rearing out of the water, too late. There had been no swan song.

Grace could feel the old, familiar jealousy. The way she had felt when Carl the elder appeared with his baby son, when she was still childless, watching them embrace each other as brothers and loving friends, and watching Ernest fuss that child, because he was a *boy*.

'It was a mistake, wasn't it, not to tell Ivy at once. About how it had happened. To let her have dreams of Cassie being turned into a swan.'

'I'm glad you remember that much,' Grace said caustically.

'I heard you with her. I suppose it helped to get her to sleep.'

May heat waves. A sudden spurt of August-like warmth which made them all want to peel off winter clothes. There could be snow in April, heat fever in May, but never for long. *Hottest bank holiday on record since 1899*. They always said that.

'It wasn't Carl's fault,' Ernest said. 'I wish he'd come back.'

He always missed the point, Grace thought, curling her fist around a clump of grass. Of course it had been Carl's fault. She remembered him coming into the house, clutching that bawling, abominable boy, as if he could not walk, throwing him towards his mother, who was having a well-earned rest at the kitchen table, sharing motherly moans over tea. All *he* had had to do was supervise them down by the lake. He couldn't even do that. The boy got fractious, so he brought him back. OK to leave Cassie. Actually, it did seem OK to leave Cassie; they all thought so. She could swim like a fish; the lake was shallow; she could run home in her bare feet in three minutes. Only she didn't. She hadn't. Grace could never understand how Ernest did not hate Carl the younger for the casual, wilful destruction of his wife, Ernest's daughter, which followed.

'She must have been on her back, with her neck extended, for the cob to bite her like that,' Ernest said. 'And make that mark. She must have swum too close to the nest.'

As if she did not know. As if it hadn't been gone over again and again.

The lake was calm and dark under the fitful cloud. It was hardly a lake, more a pond. It was difficult to imagine the water churning, the swan's beak around that tiny neck, pulling her under, making her panic, drowning her noise. Such a noisy, determined, talkative thing.

'He shouldn't have left her,' Grace said stubbornly.

'I'm hungry,' Ernest said. 'Is there anything for lunch?'

He was like that now. A narrow concentration span, skittering away and taking refuge in the dreams she would love to fulfil for him. She put out her hand, took his and hauled him to his feet, feeling the weight of his bones. He still saw so much more than he ever shared. Sometimes she thought she scarcely knew him at all. The path back to the house seemed long. He would have to deal with the cow after lunch, even it meant there were more flies. Otherwise, he would not eat.

'Ivy's all right now,' he announced.

Her belief in his insight faded again. He had heard her that once, ten years ago, telling Ivy that Cassie had merely turned into a swan. He had never heard Ivy screaming in the night, never gone to hunt for her in the meaner streets of London, never known what ailed her, or the only way it could be cured. Revenge. He did not understand the coldness of anger, only the brief heat.

'I like that Rachel,' he said. 'Lovely girl. I don't like Ivy going to live with her, though. It isn't really fair on her, is it? You're using her, both of you.'

Yes, he did understand. She should never underestimate him.

'We must give her a better time when she comes back. Take her to the pub instead of talking her to death,' Grace said. 'No, on second thoughts, not the pub.'

He sighed, ignoring her again.

'Just as well he sends back the letters, really. The boy will come when he's ready. He'll find his own way. Just as well we don't know where young Carl lives any more. Just as well we don't have any way of finding out, nor Ivy either. We don't have the right, you know.'

'No,' Grace said, meekly. 'We can't find out where he is. Not without spending money we haven't got.'

'He said he would look after us,' Ernest complained. 'He *promised*.'

'That was when he married Ivy.'

He lived on another planet. The computer was only for the cows and his records, and he did that with difficulty and resentment. Of course they could find out where a man whom she knew had become a judge *worked*, if not where he lived. If they knew how to access internet directories, libraries, had the courage. Of course there were ways, but she did not know them. Nor could she leave him for long enough to find out. Ivy neither. Ivy had given up, hadn't she? That was what she told Ernest.

Rachel could. It would be easy for Rachel, belonging to the same world. Rachel could find him, flash a card, demand to see him, and they would let her in. Rachel had all the qualifications. Rachel could.

Yes, Rachel could. She knew Rachel would.

Ernest stumbled and took her arm, smiled his sweet smile at her, as if there was all the time in the world to get home, to deal with the cow and the future and the collapse of dreams. As if there was time, with his fading mind and Ivy needing to be made whole again. Wanting to be restored to her former self, and always wanting to please him, for not being a boy. There was precious little time.

'Such a clever little thing,' he said. Grace did not know if he was referring to one of the cygnets, to Cassie, to Ivy. He was probably referring to Carl's son, Carl. The boy. He looked at her; she wished her misjudgements of him were not as frequent as the times when she guessed his thoughts exactly right.

'I mean Ivy, sweetheart. I was hard on her, wasn't I? Expected her to do so much. Clever isn't the right word. She took everything to heart and learned it. She knew she had to practise and learn and memorise, and she did.'

'Yes, she did. She does.'

She put the thought of the drowned guest firmly from her mind.

Rachel opened the personal file on her private organiser. *Dear Diary* . . . She wrote to herself most days, usually in the office. *Do you know, there was never a more opportune time for a clandestine affair in a crowded place? Except for finding somewhere to lie down. In the middle of an open-plan office like this, where everyone is isolated with their own screen, the lovers can e-mail in code, or pick up the mobile and text, without noise. Never has so much been done and misunderstood without speech.*

I went into her room this morning, after she'd gone to clean offices. I wish she wouldn't. I didn't linger, promise. I just wanted to see if there was anything she needed which she wouldn't ask for, like a better bedside light, because she sometimes draws in there and looks at her books. Why was I so slow to realise she can scarcely read? How will she ever get a degree? She's so generous, and so proud. She's made it into a nest, pinned up a couple of drawings. I shouldn't look. It's her private space. I won't do it again.

Grace phones at eleven-ish, most days. Here. Otherwise, in the middle of the afternoon. Her fallow times, and mine too, I suppose. We don't discuss Ivy, we talk about me. Which I like. She's very tactful. She doesn't want Ivy to be a nuisance, as if Ivy was a child and still her responsibility. She didn't ask me to find out where that bastard Schneider lives or works, but I have, it's easy. He's in the Law Directory. I've already phoned up from here, said who I was and how I'd got a personal delivery for his home address, can they give it, and bless them, they did. I'd have got him off the electoral roll, anyway. I can't picture where he lives. What he's got to hide . . . I KNOW what he's got to hide. Cruelty and desertion. I just want to know a little bit more, then I'll find him.

We've got Dad for supper tonight. Sound like we're going to eat him, ha, ha. I've just got this awful feeling about it. Hers are so colourful, mine are so plain. Grace keeps telling me I'm beautiful: she makes me feel it. I can't wait to go back and tell her I've found him. No, I won't, I'll go and meet him. The bastard. The cruel bastard. I'll go to his office, chambers, whatever. Someone, some man, like that should be exposed. He's a judge!

It must be easy to divorce a person who cannot read. I went to the divorce registry yesterday, looked it up. On the grounds of adultery, I ask you.

She was wearing new clothes today. Her head ached; she wanted the sea and the lake, and she wanted justice.

OK to tramp the streets, though Donald did want to be home. It was not a day to be catching sight of himself in shop windows, especially in Soho, unless what was on the other side of the window was food. One of his favourite areas. It had always had people like Blaker. Soho changed its spots, but not its disposition. Sex and food, food and sex. Having lost interest in both, he was less than charmed. Sometimes he wondered if everyone had done as he did, i.e. short-circuited the whole process of judging human nature and come straight to the conclusion that everyone was vile. The effort of proving otherwise was scarcely worth it.

He saw her flitting round the stalls in Berwick Street, and knew he had seen her before. Tall, slightly gaunt, handsome, buying in vegetables and garlic, arguing the price. A tart if ever there was one, but a tart who cooked.

Donald really did not want to know about daughters and sons and wives. He was looking for Blaker. This was his patch, as it always had been. Blaker was a gentle mugger, only hit them when necessary, i.e. when they noticed they were being robbed. A daylight man who only ever got them when they were shopping. Favoured the good handbags, carelessly worn with the mind of the owner concentrated on shopping, that was his favourite modus operandi. He watched them first here on the stalls, and then in the silk shops. Theatrical types and curtain-makers went in there, foodies stayed outside. On the outside stalls of Berwick Street they had metal bowls with exotic fruit and veg at one pound a time. There was ginger and mangoes, one stall avocados only, another purely for pink apples, and the shops on the far side of the caffs sold silks, satins, videos and cheap, flashy jewellery, where the stallholders could stand outside, play cards and swear.

This was as far as the tarts from the other side of the river got in the 1870s. Over Waterloo Bridge, away from the drovers and market men worth a shilling a time, up into Covent Garden where the prices were higher. The unlucky ones went back in despair, some of them preferring to drown themselves in the river rather than return empty-handed. They called Waterloo the bridge of sighs.

The woman buying vegetables was streetwise. Her bag was strapped across her body and tucked into a belt, leaving hands free. No one would part her from her money without a fight. She tested the vegetables, disturbed the display, and no one argued back. She was a sight for sore eyes, if you liked them Amazonian. Donald had come here looking for Blaker. It was still a better bet than handling all that stuff about missing wives and old grievances. He could clock up the hours, looking for Blaker in the confident hope he would not find him in a hurry.

The woman stepped away from the stall, all negotiation done. Cash was king here, credit cards a no-no. This stall faced one of the few caffs down this stretch, ranging from bistro snacks to burgers. She waved towards the window. Donald looked in the direction of the wave.

Fuck this for a game of monkeys. The man in the window, being waved at, looked like Blaker.

Such a small world, and way too soon. Couldn't be right. He wanted this job to last.

CHAPTER NINE

The bad thing about being stuck in a rut, and the last thing she had noticed, was the habit of taking the same route to work in the morning and never varying it. How could you ever do that in London? Ivy had said. There's so much to discover if you go a different way. The habit of extending the route and thinking of more than simply getting there had begun ever since Rachel started the first drawing classes, because she found herself wanting the opportunity to look at faces and bodies with a new, almost prurient fascination. She wanted to linger, checking human proportions, the elegance and the lack of it in all of them, wanted to notice how each one sat differently on Tube or bus, walked at a different angle, how some would relax with a newspaper in a queue, others could not, stood twisted. How some were stiller than models, others in constant movement. Rachel no longer kept her head down, varied the route to and fro to make it longer, and looked, boldly.

Keeping her head down in all senses had become a way of

life; she was accustomed to it. She was still isolated in her relatively new job in the offices of Stirland and Co., because everyone knew she had been a whistle-blower in the job before. The smart, sanctimonious bitch who had revealed a major scam and could not be loved for it; the one who refused to ratify a company's accounts because they were as false as they had been for years, and refused to keep quiet about the fact that a senior consultant had been bribed to maintain a deceit. Management had been ostensibly grateful for the information, received in time to prevent a scandal and to turn what was corruption into a mere mistake, but they had lost money in the process, which was not easily forgiven. And everyone there, and thus everyone here, knew that she had got her lover the sack. She had not been particularly popular before: a beautiful, numerate girl who worked harder and quicker than anyone else, was socially timid but deadly obstinate, with ambition worn on her sleeve. The fact that she had championed the cause of the unqualified females groped and bullied by the overfed male of the species did not make her top favourite with either. She was bred uncomfortably honest; she hated bullies and arrogance, nothing could change it. It was simple conviction. The partners did not like to be reminded that they were only well-paid servants, oiling the legal and financial wheels of larger corporations, and that while vital to the life of the client, they were not as important as the rules they were paid to uphold. Not a good thing to be right all the time. Rachel Doe was too reserved for the men, too severely good-looking for the women, and she had to live with her reputation going before her. It was better at Stirland and Co. since she had lightened up and wore her hair down sometimes. She was more approachable. The firm had a high turnover of staff. Some of them had forgotten she had the makings of a traitor.

"Lo, Rache, can you help me with this?"

She had always wanted to make partnership; it was no longer important and it showed. She thought she was easier to get on with than she had been, that the mark of shame on her forehead had faded, but she did not really know what they thought, and while she had once cared so much she had shrunk into herself more and more, she now cared less and less, even though she was exasperated by the corporate refusal to see that long-term profit meant *never* doing anything underhand. She was still her father's daughter. It was her weakness and her strength.

A small hangover today. Rachel wished she had been a lawyer, rather than the number-cruncher she was. They were more important. She did not want attention, but would have liked influence. The lift took her straight to her floor, the fifth of ten. The other floors were different capsules, like decks in a ship. From her window she could see the street below, saw people spilling out from the station opposite, near and far, wondering if she would actually recognise anyone from this safe distance. She thought she would, and never had. These days she watched before getting down to work.

It was early. She sat at her desk and considered the personal file on her organiser, labelled DIARY. The débâcle with the dishonest consultant who was also her lover was what had made her keep this in the first place. She, who would never again trust any incriminating or confidential information to an office computer system, had recorded his, printed it out; and when he would not admit it, had called her a silly, treacherous bitch, she had shown *them* in logical sequence what he had done. The habit of keeping her personal file remained.

The diary file was thinking time. As for work, there seemed nothing which could not wait. They all exaggerated their own importance and the need for urgency. It was time to do something else which could not be postponed.

She wrote down all the things she knew Judge Schneider had done. She was enraged by the fact that he was a *judge*. The more the simple internet research told her about him via the chambers website, the more she was angered. *Called to the Bar in 1973. Specialised in family law/criminal law/human rights issues. Judge: 2000.*

She knew enough about the system to know that Schneider was not at the top of his tree. He had avoided the brinksmanship of commercial law, as well as the high earnings. Might have taken a judgeship for easier hours and a pension. Not an ambitious high-flyer, so occupied the moral high ground of family law and crime instead. Opted for the anonymous, virtuous role of judge because he had something to hide.

This was what he had REALLY done.

Seduces young girl/wife.

Neglects child; lets her drown.

Shuns wife, shuts her out. Beats her up. Lets her drown too, in a manner of speaking.

Fixes a divorce.

Neglects grandparents. Denies rights of access.

Prevents son from maintaining/making contact.

Is cruel.

Shame on him.

Tomorrow, she vowed, tomorrow I shall try and find him. Phone? Yes, but why would he speak to me? Now wait a minute. I know Grace wants me to do this, she doesn't ask, but I know anyway, and I also know she doesn't want me to alienate him, just get him to . . . What? Grace really does know Ivy best. She knows Ivy will never be whole until her son sees her for what she is outside the ghastly picture his father has painted of her . . . Rachel worked on her rage. How dare he do this?

Still she prevaricated. And what would Ivy think? Ivy must want to see her son; Ivy cried in her sleep. There were sketches, pinned to the walls, of a boy child, a boy, the young man he might have become. And what of him? What of the son, what did he want, which no one else knew?

She told herself that all she wanted to do was find the judge and explain, but before all that there was her father, and Ivy, this evening, to which she was not looking forward. It was always like that with her father: she was proud of him, and his ridiculous standards. It made her ache.

As the others filtered in to work, she greeted them cheerfully. The hangover headache was secretly supplanted by a certain joy in being alive, which did not quite stop her noticing that the waste-paper bins had not been emptied since yesterday and the desk and floor bore the traces of yesterday's dust. Things often went wrong with the contract cleaners who came in at night. It made her wonder, with a smile, what Ivy was doing. Ivy would do better than that.

This was simply not fair. Blaker, the leading joker in a not very convincing pack, was not supposed to be so easy to find. It was meant to take days. Donald put the lid on his frustration. For a start, he did not know what to say to the man, since nothing was remotely rehearsed yet, and he could not think of anything he could do to set the ball rolling. Such as, look here, Terry, there's a bloke threatening the last judge who sent you down, is it you, by any chance? I don't really think so, but it makes a good theory, and I've got to find someone and it might as well be you, so would you kindly oblige with a confession, and would you mind leaving it until next week? Or at least give me an alibi which takes ages to establish and comes back solid? No offence, mate. OK, do you have access to a computer, knowledge of medieval images, can you draw? There's a good man.

Donald watched the woman walk away. Not a good handbag, cheap and cheerful. He stood still, watching with conspicuous uncertainty, and then went in the door by the window where the man who was a dead ringer for Blaker sat. He had to do that, at least, to make sure; maybe he was wrong and, hope against hope, it wasn't Blaker after all. Identification via mug shot photograph was not the last word in reliability, even if blown up on a screen to show the skin pores and the sullen mouth. No one smiled for a mug shot.

The setting made it clearer that it was indeed Blaker, or at least it did to a suspicious mind with an in-depth knowledge of Blaker's repertoire. This was an upmarket, no-smoking patisserie, redolent with good smells of fresh coffee substances, sweet pastry, anxiety to please, clearly favoured by the better-off of the consumers who used Berwick Street, in preference to the other caff, with its solid sausage rolls and bacon sandwiches, which was the haunt of the stallholders in the cold. The stall men were up with the lark; they were always hungry. No point trying to rob them; they would see you coming out of the back of their heads. This, on the other hand, was the perfect place for Blaker to sit and survey those who had, or were about to spend, money. The ones on the way to buy silk or ginger, pausing to check the list and speak into tiny, shiny mobiles. A stressed-out, multitasking female, juggling the luggage of shopping, job, self-consciousness, ambition; that would be his chosen type. Judged first by clothes and attitude, good hand-bag next, with cash in it, because that was the coinage here. From this vantage point, a thief like Blaker could seek the quarry, watch them shop, watch them pause with their espressos, and, if he was working, follow. All the short way to Shaftesbury Avenue, Theatreland, which was his other stalking ground, even if he always began here. They would be waving for a taxi, waiting for a bus, when he struck. And, blow me, if it wasn't an internet café, also. It had to be him. It was.

Donald sat with his coffee in the seat level with the window, with his back to Blaker and a sideways view of his reflection in the glass. The pavement outside was slippery underfoot as the rubbish increased.

The tall woman came back. There was a parcel of asparagus she had forgotten. Not so efficient then. This time she did not wave. Donald could allow staring at her to be his alibi. It was her height and strength which was interesting, rather than any hint of glamour. Amongst the discarded rubbish of the busy market stalls, she seemed conspicuously clean, like a polished apple. He could not have guessed her age. Ever since his own daughters grew into adults, he had lost his knack for gauging the ages of women. They came in swathes of the eighteen-to-thirty, thirty-to-over-forty, when they all looked the same. He told himself he could still tell something about their lives, from the faces and the hunch of the shoulders, the way his wife had taught him, what they shopped for and what they wore, but never how old they were. The coffee was good. He would settle for that for now. He could smell the man behind him, made the mistake of checking the reflection to see if he was still there, almost jumped out of his skin.

'She's a piece of work, isn't she?' Blaker said. 'I wouldn't try, if I was you.' He turned sideways in his chair, presenting a broken-nosed profile and a waft of dirty hair. 'She's a model, you know.'

Donald turned his own, harmless face with its fine, clean hair, glasses, combed moustache and caught a glimpse of brown teeth. It was a mistake to imagine that a con of Blaker's experience could smell a copper from forty paces, because they simply couldn't. Or if they could, which was as likely in Blaker's case, they simply didn't care, because they had nothing to fear. Or they were the sort who got on fine with those who hunted them so ineffectually, most of the time. They were simply two men, caught in the act of staring at the same woman.

'I thought she must be,' Donald said. 'Figure like that. I wouldn't mind bumping into it, slowly, if you see what I mean, but I'd be too scared she'd eat me alive. Model, is she? Since when do they do their own shopping?'

Blaker sniggered. 'She's not like that,' he said. 'She's the down-to-earth kind. She's come up in the world. You would-n't want to know what she did before that. We were an item once. Still friends. She bought me this coffee. Buys me a drink now and then.'

There was a lingering note of pride in his voice. He tapped long, horny nails on the table.

In your dreams, Donald thought. Why would that shining woman with the figure of stone buy anything for an odorous loser like Blaker, but then there was such a thing as simple kindness. Donald scratched his head, adjusted his glasses, grinned. He knew it wasn't his open face. The man was lonely and bored; he would talk to anyone. He needed to protest that he was better than he looked; nothing to boast about and therefore needing to boast.

'I never get to meet women like that, not in my line of work,' Donald said. 'How come you get so lucky?'

Blaker sniggered again. He tapped his coffee spoon on the table. He smelt musty and his thin thighs were pressed round the leg of the table as if somehow restraining it from moving away.

'I tried to rob her once, matter of fact. Not slowly, either. I was good then.' He smiled sadly. 'But she saw me coming, belted me round the head. Then she gave me some money. She said, if you need it enough to do this, you'd better have it. Turned out she'd even less of it than me. We got to be mates. I used to read the newspaper for her. Those were the days.'

The clock on the wall said eleven thirty. Between the stalls, Donald could see the stallholders' pub on the other side of the road.

'How about a drink?' he asked. Oh God, it was so clichéd, it was a giveaway.

Blaker smiled, showing more of the teeth. 'If you want information on our lady friend, copper, it'll cost you more than that.'

Donald sighed. It was so galling to be wrong, and so nice to be given an opportunity, even when you did not want it. Always take the sideways option. They could talk about his lady friend, someone, something else, work backwards to him.

'Such as what?'

'A really good fuck up the arse,' Blaker said, and roared with laughter. They both did, as if it was really witty. Blaker wiped his eyes with a grubby fist. The dirt was ingrained. Donald could not see those fingers tapping on a computer keyboard. Blaker leaned forward.

'If you're looking to bump into that one slowly, don't even think of it,' he whispered. 'She's a judge's wife. A fucking judge, I ask you. We get all sorts here.'

Donald felt his world begin to spin.

'I've got fuck-all to do,' he said. 'Let me buy you that drink.'

He was the man.

Rachel's father arrived at six, resentfully early, out of place and feeling outmanoeuvred by the invitation in the first place, slightly sullen and anxious to get it over with. He carried his worry like a sack on his shoulders, looked like someone who had never gazed up at the stars and waited instead for them to fall on his head. Ivy bore his coat away to her room out of the way; he seemed to miss it. She towered over him. Dislike settled on his features. He said he was not feeling well. The preponderance of flowers in the small living room made him sneeze. He had bought a plant. He stared at Ivy, dwarfed by her, then stared at her again, as if she was a specimen.

The occasion was less disastrous than uncomfortable at first. They ate roast chicken, new potatoes, and asparagus which he did not like because he knew it was expensive, and he stared at Ivy.

'I'm sure I've seen you somewhere before,' he said.

'Must have been my starring TV role,' she answered.

She was making an effortless-looking effort; she could have charmed blood out of a stone with the way she fussed over him. He forgot to ask questions. Mid-meal, he put down his knife and fork, turned to Rachel.

'I bought my stuff so I can fix that tap in the bathroom. It was leaking last time.'

'Oh, Ivy fixed it.'

'And that dicky cupboard in the kitchen, the one with the hinge . . .'

'It's OK, Dad, it's been fixed. Ivy . . .'

Silence fell. There was the scraping of cutlery on plates.

'Place could do with a coat of paint,' he said at last. 'I expect Ivy could do that too.'

They removed from the dining table to the living end of the room, with coffee and chocolate. His temper had gone.

'She needs a man about the place,' Rachel's father said to Ivy, still staring. 'Only she can never get them to stop still. She puts them off. And now she's living with a lesbian,' he said, choking on his words, talking about Rachel as if she was not in the room. He was bitter with hurt. 'That's not how me and her mother brought her up. I know where I've seen you before. At Euston, wasn't it, a few years since? Begging. Not many tall, blonde beggars. I never forget a face. I try not to look at beggars, never give them anything, but I noticed you. I thought, she's young, she looks fit, why doesn't that girl get a job?'

'Dad . . .'

'I think it might have been King's Cross,' Ivy said smoothly. 'And I'm ever so respectable now. On my way out to work, as a matter of fact. Can I get you more coffee before I go?'

He seemed surprised by his own outburst, shocked by his anger but unable to stop it.

'At least you work,' he said. 'That's something. At least you're not living on handouts. Unless you're sponging off my daughter. What is it you do again?'

'Clean floors and lavatories, mainly, wait on tables, and strip,' Ivy said.

'You what?'

Ivy got up and cleared the table. They could hear her in the kitchen beyond, then her footsteps going towards her room, scarcely audible in her rubber-soled shoes.

Rachel sat, stunned by her father. He was like a small child, shrill with temper. She was so angry she could not speak. He turned to her, moved by feelings he could neither understand nor control.

'You fool. You silly fool. You always were a fool. You don't know good from bad. You're green as grass, you. She's a bad 'un. A sponger.'

She left him sitting, and moved the few paces to Ivy's room, where she knocked at the half-open door. Such simple rules of privacy had been easily established without discussion: knock before entering. This was the room where Ivy confined herself. Apart from the little improvements, the fixing of the tap, the cupboard hinge, and the influx of flowers, her presence was difficult to detect in the rest of the flat. An untidy nest in here, everything left tidy elsewhere, her own space deliberately small. Ivy was sitting on her bed, looking at the timetable she made each week to remind herself of which job to go to next, all written out in messy block capitals. She was crying. Rachel's father's unnecessary coat lay on the bed where Ivy had carried it when he first arrived. The first action of a hostess: take the coat, make him comfortable without it.

'I'm sorry,' Rachel said. 'I'm really sorry. I don't know what's got into him.'

Ivy dashed tears from her cheek with her fist, attempted to smile. The room was tidier than it had been that morning, Rachel noticed guiltily. Ivy was up at five, while she herself slept, out again to work at nine forty-five tonight, shopping and cooking in between, only to be insulted. She had taken her sketches off the wall, replaced them with a poster of Matisse's *Leda and the Swan*.

'Don't worry,' Ivy said. 'Please don't. It's not such a bad thing to be reminded of a past life. Any right-minded person would be suspicious of me.'

'I could kill him,' Rachel said.

'Enough,' Ivy said. ' He's maybe just a bit jealous.'

'Jealous of what?'

'You're all he's got, Rache. Try and understand. Don't be hard on him on my account. He's nice. At least he says what he thinks. He's not very well. I'd better go.'

She slung her bag across her body and began to whistle, stuffed the timetable into the bag and left the room. Rachel followed slowly, returning to the living room to see her father cowering, as if waiting to be hit, hating him for that too.

'Don't get up,' Ivy was saying gaily, bending to touch his shoulder. 'It was nice to meet you, Jack, honest it was. Don't mind me, will you? I look worse than I am.'

'I'm sorry,' he muttered. 'Sorry.'

Rachel was dumbfounded. She had never known him say sorry before. About anything, ever. The door closed behind Ivy, leaving them alone. He looked small, hunched and miserable and he was not going to say sorry again.

'Well, Dad. You were on good form. Are you all right to get home?'

'Course I am. What time is it?'

There was no losing face in front of a daughter. He looking distressingly pale. No point discussing it. She fetched the coat and walked him to the Underground station in silence, watching dark fall around them. Wishing it was different, annoyed, wanting to run after him as he moved out of sight. He was so stupid and so small.

The theatre at the north end of Shaftesbury Avenue was showing a musical, with a *Pop Idol* guest star whose name was on the lips of everyone under twenty. The small cleaning team for backstage had arrived on foot, their arrival timed for shortly after the audience and the last of the cast were gone. They stood around smoking fags, waiting for everyone to disappear so they could get in. The show had overrun; it was the last night; there was a crowd of autograph-hunters and semi-frantic fans crowding round the stage door, jostling and chanting one of the songs, half hysterical with anticipation. Fuck them, one of the cleaners murmured under his breath, moving forward. If we can't get in, we'll still be here after the last train. Come on, shove through. The fans did not like it. They, too, were kept waiting.

The cleaners were undistinguishable from the other, larger crowd at first sight, which was why there was trouble. There were the same hoodies and hat-wearers. Closer up, the working group were generally older, scruffier, and free of the adrenaline rush that follows watching a performance. They were not as lightly dressed; no music beat in their ears. The chanters could not see why anyone else should be allowed inside as they waited. Their number was swelled by others drawn by the sound and the spectacle of a crowd. The night had not yet started.

They had to get in; they had a timetable; they would not be paid for being kept late. The cleaners were jostled and abused. One man in particular, shielding a half-clad girl who bellowed out the last song of the show, pushed forward. Where the fuck do you think you're going? It was hot.

Aided by the stage-door staff, the group slipped through, jostled as they went, the man pulling at clothes. Only as the last of the six disappeared into the lighted doorway, and the loud girl began bellowing louder, and the Idol appeared, and the noise turned into hush and then into applause, did she notice her bloke, saying again, what the fuck, slipping to the ground and staying there as they surged forward and lost him in the roar of welcome.

Tomorrow's headline. *Man stabbed to death by rival fan.*

Rachel went back into Ivy's room. Looked around its smallness. It was not fair. It wasn't bloody fair. Too many people had spat upon Ivy. Her father's reaction was the same as many. It was not fair. Ivy deserved better.

Rachel's father felt bad. What the hell had got into him, except a feeling of being made redundant all over again? At his age? It would have been the garlic in the chicken; he could have sworn there was something in it. She was a bad lot. He felt ill.

One train cancelled, a crowd on the next. It was later than he liked it to be. The crowd in his carriage were carefree and singing. The windows were stuck shut. He was sick and old and tired and ashamed, and horribly breathless, overheating in the coat. He fumbled in the pockets for the inhaler, then for the pills.

There was nothing there.

CHAPTER TEN

Friday. Do it now.

Hello, my name is Rachel Doe. I'm a friend of Ivy. I need to see him.

No, that was not going to do. Appeal to self-interest.

Hello, my name is Rachel Doe of Stirland and Co. I need to set up a conference with Judge Schneider in his chambers, if that's convenient.

Can I ask which case? He doesn't do cases any more. He tries them.

Yes, of course, I should have said. It's an old matter in which he was involved several years ago. It's now the subject of a compensation claim between victims, and we wondered if we could trouble him for a few details of the criminal case which we seem to have missed. We need his memory. We will pay for his time, of course.

That won't bother him, honey. What was the name of the case?

Wiseman v. The Ivy League. R. v. Wiseman originally, I think. I'm sure he'll remember. To whom am I speaking?

I'll check and get back. Give me your e-mail and mobile. Judge Schneider's busy right now.

How the hell did anyone get anything right? What if he answered and what if he didn't?

Easy to find the court, easy to find the way in if you spoke with a degree of authority. Not so easy to cope with no reply.

It flashed up on her e-mail, two hours later.

He says, of course. Temple. Paper Buildings, name on the door. Four thirty this afternoon would be fine. He's in court until then. Please confirm.

If the judge had something to hide, or wanted to hide, he was bad at it, or else whatever method he had used to hide himself from his wife and his wife's family was only effective because they did not know how to look up a directory. Did not have the right voices, the right technology, the means, or even a telephone directory. The huge divide between the lives of the Wisemans and her own was humbling. They did not have the tools.

Rachel sat back and wondered how easy it was to fool some of the people some of the time.

Ivy was modelling this evening, out until late. There would be no opportunity to explain on her return. What did she want to achieve?

I wanted, she wrote in the personal file marked DIARY, *to know. I want them to resolve it. I want Ivy to have respect. Her rights.*

Every day had a regime. She and Ivy were going to the farm, early tomorrow. Something had to be achieved by then. She phoned her father. Peace could be established by pretending nothing had happened. There was no reply. He would take days to come round. He would not be saying sorry again.

She had been careful about her clothes, mainly Ivy's choices from shopping with her. Ivy positively enjoyed the process of pointing out things she could not afford but wanted to see on someone else; she enjoyed being a style consultant. No one does power-dressing any more, Ivy said. I clean more offices than you ever see, so I know what they like. They wear their training shoes all day and leave their high heels stuffed inside their desk drawers. Rachel was informal with attitude today. Linen trousers with loafers, pale, unstructured linen jacket, her hair long and loose. She was not going to wear black simply because she had the chance of meeting a pitiless judge. Tomorrow they would get in her car and go to the farm, early. Kick off shoes, run around barefoot.

Once the meeting was set, far more easily and immediately than she had thought possible, Rachel found the morning stretched like elastic, minutes taking hours. It was moving towards the holiday time of year, the place half empty while those with young families queued at airports. She did not envy them. By one o'clock she could not bear it any longer, tidied up carefully and left. Someone had complained about the cleaners; their efforts had been redoubled. Her computer printed off the right section of the map on a clean page. Middlesex Crown Court was right in the heart of London, and she was becoming a specialised form of tourist.

Since justice must be seen to be done, she knew that there was public access to all trials and most courtrooms, except where security was paramount, and even then, as far as space allowed. The few visitors to the public galleries of Middlesex Crown Court were directed through X-ray pergolas, as if at an airport, and once through could wander at will. After a morning's worth of justice procedure, the public waiting areas outside each court were lightly littered with dead paper cups, a Coca-Cola can under a plastic seat, waste-paper bins overflowing. A posse of people were standing outside, smoking; the smell had drifted in with them. Rachel found her way with confidence; she knew she had the right to watch. Court Five had a small public gallery at the back, reached by a separate entrance and a flight of stairs; once there, Rachel looked down. There were three other people, watching listlessly, apparently unconnected with the slow theatre played out below. They looked as if they had come in simply for something to do. Rachel wanted to watch the judge at work, and sneer at him. She wanted everything she knew about him to be confirmed, and she wanted to know what he looked and acted like before she met him at four thirty.

There was no jury. There was no on-going case. The usher informed her that it was an afternoon devoted to passing sentence on those already convicted, those who had pleaded guilty or been found so, cases adjourned for social enquiry reports into background circumstances, recommendations as to sentence and the preparation of speeches in mitigation, appealing to His Honour's discretion for leniency. They could all go to prison, or not.

The first defendant shambled into the dock without assistance, with the air of one sick of waiting, feigning nonchalance. It was only as he gripped the rail of the dock firmly enough to break it that she could see how frightened he was. A persistent daytime burglar, unsuccessful by definition. When he was asked to confirm his name, he could merely nod. She could sense a desire to be sick, to run, to escape. As someone spoke for him, facelessly, from behind a wig, about how he had turned a corner, about how he no longer felt driven to steal, how well he had responded to his drugs treatment, she could feel the stirrings of cynicism. Yeah, yeah, yeah. He'd stolen since boyhood; he would do it again. Prison was right. Tick the box, she heard herself saying, waiting for him to be dismissed. As the speech ended, the man began to shake. The judge spoke to him directly.

'You haven't had much luck, have you?' he asked.

A nod.

'Well, maybe it's time you did.'

It surprised her, the soft, brief pity of it, the lack of judgement and lecturing. The next was different, the approach the same. Bailed for reports as to why he should not be imprisoned for three counts of actual bodily harm, all done in drink. Off the street, alone in the dock, stripped of everything, his defiance pathetic, he shook with dangerous nervousness. Someone spoke briefly and condescendingly on his behalf, going through the motions, patently weary of him and his kind. Tension snapped; the defendant yelled that he had had enough of this, pushed his way out of the dock. Then he seemed to hesitate, as if knowing that this would seal his fate, half turned back, and in that split second, Rachel could have wept for him. It was so futile and so foolish, made everything worse.

'Going so soon?' the judge said. 'Aren't you even going to say goodbye? Please come back. We'll miss you.'

As if he had a choice. There was a brief underswell of laughter, but it was the judge who absorbed the ridicule and looked a little precious.

The same with the next, a fat recidivist benefit fraudster. His Honour invited her to sit. Tell me, he said, what I ought to do with you. It all flowed like silk in that hateful, barren room. One after another, prisoners and lawyers, whatever their sentences, however bad their speeches, left with their dignity. It was quietly impressive. It was not what she expected. Everyone here got a hearing.

Rachel shivered on her way out in the sun, hurrying down to the Embankment for the ten-minute walk to the Temple, passing Big Ben as it struck four, telling herself that surely it was easy to be magnanimous and even pleasant as a judge, when you had the support of all that regalia, a throne upon which to sit, a wig and gown beneath which to hide and someone to guard you if anyone produced a gun or a knife which had not been discovered by the X-ray at the door. She was trying to argue herself into feeling critical. A judge did not do his duty by being lenient and kind. He had to weigh the need of society to be protected against the hope of the individual to be spared, and it wasn't the individual who was paying him. What struck her most was how ordinary and diminished those people in the dock were, in relation to the damage they could do. Who lost most? Who won, who gained? The other abiding impression was how lonely the judge looked on his pinnacle, below the sign, *Evil to him who evil thinks*. Did he dream of them, these flotsam and jetsam who floated before his throne? Maybe it was they who had made him human. Maybe his red sash of office had given him a heart.

She had hardened her own heart by the time she turned into Middle Temple Lane and entered the quaint tranquillity of the Inns of Court, a series of cobbled lanes and squares, moving uphill away from the river, as if meandering without purpose. Ancient stone buildings bent towards one another at the beginning, opening out into shaded squares, then into colonnaded walkways, then into another lane and then into the openness of Temple Gardens, reached by steps descending to a lawn, shrubs and trees, so surprising in its secret, spacious loveliness and dizzying show of flowers, she stopped to breathe. Busy footsteps on paving stones seemed impertinent here. The larger buildings spoke of grandeur, the smaller warrens of cosiness and secrecy; she had forgotten how beautiful it was.

Rachel paused to remember the last time she had been here, remembering a wintry landscape, with the hidden gardens clad in a rare blanket of snow. Ah yes, Ivy had brought her here. It had been part of her winter education. One of those many city places which do not look open to the populace, but really are. No one was going to invite you, but all you had to do was walk in.

It was Ivy who made her look at a building and want to turn it inside out, as if it was a doll's house, the front of which could be removed to reveal the complexities, eccentricities and practicalities which lay within. Like taking up a curtain on a stage. Paper Buildings was pure Dickens. The rooms at the front would overlook the trees and the river; the entrance at the back with the hand-painted names of the occupants inscribed in order of importance, in glossy, old-fashioned red-and-black script, exactly as they would have been in Dickens' time, some looking as old, led on to stone steps, curling upwards and out of sight, with a black iron banister, knobbled from a dozen coats of rust-disguising paint and cold to touch. Even in August, the steps were slightly damp, bringing back the smell of winter. There was no room for a lift to the fifth floor, no such luxury. The walls were cold. She reached the top, passing separate nests of rooms on each floor, where stone gave way to carpet and the same script said Knock and Enter. Another world.

He was waiting for her inside the door. Behind him she could sense the familiar hum and smell of a twenty-first-century office, hear the sound of a fax machine, the ringing of phones, the burr of a printer and voices arguing.

'Miss Doe?' he said, extending his hand. 'Wiseman and Ivy League? I'm so sorry. We're very short of space here. There simply isn't any room. Do you mind if we sit outside?'

She could not shake his hand; she simply could not. The hand that had struck Ivy, shut the door against her, NO. They went back down; she knew she was being outmanoeuvred somehow, and all she could do was lead the way until the gloom gave way to light again and they were sitting on a shady bench, facing the gardens, him taking the lead. The first sight of him without the wig shocked her. His hair was flat against his head, and glinted in the sun. His presence in this outdoor space was twice as potent as it had been in the courtroom.

'I watched you in court this afternoon,' she said.

'Yes,' he said. 'I know. I saw you. It's unusual to have a single woman in the public gallery, unless it's a mother, crying. Or anyone beautiful, for that matter. I wish more people came.'

'I thought you were very . . . . fair.'

He turned a pleasantly surprised face, smiled. The effect was paralysing.

'A pushover, you mean? Fairness is the least they deserve. Most of them have had a rotten deal in life.'

He did not ask, *Why?* Nor did he say, *What are you here for?* Of course the name of that fictitious case, *Wiseman*, was a clue. He was not defensive, or obviously curious, none of that. He simply sat and waited. She was trying to summon up the anger and found it difficult, wanting him to start, getting more flustered as he refused to oblige.

'We've had the best of the year,' he said finally, waving an arm in the direction of the garden. 'Maybe not yet, though. If there's nothing to say, perhaps I'd better go and let you enjoy the view. But you have to start, you know. I've absolutely no idea what you want, and it isn't *fair* to put words into other people's mouths.'

She stared at a vibrant fuchsia plant, thought, yes, the best of this summer is beginning to be over, and began slowly. The carefulness of his speech was infectious, like the protocol of the court procedure she had watched. The script she had rehearsed was already abandoned. There was nothing to do but be honest. He wasn't a judge; he didn't deserve to be a judge. He was just another dishonest man. She reminded herself of that.

'Your wife, your ex-wife, is Ivy Wiseman, right? You divorced her two years after your daughter, Cassie, died, ten years ago in May?'

He inclined his bright head. He did not wince at the mention of their names.

'We divorced each other,' he said. 'As one does.'

That was her trigger.

'It's hardly mutual if it's done on paper and one of you can scarcely read.'

He inclined his head again. It was neither negative nor affirmative, simply an indication that he was listening.

'And your son, Sam, nineteen now, has had no contact with her, or with his grandparents, Grace and Ernest Wiseman, since just after Cassie's death?'

This time a bloodless nod. The shadows were longer over the gardens. It seemed so unfair that there were tracts of lawn and roses and shade which no one used on a sunny afternoon. He looked as if he was nodding acquaintance towards the flowers rather than anything else, listening intently to another voice.

'Because you prevented it,' Rachel went on. 'As you still do. Breaking all their hearts, especially Grace's. Perhaps her husband's even more. It isn't right.'

'Whose heart?' he asked, as if coming back from a distance. '*Ivy's* heart?'

'Yes, Ivy's heart, and I do know. I'm her friend. She shares my flat. She's my friend. She befriended me, we befriended each other . . . Oh, shit. And her parents.'

He turned right round towards her, regarding her carefully, as if memorising every detail.

'Are you her only friend?' he asked.

'Yes . . . I . . . No, of course not.'

'Perhaps you should ask yourself why. Why it is you're the only one. And tell me what you want.'

What did she want? She was completely out of her depth. She faced the fact that she had expected someone demonic and Germanic. A guttural Nazi in sheep's clothing. Yes, she was prejudiced.

'Do you love her?' he asked gently.

'Not . . . like that. As a friend, yes. Very much.'

'I didn't mean *like that*. I meant as a friend. Highly underrated, isn't it, asexual love? Just as powerful as any other. Puts sisterhood and brotherhood to shame.'

That sounded pompous and got her back on track. She resumed with a machine-gun blast of questions and accusations which had been reverberating round her head ever since the last weekend.

'It was your fault Cassie drowned. No, I'm sorry, I

shouldn't have said that. But you drove Ivy away, you locked her out when she was vulnerable. Look, no one's responsible for someone else losing their mind, no one says you fed her drugs, but you left her. And she went over the brink and dragged herself back, and I bet you don't know what that takes, and she's fine and . . . and . . . It's just that I know she'll never be entirely fine, I can't imagine she will, anyway, until she can, sort of, have it out with you. And explain it to her son. She wants him to be proud of her, not ashamed. She can't initiate it; she daren't, but Grace tries, with all those letters she sends to your solicitor and you crumple up and send back. Now that really is despicable of you.'

The last, jumbled sentence startled him.

'Recently?'

'Of course recently. Over the last year, dammit.'

'Oh. Those.'

The carelessness of the response infuriated her.

'*YOU* kept them apart. You keep them dangling. You prevent any resolution. Grace can't live with it.'

'Do you mean closure?' he said. 'Dreadful word.'

'Not closure,' she said angrily. 'An opening. The chance to make amends. The chance to see things for what they are, oh, I don't know. Ivy blames herself, for everything. She wants forgiveness. She's done absolutely marvellously.'

He was nodding again, as if he entirely understood. A good trick. He probably did it with witnesses, to get them on side, make them think he was with them somehow, stuck right in the middle of their point of view.

'You aren't a lawyer, Miss Doe, although your firm . . .'

'You looked me up?'

'I didn't, my clerk did. That aside, have you ever heard of the hearsay rule?'

'Even accountants know a little law.'

'There's a rule which says that reported conversations between third parties are not admissible as evidence in a criminal court, because they themselves do not prove the truth of their own content. Just because one person says to another, so-and-so dyed their hair black yesterday, that cannot be evidence that they actually did. So we don't let it in. I often think it's a rule applicable in real life.'

'You condescending sod,' Rachel said. She was suddenly as angry as her father had been; indiscretion came upon her just as quickly. 'You just don't want Ivy to appear in any way, shape or form, in case your hypocrisy comes out with it.'

Neither moved, sitting on the bench, staring ahead, like lovers having an argument, with the difference that he still seemed at ease. The truth was that there were several reasons why she could not look at him. She was embarrassed because she had flunked this self-imposed test of sangfroid, because he was so composed and unashamed, because she was waiting for him to laugh at her, almost wished he would. And because she could feel this great gravitational pull towards him, a horrible desire to impress him with her own honesty, somehow, to be able to say to herself, later, that she had walked away intact, like one of his defendants. He made *her* feel guilty.

It had been a lousy idea to see him in court, discover in advance something of that ingredient which might have made Ivy fall for him hook, line and sinker in the first place. The stinking, cruel, cunning, bully-boy hypocritical bastard, the worst kind, honed into charm by sheer bloody practice. The shit. Dead right. The obverse of a talent for putting people at ease and granting them dignity was the subtle ability to humiliate. She wanted to snarl and grind her teeth, snap at his ankles, and above all, make him smile at her.

'If you don't mind my saying so,' he said in his quiet voice, which was surely honed, and practised too, to carry such resonance at so low a pitch, 'I do think you're very brave, doing this. I mean, it takes some doing. It's not everyone who can wade in and interfere in the name of friendship, duty, love or anything, and confront someone else's tragedy for them. Try and fix it, instead of doing that very English thing of *nothing*. To act as a friend as only a parent does for a child. It's brave. It's unusual. So are you. What I meant to say is it deserves hearing. Do you think we could start again? And before we do that, I should say I quite understand how and why anyone would love Ivy in whatever fashion they do. You'd have to be out of your mind to resist it. Such a capacity for giving love. Hatred, equally. Am I going on?'

She felt suddenly tearful, a child admonished and forgiven, bent her head in a kind of 'yes'. Let's start again, please. Please like me.

A series of people had passed in front of their chosen bench during the time they sat. The to-ing and fro-ing of the Inns, coming back from court, hell-bent on the work which preceded the next day or week, more time inside a court than out, always. She let herself relax, ever so slowly and unsurely, fraction by fraction; she was going to be let go without looking a fool. Footsteps came quickly towards them, from behind.

'There you are, Mr Schneider, sir. They said inside you'd be here. Sorry. Can I have a word, sir?'

He was like the setting, a relic of Dickens, with a droopy moustache, so harmless and sedulous he was almost laughable. Padding along in this sultry heat, as if there was any rush, trying to make a virtue out of a hurry.

'We could have dinner and go from there,' the judge said, peeling a card from his pocket and placing it, adroitly, inside the rim of her handbag. She had given him hers, with all the numbers, dammit. 'Or if that's too loaded, a drink whenever you please. Do give my best to Grace. It isn't me who crumples up the letters. Hello, Donald! Do sit down. Please, don't go,' he added, turning back to her with the smile she had not realised she craved.

He waved at the intruder. 'This,' Carl said, 'is Detective Sergeant Cousins, known as the Don. And this,' he nodded in Rachel's direction, 'is Miss Rachel Doe, of Strickland and Co., a great friend of my ex-wife's.'

Donald sat heavily, recovered his breath.

'Oh, that's helpful, ever so helpful,' he said, pulling out a handkerchief and mopping his brow. She had a feeling they were acting out a scene, as he might have done in court. Donald settled back into the bench, downwind of the judge. A breeze had developed, wafting over the gardens, funnelling in the direction of the Inns' narrow exits. There was absolutely no need for him to have run, or to perspire as he did. He could have stood and cooled.

'Just what I needed,' Donald wheezed. 'That'll save time. Bit of a development, sir. Might be a good idea if I had a word with your ex-wife. You've always said you don't know where she is, but perhaps this lady could help us? If she's a friend, that is. Save a lot of time.'

Rachel loathed him on sight, and felt caught in a trap, as if she were squeezed between them. She turned to Carl.

'Why do you want to find her? You never did, and you always could, so why the hell now?' she asked him. 'What is this?'

'It's nothing really, sir,' Donald said, looking to the judge first and then to her. 'Only it looks like she might be involved in our business, sir, simply because she may know someone who is, and it may just be useful to . . . to . . . have a word. Eliminate from enquiries, so to speak.'

He looked as if he could nod and wink at the same time, like a dozy donkey invested with cunning, pretending to shake his head to get rid of the flies. Oh my, what a good double act.

'So where is she?' Donald said, leaning across Rachel, looking as if he might be about to pat her knee. She recoiled, felt oddly exposed, sitting on this bench in the early evening sun, as if she had been placed there deliberately, for a purpose she had not understood. Placed here like a target, because as soon as the names Wiseman and Ivy had been mentioned on the phone to his clerk, Carl would have guessed she would at least know Ivy's whereabouts.

'Why does a policeman suddenly want to know where Ivy is?' she asked him, ignoring Donald. 'All he has to do is ask you. You could always find her. You always could have contacted her, either directly or through Grace.'

'Ah yes,' Carl replied smoothly. 'But as you've just pointed out, I haven't been looking. I haven't made the effort, therefore I don't know.'

Ivy was going to be blamed for something again. Rachel could feel the closing of a trap.

'Is this a set-up?' she asked him. His eyes were fathomless blue, locked in a brief gaze with her own, saying I don't know. She did not believe him; rose and brushed imaginary crumbs off her trousers, listening all the same. Carl turned to Donald.

'My wife's friend was only saying just now,' he said, in a chatty tone she automatically mistrusted, 'that although she's a friend, she hasn't the faintest idea where Ivy is. Isn't that right, Rachel?'

She nodded. It was true in a manner of speaking. She had no idea what he was playing at.

'There's no urgency,' Donald said, sensing something on the wind, addressing her with a winning, repellent grin. 'Only that I came across someone who used to know her. Or she used to know him. She just might be able to tell me something useful about him, that's all.'

The lameness was embarrassing. She adjusted her handbag, stepped backwards, as if she had just realised the time and had to go, now.

'I must . . .' she said.

'Go.' Carl said. 'But we're meeting next week anyway, aren't we? I'll phone the office. Tuesdays are good for me.'

She was about to say yes, and then, startling in its irrelevancy, there came into her mind the comforting vision of the life drawing class. The weekly commitment, never to be missed, the start of all this. The last class of term.

'Not Tuesday. Or . . . it would have to be late.'

'We'll speak, shall we?'

'Yes.'

She walked away, and once round the corner found herself running. Once she was out of the Inns and hit the roar of Fleet Street at the top end, she paused for breath and went into the nearest bar. Her face in the mirror blushed red. She had bloody well said yes.

Rachel drank the indifferent glass of wine she had ordered as if it was water, sat in a crowded corner as though waiting for someone. No one ever quite mastered the art of being alone in a bar.

On the table in front of her, someone had abandoned

the *Evening Standard*, flourishing a dramatic headline.

Yob culture hits the middle classes! Man stabbed in Theatreland! Young fans run amok. Is nothing safe?

She ignored it. She felt she was conspiring with the enemy.

CHAPTER ELEVEN

Quick, quick, get going. She was being shaken awake. Come on, Rachel, there's a love. It's a gorgeous day. Let's go, if we're going to go, before we get stuck in traffic. If we go now, we can get to the sea first. Sorry, were you dreaming?

Rachel had been asleep when Ivy got home, whenever that was. There was a mug of steaming tea in front of her eyes, and Ivy, imploring her to move, like an impatient child waiting to be taken on holiday. Ivy, who coasted on four hours' sleep and ten hours' work, brimming with infectious energy, because life was good, life was rich and you had to enjoy every minute. That was her gift. She could give away some of that energy even at six in the morning. She was nobody's victim in the mornings and took no prisoners.

Rachel had been dreaming of the farm again. Imagining the figure of Grace and being hugged by her in the kind of embrace which said, nothing else matters, you're safe here. Carl, hugging Grace.

Once on the road, it was singing all the way. Whizzing through the deserted streets of London as if they owned it and everything had been cleared and cleaned for their benefit, and even the traffic lights deferred to them, the skies lifting as they hit the motorway stretch and left it all behind. The first hour was nothing. The radio blared and they sang to that.

The lane going towards the house; the joy of it. Bluebells in May, Ivy said, blossom in June, every shade of green in July. August is for yellows. Snowdrops in February. *Ivy said, Ivy said, Ivy said.*

Grace was tending the tubs of lavender and herbs outside the kitchen door, but really waiting. The purple hair complemented the shocking red of her pelargoniums and the pink of her cotton shift, which looked as if she had sewn it the night before. She was barefoot and jangling with multicoloured beads. Follow the noise. The shriek of welcome could have woken the dead, and it was Rachel she hugged first, Ivy next, then both together. You made it, she kept saying, you made it, as if it was a miracle. I've been reading the newspapers, she said. I've been so worried about you. All those terrible things happening in London. It isn't safe. You can't queue for an autograph, or get in an ambulance, awful.

'I had a plan,' Ivy said, interrupting the flow.

'To go to the sea,' Grace finished. 'I've been craving it all week.'

'That's why we're early,' Rachel added.

'Party time for Mother,' Ivy said. 'The sea and the pub today. We've all been working too hard. Dad can make hay while the sun shines. We're going to bring Rachel's dad to keep him company next time.'

That had been discussed in the car. Ivy had suggested it.

'Just to warn you, darling,' Grace said to Ivy, as they bundled back into the car, Rachel relieved that she was designated driver, 'I mustn't be out too long. We have a slight problem at the moment. Because of the hay, they always arrive when he cuts the hay. Not to worry. The man's coming sometime, with the dog.'

'Is this code?' Rachel asked. 'Or can anyone know?'

'We've got a rat in the house,' Grace shouted from the back seat, yelling as loudly as she would in her own, deafening Volvo. 'Ivy's never liked them much. Oh look, we're nearly there. This bloody thing goes so much faster than mine.'

'I can't go into the house if there's a rat,' Ivy said. 'I can't.'

Rachel paused at the mention of a rat. Such a nasty word. She was not going to tell anyone, not about yesterday, or anything, not yet, and it felt like being a rat, all dispelled by responding to the instructions they yelled at her to take a different route, no, right, I mean left, did I mean left? No, I meant that way, to a different stretch of the coast which was over there, the five miles separating it from the farm and the fields like crossing the Gobi Desert, the same difference as the City and here. Another secret place they knew, reached by a series of back doubles, hidden under cliffs, with a railway line snaking above their heads into a tunnel. The City was another country, and the railway, hugging the coast, was only a reminder that there were people unfortunate enough to be going somewhere else. A tiny cove, hidden beneath a mysterious cliff, which hung above it more like a guardian than a threat. Mid-morning, empty, and still the same old glorious sea. This was the precise point where I learned to swim, Grace was saying, but then again, I'm not sure. We knew every scrap of this coast, Grace said, when we were kids. We cycled for miles. We were shoved out in the morning with jam sandwiches wrapped in greaseproof, and told to come back when we were tired. I thought we might try it. The sandwiches, I mean. There is really nothing quite as disgusting as a jam sandwich made with margarine and red pulp with woodchips in it.

'Golden syrup on toast,' Ivy said. 'Treacle sandwiches. Butter and sugar on fresh white bread.'

'Go on,' Grace said. 'You were way too young for that.'

'I know, Mum,' Ivy said. 'But old habits die hard. That's what you fed me.'

There were no waves like before, simply a breeze which ruffled the surface of the water so that it mimicked a smooth lake. It was like approaching a different, friendlier animal, which would embrace softly, rather than a rough, challenging hug. It was markedly warmer than the week before, a different stage of summer. There was the same rushed changing into swimwear, although Grace and Ivy had no shame. Grace simply stripped naked, hauled on the baggy swimsuit; Ivy did not bother with changing and reached the shoreline first, clad in her bra and knickers, ran straight in with a noisy splash. Rachel followed, wading gingerly to waist height, testing the ground for the way back, automatically looking on the way for jellyfish and monsters, laughing at herself for doing it, while Grace squealed and flopped and decided it was best to go in backwards, tripping and splashing, yelling, watch out, it's fucking freezing, Oh bloody hell fire. They were there to play, Ivy to swim. She outranked everyone as a swimmer; she moved away from them with natural speed in a graceful crawl into the distance, and only turned back to shore when Rachel and

Grace were sitting in the warmer shallows, feeling virtuous, kissing the last week goodbye.

Grace did it again as they were towelling dry, dropped a small stone of conversation into the flurry of movement, as if tossing it into the sea and getting rid of it. It was directed at Ivy.

'You remember that paying guest, Joe his name was, the one in May who got drunk all the time when you were here that week? Well, he died. PC Plod had to bestir himself and come and tell us.'

'Oh, what a pity,' Ivy said with careless politeness, wrapping her head in a towel, then balancing to pull on her jeans over bare skin with the ease of practice.

'One of your guests?' Rachel asked. 'How awful. Wasn't your food, was it?'

'Don't think so,' Grace said. 'Though he ate enough of it. No, he went and drowned somewhere after he'd left. Remember him, Ivy love? He wanted to swim in the lake and we told him he couldn't. Because of the swans still nesting.'

'Yes, that's right. Anyway, he preferred the pub. He was bloody rude to you. He was always trying to do things he couldn't do, wasn't he? Probably took up sailing next. He never could see the need to practise. Like that lot.'

She pointed to the horizon, where a small flotilla of yachting dinghies with yellow and pink spinnakers tacked about like waterborne butterflies, chasing each other. Grace shielded her eyes with her hand, and sighed.

'I wish I could do that,' she said. 'But perhaps not. I'd rather be in it than on it. God, I feel better for that. It's like taking the cure. What time were you up? You must be bloody starving.'

No unpleasant news was going to disturb this day; that had been decided. No paying guest stayed long enough to form himself into a ghost.

'Poor Jack the Lad.' Ivy finished it, picking up towels and bra. 'You know who he reminded me of, Rache? That Plonker in the life drawing class. They could've been twins. He's one of Rachel's fans,' she explained to Grace. Rachel laughed.

'One of yours, you mean.'

Grace threw her hands into the air. 'And what about me? Where are mine? Any left over for a woman in her prime? I don't care if they're stupid.'

'She can still pull them, you know,' Ivy said, 'The ones who want mothers. And she can swim better then me when she tries.'

'Here she is,' Ernest said to Rachel when they got back. The salt had dried on their skin from the air blowing through the open windows of the car. 'Here's my favourite girl. Are you coming out to make hay with me this afternoon?'

'Food,' Grace said. 'Food first. Followed by no decisions at all.'

There was smoked ham, a salad of herbs, raspberries with yellow cream, eaten in the garden. Ivy would not go into the house.

'The lake's murky today,' Ernest said, with a mouth full of food. 'You were better off with the sea. When's the rat man coming, love?'

'You never know with him,' Grace said. 'We may as well all sit in the sun. You never know how long it's going to last. You see to him, will you? I hate it. Ivy hates it.'

'My little phobia,' Ivy said. 'Bloody rats.'

Rachel and Ivy lay on blankets on the unmowed lawn, listening to the humming of insects, and Rachel drifted into sleep. The sea did that. There seemed to be all the time in the world for everything; it was an excuse for saying nothing and she was pleasantly tired. Before she slept, listening to the buzz of the semi-silent life which went on all around her at ground level, regardless of human beings, she was thinking, solutions find themselves for insects, why not for us? The solutions to dilemmas were often so much simpler than the problems themselves. The bees and the flies went on fine without much obvious thought. It was wonderful here. All she needed to do, surely, was to get Judge Carl Schneider. Get him to come back here. Him first, then the son . . . Yes, that would work. She felt a twinge of excitement. Get him to come to this place, be charmed by the goodness he had forgotten, and then everything would follow. He had loved them all once. He and his children and his father . . .

She woke, warm and heavy, the sun still hot on her back, her chin level with the long grass, her mouth dry and the salt on her skin itching. Something crawled on her calf; she twisted round to slap it. Ernest was sitting beside her, slumped in a very old striped deckchair. Half asleep, she noticed that the visible stripes of the cloth around his head were as faded as the wood of the chair, bleached into the colour of a pale mushroom, and he was wearing a vest, and he and the chair suited one another. *Old man in deckchair, wearing vest and knotted handkerchief,* like a postcard from the 1950s, still dressed the same, better in sepia. The weeks of sun, however intermittent and easy to ignore in the City, had turned his face, neck and forearms deep brown, with a sharp demarcation point above his elbows and below his chin, showing the precise point to which his shirt sleeves had been rolled up and his collar left open when he was out and about. Farmers did not care about nice even tans. Rachel thought of the builders seen from her high office window, stripped to the waist with evenly brown backs and builders' bums, a perk of the job, and then, looking at Ernest's milky-white shoulders, had a stark image of her father on holiday. She should have tried to phone him again; she tried to remember where she had left her mobile.

Ivy's blanket was empty. The lawn was small but seemed vast.

'Oh, hello,' Ernest said. 'You're awake then. I was sitting out here waiting for him to do his business. They had to go, Ivy and her mother. They can't stand it. Don't know why, when they're so good at killing things. Maybe they don't like to defer. But the rat man's indoors. I thought you might be interested. Shall we go and see?'

He began to haul himself out of the deckchair, the seat of which sagged ominously, and then gave up the attempt. The bottom half of him was still clad in his baggy canvas trousers, without boots or socks, showing feet the same milky white as his shoulders. He retrieved his shirt; the demarcation lines of white and brown disappeared. Rachel thought of a model in the life class. Saw through the wrapping to the way he might have appeared, stripped of his clothes and his role, emerging as a gnarled old tree trunk, already struck by lightning, discoloured by fungus, growing weaker.

'He's a very clever beast, Vernon. If he were half as sharp as the ferret, they'd have made a mint.'

She had been disconcerted to be found asleep in her shorts and cropped top, beneath Ernest's innocent gaze. She sensed that he had been willing her awake, simply because he wanted company, and she was slightly hurt to have been abandoned by Ivy and Grace, her chosen companions for the afternoon, and then she could hear them saying, she's sleeping, poor lamb, leave her, and thought, yes, that would be the reason.

'No rush,' he said. 'It's not the best time of day for it.'

'For what?' she asked, still fuggy.

'Flushing out the rat.'

'Why's Ivy so scared of them?'

'Got locked in the cellar with them once. Don't have a cellar any more. It spooked her.'

Rachel sat up, reached for her bottle of water and drank, resisting the urge to pour it over her head. Then she put on her hat and felt as if she had rejoined the world and looked around from a new angle. The garden was more like a meadow, left to run wild, apart from the lavender and flowers by the back door, and the obtrusive row of rubbish bins. It had resisted any kind of makeover. The back of the house was creeper-covered, mellow red brick. It seemed timeless.

'Tell me what it was like here, oh, twenty years ago,' she said.

'That's not long,' he said finally. 'I remember much further than that. Not much changes, only the way we use things. The way it was. All those people, all that company. That's what I miss. Used to be everyone in on it when we harvested hay. A gang of us, always a gang. Grace was feeding the whole lot. That's the difference. The company. Three of us for the pigs, four for the milking, ten for the hay. Now it takes me and a machine to make hay, all by myself. A farm gets run by one man and a Polish cowhand who can't speak English. It's lonely, that's the difference. Now most days are the same and always will be. Unless Carl comes back.'

He began to struggle out of the deckchair again. Deckchairs like these were traps for the unwary, lessons in indignity; his efforts were almost comical. He was not used to sitting anywhere for long except on the upright chairs of the kitchen, or perhaps in the comfortable armchairs in the living room which Grace told her only really came into its own in winter, when on wet days Ernest would watch wildlife programmes on the TV.

'Come on,' he said. 'Let's see how he's doing.'

Still mystified, she followed him back through the ever-open kitchen door, through that room, down the corridor which bisected the house. The living room faced the front of the house, next to the front door no one seemed to use. It was as if the kitchen entrance was the mouth of the house, through which everything and everyone passed, where everything was prepared and digested, debated and decided until it was time for bed. The living room door was closed. Ernest knocked very softly, entered on tiptoe, ushered her in behind him and closed the door, nodding to the man who sat at his ease by the dead fireplace with a dog at his feet.

'That's Vernon,' Ernest whispered, pointing at the dog. No one else required an introduction. They sat on a sofa, in silence. The room was cool; she shivered. It was odd to be sitting still and silent with two men and a dog on a glorious day; it made her want to giggle. The dog raised its head and cocked its ears. The strange man in the chair played with a soft leather pouch, squeezing it between his hands like a man with worry beads, keeping his fingers occupied. It was all rather peaceful.

It was then that she began to hear the sounds, at first from above her head, then from one corner of the room, then another, then almost under her feet. Scrabbling, scratching sounds, the pitter-patter of ghostly feet, a series of minute thuds, the sound of running, which made her turn her head to try and follow, detect the weird, unseen source. Then more silence; then the sounds resumed, *scritter, scratter*, running, bumping, something twisting and growing behind the skirting boards or under the wooden floor. She was struck dumb by the sounds.

Ernest leaned towards her and whispered, 'He's got him on the run.'

'Who's *he*?'

'The ferret. Look at old Vernon.'

The dog sprang to its feet and stood, quivering. The sounds grew louder, echoing into the room, a race coming closer and closer until it was focused on the furthest corner, where the old skirting board failed to meet the floor. It was a crooked room, she remembered, full of gaps and draughts, warped into its own shape, the dark side of the house.

She imagined something screaming, saw a brown shape squeeze through the hole and catapult into the room, a live creature running. Until the dog sprang, snatched it up mid-flight, shook it and tossed it twice, let it drop broken-necked, then picked it up and carried the trophy to his master's chair with the sedate, brisk movements of a well-rewarded servant. The dead rat was deposited with dignified indifference. The man patted the dog. The efficient brutality of the death took her breath away.

Again they waited. She followed the direction of Ernest's gaze to the same corner of the room where the rat had emerged. A sinuous, slinky animal, almost ash blond, emerged into the light and began to wash itself. The man crossed the room in his stockinged feet and picked it up with one enormous hand around its neck, so that its head protruded from his fist and its legs dangled. The man came back towards them, proffered the ferret in his fist for Rachel's admiration.

'You can stroke him if you like,' he said. 'Just the back of him, like. Not his head. He bites.'

She touched the spine of the thing gingerly, with a single finger, feeling shiny silk.

'He likes a good hunt, this one,' Ernest said admiringly.

He picked up the dead rat by its tail, moved out of the room, down the corridor into the kitchen. She watched him fling it into the ever-burning fire of the Rayburn, without ceremony.

'It's a lot more humane than making the poor bugger eat poison and die in agony. At least he gets a fair fight. Anyway, that's what happens to rats in this house. Doesn't work quite so well in the barns.'

There was no ceremony in the brief exchange of a note, taken from Ernest's pocket, palmed by the man and tucked into his own. He grinned a toothless grin, whistled for his dog and went out of the back door. She could think of nothing but a character from a film, utterly believable at the time of watching, but better never seen in real life. The strong smell of animal remained behind him. There was an insignificant sound from the Rayburn, as if it had belched. Ernest ambled around from sink to stove, filling and placing a kettle for tea, chatting as he went.

'Don't take it unkindly that Grace and Ivy upped and left you asleep,' he said. 'Grace said you looked so sweet it was a shame to wake you, and Ivy can't be around the rat man. They've only gone to the farmers' market. Not that they needed anything, just to get out the way. But I took the liberty of waking you because I know you like to know how things work.'

She began to relax a little, realising that she had been wound up by the shift from the sun in the Garden of Eden to the relatively dark, animal-smelling area of the silent living room, with its gap-filled skirting boards and the hollow floors and walls with conduits to all parts of the house. A rat could come and go and hide as it pleased in a house like this. Her father would have stopped up those cracks, those holes, years ago. No rat would ever be allowed in. He would have covered every board with carpet, fitted every hole and crack with plaster and wood cement, made everything smooth. The making of tea reminded her of all those things for which she felt gratitude. Maybe it would not be such a good idea to bring him here, as Ivy had suggested, after all, although he would revel in a certain kind of superiority which he might enjoy. At least his humdrum little house was hermetically sealed against draughts and pests, down to the smallest fly, and he did not have to take in paying guests in order to finance his pigs and cows. Grace would charm him, Ernest would reassure. It would be fine.

Ernest made the tea, handing her a mug already laced with milk and sugar, and it seemed churlish to ask for another without it. Nice to have sweetness, once in a while. She found her voice at last, heard it sounding clipped in this quiet, ticking, humming room, which was always warm, never hot, even with the Rayburn always about its business of heating the water, the oven, the whole house. The sunshine outside no longer appealed. How lovely it would be in winter. She was already thinking of the pleasures of winter.

'Well, fancy Grace and Ivy being scared of the rat man and

the ferret. I thought those two weren't frightened of anything.'

Ernest grinned and scratched his head. 'Reckon it's pride. They could neither of them kill a rat. They're too quick. Target's too small, however you practise. Me, I can't kill anything. So them two had to learn, but they never could manage a rat. That's why they scare them. You can only get it right with practice. Like that ferret. No finesse, my girls.'

'Wouldn't a cat be better?' she said.

He shook his head. 'Maybe. We don't have cats or a dog any more. Can't risk it. That's where Ivy got her first practice.'

'Got her *what*?'

'Practice, I said. What did I say?' He shrugged and drank his tea, forgetting where he was, drifting away and coming back.

'Not that there's any choice, you know. There never is. If the beast's got to go, it's got to go. Like road kill. Kinder to everyone in the end. He shouldn't have killed the swans and made such a mess. Would you like some more tea? What time is it? They said they'd buy a leg of lamb for supper, that'll be nice. Crazy that we can't eat our own cows.'

There was the sound of the car, heard from a distance, stopping noisily outside. Slamming doors, laughter, a flurry of footsteps over the gravel, the omnipresence of Ivy and Grace laden with bags, coming in with a chorus of apologies, chirping like the sparrows which had started their own early evening chorus in the creeper round the door. They exploded into the kitchen, bringing in colour and warmth and noise. Trailing behind them, as if uncertain whether they should, were two blond young men with knapsacks. Paying guests.

'Oh Lord,' Grace said. 'We thought we'd only be an hour, and the pair of you would still be asleep. Sorry. The rat man's gone, hurrah! Saw him on the road. Just as well we're late, because we picked up these two in the lane. They came in late last night, and they've been walking since dawn and they're shagged out. They're German, by the way,' she added.

Ernest beamed at them.

'*Guten Tag. Ich hoffe Sie hatten einen schönen Tag. Aus welchem Teil Deutschlands stammen Sie?*' he said slowly.

'I got some organic wine,' Ivy said, flourishing a bottle. 'Therefore entirely harmless. Anyone?'

'Do you have beer?' the blondest of the two asked. 'We are from Berlin.'

Ernest clapped his hands, looking delighted.

'*Berlin ist eine sehr schone Stadt,*' he said.

'Do we have beer?' Grace said. 'Do pigs have wings?'

'What . . .?'

'Never mind,' she said. 'Sit down, sit down.'

'Berlin people are very nice,' Ernest said.

A party atmosphere was prevailing, as if the departure of the man and his dog was an excuse. Not that Grace or Ivy ever needed an excuse to celebrate. Ernest needed company and they had brought it home. He was lit with smiles. Rachel wanted to join in, wanted to please. One of the paying guests was looking at her shorts with frank appreciation, and it was that and the remembered smell of the ferret which made her murmur she must have a shower before a drink. She went upstairs to her room, washed in the tiny bathroom, and found a clean shirt in the bag she had dumped on the bed. Her mobile phone lay accusingly beneath it, reminding her that she must check on her father.

Two messages. The surprise was that the first was from her father. He hated leaving messages, hated mobile phones and refused to have one. The sound of his stuttering voice alarmed her as much as the fact of the message itself.

Been a bit poorly, his voice said. Someone picked my pocket on the train. I had a turn, had to go to hospital. I was there all night, or was it two? Can't remember. I'll be all right. Just wanted to let you know before anyone else does. 'Bye.

He never told her when he was ill. Rachel checked the number. Number not available. She pressed out his home number: no reply. He was not at home; where the hell was he? She was furious with him. Typical to leave a message to worry her sick, without giving her any opportunity to do anything about it. Maybe he was at his neighbour's; he had one good neighbour; they went shopping on ebay for fun. They would shop for a bag of nails. She did not have the neighbour's number. It was in a book, in the flat in London. Damn, damn, damn. Maybe the second message would explain, but the second message was not from him. It was from Carl Schneider.

Any evening next week would suit him fine, for dinner or drinks or whatever she wanted. Please.

Rachel sat on the bed with the phone in her hand, hearing sounds of laughter through the open window, wishing she had not touched the thing, wanting to go back downstairs and join in and knowing she could not. She found herself shoving the phone out of sight. Ivy stood in the doorway, proffering a glass of wine.

'What's the matter, love? We're missing you down there. Dad's embarrassing everyone with his little bit of German. He's probably going to give them his version of the war. We thought we might take a stroll to the lake, but it'd be pointless without you.'

'It's my father. Left me a message. He's ill, or he wouldn't leave a message at all.'

Part of Rachel wanted to ignore it. Then she remembered how he had looked when last she saw him. Old and grey. She had forgotten everything else. He was her father.

'What exactly did he say?'

'Something stupid. He said someone picked his pocket on the train. He must mean the other night, going home from us. Says he went to hospital.'

Ivy slumped against the door, then came and sat down beside Rachel.

'On the *train*? Oh, poor thing,' she said. 'Are you sure he said the *train*? He didn't say anything else?'

'No.'

'But he's all right? He must be, surely, to phone at all.'

'He probably is. It's just that I can't get the number he called from. I'll have to go back and find out where he is. He's not at home, probably at the neighbour's and I don't have the neighbour's number with me. If he's in hospital I don't know which hospital. If I go now I'll be back at the flat by nine. Sorry, sounds like I'm missing a party.'

Ivy handed her the wine. Rachel shook her head.

'Wait until the morning and I'll come with you,' Ivy said.

'Shit, I forgot that. How will you get back tomorrow without the car?'

Ivy put her arm around her. She felt hot from the sun and there was the dry sweetness of wine on her breath.

'Same as I always do without you. Lift to the station, train. Are you sure he said he was pickpocketed on the train?'

'Yes.'

'The bastards. The fucking parasites,' Ivy said, sounding somehow relieved, and then hesitated. 'I could come with you now, if you like.'

Rachel felt grateful for that, but shook her head. She had heard the hesitation and that was enough.

Your father is yours, and mine is mine.

CHAPTER TWELVE

It turned out Blaker had been a country boy, once. Came
from somewhere up north, territory unknown to Donald,
who was London born and bred, although he could understand why someone might want to live anywhere else, the
way it was now. He wasn't a bad chap really, by which
Donald meant he was interesting, he could talk, he was educated enough to have a nodding acquaintance with history, so
therefore he passed. It did not make Donald approve of him,
which was another matter, but in general he found thieves
easier to understand than their more moral, less articulate
counterparts.

All he had established that first time was that Blaker had
the skill to threaten the judge in the way the judge had been
threatened, and that by some weird coincidence he was
enamoured of the judge's ex-wife. The coincidence wasn't so
great when he considered the territory. The West End of
London was still the uncomfortable but manageable refuge
for runaways, thieves, opportunists, drug addicts, homeless

drop-outs of all types and ages slipping through the social net. There was the official Centrepoint refuge in Tottenham Court Road, dumping ground for the displaced youth of several boroughs, there were the favourite places of shelter all around Charing Cross, with the warm underpasses for sleeping; there was the endless opportunity of casual, cash-paid labour; there were doorways and nearby hospitals and above all, millions of consumers. A person could live on what was dropped and left and a person could be paid to pick it up. Get to London, like Dick Whittington, because the pavements were paved with gold, flee inland from the coast, downhill from anywhere, get lost or found, and survive, for a while. Huddle together with kindred spirits, make friends and allies, or shun them. Celebrate a fresh misery or a win. Keep the cold out.

'I reckon some of us blag our way out of the homeless shit out of sheer boredom,' Blaker said. 'Either that, or you lie down and die. I've known Ivy a long time. She was always going to rise, like a cork floating on the muck, because she had the will, and she never quite dropped out of the system. She had support. She chose the street. She shared stuff, though most of us don't. I'd just got out of prison for the third time, back here like one of those bloody pigeons. Either here or down Embankment Gardens if the weather's nice or I want a change. Ivy's the same, but she has other places too. I saw her again when I was on bail for the last lot. Told her I'd come up in front of a German judge – is that what we fought the fucking war for? – but at least he gave me bail before the trial, and she said, You what? What was his name again? Then she laughed and laughed. Oh, he's a judge now is he, now isn't that rich? He wasn't one of them when I was married to him. A fucking judge. You could have knocked me down with a feather and I laughed back at her, didn't believe a word of it. Ivy doesn't like being laughed at. Nor being pushed about, or touched. You've got to be careful about that. You have to give it to her. She worked her way out of it. Said it was the only way. She said if you don't earn the money, someone's going to take it away; if it's nicked, they nick it back. I wish I'd listened, but work and me, we never got on. Now I've got no fucking choice, because I've lost my bottle for the other. She got me a job on a night shift.'

'What sort of shift?'

Blaker looked at him scornfully.

'There's all sorts of shifts. Honestly, you people don't know you're born. There's shifts for loading and unloading, shifts for cinemas, theatres, lavatories . . . when do you think they clean the shops? Pubs, clubs, shifts for packing sandwiches and scrubbing decks, gettit? A lot of them are sewn up, but they'll always take Ivy. Pity she couldn't have got me a job as a model, too. That'd be a treat for them.'

He sniggered with laughter at his own joke. Donald did the clichéd thing and got up and fetched another pint. They had not moved far from where they had first met. He was still smarting from his attempt to tell the judge his big discovery about the Blaker connection, storming up to his chambers at the right time of day, finding him out there on that bench. But the judge had been in a state at first, then cool and dismissive, listened and said, that's fine, but don't you need to know a little more? Has he admitted anything? I'm sure lots of people knew my wife. He had not liked his tête-à-tête with the girl on the bench interrupted. They had looked close; Carl had kept his eyes on her as she walked away, as if following a dream and wanting to run after her.

On second thoughts, he might have been right about

Donald not knowing enough and getting overexcited about finding a connection which could be nothing. Yes, Blaker had said he would do anything for this Ivy woman, but so what? That was as far as he'd got, apart from establishing that Blaker was lonely enough to be up for a longer chat any time and seemed to have nothing but regret on his conscience. Thus, today, Donald was doing his policeman's thing of buying pints for an old con and enjoying it. Saturday counted as overtime; Saturdays and Sundays were bad days for Blaker because there was less to watch. The pub in this street could have done with a spring-clean. They were like ladies, meeting for lunch, and Donald was resenting the money. Blaker could run just as well on coffee, not that the price was so different.

'Don't mind my asking,' Donald began, 'but you know after you mugged those girls, why did you phone them up? Why keep the keys? They'd have changed the locks. You were never going to go stalking, were you?'

Blaker shook his head.

'It was something to do. I was bored. Made sense at the time. I liked the idea of the silly bitches being frightened. Remembering me when no one else would. Silly. And the keys were just an insurance against some time when I might have nowhere else to go. Gave me a kick, having keys and addresses, rainy-day insurance. And anyway, they wouldn't all have changed the locks. It's expensive. Ivy said she probably wouldn't have bothered when she was married with a house of her own. It might have been worth a try sometime. Silly; it got me a bigger sentence from that bastard. I couldn't believe it was him sending me down. Fucking Kraut. Because I knew all about him by then. How dare that fucker sit in judgement on *me*?'

Donald wanted to seize his thin shoulders and rattle him for information; instead he moved his feet on the sticky carpet and imagined rats in the cellar. The beer was warm, the heat outside stultifying. There was no point in hurrying anything.

'Like I said, how dare he? All I'd ever done was steal from silly bitches who could easily afford it and it's them gets the sympathy. Losing your fucking handbag won't make a jot of difference the day after. What about the poor sod who's got no other choice but to take it? Once you start, you've got to go on. Not like him, a fucking Hun judge, been given everything, with nothing taken away. Just like the Germans after the war, innit? They got everything, we got nothing, and who got rich? Them. Aside from all that, I couldn't believe him being a bleeding judge, after what he'd done to her. He's a fucking murderer, for God's sake. I bloody told him what he was. Him sending *me* to prison? The cunt.'

Ah. That explained that.

'Bit extreme, isn't it?' Donald suggested chattily. 'Calling him a murderer. I mean, judges can't actually hang you any more, even if they might like the idea. There's probably some of them gagging for the chance to give out a death penalty, but they're not allowed. Not since the sixties.'

He was recalling the irrelevant fact that the last public hanging was in 1868, abandoned after that for the avoidance of litter, public unrest, and the awkward dispersal of the thousands who gathered to watch. He wondered if they would now. Probably. Blaker had calmed down again. You could never make anyone tell you a story in chronological order. History was not like that either. The only consistent thing was that the most civilised of men remained savages, and women could be worse, and that Blaker personified an individual episode in the Industrial Revolution where men drifted into cities because there was no longer work on the land. *Plus ça change.*

'Like I said,' Blaker went on, 'I didn't believe her when she said she'd been married to the judge, even if he wasn't one then. She told me all about her bastard old man. Never thought I'd meet him. Killed the kid and locked her out, he did. I thought she was making it up, but then we used to talk about lots of other stuff, like home. I worked on a farm, see, when I was a kid, would be now if there'd been a job; no, I lie, I wouldn't, but I know how to bale straw and make silage and what pigs eat, all that shit, and so did Ivy. She wasn't kidding, she knew what she was on about there, so I got to believe the rest of what she said about the marriage and *him.* I used to say to her, why don't you just go home, and she'd say, why don't you, and I'd say, there was nothing there to do when I left, why should there be now? And she said she'd never go back until she could hold her head up. But she did, because she could. She's been good to me, Ivy.'

He sipped at the pint with great delicacy, making it last. Another thing about him Donald quite liked. He wasn't greedy or demanding, except for someone to listen.

'When I was on bail, the last time, all that shit about phone calls and keys coming down on my head, oh, when was that, three years ago now, I said to her, wouldn't it be odd if it's your old man in the judging seat again. There's not that many to choose from, you can't choose, it's always the same bloody court you end up in. She was on the way up then, got a room; mind, Ivy always had a room if she wanted, and jobs and a modelling job, and said she was a student, but still she'd find me, somewhere near here, or down in the Gardens with the others. Not often, often enough to give me money if she had it. I don't know when she told me that her old man had killed her daughter, and that's why she hit rock bottom and got chucked out, that was long before. Couldn't be seen wedded to a crackhead, could he, wanting to be a judge and all? Drowned her and killed her.'

'Both?' Donald said faintly.

'That's what she said. And chucked his wife out on the streets, I ask you. Makes her go mad, so no one will know what he's done. The bastard. Hypocritical cunt. I was so fucking angry when he sent me down, I screamed at him. People should know.'

'I don't know how you can drown someone *and* kill them,' Donald said.

'Drowned her and shot her ghost, she said. Let's go out, Don, whatever your name is. I need a view. I know all you coppers think drink's the thing, but I need a view.'

They moved into the light and Blaker, totally unaffected by three pints, led the way. Donald followed him on to the hot pavement outside and felt disorientated by his own pint of gassy ale and the afternoon itself, found himself seeking the shady side of the street and dreaming of trees. Blaker led the way, Donald wondering if there was any greenery within a mile of here, or any place not thronged with people. They did not go far. Blaker was not seeking a rural view and was suddenly tired of him. He pointed to a café with tables outside in Wardour Street.

'They used to let us sit outside here for hours when they were Italians,' he said. 'All day if we wanted. Now it's fucking Starbucks, so I reckon it'll be ten minutes max before they move us on. Want to bet?'

Donald did not even want to know about the sensation of

being moved on. He left Blaker on the seat with a view of the newsagent's on the other side of the road, a place famous for selling every newspaper under the sun, and came back with two bottles of overpriced water. Blaker ignored the offering and belched noisily.

'We used to sit here and read the newspapers people left, still do, occasionally. Or at least, I'd read it and she'd ask me what I was reading. Ivy's as clever as all get out, but she can scarce read, you know. Knew everything by heart, though, a real learner.'

He adjusted himself on the metal seat and stretched his legs, challenging anyone who passed by on the narrow, ungolden pavement to manoeuvre round him. Donald curled his own legs beneath the chair, adopting the habit of the non-confrontational.

'Ivy'd changed by the time I came out last time,' Blaker said. 'Cleaned up altogether, not that she wasn't well on the way when I went in. Only person in my life I've ever worried about, or worried about me, for that matter. But you know what? It was always as if the more she cleaned up, the more she worked, the more she realised what had been done to her, and nothing was ever really going to cure it. Nothing could give her back those years. Couldn't give me back either, not after he'd sent me to prison. Two years! For nicking hand-bags! I couldn't be there for her then. She wanted to make him pay, she said, for what he'd done to both of us. And her mum and dad, and everyone else.'

'Revenge, you mean?'

Blaker nodded. 'Something like that. She said it would make her complete. Get her soul back. An eye for an eye. She said it would fix everything if he were dead. She hates him. It's only natural, isn't it?'

'If you say so.'

Blaker was angry at that. He moved from voluble passivity to rage and back again in seconds, his voice rising to a shrill whine.

'What's *natural* to you, you daft bugger? How do you know? I bet you've never even seen grass grow, let alone anything edible.'

'Sorry.'

The thread of narrative was running out; Donald could feel it slipping through his fingers and knew that if he pressed him now, he would only invent, as perhaps he was already. Giving him water had been tantamount to an insult; Donald knew he had no more bargaining power, no influence, nothing he could offer apart from company, no threat he could make.

'Death to all lawyers,' he said.

'Too right,' Blaker said. 'Too bloody right.'

'My wife says I'm a patronising git,' Donald said. 'But I think if she chucked me out, I might want to kill her.'

Blaker nodded sympathetically.

'Used to think that myself, about the bloke I ran away from home for, but shit, I would have gone anyway, and they all leave in the end. You're only going to get caught, so why bother? Since when was a fuck worth a lifetime in jail, and who'd get the sympathy vote? Him.'

The afternoon stretched before them. Like ladies who lunched, neither had better things to do, and the curiosity and mutual need which blossomed between them into mutual tolerance made Donald want to go as well as to stay, extend it or finish it, he was not quite sure which, but it was worth the gamble. He was wondering what his wife would think, and what she might have done if he had ever tried to part her from his daughters, yes, she would have killed him . . . Love was a many-splendoured thing. It was the gut ache he had now.

'If you want to know how come I got out of prison so early, you could always ask,' Blaker said.

'I was curious. None of my business.'

'I'm HIV positive, see? They don't really like us hanging around. You might like to think of it before you give me a hug. Ivy doesn't.'

Donald tried not to react.

'Fancy a walk?' he said. 'I know I know fuck-all about the way the world works compared to you, but I do know another garden where you can sit for free. Supposed to be private, but it isn't, not really. It'd take an hour at least before anyone moved you on.'

'How come you're not busy, copper? All those fucking murders I read about. That poor bastard in the ambulance, the other one outside the theatre . . . Shocking. What's the world coming to?'

'Rumour has it,' Donald said, 'that it's better than it was.'

What a waste of time. She was more than halfway back when her father answered the mobile calls she made every ten minutes, and just as she neared London, they spoke. Yes, he was at his neighbour's and very nice it was too, thank you. What was the problem? She was at the end of the motorway, mounting a three-lane slope which took her past the high-rise places where she would have hated to live, thinking, how do they do this, wanting to be by the lake, but not wanting, not capable of anything until she had heard his voice. She almost took the car off the road. The summer night had given way to near darkness, a sky beautiful and streaked with colours, magenta, blue, grey, purple, misled by artificial lights into a backdrop of marvels, the stage set for Act One of the night. Ten thirty, all at once in reach of home, and no reason to be there. He was fine, he said. No, he didn't want her coming to see him right now. He'd had an attack on the train, had a day and a night in the hospital, which was more than anyone got these days. Should have gone home sooner. It was because of the crowds on the train, someone picking his pocket, taking the Ventolin and the pills, and it was hot and scary. He kept repeating that, like a litany. Oh yes, all right, if she was free she could come tomorrow, but there was really no need. He'd rather not. Yes, he had thought he was going to die, but he hadn't, had he? He wanted to look better. Get back on the rails. Please. She thought of the crowds jostling that small man, the panic as he felt for his inhaler and the pills, and the humiliation, the hating of help, and she wanted to cry.

Bathos and pathos hit like a blow. Her car was parked with hazard lights flashing on the hard shoulder of a spaghetti junction of converging roads, ready to be hit and bounced over the crash barrier, and she did not care, as long as he was all right. The relief of hearing his voice was overpowering, however petulant he sounded. He was alive and that was all that mattered. The sound of a car horn brought her back to the present. One and a half hour's drive from Paradise; she found the gears and carried on.

Why had he not phoned her when he was first ill? Why was she the last point of contact when he was in need, rather than the first? What had happened? Who would pick the pocket of an old man in a train, hardly rich pickings. What was the exchange value of an inhaler? The thought of him wheezing and falling, scrabbling for breath in an over-crowded carriage had haunted her all the way. She should have gone with him; she should not have let him leave, she should not have upset him. She should not . . .

Inside the flat, it was dusty with trapped heat. She was tired and fretful, went round opening every window, tidying as she went, straightening a chair already straight, washing the already clean mugs in the kitchen, feeling as if she had been away for a week instead of a matter of hours. It was a way of maintaining control. Had he meant to sabotage the weekend? Didn't he know she would rush back in his direction as soon as he sounded the alarm? Did he have any idea how much she loved him, the cantankerous, miserable old bastard, with all his prejudices? Did he know she only wanted him to be happy? Which was, she reflected, all he had ever wanted for her. He just thought that contentment was dependent on status and success and the right kind of friends, all of which had evaded him. She looked at the shelves he had made in her kitchen, and wanted to weep again.

Dad had liked her lover. Dad thought Rachel's man was the best she could get, and he only wanted the best. Or maybe he wanted her safe. But the lover had been a thief, and Rachel had betrayed him. She had never told him that; she could hardly complain if he told her so little, the way they protected each other from the reality of one another. Maybe parents did not know their children and children never really knew their parents until after they were dead and they watched themselves turn into them. That was the dread of her life. But her father had liked her lover, and detested Ivy on sight; he had no judgement. Yes he had: he was a shrewd, if oversuspicious judge of character, and after all, the lover had been good, once, and she had loved him for years. His judgement was only as flawed as her own; how did anyone ever know? She had a memory of her father cross-examining her teachers at a school evening, not letting them get away with anything, and smiled at the image. He was small but he could make them cower; she had been embarrassed and proud at the same time. The house on Saturdays had been full of the sound of his hammer, fixing things, trying to make things better.

He did not *seem* to need her. He knew she hated his small life and his little house. At the moment she disliked this one too and felt that, modest-sized though it was, she was rattling round in it like a pebble in a can, and her skin was still sticky with salt. She had never had the shower at the farm, and she had missed a party, no harm in that, although she wondered what they were doing now. The flat without the presence of Ivy in it seemed horribly empty. Ivy had only been there for a couple of weeks and she was out most of the time; it was not as if they were inseparable, indoors or out, or that Ivy had colonised the place in any noticeable way, it was simply that Rachel knew she would always be coming back, sometimes late but always before the night was over, and that if anyone else unlocked the door, it would be her. They had come to spend the bulk of Sundays together long before Ivy took her to the farm. It would be strange to have that long day to herself, go back to the endless Sundays which had preceded the advent of Ivy and her unqualified friendship and her mountains of ideas of what to do and see for next to nothing. Back to the loneliness which had driven her to the life class.

She found her sketchbook and got it out, looked at last week's work critically, and put it away. She could draw all day tomorrow; she could take the book and show her father, and he would say, Why? She could regard the otherwise empty day as an opportunity. Rachel found her mobile and listened to the second message again. The one from Carl.

Ivy needed her. The Wiseman family needed her. Ivy would not be back until late tomorrow. She was no use to her own father, but she could be of use otherwise. It would be so much easier to meet the judge when Ivy was not around, rather than an evening in the week when she would be coming home and there would be the temptation, the obligation even, to tell her all about it, and instinct told Rachel this would be a bad idea, however awkward it would be keeping silent. She had no idea how Ivy would react to what she had already done: gratitude in the end, perhaps, if it all worked, but not immediately. She would have to work it out; she might have to tell Grace first, oh what the hell, do it. Think later, that's what Ivy would do. Make something out of disaster, use the time.

Eleven thirty, Saturday night. Was that too late to call? She dialled, quickly, knowing that if she hesitated she might not do it all, wanting him to be out.

It was as if he was waiting, picking up on the first ring, unflustered.

'Hello, Carl here.' Not too late, not asleep. Courteous and welcoming in two words.

'Oh, er, hello. It's Rachel Doe. Look, I'm sorry it's so late, but . . .'

'Not at all.' Waiting for her to continue.

'Do you have any time tomorrow? Could we meet then, do you think?'

'Yes, of course. I should like that very much.'

Later, when the conversation was over and arrangements were made and she was bathed and scrubbed and trying to sleep, she realised the source of her confusion. *I should like that very much.*

Yes, she would. Whatever the circumstances had been, whatever he was, she wanted to see him again. Very much.

CHAPTER THIRTEEN

Where we met before, he said. I can always come to you. The bottom gate, from the Embankment, is always open, even on Sundays. I'll bring the car, pick you up. Easy on Sunday. Then we can go wherever you'd like. We could lunch, we could walk, I could drop you at home.

Proprietorial, organised.

Do not ever get into cars with strange men. No. Certainly not to be brought home. That would mean he would know where Ivy lived. Wasn't that the whole idea?

No. What was she thinking of? He could always have found out where Ivy lived or had lived, if he wanted. Grace would have told him, if he had not been avoiding Grace. Maybe he did want to know where Ivy was.

In the long reaches of the night, when she woke from the dream of the rat being pursued across her own room, she tried to think it through logically.

Carl had long since abandoned his wife. He did not want to know her family. He might have remarried, repartnered.

He was doing all he could to prevent his son from seeing any of them. It would be better for him all round if Ivy and her kind did not exist. Maybe Rachel was acting the role of the ferret, flushing him out of his hole. Maybe she was the decoy, the deliverer of prey. Maybe she was not helping Ivy or Grace at all. Maybe she was simply exposing all of them.

She had put out of her mind the memory of the panting policeman who had interrupted them on the bench, the one who wanted a word with the judge's wife. Did they intend to frame her for something? Why would a policeman want a word with Ivy? Was he the judge's pet poodle?

Had Rachel disturbed a hornets' nest? She remembered with shame the careless way she had revealed to Carl that Ivy shared her flat, and the deft way Carl had sidestepped the policeman to deny she had any knowledge of where Ivy was. It had been smooth; it had somehow felt kind, at the time, as if he was sparing her something, and yet it was only proof that he lied with ease, whatever the purpose. Still, she treasured that memory, alongside that of his courtesy in court.

By the time she arrived at the Embankment gate to the Temple, she could no longer admire the view of the river behind her and the narrow cobbled road which led into the labyrinth of courtyards before her. She was wishing she was not there, uncertain of why she was there, feeling guilty, suspicious, nervous, impertinent, and yet, through it all, she did want to see him again.

As he pulled into the entrance and jumped out of the driving seat, neither his car nor his clothes was designed to impress. An old Ford, with a conspicuous dent in the rear left wing. He was dressed for the sticky, humid weather carelessly, in the clothes of a man who wore a daily uniform and did not otherwise care. A half-pressed check shirt, creased cotton trousers, shoes, no socks, no obvious thought behind what he wore. The clothes were clean and solid, like himself. They fitted his bulk. He smiled that radiant smile of his, the one which so discommoded the defendant in the dock, even when it came from behind that ridiculous wig. It was a grin which said, I know what you mean, and she hated herself for responding to it. She had a painless flashback to the last time she had got into a car with a man. Her lover would have selected every item of his expensive apparel with care, concentrating on the overall effect. The car would have to be a BMW, at least. He had liked money too much.

'I didn't bring the Porsche,' Carl said, 'in case it got wet later.'

A joke, she realised. He looked better suited to a tractor than a Porsche. 'My son is so ashamed of this car,' Carl said, opening the door for her, 'that he almost refuses to borrow it. Almost.'

They could have been a man and a woman interested in one another, going out for a drive and a meal, like thousands of others across the city and beyond. Simply seeking entertainment. Could have: it was a nice illusion. She was trying to guess his age. Mid-forties, minimum, the kind who improves with age, except she could not imagine there had ever been anything callow about him.

'Was it him or you who backed this heap into a wall?' she asked.

He manoeuvred the car back into the slow Sunday traffic, across three lanes, turning back at the next junction to go in the opposite direction, entirely certain of his route.

'It was him this time,' Carl said. 'But for the sake of good neighbourly relations, it's always better to be me. I thought we might find somewhere near the river. The Tate? A view of the water always helps.'

She was not being given a choice, and since she was so confused about the nature of the occasion, she was glad to have decisions made for her, simply nodded, fine.

'What freed you up for today?' he asked. 'Nothing unpleasant, I hope. Nothing disastrous.'

Rachel had decided on sight of him that any kind of subterfuge or messing around was beyond her today, especially since she did not know what game she was playing. She had never been good at games.

'I was at Midwinter Farm, with Ivy and her parents. My father was ill and I had to come back last night.'

'Oh,' he said, slowing down almost to a standstill. 'I'm so sorry. Where does he live? Shall I take you there? Is he all right? I could take you, that's what cars are for.'

It was so disingenuous, she laughed out loud.

'He lives in Luton, and he doesn't want me there today. An asthma attack. Nothing terminal. He just wanted me to know.'

'You're sure? My son was asthmatic; luckily he grew out of it. It's terrifying. Are you really sure? Doesn't matter where it is. I can take you.'

'Yes. I'm sure. Or at least I'm sure he's sure. If we're going to Pimlico, it's the next turning on the right, there.'

She was glad to be able to give directions, relieved that he had almost gone the wrong way. It made him fallible. In profile he looked so much like the photo of his father in the Wisemans' underused living room. Carl the younger, the image of his dad.

'What's your father like?' he asked as if guessing her thoughts.

She was surprised into replying.

'Mine? Oh, stiff-necked, proud of it. High standards, low prejudices. Finds it difficult to relax. Has to be busy.'

'Sounds a little like mine was. I wonder if we all make life difficult for our children. It's the only reason I dread being old.'

The car was parked; they walked towards the river, another section of it with a different view. He was saying how he was never quite able to get away from the river, and wondered why. He hated getting wet, but there was nothing quite so wonderful as the spectacle of light on water, and had she ever been to the Tate at St Ives? Yes, she said, she had. She had been everywhere and seen nothing; the knowledge surprised her. Years before, she had gone. Maybe the drawing class had not been such a random choice. Even before Ivy she had always been attracted to shape rather than nature. The interest in drawing had always been there, or maybe she meant an interest in lines. She told Carl where she had met Ivy. I would kill to be able to draw, he said; my father thought any such thing frivolous. Mine too, she said. If he knew, even now, that I went to a life drawing class, he would think I was crazy. He'd say, what for?

'Mine,' Carl said, 'would have said, *for what?* He took English as his second language very seriously. He learned how. Never put the preposition at the end, nor split an infinitive. I grew up speaking like a grammar lesson. Composing sentences in my head in advance. *You must get it right. Don't speak as I do, people will know.* He never did get it right. If he were here now he would say, at which place lunch are we having? Let's be sitting, shall we?'

'Mine would say,' Rachel said, laughing at his mimicry and the speed of his speech, 'I don't care where we go, because I'm not going to like it.'

'Well,' he said, 'I hope the same thing doesn't apply to you.'

They were under a blue awning on a balcony, the colour casting shade on their faces, before she remembered he was the enemy and that an ease of manner, masquerading as charm, was part of his profession. No, that was not true; she knew many an ill-mannered lawyer. It seemed a shame not to enjoy it: she wanted to postpone the shattering of the temporary illusion and the going back to the knowledge of what a shit he was, the picture of Grace weeping over the crumpled letter in the kitchen and Ivy working so hard so that she might be fit to see her own son. It would be nice to be out on a summer's day with a man whose face she liked, and who, it seemed, liked hers, talking about fathers in the shade, with nothing to do but eat and fill in the blank spaces of each other's histories, which in his case, right here and now, she would have liked to forget. She looked round at the place he had chosen, and remembered that Ivy would have to work two long night shifts to pay for a meal in a place like this.

'Shall we get down to business?' she asked more shyly than assertively as the waiter went away with an order. Just a drink for now, thanks.

He became businesslike.

'My pedantic father would have said business always involves money. Everything else is personal. On second thoughts, maybe it *is* about money. Is that what Ivy wants?'

'No. *No.*'

Rachel was immediately defensive. The pleasantness had been too good to last.

'It was a question,' he said, 'that's all. A question. An entirely pragmatic question. *You* aren't on trial. It's me who's on trial. I never thought of you as an emissary with instructions, and I have thought about you, incessantly. Maybe because you're beautiful and I liked you on sight. As I said, you're brave.'

'Oh.'

Crisp white wine under a shaded sky. Praise, of a sort. Rachel steeled herself. Praise instead of criticism; being listened to, waited for. The preposition was in the wrong place. She knew her weaknesses, rallied to attack.

'There's nothing brave about it. It's . . . necessary. And no, it's not about money. It's about dreams. I love them, you see. Ernest and Grace and Ivy, Ivy first.'

'And I,' he said, 'have loved them longer. Since I was a boy, and my father before me.'

'You've a fine way of showing it.'

'When you have children, you might, just might think differently. You have to have priorities. Them first and always. If there's conflict, something has to go. The child is always first. You must keep their innocence as long as you can, I think. Even if you have to sacrifice someone else.'

Now she was really angry, inhibited because she didn't really know, had no experience to quote, except her own. She felt ignorant; the selfish, childless one who only dreamed of having children.

'When I married Ivy,' he said, 'it was the most natural thing in the world. Shotguns weren't necessary, although the gun had been jumped, if you see what I mean. I wanted Cassie. My father wanted Cassie. I wanted lots and lots of Cassies, boys and girls. I'm an only child of an orphaned child. Boys for my father, boys for Farmer Wiseman, girls for me. *Success* for me, so that I could keep them all. I don't know how much you know about all of this, but . . .'

'Quite a lot. From Grace. Just tell me the story.'

She was reasserting some semblance of control. He looked away. The sky beyond their blue canopy darkened.

'Ivy was eighteen, I was twenty-seven, when Cassie was born. Ridiculous. She was the most beautiful thing, *they* were the most beautiful things. I wasn't a good father, not with babies. I didn't know any more about shared responsibility than Adam and Eve. Old-fashioned, work-obsessed. I didn't understand why Ivy still wanted to kick over the traces. Go out, behave like eighteen, as if motherhood changed all that, instead of imprisonment, stretching away, for ever. I don't know, I wish I did. Sam was born the next year. I really had put her in prison. We were a big old battleground. Cassie clung to her, Sam to me. We fought.'

Like cat and dog, she finished. Something came into her mind. Ivy practised on the cat and the dog. Can't risk having pets.

It had become warm and muggy. Maybe Ivy and Grace would have gone back to the sea. Or down to the lake. She must swim in that lake. She wanted to dive into the dangerous river Thames, get cool. It was pre-thunderstorm, oppressive heat.

'All I want,' she said, 'is for you to meet Grace and Ernest. That's it. That's all I have to do, all I want to achieve.'

'All? And for what purpose?'

She had thought about this, scaled down the ambition of whatever it was she had wanted.

'Ernest is getting old and uncertain. He dreams of you, or your father, coming back. I've done the sums, unofficially, on the farm. It loses money. Grace has a bed-and-breakfast business which just about keeps it afloat, but not for much longer. It might . . . reconcile him, them, one way or another.'

'It might enrage him. He might ask me for money, in advance.'

Money, again. She knew what judges earned. Not bad, but not mega-riches either. She could not help but be interested in the money aspect of everything. It was her job. It was natural to be preoccupied with money.

'What do you mean, in advance?'

'Ernest has always known that if I die, prematurely or otherwise, half of what I own will go to them. My money, such as it is, is never mine. Unfortunately, everyone has to wait until I die, and I'm only forty-five. Ancient, I know. That was a provision in the will I made when I married and I haven't altered it. Prudent people make wills when they marry, as you know.'

Yes, prudent accountants always advised it.

'I made that provision because of my father. He wanted me to look after them. He said we owed our start in life to the Wisemans. It was his home, you see. But I can't help them yet. What I earn is earmarked for Sam.'

'Carl the elder,' she said.

'I see you know the history. Or some of it. Why are we talking about money?'

'It's always . . . relevant. But not the point here. Ernest has to work out what to do, and dreams get in the way, perhaps. As for darling Grace, I think if she clapped eyes on you, all would be forgiven. If she could get to see her grandson, *once*, all would be forgiven. There would be an ending and a beginning, and from there you could all work out how to get Ivy and Sam together.'

It sounded depressingly optimistic and naïve, even as she said it.

'And Ivy would have no part in this initial meeting?'

Rachel shook her head, sure that that was right.

'No. She wouldn't know. It would be a . . . strategic meeting. Tell her afterwards. Let Grace tell her.'

He poured more wine into her glass, scarcely touching his own. He did not fidget. She noticed the way he applied his full concentration to everything she said, and everything he said himself. Not a man for the ill-considered remark. Rachel was trying to remember his cruelty. Beyond the awning, the sky darkened.

'All right, I'll do it, on those terms.'

'What?'

'I said, I'll do it. Or at least I'll consider it, as long as you do too, because there's something you have to understand. Wisemans don't do forgiveness, at least not the female of the species. I don't think Ernest would ever forgive me either; God knows, I've a lot to be forgiven for. And Ivy herself may never forgive you at all for your part in it. The result could be as hurtful as the hurt it intends to avoid. Especially if I have to explain that Sam is so absolutely adamant that he does not want to meet his mother, or his grandparents, that he resorts to deceit to avoid it.'

She did not believe him. How could anyone not want to know Ivy and Grace? How could anyone not be better for knowing them? This was the man who had virtually killed his own child by neglect, left her to drown, blaming his other child for not wanting to make amends.

'It's always useful to have someone to blame,' she said.

'You could,' he said, 'apply that to Ivy as well as to me. Are you sure she would like this to happen?'

All of a sudden, she wasn't. She fell back on it being, feeling, the *right* thing to do. It was all too easy. He was too damn straightforward, too *likeable*. The images simply didn't fit with that of a man who had thrust his wife out into the cold because she was mad with grief. But then she herself had loved a man corrupted by greed, and that had not shown either.

'Look,' he said, 'will you come home with me? I've got better wine than this, and if you really do want to remain involved, there's a couple of things I'd like to explain. You might meet my son, although I doubt it on Sunday. Alternatively, you can back out now and we never had this meeting. Ivy need never know.'

She did not want to go to his home with him, and yet she did. It seemed an insane, risky thing to do, but the curiosity was stronger. So was the challenge. She had wanted to be involved, and that meant being willing to be involved up to the neck. What kind of friend backed out now? And there was that inconvenient visceral thing. She did not want to leave him yet, not for a long time. He smiled that smile which had surely duped dozens of people into thinking he cared about them. She hesitated. Going back alone to the house of a man with a record of violence was a stupid thing to do, and she shouldn't even think of doing it. Better stay on neutral territory. Then she thought, sod the risk, don't flatter yourself, and besides, he's already conceded a lot, so why not? She thought of all the things Ivy would risk for her without counting the odds. Ivy would jump into a pit of rattlesnakes for her. Besides, she dearly wanted the explanations, whatever they were. She wanted to give him a chance. He saw the hesitation.

'Don't worry,' he said. 'As a judge, I have a reputation to keep. I shan't do anything nasty. Not to a successful professional woman who would report me anyway.'

But you would to a woman with no qualifications or status. Like a wife.

The thought was ironic but reassuring. She was protected by a certain status; shameful that Ivy never had been. He had too much to risk. She made up her mind. The whole scenario was bizarre; let it be more so. She was helped by the conviction that this simply was not planned.

'By all means phone someone and tell them where you'll be, if it makes you feel safer.'

She shook her head.

'Where do you live?'

'The other end of the river, by the water. Not far, on a Sunday.'

It began to rain. He took her arm as they ran back to the dented car, and she shivered.

Back through the centre in the pouring rain, keeping to the river, then into the hinterland she had never known, all of it obscured by the rain on the windscreen. Diving into the half-empty streets of the banking district, which she knew, out the other side towards the east. The territory of old markets, tide upon tide of immigrants who stayed and colonised, laid waste, rebuilt, moved on. She had never quite understood the romance of the East End and the old Docklands, apart from it being a route somewhere, and looking at it through the rain, she could understand why it impelled each new generation to get out.

'This was where I grew up,' Carl said. 'At a time when no one was quite sure what nationality they were, or wanted to be. The main division was white and black. There were two many races for anyone to be racist. It was a good beginning. My father was a cleaner. Rose to supervisor.'

That jolted her. The judge had come a long way.

'Did your father ever go home?'

'He had no home. He never wanted to go back to see the

ruin of what had been his. Berlin was razed to the ground. He thought it would make him feel angry, and he couldn't afford that. Something he taught me. Keep your anger dry, boy. Otherwise it rots you.'

She forgot the route, and once the decision had been made and caution put to the back of her mind, she felt oddly comfortable in the passenger seat, being taken somewhere she did not know, like a patient, curious passenger on a coach trip. Nothing to do except say, Oooh, look at that, and wait to arrive. The destination, any destination became desirable as the rain increased into a torrent, beating against the car. There was a moment of anxiety when they entered an underground garage which looked like a prison, reassuring to find it light. She followed him up endless stairs into his flat, stifling the recurrence of unease, thinking how clever he was. This would be hard to find. It felt like entering a fortress.

A comfortable fortress, with attractive minimalism, the bare necessities of furnishings, wooden floors and rugs, enough clutter to show signs of life, and the luxury of silence. It was both domesticated and orderly and made her feel better. She scarcely noticed the details except for the cool clarity of it all, the balcony and the mesmeric presence of the water beyond that big window. That did it. Assessing it simply as a place, Rachel could have gone home, packed up her bags and come to live here tomorrow. She almost said so.

He came back from the kitchen with wine, olives, roughly cut cubes of bread and cheese, the work of minutes. Better than lunch, a mere relaxing ritual. The eating of something made her feel better. So did the realisation of knowing that it was he who was nervous and anxious to please, and what he provided was leftovers. Kind, but hardly part of a grand master plan. This was not quite what he had expected to happen. He was not used to entertaining at home. No rings on his fingers. The bathroom she had used was notably free of feminine smells. The wine had gone to her head. Stop it, she told herself. Listen. Remember who he is. He is trusting you. Now you know how *he* lives, it makes us more equal.

Why is he being so nice to me?

Carl wiped his hands on a napkin.

'What I wanted to explain is something you may not know, but it is the clue to rather a lot more. Ivy is . . .'

'If you're going to badmouth Ivy to me, forget it. I won't hear it.'

He drew breath patiently.

'I was going to say Ivy's complicated. I've never criticised my wife, least of all to another woman. I've had to point out certain features of her, but that's not the same thing. I don't criticise her to my boy, or to anyone else. I tell people she had her reasons, as she still has. You'll know better than me about that. But I do want to point out her *unreason*. If Ivy ever worshipped any god, it would be the great god Pan. Or some marvellous creature of a mythological world, Thor, or Diana the Huntress. A vengeful god at any rate, one with the power over life and death, although I suppose all gods have that. What I mean is that hers is a primitive soul, with all the sophistications that follow. Conventional morality simply does not matter.'

Rachel tried to stop him.

'That doesn't prevent her from being the kindest, most generous person alive,' he went on. 'But her head is full of images you and I might not be able to guess at. And a binary set of rules. She loves you or hates you. White or black, no shades of grey. Perhaps because she's never mastered more than rudimentary reading – and no, I could not make her do that – she has less chance of analysis. There's nothing to mitigate a fixation. She was reared on fairy stories. Love, death, revenge. Unless you read, you don't shift the imprint of what you've, literally, learned by heart. You don't change your own maxims. Practice makes perfect was one of hers. I can see why now.'

'There are other ways of learning and analysing. Like drawing and listening.'

'Yes, sure.'

'You're saying Ivy's thick and irrational.'

'No, I'm not. I'm saying she has a very literal mind, even if it isn't literate. She'll choose a single track and stick to it. She's had to fight her way to what she knows. She sticks with what she's good at. You're right. Of course I don't know what she's like now, and I'm only saying anything at all because I don't want you to risk Ivy's hatred. It's awesomely determined, especially when turned on herself. Oh, hell. That isn't what I wanted to explain, though, even if it might be part of it.'

He moved across to the desk which dominated the room and came back with a folder of photographs, selecting a couple as he moved.

'I wouldn't wish these on anyone,' he said. 'They aren't exactly holiday snaps, but if you really want to stay involved – and you can stop, whenever you like – then you must know how my daughter, Cassie, died. It's the only way to get a grip on who has to forgive whom, and for what.'

He sat beside her. Her skin tingled. She felt as if the sea salt lingered from yesterday.

'Police photos. Only the setting is aesthetic. You know the lake. You didn't know Cassie.'

A pale, dead face in close-up, turned to one side, blood in

the nostrils, red-blonde hair, and a triangular mark on the neck. Rachel wanted to turn away, and disliked him for being able to hold the photograph with a steady hand. He withdrew the last picture and turned it face down on the table beside the remnants of the food, watching her reaction with concern.

'I'm sorry, I've looked at these so often, and judges see photographs of injuries all the time, I forget other people aren't used to it. One more.'

A photo of a piece of excised skin, pinned and stretched on to a grey surface, the same mark, stained brown. Revulsion was at war with curiosity. He pointed at the mark.

'Exhibit A. A section of skin, taken from the neck. No one could understand why Cassie drowned. All right, she was left alone. I was in charge, impatient father that I was, half asleep, time for tea. She wouldn't get out of the water. Sam was furious with her: she was ruining his afternoon and he was hungry. He went down to the edge and threw stones at her. Pebbles, really, pathetic aim, no chance he would hit her, but she swam further out. I caught him and spanked him, yelled at her to do what she damn well liked and carted him back home, yowling all the way. I didn't worry about leaving Cassie. She would come out as soon as she wanted; she was like an eel and the lake was her playground. Not usually so early in the year, because it would have been too cold, but it was a May heat wave. I didn't know about the swans. Ivy's father's precious swans, the descendants of those which Ernest and my father had reintroduced to replace the ones Carl and his hungry mates had killed to eat, years before. Another story that was always on his conscience.'

Carl the younger was speaking faster and faster, as if to minimise it without omitting anything and get it over.

'There were no injuries to Cassie, no third parties. Only that mark on her neck. Ernest pointed the police in the direction of the swans. It was too early in the year . . . she went too close to the nest. They trapped the adult swans, made beak imprints. One of them matched. Daddy Swan had done for her. It took quite a while to establish that.'

He took a deep breath and steadied himself. There was a slight sheen of perspiration on his brow. Rachel wanted to wipe it away. He put the photos back into the folder.

'Ivy stayed with her mother, who tried to calm her. It simply wasn't possible. Sam wanted to be with her. He cried in her lap and told her about throwing stones at Cassie in the water. She went ballistic. I took Sam back to London with me. My father was dying, then. I was trying to comfort them both in my ham-fisted way, and trying to keep myself under wraps. I had to stay in control at all costs. Then, a fortnight later, when I finally heard from the police that Cassie's drowning was caused by the swans, something in me snapped. I drove down overnight, got Ernest's rifle – he had a licence for one then, never used it, someone else always had to do the killings; my father had taught me, like Ernest taught Ivy. Anyway, I'd lost my mind. I bribed the swans with crumbs, and blasted away like a madman. I shot them all.'

He stopped abruptly. Pushed the folder away and gave a short, mirthless bark of laughter.

'I don't know quite why I'm telling you this. It makes me a helluva lot more primitive than Ivy. As stupid and wicked as a seventeenth-century judge, presiding over the trial and execution of an animal, as they did. Sanctioning the hanging of a pig for harming a baby, the ritual slaughter of a goat for damaging property. I've never been more ashamed of anything.

More ashamed than I was of leaving Cassie. I hated them and I shot them.'

Rachel was silent. She wanted to touch him. He turned to her, as if imploring her to understand. She thought she did. She wanted to take hold of his hand, and didn't. The silence seemed to relieve him.

'*That's* what I wanted to explain, because I never have. And also to put your very kind master plan into perspective. Ernest took the blame. The police sympathised and did nothing except take away his licence for a rifle. Only handguns left with a three-foot range, I expect. I think of it every day when I sit on the bench. It's not so difficult to forgive people really, not when you're me. I not only let my beautiful daughter die in terror, I killed her ghost as well as Ernest's swans . . .'

'They've come back,' she said. He was not listening.

'So you see, there's rather a lot to reconcile, more than possible, I think. And if you should ever meet my son for long enough, don't ever mention he threw pebbles into the water at his sister. He's a nice boy, he doesn't deserve to remember that. It had nothing to do with anything in the end.'

He turned back into the considerate judge, clicking his tongue, tut-tutting at himself, agonised with apologies.

'I am *so* sorry. I've burdened you with more than enough. You look pale. It isn't fair. Look at the time. I'll take you home. Public transport on a Sunday's a bugger from here. I shouldn't have invited you here. I'm amazed you accepted, amazed you listened. I don't want you to regret it.'

She wanted to say, yes, I'm amazed at myself, and I've got no problem with anything you've said. I'm just gobsmacked that you trusted me with it and I don't doubt a word of it. I'm lost. And I'm also thinking, I've got no issues with that piece of history, only with what you did next. Did you apply all that leftover anger to Ivy? Is that why she had to go? Is your son frightened of you? I would be. Ivy was.

There was the sound of a door slamming, a noisy entrance into the place, whistling, the banging down of something. Someone wanted to be noticed. The door to the main room of the flat burst open in response to a kick and he shambled in. He was, she thought later, a rather beautiful sight. Better than any view of the river. He was long and rangy with an elegant slouch, brilliant blue eyes, black jeans and vest.

His own view took in the scenery, from the rainswept balcony to the half-eaten olives and empty bottle of wine, to Rachel's face, figure and clothes, right down to her feet. The boy and the man gave each other a look of quizzical affection. Sam winked at him.

'Cool, Dad,' Sam said. 'Is this your new squeeze? About bloody time.'

He went over to his father and hugged him briefly. Then turned to Rachel, smiling.

'I wish,' Carl said. 'Sam, this is Rachel, Rachel, Sam. She's only my accountant, unfortunately. Recently demoted to being my confessor, poor woman.'

Sam shrugged his shoulder in mock despair.

'Shame,' he said to Rachel. 'It's been *years*. I have my hopes, but he never delivers. You're very welcome. Are you sure you don't like him? Even a little bit?'

Rachel found herself laughing. He was entirely infectious. He had his mother's ranginess, and Grace's outrageous smile.

'Mustn't keep you,' Sam said. 'I'll get out of the way, just in case anything develops. Can I borrow the car?'

'Not if you've been drinking.'

'You joke. On the Sabbath? I mean, not yet.'

'Depends on where you're going.'

'Up west.'

'Fine. Provided you take Rachel home.'

Sam looked at her steadily and grinned. She could not help but grin back.

'Cool,' he said.

She turned to Carl, still grinning.

'I promise I won't reveal *all* your financial affairs en route.'

'Feel free,' Sam said. 'I love gossip.'

'Hope not. We'll talk in the week about the meeting, when you've thought about it, if you like.'

'Fine,' she said. 'Fine.'

He *trusts* me.

CHAPTER FOURTEEN

Sam drove the dented Ford as if it was a taxi, complaining about the fact that it did nothing for his street cred. He knew every back double between the Isle of Dogs and the West End, and every road-checking camera. It was not simply the speed of it, before they reached the City outskirts, which made Rachel feel old; it was the confidence. He chattered like the dawn sparrows at Midwinter Farm; he seemed to have a talent for confiding which reminded her of both Grace and Ivy, as if it had never occurred to him that anyone would disapprove, and everyone he met was a potential friend who would like him as much as he liked them. Self-absorbed, yes – who was not, at nineteen? – but likeable and beguiling and artlessly funny. He had a beautiful profile. A strange thought arrived unbidden, namely that she was at risk of being at least half in love with the whole damn family.

'Pity you're Dad's accountant. On a Sunday! Just get him to up my allowance, will you? He's really tight. Wants me to discover financial necessity before it's too late and I'm totally corrupted. Wants me to move out, for the sake of worldly knowledge. Preaches a lot. I want to stay 'cos I don't want him to be alone. Are you sure you wouldn't like to move in? Pity. So how much is he worth, then? No, don't answer that. Don't Sundays go on and on? A day for the movies. At least you can park. Not near Leicester Square, though. Did you read about that bloke killed in the ambulance? And the one behind the theatre. Awful. We don't need terrorists, do we, got them already. I suppose there's a difference between one at a time and fifty all at once. Where do you live again? Cool, that's a really cool place to live.'

Rachel remembered that she had not read a newspaper for weeks, and felt vaguely ashamed of the loss of an old habit, but she was concentrating on the opportunity she was being given. She adored the chatter, but wasn't going to give up a chance. Surely Carl knew he was either misguided or overtrusting to leave her with his gloriously garrulous son. Perhaps he intended it; perhaps it was planned: either way, it was fun and she did not care.

As they bowled across London Bridge, she said, 'I know your father's divorced. Do you ever see your mother?'

Sam slowed down for the red light on the far side of the bridge. Beyond that, she could see the inevitable queue of traffic, scaffolding and building works narrowing the road into a funnel. Good. People of all ages talked in cars. It was turning into a lovely evening, with the vehicles ahead still shining wet after the rain. She wished she had not left that balcony with its view of the river.

'No,' he said. Then laughed. 'You want to know about my mother? Cool. Could this mean you're interested in my old man after all? Isn't that the way? Scout the scene? See if there's any opposition lying around? Old or new?'

'You're a very impertinent young man,' she said, mimicking a pompous voice, and laughing at the same time, because Sam made her laugh. Like his grandmother, like his mother.

He punched the steering wheel, veered to the left and up through the City. Confident and sure and just in control. He would worry me to death if he was mine, she thought. I would worry about him getting cold. The traffic remained stalled.

'Well, you're in with a chance,' Sam said with his infectious grin. His hair glinted chestnut. His skin was sallow. He would tan easily, like his granny. ''Cos there's no one on Dad's scene. The ex least of all. *We* haven't seen her for years. He likes clever women, see, preferably blonde. Short supply. Can't bear junkies. And all I remember about my mother is her trying to kill me. And telling me how she was going to kill Dad one day. She grew up on a farm. She knows how to kill things. She's really, really good at it. Made me learn to swim. She was barking bloody mad. She stuck pins in me. She hit me. I hit her back. I had asthma. I could pack a punch when I was nine. Do you know we're three-quarters grown at nine? Couldn't do it now, though. Don't like to think about it.'

He hit his fist against his forehead in a dramatic gesture which neutralised any hint of self-pity and made it all seem contrived for amusement.

'I was a *tortured* child. Does it show?'

'Not that you'd notice, no.'

'Shame. You might feel sorry for me. That's a great linen jacket, where did you get it?'

'Camden Market,' she said, nearly adding, with your mother. Your mother knows where to find things. Didn't say it. Not all of Sam's remarks were in the best of taste. He exaggerated, fancied himself as a comic clown. She bit her tongue. Sam looked at his watch.

'Film showing at six. I'm going on holiday next week, courtesy of Dad. Have you been to Crete? I've got the end-of-term high. I'll miss that when I have to go to work. Don't you love Sundays?'

'I certainly liked this one.'

'Good,' he said, pulling out of the traffic and down a side street. 'Goody good. So he's *really* in with a chance, is he? Don't worry about my mother, she's long gone. Hope it stays that way. He's got the police on the case anyway.'

You rotten little lying hound, she said to herself, without quite the fervour she meant, and without, quite, being able to lose the instinct to like him. That profile, so unlike his father. Life drawing class, creating new tiers of judgement and appreciation. Too much information today. The traffic unsnarled and they raced through the city like a bullet. As they drew closer to Clerkenwell, with Sam chattering about which film to see, what did she think, Rachel thought, why don't I ask him in to the flat, maybe Ivy will be back, and I'll say, Ivy, this is Sam, Sam, this is Ivy, and maybe they'll fall into each other's arms and he'll see she's not what he thinks. Or what he might have persuaded himself to think, in order to dramatise himself. It'll be love at second sight. Instead, Sam found her street without further directions, as if he had a map of everything in his head. He knew it, he said, because there were some really cool bars nearby, did she ever go? She didn't, but she would now, she said. He bowed her out of the decrepit car with a flourish and roared away, tooting the horn, leaving her on the pavement, smiling.

The rain was in abeyance, replaced by the muggy, damp warmth which signalled more, and the flat was as empty as a plundered grave. Rachel checked the messages on the land-line. Ivy knew she preferred it. None from her father. One from Ivy, warm and concerned. How's your father? Don't forget we can bring him here next weekend, or the week after. I've got to help Dad this afternoon, coming home on early train tomorrow, straight to work, see you. Phone if you need. Love you.'

Rachel was dizzy with impressions. She did not quite know what to do with herself. The curse of Sundays descended. Confusion, dread, the ordinary desire to push the next week back, clear up, prepare, a reluctance, a horror of facing the dead space for thinking which yawned now. The flat seemed subtly different, as if a breeze had blown through it. She could not find anything, looked for something to occupy her hands, and where had she put the mobile phone? Safely in her room, instead of leaving it lying around, why?

Thinking time. Dangerous. Tough day, Monday, meet-ings wall to wall. He had said, *Let's discuss meeting after we've thought.* She just wanted to see him. She was a stupid, cred-ulous idiot, bearing the impression of the last person who had sat next to her, with a history of being duped by men. She *liked* him, that was all. And they were *wrong,* so wrong, about Ivy. That boy said shocking things. She was begin-ning to feel suspicious and wanted to put that somewhere else too. She wrote a list for the week in her clear, strong handwriting.

Monday, Tuesday, full to bursting. Wednesday evening, last life drawing class. Shit. Her sketchbook was full. Meant to buy another. Drawing was therapy. The pencils she had used were down to stumps, too small to sharpen. She did what she often did, hauled out the sketchbooks and examined what she had done these last evenings in class. She could see her own progress, her own increasing freedom. Looking at what she had done over the last term cheered her. There was the Plonker, there was Ivy, there was all the in-between. She wanted to draw; she did not want to listen. She had run out of paper. She wanted to draw *him*. Drawing soothed her. She had first wanted to do the drawing because of endless Sundays. It used up her brain and cleansed it.

The landline phone rang. She answered. Dad, Carl, Ivy, Grace, anyone please.

'Hello. Is that Mrs Schneider?'

'Mrs Who?'

She was late in recognising the name. There was no Mrs Schneider here. There was Ivy, Ms Wiseman, and herself. Get the names right. Mrs Schneider? Ivy was that person once, not any more, he meant Wiseman. She spoke without thinking, Ivy always on her mind.

'Nope. Sorry, she's out at the moment.'

Then she put her hand over her mouth. It was as good as announcing Ivy lived here.

'Oh, sorry. Is that Miss Rachel Doe? It's DS Donald Cousins here,' he said. There were the sounds of a TV in the background, the sonorous voice of someone talking to camera about live things in jungles. 'We met the other day.'

'Did we?'

She remembered him, with fleeting dislike. There was an uncomfortable pause. The TV sound droned on. She looked round wildly, imagining it was hers. The blank screen looked back.

'Well, if she's not there, that's that. If she should happen to come back, would you tell her that her friend Mr Blaker is asking after her?'

'Her *friend*? Mr Who?'

She has no friends. Her hands felt slippery wet on the phone she held. She was suddenly angry.

'I'm not a message service,' she said. 'Get lost.'

She put the phone down. She was furious. She had been set up again. Bastard.

The swine, the *shit*. That bloody judge, using her and her emotions, all that trust-me, shite. Treating her sweetly, leading her on, food, wine, fucking *trust*, and then he goes and gives out her number to a wet, sedulous policeman with a moustache, who wants to find Ivy for some miserable purpose of his own, how *dare* he? Somehow it followed that neither Carl nor his son was capable of saying anything which was true; every single bloody thing was all contrived and engineered, for WHAT? She found herself shredding the last piece of useful drawing paper out of the sketchbook, tearing it up into ever smaller pieces. Thinking of Carl warning her against Ivy's hatred, the *shit*, Sam speaking casually of maternal violence for something attention-seeking to do at a traffic light, and she, silly child-free ignoramus, had listened and swallowed as if she was being paid for a blow-job. What they wanted was for Ivy to be abandoned and given up, like before, for something she had not done, like before. As if they could not stomach the sheer fact that Ivy had emerged from her chrysalis as good and strong as she was, and that she had a *friend*. They wanted her to buried all over again, and they could fuck off, because it was not going to happen. It was not going to work because *she* knew what she knew and she was not going to be deflected from what she knew. Which was what was right and just, what Ivy deserved, what Grace wanted.

When Cassie drowned, Carl had lost a child. Ivy had lost everything.

Rachel prowled. She wanted to talk to somebody, but there was nobody. She wanted to pick up the phone and shout at Carl. Instead, she dialled 1471 and wrote down Donald Cousins' number. Then she sat with the full sketchbook on her lap, turned over the pages. She had drawn Ivy several times in the last term; she would do it again, this week. She had an overpowering desire to scribble, she felt the urge to etch graffiti on the walls, make herself concentrate on something in order to clear her mind. The very act of drawing anything had that effect of release, whether she did it well or badly. She wanted to draw what was in her mind. Sinuous shapes, slithery ferrets, rats, swans. There was nothing better to do, but she had torn up the last sheet of paper and the pencils were stumps.

Ivy always had pencils and paper. She never used a pen, only a pencil. Ivy was always willing to share what little she had. She would give you her last penny. Rachel went into Ivy's nest, looking for the pencils and paper she knew Ivy kept in her pink folio.

The room was tidier than when she had seen it last. There were traces of Blu-Tack from where Ivy had detached the sketches she had used to decorate the walls, replaced with the poster of *Leda and the Swan*. The folio case stuck out from under the unmade bed. Rachel moved to straighten the duvet, an automatic reaction which was the same as the one which made her pick up anything which had fallen to the floor, an instinct for tidying up as she went along for which Ivy had teased her. Ivy would leave the dropped object where it was until she needed it. Rachel stopped herself. How Ivy left her room and her bed was entirely up to her. Rachel had given her this room for her own. She pulled out the folio case, opened it and searched inside for pencils and paper.

That was all she wanted. She would always resist the urge to look at the rest. It would be like reading someone else's post. In the middle of this slow activity, she had a mental image of Sam crumpling up the letters from Grace which might have been addressed to his father, posting them back. She could see him doing that.

There were no pencils in the untidy mess of the folio case. Rachel sat down on the bed, suddenly weary beyond belief. There was a lump under the duvet, a sound of crackling plastic. She got up and pulled the duvet back, concerned that she had sat on something breakable, found a polythene bag bearing the legend of a shop she did not know. She opened it to see what she might have broken. Inside she found an inhaler, and two small brown bottles of pills, folded into a handkerchief. She held one of the bottles up to the light. Prescribed pills, with a white label almost worn away from contact with the material of his coat, and her father's name still legible.

The room began to spin around her. She put the bag back.

Donald Cousins was thinking to himself that maybe the phone call to Rachel Doe had not been so very clever, and he was still trying to work out why he had done it. Perhaps because there was no one at home on a Sunday evening, the whole lot of them round at his mother-in-law's, and he was bored, and Blaker had been haunting him. Despite the hours now spent in Blaker's company, he had never managed to pose a direct question which was relevant to his investigation, never quite summoned up the nerve. Since Blaker had told him that he was HIV positive, it seemed cruel to do anything other than chat, sit in the sun in Temple Gardens, as if it was really open to the public and they owned it. Very private, better than Embankment Gardens, Blaker said. Donald did not doubt that what Blaker said about being HIV positive was true: people did not announce their own death sentences unless they really wanted attention, and Donald did not think that Blaker wanted that kind. He could check anyway, and it did add another dimension. What did the poor bastard have to lose by issuing threats to a judge, either on his own behalf or someone else's? He was looking at a short life where all the major risks had already been taken and the gamble lost, however long it took the Grim Reaper to call in the debts. He could murder and threaten with impunity; what could punish him now that the worst had happened? And no, he had not asked Blaker if he used internet caffs to send threatening images to a judge; Blaker might tell him, in time. Instead they chatted about Blaker's old friends, and the changing history of Soho. Blaker looked sixty and he was scarcely forty. Donald counted his own luck.

She was a brave lady, Mrs Ivy Schneider, to embrace and befriend an HIV-positive man. Blaker had been diagnosed three years ago, before the last prison stint. Ivy made me check it out, he said. When I found out it was yes, she hugged me. That's as far as we ever got. I reckon she would have shagged me to prove a point, but she knows my preference. Big, dark buggers, who know where to go. The disabled lavatory in Starbucks, more room in there. Donald knew he was not really a citizen of the real world. He belonged in the suburbs, thought he knew about London, but he didn't. He only knew it as it had been, through the pages of history books, which told him it had always been a den of iniquity and delight, not always in equal shares, and not all of those drawn to it survived it.

The different dimension added by Blaker's liability to AIDS was an additional interest in Ivy Schneider or Wiseman, simply because it made her more compassionate. Blaker said she came into Berwick Street once or twice a week, or Embankment Gardens, at no prescribed time, on her way to or from whatever work she was doing. Couldn't stay away, he said, it's my charm. There was something Blaker wanted to tell him about this woman, namely that for all her restored status, he was desperately worried about her and what she might do. It all meant that Donald could not ignore the Ivy connection, or at least it gave him an excuse to protract his useless investigation for a few more days of summer by including her. He could not allow himself to think that such a long-divorced wife who by choice and design maintained no contact with her estranged son could really pose a threat to the good judge, but Blaker had said she hated the man, so he'd better talk to her. Maybe he was barking up the wrong tree with Blaker, and all the threats really came from somewhere else, and she might know about that. She would know about the distant past, not the obvious present.

It was later he remembered the hurried introduction to Rachel Doe, *a good friend of my ex-wife,* and the judge's shifty insistence that this beautiful girl, who looked at him with such undisguised contempt, did not know where said wife lived. Oh yes? What kind of good friend was that? He felt better about the phone call now. A brilliant ploy, an impulse rewarded. Of course he could have hung around Berwick Street waiting for the tall woman to come back, but he was sick of the place. It was dying on its feet. Tesco Metro would bury it. Not that knowing where Ivy Wiseman lodged was an instant answer to making contact, but at least it was a start, as well as a change of scene.

It distracted him from tending to his wilting garden, a domestic task he loathed but that was his by default. Mine's the house, yours is the garden, his dear wife said, and was kind enough not to hold him to that too strictly. Snaresbrook was a nice place to live, convenient for the Central Line, which went straight into the heart of the City, bisecting it from beneath, and from which he emerged, blinking like a mole to breathe the polluted air he preferred, wondering why anyone would be daft enough to imagine Londoners being deterred by bombs. What they did to one another on the street was far more frightening.

Another Sunday task was reading the papers and catching up with the news of what the wider world was up to, as well as what his comrades in arms were doing. Police bulletins, issued daily, including details of the unsolved and the unsolvable. Trying to get better at identifying terrorists made them so much worse at everything else; there were only so many experts to go round. Computer literacy required, far in advance of his own. Good. Leave me alone. Better being an old has-been than being out there with a smoking gun.

He read in the bulletins now e-mailed to him at home about new credit-card scams, exotic thefts and unsolved deaths. No one was any further forward in discovering who had garrotted the injured bloke in the ambulance, except it might have been the product of Albanian gang warfare. Well, maybe; no one wanted to know if it was all home-grown. He read about a man who drank bleach in an office, about another man stabbed in a queue waiting to get an autograph, no progress in any direction, and the only grateful feeling which came to mind was his own huge relief not to be on the night shift which found the bodies.

Night did indeed shift, uncomfortably into day and back

again, like a thief, taking hostages under cover of darkness. It grew cooler as he sat in his untended garden, hoping they would all come back and hoping they wouldn't, grateful for the fact that the afternoon rain meant he did not have to water the plants. It was early yet; they could be hours, those beloved, so often discontented, daughters of his, and their mother who liked to be out of the house.

A woman's rage . . . night shifts. Did anyone notice that the unconnected deaths, two murders and one apparent suicide, all happened around the same time of day? No great force required, two shifty killings, a knife, a garrotte, a woman could have done it. Come on, man; hardly coincidental; homicide usually favours the cover of darkness, unless done in the name of war. How comfortable to reflect upon it in the safety of his own garden. The whole problem in his own little investigation was that the judge was only telling him half of it, and the other half he might not actually know.

The judge, Donald feared, suffered from an unhealthy belief in the essential goodness of human nature, believed everyone deserved a second and third chance. He had that look about him; he was a light sentencer. He had acted upon the threats made against him only for the protection of his son. He did not really believe anyone, apart from a religious fanatic, could nurse purely individual hatred for long, for years if need be, because he could not have done it himself. He would not see the point, any more than his father would dwell on losing the war.

Since meeting Blaker, Donald had reluctantly looked into the matter of Ivy Schneider, née Wiseman, and she had thoroughly taken hold of his imagination. He had the date of the marriage, more than twenty years ago, the date of the death of the child, Cassandra. He knew where Ivy had been born.

He knew she had acquired a minor criminal record in her late twenties, early thirties, drug abuse, clogging up pavements, that kind of thing. No theft, no dishonesty. He knew she had redeemed herself, been rehabilitated, and remained a friend to an HIV-positive loser, and that raised her in his estimation. And what the earlier phone calls of the evening had told him was that the Wisemans owned a farm-cum-guest house in Kent, and apart from the accidental death of the child, nothing was known to their discredit. It was only very recently that they had come to police attention, on the periphery of something else. A young man who had stayed as a paying guest at Midwinter Farm, a Londoner, had disappeared, only to reappear as a drowned corpse on the nearby coast. The last known sighting of him had been in the local pub, getting drunk in the company of Ivy Wiseman and her mother, Grace, before setting off back to his London home. It took three weeks to identify him.

Donald did not know why this stuck in his craw. He was haunted, daily, by the thought that one of his daughters would leave the house one day and never come back. There were plenty of Londoners who thought that with good reason. But not to know what happened and why, that was hell.

Slowly it was coming to him that he might just have to go and find this damn farm, if only because that was where the daughter had died and that provided enough of a link to justify the time in the final report. Donald hated the country-side, but a day out in this weather could be fine.

He heard the phone go from his place in the garden and ambled indoors to answer it without hurrying. Nothing could be terribly urgent on a Sunday evening, except his own business.

'Hello?'

'Rachel Doe. You rang me.'

He was surprised. 'So I did. You told me to get lost.'

She ignored that. 'I want to know why you want to contact Mrs Schneider, and she's called *Wiseman*. You can't just phone up out of the blue and demand to know where someone is . . . why do you want to know?'

She sounded as if she might have been crying. 'I need to know,' she said. Her belligerent voice began to falter. 'And I need to know who gave you this fucking number. It's outrageous, you've no right. Bloody Carl gave you the number, didn't he? *He's* no right.'

Donald drew a deep breath. God save me from wailing women, some king had said.

'As a matter of fact he didn't, Miss Doe. I had your name, and your telephone number's in the directory, if you must know. And I didn't know the lady frequented your establishment until you confirmed it for me.'

There was a pause before her voice resumed with more determination, half belligerent, half pleading.

'I *must* know why you want to contact her. What's she supposed to have done?'

Another deep breath. She was a professional woman, well dressed, well set up, he remembered. He could see a complaint winging in from the side. Something which was not going to improve his already diminished career. Interference with the civil liberty of another, invasion of privacy, blah, blah, blah. He spoke in a conciliatory rush.

'Why, absolutely nothing, madam. Nothing at all. In fact, from what little I know of her, she appears to be a kind woman. It's just that we' – always hide behind 'we' – 'are making enquiries into an unrelated matter which, in which . . .' Now it was he who began to stutter. The jargon failed him. It always did when he was at home.

'Look, Miss Doe, I acted out of turn in phoning you. We are *not* investigating Mrs . . . Wiseman for anything, but we are investigating an acquaintance of hers, from the distant past I believe, and I hoped she could help. That's all.'

'Oh.'

Another pause, then she went on with ever greater certainty.

'So what is it he's supposed to have done? Why should Ivy be able to help?'

'I'm not at liberty to say, madam. Except that it isn't anything particularly serious.'

'Serious enough to be trying to find her on a Sunday evening?'

'Police work knows no set hours, Miss Doe. Sunday evening's a good time to find people at home.'

'This isn't her home. I've no idea where she is. She has stayed here, she doesn't now.'

Too hurried to be truthful, but communicating. It didn't matter. The prospect of a complaint receded. He chanced his arm a little further.

'Could you tell me where she works? I could maybe trace her there. No urgency.'

'Works? Ivy? No one works like Ivy. She works all over the place. West End, City. Night shifts, cleaning, modelling, anything . . .' This, he noted, was said with pride, before another pause. He waited it out.

'Why did you say you thought she *appeared* to be a kind person?'

He thought about that.

'Because she has been conspicuously kind to the person

who is the subject of our enquiries, and believe me, Miss Doe, he's not someone a normal person would want to touch.'

Night shifts.

'Thank you,' she said. She sounded enormously relieved. 'If I see Ivy, I'll think about giving her the message.'

Ivy was the kindest person she had ever met. Rachel told herself she must remember that.

Then why had she done *that*?

Done *what*? The pills must have fallen out of his pocket when the coat was thrown on the bed, but he never kept them in a polythene bag, he wanted them accessible all the time. He always wanted to be able to touch them.

CHAPTER FIFTEEN

Rachel could not think of anyone but her father. His coat and his medicines.

She phoned him, simply to hear his voice and to say good night. He was drowsy and did not want to speak. Then she drew his face as best she could remember it on the back of the other drawings, trying to remember the salient details of it, but oddly Carl's face became superimposed on the older one. She was using a pencil stump, which she broke, and the breaking of it made her cry.

She stayed beneath the shower, scrubbing herself pink, trying to wash away the contagions of the day, went to bed.

Nothing had changed over the course of the day, nothing. *There must be some mistake. Dad's pocket was not picked for his drugs on the train; they fell out . . . How?*

She was exhausted and fell into a fitful sleep. Nothing would change what was going to happen on Monday. There was always work, and without it there was no life. She was wishing she had not deviated from that single track and was still the work-devoted, isolated, priggish bore she had been a year ago. Dreams intervened, nudged her awake. This time it was snuffling piglets, nuzzling at the multiple teats of a mother pig who was held by bars so that she could not suffocate them. A rat sneaked in alongside. Someone placed a hand on the back of her neck. The hand was cool and dry, soothing, feeling for a pulse beneath her long hair. Her father had done that once. There was a shuffling in the darkness, a rustling, followed by the sound of the door of her bedroom clicking shut, softly.

She remembered she had left all the windows open at the front. One floor up was all, easily climbed, warnings given all the time about neighbourhood burglary. She might not even have double-locked the door; she never did that now, not with Ivy here. Ivy was far away, Ivy was not here. There was no one here. When Ivy called out in the night, there was always someone there. Rachel repeated her name out loud now, louder and louder, accusing her for her absence. *IVY! Ivy! Ivy!*

The door opened quietly. Ivy, barefoot in a long T-shirt, stood there, framed by the dim light filtering from another room, coming towards her from the light into the dark, her voice a soothing whisper.

'What is it, what's the matter? It's me, only me. Can I come in?'

Yes. Anything, anyone, please. Anyone was better than no one. Rachel lay there stiff with fear. Ivy was matter-of-fact.

'Look,' she said, 'I didn't mean to wake you, but now you are, there's something I've got to tell you. We could leave it until the morning, only it's almost the morning already.'

'I thought you weren't back. I thought . . .'

'That I wouldn't be back until later? I'm here now. Thank God I'm here now. You were dreaming. Can I come in?'

Rachel turned and saw Ivy's profile against the corridor light, her hand with a protective hold on the door, the glint of tears on her face. There was a cool draught from the window. She had been sweatily hot; now she was cold. She buried her head in the pillow, and smelled the scent of fresh soap. The back of her neck itched. She could hear the sound of rain, and shivered. She was naked; the duvet had fallen to the floor. Ivy picked it up and put it back, then peeled off her T-shirt and slid into bed beside Rachel, tucking the duvet round them both. They lay like spoons, Ivy holding her, her body pressed into Rachel's back, her bosom against Rachel's shoulder blades, her chin on Rachel's head. Rachel stiffened, then, slowly, relaxed. The sudden warmth and feeling of safety was utterly seductive. She lay very still, not daring to move. They had never been intimate like this, never unclothed. Hugs and pecking kisses on greeting, easy togetherness, massaging each other's feet at the end of a long day out, but never lying in the same bed, skin against skin. She wondered why. It was nice. She needed it, did not want it, might never want it again, but it was nice.

'This is how Grace used to calm me down,' Ivy said. 'She calls it the human straitjacket.'

'There was somebody else here,' Rachel said. Reality was coming back. Remembrance of the last things she had thought of before going into that awful sleep. She had thought of her father, and of what it would be like to sleep alongside the lovely bulk of Carl. She had imagined his heavy male hand on her neck. Shame on her.

'No, lovely. There was no one. Only me. Unless there was a ghost, escaping the rain. Ghosts don't like rain.'

That was what this was. It was Ivy being mother, acting like Grace, the human straitjacket, making everything right with her warmth, operating on the same instinct to look after someone with the whole of her body.

'What was it you wanted to tell me?'

'I want to tell you what I think happened with your father.'

Rachel stirred, pressed her head further into the pillow. Ivy's weight was light against her. She could move whenever she wanted, waited, breathing hard. Ivy had been crying and her speech was clear and urgent.

'I don't think anyone picked his pocket on the train back. I think he left all his stuff here, in my room. Must have dropped out of his coat pocket. I put his coat in my room, out of the way, remember.'

Rachel was silent. Things did not fall out of pockets, not out of her father's deep pockets, not precious, life-saving objects like that. There was, all the same, a great relief that Ivy was talking about it, not hiding anything, because there was nothing to hide; that Ivy was introducing the subject before she did, and she would not have to admit sneaking around her room and the suspicions which had been the final blow in what felt like a day of treachery. Ivy seemed to sense the slight shift of Rachel's body. She moved her hand and softly eased Rachel's hair away from her face, and stroked it back. That was nice too.

'I found them, I think it was on Friday. You know what a mess my room is. Thought nothing of it. I should have remembered it when you said he'd phoned and he was ill, but I didn't connect, wasn't thinking, so I only remembered halfway through yesterday afternoon, because I was worrying about him. That's why I came back. I thought, supposing Rache finds that medicine, supposing she's looking for something else, what would you think?'

'I don't go into your room,' Rachel lied.

She had a vision of the living room as she had left it. Had she tidied it all away? That would be normal, even when drunk, *especially* then. She had not been drunk on wine, but something else entirely, like the shock of what she had found, and put back, and not being able to remember quite what she had done. Not being able to remember frightened her.

'But if you had,' Ivy continued, still stroking her hair, 'and found your dad's medicines, you might, just *might*, think I had taken them. And I really couldn't bear the thought of you thinking that. I couldn't bear it.'

'Why ever would I think such a thing? I wouldn't.'

She was lying again. That was exactly what she had thought. It was why she was lying here, rigid.

'Why would you think it? Because he was mean to me, because in the past I've done very spiteful things. Because it would be *natural* to suspect me. I'm the loose cannon, remember? I'm the one accused of abusing my own son. God, I was even accused of killing the cat. So it's just what I might do, isn't it? Something spiteful like that. It's what junkies do.'

Ivy began to cry. A large tear fell against Rachel's forehead. The sound of her sobbing was unbearable. Rachel felt ashamed and did not know what to say. Ivy propped her head on her hand, brushed away the tears.

'Sorry. This isn't about self-pity. It's about your dad. He's got to know that he wasn't the victim of a dipper in the train, or he'll never get on a train again. He'll never come back, and he's too insular already. You want him to come back, he's your father. It would be terrible if he thought there were thieves everywhere, even more than he does now. It isn't fair, because it isn't true. He might have been mugged, but not for his pills.'

Her voice was back in control, warm with worry. *She seems to me to be a kind person. Nothing stops her being the most generous person alive.* Things do not spring out of the pockets of a coat left on a bed.

'But on the other hand,' Ivy said. 'I don't know if it's better that he thinks he was stolen from, rather than admit he left the stuff here. He'd hate to admit to being forgetful, wouldn't he? He'd hate to think it was his own fault.'

How observant she was.

'Left them? Not dropped them?'

She could feel Ivy nodding. They were whispering, as if there was someone to hear.

'Yes. Remember when he started getting so cross, and he went to the lavatory?'

No, she did not remember. Only that her father needed a lavatory at any given time. Blamed his age. Ivy's arm crept back round her waist.

'I think he must have gone and found his coat, had a puff, maybe a calming-down pill, and left them out in case he needed another. Then he was mortified by losing his temper, poor thing. It's awful to feel like that. He wanted to go home so much, he forgot. You fetched his coat.'

It made Rachel feel partially to blame. It also rang entirely true. Relief flooded through her like a warm wave. Her breathing had slowed to normal.

'So what will you tell him?' Ivy asked.

'I'll tell him to keep his bloody Ventolin on a chain round his neck.'

They both snuffled with laughter. Rachel relaxed entirely. Ivy's callused hand stroked her hip. Their breathing seemed to have synchronised into one peaceful breath. She wanted this to go on, wanted it to stop. Sleep beckoned, hormones stirred, sleep was winning. She knew with absolute certainty that Ivy would make love to her at the slightest invitation, and was not threatened by the thought. Ivy wanted to strengthen the bond; Ivy wanted to please, and there was no need. The desire for sleep was stronger than anything. One last thing.

'Ivy . . .'

'Yes, love?'

'I do know you, don't I?'

'Better than anyone. But I have lied to you once.'

'Did you?'

'I said I could wait to see my son again. I said it didn't matter. But I think of it all the time.'

'Ivy . . .'

'Don't say it. Go to sleep. I'm here to keep you warm, that's all. I'll always be here for you.'

When she woke, Ivy was gone, the imprint of her left on the side of the bed nearest the wall. The way she had lain meant Rachel could have moved away whenever she wished. She was grateful for that too. Grateful also for the emptiness of the flat she had so loathed. Invigorated, even. Washed and dressed and on the way to work by the time Ivy had been on her morning shift for two hours.

Ivy, in sleep, had the gentlest of touches. She did not hog the bed; she remained still, smelling of cleanliness and soap. Rachel had woken once, watched her for a second. Her face in repose was both hard and vulnerable, giving up to sleep, looking like a picture of the lowest of Victorian household servants, exhausted by hard work, sharing a bed with nothing but honest labour to look forward to, and yet still accused of stealing the family silver. It made Rachel feel an additional bond to her, the simple fact of sharing her bed. Made her realise how much she yearned for skin upon skin, the weight of another body. And a new determination to make things right, not only because she had doubted Ivy's transparent honesty, but because of guilt. The guilt of suspecting her of malice, and the guilt of knowing . . . knowing what? Simply that she wanted to see *him* again. She had dreamed of him, when she slept alongside Ivy, wanted it to be him. The guilty knowledge made her blush in the bathroom mirror, hand poised still with mascara brush, looking at her own dilated eyes.

In the living room it was as tidy as she usually left it, the bag ready with the full sketchbook leaving room for the new one and the new pencils and charcoal she would buy somewhere en route before the last class of term, which would leave the rest of the summer curiously empty. Mid-July now, schools out for summer, that end-of-term feeling. Who had said that? Sam. In all the years since leaving school and university, there had never been a summer when she had not woken, dreaming of taking an examination and not being prepared. Training courses ever since, all culminating in one month of the year. It was what had typified early summer, until now, when the rest of July and August spread forward without punctuation marks. Such small nightmares she had had until now, such small services and mercies she had rendered to anyone else, intolerant, overprivileged, a bit of a shallow bitch, overeducated in everything but real life and the obligations of love.

So thought Rachel, who did not like herself, or much notice how much effect she had on others, getting into gear for Monday morning, dismissing everything irrelevant to the task and only remembering to look as if she mattered. Seeing that in the tidiness of the living room she had left the torn piece of paper which said, *Who is Blaker? DS Cousins? called.* Ivy couldn't have seen that.

She put it into the kitchen bin, tidily. She was back in control. An ache in the heart for Dad, but Dad was all right, and Ivy had not picked his pocket, and everything else she would think of as she went along.

She had dressed for the day in the wrong clothes. It was cool out there. She went back for the older, warmer jacket she had worn to the farm. Clouds filled the sky as she looked up, pacing herself for work, taking the favourite, shortest route, but still looking up and sideways. Looking with pleasure at what she could see. Handsome people, moving with purpose, refreshed by rain in the night and the drop in temperature, like plants in a busy garden.

Grace and Ivy, Ernest and Grace. Bugger the swans, I don't care about swans. And I found my mobile phone after all, back where it belongs, in my bag. She strode along with the bag across her body, one hand in the pocket of her old jacket, felt the tiny piece of bone which was still there from when Ernest had presented her with it as his souvenir. Some of it had fragmented into sharp crumbs which felt like sand. A reminder of time passing, making her feel clear and urgent about what she was going to do. It could not wait. If Ivy had still been beside her when she woke in the morning, she might have changed the plan, told her everything, confident of the response while they lay tucked up and close like that, but now she was glad that Ivy had gone.

Yesterday's plan was still the best. Get Carl to come to the farm, meet Grace and Ernest, take it all from there. Mission for today, suggest this to Grace, as a theory at least. It was the bone that reminded her about the strange sense of running out of time, like summer did in July, before it had scarcely started.

All the same, she would wait and see if Carl phoned her. He had made some kind of commitment, wanted time to think, wanted her to have time to think of the wisdom of her own suggestion. So be it. She would be patient, let things take their course. But by the time Grace phoned in the afternoon, patience was wearing thin.

'How's your father?'

'Better, thank you. How are you?'

'Thank goodness for that. I've been so worried. Tried to phone all day yesterday, but you were out, and I knew Ivy was coming back, so I knew I'd hear one way or another, and I would have heard if the news was bad, because bad news travels fastest. Look, when can you bring him here for a holiday?'

It was a headlong rush of words.

'I know all about asthma. Sam had it when he was little. I'll be able to look after your dad wonderfully.'

'He's not so easy to persuade, Grace. I'll try and talk him into it. He's embarrassed and avoiding me.'

'I can dream. I wish you were here. It's a perfectly glorious day. I want someone to go swimming with. Saturday night turned into a bit of a party. We all need those sometimes. Ernest is in the dumps. Well, something like that. He put his boots in the freezer, God knows why.'

'To cool them down?'

'That'll be it. I almost got them out and roasted them. Are you coming next weekend? Please say yes. Ivy can't, she's got another end-of-run theatre job that lasts all weekend, and pays a fortune, she says, did she tell you? Only I don't want her doing it. I heard on the radio about the man getting stabbed outside.'

'That was last week, Grace. There'll be something else this week.'

'You will come, won't you? I don't want you being in London on your own either.'

It was a little proprietorial. Rachel felt she loved Grace without reservation, but perhaps Grace was taking her role as mother substitute a little too far. Typical Grace, she guessed it.

'Oh Lord, I'm being bossy, aren't I? And talking too much and interrupting your work, just because I've got nothing interesting to do and Ernest is wandering round, lonely as a cloud, somewhere. I'm not your mother, I just wish I was. What's the weather like?'

She was instantly forgiven, the warmth of her lapping round Rachel like a cloak, making her laugh again.

'Cool,' Rachel said, and thought of Sam. 'Listen Grace, I know this is a surprise, but I've found Carl. Carl the younger.'

'Oh my God . . .'

'Now, supposing he could be persuaded to meet up with you and Ernest, just you two, or just you, maybe, at the farm, do you think that would be a good idea?'

Grace choked on a jumble of words, Oh my God, oh dearie me, oh fuck, oh bloody hell, yes. Then stopped abruptly.

'When?'

'I don't know. I'm only supposing. I don't know if it can be done. Soon, perhaps.'

Grace was crying. She made the same crying sounds as Ivy did, recovered quickly.

'Oh my wonderful, darling child. It would make Ernest so happy.' She paused. 'There's no one else here next weekend. Cancellations.'

'I can't promise anything.'

'I know you can't, darling, but I do love you for trying. What have we done to deserve you? Oh, it's all going to be fantastic. I know it in my bones. Just Carl and Ernest and me, working out where it all went wrong. Oh, darling.'

If it made Ernest happy, and that was all it achieved, it was worth doing, Rachel thought. She reminded herself to keep her ambitions small, her excitement under control, because she had no power over anyone or anything, whatever Grace thought. It still felt like progress.

Carl phoned at four thirty. Was she free this evening? He had done enough thinking, he said. Yes, of course she was.

Grace sat in her kitchen, staring at the Rayburn. The domestic machinery hummed, dishwasher and washing machine together making music which was satisfying on a good day, irritating the next. What would she feed him when he came here? What was it he used to like, a dozen years ago? He must come here, he must. Otherwise Ivy would never stop, and Cassie's immortal soul would continue to haunt the lake. He must lay the ghosts to rest, and take his punishment.

Ernest had been busy. He had made the appointment. The lorries would arrive sometime in the next fortnight to take away the cows for sale. Milk did not pay for its own production. The knock-down price of the good cows would pay something towards the debts. The Polish herdsman would go to a bigger herd, saving his salary. It would come to that, unless, unless.

She could hear the sound of Ernest scraping his boots on the mat outside the door before opening it and coming in. He looked clear-eyed and himself today, damp from the rain, sniffing the air for familiar smells, even now always looking round for the old dog he no longer had, or the cat which would spring into his lap as soon as he sat down. Both of them long dead, killed and never replaced.

He washed his hands and sat down expectantly, waiting as he always did for something to be given to him, ever hopeful that something nice would happen, with the optimism which always touched her heart and also made her want to scream. You have to work in the right way for what you want, she had yelled at him once, and work even harder for what you must have. You have to plan for it, and you always left the killing to me until you trained Ivy to do it and made a man of her.

Grace poured the tea. Since this was a good day, he could sense her cautious jubilation. He noticed moods, details, undercurrents only when he chose. He also had ears like a bat, when he chose.

'So you've got him then, have you?'

'Might have,' she said modestly, turning her back on him so that he would not see her face. He drank the damned tea. Grace thought she could have lived for ever without drinking another cup of tea.

'You reckoned that since he couldn't resist our Ivy he'd not be able to resist her friend? You might be right at that.'

'I don't know what you mean, dearest.'

He poured more milk into the mug of tea, and two sugars, for strength.

'There's the difference between you and me,' he said. 'I never could hate anyone for so long. Not like you. Not like Ivy.'

It sounded like an accusation, and she knew it wasn't. It was a sort of wonder.

'No, dearest. But you will do as you're told, won't you?'

He shrugged. He was bent these days, but his shoulders were still broad, even if his belly was soft.

'Don't I always? Don't I know I owe everything to you? I always do what has to be done afterwards? I got rid of that cow, the dog, the cat, how long ago was that?'

'Longer ago than you should be remembering. It doesn't matter now.'

'Why, Grace, why? Why this time?'

It was her turn to shrug. She wanted to brain him with the teapot she carried towards the sink, signalling the interrogation was over.

'Things have to be paid for, darling. In all senses. And I can't have Ivy going on with her practice and getting caught. And because it really is the right time to put everything right. Make a new beginning.'

'Practice makes perfect,' Ernest said.

'Not always,' said Grace. 'Can you think of anything that would put people off going to the lake? I know they're few and far between, but no one at all would be better. A notice, I thought. And something blocking the path. And you could choose a site for the dust.'

'Ding dong bell, pussy's in the well,' Ernest intoned rhythmically. 'What's for tea?'

CHAPTER SIXTEEN

It was the funny feeling in the pit of the stomach, the same as it was when she had first encountered Ivy, that there was everything to say and nothing she would be ashamed to admit. Weird in these circumstances, where there was hardly an element of trust, except, self-evidently, his towards her. Could she like a hypocrite, a bully, a multiple offender? But men changed, didn't they?

He was everything she suspected, including his authority, his history and his charm, and yet she approached him with as light a step as if he was real, and as if she had known him for ever. It felt both right and utterly wrong.

They met at St James's Park Underground station, closer to his place of work than hers, an easy passage for her on the Circle Line from the City. A grey day like this was ideal for a walk in the park, he said. Did she like to walk? Yes, she did now, she told him, although she had not always. She had been the one who took the fastest route to the next stop, ignoring the scenery. It was Ivy who encouraged the walking in winter and spring. All the better for feeling free, seeing things, and besides, it's the cheapest way.

On a cooler day, with a troubled, rain-filled sky, the glories of St James's Park became more exclusive to dozens of admirers, rather than thousands. On a hot summer day the grass would be littered with wall-to-wall bodies, sitting on deckchairs, lounging on the ground, clogging the curving pathways which led around the lakes in an inner circle, while on the outer circle people moved purposefully and joggers moved ahead beneath a canopy of trees.

They began at Admiralty Arch, looking down the Mall towards Buckingham Palace in the distance, then walked into the park itself, drawn towards the irregularly shaped lake which meandered the length of the valley, the territory for ducks and swans. Willow trees drooped gracefully from the bank; there was a bridge for standing and dreaming, and halfway down, a mysterious island rising out of the water in a million shades of green, yellow and rust where she some-how imagined all the birds went at night. Seen from the bridge, the ducks were iridescent in shades of turquoise, white, black, brown, comical and ever busy, while the swans moved slowly, pausing as if to acknowledge an audience without any gesture as vulgar as waving.

Carl bought coffees for them both from a stall, and joked as they sat on a bench that it looked as if he certainly knew how to give a girl a good time. A walk in a park, and a cup of coffee. Rachel said that was fine by her, and this was surely the most beautiful park in London, a user-friendly park made for exactly this, sitting on a bench and enjoying. The cool of the evening made her glad of the old jacket, all the same, and she felt for the fragment of bone in the pocket to remind herself of a sense of urgency. They were not addressing the subject matter of their meeting, and yet they were strangely at ease, as if both of them were content to avoid it for a while, and simply *be*. It was a good sensation, and could not last.

'Did we come here to watch the swans?' she asked.

He shook his head. There was energy in all his movements and gestures, but he looked tired. She hoped it was the result of a sleepless night – he deserved that, at the very least – but all the same, she wished he was not tired.

'I come here for all sorts of reasons, I suppose. Principally to see people at peace, enjoying themselves and recuperating. It's an exercise in harmony, isn't it? A walled park, a safe place, mimicking the countryside, but very far away from the rigours of that. Wildness tamed. I wish I could achieve that in my courtroom. I keep saying we should have flowers.'

He waved in the direction of the yellow palace, half hidden through the trees.

'I also come here to admire my inheritance. Palaces, kings and queens, a constitution which still works better than most; it brings out my not so latent patriotism. Makes me proud of what we have. Odd, how unfashionable it is to be patriotic, even at times like these.'

'Part of your own inheritance,' she suggested. 'To have a need for patriotism.' He nodded, and smiled at her, self-conscious and wanting understanding. Rachel did understand. She had taken to counting her own privileges, which included a vote.

'Yes. My father chose to be here. He embraced it. He could take nothing for granted, and nor can I. And I'm so sorry, I forgot to ask, how is *your* father? Better, I hope? When will you see him?'

'When he wants to be seen. Pride, you know.'

She found herself explaining how her father had left his

inhaler and his emergency pills in her flat after he had come for supper and how he had no remedy on the train for an asthma attack. Even as she explained this, as she already had to people at work that day, several times, she wondered if she was repeating it to reassure herself. Embellishing it and adding details to the story to make it ever more true. Such a nice supper too, she added now. Ivy cooked it, she's good at it. She bit her lip; he would know that.

'Did they get on well?' he asked.

'No, not now you mention it, but that's my father for you. He doesn't take to anyone easily.'

He was silent for a minute, nodded in sympathy, then suggested they get up and walk. Finally they were back to Ivy. Rachel noticed how he adapted the pace of his walking to hers, slowing his faster footsteps to match. She wished they could postpone talking about Ivy, Grace and Ernest, and talk about themselves and the colours of the park instead. Sit and people-watch, in shared amazement.

'I liked your Sam,' she said. 'He's outrageous, but he's terrific. He's all flash and fire and no inhibitions. He sort of shines, you know. I wish I could be like that, even for a day.'

Carl raised his eyebrows, grimaced and smiled again. There was pride in his voice.

'Why on earth do you think you aren't? You shine. You shine with beauty and purpose. Sam shines too, but the trouble with him is that he always has to impose. He has to challenge everyone, test their reactions, run the risk of enraging and shocking them, just to see if they're going to accept him. I don't know if that's part of being gay, or just insecure. Or simply mischief, he's got plenty of that. And I like him the way he is. He's acquiring confidence.'

'He can talk for England,' Rachel said. Rounding the last

curve in the lake, facing a bank of vivid flowers, she had a vision of Sam meeting Grace in a flurry of colours and noise. If only it could happen; it would happen; it must happen; it could only enrich them both. Then Ivy would come in, and they would love each other too, and she, Rachel, would slip away, leaving happily ever after.

'Look at the swans,' Carl said. 'I make myself look at the swans.'

'Ivy still likes swans,' Rachel said. 'She has a poster on the wall, of *Leda and the Swan*, Matisse, I think. It's all graceful shapes and curves. The swan is blue and Leda is yellow, all bordered in red. It's a very abstract swan.'

'Leda, wife of a king of Sparta, mother of many famous children, Clytemnestra and Helen, mates with Zeus, who takes the form of a swan and produces a god-like child. Yes, I can see why Ivy would like to have that on the wall. We had it at home.'

Rachel winced at that. It reminded her of everything she did not know. She only knew about the miseries of which she had been told, nothing of the happiness. She felt old, envious and curious.

'Another version of a virginal birth, the god sent from heaven, no choice about it,' Carl murmured. 'Impregnation appears to have happened via the ear, the swan hovering above, but maybe Leda got confused, she had children already. Perhaps Ivy would prefer that as an explanation of conception. Just as she preferred to think that Cassie did not die, but became a swan, like a daughter of Mir, surviving as long as the swan survived. Do you know, I would much rather talk about something else. I didn't bring you here to look at swans. Oh, I wish this was over.'

Obligingly the swans turned a bend on the south of the

island, out of sight. Carl and Rachel got up and moved on. He tucked her arm in his, protectively, shielded her from a boy on skates racing towards them.

'Look,' he said, 'it wasn't so difficult, thinking it over, it's all obvious, isn't it? I have to try and make my peace with Grace and Ernest, for everyone's sake. I have to try and help them financially if they're in trouble, I promised my father that, I made a will when we married . . .'

'Grace never mentioned that.'

'I know that's not the issue. I have to meet them, and from that somehow forge a way not only to persuade my reluctant son to meet his mother, but also to persuade him it was all his own idea. So much is overdue. I can cope with Plan A, so let's do it. I'll go and see them, take it from there.'

He paused. 'But what worries me is you. You're somehow inside the toils of something which has nothing to do with you, and it's going to put you in the awful bind of keeping secrets from a friend, which you must, you know. If I go to Midwinter Farm, say in a day or so, say next weekend, you're the intermediary, which seems bloody unfair to me. I shan't be able to tell my son where I'm going, and you can't tell Ivy. And I want to do this because you were brave enough to suggest it, and at the same time I dearly wish we had met each other in any other context. I want you to know I'm not the devil incarnate, and I should dearly, dearly like to know who hurt you so much that you come out, blinking like a fledgling in sunlight, lovely and shining and determined like you are. I should like to know everything about you, I should like to court you, Miss Doe, I really would, and I am not fit. Yet. And I'd love to meet your father.'

He would like him. Of course he would. The thought of that swam into her consciousness like an injection of something warm. She tried to shut it away, but a feeling of joy persisted.

'I'm not fit to be courted myself, Carl, and what a quaint way to put it. The last man who got close to me was a thief and I sold him down the river. I'm no good at selecting the male of the species, no good at judging, Judge, and I harm the men nearest to me. Are you really saying you would do this, I mean meet Grace and Ernest on their own territory, for the sake of my good opinion? Or is making me blush simply another tactic in your armoury?'

He was serenely unoffended, sat back and considered, smiling.

'The lover-thief might explain a lot about you,' he said.

'I worked with him,' she said. 'He was a . . . colleague.'

Carl stopped smiling and touched her hand.

'Poor you. That must have put you on quite an island. You must have been very lonely. But yes, for the record, I'd go a very long way to secure your good opinion of me. As a preliminary. Anyway, Sam likes you. We do instant liking, Sam and I, instant judgements. Unfortunately for those concerned, they tend to last.'

'So, if he likes me on one meeting, *I* might be in with a chance of persuading him to meet his mother?'

'Play your cards right.'

He was smiling at her, teasing gently, trying to make all this less serious than it was. She could not resist it and smiled back.

'Tell me about the lover-thief.'

Rachel sighed. She wanted to do just that, say what it was like to be a whistle-blower. But it was not the time or the place to describe cynicism and loneliness, unless to say how it was Ivy who had made her change.

'The lover-thief glamorises him rather,' she said. 'I think, in retrospect, his greatest crime was having no sense of humour, and gradually depriving me of mine.'

'But not taking away your ability to do what you thought to be right?'

'No. Not yet.'

'That's my kind of woman. Enough. Now, when shall I go and see these two in the lion's den of Midwinter Farm?'

YES! She took a deep breath.

'Saturday. Ivy won't be there.'

He took a diary out of his back pocket, and then put it back without looking at it, nodded.

'Yes. I know that's good. Free day. Sam's going to Crete on Thursday, so he'll be out of the way, and I'll be able to resist telling him. What about you? Will you be there?'

She hesitated. 'Yes, if you want me . . .'

'Yes, I do.'

'. . . to be there,' she finished.

'Yes,' he said again. 'If I knew you were in the background, it would make it so much easier for me, even though it isn't fair to ask.'

'We've done that bit. I'll be there as a friend of Grace and Ivy and Ernest.'

'And me,' he added.

'Yes,' she said. 'All of you.'

Carl got up, held out his hand, and said, shall we walk and talk of other things?

Of shoes and ships and sealing wax, of cabbages and kings.

It was later, when they parted, with a mutual reluctance they were both trying to hide, that he ruined it all. Ruined the dream that they were two normal people, walking, talking, eating, drinking, enjoying one another.

He insisted on getting a taxi to take her home. It was as quaint as courtship. She didn't want it, but he put his foot down, and while they waited by the side of the road, watching black cabs with orange lights swim by, but quite unable to part, he said, 'There's something else . . . I ought to tell you. Your father and his inhaler. It reminds me of Sam. She used to hide his inhaler, she used to take it away. That was the last straw.'

And then the taxi arrived, and she got in, and he paid, like an old-fashioned gentleman, ignoring protests, making it a courtesy rather than condescension, and leaving her sitting in the back, suspecting him again. He couldn't leave it alone, could he? He had to make an unpleasant suggestion, an implied criticism of Ivy, and leave it lingering, the German bastard. He had to resurrect an image of Ivy as monster mother, to justify himself. Bastard. Rachel was triumphing in what she had achieved, she had been happy, and now she felt limp as she stumbled out of the taxi in front of her house, which no longer felt like home.

Must phone Grace. Must not ever again look in Ivy's room. Must never again betray anyone. Must not divide loyalties, all men were shits, especially charismatic judges, but her eyes in the bathroom mirror where she rushed to wash her face, were shining with hope and doubt.

In the event, as policemen and lawyers are liable to say, Donald Cousins went nowhere that Monday, except to West End Central Police Station, in response to a direction to postpone his hopeless little enquiry into the matters of a lesser judge of German origin, because there were better things to do, even for him, who was so often the last chosen for a team. What was needed, this weekday morning, was old-fashioned skills, of checking and cross-checking, finding and interviewing. They might have remembered he was good at that, but Donald was not kidding himself. He had been hauled back into real work because there was a panic on, the sort of panic started by a tabloid newspaper article the week before, which in turn provoked the sort of activity designed to head off yet more adverse publicity for the police. The subject of the article, copied by other articles on the no-news days which followed the commencement of the holiday season, was inner-city violence, and the disgraceful level of non-detection of apparently casual, apparently alcohol-fuelled murders. Such as the awful death of the man in the ambulance, the death in the autograph-hunters' queue, and one in an office. Some brilliant mind on a computer had come up with the notion of a connection between the latter two. They had both happened at night. The same cleaning company had featured. Not much of a link, and only slightly better than nothing, but it was one of those days when something had to be done.

Donald had been expecting something of the kind, because that was what happened at this time of year. There was a briefing meeting, the necessary flurry of activity. They were like bees, buzzing. He thought of his proposed trip out into the country; he thought of needing to see Blaker, and sighed. It was ever thus. He was never allowed to finish anything, and now, to his own surprise, he needed to finish this little enquiry, even though he had resented it in the first place. He put in his two pennys' worth, his own little mite of observation, which wasn't much. There were all sorts of night shifts, for theatres, offices, shops, bars, pubs, and what did that have to do with anything, he said sagely, and was dismissed as negative. What was this company called? Clean Co. Was it worth pursuing?

We need to find someone who does the theatre shifts, someone said. Can't find a boss, gone on holiday. Donald wanted to say they could never find a needle in a haystack, and thought of haystacks. Then he thought of a way through it. He was skilled in getting what he wanted. Feeling ever so slightly treacherous, he raised his hand and put Blaker in the frame. Said out loud that he knew a parolee, a man with a vicious record and nothing to lose, a man known to work these shifts, could he start with him? Not a suspect, no, but a talker.

It took all day to get that far, to make Blaker officially his. Until he had licence to do what he had wanted to do in the first place. Go and find him, alone. Invite him to assist with enquiries, at least as a general part of rounding up the usual suspects. The day had spread well into the evening before he found him.

Which was why, at nine on a Monday night, he sat with Blaker in the waiting room at Accident and Emergency, with Blaker's mumbling, blood-streaked face in his lap, the grime of mucus making a real mess of his trousers. It was like dealing with a large slobbering dog in someone else's house: some code of manners dictated that you had to let it happen to you. The mumbling had followed the sobbing which followed the other mumbling, and if the body was the temple of the soul, as Donald had been told, this one had been bombed. The injuries were superficial enough, a bang on the head and awful scratches round the neck. It was the damage to the soul that did for him. Donald was rubbing Blaker's back, saying, there, there. Oh, she did, did she? Thinking at the same time that this really was over and above the call of duty, and then thinking maybe not, since Blaker's woeful condition was really his, Donald's fault.

Somewhere along the line he remembered Blaker telling him that a favourite hang-out of his was Victoria Embankment Gardens. The gardens were hidden from view by railings and stretched alongside the Thames by Hungerford Bridge. They were long and narrow and evergreen, good for loitering in any weather because of the shelters. It was too crowded, though, because there was musical entertainment in the summer and too many hobos coming from both sides of the river, too many hot bodies on a hot day, like everywhere. It had not been a hot day; it had been cool and wet when Ivy had found him in the late afternoon, two hours before Donald did.

'She knows I come here most days,' Blaker said. 'I always tell her where I might be. Believe it or not, I try to plan my day.'

'What happened?'

Blaker had been sitting on the ground, recognisable with one swollen eye and only as much ignored by passers-by as the other dozen or so of the walking-wounded homeless who hung around, sleeping off the day's bottle and looking bashed about by falling over. Self-harming, injured people were part of the scenery, to be walked around without eye contact most of the time, pity not something to be wasted on hopeless causes. Nor was anyone likely to interfere in their squabbles, the drunken debates turned sour and the half-hearted spats and blows, the raucous laughter.

'She was angry,' Blaker said. 'I was sitting on a bench by myself, and she just came up behind me, put one hand on my neck, and punched me, then she put both her hands round my neck, and . . . shook me. I didn't see her at first, but I smelt it was her, and I started to choke. I was saying don't, what's the matter, and she just hung on like grim death. Look.' He fingered his own neck, where a line of grazes decorated it like a red and purple necklace. 'I thought she'd kill me. She didn't care who saw. I got my hands on her arms and tried to fight her off, but I was dying there, man, dying, without being able to ask why. And then she stopped. Like all the anger went. She let go. I sort of slumped forward, and . . . and then she came and sat beside me and said she was sorry. And I said, what did you do that for, Ivy? and she said, you know what you did. You've been talking to someone about me.'

Blaker raised bloodshot eyes to Donald's face, the intensity of his gaze shocking in its sorrow.

'I think we'll maybe get to a hospital and get you checked out,' Donald said.

Blaker did not want that, but above all he did not want to be left alone. So they were sitting in the queue, and Blaker, fuelled by burbling sorrow, soreness and the whisky his attacker had left him, began to snore in Donald's lap, and Donald detached him to curl up in the plastic chair next to his own. Then he took out his notebook and started to make notes.

He always wanted to begin, like an old Victorian copper giving evidence, by saying, *As I was proceeding in a westerly direction* . . . he always wanted to write his notes like telling a story, but all notebooks had issue numbers, all had to be accounted for, returned and examined, they were not the place for putting down what you thought. They were for writing a précis of facts and dialogue. He put back the official, date-stamped, serial number 1366197 notebook and took out his own, wrote in that because he could use his own language. He could make up an official record of events later, if ever.

Blaker is a persistent offender, HIV positive, with not a lot to lose. He was attacked today, in the open, by an angry woman he has known for years, simply because she found out I had spoken to him and thus knew of her. She knew this because she stays with Ms Rachel Doe, whom I had phoned because I was idle and in the mood to set a red herring to catch I didn't know what. It follows that Ivy W. has something more than usual to hide about a strange and tragic background. I believe that Blaker (who's a lovely old queen, whatever he's done, including robbing women because he fancied their handbags as much as anything else) is complicit with Ivy, and that Ivy used him to send e-mails, with images, to her ex-husband. I have absolutely no proof of this, but I think it. I also believe that Ivy is violent but not uncontrolled. Blaker bears witness to this. It's a very bold move to attempt to throttle someone in public, very bold indeed. It wasn't her hands she put round his neck . . . looks to me like it was some sort of rope, there are grazes and scratches. A sort of garrotte.

Blaker also bears witness to her kindness. Is this consistent? He says she left in tears and full of apologies after what she had done, giving him a half-bottle of whisky. Kindness, or a short route to oblivion. She left him saying she was very, very sorry, but she had things to do, and he must not talk about her to anyone. Talk about what? What's so bad, that Blaker knows?

Blaker stirred and Donald scribbled.

What is she like? I know this much. She's potentially murderous. She loathes her ex-husband, the judge, so Blaker says. According to the son, she was violent to him. Is either telling the truth? And she's worked endless night shifts. Supposing she has a vendetta? Against men? Or a particular kind of man?

Garrottes. I brought him here because when you've got grazes, however shallow, you risk things getting septic, and I don't know what an HIV bloke should risk. She wasn't trying that hard, not as hard as it looked, she was making a point that she could do far worse, and she could, you know. No one would notice in Victoria Embankment Gardens.

He paused for an irrelevant thought. Queen Victoria had brought the German influence. Through her, the Germans did so much for this particular city. Victorian morality. There was always a down side to the up side of achievement. Poverty, prostitution and monuments went together somehow. Then he shook himself and went on writing.

Ivy W., a girl brought up on a farm. She might know how to kill animals, but not how to kill human beings. Am I missing a trick here?

She's a night-time animal who works and befriends. She is as kind as she is vicious. Blaker keeps talking about practice.

He swapped the private notebook for the one with the serial number, and began again.

I found Mr Blaker, who was poorly and intoxicated. He was unable to tell me anything about Clean Co. because of this. He told me that he had been attacked. I took Mr Blaker to A and E. I am pursuing enquiries into the matter of his alleged assailant . . .

He was full of an unholy sense of glee, yes, yes, yes, because whatever he had seen, he had perfectly legitimate grounds to arrest the ex-Mrs Schneider for assault on Blaker. And he knew where to find her. He could go and haul her in, question her about why she had done that, and about night shifts.

No, he couldn't. The correct course of action would have been to take Blaker to the nearest nick, West End Central, as it happened, and let the locals deal with it, or call someone straight to the scene. Pursue it as just another street crime.

He was perverting some course of justice; he was already hopelessly compromised by what he had done. He was not doing anything like his duty. He was doing what Blaker wanted and shielding him.

Blaker stirred, nuzzling his shoulder, like a child.

'She didn't mean it, you know. Fuck this, can you take me home?'

'You need looking at. Cleaning up. Antibiotics.'

And I need evidence from a doctor.

'You're not going to report her, are you? You're not going to tell anyone what Ivy did to me? I don't want her in trouble. If you do anything like that, I'll just deny it, I'll say it was someone else. I shouldn't have told you. Why the fuck did I tell you? I've been out of it, haven't I? *What else did I tell you?*'

Donald was deliberately silent, for a long time, until Blaker nudged him, hard.

'Promise, fuck you, or I'll get you in trouble.'

Then he began to cry again. 'No, I didn't mean that. Oh please, Don, don't do nothing. I want her to come back. I wish she'd killed me.'

'Why on earth should she do that?'

Blaker shut his eyes.

'Did you e-mail stuff to the judge, Blaker? I thought I heard you say that in your sleep.'

Blaker nodded. The pain was beginning to kick in, along with a dull, defeated, overdue anger, at himself, at everything. This was good, Donald thought, although what the hell he could do with anything Blaker said was another matter. He wished he did not have to react like a policeman and could recover the other instincts of a normal human being and just do something kind, because that was what he wanted to do.

279

No chance.

'Sending that stuff, pictures from books, is that what she didn't want you to talk about to someone like me?'

Another nod, then a violent shaking of the head, which hurt.

'That's not much to worry about, is it? Or was it something else?'

Blaker was sobbing again, clutching his throat.

'She's going to kill him,' he said at last. 'She's been practising. She boasts about it to me, because no one would believe me. She's going to kill him, one way or another. She says she's got someone to help her.'

Oh, shit. Donald wanted to shout. Here he was in collusion with a fantasist with a death sentence and a horrible knack of telling the truth. Maybe he could restore his reputation with this one. Maybe this was a coup. But Donald had never had a coup in his life, and who would believe Blaker?

What would his wife think if he brought Blaker home? If he turned Blaker in, he'd be bailed by the morning, off and away as soon as he'd retracted everything he'd said, and Donald would look a real Charlie.

A nurse was coming towards them. She looked long-suffering, faced with her twentieth drunk today.

Donald thought it was time he took advice from the judge. Maybe not. The judge would not want Donald going anywhere near his ex-wife, he knew it, otherwise he would have mentioned her in the first place. He nudged Blaker, who was shrinking away from the nurse.

'He's HIV positive,' Donald said to her, wondering if this was information Blaker would have volunteered.

'Oh,' she said. 'I'll just get some gloves.'

Donald settled back.

'Well that's put me to the back of the queue,' Blaker said spitefully, quite cheered by her reaction. 'Thanks.'

No, Donald could not take him home. He wasn't that good a man. He had daughters to consider.

'It'll be all right,' he said. 'Now, my friend. You said this Ivy was a model. When she's not doing something else. Where was it you said she did the modelling?'

Blaker looked up in surprise, confusion coming down again. He could not remember telling Donald that.

'Just up the road. At the art school. She wasn't going to go far away, was she?'

CHAPTER SEVENTEEN

There was definitely a pattern to Rachel's dealings with the judge, rather like the patterns of a dance. She would be on the one hand appalled by him, or reports of him, then she would see him and feel attracted first, before being repelled again. She had begun by loathing him on the basis of what he would call hearsay evidence, then she admired, then she was hopelessly attracted, then she was repelled, then she was attracted, and then she was confused. She could not believe he was the good man he seemed to her, and the wicked one he seemed to others who had known him so much of his life. Rachel was a novice in the affairs of the body and mind, but she knew that if she had met him without knowing anything about him, ignorance would be bliss, and she would have admired him. But even something as innocent as respect felt like treachery and she could almost have wished she hated him.

She referred to him as 'the judge' in her own mind when she thought of him, which was most of the time during the

Tuesday and the Wednesday, simply to put him at a distance, make him a man without a name, and encourage herself to analyse objectively, instead of saying *Carl*. She tried to put her own feelings in a box marked *Anonymous* and close the lid, instead of spreading the contents out all over some clean floor, like she sometimes did with work documents, to see what caught her eye, to see a sequence, to see what did not fit, to notice what jarred, undistracted by what should have been there. Look at what she saw with her own two eyes, instead of assuming that what she had been told was true. But then she had never felt like this before. She had never felt drawn to the hideously selfish husband of a best friend before. It skewed everything.

I am so insecure, she wrote in the diary at work, *that I fall in love with anyone who pays the slightest bit of positive attention to me. Anyone who takes me seriously. I'm a thirty-two-year-old virgin.* Delete.

She looked out of the window of the office, and watched the people pass, far below. Too much time spent doing this. She kept looking because she was sure, early this morning, that she had seen Grace, stepping out with the rush-hour crowds disgorging themselves from the station, and she had been so sure it was Grace, because of the metallic hair and the way she walked, she had wanted to shout, STOP, and then run downstairs and find her, but waited instead for the figure to pass out of sight. Whenever she thought of Grace, she saw her walking with her own shadow trailing behind, the way she thought about Ivy. A person with a tall and elegant shadow.

It could not have been Grace. Grace was at home, mid-afternoon, when she rang, full of tales of the weather, until they began to speak in a strange kind of code, as if Ivy was listening.

Saturday OK, Grace? Oh, yes. But you're coming Friday, aren't you? Yes, I think so. Are you sure? If you want . . . Yes, I do want.

Have you *met* him? (This was Grace.) No, not actually, but we've spoken. How did you persuade him, darling, oh you are marvellous.

I didn't persuade him, Grace, I threatened him, and then he volunteered. How easy it was to lie.

I shall have a splendid lunch, Grace said. Ernest is not quite himself. I long to see you. Is Ivy as busy as she says? Yes, thank God. Grace, did you ever meet any of Ivy's friends? No, darling. I don't think she had any other than lowlifes before she met you, I told you. Can you come soon, on Friday, I'm so nervous. And how's your father? Truculent and uncommunicative. Oh my God, aren't they all? Men, bloody men, I love you, dearest. I shall colour my hair scarlet, just to scare him. Take care, talk soon.

Is Ivy as busy as she says?

Two points, which she counted on her fingers. Ivy and Grace clearly chatted like starlings every day, imparted news back and forth in a way she had never guessed and Ivy never said. Ivy had always had friends, but no one Rachel had ever met. Like someone called Blaker.

She took Sam's inhaler . . . it was the last straw.

Ivy had been out when Rachel got home on the Monday night. She was back late and left a note next morning. *See you at drawing class on Wednesday . . . be good.* Where did Ivy go when she did not come home?

Last class of term, and Rachel could not look forward to it

because Ivy would be the model, whereas before it would make the evening. It was the keeping of secrets that made it different, that was all. The spasmodic sightings of Ivy, the communication by note and text which typified their shared existence was only normal flatmate stuff, with one working days and the other, more often, nights, but at the moment it felt as if they were avoiding one another.

Rachel's father remained aloof, as if he too had something he did not want to tell her. He would like her to visit next week, please, when he had finished renovating the bathroom. And how was that friend of hers? Ivy whatsername?

Fine, Dad, fine.

Don't you miss that class of yours.

She took Sam's inhaler . . . it was the last straw. Things don't fall out of pockets. She must focus. The week would go in a flash. She was sure she had seen Grace. No, she was not sure of anything.

She read a newspaper she found lying around, for distraction, and then put it down. Full of the usual crap. *Death in ambulance unsolved.* It was easy to read about London being a dangerous, violent place, and ignore it entirely and effortlessly when you lived in the heart of it. She threw the paper away. That was the London her father feared, not the London she knew.

Towards the end of the long Wednesday afternoon, Rachel was called down to the front desk of her office building, two floors down, with a message that that there was a delivery for her, and the delivery person would like a signed receipt. Unusual, but she went, anything to move.

In the foyer of the building she saw a bright bouquet of flowers on the desk, and beside it, dwarfing it in colour and size, stood Sam Schneider, dressed in white and looking dazzling. She could not help it: his presence created a frisson of shock and a feeling of being intruded upon on her own territory, but he was also instantly familiar, and he made her smile.

'What on earth are you doing here?'

He made an exaggerated bow, scooped the flowers off the desk, handed them to her, and spoke as if he was running in a race.

'Dad sent me. He's got me doing errands, since I'm freed up and he never is. In return for which he may have to pay me back with menial work, such as washing and ironing, at which he excels, did you know that? And basically he trusts me slightly more than Interflora.'

'They're lovely,' she said, burying her nose and her embarrassment in the sweet scent of the flowers. There were jasmine and roses in there. She did not know what to say.

'Or rather,' Sam said, 'he trusts my taste in choosing floral tributes for beautiful women better than his own, done over the phone. Do you really like them?'

'Of course I like them,' she laughed. 'How couldn't I? Can I buy you a drink or a coffee, or would you prefer a more conventional tip?'

Sam doffed an imaginary cap and grinned at her.

'I'm not allowed to take bribes, miss, honest, and I don't usually demean myself with errands either, except when I'm curious. The old meanie hasn't sent flowers to anyone except his clerk in a million years, so please don't send them back.'

'I shan't, I promise, but surely I can give you some reward?'

Sam winked, ludicrously.

'Nope. I'm off on holiday. You could, you know, look after him while I'm away. You're definitely in with a chance.'

Then he waltzed away, leaving her extraordinarily light-headed. She never knew quite what to do with someone who was pleased to see her. There was a note with the flowers, which said, *Thanks for being yourself. See you Saturday at twelve, or before?*

Better not before. When she phoned Carl to thank him, half hoping not to reach him, they talked for an hour, about very little other than the flowers on her desk. What a pity she could not take them home. Ivy would want to know who they were from.

She stayed late at the office and got to the drawing class early, light in heart. The corridor leading to the designated room through the labyrinth of the college was cool and dusty, but the room itself was hotter than an incubator. The flowers would have wilted. Sweaty, bad-tempered, hot-from-mal-functioning heat, left on for the last model with no clothes, still going full blast hours later. Rachel switched it off. She wanted to open the windows, which were set high in the wall, and unable to find a way, left the door open for a faint draught to flow through. In spite of her distractions and the ridiculous heat, Rachel looked at the unkempt, scruffy, paint-smeared place with great affection. In those black old days when she had first sidled in, it was a place she had loved on sight, so much so she liked being early, breathing it in and being the good girl who put out the chairs for the majority who were late, as long as she could avoid the Plonker, who was often early too, on account of not having much more of a life than she did then. It was the last day of term; she did not know if she would ever come back, but she thanked this room for what it had done for her in the dog days of winter and the darkest days of gloom. In this ugly, beautiful space, she had discovered a talent and a whole new world. She began to put out the plastic chairs, looked around for the equally filthy plastic stands on which they would balance the boards, and then she noticed that the room was even more untidy than usual. Chairs had been knocked over by the last class in a stampede to leave; must be the heat. Rachel was back on familiar, if borrowed territory, saying *tut, tut, tut,* under her breath, laughing at herself, looking at the clock, which told her she had ten minutes before the teacher came in, and why was she always such an early bird? It had been nerves, at first.

She heard him before she saw him. A moaning sound, coming from the makeshift little cubicle where the model disrobed behind a limp curtain and came out, into the heat, waiting for instructions. The cubicle was nothing but a corner, conveniently close to the washbasin and its single cold tap, behind the same curtain. The moaning went on. Rachel yanked back the curtain.

The Plonker was behind it, sitting there with his head between his hands and his elbows on his knees, keening to himself. His summer uniform for a hot day was baggy shorts and sandals, exposing large white thighs and hairy calves, and he was a man who should never have worn shorts in public. Winter and summer, he always wore the wrong clothes. Too many, too much, or too few. The wrong clothes, chosen with care in furtherance of a long-dead image taken from a film he had loved featuring a hero with a different figure, and jazzed up by a silly scarf.

'What's the matter?'

'Agghhhhh!'

It was a loud yell in the quiet room. Norman put his hands round his neck and jumped to his feet, then slumped back down heavily on to the stool on which he sat. He wound the silly scarf tightly round his neck with trembling fingers, and coughed loudly. Then he removed one hand from his neck and waggled his fingers. Rachel did not know if this was an apology for the scream, or what it meant. She had a sudden image of what her father might have looked like as a young man. He would have been the sort everyone labelled fusspot or plonker, or something of the kind. It didn't make him bad. It gave him a futile bravery. Norman, the Plonker, looked sad.

'What's the matter?'

He looked up at her beseechingly and made a pathetic attempt to shrug.

'I thought it was Ivy coming back,' he whispered.

'What do you mean, coming back? She'll be here any minute, along with everyone else. What are you doing in there? Come on out.'

He shook his head.

'You don't know, do you? You really don't know. You don't know anything. I'm glad it's you, I thought it was her, coming back. She came ten minutes ago. She told me if I said anything she'd kill me, and she would, I know she would, I . . .'

'What the hell are you talking about?'

'I was with her that night,' he gabbled. 'She ran away from me, she got in the thing, she did it. It had to be her. You've got to tell her I'll never tell anyone, never, ever, ever. She put her hands round my neck and she squeezed.' He fingered the scarf, scratching at it. 'She said . . .'

They could hear footsteps coming towards the open door. He began to stutter. 'You've got to know what she's like. She said if I ever . . .'

Rachel hauled him to his feet and out into the room.

'Don't you mean,' she said, 'that Ivy said she wouldn't go

out with you or sleep with you at the point of a gun? Isn't that what she said when she found you hanging round, waiting for her? Isn't it?'

He looked at her helplessly. He had the expression of a man who was never believed.

'Tell her I won't tell,' he muttered.

Ivy and the teacher swept into the room together, he small and squat, she tall and lithe, an incongruous couple. Ivy knew all the gossip and could talk the teachers' talk. Ivy could talk anyone's talk; she remembered everything they said. She beamed at Rachel and Norman, embracing them both with her smile, stepped across to Rachel and kissed her on the cheek.

'Hello, hello, here we are again, end of term too. Fun time. We've got crisps and wine for the interval. It's a very cheap and refreshingly nasty red. We'll have to make up for it later.'

The Plonker turned away and picked up one of the fallen chairs. He was trembling again. Ivy caught Rachel's eye and raised her own eyebrows, as if to say, what's this about? and Rachel responded with a 'search me' shrug.

'I'll think about that,' Rachel said, grinning back. They had always been conspirators, Ivy and she. It was good to feel that way.

There was a clatter of more footsteps, the main posse arriving with a minute to spare, bringing in a draught of sound and the reassuring presence of the outside world, sorting out easels and stools and boards. Rachel found her familiar place. Out of the corner of her eye she saw Ivy detour on her way to the cubicle, to touch Norman on the arm and smile hello. He flinched away from her, then smiled back. Nothing wrong then. Just besotted.

She tried to will herself back into the state of utter

concentration on the class and the sheer exercise of drawing which had so beguiled her in the first place, and the magic worked, as the still overwarm room fell silent, apart from distant outside noises and the shuffle of bodies and paper. She was sitting opposite the Plonker, who had deliberately placed himself at the far side of the room, not close to anyone else for once. He seemed to have pulled himself together.

'Three-minute poses, please.'

Ivy stepped out of the cubicle, jumped up on to the wooden podium and smiled at them all. She stood stock still with her legs apart, one hand on her hip, the other hanging by her side, head in profile, looking away from Rachel. They had agreed a long time ago that whenever Ivy was the model in this class, she would never look directly at Rachel, because it made them giggle, and when that started it could not be stopped, like laughter in some holy place. Ivy always looked away. Rachel began to draw quickly, get down the outline and place it on the page. It was an easy pose, Ivy knew to begin with easy poses. A quick glance to memorise it, mark the outer dimensions of head and feet and centre body, then go. She glanced up, past Ivy, and saw the Plonker's face, gazing up. His mouth was open; the gaze was one of fear and ador-ation, like someone imploring a favour from the effigy of a cruel saint. His scarf had slipped; in the harsh light, Rachel could see that his neck was red and his face was pale. She looked away.

'Change pose.'

Ivy moved slightly, changed the angle and let both arms drop by her sides, head flung back. She flexed her fingers but was otherwise still. Rachel could see scratches on her upper arms, red against her tanned skin, shockingly bright scratches which must have bled. The words *road kill* came into her mind, Ivy washing blood from her hands. When and where had she got those? Where had she washed the blood away? Not in their bathroom, surely. Looking at the whole figure, Rachel had a sudden, alternative picture of her, startlingly different from the first. Not an animal, not the hunted running creature she had first seen, but a fighter, curling and uncurling her fingers, ready to do battle, poised and trained. A Boadicea who would cut off her own breast the better to hoist a weapon. A ruthless physical opponent, something merciless. For one brief moment, watching those large hands moving slightly, and the back held taut, Rachel was frightened of her.

The class went on. The image faded in the long poses, when Ivy knelt and leaned forward, exposing her long back, her face concealed, her arms stretched before her, like a supplicant making an obeisance, utterly defenceless. Abused, waiting to be kicked, the scratches on her arms making her victim rather than predator. That was the image Rachel wanted to keep and treasure. The class went on. The interval was spent drinking bad wine; the temperature cooled and Ivy made them laugh. When they resumed their seats for the delayed second half, the Plonker had gone.

'Good,' Ivy said, passing Rachel's seat. 'Are we having a drink? I feel like getting absolutely plastered. Let's.' She held out her arms. 'Look at this. We had to take out some hideous dead plants from the back of an office. Prickly stuff, the bastards. Look what it did.'

The words echoed in Rachel's head. *I don't believe you. I just don't believe you.* You were fighting. You don't get nail scratches at work, not even your work.

She found herself repeating to herself the words *I don't believe you,* to stop herself saying them out loud, and saying instead, 'Honestly, Ivy, if you go round hitting people, you've got to make sure they don't fight back,' and turning away to gather her things, feeling a huge sense of loss because it was such an obvious and glib lie. Ivy grabbed her by the arm. She could feel her hand burning into her bare skin, like being held by hot steel.

'I didn't say anything about hitting people,' she said angrily. 'I said I was moving prickly rubbish.'

'Well I don't think you should be asked to do that on what you get paid,' Rachel said briskly. 'Five pounds an hour doesn't include danger money. Or having fifteen people in a class wondering if you've been snuggling up to a tiger.'

Ivy's eyes lit up with delight at the very idea.

'That's what I hoped they'd think,' she said. 'But they're so polite, aren't they, they didn't even ask, not even Teacher. C'mon, let's go and forget the taste of that red stuff. Drown it in something better. Did I tell you I get ten pounds an hour for the next weekend? Three days solid, they want. I'll be worth a fortune, so I'm paying.'

Go with the flow, it would all be fine. Get down a bottle of wine, wish the week away, stop consulting that little nag in the heart which felt like a stone, the feeling she had seen something she should not have seen, and wished she hadn't. They went out into the light sky and the traffic sound, lulling now at nine at night, with the imprint of Ivy's vice-like fingers still on her arm, and the temperature rising again with the pressure of hundreds of people out there, hunting for a good time.

And there, by the entrance, was DS Cousins, with his droopy moustache and a cigarette in hand, waiting to one side and leaning against the wall like a person waiting to catch a bus from the nearby stop. Rachel recognised him instantly, saw his face and somehow heard again his voice on the phone. He was not looking at her; he was looking across the road. Her response was instinctive. At first she had the absurd desire to barge into him and push him out of the way, and then all the protective urges she had ever felt towards Ivy came in to play and the rest was forgotten; she linked arms, pulled down Ivy's cap, and marched her forward, staring ahead herself, talking hard, until they were well past him. Then she shuffled Ivy along even faster, until the West End pavement crowds swallowed them. Ivy allowed herself to be carried along, laughing that Rachel's enthusiasm for a decent glass of wine was a bit extreme, wasn't it, had the end-of-term class been that bad, and what was the matter with the Plonker, until they detoured left and right and then into the basement bar where Ivy had taken her first.

Ivy pushed through to the front of the crowded room; people made way for Ivy. Rachel grabbed a seat, sat down heavily with the drawing bag banging against her knees, and drew breath. She felt less rage than disappointment. Judge Carl's tame policeman, his sad-looking jackal, had been sent to wait for them. He wanted Ivy; he had been primed, twice, as to where he might find her. And if DS bloody Cousins was to get to Ivy now, whatever innocent thing he wanted to ask, Rachel's underhand dealings with Carl would be revealed. Sure, they would have to come out sometime, but not yet, not until there was a tangible result.

Why hadn't she asked Carl about that damn man? She had simply forgotten. DS Cousins could ruin the plan. Rachel looked towards the door. No one had followed them. DS Cousins in his shirt and tie would stick out a mile in here, and still she felt they were both pursued.

She was so tired, so very tired. Anxiety sapped energy,

but more exhausting still was the solid knowledge of what she had observed in Ivy's naked, speechless body, in Norman's face: that Ivy might be sweet, generous and kind, but she was also a savage; she had never been entirely powerless, and she had done something terribly wrong and was revelling in it.

Ivy was as high as a kite, sailing on nothing but city air and two hours of being admired, pushing her way back to their table with a bottle of wine and two glasses, in party mood, the way she often was after modelling. She sat down and leaned forward confidingly, full of mischief.

'Now, shall I tell you what really happened with the Plonker? What an idiot! Why are we feeling sorry for him?'

'What happened? Why's he so scared of you?'

'Oh, pooh, he's not scared, just embarrassed. I dropped my kit off in the room before class. I was going to go and get a coffee. And he was in the damn cubicle. Waiting for you.'

'For *me*?'

'Yes, darling, for you. Wanted to leap out and say boo and charm you, I expect. You're the only other one who's always early. He was waiting for *you*. A joke. He wanted to play a joke. Fancy him waiting for you. You've got a major fan there.'

Despite herself, Rachel laughed.

'What is it he wants you to know he'll never tell?'

Ivy's expression changed, fleetingly, and then she grinned.

'He knows my dark secret. He hangs around. He saw me,' here Ivy put her hand to her brow in a gesture of profound and dramatic shame, 'pinching the stationery. Yes, I confess it, I also pinched a pen. And do you know *his* sad secret?'

'Nope.'

'He wants to be a . . . model.'

There was a sudden common vision of sad, slack Norman standing on the podium with no clothes and everything pointing down. Cruelly, they both laughed. *I don't believe you* still echoed in Rachel's mind, but she laughed and searched for oblivion via Chardonnay.

Donald watched them go. He nodded to Blaker across the road. Blaker made a thumbs-up signal. ID confirmed. *She's going to kill him, and she has someone to help her.* Well, God help the poor sod, with two furies like that after him. Donald could no more have tried to split up those two than he could have climbed Everest, and it had never been his intention. All he had done was gone in and enquired if a model of that name worked at the college, to be given the information that yes, she did, she would be here later; and then he had gone away, and come back just to get a look at her, and he'd been lucky in that. Rachel Doe being there as well had surprised him. Were they inseparable, as well as living together? She didn't look like a dyke, Miss Doe, but you never could tell. What kind of a bitch was it cosied up to a man and his ex-wife, and pretended to the man she didn't know where the ex-wife lived? For what?

The depth of Donald's wife's friendships with other women never failed to surprise him. Women, it seemed to him, would do anything for one another when push came to shove. It was what made them so radically different to men. Men had limits.

Better get along and keep his appointment with the judge. Sorry about the lateness of the hour, sir, but I've got to be doing this in my own time now. There's another panic on.

Thank you, said the judge, I appreciate it.

But I bet he won't listen to me. I must temper what I say, keep it to facts and questions.

Such as why does your wife want to kill you, and who is it who is going to help?

It looked like Rachel Doe. Shame about the evidence.

CHAPTER EIGHTEEN

It was a long haul out to the judge's flat on the rail link. He'd said he didn't mind how late it was. Up to him, really.

When he got there, getting himself into the citadel in the darkening light was bad enough, and once through the front door, it was refreshingly untidy. It turned out that Sam was using the living room to spread out his packing for a week's holiday. The severe lines of the place were improved by washing hanging over the balcony. Carl led Donald in, smiling welcome.

'Don't you have a home of your own to go to, Donald, working these hours? Come in, come in, have a drink.'

'Yes, I do have a home, but my wife usually takes the daughters on holiday this time of year. Sun and sand's not for me, so I've got all the time in the world.'

'My good fortune, then. I'm honoured.'

'Maybe not, sir. I'll have a beer please.' He pointed at a pile of shirts on a chair. 'Is your boy expecting his clothes to be ironed by the time he comes home?'

'Probably. The worst of it is, he's probably right.

Donald nodded, understanding. They sat with ice-cold beer, relatively at ease and quite pleased to see each other, apart from the business in hand. Pity it wasn't social, maybe another time. The world would be a better place if judges and coppers drank together.

'I've found the man who sent the e-mail stuff. It *was* Blaker, the man I told you about who knows your ex-wife. I haven't arrested him, there's no official admission, and he's a poor sick creature.'

'Is he the one who got into the office at my chambers?'

The beer was Belgian and delicious, if only he wasn't so tired. Donald had been dreaming strange dreams recently, instead of sleeping. Might be sickening for something. Felt poorly since Sunday night.

'No, I don't think so, or at least if he was, I don't think he was alone. I think that was someone else. Possibly someone with a cleaning crew.'

Donald was making that up, but it sounded plausible, and it was what the other team were working towards. 'I don't know about that, but it's the motive behind the whole thing worries me. Blaker talks to me; he might talk to you if I ask him nicely, and for a reason which might surprise you. He seems to be genuinely worried for your ex-wife . . .'

'Ivy.'

'For reasons beyond my understanding, he's worried about her.'

Carl was silent. Donald took a slug of his beer. The second mouthful was never quite as good as the first.

'Blaker sent the e-mail stuff because Ivy's not so hot on that, although I reckon she was standing over him in the art college where she works, part-time student and model, maybe tore the stuff out of books. Blaker's not fond of you because you sent him down, and Ivy, well, she doesn't like you at all, to put it mildly. Blaker thinks it goes way, way beyond that. Now, sir, could you help me out here and just tell me about your relationship with your ex-wife? Begin at the beginning, it's always easier.'

Carl had left his own beer untouched, listening intently, thinking up an answer which would be both honest and brief.

'Once it was good, in the very beginning, passionate and absolutely hair-raising, then very bad. It would have fallen apart even if my daughter hadn't drowned. I haven't seen Ivy since before we divorced. I settled money on her. She's never asked for anything more.'

'I know about you shooting the swans; your boy Sam told me about that. He also told me his mother mistreated him.'

'He probably thinks I do too. What a trustworthy boy he is. I'm afraid she did. She hated me then, blamed me for the death and especially for the swans. That bit's really too complicated to explain, but she blamed Sam even more for just about everything, for throwing stones, for his very existence. She'd already been experimenting with drugs before the accident . . . making up for stolen youth, poor thing. Ivy's an obsessive personality, she does nothing by halves, and then grief made her go over the edge. I couldn't blame her, or reach her, poor thing, but she was very cruel to Sam, hurt him quite badly.'

He swallowed. 'Poking, pinching, slapping. Took me a while to notice him cowering away. He couldn't say; believe it or not, he was dangerously asthmatic and a deeply introverted boy. I lost count of the times I took him to hospital. Ivy was often out, or out of it. It got to the point where she simply couldn't be left alone with him. She took away his inhaler, she could have killed him. That was the last straw. I got her committed on to a treatment course. She ran away once or twice. Then I couldn't let her come home.'

'So you shut her out.'

'It was her or Sam. He was ten years old. What would you have done?'

Donald got out his cigarettes, and crushed an empty packet.

'I don't know, but if you don't mind my saying so, you could have mentioned some of this at the beginning, because personally, a violent ex-wife is the first person I'd think of when it comes to death threats. I asked you if this could be something personal rather than professional, some woman scorned or whatever, and you said no.'

'Donald, if you haven't seen your ex-wife for nearly a decade, and you know she's turned out all right because you've been in contact with her parents, you don't actually imagine she'll come back out of the blue and send vile messages, especially if she's not exactly literate. She wasn't bad, she was mad, and she surely came to know that. Yes, I know she hated me, and I gave her cause, but she made an alternative life, and hatred dies, doesn't it?'

Donald was patting his pockets, looking for the other packet of cigarettes. He had never been able to stand waiting in a street without smoking a cigarette. The last one had made him light-headed; he really did not need another.

'No, sir. You're way too rational. Hatred doesn't always die. Most of the time, yes, but other times it grows and grows until it becomes all-consuming, people feed off it. Supposing she blames you for everything that happened in her life, the whole mess she made of it was because of you, and the only way out of the mess is revenge. Remember *miasma*. No honour without revenge, the soul rots without revenge. Supposing she thinks you deprived her not only of her daughter, but also her son, and you remain the sole barrier, to what? To him loving her again, to her feeling, how can I put it, *whole*? Back to what she was, with a clean slate?'

Carl walked out of the room and came back with another beer.

'Thanks. It's OK, I'm not driving.'

He felt he had to say that to a judge.

'Sam's the barrier to any reconciliation,' Carl said. 'Not me. As for the rest, with the greatest respect, Donald, what you've said sounds a bit psychobabbly to me. And how does she get her revenge, her *liberation*, by simply making me feel foul with a few futile gestures? What does that show about her feelings for Sam? It certainly doesn't help Sam to hurt me. And why is this man Blaker worried about her?'

Donald wanted to down the beer in one. He deliberated briefly about doing it, and then did it anyway. It was strong stuff.

'Blaker says she wants to wound you. Literally. The e-mails are only to prime you, make you frightened, sort of flush you out into the open. She knows where you are, she knows where you live, even though you've tried to duck and dive for the last few years.'

'*Sam's* tried to hide both of us for the last couple of years. He doesn't want to remember and I don't want him to either.'

'Well, it looks like you. Blaker says he thinks she's enlisted some help, some real muscle apart from him. And she's been practising . . . techniques. Blaker thinks she wants you a dead judge, soon.'

It was Carl's turn to toss back the beer, very quickly. He stood up and paced over to the balcony.

'For God's sake, this is ridiculous. Enlisted help? Ivy can't have much money, unless she's found someone rich. Hitmen don't come cheap. And what could she do on her own? She's a woman. And WHY?'

He stopped short of the balcony and laughed, briefly. 'Maybe she thinks I've still got money, but I sold the house, for God's sake, Ivy got her share, it all went on treatment and whatever. No, they can't think that.'

'Money's the root of all evil, Carl. And who said anything about a hit*man*?'

'Money never meant much to Ivy, and whatever her parlous mental state, I don't believe she could ever carry out a plan to do serious harm to me. She's essentially incredibly kind, and anyway, it would take such *nerve*.'

'Unless she practised,' Donald murmured.

'What did you say?'

'Practice,' Donald said. He was suddenly a bit dizzy and felt awful. 'Dress rehearsals for murder. Have you noticed, everyone gets it in the neck? The man in the office, the man in the ambulance, poor old Blaker. The man off the coast, who'd been staying with them, seaweed all round his neck. A girl bitten by a bloody swan. Always the neck.'

The beer and the earlier drink had finally gone to his head. He realised he was mumbling and incoherent. Bloody Belgian beer, too strong, and himself feeling tearful and stupid. Just as well the judge wasn't listening, because this was a pathetic performance, moving into the realms of conjecture and nightmare he had been hoping to avoid, the same nightmares which ruined his sleep. Carl was still pacing around, making him feel dizzy. Donald sat up straight and tried to control himself. There was another beer in his glass.

'Listen,' he said, 'I agree with you. Bloody women. Fit for

nothing. Murder's a man's job. But what would you do if you were determined to get away with it? Practise. I bloody would. And I wouldn't be worried, Carl, if I hadn't seen already what she might be able to do. I've seen it with Blaker, just like you have with your son. Only he was little then, wasn't he? You've been warned, that's all. Suggest you alter your route to work. And Sam's not your son, is he? He doesn't look like you.'

He still wasn't listening. Donald was looking at the washing hanging around, and it made him feel sad, at the same time as realising his chin was on his chest, and he wanted to blub into his beer, and that he liked this man, very much, he was a good mate and a good dad, which was what counted in the end. It was the washing did it, fucking washing. A man ready to iron clothes for a boy who was not his flesh and blood.

'This is very kind of you,' the judge said, still at the end of his first beer, the bastard. 'If a little extreme. Ivy always fantasised. It's a way of dealing with impotence and frustration when you can't analyse facts. And if she's been fantasising about revenge to a friend, playing with the idea, so be it. As it is, fate's intervened. I think the end may be in sight. There's another way round it. I have been hiding, but I'm not any more. I'm doing the right thing for once. I'm going to meet her parents at their farm on Saturday. Try to bury the bad news of I don't know how many years. See my dad's best friend. My dad was Ivy's father's hero. Difficult to imagine, isn't it, that a German prisoner of war, ten years older, could actually be the soul of glamour. An exotic foreigner, my dad was. Ivy adored her dad. Her dad adored mine. Anyway, I'm digressing. If Ivy's got a bee in her bonnet, I'll find out from them, see what it's all about. If these puerile threats are a plea for help, we'll get the help. Head off trouble. The situation will be defused, and I'm not a humble judge for nothing, diplomacy goes a long way. I'll find out what's up with Ivy, what she wants . . . Why can't she just say what she wants? Rachel was right, approach sideways, via Ernest and Grace, and it's absolutely the right time. Oh shit and damn. If Ivy's really sick, what about Rachel? What have I got her into?'

'You don't want to trust that Rachel, you really don't.'

'What else did you say?'

'Rashell . . . Dow.'

'No, not that. About Sam not being my son.'

Donald felt suddenly faint, the words difficult to articulate, and the judge was looming over him saying, are you all right, are you all right? When did you last eat, for God's sake, I'm so sorry, what an idiot I am, look, what do you think you need? And then Donald leaned over the side of the chair he was in and was gracelessly sick on the laminate floor, immediately better, but weak as a kitten. A long, hot day, and yes, he was hungry. Not much since morning, and far too stressed out and sad to be the inefficient bearer of bad news, even before he got as far as Rachel Doe, and he wasn't going to elaborate on that, and he felt hollow. A hollow man, from his toes to his head. Not good in heat, with only an empty home to go to, and the long-forgotten remnants of a West End doner kebab, still doing damage.

He was left in his chair, drowsing, until a cheese sandwich appeared on a low table by the side of his chair, where a glass of water had materialised minutes earlier, and the sick efficiently removed, so that there was not even a sniff of it. His feet were propped up on a low stool. The judge would make a good wife. Donald wolfed the food. It was like an injection of adrenalin, normality, everything, and left him still awash with the seedy sediments of sentiment. That bloody washing hanging around, that was what did it. Like just before a holiday at home.

'Look, it's late,' Carl was saying. 'You're really welcome to stay here, more than welcome, and I'd rather you did, you look awful, but what will your wife think? Can I phone her and say it's all my fault?'

'I haven't got a wife,' Donald said wearily. 'She died two years ago. Breast cancer. I just go on thinking and acting and pretending as if she's still here. It's the only way.'

'Ah,' Carl said, as if there was nothing wrong or odd about such a statement. 'And the daughters?'

'Oh, they're real all right. Flown the coop, keep coming back. Perhaps makes me understand some of this shit. I wanted to kill the doctors and the nurses when my wife died. As for the kids, if anyone had barred me from one of them when they were small, I'd have killed the bugger and gone to the gallows with a clear conscience.'

'Are you sure you haven't got a nice gay son I could introduce to Sam?'

'No, sorry.'

'They tell me,' Carl said, presenting a snifter of brandy now that the matter of going or staying seemed to have been settled, 'that it's better if your wife dies on you than if she leaves you for someone else. I've always wondered if that was true.'

Donald thought about it and shook his head.

'Don't think so. I think I'd rather she was alive, whoever the hell she was with. Cheers, Judge. Do you want some help with that ironing?'

'No, you're all right there.'

He went into the kitchen and came back with an iron and

board, selected a couple of vibrant shirts. 'The hell with it,' he said. 'You're only an irresponsible, feckless boy once. OK, Don, you talk or sleep or whatever, I'll do his bloody ironing. I quite like it, as it happens.'

'You'd make some woman a lovely husband.'

'I'm thinking of it,' Carl said.

'And you're a Grade A dad. You iron his clothes and spoil him rotten, and he's not even your son.'

'Is that guessing or simple deduction?'

'Guessing. Allowing for appearances to be deceptive, of course.'

Carl was dashing away with the smoothing iron as if he was well in practice. If only his courtroom could see him now, they'd never be scared of His Honour again. His Honour, ironing in a wig, now there was a thought.

'You're quite right. He isn't biologically mine. My fault, and mine by default. Ivy and the horror of motherhood didn't quite gel. She was still a wild child herself. Went straight out of the cage as soon as Cassie was weaned, and as far as I know, shagged everything in sight. Hormonal madness, I think. Hypnotised by living in London. Went to her head.'

He folded shirts with quiet precision.

'Must have taken some explaining.'

'Yes. Evasion, horror, forgiveness, acceptance, and explanation, not necessarily in that order. The most novel explanation was that she'd been impregnated by a swan, all done by magic. I told you she fantasises. She knew I wouldn't walk away and she was more terrified that her parents would find out, especially her father. They never did. They would forgive her anything but that, especially Ernest, who was over the moon about the prospect of a son. Sam was convincingly blond when he was small. He's really quite dark and bleaches

it all the colours of the rainbow now. He just got born, somehow.'

'And?'

Carl spread his hands.

'It was love at first sight.'

Donald was now thoroughly drowsy, with sheer, appalled
curiosity the only thing keeping him awake.

'I thought it was always the woman who was left holding
the baby.'

'Someone has to catch them,' Carl said lightly. 'Every boy
deserves a father. And it's been a privilege and a pleasure.
Maybe not the next bit, but most of the time.'

'You're a good man, Carl. Does anyone know how good?'

His eyelids drooped. A voice came from a distance.

'First on the left after the kitchen, bathroom on the right.
Pyjamas on the bed if you need them.'

Donald hauled himself to his feet.

'Thanks, Dad. I needed that. What are you so fucking
cheerful about?'

He was putting away the ironing board.

'It's not been a bad week, Donald. My son's happy, I've
met a beautiful woman, we may be on the way to solving a
big problem by peaceful means, and I think I've made a good
friend. Can't be all bad, can it?'

Donald wanted to cry, smiled slowly instead. If he talked
about Rachel Doe now, no one would listen.

'Speaking in my official capacity as a bodyguard, Mr
Judge, I shall need to know your movements over the next
few days. And I don't think you should go and see your in-
laws all by yourself. It's never a good idea.'

'If you don't go to bed,' Carl said, 'I shall give you a good-
night kiss.'

Donald hesitated, one last question hovering in his mind.

'Did you really *never* suspect that your wife was behind the threats? She was always artistic, wasn't she?'

Carl shook his head.

'Yes, of course I did. Then someone delivered a rat. A dead rat, remember? I was convinced then it couldn't have been Ivy. Ivy would never go anywhere near a rat. She's terrified of them.'

Chapter Nineteen

What was false and what was true?

Thursday was endless, moving forward in jerking movements, and there was no doubt about Ivy avoiding her. They were avoiding one another. A nice bit of bonhomie engendered through alcohol and cruel laughter, and then to bed, and she had lost her mobile phone again, somewhere in the flat.

A longing for Carl, a conversation with Grace, an avoidance of newspapers and discussions about scratches. Ivy repeating how sorry she was not to be going home that weekend, but perversely excited about the prospect of ten pounds an hour for a whole weekend cleaning out a theatre between productions, if only Clean Co. would confirm, and they had. Never mind how the story slipped and slid a little as they talked in the bar after the class; Rachel was not sure if it was an office or one of the bigger clubs, the Dream Factory, the Lotus, the Shadow Place or whatever. Ivy, briefly seen on the Thursday, first thing in the morning, glittered with unholy happiness, and Rachel could only pity the enthusiasm for earning three hundred pounds cash, which was what she herself earned in far less than a day. Guilt.

Carl phoned. It was becoming a habit, but the phone calls lasted an hour. Grace phoned to discuss the menu for Saturday, sounding sunny and carefree. Her father phoned to say the bathroom was almost complete.

Why should she worry?

Dear Diary, I know he's a good man. I know it.

The flowers glowed on her desk.

It was with huge relief that she drove out of London on Friday afternoon, the car on automatic pilot, Ivy further to the back of her mind, and a box full of goodies in the boot. As if to a family reunion to which she belonged. As if she ever would. Her small family never had any of those. Whatever relatives they had, Dad ignored. Rachel had always felt ignorant of the secrets of family life, always romanticised it.

The further she went from the city, the better she felt. Even the driving held no irritations, because it was a day when everything had worked and looked as if it would continue to do so, from getting up early in the empty flat, to moving unimpeded through the London streets on another fine, clear day which in itself seemed disposed to be helpful, to being able to leave work far sooner than she had hoped, to driving on roads which seemed to make space for her. Since this momentous weekend was arranged, she had suspected something would prevent it, and now it seemed nothing would. She was excited, the way she was the first time she went to the farm, was remembering the associations of pleasure rather than the darker side, determined that Carl and all of them would too. She had planned to use the extra time to detour to the sea, to borrow some of its energy, had left a towel in the back, but the urge to get there was too strong for that.

The countryside had changed subtly in a month; the slender branches which trailed against the side of the car as she turned down the narrow road to the farm seemed thicker and more determined, and the effect of plunging from light into darkness and then into light was more pronounced and exhilarating in this obscure road to a glorious place, making it seem hers and hers alone. She wondered if Carl would remember the way after so many years when he drove down tomorrow, and then thought, of course he would: it was unforgettable and nothing would have changed. Carl, stop thinking of Carl, and knowing full well that part of this excitement was wanting to see him again.

What would Ivy think if she knew was another recurrent thought. Rachel no longer knew what Ivy thought, told herself it was Grace who mattered more at this point. It was Grace who would carry it forward, and Grace was overjoyed with the chance. She would be there, setting the scene, ready to reconcile, smoothing everything, ready to embrace. If Rachel had doubts, and she did, many and various doubts, Grace on the phone dispelled them and treated it all like organising a small party, and it was Grace who said, nothing but good can come of this; there is no bad result, even if it's upsetting. And Ernest is so pleased. You are doing good things, Rachel, you are putting salve on ancient wounds, and I am longing to see you.

Except, when she got there, pulled the car to the side of the road under the shade of a tree about fifty yards from the house and walked towards it, it was all completely quiet. She walked round the house to the ever-open kitchen door and found it shut. The garden was tidy, the yard was swept, and there was no sign of life, not even the rattle of Grace's radio, no yell of welcome, simply an empty house. Rachel knocked on the door and tried the handle; nothing yielded or answered.

She stood back, shielded her eyes and looked up at the windows, which stared back blankly. The house seemed utterly dead, and the only sound which came to her was the humming of bees, busy round a lavender bush nearest the door. The sense of disappointment and mistake was almost overwhelming.

She could imagine the place the way she had never seen it, cold and uncomfortable in winter, with everyone locked inside. She looked up at the crooked chimney, at the mellow brickwork of the walls, which needed repointing, the broken gutter, smelt a faint whiff of rot in the air and remembered the rat, flung into the fire, and for a moment it was as if the whole place was an illusion and had never existed as she remembered it, except in her imagination, and the back door into the magic kitchen had never been open at all. No one lived here really. She shook herself, but could not avoid the feeling of how shabby it was, and how it was a place from which a teenage girl would have wanted to escape.

By now, she wished she had detoured to the sea. She was early, that was all. Perhaps she should drive away and come back, begin all over again, reverse the film. Instead she found herself trying to imagine what Carl would think, and how he would have seen it as a young man. Waiting there, rooted to the spot, she was also trying to reverse the clock on what she now knew about Ivy, what the life drawing class and the evasions so unwittingly revealed, a knowledge so negative and diffuse it amounted to nothing more than a glimpse of something savage which should be ignored, because who would not be so in Ivy's shoes, with Ivy's life, which had never been far from the endless, brutal cycle of life and death, nurture and slaughter which was the real business of life on a farm with animals.

Rachel went back to the car and fished out the towel and T-shirt she had left in the back, and walked in the direction of the lake. The day had grown hotter, the evening would be balmy; she would test the water and try at the same time to see the lake as Carl might see it, and then, when she came back, the slate would be clean, and Grace would be there and the house would take on the warm colours of its owners. Remembering the way as if she had done it a thousand times, already feeling the healing sensation of water on her skin, she halted at the last bend in the path, ready to savour the view, closed her eyes for a minute. When she opened them, she saw a new innovation, a large, hand-painted sign stuck on a stake, reading DANGER. KEEP OUT. POISON WATER. Then she could see Ernest in the near distance, crouching at the edge of the lake. He held out his hand to a swan which floated close to him in the shallows. The swan pecked at whatever he held in his hand and swam away gracefully. Ernest remained as he was, with the breeze off the water ruffling his white hair. It was a pretty sight; Rachel quickened her step and shouted hello. Ernest did not move; he was as unresponsive as the house. She came up behind him and touched him on the shoulder. He turned and smiled sweetly and vacantly, squinting in the sun, as if he did not recognise her at all. There was another stab of disappointment, then of anxiety: was he all right, had his memory gone, was she not important enough to remember, and was it too late for Carl to make any difference?

'Is it safe to swim, today, Ernest? It's me, Rachel.'

'Hello, love, lovely to see you. Do you know, for a minute I thought it was Ivy. Sit yourself down, girl.' He patted the ground next to him.

'Ivy's not coming,' Rachel said, wanting to remind him who she was. 'Not this time.'

'I expect she'll be here later,' he said.

He continued to pat the ground next to him, and she sat. Ernest gazed back over the water to where the swans and their cygnets glided towards the opposite bank of vivid greens. Rachel's desire for immersion in the water faded; she could not share the space with the swans, because of what she knew, and whatever the season of the year, she would always be afraid of them. Nor did she want to undress with Ernest watching, so she sat with him, trying to see the calmness of the lake and not imagine the sound of gunshot, the presence of blood and feathers drifting up to the bank.

'Lot of feathers earlier in the year, when they moult,' Ernest was saying. 'Not so many now.'

'How do you get them to eat out of your hand?'

'Practice.'

'Where's Grace?'

'Oh, she's making ready for the slaughter, or going shopping for knives, or something like that. She keeps leaving me alone just when I need help,' he said, sounding petulant. 'Ivy and her keep arguing about exactly what it is they're going to do. You'd think after all this time they'd know. They want me out of the way, and then she wants me there. Sometimes she talks to me, sometimes she doesn't. Bugger them.'

'Ivy's not coming,' Rachel repeated. 'She's working this weekend.'

'Is she?' he said, suddenly confused. 'Oh, that's all right then. Because Carl's coming, you know. Poor Carl.'

He snorted into a large handkerchief dragged out of his pocket with an effort.

'I loved him, you know. Loved the elder and loved the younger. Should have been my son. He loved me, that Carl, we used to love each other, down here, that Carl, poor lonely sod, never forgot it. We were boys, although he was a big boy, yes, very. Rachel's bringing him. That boy should have been my son all right, though it was only his father knew anything about pigs. And this lake. It's his lake. I want him to see it before they kill him.'

'Kill who, Ernest?'

He looked at her, puzzled, and then back out over the water. The swans had disappeared and half the lake was in shade.

'They want to kill Carl, sweetheart. And the soldiers wanted to kill him. They want to drown him here. Like Cassie drowned. Only the swans won't care, it's the wrong time of year for caring about anything. I told Carl he was wrong for never teaching his boy how to swim.'

He got to his feet, and Rachel did the same. He pointed.

'It never gets much deeper than eight foot. Only in the middle. If he wants to get away, he stays out of that. Goes towards the swans, not away. As long as he remembers he can't swim. When he shot the swans, he waded in, nearly didn't get out.'

He sniggered.

'She doesn't know about the rats. I got Vernon to collect some rats. Lots of rats from the barns, still plenty left.

Couldn't afford that poison, too much money. One got in the house too. There's rats on that bank over there. She'll not go near a rat.'

'Are you feeling ill, Ernest? What the *fuck* are you talking about?'

Rachel did not know if he was talking in the past or the present, listened to his rambling with increasing alarm. She was tempted to feel his forehead in the hope of finding evidence of a raging temperature, but for all Ernest's wholesomeness, she did not want to touch him. He shifted his gaze from the far bank, stared at her as if only just noticing there was anyone there, and then put his head in his arms.

'All this planning and practice,' he muttered. 'Makes me so tired.'

'Planning and practice for what, Ernest?'

He raised his head from his arms and winked at her.

'Doing away with the enemy, my dear. You always have to keep a weapon. You always have to do that. The soldiers are going to do it. Should always have been woman's work, so much better at it than the men, but so much more cruel. I'd just have shot him, more in sorrow than anger, you know, but that's not how they want to play it. They want him to know what it's like to drown. There was never any time for that sort of revenge in the war. My father told me. Better to kill them quick and be done with it. Besides, he'll be harder to burn if he's full of water, heavier to lift, too.'

He plucked a blade of grass, held it between his two thumbs and split it cleanly. Then he did the same with another, and wove the two together.

'Should be using a gun,' he grumbled. 'I've still got that old rifle left. The one Carl learned on with his dad; me too.

World War Two rifle, that; my dad kept three of them. Had to hide that one, so old no one noticed. Grace doesn't know about that.'

He turned to face her. 'When's Ivy coming?' he said.

'She's not coming,' Rachel said for the third time.

'That's a pity. Never mind. I expect she'll get you to help. She's good at that.'

He patted her bare arm. His hand felt cold and left a green mark on her skin.

Rachel scrambled to her feet, left the towel and ran back in the direction of the house. She wanted to run further away than that, back into the womb of the city, anywhere far away from the lake and the sinister ramblings of an old man. Kill who? Who did he mean, was he talking about Carl the elder, Carl the younger, had his addled brain gone back to the war, thinking of death and killing and drowning, not reconciliation, peace or the sight of a once-loved face? She was full of horror for what was in his mind; it couldn't refer to the present, it *couldn't*.

She drew breath near the house, slipped through the gate into the back garden, and there all was normal. Grace's car was parked at a crazy angle to the gate, there were supermarket bags in the yard, the kitchen door was open, and as she drew closer, she could hear Grace singing to the radio. She emerged through the door, bent to pick up her shopping, saw Rachel, dropped the bags and threw her arms open wide in a jangling of bracelets. The shopping seemed to contain a record number of plastic sacks and cleaning stuff, enough for a year.

'Gorgeous! You're here! I saw the car, and I thought what the hell . . . Oh darling, you came to an empty house, I can't bear it . . . how awful.'

Then there was the almighty hug, the sweet smell of her, one hand grabbing Rachel's loose hair, smoothing it, the other hand rubbing her back as if to make something better. Back to normal, the whole world spinning back to normal.

'Good journey, darling? Must have been, to be so early. Where did you go? Are you starving? Is it time for tea, can't be too soon for a drink, come in, come in . . . oh, it's so nice to see you . . . What's the matter, sweetheart? You look like chalk.'

She had to respond to the hug, she could not resist, but then her body went wooden. Grace held her at arm's length, studied her.

'What *is* the matter?'

'I've been down by the lake, listening to Ernest. Has he lost his mind, Grace? Tell me he's lost his mind.'

'What was he saying?'

'About killing . . . someone. He was rambling . . .'

'Oh, my poor darling,' Grace said. 'It was one of those moods, was it? I'm afraid, yes, his mind's been wandering all over the place. Overexcitement. It's because of selling the cows next week. Yes, dear, I'm afraid the decision's been made, sell the cows and keep the pigs. I've been trying to keep him away from the lake, but he keeps on going back. Makes him maudlin. Oh, I wish you hadn't been early and had to face that. It's all very tiresome. What exactly did he say?'

She turned away and bustled into the kitchen, tripping over bags. Moving about automatically, Rachel began to help, picking up bags from the floor and heaving them on to the table.

'None of it was very exact. About drowning someone in

the lake . . . rather than shooting them. He mentioned
Carl . . . a rifle.'

Grace nodded understandingly. The kettle on the hob was
boiling noisily, the washing machine hummed in the corner.
The sinister images began to fade, but not disappear.

'Yes,' Grace said. 'That's the way it usually is, and it's not
getting any better. Can you see now how urgent it was to get
Carl here sooner rather than later? Before my darling husband slips his moorings completely? Seeing Carl might
change all that, of course, I'm hoping it will, because most of
the time he's entirely rational and normal. We went to the
doctor during the week. Alzheimer's creeping in, but slowly
so far. An early stage, still plenty of time for happiness. The
mind goes back to the distant past all the time, can't hold on
to the present.'

Tea was made in between her hurried but precise words.
She cleared a space on the table with her elbow and put
down two mugs.

'This really isn't fair on you, darling, when you've been
such a complete brick. He's fine as long as he's away from
that damn lake. I've got a theory that something horrible
happened there when he was a boy, just after the war, when
people would kill one another for food and horrible things
were happening everywhere, something he'll never say, long,
long before Cassie and everything else. It keeps coming up
and drowning him.'

'Featuring Carl?'

'Yes. Carl who he always adored. Boy worship. The glamour of being *foreign*, all that shit. And whatever he said,
darling, he's not talking about the here and now. I've told him
Carl's son is coming to see us, coming home, but I didn't tell
him when. He doesn't know it's tomorrow. Oh, bugger this

tea, it tastes awful. Let's have a good stiff gin. You deserve it.'

'I thought I saw you in London last week,' Rachel said. 'I must have been thinking of you.'

Relief was washing over her, like a cool shower.

'Fat chance,' Grace snorted. 'I just can't leave him, but I'm telling you, lovey, when this is over, wild horses won't keep me away. Now, tell me all about Carl. What does he sound like? Do you think roast pork is the right thing to give him for lunch? Rather wintry, isn't it?'

There was nothing more comforting, more distracting than domestic detail. It banished anything fantastic. When Ernest came in, he greeted Rachel affectionately, as if she had never seen him by the lake at all. And then she thought, Grace is going to need Ivy and me and a grandson to help her through this. There had to be something good in the future for Grace, and that was all that counted.

And Carl would be free of his past.

Donald Cousins sat with Judge Schneider in his tiny retiring room off Court Seven, arguing quietly. Not quite an argument, but a sort of debate, slightly at cross-purposes, and with the inevitable gaps. Certain fictions had to be maintained between the best of friends or enemies; Donald knew this from having children.

The first fiction was that Donald was not a cunning, underhand bastard who took advantage of hospitality and sneaked around other people's personal documents in the very early hours of the morning, thus knowing the route to the Wiseman place from the road atlas which was open on the desk. He also knew the contents of the judge's last will and testament.

The other fiction hanging round Donald's Friday-afternoon conversation with Carl was that Donald had done nothing in the meantime except become reacquainted with the ordinary day job and its unrelated investigations. Under cover of that convenience he had discovered that Ivy Wiseman was on the books of several cleaning agencies, and her name featured all over the shop. The same researches, conducted by others, had her placed, possibly, at the back of the theatre where the man had been stabbed, as well as, possibly, in the office where the man had drunk bleach. There was no connection with the man in the ambulance in Leicester Square. The Wiseman name came up nowhere else, except as a peripheral part of that dead-end enquiry featuring the young man from London who had drowned in circumstances no longer regarded as suspicious. Donald had found this connection interesting, but did not mention it. Never mention anything to a judge unless you have the evidence for a warrant, and he didn't, even if the same judge had given him a comfortable bed.

The last of the fictions was that he was not worried, and that he did not like Carl Schneider very much indeed. He was not going to tell him what he thought of him, probably ever, but he would have liked the chance. You are naïve, and honourable, and pig-headed, and you know fuck-all about women.

'Two things, Carl, about going to this house in the middle of nowhere. Are you sure your ex isn't going to be there?'

'Yes. Rachel said. That's the whole idea.'

Rachel said, Rachel said . . . Didn't he know Rachel could be part of the problem? *Was* the problem? A cunning bitch, dyke or not. Carl was not going to be told.

'You're absolutely sure?'

'Yes. Ivy's working. Ivy never misses work, Rachel says.'

OK, Rachel says it. Donald believed it because Blaker had said the same. Ivy never missed the chance of work, matter of pride.

'OK, Carl. Good luck. Keep me posted. Families, eh? But what you don't want to do is fall in with what everyone says. Don't be a complete patsy, obeying orders. Be early, be late, be something. Take control.'

'Will you ever stop being a policeman? Are we going out for dinner next week, man to child-free man?'

'That'd be nice, Judge. I'll show you the real world.'

It was only several hours later in his empty Friday evening, when he returned to the police team which had done so much more to so little effect, because all they had unearthed was the fact that there were several people who had been present together at the scene of the theatre and the office, that Donald took advantage of their work after everyone else had gone home. Heads had been knocked together to get agencies and companies to reveal the names of their legal workers, their illegal workers, the lists and shifts of the non-cohesive casual labour they planned to use for the next three days. He studied these with interest.

Ivy featured on two lists as a regular and reliable worker, and on one she was booked to work the whole weekend, as she had done before. But this time her name had been crossed off.

Ms Wiseman, it seemed, had phoned in and cancelled.

CHAPTER TWENTY

Supper was early at the house, just the three of them. It consisted of an assembly of cold foods, hustled together with limp salad, Grace saying it was too hot to do anything else. Ernest was in charge of the wine, the homemade variety with Grace's own label, which tasted as if it was made of acorns. Rachel did not like it much, but Grace was edgy, so she praised it all the same and Ernest filled her glass again. The second glass felt heavy in her hand. By the end of a solid cold pie, all appetite had gone. A scratch meal, without much of the festive feeling which had been present in the other meals eaten here. The effort was being saved for the next day and Rachel thought that perhaps this was what it meant to become a true member of a family. Eating the leftovers, like real family members did, and following instructions to hold back for guests. It could have felt like really being accepted, but it didn't quite. Grace said she felt tired, and blamed the heat; Rachel simply felt dull. There had been talk of maybe going down to the pub, but that faded. Ernest had to milk the cows later, on his own this weekend because the cowman was away. By tacit consent, talk of Carl was left until later.

The only cause for celebration was Ernest being so entirely himself, in full command of his memory, as if everything he had said down by the lake really was part of an ongoing dream he visited in that particular place and nowhere else. Ernest, at least, boded well for tomorrow. He was sweetness and light, talking intelligently of how he would miss the cows when they were gone, but really he was too old for milking at midnight, and he would still have the pigs. They could maybe develop the barn, what did Rachel think? There were grants for such things. They would simply do what the government wanted farmers to do, which was to cease farming. They could develop the lake. He talked of the future, and did not mention the past, as if food restored him to hope. He smiled at them both, looking for approval, particularly from Grace. She patted him on the head, and fetched his boots, and at about ten o'clock he set out to do the milking, as the last of the light finally fled.

Rachel wanted to talk to Grace about Ivy, but the tiredness seemed to mushroom between them into apologetic smiles; there was suddenly little to say, punctuated by awkward silences, without Ernest. Grace did not ask her about Carl, and Rachel did not say what she wanted to say, and it seemed as if Grace wanted her out of the kitchen. Grace was ashamed of being tired, so sorry, love, not like me, it's the stress, you see, and I've been so worried about Ernest. It's sometimes hard to be cheerful. At least I can be tired with you. It's just *this*. You being in the kitchen, like Ivy was, when he came back into the house without Cassie. Him coming here, it's like an anniversary, brings it all back. Makes me stupid and sad. I can't think of anything else. I haven't been sleeping. Let's call it a day, shall we? Tomorrow, well, tomorrow, this time we'll really be celebrating something, won't we, love?

'Tired' varied from flu-type exhaustion, to nice exhilarating tiredness after a long swim, to this kind of tiredness which was like amnesia, and felt like being drunk, although Rachel wasn't. Just tired, from anxiety and relief, punching from different sides and making bruises, tired from the effort of suppressing unease. She was glad to be back in her very own room, with a spray of lavender by her bed. It reminded her of Carl's flowers. She struggled to stay awake; she had a huge desire to phone him and say, It really is nice here, it will all be fine, then she fell asleep. Everything was taken care of, everything.

She was halfway awake, then dozing again, dreaming of voices and closing doors and the sound of an owl. Her eyes opened wide and recognised the clock by the bed, reading three a.m. Grace was shaking her shoulder, jolting her awake, her voice high with anxiety.

'Rachel, love, can you help me? Ernest hasn't come back. Sorry, sweetheart, we've got to put on our boots and go and find him. Sorry, petal, it shouldn't take long, he's probably fallen asleep somewhere. Come on.'

Grace was clad in a floor-length nightie and a very old dressing gown. She held out another one to Rachel. Rachel got out of bed and put it on.

'Boots downstairs,' Grace said. 'What a bugger. Sorry.'

They went down, down, down to the kitchen, which felt as warm as toast. Tired as she was, Grace had cleared it, and it was as clean as a surgery.

'Won't take a minute,' Grace repeated, proffering a pair of boots, which Rachel scooped over her feet. They were too big, her feet slopped around in them, and they were out into the night, the air chill after the kitchen, flapping along with Grace in the lead, talking over her shoulder.

'Wouldn't have bothered you, lovey, but it might be a bit difficult to rouse him by myself.'

'Does this happen often?'

'No. Once or twice.'

It was all different in the darkness; she would not have known the way. The path seemed smooth; Rachel followed, trying to keep up, infected by Grace's urgency. Grace carried a torch which wavered ahead, scarcely piercing the darkness. Rachel remembered the route to the cow barn and milking parlour as being a couple of hundred yards, tried to remember the layout of the place, wishing she had paid more attention, the cow barn first, the pigs and their stench furthest away, the hay barn to the left, and then the buildings looming ahead of her, with the milking parlour first, lit up like a ship floating on a dark sea. They drew close, Rachel stumbling and Grace sure-footed.

The milking parlour was empty. The well of the room, surrounded by the higher railings and stalls, was sluiced down, clean and wet, achingly silent apart from the hum of machinery. It smelled of milk and detergent and the lingering presence of animals, a factory at night, with all the contours stark in the harsh overhead light.

'Ernest!' Grace yelled.

She went through to the anteroom with the milk tanks, from which the humming sound came. Then she came back. She was trembling.

'Come on. Maybe in the shed.'

They went down the ramp into the cows' barn. Semi-lit, it seemed far larger than it had looked in daylight. The sweet smell of hay, silage, molasses caught at Rachel's throat. The standing cows stirred; the place was suddenly full of the subdued noise of shuffling movement, and all she could see was a series of enquiring eyes, resenting disturbance. Her feet moved awkwardly across the hay-strewn floor, clumsy in the boots. Grace shone the torch around the feet of the cows as she walked past slowly. Perhaps she thought Ernest had lain down with his beasts. Rachel kept close. The cows lumbered towards them; Grace shooed them away; they came back. Rachel could feel the presence of tons of flesh and bone ready to walk over them, mash them into the ground with the hay and the shit, and she wanted to scream. She clutched at Grace's sleeve. Grace pulled away.

'Don't be silly,' Grace said angrily. 'They're only curious. Where the hell is he? Come on.'

The cows were so close, Rachel could smell their breath. It made no difference that they meant no harm; it was the crushing weight of them. They reached the far side of the barn, facing open fields and fresher air. Grace paused.

'The daft sod'll have gone to say good night to the damn pigs. That's where he'll be. Come on.'

'I don't want to go there,' Rachel said.

The smell of the pigs was already in her nostrils and her legs were trembling. Grace turned on her and shone the torch in her face.

'Oh *come on*, Rachel love. Don't be so selfish. You really don't know much about the real world, do you? Do you want me to go by myself? If he's in there, we've got to get him out. What kind of daughter are you?'

She moved off, confident that Rachel would follow, and

Rachel did. There was another faint sound of humming as they passed the incinerator of which Ernest was so proud, heating itself at night, for what? The small box of stone radiated heat as they passed. She remembered it was like a safe containing fire, remembered the small particle of bone Ernest had given her. She was ashamed of her cowardice. It was all beginning to feel like a bad dream, and yet she was stung. *You really don't know much about the real world, do you? What kind of daughter are you?*

She stumbled again on the steps leading into the pig barn. Grace pulled at the great wooden bolt of the door, a piece of rustic efficiency Rachel had admired for its simplicity before she had been stunned by the smell. Pig smell, a reeking, penetrating, throat-filling acidic stench which clung to clothes and hair worse than any real filth. Such clean animals to stink like that with their own unforgettable smell and revel in the way they repelled those who did not love them. A pig was a pig was a pig. It knew what it was, and loved no one but its own. Rachel thought of Ernest, talking about pigs. Maybe he *had* come to talk to them.

'Ernest!' Grace yelled. 'Come on out, you daft sod.'

The pigs had none of the silent curiosity of the cows. The sows and the piglets in the ten pens, ranged five each side with the aisle in the middle, reared in their confinement and squealed and snorted. The long, narrow barn was lit by two wavering lights, which moved in the draught from the open door, and the light of Grace's torch, which showed the exit door at the far end and the contours of the metal pens, full of writhing, moving, stinking shapes, pushing snouts through the bars of their cages. They knew no reason for human presence other than food or violence. Someone was there to give food or take the babies away. Rachel felt a snout, protruding through a metal bar, making contact with her bare knee, and heard deafening squeals underlaid with a cacophony of grunting. She swayed on the uneven wooden floor, steadied herself on the nearest rail, and felt another pig nuzzling her hand, and she recoiled as if stung, her scream inaudible above the din, the stench of them making her gag. She crossed her arms and took a tentative step forward, telling herself, they're pigs, where's Grace, where's Ernest, this is hell, and why . . . are they always hungry? What makes them so angry? Why am I here?

She screamed for Grace.

Then it grew quieter.

'If you stay still and do nothing, they'll stop in the end,' Grace said. The voice seemed to come from a distance.

Grace was sitting at the far end of the barn on the step which led to the other door. The light of her torch played on her feet; the light of the building showed the glow of a ciga-rette. Rachel moved towards the light and the boots, which was all she could see.

'Just stay still, would you?'

The pigs shuffled, disappointed, resigned, grumbling.

'What I really want to know is are you going to help us?' the voice said. 'I thought you would; now I'm not sure. C'mon, darling, give us a hug. Everything's going to be all right.'

Rachel tottered towards the end door. The torchlight swung towards the ceiling. The pigs began to squeal again. She felt a fist connect with her stomach, and all the air went out of her as she stumbled over the boots and fell to her knees and stayed there, clutching herself.

A door slammed, far away. Everything was quiet. Someone was stroking her hair. She was crouched at the foot of the step, still curled. The torchlight played on booted feet. Not the same feet.

'Honestly, Rache, you're such a patsy. Fancy believing a single thing my bloody mother says. Or anyone else for that matter. But you do, don't you? Because it's all true. In a way.'

Ivy.

Rachel raised her head and stared. She could do nothing but stare and saw nothing when she did. She was crouched at Ivy's feet, saying nothing, doing nothing, listening.

Ivy lifted her, effortlessly, so that she sat on the step with her torso grasped between Ivy's knees, Ivy's big hands on her shoulders, pinning her down, and Ivy's hand on the back of her neck. She remembered that. She had a dim memory of when that was *nice*.

'Cat got your tongue?' Ivy said. 'Nothing to say? Well, I bloody have, you bitch. Who's been cosying up to my husband with lots of chummy mobile calls, then? You. Who's the one person I love best in the world? You. Who do my mummy and daddy love so much? Who wants to manage everything and goes in my room when I'm not there? You. Who's sorting everything out where I can't? You. Who's sicked some fucking policeman up on my doorstep, making old Blaker spill his guts, and you don't even tell me except by mistake? You.

'You were supposed to help, you bitch. You were supposed to *stop* me.'

Rachel leant back against her and nodded. The world and the stench of the pigs came back. There was no sound except shuffling, grunting. Ivy's granite knees increased their grip, forcing Rachel's arms to stick out in front from her hunched shoulders. She could see Ivy above her, adopting a pose.

Venus clutching a serpent between her knees. She wondered why she was not so surprised. Ivy the savage, what a nice word that was. She could see her own hands, resting on her own knees; she looked down the alley of the barn. Cows were nothing. Her head could not stop nodding. She was beginning to get the picture she should have got. Bile filled her throat. She hurt all over. Grace loved me. She said I was a daughter.

'So are you going to help us, or what?'

'Do what?'

'What I was always going to do. Kill Carl. Oh, sweetheart, you've been very good. You've got him to come here, do you think I didn't know? I've been practising to kill Carl for months now, ever since I found him. Knew I didn't have the nerve, not without practice. Animals are one thing, humans are another. You're not *supposed* to do it, for a start, can't think why. Killing the thing you loved takes nerve, you know. I've had to learn cold blood. They were all a waste of space, why not? They steadied the hand. But I've got to get away with it, which is all that matters. I'll get away with this now, and bring Sam back. You're my friend, Rache. You should have stopped me.'

Rachel bent her head. There was a *click* as Ivy lit another cigarette.

Rachel heard the sound of her own, controlled, admiring voice.

'You're amazing, Ivy. I love you. Who did you kill for practice?'

'Got in the neck, like Cassie? Oh, one by persuasion, a man who stayed here. He was awful, he had no respect, you know, couldn't swim as well as he thought either. Shit face. Carl can't swim at all. A man in an office who wanted to die, so I

332

helped him swallow it. That one in the ambulance, had to be
so quick, I just had to do it, so I'm ready and skilled, Rache,
for the main kill. Nerves like steel now. Not quite sure of the
method, sure of the nerve. Everything's gotta be learned. So,
are you going to help? Are you with us or against us?'

'Does Grace know?'

It was a stupid question.

'Does Grace know what, you silly little thing? It was Grace
wanted you here in the first place. Grace suggested it. Grace
thinks ahead, see? She said dear Carl would like someone like
you. Far less risk if we got him here and killed him than if I
killed him somewhere in London. That was the original plan.
Flush him out, scare him, kill him, as soon as I knew I could
do it. But not good enough, do you see? Not after he sent
back Mummy's letters and we knew he would never let me
see Sam as long as he was alive. He'd stop Sam coming home
to Granny, it would be over his dead body . . .'

'That's not true.'

She could feel the stirrings of anger. She could see more
clearly now, wanted to explain, kept her voice low.

'It's Sam who doesn't want to see you. Carl's a good man,
he'll do everything reasonable. He must be a good man,
because he agreed to this. Oh, Ivy, have you thought . . .'

'So you admit it, you bitch. You've got into bed with him.
Yes you have. You've fucked my husband, you've got it out of
him. Well, you weren't quite supposed to do that. Christ,
you've probably fucked my son as well. I've watched you,
Rache, this last week, ever since you snuck out on the
Sunday, you've been in some fucking dream. His number on
your mobile, messages from coppers you don't tell me about.
Quite funny, really. I should kill you now, but I love you, you
know, and I thought you loved me. You're a thief.'

'I do love you. If you love me, let me go. Let me tell him not to come. Let me stop you.'

Ivy stroked her hair. She tried not to flinch from the touch, and failed. Ivy noticed.

'Oh no, my darling. Too late for that now. Things have changed, ambitions change, you said that once. I don't just want him dead, I want him to know. I want him throttled and drowned in the lake, and I want him to know, right to the last minute. Like Cassie did.'

'Why? Ivy, why?'

'Because it was all his fault. Because he killed her, and then he killed me. He shut me out and shut me away. He poisoned Sam against me, he made my life hell, he sent me right down to the bottom of hell. And when I got better, when I got to know he was a fucking *judge,* well, that was it. I tell you, Ivy love, it's like having a cancer eating at me, just knowing he's strutting around there, and I can't *live* knowing that. Strutting round in the big wide world, with *my* son. Not *his* son, my son. I can't live with that.'

Not his *son, my son.*

Ivy giggled. It was a horrible sound, worse than the pigs who looked on, quietly now, still hoping for food. Rachel could feel them breathing from the shadows of the pen.

'You'd better not tell anyone else I said that,' Ivy said. 'Ernest only wants Sam because Sam is Carl's. Grace'd go demented. Carl's fucking grandson is all he wants. Now, are you going to help or not? I think I know the answer. Ernest said you wouldn't. Grace said you would. She didn't know you'd fucked him.'

Rachel knew she was damned either way. Ivy was strong and Ivy was mad, and the pigs stank. All she felt in the semi-darkness was an overpowering hurt.

'Didn't I make any difference?' she said. 'Didn't knowing me make any difference? Didn't I make anything better for you, the way you did for me? Did I really not make a difference to that *cancer* of yours?'

The stroking of her hair had stopped. In the silence that followed, she began to hope that Ivy was pausing for thought. Ivy laughed. She laughed like a hyena.

'Of course you made a difference. It was through you that I could see what it would be like to have life without a curse on it. Not a care in the world, a father who loved you instead of wishing you were a son, no real losses, no mistakes, nobody's victim. Lucky you, no scars to speak of, just your pathetic little tragedies and pathetic little morals. I doubt if you've ever made any difference to anyone in your life.'

She laughed again.

'Although you'll certainly have made a difference to Carl's. God, you useless, innocent women make me sick. Besides, you didn't really love me. You don't know what love is.'

She bent forward and whispered in Rachel's ear, her breath on her neck.

'It means being willing to do *anything* for that person, *anything* to make them better. I would have done that for you, Rache, but you're not going to do it for me, are you?'

Rachel jerked her head away. She felt icy cold, but she could speak. She could open her silly big mouth.

'You're mad, Ivy. Madder than you know if you think I'd watch you kill another human being and not try to stop it.'

She could feel Ivy nodding, rocking, still gripping her and holding her still.

'Grace realised that. She said you didn't love us enough. Well, I'm sorry about it.'

She got up to her feet, talking as if to herself. 'Strange, isn't it, I can't actually kill you myself. I can only do it to men. Big mistake, you being here, but Grace didn't think Carl would come unless you were here first. Sorry about that. Shame you don't love us enough.'

Rachel did not move. She wanted to plead, she wanted to spit at Ivy, she wanted to fight, but she did not move. She felt a massive punch to the side of her head and sprawled forwards to the floor. The pigs began squealing again. Rachel was lying with her face against the rough wooden slats of the aisle between the metal pens, facing the curious snout of a huge young pig. They were touching distance.

'It won't hurt much,' Ivy said, almost sorrowfully. 'But the pigs haven't been fed today. Ernest'll come back in a couple of hours and let them out. He just has to press the button outside to release the traps. He said you were scared of them. Don't worry, they won't eat you until they've trampled all over you, you won't be conscious. Don't fight it, but then you never do, do you? You've never had to fight.'

And, as the final valediction, Ivy bent forward and touched her hair one last time.

The door slammed and Rachel heard the heavy wooden bolt slide across. It was the same noise she had scarcely registered from the door she had entered with Grace. Grace had gone out the same way as Ivy came in, her part in it done. Grace might have listened, might have waited behind the heavy door, made to contain an army of giant pigs, which moved about her now, sniffing hungrily. The stench at floor level was overpowering. Her head was thumping; she could feel the imprint of Ivy's fist and she wanted to weep, for everything. For sheer fear, for being hated and loved and betrayed and left to die like this, for what was to follow, until gradually, it was the horror at what she had done that paralysed her most. She had led Carl back to be slaughtered. She rehearsed in her mind all that Ernest had said by the lake, all the lies Ivy had told. How she had ignored what she really knew by instinct, again and again, for the sake of being loved. Ivy had tried to kill her father, Ivy had stolen his pills and inhaler, and she, Rachel, had believed her.

Ivy told lies: that thought comforted her for a moment. It could not be true that hungry pigs would eat a live human being; they ate processed protein, already mashed into pieces. That must be a lie – how could hatred be so extreme? – but she did not know if it was. *You don't know anything. Pigs eat anything.* There was a memory of a woman minced and fed to pigs.

Lying there, it was her own ineffectuality and awful grief which finally angered her into movement. No, she had never had to fight, Ivy was right, but she would fight now. She had to get out before Ernest came and released the pigs to fight over her. She got up and walked unsteadily towards the door, keeping her arms crossed and avoiding touching the railings on either side. As soon as she moved, the pigs squealed; if she stopped, they stopped. She reached the door, pushed it, found it immovable. Then she retraced her steps and went to the other end, accompanied by more racket. It was tempting to stay still, just to stop the noise. She began humming to herself to drown it out. The second door was immovable.

Wearily, Rachel sat down on the step where Ivy had sat, and kept very still.

Silence fell again. Then she was violently sick.

The supper she had eaten in Grace's kitchen spewed forth in volume, hitting her oversized boots and then the planks of the floor. It felt as if she was ejecting poison, and she heaved again and again, feeling the wretchedness of being sick, distant enough to wonder how her own small body could manufacture so much bile and junk from the small amount consumed. It was as if whatever she had eaten and drunk had trebled in volume and gushed forth in a projectile flow. Rachel watched her own emissions with objective distaste. Then she felt slightly better, as if she had at last done something positive. Ejected indecision along with the homemade wine, which had tasted nasty and sent her to sleep, making her biddable and ready for Grace. At least she had got rid of that. There was a glimmer of daylight in the cracks round the far door. It must be cold and bleak here when the wind blew; she supposed pigs made their own insulation. Pigs insulated themselves, pigs were clean, even if they smelt; they would not lie in their own shit. They lay on open slatted wooden boards, cushioned only by straw; the shit and the urine fell through the slats into the cavity beneath to be hosed and swept away, as and when. Not a task for a rainy day, Ernest had said. Dirty straw was swept away, also through the floor.

Rachel lay down and peered through the slats. Dawn was breaking. She could see the dull glimmer of liquid a few feet below. A lake of ordure. That was the way out. She swallowed. The only way out.

Ignoring the piggy protests, grateful for the extra light, which also added to the urgency, Rachel felt for the edges of the boards, looked for the joints. Went back to the other end, worked forward, looking for anything loose, trying to remember where the floor creaked most, trying to recall what Ernest had said about sweeping out the straw: he carried it in, he swept it not out, but down. Not a board in the end, a metal drain in the centre of the aisle. She tried to prise it open, broke her nails on the edge. Worked round, felt for each corner, tried again. Ernest would use a tool; she had no tools. She finally stood on one side of the drain, felt the other side lift slightly, grabbed it and pulled. It fell back, trapping her fingers and she shouted in anger, freed her hands and did it again, held it and danced round, put her boot in the space and heaved. The metal moved with a sticky sound, revealing a hole and intensification of the smell. Rachel paused, then sat on the edge of the hole, her booted feet dangling, her empty stomach heaving.

You've never made a difference to anybody's life. They really are going to kill Carl. Never mind you, you have to warn him. Even if it's the very last thing you do. All this is you own fault.

Rachel dropped through the hole, to the sound of enraged piglets, and sank into liquid manure.

CHAPTER TWENTY-ONE

She landed in a shallow lake of faeces and bodily waste and straw, mercifully upright until she began to wade her way, muck oozing over the boots, and then her feet were stuck as she tried to move and she stumbled into the filth, covering herself with it, trying not to breathe. There was life in the tank below the pig barn; she could feel something running over her arm, kept her mouth closed against the scream and waded to the side, watching the progress of small creatures scuttling ahead, swimming over the top of the slimy debris leading to daylight. Rachel reached for a beam over her head, the floor of the barn where the pigs were inaudible, and, hanging on to it, pulled one foot out of its boot, and then the other. Dense, fetid liquid squelched between her toes, but she could move. She followed the rats towards daylight and the stony surface of the muddy yard. Pure mud was good. There was something reassuring about the rats she had heard scuttling away. They were more frightened of her presence than she was of theirs. They were running away from her.

She stood by the side of the barn, not looking back at it, shaking her filthy, dripping arms, blinking in the light, breathing through her nose, not daring to wipe at her face with her poisonous hands and wanting nothing but water. Shuddering with revulsion, but free. She began to walk back towards the other barns, remembering that Ernest was due back to release the pigs and he might come this way, any time now. Ivy might have lied about that too; Ivy might only have meant to frighten her, but she would not wait to see. Ernest, she hated Ernest, the passive deceiver who let his frailty be used as bait. Grief was giving way to anger. She hated them all.

Rachel did not know a way back except by the main route, short of crawling through the fields on either side. If she saw him, she would simply run. Even barefoot, she could outrun Ernest in his heavy boots, and she thought, I could never outrun Ivy. Supposing it was Ivy who came back and found her gone and the drain open. Rachel stopped and looked around wildly, seeking shelter off the track. Somewhere just for a minute, to stop and think.

She crossed to where the incinerator stood, the hum of its engine only audible from very close, went behind it and crouched down in the nettles which grew at the back. From there she could see the track leading to the cow and hay barns and the house hidden a hundred yards behind. It was a treeless landscape, the hayfields flat after the last mowing, the trees only beginning where the land dipped towards the valley of the lake. Rachel thought longingly of the cows' trough in their barn. She would not be afraid of the bulk of the cows; she would shoo them away with curses to get in their water. Rank as it was, it was better than this.

She had the irrelevant thought that she could now see why

the smell did not matter to those who were accustomed to it. She would never in her life be as repellent as this, if she lived that long. If. If that mattered any longer.

Rachel ducked down. There was an advantage to being covered in ordure. She would merge with the landscape. It took several, itching minutes to be utterly sick of hiding. The filth was drying on her skin.

She had reached the dry stock barn and discovered her second good idea. Sanity was beginning to return, along with a slow-burning fury. She went into the shade of the barn, pulled hay from the nearest unbaled pile and wiped herself with it. Hay and straw kept animals clean. It would do for her. She plucked at more hay, rubbing herself with it. It scratched; she stopped, began more gently. So far she had not bled. Oh for water. The silence of the barn was soothing. A cooling breeze fluttered around it, echoing against the roof. Then, from nearby, she heard the sound of whistling, flattened herself in the shadow of a wall.

Ernest came into sight, plodding along the path, from the direction of the cows. He seemed entirely unperturbed. She watched as he paused in the middle of the barn and scratched his head, as if he had forgotten why he was there, uncertain of his purpose or his direction. Then he nodded to himself, looked at his watch, and plodded away again, not in the direction of the pigs, but towards the milking shed and his cows. Before leaving the barn, he moved to one side and fetched something from behind the drawn-back, roller-driven doors, and then, leaving the place as open as before, moved away out of sight, not whistling this time. He seemed so preoccupied, it seemed safe to follow. He disappeared into the milking shed. Closer, she could hear him calling to the cows. The thought of the cow trough and a depth of water receded into a dim hope. He was too close. Rachel was not afraid of Ernest out in the open because all sorts of dimly remembered lines were coming back into her mind. It would never be Ernest who did the killing. She settled back into the hay with her itching skin which she could no longer smell, and remembered a few things, all coming to connect.

Ernest never killed anything, was Grace's complaint, but Ernest could deal with the result. He could butcher a carcass, he could put it in his precious incinerator and reduce it to fragments of porous bone meal in a matter of hours. It took a long while to get the incinerator up to heat, he did not waste money. It was humming away, ready to receive the human sacrifice of Carl. That was what he had more than hinted at down by the lake, when his mind was not so much fuddled as clear. He knew Carl was coming; he knew his instructions, or if he did not know, he had guessed, he had watched, he had listened as Grace and Ivy planned.

She thought of Grace, dry-eyed, with a cold anger and something like bitter admiration. Grace the consummate actress, so full of love it could be dissembled and turned off, who had such generosity, colour, warmth and utter devotion to no one else on earth except her child. Had Grace meant any of her warmth, ever? Sitting there, feeling the insects in the hay, Rachel wondered if Grace really knew all about Ivy. Or if anyone ever knew all about Ivy. She was coming to conclude that she did. Grace was the diplomat, Ivy the warrior. Grace would use anyone, anything for that child. She could never love anyone else, except useful strangers.

For Ivy, Rachel felt a passionless hatred and primeval fear. She remembered the lines of her naked body, and all she should have known and sensed. She felt bitterly angry for being such a fool, for ignoring what she had surely sensed, again and again. But this was not about her. She rubbed the brown skin on her arms, and saw a bloated insect settle on her bare knee. She was wearing a long T-shirt which had been white when she went to bed. The loaned dressing gown was long gone. Rachel tried to think if she had abandoned it somewhere visible.

This is not about me, or my feelings. If I don't stop them, I may as well die now. I've got time.

There were so many places on a farm to hide and wait, and it was tempting to do that, sit it out. She could not tell the time by the rising sun, or work out how long she had spent in the barn, because it could have been hours. She remembered the clock by the side of her bed saying three a.m., and that was all. So by now it was morning, but not advanced morning, still early. Certainly plenty of places to hide, but none of any use, because Ivy would know them all. Rachel was the stranger here; she had no routes but the obvious, and if Ivy knew she was loose, Ivy would find her, long before Rachel could intercept Carl.

She roused herself. The main thing was to intercept Carl, for which she needed a phone. There was time; her gradually less fuddled mind, beset with images of Ivy, and Ernest, and Grace, and the contempt they felt for her, gave way to him. Carl was the reason for getting out of the pit. A good man, who had raised and saved a child not his own, travelling towards an undetectable murder by a couple of madwomen who blamed him for everything in their lives and wanted to kill him in some insane ritual which would somehow redeem them and bring back the dead. All of it fed by delusions and illusions. That this death would enable them to capture and bring home a beloved grandson for Ernest, resurrect Carl the elder, and snatch back time. They were primitives, nurtured on legends and myths, as if the century in which they lived did not exist. The sheer malice of the enterprise was as breathtaking as the delusion behind it. They did not live in an age where a boy could be suborned against his will. It did not follow from what they planned that Sam would ever love them; exactly the opposite. Would they wait for Sam to grieve for the mysterious disappearance of his father, and then appear with irresistible blandishments and condolences? They were not thinking at all. It was only revenge. They wanted revenge to relieve themselves of the curse of themselves.

And money. What dead Carl would leave, what he had promised, which would only take effect if he died. Money always played a part, but how did they think they would manage the business of getting hold of it? It was with an extra frisson of horror that Rachel realised that in their mad way, Grace and Ivy had come to believe that she might help them in that too, with the professional skills and influence in which they had blind faith, and she wondered, again with horror, what she might have been persuaded to do if their combined seduction of her had been completed, if it had gone on for longer, if her father had died. If she had been absolutely isolated, if she had no one to believe but them. She had taken the initiative too soon and what a terrible disappointment she must be to them, what a mess she had made.

She had a vision of Ivy appearing on Sam's doorstep in all her glory, offering comfort, love, condolences, apologies, a significant part in his future, with sweet-smelling Grace standing beside her. They would be utterly convincing. She could see poor, confused Sam stepping into their arms, dazzled by them and their style, just as she had been. He might not stand a chance.

Rachel was thinking calmly now. Logic came back.

The fact that the Wiseman plan was insane and impossible to fulfil did not mean that they would listen to reason. They were hell-bent on murder; Ivy had dreamt of it, rehearsed it, and Ivy would have her dream. Rachel believed that absolutely. Carl would be held by the neck until he was dead, this very day, unless she stopped it, and if they did not also kill her, they would implicate her.

The Polish cowman was away. There was no one within a mile. It was still early in the morning. Carl was due later; there was still time.

Rachel walked round the cow barn. Ernest had been there for half an hour. After that he would go to the pigs, perhaps, then he would report back, wouldn't he? Then Ivy would come hunting, perhaps. She walked back in the direction of the house, and into the garden. She was trying to think what she had done with her phone. She could see it in her bag, the phone Ivy must have held, looking at Carl's number, working it out, as if she could not already read Rachel better than she could read any book. Get into the house, get the phone and the car keys, get shoes to drive, phone, go. It seemed simple before she was in sight of the back of the house and took shelter behind a tree to watch. Then she could see it was impossible. The back door was open. The sight of that open door made her shake. She imagined the sound of her own footsteps, manoeuvring her way up those stairs, which would creak, barefoot or not, even if she could get past the kitchen or in at the disused front entrance. Even if they did not see or hear her, one of them would smell her. Her own stink would go before her. It would fill the place.

She turned back, and went down the other path which led to the lake. Surely they would not look for her there. She felt she could do nothing, and there was no hiding place from which to strike back as long as she was damned with this smell. There was still time.

The morning was mild, but not warm enough for bare feet and skimpy clothes, and she hugged her arms around herself. The lake looked innocently beautiful in the morning light, although she could not appreciate the loveliness of the water, only the sinister shadows, and the posse of swans, hugging the far bank. Even they held no threat any more. Anything which did not have the shape of Ivy or Grace was nothing. She jogged down the path, and saw by the bank where she had sat with Ernest the shirt and towel she had left the day before. She picked them up: they were damp with dew, but so clean she could have shouted with joy. It was like turning a corner. Rachel peeled off the filthy shirt and waded into the water.

It was icy cold, stinging the grazes on her feet, making her gasp. She waded further out to where the water was deeper, sank down and swam towards the swans, stopping after twenty strokes, which she counted, carefully, to see if she could feel ground beneath her feet. Ernest was right: only the centre was out of her depth, and towards the swans' bank, the ground grew shallow again, and she knelt in clean mud, scrubbed herself with her hands. Then she floated, pushing her hair back, running her fingers against her cold scalp, washing it cleaner. She knelt again, watching the roots of the trees stretching into the water, and kept very still for a moment. What was it Ernest had said, that he had taken rats to the lake? Ernest was the only person who told the truth. Ernest had a rifle.

She could hear and see nothing, swam back, stopped, scrubbed again.

She was not clean, but it would do. Now she could be positive. She was, at the very least, alive and kicking and out in the open. She was revived as she always was by the water, and the shaking with cold and dancing up and down to shake off the moisture and get warm. It did not matter that she would smell for ever.

Wearing the clean shirt and the wet towel tied round her middle, she retraced her steps towards the house, looking for a vantage point from where she could watch. One or other of them would leave it in the course of the morning, especially if Ernest came back with news of her escape. There would be a time in the next hour when she would be able to get in. She looked longingly at Grace's old car, parked near the back door. The keys for that were on a hook in the kitchen. She wished she had the skill to jump-start a car, do anything useful. She wished she had shoes. Even get to the boots in the corner of the kitchen by the washing machine.

Think. Think clearly, think rationally. Ivy and Grace would go nowhere else this morning. They would assume Ernest had done what he was told, and they would cling to one another and get ready. Even if Ernest had not let the pigs out, they would assume that she was safely locked away, to be dealt with later. It was difficult to second-guess their minds, but she had to try. They had everything they needed; soon they would begin to prepare a meal. Then Ivy would hide upstairs; she was not supposed to be there, it was Rachel he would be expecting to see. It was the thought of what he would think once they had got him inside with the wonderful Grace welcome and Ernest's handshake, what he would think when Ivy appeared. Carl would think, Rachel has led me to this. Rachel is Judas. That thought was unbearable. Judas betrayed with a kiss.

She wished she knew what time it was. Think, do what she should have done before, the obvious thing. Skirt round the place, go back in the direction of the lake, take the other track through the woods, cross the field, reconnect with the shady lane which led to the farm, go to the main road, stand in it until someone was forced to stop, get them to call the police. They would have to stop for a deranged woman using a towel to cover herself. Who would believe her, would the police actually come? She would say she'd been raped. Or better still, simply stand and wait at the top of the track, and intercept Carl in his car. Whichever was first. Grab a mobile and call his number, except she could not remember it, it was stored in her phone, not in her memory.

She stumbled back in the direction of the lake, taking a wide detour round the fields, moving slowly on bare feet. She wanted to be as far away from the farm as possible, in case of pursuit, but to get to the road she could see across the field in the distance. She remembered some of the layout of the land she had seen that second time, from the top of the hill. She lost her way, backtracked a bit and started again, hit an insurmountable hedge, then a field of wheat, waded through it and finally reached the road, where she walked back on the grassy verge towards the junction with the track. To call this a main road was an overstatement; it was a lonely country lane where something should come along every five minutes, but nothing did. It would, she was sure someone would. She was hobbling, trying to ignore the cuts and bruises to her feet, panting with effort, but faintly triumphant. She got to where she needed to be, at the point where the only vehicle access to Midwinter Farm met the road, where Carl was bound to pass and see her standing there with the frayed towel wrapped and knotted round her middle.

Then she looked down the narrow green avenue of trees sloping out of sight towards the farm, and there was his car. She walked towards it, staring at it, touching it to be sure. Unmistakably Carl's old car. She knew it from the colour and the unmended dent to the wing. He had parked it carefully on the bank so that it stood at an angle, leaving room for anything else to pass. He must have decided to walk the rest of the way.

Rachel groaned out loud. All that and the judge had out-flanked them. Carl Schneider had decided to be early. Yet again, her own stupid manoeuvres had failed. She stood in the road and screamed his name. The hawthorn branches waved back in silence. There was not another vehicle in sight.

Rachel ran back towards the house.

There was nothing else she could do. If they were going to kill Carl, they would have to kill her too. It would not be worth staying alive.

Her feet gave out before her breath, a sharp stone from the recently mended potholes in the road digging deep into her bruised instep, making her wince and lurch to a halt, then go on again with a limping gait until she reached the front of the house, which gazed back innocently, that utterly hateful house which had once seemed heaven. The pain in her feet reminded her of new school shoes. She staggered into the back yard, where the kitchen door was now closed. Windows open, door closed. All quiet, as if no one was there, a faint echo of what it had been like yesterday. Hope sprang: Carl was early, they had gone out, Ivy had gone out hunting her.

Carl had been early, just as she had been; Carl had detoured down to the lake, just as she had done, they were thinking alike, it was all right.

She moved to the side of the house, where the little-used living room was, the windows almost covered in ivy. The room of the rat. *You know what happens to rats. The only thing Ivy's afraid of is rats.*

There was no one in that room. It was as disused as ever, the place for rats.

Rachel crawled through flower beds, round the side of the house towards the back door. Grace's car was where it had been before, ergo, Grace was there. The towel fell off again. She knotted it back, and moved slowly round to the kitchen door, ducking below the window, trying to think. Behind the lavender bush to the left of the door, she saw what looked to her inexperienced eye like an ancient rifle, hidden behind the buzzing of the bees, and then from inside she heard a bellowing scream.

'Where's Rachel? What have you done with Rachel? Where's Rachel?'

Carl's voice, pleading and screaming. For her.

Ivy spoke loudly, with calm precision, as if he was a mistaken child.

'Your lovely Rachel? She should be finished by now. She's *my* friend, you know. She's mine, she was never yours. She was simply there to get you here, have you got that? She hates you like we do, she was only the bait.'

'No,' he said. 'No, no, *no*.'

Rachel launched herself towards the door. If both of them were going to die, the most unbearable thought was that he should go thinking that. She hated Ivy like poison, hated her, hated her, hated her for what she had just said.

Everything that happened in this house happened in the kitchen. She should have known. The towel dropped as she went in.

There was a brief view of the tableau, before Ernest came towards her. Carl, tied to his chair by his feet, looking towards the door, one eye contused into a vivid bruise. The tying-up was improvised, not according to plan. The plan would have involved wire or rope, rather than Grace's old washing line, but Carl had been early. Carl looked at Rachel; Rachel looked at Carl. His eyes travelled from face to groin. She had lost the towel. Grace was on the other side of the table, panic in her eyes. This was not her plan either. She screamed like one of Ernest's pigs and put her hand over her mouth. Only Ivy was calm.

'I didn't know,' Rachel said, looking straight into his eyes. 'I didn't know, honestly.'

He nodded. It was his feet which were tied to the chair. His hands were free, spread palm upwards on the table. There were slashes to both his wrists, which oozed blood, quietly. Ivy had the knife. She seemed to need to explain, as if recounting her symptoms to a doctor. There was no tremor in her voice, no shaking in her hand.

'I wanted him to lose blood,' she explained. 'Make him weak, you see? Could have injected him with the tranqs we use for the cows, but this is better, isn't it? So glad you're on side.'

She seemed to be looking for approval.

Rachel turned to both of the two witches, standing either side of his chair, put her hands on her hips, spoke as if she was managing a financial strategy meeting, where she was supposed to be on the side of everyone. Nodding at them both, laying down the law.

'That's enough. That's more than enough. Let's wrap it up here, shall we? No more time. Strategy failed. This is nonsense. Load of crap. Just get him out of here, he's learned his lesson, he'll do whatever, give me the knife. I'll take him home, sort him out, never a word. OK? I'm on your side. Why did the silly fucker have to be early?'

It almost worked. There was a split second when it might have worked, until Ernest came forward and spoke.

'It's that Rachel,' he said. 'Got no knickers,' he said. 'And she smells. She's been fucking a pig.'

He stood up close to her, his eyes close and confused.

'She was supposed to bring Carl. Little Carl. You get rid of big Carl, that murdering man who killed Nina and Hans, and you leave the little one behind. Where's young Carl, then, where is he? Where's my boy? Where's my little man? You promised.' He wheeled round towards Carl, pinioned in his chair, stabbing his finger towards his face. 'Where's Carl's son, where's my boy?'

'He's somebody's boy, but he isn't Carl's,' Rachel said crisply, full of anger. 'Sam's her bastard. A glorious bastard, but not Carl's. Grandson of you, sweetheart, but not of Carl. You should see him. He's queer as a nine-bob note, with skin darker than a gypsy, and I tell you, to know him is to love him, but he isn't Carl's.'

Grace began to wail.

The kitchen smelled. The prevalent smell was roasting pig. Pork, sizzling in the oven, cooked early, maybe to be eaten cold. A bowl of apples on the table. The clock on the wall said ten.

'Well, time flies when you're having fun,' Rachel said with a gaiety which sounded completely artificial even to her own ears. 'I'll just go upstairs and put on some clothes, take this man away, and then you can get on with lunch. Or I'll take him for a walk and then bring him back if you like.'

The moment really had passed. Ivy shook her head sorrowfully.

'What, go and get your phone, dearest? When I've got it here? Anything else you want to say, you sanctimonious bitch? You BITCH.'

'Wait a minute . . . He's not Carl's boy?' Ernest kept repeating. He looked towards Grace, who was ashen. 'Not Carl's boy? Not my Carl's boy? Where is he?'

'Shut UP, Ernest, SHUT UP. Shut your stupid fucking mouth. Do as you're told,' Grace screamed. 'It isn't true, you silly fool. She's lying.'

'Rachel doesn't tell lies,' Ernest murmured. 'Not . . . Carl's boy. She did it with someone else. Not my boy.'

Rachel moved towards Carl. His eyes were glazed with shock, but he managed a lopsided smile. She put her hands on his shoulders and kissed his cheek. There was a length of rough rope round his neck. She bent down to untie his ankles.

Ernest grabbed her round the middle and dragged her away. Rachel kicked and screamed and over the din of her own screaming heard Carl calling her name. Ernest was stronger than her, even though his hands slipped on her skin. He dragged her out of the open door, and stood, holding her, speaking quietly as she writhed in his grasp.

'They don't need us, dear,' he said. 'They never did.'

From inside, there was another guttural, choking scream.

CHAPTER TWENTY-TWO

Ernest held her head down with the massive hand which was Ivy's true inheritance. Strength, without reason.

She could hear Carl's voice, low and pleading and choking.

'Whatever you want,' he was saying. 'Let her go, please,' followed by Grace's voice, saying no, uncertainly. I left her somewhere safe, Grace said. I left her locked in somewhere safe, it's her own fault she left. There were sounds of chairs being moved, and Grace saying, prosaically, I must turn down the oven, or the meat will spoil. Pork never spoils, said Ivy.

Then Carl's voice, saying, 'As a judge, I think I'm entitled to an indictment, at least, before sentence. What exactly have I done?'

'You killed Cassie,' Ivy said. 'You waited until she turned into a swan, and then you killed her. Then you drove me away and buried me alive. You sentenced me to death.'

'Your father made my husband love him more than me,' Grace chanted. 'You stole my grandson.'

'I saved him, Grace. And what about you, what is it you've done? You knew what your daughter was. You couldn't wait to give her away, even to me, Carl's son. You knew what she could do.'

'Shut up, Carl, shut up, shut up, shut up . . .'

Ivy's voice was cold and definite.

'You didn't try to save me, husband. You didn't love me.'

His voice was sad and resigned.

'Oh yes, I did. But not enough. I loved someone else more. I plead guilty to that.'

'Drink up, come on, Mother, give him the drink, hold his head. This is for Cassie, your little anaesthetic. Drink it all.'

There was an unbearable sound of futile struggle, coughing, spluttering, groaning. Then equally unbearable silence.

Beyond the door, Rachel stood trapped in Ernest's sexless embrace, with tears coursing down her face, sick with rage and weakness. After a minute, he seemed impatient with the tears, let her go abruptly and pushed her aside. The freedom was temporary; she staggered, blinded by tears, and then his arm was back round her neck, holding her effortlessly. Something cold prodded into her back. He was old, but a foot taller and still stronger.

'Come away, girl,' he whispered. 'Come away to the lake. They'll come with us. Let them do what they must.'

Grace led the way out of the house. Carl followed with the noose round his neck, tight, loose enough to breathe and swallow without comfort. Liquid dribbled from his slack mouth. Whisky. Ivy was behind him, holding the end of the rope, like walking behind a dog on a leash. Then Grace took Carl's left arm by the elbow and Ivy took the right and they walked away, holding him close to their own bodies. It looked almost affectionate, like a convalescent patient supported by family. His face was purple, his breathing laboured, his wrists were bloody, he looked a sick old drunk and he swayed, but they held him firm and marched him forward. He did not try to resist. Primitive methods of subjugation, no training needed: rope, blood loss, alcohol, enough to make him incoherent, but not enough for the mercy of oblivion. That was the last cruelty. Rachel knew exactly what they were doing, and what they had always intended to do.

They walked and stumbled along in a macabre procession all the way down to the lake, the trio in front, progressing with efficient speed, Ernest and Rachel following behind. She watched Carl sag between them and wanted to believe he was shamming, and that in a minute he would find the strength to break free, cast them off and run back, but they hoisted him straight and on they went. Stop them, Rachel muttered to Ernest as he pushed her forward. He did not reply. Someone will see, she said, someone will come. No they won't, he said, finally, I put up the notice and blocked the path. Rachel looked down at her own feet, and then watched Carl, willing him free. Minutes were the same as hours, but it was only minutes before the two women, by now more urgent in their movements, as if wanting it done, reached the edge of the lake at the shallow bank which was the easiest point of entry. Her own footprints were still upon it. The sun had risen in the sky; she was cold to her bones, yet slippery with sweat, and the gun poked bruises in her side, and she was trying to think and all her effort went into breathing.

They were going to drown him, and he would know what was happening. Ivy would lead him into the lake, push him under the water where it got deep, hold him there. She had the nerve, she had the killing practice, she would not falter now. She had not faltered when she took the vital medicines from Rachel's father's pockets. Again Rachel was full of rage and struggling. Ernest held her back, twenty yards from the lake, close enough to watch.

The movements of the women by the bank were almost graceful, as if the ritual were rehearsed and dignified. Ivy left Carl to Grace and stripped out of her own clothes. Then all three of them, Carl in the centre, waded out into the water, still holding him. At waist height, Grace let go and came back, while Ivy relinquished her grip and twisted the tail of the noose round her arm before wading forward again, yanking it. Carl's whole body jerked; he stood uncertainly; she pulled again and he floundered, bellowing like a wounded calf and coughing. The water was level with Ivy's chest when she yanked the rope again. Her strength was awesome and his weakness awful. Rachel thought of Ivy naked, savage and . . . afraid. It was eerily silent now, only the lapping and splashing of water. It was only deep in the middle, shallow round the edges, a muddy pond for drowning. A little deeper and she would pull or push him under. Or leave him. Ivy pushed him. He sank out of sight.

Ernest took a deep breath. He was whispering something, *Get them apart.*

Rachel tore herself out of his grasp and ran towards Grace, cupping her hands round her mouth and screaming at the top of her voice, 'Ivy! Look out! There's RATS, Ivy! Thousands of rats, LOOK OUT. They're coming for you from the bank, LOOK.'

At the same moment Ivy turned to look, a single swan appeared from the shadow of the far bank, speeding towards the noise. It seemed to bear down upon them fast, wings arched over its back. Carl rose to the surface in its path and sank, choking.

'Rats!' Rachel screamed. 'Rats, rats!'

Ivy was looking towards the swan, listening, reacting. She dropped the rope and half swam half waded back towards Grace. Rachel ran in a straight line through the reeds blocking the nearest edge of the water, well away from them, and splashed in, swam towards the form of Carl thrashing in the deep centre. The strokes felt like slow motion, swimming through treacle with arms like lead, until she reached him.

He struggled as if wanting to pull them both under. She remembered slapping him, stunning him, then holding his head free of the water, kicking back furiously to tow him out of the deep. Not far, she told herself, not far, only a small lake, remember how small, it isn't the sea. Then they were there; she could feel muddy ground beneath her feet. Put your bloody feet down, Carl, yes you can. She looked back and saw Ivy, standing alone in the water, shouting, NO, NO! Then Rachel was holding him up in the reeds, with his body slumped against hers, cursing him, as she heard the sound. That great booming blast of gunshot, echoing away, and then Grace screaming, and Rachel looking back again, and Ivy no longer there.

She would never be able to remember later how she dragged Carl through the obstructive weeds and on to the bank with his heavy body and heavy clothes, or how her nerveless fingers fumbled with the rope which had swollen tighter round his neck, or when it was she realised it was not so much a noose as a simple halter for a bigger beast than he. Or at what point it was, as she began to chew at it with her teeth, listening to his breathing, that someone came to help, or even who that someone was. It could have been Ernest with his knife, sawing through the halter knot; it could have been anyone. It was simply herself and an unknown man who were slapping Carl on the back, making him spew forth pond water and whisky like a fountain. She heard a voice saying, You gotta learn to swim, Judge, and then the same someone told her to sit with her head between her knees, which she did, until she looked up, and wished she had stayed staring at her own muddy groin.

He was strong, old Carl, he got better quick. Donald Cousins rarely acted on instinct unless his sympathies were thoroughly engaged, which they were, and unless it was a bright sunny day, which it was, and unless his conscience really troubled him, which it did. They might even give him something to eat if he got there by noon. Rachel Doe might be a bad girl, and a dangerous combination with Ivy Schneider, but at least she was a professional woman and would exercise caution if he was there. It was the likelihood of the two bitches together in a remote place with the judge which scared him. The old folks didn't count. Two conspiring women did.

He had followed the map and found an empty house, a kitchen smelling of roasting meat, and followed the small spots of blood and his nose. When he came upon the famous lake, he saw from a distance a woman and a clothed man apparently frolicking in the water, moving away from a tall, naked woman, whom he recognised, standing alone with only her feet in the water, shrieking at a swan. A scene of bacchanalia, everyone having fun, no problem at all.

Then he saw an old man raise a heavy rifle and shoot away at Ivy Wiseman from the close range of the bank. He didn't need to have much of an aim to hit a target as near as that, only a few feet, and a helluva blast. The noise was eerie, it bounced about longer than the screams.

Donald ran full tilt towards the old man, and it was as if the old man could hear the vibration of his footsteps as the echo of the murderous sound died away. He turned and pointed the barrel of the gun at Donald's chest.

'Go and help Carl,' he said, gesturing with the gun. 'I can't do this twice.'

Donald would write in his notes later that the old man had a firm grip of the rifle, even though he was weeping and seemed bewildered. At that time, he was only glad that he had brought his mobile and knew the map reference. He was way out of his depth here.

What Rachel remembered later was that they left her alone. That Carl came to his senses far sooner than she, and that he and his friend left her where she was, sitting mostly naked on the bank, and then, not so much later when she stood up, she could see all of them, except for Ernest, pulling the body out of the water. She did not notice the rest of them, except for Carl, sitting on the bank, cradling his dead wife in his arms as if he could not let go, with the crater of a wound in her chest soaking blood into his wet shirt. She was still his wife. The whole posse of swans watched from the centre of the lake.

An ambulance and a police car were rocking down the track. Men appeared, hitting the ground running. Rachel thought, numbly, of being naked from the waist down.

Grace and Ernest stood together as she approached. They, too, were still married. Grace was pale and angry.

'You bitch,' she said to Rachel wearily. 'Why did you tell him it wasn't Carl's son?'

'Not Carl's,' Ernest said. 'Not mine. Bad girl.'

Rachel saw that the rifle lay on the ground where it had been flung. Ernest turned to Grace.

'I forgot to feed the pigs,' he said.

She had eyes only for him now. Eyes only for what was left.

Rachel needed clothes. She did not need recognition. No one noticed as she walked the hateful route back to the house. Ivy was the focus. Passing through the kitchen, she turned off the oven, as Grace would have done. She went upstairs to the room with the lavender by the bed, found her trousers and shirt and car keys. Her feet looked like swollen balloons. She forced them into her sandals, and then, summoning up her last reserves of strength, walked back out of the house for the final time and left.

Driving away was the easiest part. She could drive on automatic pilot. The first hour passed without her noticing. As she got closer to London, instead of going home, she detoured north, following signs for the motorway to Luton.

It was high time she visited her father. She needed him, very much, and that was all he had ever wanted. He was wiser than her after all.

The last image was Carl, holding his wife, trying to coax her awake.

CHAPTER TWENTY-THREE

By the end of August, six weeks later, the long, hot summer had finally died.

'Never a good idea to run away,' Donald said to Rachel. 'But I can see why you did.'

'I didn't run, I drove, Don. And I made it easy. I left my phone. I let you know where I was.'

'Very useful it was too. You know what, Rachel? I think you were thinking like a man. It's this awful control and time management thing blokes have. If they've done all that could possibly be done in the circumstances, and nobody needs them at the moment, they tend to fuck off. I used to do it with my wife, before she told me what I was doing. What could I do about her giving birth, for instance? Sweet nothing. I went to the pub. You've lost a bit of weight.'

'Did I ever tell you, Don, that the one thing I loathe and despise is someone telling me they know what I think. Or they think they know what I think.'

He was very cheerful indeed today, at his most irritating.

363

So he should be, he thought to himself, for being someone who had redeemed a failing career by solving a murder or three by complete accident. On the back of other tragedies, for sure, but never mind that for a minute.

They had advanced, in the first few hours, only as far as her preferring him to anyone else, and how had he done that? Her dad liked him, and he liked her dad. One look at a dad like that, and you knew what she was about. Smashing kitchen he had. Donald became her interrogator of choice, the only one she would talk to, and she had, in police speak, been very helpful.

'My daughter,' Donald said, 'wants to be an accountant. Get rid of the going-nowhere job. Will you talk to her?'

'She's only twenty. Tell her she needs her head examining. Tell her to go and see the world. And tell me what's going on.'

It was he who found her, *not Carl*, and it was he she would rather have round her shambolic, searched-from-top-to-bottom flat. Such a haul, they had, but only from the one room, which was good for her, not so good from the point of view of anyone else who would have preferred the murders to be a conspiracy with two glamorous dykes in the frame rather than a single oddball divorcee who hated her husband so much she went into training to kill him. Donald would have liked to have told her quite how much he had deflected away from her, but he did not have the heart, and besides, she already knew.

'Nice flowers,' he said.

She shuddered. She was good at that. She could shudder from her heels to her head, like a dog fresh out of a pond, sorry, perhaps better not add that to the list of things he admired her for at that point. He and his wife had a dog once. It died. He would get another.

'No charges,' he said.

In Ivy's room there was a bag. In Ivy's bag there was a gar-rotte and rope, a scalpel fit for an assassin or a barber, and on Ivy's scant supply of clothes an interesting selection of DNA. Then, courtesy of Rachel, there was the Plonker, and what he had seen, namely Ivy, testing her skill and nerve in the back of an ambulance. Then there was Blaker, currently safe and spinning his own story. Not a cat in hell's chance of him being a reliable witness, or a witness at all.

'It's all terrorism now,' Donald said kindly. 'We bury what else we can. So's we can pretend to cope. Things change.'

'No charges?' She looked relieved. 'Really? No charges?'

'Nope. Use your brain. Ernest Wiseman is a bit doolally, but not all the time, prognosis not good. When he's up, he's up, when he's down, he's down. Then when he's halfway up, he falls all the way down. Such as, the pigs wouldn't have eaten you, but then they would, then they wouldn't, that kind of thing. He's never going to be fit to stand trial or give evidence. Grace is a different ball game. She changes her tune all the time. Grace is totting up all the angles, fighting to survive. There's nothing she won't say or do.'

'And?'

He counted on luck as he recited.

'Grace said, at first, that you were implicated. That you set out to get the judge to a place where they could do their business, and you knew all about it. Just as you knew all about the other murders. Stop, don't wave at me like that, I know, I know, I know.'

She was smoking for England. They both were. The smell of nicotine was well absorbed by flowers. Lots of flowers.

'I got sacked, you know,' she said. 'Two weeks off work, whistle-blower to boot, you get sacked. It's pretty easy when you don't fight. And you know? I don't give a shit.'

'That's good. Always another job for someone like you. Sandra . . .' He stopped in confusion. He had just spoken his wife's name. 'Sorry, that just slipped out.'

'You mean, your wife would say it doesn't matter, and she'd be right. And I do understand why you do it.'

'No you don't. And when you say you understand, you should swallow the words. It's as offensive to me as me telling you what you think. Sorry about that. And don't go thinking you understand Carl, either. Not unless you try.'

'Point taken. I understand that my own tragedies in all of this are very small ones in comparison to those of everyone else. I am not related to anyone who was killed on Ivy's practice run. I am not dead or disfigured. My losses are minimal; I must think of others. That's the lucky story of my life. Tell me again why no one will be charged with anything.'

'Because it's better that way, although hardly justice. No charges unless you insist, and if you did, Grace is the only one in the frame, and she will pour shit all over you. And Carl. She'd say you knew all along, and someone will believe her. Beautiful accountant implicated in murder conspiracy. It'll do as much for your career as it will for the judge. Lovely media coverage. And again, there is this little matter of a lack of evidence. It's always the same when the prime mover dies.'

'Ah, I see you've been taking advice from Judge Schneider. An in-house expert on what'll work in front of a jury. How unusual. The victim as expert.'

She knew she sounded bitter. It was the aftermath of two weeks' solid crying. The crying had started as soon as her father had told her how he knew that Ivy had taken his inhaler and his pills, but had not wanted to tell her for fear of causing further offence. That he had known instinctively that Ivy was dangerous, but didn't know how to say. The pathos of that made her cry, and she had not been able to stop. She had grown to appreciate the safety of that little house in Luton, where the floorboards did not creak and the windows stayed closed.

'Grace *not* being charged with conspiracy to murder is, I admit, an absolute disgrace. But where's the evidence? And consider the spin she could put on it. How does it look? She's cunning as a cartload of monkeys, determined not to be parted from her husband. She is, for the sake of the defence argument, completely under the thumb of her psychotic daughter, who began on her homicidal track a long time ago. Ivy killed the pets before she was ten. Ivy's instincts were always there. She killed what she considered to be superfluous, just as Ernest taught her, because he hated to do it. Grace will say there was never any real intention to drown Carl. It was a game. Ivy wanted to make him suffer his daughter's fate, almost, but not quite, and then they would haul him back safely. Ernest, poor soul, got it all wrong. He wasn't told to bring the rifle. He was suddenly, irrationally devastated by the recent news of his daughter's infidelity, and went back into the past. At one point Ernest said he was trying to kill the swan, because it was going for Ivy. At another point he was defending Carl, like he defended him once before. Either way, it was spontaneous. It was a World War Two rifle, a carefully preserved Lee Enfield, and he hadn't shot a rifle in years. It was an accident he hit her at all.'

'He must have known how to shoot once. He shot Ivy as soon as she was a clear target. As soon as she moved away from Carl.'

'I know,' Donald said. 'I saw. But then again, I might not have seen right.'

'And what about Grace locking me into the pig barn?'

'Ah well, the only witness to that apart from you was Ivy, and Ivy is dead. And you yourself washed away all the traces.'

'I've been scrubbing myself every day, twice a day, ever since. Please tell me there isn't a trace, and I'll make some more tea.'

Tea, the panacea for all ills. Donald liked his with two sugars.

'You were very brave,' he said.

'I don't think so. I did everything wrong. And then Carl was early.'

She liked Donald. He was easy to be with. He never once suggested that she had been a fool; he apologised for suspecting her, but added that it was just as well he had, otherwise he would not have arrived at all, to protect the judge from a pair of harpies. Nor did he say that he thought the end result was all that bad. One way or another, Ivy had to die before she killed anyone else, and it was fitting that she died where she did.

'Ivy told Grace about the other murders, and why. The man in the office, for practice. The man in the ambulance to see if she had the nerve. The man in the theatre queue, ditto. These poor people's families have to know the miserable nature of the motive. Practice.'

Rachel nodded. Another reminder that other people's tragedies made her own seem small.

'And the young man who drowned? The paying guest?'

'I don't know. But it wasn't Ivy who left the pub with him, it was Grace. They were supposed to be going swimming.'

She was crying again.

'You couldn't have prevented any of it,' he said.

'She wanted me to stop her. I didn't stop her. I just wish

you could have seen what she could be like. She was beautiful. She made life *glow*.'

'I know,' Donald said. 'Carl told me.'

There was a pause.

'Without a trial, Sam Schneider is better off. That's Carl's problem at the moment. It's bad enough having to tell your son that his mother was a serial killer; it would be worse if it featured in the news over several weeks. Oh, and yes, your dad isn't your dad.'

'Oh, poor Sam. How on earth do you react to that?'

'Interestingly. He said he's always known about his parentage, he'd known it from looking in the mirror, and anyway, Ivy had told him. After Cassie died, she told him, another sort of punishment. Sam says he knew exactly who his father was, and it was and is Carl in every way that matters, and he doesn't want another. And he doesn't think he's inherited much of his mother, because he hates the countryside and couldn't kill a fly. The irony is that he'll probably inherit a bloody farm some day. That's what's in Ernest's will, anyway.'

It was the first time he had seen her smile.

'And that's where you can help. Sam says talking to you would help. Someone who knew her. Knew the other side of her. Someone who can give the bigger picture, the other side of her. The good things, the life-enhancing things. The reliable worker, the missing bits from the picture. Will you do it?'

'Yes.'

'They're worth a lot, both of them.'

'Grace used to hum this song in the kitchen. I can remember a verse. *She stepped away from me, and she moved through the fair. And fondly I watched her move here and move there, And she made her way homeward with one star awake, As the swan in the evening moves over the lake.*'

'Called "The Bard of Avalon", wherever that is,' Donald said. 'I'd stop humming it, I would if I were you. It's like all those anonymous dirges, they end badly. *Last night I dreamt my lost love came in, So softly she entered, her feet made no din.* Life's a bitch if you don't take your chances. That kind of thing.'

'Donald, I don't know what I'd have done without you. I think you're the nicest man I've ever met, because I can tell you anything. You know what I'm really suffering from?'

'The grief of the abused?'

'Yes, and the conscience of the person who should have seen it all coming. I saw her naked, I saw what she was like. I'll always wonder if she selected me. If she cleaned my office and my desk, and found me that way. Doesn't matter. I know I'll survive, because I can't regret that year of Ivy. I'd like to undo what she did, but I don't want not to have known her. I don't want to go back and forget that. I don't want to forget all she taught me, the world she opened up. I don't want to give back the knowledge and the curiosity, and the way of looking at things. And I don't want to give up trusting people. That, above all. I want to be able to say I'll take that leap of faith, because it's worth it, even if you fail. You have to take the risk, you've got to give. But I'm jealous. She was all charisma to my lack of it. And Carl, well, Carl . . . I can just see him, cradling her in the water. He still loves her. Anyone would. Ivy won in the end, you see. Ivy and Grace, they won. They got him back.'

Donald sat back and lit the last cigarette. He was trying to consider very carefully what to say, and it really was a bit tricky. A test of skills. Ah yes, no doubt the judge had wanted to touch her, one last time. Witnessed by the swans, he had kissed her forehead and murmured he was sorry. Like

Donald had with his wife, without witnesses. Since when did loving one woman stop you loving another? Don't argue with ghosts, live with them. Think of what it was like to clear up after the war. He shook his head. He felt better for shaving off his disguise of a moustache. It made his face even more ordinary and guileless.

'I don't think that had much to do with love, you know. He was on his last legs himself, but I had the distinct impression he was trying to reassure himself that she was really dead. That's what that was about. And I couldn't get her out by myself. And he did come to see you when you were out of it, you know. And there's all these flowers. You're on his mind.'

Her smile widened into a brief laugh.

'How useful to be able to lie,' she said. 'Will I ever learn?'

'Take your chances,' he said. 'Good men are hard to find. I know one when I see one. He really wants to see you. But there's a lot going on there, aside from Sam. Same things as you. Regret, shame, feeling foolish. Failing to see what he should have seen. Worried to death about you. Also that ego thing. Not exactly looking his best when you saw him last, was he? Has to be fucking rescued by a woman, when he's stinking with whisky himself. You know what that does for a man? And at least,' he added, 'you don't get a pig in a poke – sorry I said that, but you know the history – which is more than you usually get. Better watch it, though. He knows fuck-all about women, always the same when the mothers die young. At least my wife stayed the course. And he's seen you in the raw.'

It was not in the best possible taste. He sighed as he left her. That was what being a friend was about. He could have been in with a chance himself. We men, he told his daughter, we're just calculating animals. You want to watch out for us. We need looking after a helluva lot more than you.

They met in St James's Park. The end of summer, recovery time, everything beginning to go back into the ground and change colour. The calm lake mirroring luxurious browns and yellows and greens, the view different and better for the shrinking foliage. Nature tamed beyond danger into harmony, and an early autumn sun, placid, beyond burning the skin. People getting on with it. Everything around them was taking the risk of dying, in order to come back and live again. Ivy had loved beauty as well as ugliness. God rot you and God save you, Ivy. May you not be in hell.

She might never be the first in anyone's life. Second or third would do.

His quiet footsteps came to the bench beside her. He took her cold hand and kissed it.

'I would like it very much,' Carl said, 'if you would teach me how to swim.'